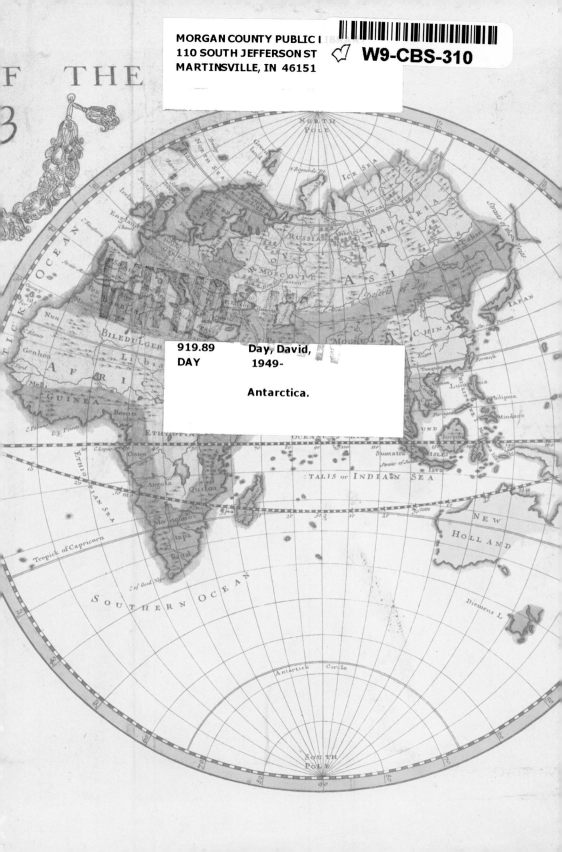

W9-CBS-310

ANTARCTICA

ANTARCTICA

A BIOGRAPHY

DAVID DAY

OXFORD
UNIVERSITY PRESS

OXFORD
UNIVERSITY PRESS

Oxford University Press is a department of the University of Oxford.
It furthers the University's objective of excellence in research,
scholarship, and education by publishing worldwide.

Oxford   New York
Auckland   Cape Town   Dar es Salaam   Hong Kong   Karachi
Kuala Lumpur   Madrid   Melbourne   Mexico City   Nairobi
New Delhi   Shanghai   Taipei   Toronto

With offices in
Argentina   Austria   Brazil   Chile   Czech Republic   France   Greece
Guatemala   Hungary   Italy   Japan   Poland   Portugal   Singapore
South Korea   Switzerland   Thailand   Turkey   Ukraine   Vietnam

Oxford is a registered trade mark of Oxford University Press
in the UK and certain other countries.

First published in Australia in 2012 by Random House Australia

Published in the United States of America by
Oxford University Press
198 Madison Avenue, New York, NY 10016

Library of Congress Cataloging-in-Publication Data
Day, David, 1949–
Antarctica : a biography / David Day.
p.   cm.
Includes bibliographical references and index.
ISBN 978-0-19-986145-3
1. Antarctica—Discovery and exploration. 2. Antarctica—History.
3. Antarctica—Environmental conditions. I. Title.
G870.D296   2013
919.89—dc23   2012040014

Endpaper maps courtesy of National Library of Australia

1 3 5 7 9 8 6 4 2

Printed in the United States of America
on acid-free paper

CONTENTS

PREFACE

Like Captain James Cook, I have been slowly circling the Antarctic. While labouring on other books, the ice-covered continent kept looming into view like an alluring mirage, suggesting itself as a subject worthy of closer exploration. The chance to do so came after I completed *Conquest: How societies overwhelm others* (2008), which examined how so-called 'supplanting societies' claim territories and make them their own over an extended period of time. It was a new way of looking at the history of the world.

That book's opening chapter began with the claiming of the French Antarctic territory by Jules-Sébastien Dumont d'Urville. Only the penguins were watching the French sailors as they clambered onto an offshore islet and raised their nation's flag to claim the adjacent coastline. However, it is clear from their accounts that the officers confidently expected that the territory claimed by such customary means henceforth belonged to France. The story of d'Urville drew me to Antarctica. How was it that this simple ceremony could lay claim to a large region of Antarctica without any French citizen visiting the place during the subsequent century? How did Britain and its dominions later claim about two-thirds of the continent, only to have their claim go largely unrecognised? How has Antarctica come to be a continent with many claimants and no owners? One question led to another, and a book about the claiming of Antarctica became much more than that.

The researching and writing of this book has been a long journey, and one that could not have been completed without the assistance of many individuals and institutions. My home institution, La Trobe University in Melbourne, provided some research money that helped fund travel to archives in Britain, the United States, Norway, Australia and New Zealand. The University of Aberdeen was most generous in its assistance, providing me with a visiting position and funding to visit archives elsewhere. I would particularly like to acknowledge the support of the then Principal of the University of Aberdeen, Professor Sir Duncan Rice, and Vice Principal, Professor Bryan MacGregor. Some of the ideas in this book were discussed at seminars in Aberdeen and Melbourne and I am grateful for the feedback from participants.

I began and ended the research at the Scott Polar Research Institute in Cambridge, where the library and archive staff were unfailingly helpful and where I was able to discuss Antarctic history with Bob Headland over a lunchtime pint or two. Many thanks are due to Hilary Shibata of SPRI for kindly providing access to her translated account of Shirase's expedition prior to its publication.

Several wonderful weeks were spent in New York where Dorothea Sartain helped access the files of the Explorers Club and Mary Lynne Bird and Peter Lewis steered me towards many interesting records held by the American Geographical Society. Paul Chaplin of the Antarctic Heritage Trust was very generous with his time during a visit to Oslo, as was historian Susan Barr at the Directorate for Cultural Heritage. Jan Erik Ringstad provided valuable help at the Whaling Museum in Sandefjord, where the language barrier might otherwise have made research difficult.

In Hobart, Andie Smithies, librarian at the Australian Antarctic Division, guided me around its valuable collection. Laura Kissel, Polar Curator at the Byrd Polar Research Center in Columbus Ohio, cheerfully fielded many requests for files. In Washington, Claire Christian of the Antarctic and Southern Ocean Coalition, pointed me towards much that was relevant in the ASOC office, while Jim Barnes reflected on his years of advocacy on behalf of Antarctica.

Thanks are also due to the archivists and librarians at the Alexander Turnbull Library in Wellington, Archives New Zealand in Wellington and Christchurch, the National Archives of Australia in Canberra and Hobart, the National Archives in London, the National Archives and records Administration in Maryland, the Auckland War Memorial Museum, the Churchill Archives Centre in Cambridge, the Canterbury Museum in Christchurch, the National Library of Australia, the Dartmouth College Library in New Hampshire, the Library of Congress, the Royal Geographical Society in London, the Roosevelt Library in Hyde Park, the Smithsonian Institution Archives in Washington and the State Library of South Australia.

Once again, my literary agent in London, Andrew Lownie, found enthusiastic and supportive publishers when the book was little more than an idea. At Random House, Meredith Curnow and Elena Gomez guided the manuscript through the press with patience and good humour, while my long distance editor, Julian Welch, working from Uppsala in Sweden, now knows more than he ever thought possible about the Antarctic.

Friends also helped lighten the load along the way – Håkon Lie and Karen Mosman in Oslo, Claude and Irene Wischik in Aberdeen and Richard and Danielle Weiner in Providence. My children, Michael, Emily and Kelly, provided inspiration and stimulation in equal measure, while my wife, Tsila, was a constant presence on the journey and of immeasurable assistance with the research in countless archives. It is to Tsila that this book is lovingly dedicated.

David Day
La Trobe University

CHAPTER 1

'Farther than any man has gone before'

1770s

Captain James Cook had the look of a disappointed man as he carried his charts and journals up the steps of the Admiralty building in London in August 1775. The son of a Yorkshire farm labourer, he had become one of the world's great explorers. Yet he had failed to fulfil the great quest of the eighteenth century.

Cook had been instructed to find the missing continent that was said by the ancient Greeks to dominate the southern hemisphere. The so-called 'Great South Land' was believed to be more bountiful than the Americas. But the continent was a figment of the mapmakers' imaginations. Cook had scoured the southern oceans for a massive continent that did not exist.

Remaining just out of sight of Cook's ceaseless searching was the last undiscovered continent, Antarctica. Although Cook suspected that there was a sizeable land at the South Pole, he assured the Lords of the Admiralty that its ice-choked seas meant that it was not worth the risk involved in discovering and claiming it for England. Cook never imagined that his voyages in the South Seas would spark a two-century-long battle for control of those frozen wastes.

The first of Cook's historic voyages saw him circle the globe between 1768 and 1771. Crammed aboard a small barquentine, the HMS *Endeavour*, was a party of scientists and artists, led by Joseph Banks and Daniel Solander. Their expedition was to Tahiti, where they were to observe the transit of Venus across the sun. It was an important calculation for navigational purposes, and observations were being made in different parts of the world by French and English scientists.

That was the ostensible reason for the *Endeavour*'s long voyage, with the publicly announced purpose being designed to put the French and other European powers off the scent. In fact, once the scientists had completed their work in Tahiti, Cook had secret instructions to search the South Pacific for the mythical Great South Land and to claim it for England. According to Alexander Dalrymple, an influential proponent of Pacific discovery who had wanted to command the *Endeavour* expedition himself, the continent was about 8000 kilometres across and probably had more than fifty million inhabitants.[1] If Dalrymple was right, it was a great prize indeed.

Cook was conscious that he was sailing in the wake of the French explorer Louis de Bougainville, who had left France in 1766 to look for the elusive continent.[2] In 1768 two English navigators, Samuel Wallis and Philip Carteret, had set sail but had also failed to find it.

The dutiful Cook did as he was instructed. After an eight-month voyage to Tahiti, he spent a further three months enjoying the delights of that tropical paradise and making the required observations. Both Wallis and Bougainville had preceded him there, and in fact both had claimed it for their respective sovereigns. Cook had to be content with being the first European to discover and claim a number of lesser islands nearby. In July 1769 he took the *Endeavour* southward to the area where he expected to find the world's last remaining continent. Wallis had been instructed to do so during his voyage, but had decided against chancing his ship in the wintry conditions of the Southern Ocean. Cook soon wished that he had done likewise.

For several weeks Cook battled the strong Pacific swell, scanning the foam-flecked waves for some sign of the land that had long been marked on European maps. He saw nothing but an increasingly cold and tempestuous ocean. He might have continued on towards the Antarctic Circle, but the rough seas and low temperatures would have sorely tested the worn sails and rigging of the blunt-nosed ship as well as the good temper of the crew. Moreover, the Great South Land was meant to extend far into temperate latitudes.

Cook steered the *Endeavour* back to the embrace of warmer and calmer climes. His sortie south had failed to find the Great South Land and had left him without any great triumph to present upon his return. Cook made a momentous decision. Rather than heading home around Cape Horn, and landing practically empty-handed in England, he decided to continue his search by heading westward.[3]

Cook knew that the Dutch explorer Abel Tasman had gone looking for the Great South Land and in 1642 had chanced upon the west coast of what we now know as New Zealand. Tasman had reached it by way of the south coast of mainland Australia and Tasmania. From their trading posts in the East Indies, the Dutch had previously charted the northern and western stretches of the Australian coastline, calling the land 'New Holland'. But they thought so little of it that they had made no serious attempt to make it their own by settling it with Dutch colonists. Their attention continued to be directed further eastward, where Tasman hoped to encounter the Great South Land of European imagination. In contrast to the aridity of Australia, the Great South Land was supposed to have a temperate climate, a large population of civilised people, rich gold and silver mines, and new plants that would produce a fortune for their finders, as the spice plants of the East Indies had already done for the Dutch. Tasman thought that he may have found such a place of boundless riches when he discovered New Zealand.

At first sight, New Zealand certainly looked like it might be the place of the cartographers' dreams. It had a temperate climate, its soils enjoyed a bountiful fertility and it was peopled by an organised society. Even though Tasman saw nothing comparable to the grand cities the Spanish had encountered in the New World, and no evidence of gold or silver among the ornaments of the native people, it still seemed possible that New Zealand could be the Great South Land. So convinced of this was Tasman that he named it Staten's Land, believing it to be joined to a land of the same name that had been seen off the tip of South America. If true, this would mean he was on the western coast of a huge southern continent.

Tasman's view was accepted by many European geographers for more than a century. In fact, each 'Staten's Land' was an island, and they were separated by thousands of kilometres of the Pacific Ocean. Tasman might have discovered this but his inspection of New Zealand was cut short by the hostility of the Maori inhabitants, who killed four of his men when they ventured ashore to get fresh water. Hastening away from what he called Murderers' Bay, Tasman was still content to declare his voyage a success, proclaiming he had discovered the Great South Land. However, he brought nothing back of any value to inspire the Dutch East India Company to follow up his discovery.

Still, the west coast of New Zealand was now marked on European maps, and there was no telling how far the mysterious land extended in other directions. Cook answered part of that question when he sailed south from Tahiti and failed to find the land that was meant to be there. Heading west, Cook expected to encounter the eastern coast of the land that Tasman had discovered. The health of his men and the success of his secret mission demanded that he find Staten's Land. It would allow him to keep the dreaded scurvy at bay by restocking his ship with fresh food, water and firewood, and to determine the true nature of the land whose coastline Tasman had partially charted. Again, Cook was destined to be disappointed.

Cook was forced to abandon his assumption that New Zealand was part of a larger continent as he sailed further and further west without encountering land. Finally reaching New Zealand's east coast and making a careful circumnavigation of its two islands, he concluded that the elusive continent must be elsewhere. Further patient investigation of the remaining blank spaces on the globe would have to be made.

Cook began by heading for the uncharted east coast of Australia, where he again completed the work of his Dutch predecessors by filling in another blank part of the eighteenth century's maps. He had also claimed both places for England, going through the customary ceremonies of the time – raising the flag, firing a salute and marking a tree or building a cairn of stones – to show that he was the discoverer and England was now the supposed owner of the place. What the indigenous inhabitants thought of these curious ceremonies, performed by alien visitors who promptly decamped, was not recorded. There was little attempt by Cook to make them complicit in their possible dispossession.

After completing the charting of Australia's east coast, Cook intended to continue to the seas east of New Guinea, where the Spanish explorer Pedro Fernandez de Quiros had in 1606 chanced upon the islands of the New Hebrides, which he thought were part of the missing continent. Having disproved Tasman's assumption about New Zealand, Cook intended to test the claims of de Quiros.

His plan to pursue the Spanish chimera came to an abrupt and almost calamitous end when the *Endeavour* was run aground and badly holed on the Great Barrier Reef in June 1770. Cook only managed to stave off disaster by plugging the hole, pulling the ship off the reef at high tide and beaching it on the muddy bank of a tidal river on the nearby Australian coast. The close call, and the seven weeks it took to repair the hull, convinced Cook to abandon his plan to check the Spanish report and instead head directly home by way of the nearby Dutch port of Batavia (now Jakarta).

After nearly three years at sea, Cook arrived back in London in July 1771. The *Endeavour* was laden with thousands of strange plants, insects, birds and animals, which Banks and Solander displayed to their fellow scientists while telling tales to the king of previously unknown islands and peoples. Cook also had much to report. He had taken the *Endeavour* around the world in a masterly voyage that had seen him solve the lingering mystery of New Zealand and chart Australia's eastern coastline. He had added eastern Australia to England's growing empire, naming it New South Wales to emphasise its agricultural and pastoral possibilities. But he could see little compelling reason for England to be any more interested than Holland had been in actually buttressing its formal claim of ownership with an act of effective occupation. More importantly to Cook, these were not new discoveries. His principal discovery was a negative one: that the Great South Land did not exist in the place where cartographers had placed it for centuries. As he rather plaintively informed the Lords of the Admiralty, he had 'faild in discovering the so much talk'd of southern Continent', which he conceded 'perhaps do[es] not exist'.[4]

Despite Cook's lament, much of the South Pacific remained unexplored. England could not let the prize of discovering the Great South Land go to one of its imperial rivals, particularly the French. Unknown to Cook, the French explorer Jean-François-Marie de Surville had been exploring the coast of New Zealand at the same time as Cook in 1769, but he had drowned off the coast of Peru the following year with little to show for his voyage. And just prior to Cook's return to London, the French explorer Yves-Joseph de Kerguelen-Trémarec was sent south with instructions from King Louis XV to locate the fabled continent.

In fact, Kerguelen-Trémarec thought he had found it in February 1772, when he came across a treeless and mountainous archipelago in the southern Indian Ocean, which he mistakenly believed was of continental size. So convinced was he that he did not try to circumnavigate the desolate land mass but rushed back to report his discovery to the king. Dubbing it 'South France', he reported that it was 'the central mass of the Antarctic continent' and capable of producing 'all the crops of the Mother country'.[5] Instructed to undertake a second expedition with three ships to confirm its much-vaunted value and begin its colonisation, Kerguelen-Trémarec returned with the disappointing news that his claims were woefully wrong. The isolated islands that came to bear his name were not part of a continent and were of little value. He was promptly thrown into prison for his deceptive reports.[6]

Although successive explorers had returned to their countries disappointed, all the voyaging had vastly expanded European knowledge of the world. By a process of elimination, large areas of ocean were now known not to contain the southern continent. Cook's first voyage had left him with some doubt about whether the continent even existed. But the English Admiralty could not afford to have a French explorer prove that Cook's doubts were wrong. So another English expedition was planned.

Cook was sent back with two vessels in July 1772 to make a more intensive search in the watery wastes of the Southern Ocean. This time, he would be accompanied by the irascible Prussian-born scientist Johann Forster and his son George. If there was a continent there, Cook was determined to claim it for England. And without the well-connected and high-profile Banks, the plaudits for a discovery would be his alone. With two converted Whitby colliers, the *Resolution* and the *Adventure*, Cook would again circumnavigate the world, this time going as far south as his ships and their crews could endure, venturing further than any other explorer had dared to go before.

In November 1772, Cook sailed south from Cape Town into windswept and increasingly cold seas, looking for a land that had been seen there in 1739 by Jean-Baptiste Bouvet de Lozier, an officer of the French East India Company. Naming the land he saw as Cape Circoncision, Bouvet had assumed it was part of the Great South Land, although no one had managed to confirm his sighting in the intervening decades.

For much of November and December, as Cook and his officers vainly scanned the horizon for some sign of Cape Circoncision, the two vessels battled what one officer described as 'continual hard gales of Wind & very boisterous weather'.[7] As for the land, there was nothing to report. Nevertheless, the two ships plunged their way further and further south, with the continual light of the Antarctic summer helping to safeguard them from the moving 'islands of ice' that began to crowd the previously empty seas. When two penguins were sighted among the icebergs on 10 December, it was assumed the vessels must be close to land, but still nothing was seen.

With the ships cloaked ethereally in ice, and the coats of the sailors stiffened by the intense cold, Cook finally became the first explorer to cross into the Antarctic Circle, on 17 January 1773.[8] However, the historic effort was for nought. Instead of the hoped-for continent, Cook was confronted by an ice-covered sea that blocked any further progress and imperilled his ships. Acutely conscious of the danger, and after having reached sixty-seven degrees south, Cook ordered the vessels to turn about.[9] As for Bouvet's 'continent', he supposed the Frenchman had mistaken an extensive, snow-covered iceberg for land.

In his persistent search for Bouvet's reported land, Cook had unknowingly come within 120 kilometres of the Antarctic coastline. Although it was just over the horizon, the continent was too far away to be seen from even the highest vantage point of the *Resolution*. Had Cook turned east rather than retreating north, he and his men might have sailed sufficiently far to have seen mountains on the jutting edge of the Antarctic continent that would come to be known as Enderby Land.

Despite his disappointment at not finding Cape Circoncision, Cook remained determined to find the Great South Land in the temperate latitudes in which cartographers had long drawn it. He was mindful that searching in the high southern latitudes was only likely to find an isolated, ice-covered land that would not be of any use to England. His instructions from the Admiralty had called on him to discover and claim for the king 'that Land or Islands of Great extent' that was located 'in Latitudes convenient for Navigation, and in Climates adapted to the production of Commodities useful in Commerce'.[10] No one believed that the world's remaining continent would be almost totally confined to the polar climes.

So Cook tracked to the north before heading east again across the southern reaches of the Indian, Pacific and Atlantic Oceans, tacking north and south in a roller-coaster fashion to ensure that any continental-sized territory would come within sight of the watchers on his ships. Twice more he dipped towards the South Pole in desperate attempts to somehow spot the coast of the Great South Land. On the final dip, he sailed further south than anyone else had ever dared, reaching 71° 10' S at longitude 106° 54' W early in the morning of 30 January 1774.

Having lost contact with the *Adventure* in New Zealand, it was only the sailors of the *Resolution* who looked with trepidation on the frozen sea that stretched away to the south. Earlier, Cook had been misled into believing that he was gazing upon the snow-covered mountains of a continent, but they had turned out to be clouds on the horizon. Now there was just pack ice and locked-in icebergs, and no sign of the continent he had expected to find. Cook was finally convinced that the Great South Land, if it existed, must lie largely south of the Antarctic Circle. The Forsters thought that the missing continent might not exist even there, arguing that there was 'little reason to suppose that there actually is any land of considerable extent in the frigid zone'.[11]

Whatever the truth of the matter, the discovery of the polar continent would have been some consolation to Cook, whose extensive voyaging had seen him find few wholly new discoveries. Yet he was again repelled by its protective belt of ice, having to console himself with the much lesser prize of claiming to have sailed further south than any other navigator. The young George Forster, who was more interested in scientific discovery than geographic exploration, noted with some satisfaction that 'as it was impossible to proceed farther, we put the ship about, well satisfied with our perilous expedition, and almost persuaded that no navigator will care to come after, and much less attempt to pass beyond us'.[12]

Cook could not be so sanguine about the expedition being blocked by the impenetrable ice. Moreover, as he turned the ship about, one of his officers cheekily outdid him as the furthest man south by making his way carefully to the end of the ice-covered bowsprit, where he flourished his hat in the cold air and triumphantly declared, 'Ne plus ultra!'[13] With the ice now behind them, the sailors could look forward to some fresh food in the central Pacific, where they would spend the coming winter in more comfortable climes.

For Cook, who was suffering the agony of what was probably an intestinal blockage, it was disappointing to be defeated once again. Discovery of the Great South Land, even if it was too far south to be of much value, would have crowned his second voyage with a semblance of success. Now it seemed that he had little to show for his years at sea. Anxious not to be viewed as a failure, Cook explained in his journal that it would have been 'a very dangerous enterprise' to have attempted to find a passage through the ice. Indeed, he believed that no sane captain would ever try to do so. He tried to be satisfied with having gone 'not only farther than any man has gone before me, but as far as I think it possible for man to go'.[14]

To ward off any critics who might question his decision to abandon the search, Cook dismissed the idea of the much-vaunted continent being of any value if it was located further south. An explorer who dared to go further than he had done could have 'the honour of the discovery', wrote Cook, 'but I will be bold to say that the world will not be benefited by it'.[15] Exploiting such a continent would require ships to find their way through 'thick fogs, snow storms, intense cold, and every other thing that can render navigation dangerous'. They would then have to confront the 'unexpressable horrid aspect of the country, a country doomed by nature never once to feel the warmth of the sun rays, but to lie ever buried under everlasting snow and ice'. Any ports on such a coast would be 'wholly filled up with frozen snow of a vast thickness'. It was not cowardice that kept him from the task of discovering such a coast, argued Cook, but the futility of finding a coast that 'would have answered no end whatever'.[16]

With the *Resolution* heading back to the Pacific islands, Cook retired to his cabin to make sense of his failure to find what had never been there. Taking up his quill on 6 February 1774, he wrote that the 'assertions and conjectures' of all the authors who had suggested there was an undiscovered continent in the South Pacific had now been 'intirely [sic] refuted'. Although that was an achievement of sorts, it was not likely to see him hailed as a hero in the drawing rooms of London.

The diligent navigator spent the winter in the tropics, clearing up doubts about the positions of particular islands and noting in his journal that he had 'little expectation of making any valuable discovery'.[17] This meant an additional year at sea for the sailors, as they recovered their health and the scientists studied the natural world at a succession of Pacific islands, including a further sojourn at New Zealand. Finally, Cook sailed back across the Pacific towards Cape Horn in December 1774. He harboured one last hope.

During this voyage, he would look for lands reported by earlier explorers to exist in those parts, which might yet be found to be part of the Great South Land.[18] First, though, Cook called in at Staten Land, the small island off the south-eastern point of Tierra del Fuego, formerly believed to be part of a southern continent and which is now known as Isla de los Estados. Whales were in such great abundance in these seas, complained one officer, that their 'blowing' would 'frequently taint the whole Atmosphere about us with the most disagreeable effluvia than can be conceiv'd'.[19]

Landing ashore, they found the rocky bays and inlets were crowded with fur seals, sea lions, penguins and birds of many kinds. The larger sea lions were shot and their blubber boiled down for oil, while smaller sea lions, seals, penguins and unfledged birds were clubbed to death and taken back for a shipboard feast.[20] Midshipman John Elliott recalled how he confronted one sizeable male sea lion as it attempted to defend its clutch of females; Elliott walked 'coolly up to him, firing my Musquet into his chest at 2 or 3 yards distance as he advanced, and then driving my Baynet into his Mouth'. Elliott then went with his companions amongst the female sea lions, 'some shooting them, some knocking them on the head with Clubs – others shooting birds of different kinds, some knocking down Penguins', which he likened to 'a regiment of little soldiers'.[21]

The reports of the rich marine life would later draw sealers in their hundreds to reap an easy harvest of the lolling animals. For the present, Cook was interested in the wildlife only as meat for his crew and specimens for his scientists. His primary concern remained the sightings of a possible southern continent. If any of the old reports proved accurate, this was where real wealth was likely to be found.

One such place, to the east of Cape Horn, had been seen in 1756 by a Spanish captain, and reported as being 'a Continent of land . . . full of sharp and craggy mountains'. When the *Resolution* reached the location of this supposed continent on 14 January 1775, Cook finally believed that he had found the object of his arduous voyaging. Misled by the 'vast height of its Mountains', Cook thought it must be part of a large land mass. As befitting a discovery of continental extent, he named it Georgia in honour of his king, before carefully charting its coastline and bestowing English names on its more prominent features.[22]

There did not seem much to recommend this place as an outpost of empire. It was bereft of inhabitants, bare of trees, beset with glaciers and rocky heights, and covered by ice and snow. It was hardly the temperate and productive Great South Land that Cook had set out to find. Nevertheless, on 17 January, after encountering a suitable bay, Cook rowed off with Johann and George Forster to investigate the new land.

Perhaps because of a glacier that was splitting off great chunks of ice, or because of the difficulty of finding a secure anchorage in the deep waters of the windswept bay, Cook decided to leave the *Resolution* in the open sea. He also decided not to explore the hinterland, as 'it did not seem probable that any one would ever be benefited by the discovery'. In his journal, he described the landscape as being 'savage and horrible: the Wild rocks raised their lofty summits till they were lost in the Clouds and the Vallies laid buried in everlasting Snow'. But there were more fur seals and elephant seals to be killed, along with penguins, ducks and other birds.[23]

Despite his disdain for the place, Cook believed that he had finally achieved the purpose of his voyage. He later reported to the Admiralty his initial excitement at having 'discovered a Coast which . . . we judged to belong to a great Continent'.[24] Accordingly, with the summer temperature barely above freezing, he proceeded to take formal possession of what one officer described as 'this new Country (Southern Continent I hope)'.[25]

In his account of their time ashore, Johann Forster was more interested in the great variety of undisturbed wildlife; he described the claiming ceremony in the most cursory way: 'The Capt took a view of the harbour & then took *Possession in his Britannick Majesties Name & His Heirs for ever*: hoisted a Flag on the Land, & fired 3 Volleys, and then returned on board.' The young George Forster thought that the three volleys invested the ceremony with 'greater weight', although he went on to describe with a degree of derision how the 'barren rocks re-echoed with the sound, to the utter amazement of seals and pinguins, the inhabitants of these newly discovered dominions'.[26]

Cook's description of the ceremony was also rather abrupt. He omitted the details of the proclamation that he apparently read out to take possession. Cook reported only that he 'landed in three different places, displayed our Colours and took possession of the Country in his Majestys name under a descharge of small Arms'.[27] Back on board the *Resolution*, Cook then continued to chart the coastline, naming the bay he had just left as Possession Bay – making it one more in a long line of places around the world that he had so named.

Cook's excitement then turned to disappointment. After he had sailed little more than 160 kilometres along the northern coastline, he rounded a point to find that the coast suddenly turned northwest, towards the point at which he had begun. It was now clear to him that the 'continent' was actually an island of limited extent, about 190 kilometres long and thirty-two kilometres wide.

Naming the point Cape Disappointment, and renaming Georgia as the Isle of Georgia, later to be South Georgia, it was obvious to Cook that 'this land which we had taken to be part of a great Continent was no more than an Island of 70 leagues in Circuit'. His scattering of distinguished royal and political names along the forbidding coastline now looked almost insulting.

Cook's disappointment was shared by his officers, one of whom wrote how he had been deceived into believing that 'we had got hold of the Southern Continent', only to find that 'these pleasing dreams are reduc'd to a small Isle, and that a very poor one too'. Indeed, it was as wretched a place as they had ever seen, bleaker and more barren even than Tierra del Fuego. Ironically, this was some consolation to Cook and greatly moderated his disappointment, since a continent of such dreary desolation 'would not be worth the discovery'.[28] In fact, the island had been discovered nineteen years earlier by a Spanish merchant ship, whose captain had named it San Pedro.[29]

With his three-year cruise of the Southern Ocean almost over, Cook still believed that he might make a significant discovery of land. He had earlier dismissed Bouvet's sighting of a snow-covered land south of Africa as having been an iceberg, believing that a land in that latitude could not be snow-covered in summer. However, his experience with the snow-covered Isle of Georgia now suggested that the Frenchman might have been correct. Cook decided to make a second attempt to find out, despite being tired of 'high Southern Latitudes where nothing was to be found but ice and thick fogs'.

He steered the *Resolution* on a south-easterly course that would edge the ship back towards the Antarctic Circle, confident that this last part of the circumnavigation would finally see him successful. Indeed, he feared that he would 'find more land than I should have time to explore'.[30] On 31 January 1775, just eleven days after leaving the Isle of Georgia, Cook's prediction seemed to have been vindicated.

As the *Resolution* probed its way through the fog-bound and ice-strewn sea, the conditions cleared sufficiently for Cook to see land just five or six kilometres ahead. Again, he thought that he might have stumbled across part of the Great South Land, but the fog and ice made it difficult to confirm. After seeing a high mountain, Cook warily kept his distance from the inhospitable coast, against which huge icebergs had run aground.

He sailed south for a time before turning north and cautiously heading along what he imagined to be a continuous coastline studded with snow-covered mountains. Not realising that he was looking at a line of islands, he named them capes and gave the southern-most one the name Southern Thule, because, at nearly sixty degrees south, it was 'the most southern land' yet discovered.[31] Instead of charting the coast and discovering whether it was part of a contin-ent, as he had done at the Isle of Georgia, Cook kept his distance from the frequently obscured coastline. He was not willing to risk his voyage to chase after what might be one more chimera.

Instead of heading south to chart what he surmised was the promontory of a continent extending from the South Pole, Cook turned his ship about and headed north to chart its furthest extent in that direction. After all, the British government wanted him to locate a temperate continent, not a frozen wasteland. That would also allow him to sail back in the general direction of Bouvet's Cape Circoncision, and then on to the comforts of Cape Town and home to England.

After sailing north until the land had disappeared, Cook remained unsure whether he had found 'a group of Islands or else a point of the Continent'. Assuming it was part of a continent, although not the temperate continent that his masters wanted him to find, Cook named it Sandwich Land, in honour of his political patron, the First Lord of the Admiralty, Lord Sandwich. The name would also create a sense of English possession.

Cook had made no attempt, as he had done at the Isle of Georgia, to row ashore to claim ownership of the land. In Cook's view, the place would not be an asset to the empire and was not worth the risk that making a formal claim would carry. As one of his officers observed, 'the shores were form'd of high rocky precipices and the Bays chok'd up with Ice . . . so that getting a foot ashore was wholly impracticable'.[32]

Future explorers would find that Sandwich Land was actually several islands separated by kilometres of sea, yet Cook's error was understandable. With visibility being poor, and with two of the islands having mountains several thousand feet high, Cook mistakenly thought the sea-ice connecting them was snow-covered land. As a result, he believed that he could be looking at 'a point of the Continent' that stretched all the way towards the South Pole, which he now correctly surmised was 'the Source of most of the ice which is spread over this vast Southern Ocean'.[33]

Until now, Cook had assiduously followed his instructions to find the temperate Great South Land. Every likely prospect had been pursued until he was satisfied that it was not part of that missing continent. But he could only push himself and his men so far. With Cape Town beckoning and his supplies running low, and the disappointment of South Georgia fresh in his memory, he was not prepared to spend any further time on his historic quest. The happiness of the crew at this decision was shown in a song, which rejoiced that:

> We are out of the cold my brave Boys do not fear
> For the Cape of good Hope with good hearts we do steer
> Thank God we have ranged the Globe all around
> And we have likewise the south Continent found
> But it being too late in the year as they say
> We could stay there no longer the land to survey[34]

Anxious that he not be censured for failing to follow this last lead to its conclusion, Cook argued that most of the continent 'must lay within the Polar Circle where the Sea is so pestered with ice, that the land is thereby inaccessible'. Predicting that 'no man will ever venture farther than I have done and that the lands which may lie to the South will never be explored', Cook pointed out that it would have been rash 'to have risked all which had been done in the Voyage, in finding out and exploring a Coast which when done would have answered no end whatever'.[35]

Cook was glad to be gone from the snow-swept and fog-bound seas of Sandwich Land, describing it as 'the most horrible Coast in the World', while one of his officers wrote that it was 'as wretched a Country as Nature can possibly form'.[36] Cook took the *Resolution* towards Cape Town, but he hoped first to sight the location where Bouvet had reported land. Again failing to find the mysterious 'Cape Circoncision', Cook concluded once more that it must have been an iceberg. In fact, Bouvet had given the wrong location for what was later found to be a small volcanic island, now known as Bouvet Island. There was nothing left for Cook to do but proceed to Cape Town to prepare his ship and crew for the final leg of their long voyage home to England.

Cook reflected on the achievements of his voyage. He could take some comfort from having circumnavigated the South Pole, and from having crossed the Southern Ocean 'in such a manner as to leave not the least room for the Possibility of there being a continent, unless near the Pole and out of the reach of Navigation'. His voyage, as he saw it, had put 'a final end . . . to the searching after a Southern Continent, which has at times ingrossed the attention of some of the Maritime Powers for near two Centuries past and the Geographers of all ages'.[37]

Still, it was not the positive achievement that he had hoped for, or that the Admiralty had expected when it sent him off. Writing to the Admiralty's secretary, Cook explained that his failure to find the continent was 'because it does not exist in a Navigable Sea and not for want of looking after'. Anyway, continued Cook, he had done more than look for the elusive continent. He had done everything that could be done 'to finish the exploring [of] the Southern Hemisphere'.[38] That would have to be his lasting achievement.

In Cape Town, Cook heard news of other navigators, both French and Spanish, who had made minor discoveries of islands that Cook had missed. In the gentlemanly culture of the time, explorers readily acknowledged the discoveries of those who had reached particular places first. However, they still wanted to be first into print with the results of their particular voyage. So it was with Cook, who was prompted by the news of his rivals to quickly compile a comprehensive map of the latest discoveries for European audiences, so that his work would be published before those of the French and Spanish. He would also write a popular account of the voyage so that the world would not be in any doubt about his achievements. Cook was still smarting from his earlier voyage, when Joseph Banks had reaped most of the public plaudits.

Cook's hopes were realised when his *A Voyage Towards the South Pole and Round the World* was published to great acclaim in May 1777. The richly illustrated volume captivated the public's attention, with its spectacular etchings of the *Resolution* being dwarfed by icebergs, and its maps showing the southerly extent of the voyage. He had circled the South Pole and lain to rest the widespread belief in the existence of a continent extending into the temperate latitudes.

If there was a continent still to be discovered, Cook surmised, it must be much further south, possibly part of the briefly sighted

Sandwich Land. From his observations of icebergs, which caused him to suggest that they came from land rather than being formed at sea, Cook had deduced that the existence of a sizeable Antarctic land mass was likely. But he had not been able to confirm its discovery.

Cook was convinced that it was impossible to take a ship safely that far south, and that any continent situated there would not be worth claiming. Although he had formally laid claim to the Isle of Georgia, thinking it was part of a continent, he had not been greatly disappointed when he found that the forbidding place was only an island. An ice-bound continent could never be an asset to England, he argued. Time would prove him wrong, and it would not take long to do so.

CHAPTER 2

'I think this Southern land to be a Continent'

1780–1820

The savage killing and dismemberment of Captain Cook on a Hawaiian beach in 1779 helped make him a cult figure among the educated classes of Europe. In paintings and popular accounts published from London to Moscow, he was celebrated as an exemplar of Enlightenment, selflessly searching for answers to the mysteries of the world. In England, he was also celebrated as a flag-bearer of the empire, adding to its territories and enhancing its prestige. Both guises brought him widespread acclaim, albeit posthumously.

One of Cook's distant admirers was the Russian naval officer Captain Gottlieb von Bellingshausen, who would repeat Cook's voyage to the most southerly reaches of the Earth and achieve success where Cook had failed – by actually sailing his ship within sight of the Antarctic continent. Strangely, the feats of this Russian navigator have remained largely unknown to the wider world.

Cook's voyage to the south had revealed a vast expanse of storm-tossed ocean, beset with massive icebergs and blocked by impenetrable pack ice. If there was a continent beyond the ice, Cook was convinced that it would be a frozen wasteland of no value to any European empire. But there was one European empire that was not deterred by the cold, and which had found wealth aplenty in similar latitudes of the far north.

Russia's reach stretched eastwards from Europe to the frozen tundra of Siberia, and across the Bering Sea to the Aleutian Islands and Alaska. There was money to be made in those far-off places, with Russian traders enslaving the local Aleut people to hunt for sea otters and fur seals, the skins of which were shipped for sale to the merchants of China. By 1812, the rich crescent of Russia's Pacific empire extended from the Kamchatka Peninsula to northern California. With Russia's imperial standing boosted by its victory that same year over Napoleon, Tsar Alexander I sought to boost the Russian presence in the Pacific Ocean, in the face of competition from the British, French and Spanish empires, as well as the expanding American republic.

In 1819, the Russian emperor dispatched two expeditions to follow in the wake of Cook's second and third voyages. One was sent to explore the northern Pacific Ocean and the other to explore the high southern latitudes that had been the focus of Cook's second voyage. The tsar wanted the southern expedition to surpass Cook in both daring and discovery, and to bring even greater glory to Russia than Cook had brought to England. The forty-year-old commander of the southern expedition was Bellingshausen, who was instructed to 'approach as closely as possible to the South Pole, searching for as yet unknown land, and only abandoning the undertaking in the face of insurmountable obstacles'.[1] The Russians would find that they were not alone in the Antarctic seas.

The publication of Cook's journals had alerted the world to the rich marine life that was there for the taking, with American, British and Argentinian sealers being quick to respond to the news. Both fur seals and elephant seals were easy for an enterprising mariner to harvest en masse from the rocky shores of the islands off the southern tip of South America. Fur seal skins had a ready market in China, while oil from elephant seals was in great demand in Europe, both as fuel for lamps and as lubrication for the machinery of the dawning industrial age.

Cook's journals and the subsequent English decision to establish a penal colony in New South Wales also alerted rival European empires to the scope of Britain's territorial ambitions in the Pacific. As independence movements brought turmoil to Spanish-controlled South America, with Argentina declaring independence in 1816 and Chile in 1818, Britain was keen to fill the power vacuum left by Spain and take control of the vital Magellan Strait, which linked the Pacific and Atlantic Oceans.

The Magellan Strait also figured in the Russians' calculations. In 1803, the tsar had dispatched an expedition of two ships to the North Pacific by way of South America. Rather than supplying Russia's Pacific trading posts by the tortuous land route from Moscow, Alexander I wanted to discover more economical ways of doing so by sea. This made knowledge of the Magellan Strait an important asset to the Russian Empire.

Bellingshausen had been an officer on that earlier voyage, which was the first Russian expedition to circumnavigate the world from east to west. Along the way, the vessels called at Hawaii to replenish their stores and explore the possibility of bringing those strategically placed islands within the ambit of Russia's growing Pacific empire. While there, the officers visited the site of Cook's murder and souvenired some of the retaliatory English bullets from beachside tree trunks. The experience helped to reinforce the heroic image of the English navigator in the mind of the Russians. Now, sixteen years later, Bellingshausen was attempting to outdo Cook's achievements by taking his two well-equipped ships, the *Vostok* and the *Mirny*, further south than even Cook had dared to go.

While the northern expedition reinforced Russia's claim to its territories in the North Pacific, Bellingshausen's southern expedition was more in the nature of a reconnaissance. It would assert Russia's growing naval presence, ascertain the power of its rivals in the Pacific and try to establish secure sea routes for Russian commerce. Perhaps the tsar hoped that the spreading Russian empire might one day control both poles. That would mean locating the land mass that Cook had suggested was still to the south of his furthest voyaging.

In the event that this land was inhabited, the Russian government had struck special medals for Bellingshausen to distribute to the inhabitants of 'any islands or shores' that he might discover, just as Cook had done during his second voyage to the Pacific. One side of the Russian medal bore an image of Alexander I, while the other bore an inscription recording the names of the ships and the date of their departure.[2] The silver and bronze medals were meant to be valued by their native recipients, making it likely that they would be displayed to subsequent explorers. Such explorers would then see that the Russians had preceded them, and consequently had a stronger claim to possession of that particular place, although Bellingshausen had no specific instructions to perform the sort of ritual claiming ceremonies that Cook had done during his voyages.

These expeditions were also designed to embellish the growing prestige of Russia's burgeoning empire. Bellingshausen was instructed to compile a journal that might later be published for the edification of the wider world, detailing everything that was 'new, useful or interesting, not only with regard to navigation, but as being of general service in the spread of human knowledge in all parts'.[3] Two German naturalists were recruited to assist him, but they apparently had second thoughts about spending two years on such a dangerous voyage and failed to meet Bellingshausen when his ships arrived at Copenhagen to collect them. Disappointed that his 'hopes of making discoveries in the field of natural history were dashed to the ground', he went on to London, where he purchased books, charts and scientific equipment and attempted in vain to recruit a British naturalist.[4]

Science was a vitally important aspect of the expedition. Plant and animal specimens could prove commercially valuable to the Russian Empire, as the spices of the East Indies had been to the Dutch and the sea otters of the North Pacific had been to the Russians and the British. As well, rock samples could provide evidence of valuable minerals, such as copper, gold or silver. Strange specimens from distant lands were also important for their own sake. Men and women of the Enlightenment valued such specimens for their private collections, or gazed with wonder at them in the display cabinets of grand public museums. They also purchased the richly illustrated editions of expedition journals, and the ornithological and other books that sought to bring order to the natural world. Adding to the sum of human knowledge was regarded as important for its own sake, and for the prestige of empires. It was necessary for nations with territorial ambitions to be able to show that they had greater knowledge of the desired territory than their rivals. To achieve this without his two naturalists, Bellingshausen would have to rely on his own observations, supplemented by the work of his expedition artist and astronomer.

Without naturalists, Bellingshausen knew he would struggle to exceed the public success of Cook, whose widely read journals had been supplemented by the scientific publications of Banks, Forster and others. Ensconced in his cabin aboard the *Vostok*, Bellingshausen would have been concerned about how he could now fulfil his tsar's expectations. He planned to follow the path of Cook's second voyage, then to attempt to venture even further south. The reputation of his expedition would have to rest on the perspicacity of his journal, the accuracy of his charts and the value of any discoveries he might make. Yet he could not have hoped to make any great discoveries in seas Cook had already explored so exhaustively.

Moreover, what would be the use of any discovery in such remote latitudes? The most that could be hoped for was to find lands similar to those of Russia's newly claimed territories of the North Pacific, with their valuable resources of sea otters and fur seals, or a port that could serve as a southern trading post and way-station for ships plying the route between Russia and the North Pacific.

Bellingshausen took his two ships to Rio de Janeiro before heading south, firstly to the island of South Georgia, where he encountered two British sealing ships. The Russian noted how the seal colonies of Cook's time had already been decimated by the depredations of the sealers. Despite the British presence and Cook's prior claim, Bellingshausen charted the island's southern coast, which Cook had neglected. Bellingshausen now 'sprinkled [it] plentifully with Russian names'.[5] Then he sailed east to clarify the position and extent of Cook's Sandwich Land, which the Englishman had thought could be part of a continent stretching all the way to the South Pole. By taking the time to chart its coasts more closely, Bellingshausen proved instead that it was just a lonely group of islands. Any lingering belief that the temperate Great South Land might still exist was extinguished. If there was a southern continent, it must lie much further south.

Heading south to search for it, the Russian ships crossed the Antarctic Circle on 27 January 1820, becoming only the second expedition to have done so. The following day, Bellingshausen reported that he could see a 'solid stretch of ice running from east through south to west'.[6] Although it was probably an ice shelf attached to Antarctica, and although he was only about thirty kilometres away from it, some twentieth-century historians concluded that Bellingshausen was unaware that he was within sight of the continent, supposedly because of the poor visibility caused by the thickly falling snow. As a result of these assumptions, Bellingshausen was long denied the honour of having been the first explorer to see any part of the Antarctic coastline. Due to the poor editing of his journals, and to later errors made during its English translation, it had been easy for historians to make this error. It was only after a re-examination of the original journals and the publication of additional documentary evidence in the 1950s that it became clear that Bellingshausen and his officers were aware of land which they took to be a continent.

One piece of evidence was a letter that Bellingshausen wrote on 8 April 1820 to the Russian minister for the navy, in which the explorer described his experiences of 28 January. He reported how he had reached latitude 69° 25' S and longitude 2° 10' W, from where he could see 'continuous ice, at whose edge were pieces piled one upon another, and with ice mountains seen at different places in a southerly direction'. Further proof came from the captain of the *Mirny*, the experienced explorer Mikhail Lazarev, who had climbed the mast of his ship to view the awesome sight. Upon his return to Russia, he wrote of how they had 'encountered an ice shore of extreme height, and that evening, which was very fine, as we watched from the cross-trees, it stretched before us as far as the eye could see'.

Expecting that the South Pole was ocean rather than land, the expedition continued eastward, trying repeatedly to find a way south past the ice barrier. However, as Lazarev later reported, 'we kept encountering the ice continent each time we approached 70°'.[7] On one such encounter in mid-February, Bellingshausen described how the sea ice was attached to 'cliff-like, firmly standing ice', the edges of which were 'perpendicular and formed bays', while the surface of the ice 'rose in a slope towards the south, over a distance whose limits we could not see'.[8]

Although the later destruction of his logbooks during the Russian Revolution made absolute confirmation impossible, it is clear that Bellingshausen and his colleagues saw the coast of Antarctica on 28 January 1820, and that they believed they were looking upon a continent of indeterminate extent. They were the first to have done so. But it was only by a matter of days.

At the time of Bellingshausen's voyage, there were also British and American vessels in the seas south of Chile and Argentina. On 19 February 1819, William Smith, captain of the British ship *Williams*, was on his way from Montevideo to Valparaíso, in Chile, when he chanced upon previously unknown land about 450 nautical miles south of Cape Horn. Smith had earlier worked in the Greenland whale fishery and could distinguish between pack ice, icebergs and ice-covered land. When he reported his finding to Captain William Shirreff, the British naval commander in Valparaíso, he was met with disbelief. Shirreff considered that Smith had most probably seen ice rather than land.

Undaunted, Smith retraced the voyage in May 1819, but was prevented by wild weather from reaching that far south. When he continued on to Montevideo and Buenos Aires, the stories of his discovery circulated among American whalers and sealers in those ports. According to Smith's later account, they offered him 'large

Sums of Money' to reveal the location of his discovery. Refusing to do so, supposedly for 'the Good of his Country', Smith sailed his vessel back towards Valparaíso, determined this time to confirm the existence of the land. Blessed with better weather, he was able not only to locate it but also to sail along its coastline for a considerable distance before sending his first mate ashore. The landing party 'planted a board with the Union-jack, and appropriate inscription, with three cheers, taking possession in the name of the King of Great Britain'.[9]

Smith had found what is now known as the South Shetland Islands. Not realising that it was a line of islands, he initially called his discovery New South Britain, thereby suggesting that it was greater in extent than New South Wales and might therefore be part of the southern continent that Cook had been unable to find. This time, Smith was believed when he arrived in Valparaíso on 24 November 1819 and reported his find to Shirreff.

Having confirmed the existence of land and numerous offshore islands, Smith also reported that there were 'seals in abundance', which made the territory a valuable acquisition for the British Empire. Accordingly, he was commissioned by the Royal Navy to return there with a British naval officer, Edward Bransfield, who took command of the *Williams*. With Smith showing him the way, Bransfield charted the coastline of 'New South Britain' and formally claimed the place for the British Empire.

News of Smith's find appeared in British newspapers and journals, with an account by a British engineer in Chile, John Miers, reporting that Smith had 'observed [a] great abundance of whales and seals', with sperm whales being 'in greater abundance than he imagines has ever been elsewhere known'. Miers also claimed that Smith had seen sea otters in abundance. In fact, no such animals exist there. Smith was also supposed to have seen trees like the 'Norway pine', but again, there are no trees there. Yet Miers asserted that Smith described the 'whole appearance of the land, the structure and shape of the hills', as 'more like the Norwegian coast than any land he ever saw'. Miers went on to suggest that the new-found land was probably connected to Cook's Sandwich Land in the South Atlantic, with the two widely separated lands forming 'two points of one large continent'.[10]

The value of New South Britain was lauded by Miers as a possible British settlement, with a climate comparable to northern Scotland.

It could, therefore, become a safe haven from which British business interests could organise their operations in the tumultuous political environment of South America. It might also provide a base for the thirty or forty British whaling ships that operated in the Pacific, giving them some advantage over the 200 or so American whalers in the Pacific. And it could provide an entrepôt port through which British goods and capital could be channelled to the growing countries of South America, as well as to India and China. Such a settlement could combine with the British-controlled colonies at the Cape of Good Hope and New South Wales to provide 'equidistant depots in the Southern Hemisphere', which might defend and command a huge trade 'with more extensive markets than were ever offered to any commercial nation at any former period of the world'.[11]

It was a grand vision of a future that would never come. This was partly because New South Britain was not the arcadia Miers had portrayed. By the time his account was published in the *Edinburgh Philosophical Journal*, Smith and Bransfield had completed their survey and found the place to be very different to that of Miers' imagination. As later visitors would attest, there was 'not a tree, not a bush, not a shrub, not a flower, in all the islands'.[12]

Bransfield had been ordered to see whether Smith's discovery was 'merely an Island or part of a Continent', with Shirreff suggesting that the latter was 'not improbable'. If it looked like being part of continent, Bransfield was to follow the coast eastward to determine whether it was connected to Cook's Sandwich Land. He was told that 'the great and leading object' was to survey 'the Coast and Harbours'. He was also to confirm Smith's report about the 'uncommon abundance of the Sperm Whale, Otters, Seals etc', to collect samples of any animals and plants and to assess the potential of the place for supporting a colony. If it was already inhabited, he was to report on 'the Character, habits, dress, customs and state of civilization of the Inhabitants'. If he met with a foreign vessel, Bransfield was to inform its captain 'that the Country has already been taken possession of'.

To strengthen Britain's rights in that regard, Bransfield had been ordered to land at several places and take possession in the name of the king, 'planting a board with an Union Jack painted on it, and words written under to the above purpose'. If his survey took more than six months, he was instructed not to return to Valparaíso but to go straight to London and report the results of his survey to the Admiralty. At any ports en route, he was counselled 'to conceal every discovery that you have made during your Voyages'.[13] Nobody could be allowed to learn of these discoveries and exploit their resources, or make a rival claim for their ownership.

In fact, stories of Smith's discovery had already reached as far as Washington. The American secretary of state, John Quincy Adams, was informed by letter from his representative in Valparaíso, Jeremy Robinson, of Smith's discovery and of Bransfield's expedition. Robinson urged Adams to send a US Navy ship to do its own exploration of the islands – and, presumably, to claim them for the United States.

As more details of the discovery became available, further pressure was applied to the American government to protect its sealers. The New York merchant and ship-owner James Byers informed Washington in August 1820 of the 'great numbers of Seal and much Sea Elephant Oil' taken by the British on South Georgia, and of how Americans had been prevented from sealing there because of the British claim of ownership. Byers was anxious that the same should not happen at this new land, and he planned to establish an American claim to the place by sending building materials with his sealing ships so that a permanent American settlement could be established. Byers argued that only actual occupancy would give the United States a legal claim to the place. But an American naval vessel would also be needed, to ensure that the British Navy or British sealers could not easily expel the Americans by force of arms. Appealing for such a vessel to be sent, Byers declared that 'it would afford great satisfaction to every American if our Government was the first to survey and name the new World'.[14] Of course, the British were already doing just that.

Adams was sympathetic to Byers' appeal, advising him to confer with the secretary for the navy about the possibility of establishing an American settlement and of 'sending a Frigate *to take possession*'. Adams told President James Monroe of the correspondence from Robinson and Byers, noting that the intended settlement was simply 'a very good expedient for protecting the real objects, to catch Seals and Whales'. With American and British sealers racing to be first to arrive for the coming summer season of killing, there was no time to lose. Monroe agreed that it was important for the United States 'to aim at the occupancy' of this new land 'of great extent'.[15] However, the small US Navy had no suitable ship to send, and so the settlement never eventuated. For the time being, America's territorial ambition exceeded its naval reach. Washington could only watch from afar as Britain cemented its hold on the apparent continent.

Meanwhile, Smith had no trouble directing Bransfield to New South Britain, arriving off its northern coast on 16 January 1820, just as Bellingshausen was charting the Sandwich Islands far to the east. While the Russian was proving that Cook's Sandwich Land was actually a group of islands and not part of a southern continent, Bransfield and Smith were trying to determine the nature of New South Britain.

Sailing north-east along the northern coasts of the island chain until no more land could be seen, Bransfield carefully charted the coast as best he could, in the face of frequent fogs and often contrary winds and currents. Rounding the land's easterly point, still unsure whether he had been sailing along a continental shore, he came across an extensive bay on 22 January. He was able to land on a narrow shingle beach that was edged by high cliffs. Hoping to collect fresh water, the naval surgeon on board described, in an article for the *Edinburgh Philosophical Journal*, how the explorers had to force their way through a tumultuous mass of penguins defending their young, along with albatrosses, gulls and other birds, and seals and sea lions.

A junior officer, Charles Poynter, noted how the 'penguins disputed our landing' and wrote that 'it was not until great slaughter was made, and a lane cut through them, that we could proceed'. Like many visitors to the Antarctic, and perhaps subconsciously emulating the imperial conquistadors who had dispossessed native peoples, Poynter invested the penguins with human qualities, calling them 'amphibious Islanders' and describing how the men had to fight their way 'thro' the Islanders' to get at some seals they wanted to kill.

Going some way inland, they found neither animals nor people, and the vegetation was restricted to patches of stunted grass and moss. But it was the pullulating life on the rocky shore that made the place a valuable acquisition. Poynter reported how they came upon many elephant seals. Even when disturbed, noted Poynter, 'they eyed us with the utmost indifference, but when we attacked them with our lances, &c., they betrayed their astonishment in a stifled bellow'. Twenty-one were killed in less than half an hour, along with some seals and penguins.[16] The rich killing gave the voyage purpose and profit.

Following his instructions, Bransfield claimed the place for the king, 'with due ceremony', formally naming it New South Britain and the landing point as George's Bay. Of course, Smith had already done so the previous year in his private capacity. Bransfield was still unsure whether he was taking possession of an island or a larger landmass, as the fogs and partly ice-covered straits between the islands gave the impression of a continuous land mass. Watching through a telescope on board the *Williams*, an officer saw Bransfield raise a board with the Union Jack painted upon it. The ship responded by hoisting its 'ensign and pendant', firing a gun to salute the occasion. Although no official journal of the voyage has survived, an eyewitness account by Poynter reported that Bransfield also 'buried a bottle, containing several coins of the realm, given by different people for that purpose'. Then the sailors were given glasses of grog, with which they toasted the health of King George.

Cook had performed these same rituals on several occasions during his voyages of exploration in the Pacific. Just as Cook and others had done, prominent geographical features were now given names by Bransfield, both to facilitate the navigation of ships coming after him and as a way of making the ownership of those places more securely British.[17] Although Bransfield imagined at the time that he might be laying claim to a continent, the ceremony was actually performed on an island, which was later named King George Island.

Antarctica had still not been sighted by the watchers on the *Williams*. For the next week, the ship sailed in a south-westerly direction, with New South Britain appearing intermittently through the mist to the north. They did not know it at the time, but they were sailing along a strait that separated the line of South Shetland Islands from the Antarctic Peninsula. It was not until 30 January 1820, seeing no more land to his north, that Bransfield turned the ship south, heading away from the South Shetland Islands through waters crowded with 'a multitude of whales'. It was then that Bransfield saw a mountainous land mass appear before him.

Like Bellingshausen, who was then skirting the Antarctic coast thousands of kilometres to the east, Bransfield now had no doubt that he was in sight of previously unseen land. Poynter described the moment that afternoon when, 'after having their attention attracted by three immense icebergs, the haze clearing, they very unexpectedly saw land to the S.W.'. Being caught in unfamiliar seas, with uncharted coasts and rocky shoals and icebergs all around, was an awkward position for a sailing ship to be in. 'The only cheer the sight afforded,' wrote Poynter, 'was in the idea that this might be the long-sought Southern Continent.'[18] It would be more than a century before the world would know for certain that this was, in fact, part of the Antarctic continent.

Naming the section of coastline as Trinity Land, and mistakenly believing that he had come to the end of a closed-off sound rather than being in an open strait, Bransfield decided to head back in a north-easterly direction, carefully charting the ice-encrusted coast as far it could be followed. He made no attempt to make a landing, thereby unwittingly passing up the historic opportunity of being the first person to step onto the Antarctic continent. He also eschewed the chance to erect a board displaying the Union Jack, which would have claimed at least that part of the continent for the British Empire.

His caution was understandable. After all, Trinity Land could have been just another island, and the often foggy conditions, swirling currents, huge icebergs and half-hidden shoals made close investigation a perilous undertaking. As Poynter explained, 'sheet-ice abounded a-head, and not fewer than 31 icebergs were counted at once. The weather was very stormy, and the fatigue of officers and men excessive.'[19] Instead of attempting a landing or charting the full extent of the coastline, Bransfield decided to answer the larger question of whether there was a connection between Smith's 'New South Britain' and Cook's 'Sandwich Land'. This had, after all, been his principal instruction.

Heading north-east along the coastline of Trinity Land, Bransfield charted it as best he could to its conclusion, until sea ice forced the ship further north. It was then that he made his second landing, this time on Clarence Island, where he performed another claiming ceremony and erected the usual board with the Union Jack. Smith was not going to be outdone by his naval companion and took the opportunity of going ashore on another small island, which he named Seal Island. It was so crowded with seals that he quickly killed more than 300, all the while desperately trying to keep marauding gulls from spoiling their valuable furs. In the end, Smith only managed to get ninety of the skins away in his small boat, while the rest of the valuable carcasses were left to the depredations of the birds or to be sucked away by the tide.

Bransfield then took the *Williams* eastward, before turning south and sailing as far as he could go, still trying to determine whether this new-found land was connected to Cook's Sandwich Land. The vessel was eventually stopped by a mess of icebergs and pack ice, which blocked the way southward. With the summer over, it was becoming too dangerous to linger so far south. Although he had been authorised to sail all the way to Britain to report his findings, Bransfield headed back to Valparaíso, via the northern edge of New South Britain. An attempt was made to perform a third claiming ceremony, but the rocky and wave-dashed coastline made it too dangerous to attempt a landing. So Bransfield headed home, confident of the importance of his discoveries. His naval surgeon noted their great value 'to the commercial interests of our country'.[20] And they had the seal skins to prove it.

But the British were not alone. The American sealer Captain James Sheffield and his first mate, Nathaniel Palmer, also had some 9000 skins from the South Shetlands, which they had collected in just fifteen days. The haul emphasised the fortune that could be made from these new sealing grounds. After hearing stories of Smith's discovery, Sheffield had rushed there from the United States in the newly built *Hersilia*, owned by Edmund Fanning, a wealthy sealer, merchant and explorer who was based in the Connecticut port of Stonington.

Fanning had made a small fortune by trading skins in China for tea and other goods, which he brought back for sale in New York. As early as 1797, Fanning had been sealing off the tip of South America. In 1812, after the seals on the known islands had been exterminated, he had convinced President James Madison to send him on an expedition in search of new islands. Although that expedition had been cancelled when the war with Britain erupted, Fanning had remained convinced that there were lucrative discoveries to be made south of Cape Horn.

Sheffield's haul of skins proved him right. It also sparked a call for the United States to challenge Britain's claim to the islands, with several American newspapers arguing that American sealers had been secretly visiting them in the years before Smith and Bransfield had arrived to 'discover' and claim them.[21] No documentary evidence has ever been produced to confirm such visits.

With reports reaching New York that there were hundreds of thousands of seals waiting to be plundered, James Byers went ahead with his plan to send a fleet of three ships to secure the seals for himself and his partners. Promising to have his American ships there by October 1820, Byers again petitioned the United States government to send a naval vessel to support the sealers and help establish an American claim to the islands. With Byers warning that there was 'not the least doubt . . . the British will attempt to Drive our Vessels from the Islands', and with the American sealing vessels being 'armed for their own defence', there was every possibility of a serious conflict developing. Secretary of State Adams was alive to the threat, again urging the secretary for the navy to send an armed vessel 'to protect the Sealing and Whaling Settlement on the Newly discovered land south of Cape Horn'. Yet the navy remained opposed to sending a ship to such unexplored and dangerous coasts, and was concerned that a tussle for the islands would lead to 'a collision with the British', with the American navy being in no position to fight a war in Antarctic seas.[22]

The British were certainly on guard against rival claims being made to the islands. When Bransfield and Smith returned to Valparaíso on 14 April 1820, they handed their charts, journals and logbooks to the newly arrived British naval officer there, Captain Thomas Searle, who, in a forlorn attempt to keep news of the discovery secret and to prevent a possible rival claim being made by the newly independent Chileans, forbade the sailors from coming ashore. Searle also changed the name of their discovery from New South Britain to New South Shetland, apparently to prevent 'confusion to other places'.

With his public service now over, Smith was eager to pursue his private profit and promptly took his ship back to New South Shetland, this time 'for the purpose of fishing for Whales and Seals'. However, no sooner had he arrived than he was joined by up to twenty British ships, and even more American ones that were responding to Sheffield's report of countless seals. All were intent on reaping a bloody harvest of the marine life. Smith later reported to the Admiralty on the 'great difficulty' that he had in keeping peace 'between the Crews of the two Nations, who were on shore' laying waste to the previously undisturbed wildlife.[23]

More were set to arrive, as news of the rich harvest spread across the world, from Valparaíso to Buenos Aires, New York and

London, and west across the Pacific to the sealers and whalers of the British convict colony of Port Jackson (now Sydney). By October 1821, maps and charts of New South Shetland were reported to be 'selling in all the principal shops in London', while a British journal was reporting excitedly on the discoveries of Smith and Bransfield, predicting that 'a very lucrative trade in seals may be carried on, as the sea absolutely swarms with these creatures, of great size, full of oil, and with the finest furs'.[24] By the time of this publication, an armada of sealers had already descended on the islands and flensed many of the hapless fur seals of their skins and boiled down the blubber of the elephant seals.

Oblivious to the activities of Bransfield and Smith and the crescendo of killing on the rocky beaches, Bellingshausen continued his daring circumnavigation, venturing much further south than Cook had done. After surviving furious gales that almost swamped his ships, and with winter darkening the days and extending the pack ice, Bellingshausen finally quit these dangerous climes in mid-March 1820 and headed for Port Jackson. The colony had grown in wealth and significance since its establishment in 1788, with a brisk export trade based on sealing and bay whaling now giving way to one based on wool, as the interior was gradually opened up. Bellingshausen spent a month there, repairing his ships and restoring the health of his crews. He then took the *Vostok* and the *Mirny* on a four-month exploration of the South Pacific, reaching as far as Tahiti before returning to Port Jackson in September 1820.[25]

As he waited in Port Jackson for warmer weather to begin his onward voyage south, Bellingshausen received a letter from the Russian minister in Rio de Janeiro, who informed him of Smith's discovery of a place that the minister called 'New Shetland'. It was a report that the Russians could not ignore. The discovery was located at a strategically important point on the strait, linking the Pacific and Atlantic Oceans south of Tierra del Fuego. The name 'New Shetland' suggested to Bellingshausen that it could be part of the much looked-for southern continent.[26]

The information would have made Bellingshausen anxious to be on his way. Departing Port Jackson on 12 November, he again went further south than Cook. Although sea ice kept the Russian vessels outside the Antarctic Circle until they were well past the Ross Sea, Bellingshausen managed to cross into it briefly twice, before making a much more extended voyage within it than Cook had done.

His courage and persistence paid off. After sailing eastward for weeks, Bellingshausen suddenly caught sight through his telescope of partially snow-covered land. It was the first such land, bare of ice or snow, to be discovered within the Antarctic Circle. 'Words cannot describe the delight which appeared on all our faces,' wrote Bellingshausen, 'at the cry of "Land! Land!",' coming as it did 'after our long monotonous voyage, amidst unceasing dangers from ice, snow, rain, sleet and fog'.[27] But the hazy conditions left him uncertain of just what he had discovered. Was it the southern continent that Cook had so assiduously searched for, or just an uncharted island of little consequence?

By the following day, as the two ships ventured as close as they dared to the icy shore, it became clear that they had stumbled upon an island of considerable height rather than a continent. With the ice keeping them nearly twenty kilometres offshore, Bellingshausen abandoned his plans 'to survey the land more accurately or to take away anything of interest which we could deposit in the Museum of the Admiralty Department'. Had it been part of a continent, noted Bellingshausen, he would 'certainly have surveyed it in greater detail'. Instead, with the crews of both vessels giving three cheers, the sailors were given glasses of punch to toast the health of the tsar. Because of the encircling ice and the lack of an obvious landing place on the steep volcanic island, Bellingshausen made no attempt to send men ashore to raise the Russian flag and claim the place for the tsar. He simply named it Peter I Island, perhaps hoping that the name would suffice to make the discovery Russian.[28] Unbeknown to Bellingshausen, however, the Antarctic continent actually lay about 400 kilometres to the south, through the impenetrable sea ice.

Convinced that there must be more land nearby, Bellingshausen ordered his two ships to continue along the edge of the ice, keeping to an easterly course that was designed to take them far to the south of South America. It was dangerous work, as they picked their way carefully through the fog, past looming icebergs and shifting ice. The vision of the officers was obscured by thick snow showers, and the work of the crew aloft was made difficult by the bitterly cold wind.

Finally, on 29 January, as Bellingshausen was enjoying 'the most beautiful day' with freezing temperatures and bright sunshine, land was again sighted. This time, there was a headland that 'stretched to the northward and ended in a high mountain which was separated by an isthmus from another mountain chain extending to the south-west'. Peter I Island had only been twenty-five kilometres long but there was no telling how far this new discovery extended. Because of ice floes, Bellingshausen was unable to get closer than about sixty kilometres from the shore. Unsure of its size, but suspecting that it was 'extensive', Bellingshausen gave the land a name of great consequence. Just as Cook had named South Georgia in honour of his king, thinking it was part of the Great South Land, so Bellingshausen called this new territory 'Alexander I Land'.[29]

While bronze monuments to the tsar might disappear over time, Bellingshausen was convinced that Peter I Island and Alexander I Land would remain as 'indestructible monuments' and would 'commemorate the name of our Emperors to the remotest posterity'.[30] He presumably believed that the grand Russian names would keep those territories securely Russian for just as long, and that, because of their barren and forbidding nature, a formal claiming ceremony was not required. But merely naming a place did not bestow ownership upon the nation that did so. Further acts of possession were required before ownership would be recognised by other nations, and Russia did not follow up on the work of Bellingshausen. It would be more than a century before another Russian expedition ventured into Antarctic seas, by which time Peter I Island had been claimed by Norway. Likewise, Alexander I Land had been found to be an island. Renamed as Alexander I Island, its ownership was claimed by both Britain and Chile.

The Russians did not linger long enough to confirm the true nature of Alexander I Land. Bellingshausen was more concerned to check on Smith's discovery of New Shetland. By approaching the close-packed line of islands from the south, the Russian hoped to determine 'whether this recently discovered land belongs to the supposed Southern Continent' or whether Smith had mistaken a number of islands for a large land mass, as Cook had done with Sandwich Land.[31] Russia might be able to claim its ownership if Bellingshausen could confirm that the reported 'New Shetland' was part of an undiscovered continent.

This was the sort of discovery that the tsar wanted Bellingshausen to make. In fact, he had instructed Bellingshausen, if 'very important discoveries' were made, to 'promptly despatch one of the ships under his command to Russia to report them'.[32] The tsar was aware that being first to report such a momentous discovery would enhance the prestige of his empire and give Russia priority of possession over other claimants. But Bellingshausen was too late. Bransfield had already tried to put the ownership of the islands beyond dispute by performing several claiming ceremonies.

By approaching from the south-west, Bellingshausen confirmed what Bransfield had found the previous year. Another supposed continent had failed to live up to the expectations of its discoverer. Yet there was no sense of disappointment revealed in the journal of the phlegmatic Bellingshausen, who did not bother landing on the first two islands that he encountered. Nor did he try to claim them, except by giving them Russian names. Not knowing that the British had already done so – naming them Smith Island and Snow Island – Bellingshausen named the two islands in memory of recent military victories over Napoleon. The first was about thirty kilometres long and was named Borodino Island, while the second was about half the size and was dubbed Little Yaroslavetz.[33]

In fact, by the time of Bellingshausen's arrival, the islands already had multiple names. The reports of Smith's discovery in 1819 had inspired both an American and an Argentine sealing ship to venture south in his wake. While only a few vessels explored the sealing potential of the islands in the summer of 1819–20, the rich harvest of seal skins that they took back to their home ports had prompted many other merchants and captains to emulate them. A small party of sealers could kill and skin around 10,000 animals in a few weeks, which was sufficient to reap a sizeable fortune.

It was not surprising, then, that as Bellingshausen approached the South Shetland Islands from the south-west in late 1820, about twenty American sealing ships from various ports in New England were approaching the islands from the north-east, along with a similar number of sealing ships from England and Scotland. There was even one from Port Jackson, which had followed Bellingshausen across the Pacific. The American vessels included the Stonington sloop *Hero*, which was little more than fourteen metres long and was captained by the twenty-year-old Nathaniel Palmer, who had been first mate on another American ship during the previous summer that had collected 9000 skins. There was also the New Haven ship *Huron*, captained by John Davis, while the British ships included the Leith-based brig *Jane*, captained by James Weddell. Their names, along with those of some of their colleagues, would be forever associated with the Antarctic.[34]

Bellingshausen picked his way carefully along the island chain, avoiding icebergs and rocky shoals as he charted the coastline through the swirling mist and fog. After reaching the eastern limit of Little Yaroslavetz, he came across a narrow strait full of submerged rocks and turbulent water, which he decided not to enter. Continuing instead to the adjacent and much larger island, which had previously been named Livingston Island by the British and was now named Smolensk Island by Bellingshausen, the Russian ships found themselves in a strait about fifteen kilometres wide. Smolensk Island lay to the north, while to the south was the spectacular sight of 'a high island, with steep cliffs and its heights covered with clouds'.[35] Bellingshausen called it Teille Island, after the Russian representative in Rio de Janeiro who had informed him of Smith's discovery. Named by the British as Deception Island, it was actually a dormant volcano, the collapsed side of which allowed the sea to form a protected harbour above the sunken crater. When Bellingshausen found the harbour, he stumbled into an area of frenzied activity.

Anchored off the western end of Livingston Island were eight British and American sealing ships, some of which had been at the islands for nearly three months, creating putrefying wastelands of rotting carcasses on the previously unsullied shores. Many of the rocky coves had become practically devoid of seals, and the competition to gain control of the remaining beaches was threatening to spill over into violence.

Just days before Bellingshausen's arrival, the crews from nine American vessels had joined together under the leadership of Captain Davis to confront a large party of British sealers on Livingston Island who had prevented them from landing on a beach where there were said to be plenty of seals. The Americans had determined 'to take Seal by fair means if we Could but at all Events to take them'. With a hundred or so Americans and sixty or so well-armed British sealers ready to defend the beach, the scene was set for a bloodbath. The battle was only abandoned when the approaching Americans noticed that the much-vaunted beach was largely devoid of seals. There was clearly no point to proceeding with the confrontation, so the Americans had sensibly withdrawn.[36]

Bellingshausen's two vessels sailed into this tense situation, having spent three months traversing isolated and dangerous seas without sighting another ship. Bellingshausen had hoped to be the first navigator to confirm the existence of the southern continent but was now confronted by the small American boat *Hero* and its youthful Captain Palmer. Invited aboard the *Vostok*, Palmer explained to the Russians how he had come in partnership with three other American boats and had managed to kill thousands of seals during the previous four months, leading Bellingshausen to note that killing on such a scale must cause seal numbers to 'rapidly decrease', as had happened on South Georgia. Not only had Bellingshausen been beaten to the South Shetlands, but the islands were rapidly being made worthless by the unrestrained killing of their seal stocks. Bellingshausen made no mention in his journal entry of having talked with Palmer about the Antarctic Peninsula, which lay about a hundred kilometres to the south. Indeed, the discussion between the two sailors took less than an hour, after which Bellingshausen continued his voyage along the southern shores of the South Shetlands.[37]

A very different account of the meeting was published in 1833 by Captain Edmund Fanning,[38] the Stonington sealer and keen claimer of new territories. In his belated account, intended for a popular audience, Fanning asserted that Palmer had told Bellingshausen that he had seen a large and mountainous land mass from a high point on Deception Island. Sailing off in the *Hero* to investigate, Palmer had been disappointed to see no sign of seal colonies and had returned without charting or landing upon the shore. If the account is accurate, Palmer had seen and investigated part of the Antarctic Peninsula.

Bellingshausen had then supposedly asked to see Palmer's logbook and chart. When the documents were fetched by rowboat, the Russian was said by Fanning to have expressed amazement that Palmer had been able to achieve in his small boat what he, 'in command of one of the best appointed fleets at the disposal of my august master, have for three long, weary, anxious years searched day and night for'. Bellingshausen had then expostulated: 'What shall I say to my master? What will he think of me? But be that as it may, my grief is your joy; wear your laurels with my sincere prayers for your welfare. I name the land you have discovered, noble boy, Palmer's Land.'[39]

This was Fanning at his fictional best, inventing an imaginary conversation to put Palmer forward as the acknowledged discoverer of the southern continent.

Although Palmer's search for new sealing grounds had probably brought him within sight of the Antarctic Peninsula, his logbook does not even mention the brief meeting with Bellingshausen and offers no support for Fanning's account. Further doubt is cast on Fanning's claim by Bellingshausen, who made no attempt, in the days after his meeting with Palmer, to sail south to check the truth of Palmer's story.[40] Instead, he continued to chart the South Shetland Islands before heading back to Russia. If there had been any hint of a continent nearby, Bellingshausen would surely have checked it out.

It is possible that other sealers may also have caught sight of the peninsula, and some may even have explored its coastline. But their feats are lost to history. Few logbooks have survived, and many of the sealers were naturally reluctant to tell the world the details of their lucrative voyages. The unresolved questions about Palmer's story did not prevent several later American geographers from seizing upon Fanning's account to support their campaign to have the United States regarded as the rightful claimant to all or part of the Antarctic continent.[41]

In fact, a surviving logbook has since revealed that the first people to record their sighting of Antarctica, to sail along a small part of its coastline and to step ashore were the crew of the small American schooner *Celia*, who had headed south in February 1821 under the command of Captain Davis to search for seal colonies. Davis had found what Bransfield had seen the year before: 'a Large Body of Land' that was 'high and covered intirely with Snow'. As the crew reefed the sails to cope with the heavy seas and snowstorms, Davis wrote in his log, 'I think this Southern Land to be a Continent.'[42]

Davis's relatively brief sighting did not justify such an assessment, just as the similar assumptions by Cook and other explorers were not supported by what they had actually seen and surveyed.[43] It would take more than a century for the increasing suspicions about an Antarctic continent to be finally confirmed.

CHAPTER 3

'In the name of our sovereign, the people'

1821–1838

The blood-and-guts sealers of New England had good cause to celebrate their fortune in 1820, as they nudged their small ships into the congested harbour of New York. After risking their lives in the fog-shrouded and storm-tossed waters of the South Shetlands, they had returned laden with hundreds of barrels of seal skins and oil. They had proved that James Cook was wrong to dismiss the Antarctic as a profitless wasteland.

Fortunes were made with the bang of an auctioneer's gavel as their cargos were sold to eager bidders. As news spread of the great bonanza, a rush of enterprising American, British and Argentinian mariners raced south the following summer to look for any untouched sealing grounds on the rocky shores of the sub-Antarctic islands. Slaughtering without thought of the morrow, it would take only two summers for the thriving seal colonies to be exterminated. Anxious to find more, some sealers wanted to prove that Cook was also wrong when he had suggested that there was no point in exploring further south, where there seemed to be only snow and ice.

Despite the frenzied activity in the South Shetlands and the voyages of Cook and Bellingshausen, most of the area within the Antarctic Circle remained unmapped. John Davis might have written in his log that he thought 'this Southern Land to be a Continent', but he had no way of knowing whether his supposition was correct.[1] Many thought otherwise. Even some twentieth-century maps of the southern polar region portrayed it as an Arctic-like ocean of ice and islands.[2]

The prospect of such islands harbouring new seal colonies made the avaricious sealers and merchants of New England and Britain keen to find them. It would not be an easy task. As the captain of a sealing vessel wrote to an American newspaper in January 1821, the 'large body of land' south of the islands is 'little known, and will probably so remain by reason of the danger and difficulty in approaching the shore, from the great quantity of floating ice with which it is surrounded'.[3] Mapmakers nevertheless tried to make sense of the new discoveries, both for dilettante geographers at home and for the merchants and mariners who wanted reliable maps for their own voyages to the region.

Mapping and naming islands and other land masses was important not only for safe navigation but also for countries making claims to new territories. Securely attaching a name to a territory was a crucial step towards its acquisition. It is not surprising, then, that British and American mapmakers depicted the new-found territories in different ways. While an American map of November 1822 had part of the Antarctic Peninsula as 'Palmer's Land',[4] a London map of the same year had the coastline as part of a much larger land mass called 'New South Shetland', the name having been shifted south to the Antarctic Peninsula from what we now know as the South Shetland Islands.

The London mapmaker had received his information from the British sealer George Powell, a friend of Palmer, who acknowledged the American discoveries by naming about sixty-five kilometres of the 'New South Shetland' coastline south of Deception Island as 'Palmer's Land'. Bransfield's 'Trinity Land' covered a similar distance to the south-east of Livingston Island. While both Palmer and Bransfield were thereby acknowledged on the London map, it was the British name 'New South Shetland' that was used to describe the overall coastline that had been discovered so far.[5]

Despite the maps, no one could be sure whether or not that coastline was just another island, as other discoveries had turned out to be. The publication of Bellingshausen's journal and charts, with his sightings of an 'ice continent' on the other side of the South Pole, might have strengthened the cause of those who believed that Bransfield and Palmer had sighted part of a continent. But Bellingshausen's return to Russia in August 1821 resulted in only brief reports in London newspapers, which merely noted that Bellingshausen had proved that Bransfield's 'New South Shetland' – the South Shetland islands – and Cook's 'Sandwich Land' – the Sandwich Islands – were not part of any southern continent.[6]

It took a decade for a poorly edited version of Bellingshausen's journal to be published in Russian, apparently without any input from its author. Again, the published journal had no mention of an 'ice continent'.[7] It was another eighty years before an abbreviated version appeared in German, and only in 1945 was an English edition edited by a polar explorer, Frank Debenham. Even then, the mistaken translation of crucial passages, and the absence of other records that have since surfaced, caused Debenham to conclude that Bellingshausen was unaware he was gazing upon a new continent.[8] As a result, it would be more than a century before geographers were certain that there really was a continent at the South Pole, and for it to be clear that Bellingshausen's expedition had been the first to see it.

As for Bransfield, Palmer and his fellow sealers, none had seen more than a small part of Antarctica's extensive coastline and only a few had stepped upon its shores. Moreover, not even Bransfield had conducted a claiming ceremony on the continent itself. Most sealers had little interest in claiming ownership of despoiled islands whose economic value they had already destroyed, although some of the British had made symbolic attempts to do so. With British naval contingents present in the newly independent nations of South America, the British sealers would have been more confident than their American counterparts in having their territorial claims supported by their government.

These different attitudes were clear when Palmer set off with Powell in their separate ships to search for new islands. When they discovered islands about 600 kilometres north-east of the Antarctic Peninsula in December 1821, Palmer declined to go onshore, noting that there were no seals evident. In contrast, Powell rowed ashore in his whaleboat to claim the islands for Britain and give them British names, with the islands as a whole being named 'Powell's Group'.[9] In 1954, State Department geographer Samuel Boggs observed, with some exasperation, that the early American sealers 'were not predisposed to assert territorial claims in the name of the young "U.S.A."'.[10] The American government of the time was more concerned with extending its existing territory across the continent to the Pacific Ocean than with grabbing inhospitable sub-Antarctic territories, whose animal resources had already been mostly exterminated.

Two months after the visits of Powell and Palmer, another patriotic British sealing captain, James Weddell, chanced upon Powell's Group and named them the South Orkneys, thereby associating them with the nearby South Shetlands and the British-owned Orkneys and Shetlands in the northern hemisphere. Weddell had served in the Royal Navy for eight years before taking command of the *Jane*, a 160-ton brig whose crew hunted for seals in the South Shetlands from 1819 to 1821. When those islands were depleted of their seals, Weddell was commissioned by the owners of the *Jane* and the sixty-five-ton cutter *Beaufoy* to search the far south for new sealing grounds. Although Bellingshausen had shown that Cook's 'Sandwich Land' was not part of a southern continent, the news had not reached Weddell and his backers by the time he left England in September 1822.

As a result, Weddell notes how he set out in the belief that Sandwich Land was possibly 'a projecting point of a southern continent, or range of land lying east and west behind the islands of South Shetland'.[11] It would be likely, therefore, to have rich sealing grounds on its extensive shores. Consequently, Weddell set course for the seas between Sandwich Land and the South Shetlands, confident that he would encounter the elusive continent. Like so many other explorers searching for the southern continent, Weddell found only sea.

Further and further south the two ships went, until, on 20 February 1823, Weddell reached latitude 74° S and longitude 34° W. This was more than 320 kilometres further south than Cook or any other navigator had managed to reach, and Weddell had not been blocked by the ice that he had expected to find, and which he had found much further north around the South Shetlands. The ice-free conditions that allowed Weddell to venture so far south were so unusual that no navigator was able to emulate his feat for more than a century.[12]

Weddell never realised that only good fortune had permitted his success. In fact, he and his crew did not count the discovery of relatively open sea so far south as a success. It was seals they were after, and there were none to be caught in the open sea. With his crew 'much disappointed at our ill success in not finding a southern land', Weddell ordered the ships to head back north. He allayed the resentment of his crew by announcing their historic feat in sailing further south than any other ship. Then, to the cheers of the men, he hoisted the colours, fired the ship's gun and doled out grog to dispel 'their gloom'. With no new lands to claim, Weddell had to be content with naming the empty sea after his king, George IV, although it would later come to bear his own name.[13]

Also in the Weddell Sea that season was a young sealer from Stonington, Benjamin Morrell, who imitated Weddell by taking the schooner *Wasp*, owned by New York merchant James Byers, in search of seals and a possible continent south of Cook's 'Sandwich Land'. Venturing south of the Antarctic Circle, thus becoming the first American to do so, he finally abandoned his southward reconnaissance on 15 March 1823, a month after Weddell had similarly turned north. Morrell had not reached as far south as Weddell, only attaining 70° 14' S, but the days were shortening, winter was approaching, his supplies were seriously depleted and there were no sealing grounds in sight.

Morrell remained convinced that, with calm conditions and open sea before him, he could have continued all the way to the South Pole, if it was not for his lack of 'nautical and mathematical instruments' and the absence of 'such scientific gentlemen as discovery ships should always be supplied with'. Although he subsequently roved around the world in a specially commissioned vessel – named the *Antarctic* in honour both of his feat and of 'the future probability of her penetrating still farther towards the south pole' – Morrell never again slipped below the Antarctic Circle. Most historians have agreed that the ghost-written account of his voyage was more fiction than fact.[14]

Despite being unsuccessful in the search for seals, Weddell's discovery of an open and largely ice-free sea beyond the Antarctic Circle had important consequences. Because he saw few icebergs at the limit of his southerly voyage, and because he believed that icebergs were generated from land, Weddell concluded that the land beyond the South Shetlands, including Graham and Palmer Land, did not extend any further south than 73° S. According to Weddell, this meant that the polar sea could be 'less icy than is imagined, and a clear field of discovery, even to the South Pole, may therefore be anticipated'.[15] It gave credence to those who argued that the South Pole was at the centre of an unfrozen sea, rather than being the centre of a frozen, southern continent.

An American writer went even further, arguing that the earth was an oblate spheroid composed of 'several concentric spheres, with polar openings' thousands of kilometres across. It was suggested that the native peoples of the Americas had originated from within these openings, while some animals of North America were said to migrate each winter to a supposedly temperate inner sphere that was bathed in almost perpetual sunlight.[16] These wild imaginings helped inspire a surge of American interest in the South Pole and led to popular demands for an official expedition to test the truth of the theory.

The fantastical theory of an Earth that was hollow and habitable originated in 1818 with the former American army officer John Cleves Symmes, who proposed that a party of one hundred men join him in trekking northward from Siberia with reindeer and sleighs to find the northern polar opening and gain entry to the temperate inner world. That expedition never eventuated, but the shy and increasingly frail Symmes lectured on his theory to thousands of curious Americans. With many remaining incredulous, but some scientists giving it credence, the young and articulate newspaper editor Jeremiah Reynolds joined with Symmes to spread the word along the eastern American seaboard.

The two men began their tour in September 1825, with Reynolds' oratorical skills convincing otherwise sceptical audiences – who paid fifty cents each for admission – that the 'facts' underlying Symmes' theory were 'so natural, so consistent with reason . . . that they almost irresistibly enforce conviction on the mind'. So convinced were many local worthies that they besieged Washington with calls for an expedition to test Symmes' theory and take possession of whatever lands might lie beyond the Antarctic Circle.[17]

This was something Reynolds wanted more than Symmes, whose focus remained on the Arctic. Reynolds became convinced that an expedition to the Antarctic had greater potential for arousing public interest and attracting both public and private money.[18] The two men went their separate ways in 1826, and Reynolds saw a chance to combine national pride, scientific curiosity and commercial expansion into a popular crusade for an Antarctic expedition, with him at its head.

In August of that year he began his lobbying of government by approaching the secretary of the navy, Samuel Southard, a lawyer and former senator who had done much to expand the US Navy and support practical scientific endeavours through his membership of Washington's Columbian Institute for the Promotion of Arts and Sciences. Southard had heard Reynolds lecture in Washington, then a town of just 10,000 people. Although he made clear that he did not believe Symmes' theory, the navy secretary was 'anxious' that Reynolds should have support for an expedition 'towards the South Pole', which 'cannot fail to be profitable to science'. Southard believed that the new nation had made little contribution to the general knowledge of humanity.[19] President John Quincy Adams, who was also a member of the Columbian Institute and who wanted the United States to be 'a great naval power', was also well-disposed towards Reynolds, describing his lectures 'as exhibitions of genius and science'.[20]

Reynolds boosted his chances of gaining political support when he abandoned talk of Symmes' theory and talked instead of new seal colonies and the South Pole as an attainable objective in the light of Weddell's voyage. In early 1828 he convinced politicians from New York, Maryland, Virginia, North Carolina and South Carolina to petition Congress for money to send 'a small expedition, to explore the immense and unknown regions in the southern hemisphere'. It was argued that such an expedition could find new islands, chart the coasts where American mariners 'frequently suffer shipwreck' and open new avenues for trade in animal fur, which produces 'an immense revenue' for the government and 'greatly augments our national strength, by increasing the number of our most efficient seamen'. The Maryland Assembly pointed to the national prestige that would accrue from a polar expedition, which would add 'to the general stock of national wealth and knowledge, and to the honor and glory of the United States'.[21]

Congress was less interested in notions of national glory, or in adding to the store of human knowledge. It asked Reynolds to explain how an expedition might benefit the nation's commerce. Being a man never lost for words, and sensing how he might yet achieve his purpose, Reynolds emphasised the growing importance of American commercial activities in the Pacific, particularly whaling, which had expanded there when whale numbers in the Atlantic became heavily depleted by hunting. He also pointed to the more than seven million seal skins that had been taken by American sealing ships.

However, seals were now harder to find, and Reynolds suggested that they had retreated to 'more remote regions'. If an expedition were sent further south, he predicted, seals would be 'found in great abundance'. There was also the likelihood that the highly profitable sea otters of the North Pacific 'may yet be found in the southern hemisphere', along with sandalwood, the tusks of sea elephants, oil from porpoises, feathers from sea birds and much more besides. There might also be valuable territories to claim, since the southern polar region had about four million square kilometres that could conceal countries corresponding in nature to 'Lapland, Norway, part of Sweden, and the northern parts of Siberia'.[22]

There were other factors to consider. Reynolds reminded congressmen of the ignominy American seamen felt at having to rely on the maps and charts of other nations. The United States was the only major commercial nation, wrote Reynolds, not to have spent a dollar adding 'to the accumulated stock of commercial and geographical knowledge, except in partially exploring our own territory'. An expedition to the unknown regions of the world would help to redress these embarrassing national deficiencies.

By protecting and promoting maritime commerce, the expedition would also indirectly assist the expanding US Navy, which relied on whaling and merchant shipping to provide experienced sailors for its ranks. In turn, modern commerce increasingly relied for its prosperity on merchants having a detailed knowledge of the world, and on the US Navy being able to protect American merchant ships from being plundered. Reynolds complained that American commerce was 'extending everywhere and protected nowhere' and the 'spirit of the nation' would no longer stand for it.[23]

While Congress calculated the commercial benefits of an American expedition, the British Admiralty was busily extending the British claim of possession from the South Shetland Islands to the mainland of the supposed continent. An expedition was mounted at the request of the Royal Society to ascertain the true dimensions of the Earth by taking observations with a pendulum at various points of the globe, with the most important point in the far south being 'New South Shetland' or 'any other land in still higher southern latitude'. Scientific inquiry, rather than acquisition of territory, was the rationale for the expedition, with the committee noting that such inquiries would help 'to sustain the high station which England at present occupies among the civilized nations of the world'. To emphasise the point, the man chosen to lead this prestigious expedition was the experienced naval officer and scientist Captain Henry Foster, who had served as astronomer during two Arctic expeditions and been awarded a medal by the Royal Society for his scientific work.[24]

On 21 April 1828, Foster took the barque-rigged HMS *Chanticleer* out of Portsmouth's harbour, heading for the seas off Cape Horn. Arriving there in October 1828 and making his observations, Foster then sailed to the South Shetlands to continue his work. But the mission was not just about making observations. On 7 January 1829, Foster threaded the *Chanticleer* through a mass of icebergs and numerous whales to land on the extensive shore of what he named Clarence Land, after the Duke of Clarence. At a place that Foster appropriately called Cape Possession, he and another officer took ashore a copper cylinder in which was deposited a document written in Latin, taking possession of the land in the name of King George IV.

The ship's surgeon, William Webster, described in his journal how the landing party soon returned from the brief ceremony with some limpets and rock samples, which provided evidence of their visit and of the serious scientific intent of their expedition. The exact location of the landing would later become the subject of fierce dispute between British and American geographers, with some arguing that Foster had actually landed on Hoseason Island – in the Palmer Archipelago – rather than on the Antarctic Peninsula itself, as one of the expedition's maps suggested. Foster might have clarified the issue by publishing his account of the voyage, but he drowned on the way home after falling from a canoe in Panama. Whatever the precise location, Webster was not impressed with England's newest acquisition, believing it was 'destined to be of little account to man', being 'clothed in eternal snow'.[25]

Nearby Deception Island, where the expedition spent some weeks taking observations, was little better. There were few of the valuable fur seals to be seen, and its brooding volcano caused venting steam and gases to hiss from cracks in the ice. The crew found plenty of penguins and some leopard seals to kill, along with seabirds of various kinds.[26] Despite the lack of fur seals, the island's sheltered harbour made it worth claiming, so two midshipmen did just that on 26 February 1829, placing a flag on the summit of its 600-metre peak.[27]

As Foster was sailing south, the US House of Representatives finally decided in May 1828 that a naval ship should be sent south 'to examine the coasts, islands, harbors, shoals, and reefs in those seas'.[28] The costs would have to be borne by the existing navy budget, since the Senate was unlikely to approve any special funding for an expedition. Unfazed, President Adams and his navy secretary used the House motion to press ahead, even though the lack of special funding would limit the scale of the expedition. Adams was anxious that the expedition should be sent before the election of his likely successor, General Andrew Jackson, an opponent of the expedition.[29]

To convince the public of the expedition's worthiness, it was argued that it would provide accurate charts for the nation's whalers and sealers and would add to the nation's store of scientific knowledge. There was support from Edmund Fanning, who had been promoting such an expedition since 1812. For Fanning, commerce and exploration were a compelling combination, although the disinterested quest for scientific knowledge and the enhancement of America's national prestige were more attractive for the public and the government. Hence, the name chosen was 'The First United States Exploring Expedition'. The *New York Mirror* thought the project accorded with the 'spirit of the age'. The rebuilt warship *Peacock* was prepared, with Captain Thomas Jones appointed as its commander and Lieutenant Charles Wilkes as astronomer.[30]

Because the navy had limited experience in the Pacific, Southard sent Reynolds to New England to gather information from whaling and sealing captains. Reporting back in September 1828, Reynolds told Southard that the whale and seal fishery was much larger than he had thought, with at least 200 American ships involved. The average size of the ships was increasing to cope with the much longer voyages that were required to find the decreasing stocks of both whales and seals. The planned expedition could address this shortage, wrote Reynolds, by exploring the Antarctic region for the so-called 'right whale', a species that was preferred by whalers as it was relatively slow-moving and rich in oil-producing blubber. He suggested that an expedition could 'advance with no great difficulty into very high latitudes', and even to the South Pole itself.[31]

It soon became clear that a single ship could not achieve the objectives of the expedition, so the plans were expanded to include two more. Southard had a 200-ton whaling vessel surveyed with a view to it being purchased as a supply ship to accompany the *Peacock*. But he needed the sanction of the Senate for this additional expenditure.[32] With sheathing of the *Peacock*'s bow about to be undertaken to protect against ice,[33] and with Adams telling Congress at the beginning of the 1829 session that the expedition was 'nearly ready to depart',[34] the chairman of the Senate's naval committee, Senator Robert Hayne, demanded that Southard provide more information on the expedition's purposes.

He wanted to know whether it was intended just to discover the true situation of known coasts, islands and reefs, or whether it was intent on 'the discovery of unknown regions'. Hayne suspected that the real purpose of the expedition was to approach the South Pole, perhaps with Symmes' now discredited theory in mind. His suspicions were confirmed when Southard conceded that it was intended to explore both known and unknown lands, with the ships being instructed to sail to 'high southern latitudes', going 'as far to the south as circumstances would permit them safely and prudently to go'.[35]

Since America's own coasts and harbours were not yet properly charted, Hayne declared, it was 'altogether superfluous to attempt the discovery of unknown lands'. Not only would it divert American energies from securing possession of North America, but the discovery of new lands would inevitably lead to the establishment of American colonies, which would have to be defended at substantial cost and would drain people and resources from the United States. Creating an overseas empire would also contravene the American image of itself as a free and democratic nation that stood in contrast to the aged, monarchical and rapacious empires of Europe. As a result, instead of an expedition to discover new lands, 'whether . . . within the opening [at the South Pole] or anywhere else', the Senate committee would only approve a small expedition to survey the already known islands and reefs 'which lie in the track of our vessels engaged in the whale and other fisheries in the South seas'.[36] This was hardly the sort of grand expedition envisaged by Reynolds and Fanning, or by Adams and Southard.

The election of President Jackson and the installation of a new navy secretary spelled doom even for this scaled-down expedition. Reynolds and Fanning were forced to press ahead with a private expedition using experienced sealing captains Benjamin Pendleton, Nathaniel Palmer and his brother Alexander. Bereft of official support, the expedition's name was changed to 'the South Sea Fur Company and Exploring Expedition'. The costs would be recouped by filling the holds of the three sealing vessels with seal skins and oil. Reynolds would accompany the expedition, along with a 'scientific corps', composed of the opium-taking and sometime alcoholic naturalist Dr James Eights – a founding member of the Albany Lyceum of Natural History – the Philadelphian John Frampton Watson, and two assistants.[37] The inclusion of the 'scientific corps' was designed to generate a level of public and official interest that a mere sealing voyage could not hope to match, although Eights would later complain that he was supplied with hardly any 'conveniences for collecting & preserving objects of Natural History'. Indeed, the expedition was so strapped for funds that a New York newspaper appealed for its readers to loan it 'Books, Voyages, Charts, (if ever so ancient) Time Keepers, Nautical Instruments'.[38]

Before departing on 16 October 1829, the *New York Enquirer* reported that Reynolds would search for 'undiscovered islands' that 'will become the property of the United States' – not that Reynolds made any direct mention of claiming new lands. He simply told a journalist that he planned to 'sail round the icy circle, and push through the first opening that he finds'. This was not the opening in the Earth envisaged by Symmes but the opening in the ice envisaged by Weddell, which would allow entry to the open sea and islands beyond. By the time Reynolds arrived at the Cape Verde Islands to take on salt for preserving skins, his ambition had been scaled back. Instead of trying to reach the South Pole, now it would only acquire sufficient 'practical knowledge' for a subsequent and 'more efficient expedition' that might do so.[39]

Reynolds' hopes went unfulfilled. Hunting for seals took precedence over exploration, although there were few left to kill. The years of exploitation had severely reduced their numbers in the South Shetlands, and repeated snow storms and freezing conditions impeded the search for undiscovered islands on which new colonies might be found. Before their departure, Pendleton had confidently assured Reynolds that there were 'many valuable discoveries to be made', but the sealer was soon forced to concede that their search for seal-rich islands south-west of the South Shetlands was proving fruitless.

The search became more desperate as the ships and the men became exposed to the worsening weather of the approaching winter.[40] Eights remained convinced that they were tantalisingly close to finding the non-existent islands. He was also convinced by Weddell's experience that the South Pole could be approached by sea. But there was little that Eights or Reynolds could do to confirm these suppositions while their fellow expeditioners were single-mindedly hunting for seal skins.[41] With no geographical discoveries, the expedition's discoveries were limited to the scientific samples that Eights gathered, mainly from the South Shetlands. These included the first discovery of fossils, which showed that the barren islands had once boasted rich vegetation. As scurvy began to affect the health of the crews, Pendleton and Palmer finally quit the icy seas and incessant snow showers for the recuperative relief that could be found in the Chilean port of Valparaíso.

When the men's health had recovered, the ships went to Chile's south coast to collect more seal skins so that the sailors might have something to show for the dangers and privations they had endured. Pendleton planned to send the skins back to the United States and to investigate possible sealing grounds and trading opportunities in the North Pacific, before making another attempt at reaching the South Pole. However, some of his sailors refused to continue with a voyage that had nearly cost them their lives and produced little profit.

Faced with desertions, Pendleton decided to return to the United States while he still had sufficient men to work the ships. There was little to show for the venture. As one American botanist caustically observed, the expedition had returned 'without having accomplished much, for it turned out just as several of us suspected, that the Expedition was destined, not for discovery and scientific purposes – but to catch seals!' Arriving in New York in September 1831, Pendleton reported to Fanning that it would require a government expedition to rescue the fortunes of the seal fishery by discovering new sealing grounds.[42]

Reynolds had been left ashore in Valparaíso when the vessels had been forced to make their hasty departure. He was eventually picked up in October 1832 by a US Navy brig, the *Potomac*, which was returning from a punitive voyage to Sumatra, where it had exacted retribution on a local ruler who had seized an American merchant ship and killed some of its crew. Reynolds was appointed secretary to the ship's commander and occupied his time on the homeward voyage by writing a popular account of the expedition, in which he called for the American flag to be 'borne to every portion of the globe' to show the world 'the power we possess'. He devoted part of the book to the disputed sovereignty of the Falkland Islands, where the new Argentine republic was challenging British title to the unoccupied islands, and where both nations were attempting to block access by American whalers and sealers. Appealing to the rising nationalism of the times, Reynolds called on the American government to ensure unfettered American access to the Falklands.[43]

The voyage of the *Potomac*, and the subsequent publication of Reynolds' popular account, helped to refocus official and public attention on the economic opportunities and strategic importance of the Pacific Ocean and the seas around Cape Horn. There was also a growing constituency for oceanic exploration, led by publicists such as Reynolds, and self-seeking whalers and sealers such as Fanning, whose 1833 book, *Voyages Round the World*, opened the eyes of many American readers to the adventure and wealth to be had in the Pacific and Southern Oceans.

British exploration of the Arctic during the 1830s also led to further speculation concerning the hidden mysteries of the Antarctic. The British naval officer Captain James Clark Ross had discovered the North Magnetic Pole in 1831, and British expeditions continued to search the Arctic for a north-west passage to the Pacific. Recently formed geographical societies in London, Paris, Frankfurt and Berlin – supported by their governments – helped to finance many of these explorations into the unseen recesses of the world.[44]

Fanning remained convinced that another expedition should be sent south. With Pendleton having found nothing to the south-west of South America, Fanning suggested that an expedition following Weddell's approach – in the seas south-east of the continent – might have better luck. Indeed, he thought that it could not fail 'in either reaching the South Pole, or making new discovery of land', the value of which 'may far exceed our imagination'. So convinced of success was Fanning that he offered to help fund the expedition, lest rival nations 'snatch it away'.[45]

His campaign was supported by the publication in December 1832 of Benjamin Morrell's long-delayed account of his own Antarctic voyaging in the sea discovered by Weddell. Like Weddell, he argued that both experience and logic suggested that 'a clear sea is open for voyages of discovery, even to the south pole'. Despite well-founded doubts about the book's veracity, its publication helped to underpin a renewed clamour for Washington to sponsor an official expedition to the South Pole, so that 'the glory of exploring' it should go to 'the only free nation on earth' and not to the 'vassals of some petty despot'. The South Pole could then be 'set among the stars of our national banner'.[46]

In November 1834, Reynolds and others successfully petitioned the Rhode Island Assembly to call upon Congress to send 'a voyage of discovery and survey to the South seas'. The call was echoed by the Salem East India Marine Society, composed of ships' captains who had risked their lives sailing the world and who wanted protection from the many dangers of the high seas.

In February 1835, the question came before the Commerce Committee of the House of Representatives, which was sympathetic to the petition after being told by Reynolds of the massive size of the sealing and whaling trade. The committee agreed that locating the position of islands that could act as refuges and places of refreshment for these world-ranging whalers was worth the cost of an expedition. There were also the 'collateral advantages to be derived in the attainment of much useful knowledge, so highly prized by every enlightened mind'. The committee was advised by Commodore John Downes, who had employed Reynolds on the *Potomac*, that there were 'immense portions of the South seas, bordering on the Antarctic circle, well deserving the attention of such an expedition'. Downes predicted that 'a speedy examination of this portion of the South seas', particularly in the vicinity of Palmer's Land, was likely to 'yield rich returns in animal fur' and add to the credit of the United States for 'promoting such an enterprise'.[47]

If Congress did not act promptly, the committee was warned, the United States might be beaten by the British. A powerful whaling and sealing company, Enderby Brothers of London, had sent a former British naval officer, Captain John Biscoe, to continue Weddell's search for new sealing grounds. Commanding two sealing vessels, Biscoe only managed to gather thirty seal skins during his two-and-half-year voyage. But his sighting in February 1831 of a coastline far to the south of Africa, complete with snow-free mountaintops, was further confirmation that a continent might be found at the South Pole.

Biscoe named it Enderby Land, and named each mountain after one of the Enderby brothers. He tried to land and claim the place for Britain but was prevented by ice from doing so. Going on to become the third mariner to circumnavigate the South Pole, he followed in Bellingshausen's track towards the South Shetlands. When he discovered more land, adjacent to Bellingshausen's Alexander I Island, he named it Adelaide Island after the queen. Further islands were passed and suitably named before Biscoe landed on the nearby Antarctic Peninsula on 21 February 1832, naming it Graham Land in honour of the First Lord of the Admiralty. 'This being the mainland,' wrote Biscoe, 'I took possession of it in the name of His

Majesty King William the Fourth.'[48] It was the first territorial claim on the Antarctic continent.

Having seen 500 kilometres of land, Biscoe informed the Royal Geographical Society that he was convinced that 'this is a large continent'. The editor of the society's journal agreed, noting that the discovery of land on opposite sides of the Antarctic Circle had revived the probable 'existence of a great Southern Land'. The society rewarded Biscoe for his discovery, while the Admiralty appointed an officer to accompany him on a follow-up voyage. It also provided Enderby with funds to finance a new vessel to make 'a further and more accurate investigation into the new land or continent'.[49]

Some in the United States were alert to the danger of Britain usurping the American discoveries. They were aware that Biscoe's 'Graham Land' was the American 'Palmer's Land', although its ownership had never been formally claimed by Palmer or the US government. Nevertheless, Congress was warned that the British were intruding upon a chain of islands that was 'entirely and undoubtedly an American discovery', with the Americans now facing the danger of having that honour 'snatched from us', along with 'the glory of naming them'.[50]

Ten years after Reynolds began his campaign for a government expedition, the tide of opinion in Congress was finally turning in his favour. In February 1836, Connecticut whalers petitioned for an exploratory expedition to the South Seas that might obtain 'a more perfect knowledge' of the oceans into which they were extending their operations. They also wanted the government to provide a greater naval presence to protect them from attacks by hostile islanders.

With hundreds of vessels now involved in the industry, and with the prosperity of New England dependent on it, their call could not be easily brushed aside. It was supported by the former navy secretary Samuel Southard, who was now a powerful senator on the Naval Affairs Committee. In a report on the Connecticut petition in March 1836, Southard reminded senators of the economic importance of whaling, the potential of America's growing commerce in the Pacific, and the necessity to protect that commerce and US citizens from attack. There was also 'the duty which the government and the nation owe to its own character, and the common cause of all civilized nations – the extension of useful knowledge of the globe which we inhabit'. Moreover, Southard argued, the Pacific and South Seas were 'peculiarly our own'.[51]

The nascent American empire was starting to take shape in the minds of American leaders.

With Southard now finding support in the Senate, the bill was sent back to the House of Representatives for approval. To boost its chances of success, Reynolds was given permission to use the House of Representatives hall on 3 April 1836 for a Saturday night address on the proposed 'Voyage of Discovery' to congressmen and their guests. His wide-ranging lecture sketched out a vision of the United States as a great maritime power, arguing forcefully against those who believed that Americans should remain 'tillers of the earth' and eschew the supposedly 'contaminating effects of commerce and manufactures'. Americans had always been outward-looking, said Reynolds, and nothing would prevent them emulating the example of the British nation, from which so many of them had come. While the British were concentrating on the north and searching for a north-west passage, Reynolds declared, 'a wider range, a nobler field, a prospect of more comprehensive promise, lies open in the south'. And it was incumbent upon the 'national dignity and honor' of the United States to expand its beneficent influence across the globe. So long as there was 'a spot of untrodden earth accessible to man,' Reynolds declared, 'no enlightened, and especially commercial and free people, should withhold its contributions from exploring it.'[52]

To attract the support of commercially minded congressmen, Reynolds emphasised the practical necessity of providing accurate charts and protection for the fast-increasing American merchant fleet that now ranged the globe. He estimated that about 460 of those vessels, operating out of forty ports along the north-eastern seaboard, were involved in whaling and sealing. They had to face both the perils of the sea and the hostility of Pacific islanders, while the American government did little to protect them. National honour and national interest demanded that Congress should send an exploratory expedition, led by a well-armed naval ship, to chart the seas and overawe the islanders with American power. And any American expedition, argued Reynolds, must be on a greater scale than 'has been attempted by any other country'. Anything less 'could never content a people proud of their fame and rejoicing in their strength!'[53]

To ensure support from the nationalists and navalists in Congress, Reynolds reminded them of Biscoe's challenge to the American claim on Palmer's Land. Despite having merely touched at 'a single spot',

Biscoe had removed its American name and given it 'an English name'. It was an outrage, expostulated Reynolds, since American sealers had symbolically taken possession of Palmer's Land – in the name of *our sovereign, the people* – some fifteen years earlier.

The priority of discovery of Palmer's Land was certainly American, but Reynolds was on slippery legal ground in arguing that it was thereby an American possession when neither Palmer nor the American government had made a formal claim to it.[54] Visiting a place and killing its wildlife did not invest a nation with ownership of that territory. But this was a political audience rather than a court of law, and Reynolds' rhetoric struck a responsive chord.

Reynolds avoided any mention of his previous life as a purveyor of fantastical theories about the South Pole, and eschewed any suggestion that the expedition was primarily about exploring the South Pole. This was an expedition with a wider purpose. It would explore the Pacific Ocean from South America to Asia, and would require at least six vessels. It was only towards the end of his lecture that he raised the question of the South Pole, 'where the discovery ships should spend a few months during the most favorable season of the southern summer'.

Anticipating political opposition to the idea of exploring in regions where the commercial imperative was not so obvious, Reynolds asked his audience whether they wanted Americans to be always reproached with the accusation that they 'can do nothing, think of nothing, talk of nothing, that is not concerned with dollars and cents'. It was only by showing 'some devotion to science and liberal pursuits', he argued, that the United States could be 'truly great'. After all, it was in these high southern latitudes that there was the most potential for discovery, with vast regions 'which have never been trodden by the footsteps of man, nor its waters divided by the keel of the adventurous navigator'.[55]

In light of Weddell's experience, Reynolds tended to believe that a ship might well be able to sail all the way to the South Pole unimpeded by ice. Not that he thought an American expedition should be sent south for the sole purpose of testing that proposition, which had faint echoes of Symmes' discredited theory. It would be all right to make such an attempt, he argued, if it was done along with 'the other great objects of the enterprise'. And what an achievement that would be, he exulted, to reach the South Pole by ship and 'cast anchor on that point where all the meridians terminate, where our eagle and star-spangled banner may be unfurled and planted, and left to wave on the axis of the earth itself'.

The image of the American flag flying at the South Pole was a potent one, with Reynolds stressing how it would 'crown with a new and imperishable wreath the nautical glories of our country'.[56] It would be a discovery fit for the great nation that the United States aspired to become. So the great republic, after breaking free of its imperial fetters, was pointed by Reynolds down a path that would gradually see it obtain an empire of its own.

In the wake of Reynolds' speech, Congress agreed to provide for a massive expedition, adopting his plan for a squadron led by a frigate and supported by five smaller ships. After a decade of agitation, it should have been a triumph for the plucky publicist. However, on the night of the decision, a jaunty Reynolds encountered the new secretary of the navy, Mahlon Dickerson, at a Washington theatre and was dismayed to hear him declare that the expedition would take twelve months to organise.[57] Dickerson had long been an opponent of the expedition in Congress and remained intent on impeding it. He was also determined to prevent Reynolds from being leader of the scientific corps.

In this, he was assisted by Edmund Fanning, who had fallen out with his former ally. On the other side were the scientists commissioned for the expedition, many of whom signed a strong letter of support for Reynolds, noting the widespread expectation of the 'whole country' that he would 'occupy a prominent station in the expedition'.[58] Reynolds had some support from President Andrew Jackson, who now supported the expedition. He instructed Dickerson to appoint Reynolds as 'corresponding secretary to the commander', with responsibility for condensing the scientific reports. This was not the sort of position that Reynolds wanted. After his ten-year campaign, he wanted to be its leader, not its factotum.[59]

To allay concern about Dickerson blocking the expedition, Jackson instructed his navy secretary to take 'prompt measures' to implement the will of Congress, which he did by sending Lieutenant Wilkes to Europe to buy scientific instruments and books, and by asking the nation's scientific societies to advise on which scientists should accompany the expedition and what their tasks should be.[60] All this took time. Dickerson caused additional delay and distraction by appointing the young and ambitious Wilkes to the command of one of the vessels without consulting with the squadron commander, Captain Jones. This provoked a heated public dispute that forced

Dickerson to retreat. More delays were caused when the ships were found to require additional alterations.[61]

Instead of being ready to sail by early 1837, the dilatory recruitment of seamen and scientists and the slow refurbishment of vessels saw the expedition still unready in June. Dickerson then caused additional delay by convincing the incoming president, Martin Van Buren, to order an inquiry into whether the expedition needed to be so large.

Reynolds was now furious. Having been at the Norfolk naval base when he heard the news, he rushed to Washington to intercede with Van Buren and alert him to Dickerson's 'treacherous conduct'. When Reynolds found that Van Buren was not prepared to countermand his navy secretary, he feared that the expedition would suffer the same fate as its predecessor. Determined to avert such an outcome, Reynolds launched a long and sustained campaign against the sixty-seven-year-old Dickerson in the pages of the *New York Times*.[62]

The first of Reynolds' many broadsides, published under the pseudonym 'Citizen' at the end of June 1837, accused Dickerson of incompetence and of allowing America's rivals to pre-empt the United States by mounting their own expeditions. According to Reynolds, Dickerson was trying to generate opposition to the expedition by suggesting that its purpose was 'to go as near to the South Pole as possible' and by omitting any mention of its great purposes to protect and promote American trading and whaling interests in the Pacific. Reynolds knew that the expedition's success would depend on it retaining its original size and wide-ranging aims. If it was just to go to the South Pole, the inquiry would have to conclude that such a substantial expedition, led by a thirty-six-gun frigate, was not warranted. But a scaled-down expedition would struggle to achieve its purposes in the Pacific, where a well-armed frigate was necessary to overawe any hostile natives. Although Reynolds remained privately committed to reaching the South Pole by ship, he continued to portray himself primarily as a champion of Pacific exploration, and motivated by commercial rather than scientific impulses.[63]

It was a month before Dickerson replied. In the first of several long letters to the *New York Times*, under the pseudonym 'A Friend to the Navy', he attacked Reynolds for 'producing an impression through the country that this is his expedition'. So prevailing was this impression, wrote Dickerson, that some officers of the navy were loath to serve with the expedition because they considered it was 'the expedition of an individual rather than of the country'. Dickerson poured further scorn on Reynolds by reminding readers of his association with Symmes' theory of concentric globes. He claimed that naval officers feared Reynolds would order the ships to approach the supposed polar opening or make 'some other movements to test the truth of his strange theories'. Even if Reynolds had 'renounced his former theory', wrote Dickerson, he now harboured a similarly ludicrous belief if he envisaged that the expedition could drop anchor at the South Pole and leave 'the star-spangled banner to wave on the axis of the earth itself', as if it were 'a huge flagstaff'.[64]

Accusing Reynolds of suffering from 'monomania', Dickerson informed his readers that the expedition would be instructed not to endanger itself by approaching too close to the iceberg-cluttered South Pole. He assured its officers that their lives would not be 'unnecessarily exposed . . . for the purpose of testing certain wild theories that had long been before the public'. They would nevertheless fulfil the public expectation of examining the 'high southern and unexplored regions' by going further south than previous expeditions had done.

While he sought to disparage Reynolds' Antarctic theories and portray Reynolds as deranged, Dickerson was conscious of his opponent's public support, as well as the great public interest in the Antarctic. Conceding that the results from the Antarctic 'will be looked to with more intense interest than any others of the whole cruise', Dickerson clearly hoped that he could deflect Reynolds' attacks by taking seriously the matter of discoveries in the Antarctic.[65] But Reynolds was not about to lay down his pen.

The ninth and final letter in Reynolds' sustained broadside was published by the *New York Times* on 23 September 1837. The paper had had enough and closed the discussion, although it praised Reynolds for his 'unbounded zeal in the great cause'. Reynolds maintained his terrier-like attack on the hapless navy secretary, noting that the French king had recently endorsed Reynolds' vision by instructing a French expedition to approach as near as possible to the South Pole. The French sailors would be rewarded if they reached 75° S, with the reward being progressively increased the further south they reached after that point. If they reached the pole itself, the king promised that 'everything will be granted to the sailors that they may demand'. Reynolds cheekily suggested that Dickerson should redeem his reputation by getting Congress to similarly reward the American sailors.[66]

With French and British expeditions now heading for the South Pole, while the American one faced fresh delays, Reynolds turned to another New York newspaper to launch a renewed attack on Dickerson in late December 1837, accusing him again of being 'an enemy to the undertaking'. Dickerson was in a bind. The funds voted by Congress had all been spent on the vessels, and now additional funding was required. To curb the cost, Dickerson announced another inquiry into how the size of the expedition could be reduced. At the same time, he blasted Reynolds for having caused the expedition to be organised on a more lavish scale than that of any other country.[67]

With the expedition becoming a growing political embarrassment, in January 1838 President Van Buren transferred responsibility from Dickerson to the secretary of war, Joel Poinsett. By no means was Poinsett more warmly disposed towards Reynolds than Dickerson had been. Indeed, he seems to have been so hostile that, when Captain Jones resigned as the fleet's commander, Poinsett outraged senior officers by giving the command to the relatively junior lieutenant Charles Wilkes, expecting that the well-connected Wilkes would ensure the exclusion of Reynolds from the expedition. The scientific corps was also greatly reduced, with James Eights being one of those who were distressed to find that they no longer had a berth.[68]

Reynolds made repeated appeals, backed by petitions from congressmen and letters from the public, to be allowed to go with the expedition. But Poinsett stood firm, even after Reynolds offered to go at his own expense.[69] Meanwhile, with French and British expeditions well on their way to the South Pole, the squadron of six ill-assorted American ships was manned and loaded for the long voyage. On 26 July 1838, Poinsett and President Van Buren visited the specially decorated vessels and gave their blessing to Wilkes and his men. Three weeks later, the first United States Exploring Expedition finally weighed anchor and set sail for the Southern Ocean, with a chagrined Reynolds looking on from the shore.

Reynolds would later assert that the expedition's departure meant his 'triumph was complete'.[70] Yet his exclusion from the expedition greatly reduced that triumph, and thereafter he slipped from public view. America, too, would find that its hoped-for triumph was less substantial than it had expected. The years of political bickering and repeated delays had given its European rivals a head start in the race to discover whether there really was a continent worth claiming at the South Pole.

CHAPTER 4

'Planting the Stripes and Stars high on the mountain top'

1839–1843

The late 1830s saw the approaches to the South Pole become the scene of intense rivalry between expeditions from the United States, Britain and France. Picking their way past icebergs, and pushing to the edge of the shifting pack ice, enterprising explorers sought to fill in the remaining blank spaces on maps of the world and find lands that might harbour hidden sources of wealth. The explorers were joined in their search by avaricious sealers and whalers, who were drawn further and further south in search of their disappearing quarry.

The various voyages found land at widely separated locations, both outside and within the Antarctic Circle. Whether these lands were linked and comprised a continent, or whether they were large islands in a great Antarctic sea remained a topic of continuing speculation among mariners and geographers. It was partly to resolve this question that the various governments had decided to dispatch their men to the South Pole.

The French expedition was led by Jules Sébastien Dumont d'Urville, the son of an impoverished and stroke-afflicted aristocrat from Normandy who had narrowly avoided the guillotine during the Revolution. An avid reader of accounts of exploration, and driven by an urge to be famous, the young d'Urville joined the run-down French navy, the vessels of which were mostly locked in their ports by a British blockade. There was little scope for gaining renown in battle, which anyway did not interest d'Urville, who could see no glory in 'killing one's fellow men for differences of opinions over things and words'. Instead, he devoted his life 'to the advancement of knowledge' and used his naval position to become an explorer. A modicum of fame came to him in 1821 during a cruise in the eastern Mediterranean, when he chanced upon the beautiful marble statue that became known as the Venus de Milo.

which he helped secure for France.[1] He would soon have a much greater claim to fame.

As executive officer on a French expedition to the Pacific in 1822, d'Urville journeyed to the Falkland Islands and on to Tahiti, New Guinea and around the west coast of Australia to Sydney. His commander, Louis-Isidore Duperrey, had been instructed to explore the Swan River, site of present-day Perth, and the commodious harbour at King George Sound in the south-west of Australia as possible sites for a French convict colony. Duperry was unable to do so, however, because of contrary winds and a shortage of food.

Anxious to be the commander of any new expedition sent to find a site for a colony, d'Urville wrote to Paris with plans for another voyage to King George Sound. Appointed as commander, d'Urville sailed the corvette *Astrolabe* on a voyage between 1826 and 1829 that saw him visit Australia, New Zealand and several islands of the South Pacific. Although the voyage proved the colonisation possibilities of both King George Sound and the North Island of New Zealand, the French government allowed itself to be pre-empted in both places by the British, who were wise to the French intentions.[2]

Sidelined upon his return to France by a newly installed royalist regime, the staunchly republican d'Urville spent five years publishing a multi-volume account of the voyage, complete with atlases and scientific volumes. He also wrote a popular two-volume history of great voyages of exploration, including his own. It seemed that his hunger for fame would have to be satisfied by his own writing.

While biding his time in Paris, and later in the port of Toulon, d'Urville never lost his curiosity about the world beyond Europe, nor did he abandon his desire to lead another great voyage. 'Haunted by the example of Cook,' he wrote, 'I would often think about the three voyages of that great navigator, and I was tormented almost nightly by dreams in which I saw myself making my third cruise around the world.' Interestingly, these dreams always had d'Urville going towards the frozen waters of the South Pole, although his preference was to sail under 'burning equatorial skies' and pursue further research into the languages of Oceania. Finally, a change of government saw the forty-four-year-old navigator selected in 1837 to lead another voyage around the world.[3]

King Louis-Philippe I wanted the expedition to go as far south as possible. He had read an account of an American sealer – presumably the unreliable Morrell – who had been able to approach close to the South Pole. The king would have been aware of the American decision to send a large and prestigious expedition towards the South Pole, and he was anxious for the French to have the glory of success where the Americans had failed. There was talk in London of doing likewise. The dispatch of d'Urville might see France get there first and garner the laurels of any discovery that was to be made.

Although confessing that he had been left 'dumbfounded and irresolute' by 'this completely unexpected proposition', d'Urville soon accepted 'that an attempt to get to the South Pole would have the character of novelty, of greatness and even of wonder in the eyes of the public'.[4] Far better for his chances of renown if he could exceed the accomplishments of Cook among the icebergs, rather than just wander among the islands of the South Pacific, where so many other French expeditions had gone before. This way, he could satisfy the king by reaching the South Pole and then explore the islands of the South Pacific during the southern winter.

The instructions d'Urville was given made clear that the voyage to the South Pole was a relatively minor part of the French expedition, which would be mainly occupied in calling at many islands of the South Pacific and New Zealand to ascertain where French whaling ships might obtain supplies and French goods be traded. The French goal was to show the French flag and publicise their presence by leaving with local people specially embossed silver and brass medallions. D'Urville was also instructed to check on the spread of British settlement in Australia and New Zealand, to see whether France might yet be able to establish a colony in one of those places.

Because the French had little experience in polar seas, d'Urville was compelled to go to London to find the latest charts. Although he was received cordially, d'Urville sensed the British regret at having 'someone other than an Englishman' attempting a voyage into what 'they considered their nation's exclusive domain'. Hurrying back to France, d'Urville pressed ahead with the refitting of his two corvettes, the *Astrolabe* and the *Zélée*. Throughout the heat of the Mediterranean summer, the gout-ridden explorer was there each day at the Toulon dockyard, coaxing and badgering the officers and carpenters to meet his demanding schedule. On 7 September 1837, d'Urville headed the ships out to sea, their decks still a shambles of unstowed stores and equipment. There was no time to waste if the expedition was to reach the Southern Ocean in time for the southern summer, the short interlude when exploring became possible.[5]

D'Urville had convinced the king to reward the crews if the ships reached 75° S, which was as far as Weddell had managed to reach. An additional reward was to be paid to the sailors for every degree of latitude thereafter. This was meant to provide some compensation for the privations they would suffer and to draw them ever further south, perhaps to the pole itself. The reward would also 'focus public attention on the progress of our expedition', d'Urville wrote.[6] A century before the media-driven expeditions of the twentieth century, the ambitious d'Urville was bringing a remarkably modern sensibility to the business of Antarctic exploration.

With Weddell having indicated that a passage to the South Pole was possible by way of the ice-free Weddell Sea, d'Urville headed there after first calling at Patagonia, where he left a plaque announcing to any passing ships that he was headed for the South Pole.[7] D'Urville was particularly anxious to show the American expedition that he was winning the race to the South Pole. As he anticipated, the news was picked up by a passing American whaler, which returned in time to notify Wilkes prior to his departure from Virginia.[8]

Having established the precedence of his voyage, d'Urville sailed south-east from Cape Horn along the track pioneered by Weddell and searched in vain for the passage that Weddell had suggested would lead him south. There was only a solid line of ice, which the vessels had no hope of penetrating. On 25 January 1838, after barely getting beyond the tip of the Antarctic Peninsula and with no sign of a break in the ice, the French headed north-east for the nearby South Orkney Islands, where d'Urville hoped to collect seals and penguins to feed the crew.

Prevented by fog and snow storms from doing so, he made a second attempt to follow in Weddell's wake, only to be brought up short again by the ice. It was 'austere and grandiose beyond words', wrote d'Urville, and 'filled us with an involuntary feeling of dread'. With the officers and crew keen to push on to earn their reward, d'Urville nudged the ships into a basin of relatively clear water about three kilometres wide. The ships were tied to the ice and the crews celebrated with punch at having 'sailed boldly into the Antarctic ice.' D'Urville alone seems to have recognised the danger they were in. With the ice closing behind them, he armed the sailors with picks and crowbars and sent them onto the ice. They barely managed to cut the vessels free and escape the clutches of the fast-freezing sea.[9]

Although d'Urville had hardly passed the tip of the Antarctic Peninsula – he was not even within the Antarctic Circle – there was nothing more to be done that summer. The health of the crew, who were beginning to show signs of scurvy, demanded that d'Urville head for Chile. It was none too soon. With more and more sailors succumbing to the dreaded disease, caused by deficiency in vitamin C, the difficulty of manoeuvring the vessels through the stormy seas of the Magellan Strait increased.

Nevertheless, d'Urville took some time to survey the tip of the Antarctic Peninsula and the South Shetlands, naming the peninsula after King Louis-Philippe I, and dubbing a large island off its tip 'Joinville Land', after the Prince of Joinville, one of the king's sons. This enabled him to report some minor achievements from this first part of the voyage, and to add several French place names to the existing British, American and Russian ones. There was little else to be triumphant about. In his account of the voyage, d'Urville conceded that his first attempt at approaching the South Pole 'was a complete failure'. It made him wonder whether Weddell had concocted his account of being able to sail through the ice into an open sea.[10]

Despite his failure, d'Urville could take some comfort from the fact that the Americans would be similarly blocked. Yet he continued to worry about his expedition being overshadowed by the Americans. When his two ships limped into a Chilean port on 6 April 1838 and anchored near a British frigate, d'Urville questioned a British officer about the American expedition. He was relieved to learn that nothing had been heard of it. If the expedition had not been sighted in Chile by then, it presumably meant that it had missed that summer's opportunity for Antarctic exploration. That was some solace, but d'Urville knew that he had little to show for the advantage he had gained. Indeed, he had to fend off malicious stories circulating in Valparaíso that 'at the first sight of ice our corvettes had fled'. At a meeting with British officers, d'Urville displayed all his charts and illustrations to disprove the allegations.[11]

D'Urville had other things on his mind. Among the letters that were awaiting him at Valparaíso were two from his wife, telling him of their infant son's sickness, apparent recovery and then terrible death from cholera. He was the third child they had lost, leaving them only one son. D'Urville's distraught wife noted that he would receive the news after 'you have finished your work in the ice', and presumed he would therefore be able to return home to comfort her. 'It is my only desire,' she wrote, 'glory, honour, wealth, I curse you . . . the price is too high for me.' She warned that she might not survive if compelled to suffer the anguish alone.

Along with these tear-stained letters was one from his eleven-year-old son, who also implored him to return and questioned why he had to make such a long voyage. Although upset by the news, d'Urville could not bring himself to abandon what would almost certainly be his final chance to win glory. After writing a letter of sympathy and explanation to his wife, he turned his attention to planning the remainder of the long voyage.[12] He spent the next year and a half visiting many of the island groups in the South Pacific to survey their harbours, showing the French flag and punishing some islanders who had attacked a visiting French ship. While his officers and men enjoyed the delights of the islands, d'Urville remained aloof, as Cook had, keeping his cabin door firmly closed to the island girls who were allowed to climb each night onto the anchored ships.[13]

By January 1839, d'Urville should have completed his work in the Pacific and reached the convict settlement of Hobart, from where he was to sail to New Zealand and back into the South Pacific for a final round of research before heading home. But a series of delays meant that he did not even reach northern Australia until March 1839, when he investigated the site of a British outpost that had lately been abandoned.[14] D'Urville went on to investigate the Dutch trading posts in the Dutch East Indies, the British settlement at Singapore and the Spanish position in the southern Philippines, before finally heading south towards Hobart.

By now, dysentery was rife among the sailors, with sixteen officers and men having had their bodies committed to the deep during the two-month voyage from Sumatra. Others had to be hospitalised when in December 1839 they finally reached Hobart; several would succumb. Such was d'Urville's despair during the voyage that he had written his will, asking for his heart to be preserved and given to his wife.

Once safe in Hobart, a relieved d'Urville rushed to refit the *Astrolabe*. He had made a momentous decision to 'again try to make some discoveries in the south polar regions', although his instructions had made no provision for a second voyage south. However, letters from friends in France had reached him in Hobart, warning that his 'first attempt on the ice' had created 'very little stir' in France. The letters 'proved to me more strongly than ever', wrote d'Urville, 'that I had to persevere in my determination to return to the polar regions'. He resolved to make a quick lunge southward before the winter, hoping that another way to the South Pole might be found.[15]

Any doubts that d'Urville entertained about taking his ship into such dangerous seas – with crew members who were barely recovered from their recent ordeal – were quashed by the news he received on Christmas Day 1839. A British official told him that Wilkes' American expedition had arrived in Sydney, where it was preparing 'to go back into the ice'. In fact, Wilkes and his ships left Sydney the very next day, having spent nearly a month there. There was no telling whether Wilkes had made any significant discoveries on his way to Sydney, or where exactly his next move would take him. D'Urville learned that the American officers had been 'instructed to remain absolutely silent, so that nothing has transpired about the discoveries and the work of that expedition'.

Further news came when d'Urville was visited on the *Astrolabe* by the recently arrived British sealer and Antarctic explorer John Biscoe, who had talked with Wilkes and been similarly stonewalled. Yet he was able to tell d'Urville of his own recent attempt to explore south of New Zealand, where he had met with impenetrable ice at 63° S. Biscoe assured him that 'several sailors presume that land does exist to the south of Macquarie Island'. D'Urville determined to head there immediately. There was no time to lose if he was to beat Wilkes to any discoveries that might be made.[16]

The British lieutenant-governor at Hobart was the Arctic explorer Sir John Franklin, who celebrated the French presence with a ball on New Year's Eve at Government House. The following day, d'Urville sailed the *Astrolabe* down the Derwent River, with sheep and pigs on board to provide fresh meat for the crew and quantities of lime juice to guard against scurvy. There were no protests from the men at the prospect of enduring another voyage to the icy depths of Antarctica. One officer on the *Zélée* declared that 'every one felt that having failed the first time, it was vital for our honour to have another try'.[17]

D'Urville believed that he was heading for an area that 'had not been explored by any navigator'. Only later would he learn that two of Charles Enderby's whaling vessels, the schooner *Eliza Scott*, commanded by John Balleny, and the cutter *Sabrina*, had preceded him by a year. Balleny had left London in July 1838 with instructions to go 'as far as he could to the south, in hopes of discovering land in a high southern latitude'. Sailing south of New Zealand in February 1839, he had gone kilometres further south than Cook, discovering five volcanic islands and a nearby stretch of coastline. The islands were subsequently named after him, while the coastline was named 'Sabrina Land' to honour the men of the cutter, which was lost in a storm with all its crew.

Balleny had landed on one of the islands and brought back a rock from an iceberg, making him the first person to have stepped ashore on land below the Antarctic Circle. However, he had not found the new sealing grounds that Enderby had been seeking, and he had seen only a small stretch of coastline. As the editor of the Royal Geographical Society's journal opined, the voyage had kept alive the supposition that there was either 'a great southern land or a vast mass of islands' at the South Pole. There was much left for d'Urville to discover.[18]

It was Cook whom d'Urville had most in mind as his two ships sailed towards the ice. Ensconced in his cabin, he marked the known voyages of other explorers on a chart of the region he planned to explore, and saw that Cook had been the only one to traverse the same area. He noted, however, that 'the great English navigator still had not tried to go deep into those regions, he had remained below the 60° parallel'. D'Urville planned to go further. Indeed, he later wrote that he had been 'hoping to beat my way south as far as it was possible to go'.

By 16 January 1840, the lookout on the *Astrolabe* reported the first sighting of a small ice floe, when the ships were only at 60° S. As the two vessels pushed on, massive icebergs began to heave into sight, with the sun creating a 'ravishing and magical effect' on the crystalline walls of the floating islands of ice. Three days later, with icebergs all around them, the crews of the two ships celebrated crossing the Antarctic Circle, even though d'Urville calculated that they were just shy of it. Nevertheless, a sailor dressed as Father Antarctic, along with others dressed as a penguin and a seal, welcomed them to his realm. Rather than ducking the initiates, as was traditional when crossing the equator, d'Urville thought it more sensible to allow wine to be distributed; he did not want freezing water thrown about the decks.[19]

D'Urville was excited by what loomed ahead of his ships. For a day or so, the lookouts had reported the appearance of land, but d'Urville could not be certain that the completely snow-covered and gently sloping coastline was not cloud, a gigantic iceberg or some other trick of the Antarctic atmosphere. It was not until 20 January that he was sure it was a coastline – only to find, as they edged closer through the jostling icebergs, that the coast was a sheer ice cliff of great height. Landing was therefore impossible.

The coast stretched east and west, seemingly without limit. It was clear that they had encountered a land of great extent. They were the first to have done so in this region. With no native inhabitants or rival claimants to consider, d'Urville was keen to lay claim to it all but could see no way of getting ashore to do so. The next day, when eight or nine rocky islets were sighted, the race was on to effect a landing. Each of the ships lowered a boat with a French flag at its prow, whereupon the sailors rowed furiously the several kilometres to the largest of the islets. An ensign from the *Astrolabe* likened the race, which took them through the protective ramparts of tall, tabular icebergs, to being 'amongst the ruins of those great cities of the ancient Orient just devastated by an earthquake'.[20] But there were no inhabitants of these imagined ruins, just a scattering of bemused penguins watching the frantic approach of the two French boats.

An officer from the *Zélée* described in his diary how the sailors scrambled onto the rocky shore of the islet and hustled the occupying penguins off, with a sailor being detailed to 'plant the tricolor on this land that no human being before us had either seen or set foot on'. There was an implicit sense that their actions were rather inappropriate. As this officer observed, 'the abuses that have sometimes accompanied this act of taking possession of territory have often caused it to be derided as something worthless and faintly ridiculous'. Accordingly, he made clear in his diary that they were simply following 'the ancient and lovingly preserved *English* custom' when they 'took possession of it in the name of France, as well as of the adjacent coast where the ice had prevented a landing'. Their 'peaceful conquest' meant that they had 'just added a province to

France', with the officer believing that they had 'sufficient lawful right' to do so because they had not dispossessed anyone.

After celebrating with a welcome bottle of Bordeaux, they set about attacking the rock with picks and hammers to collect what small samples they could as evidence of their landing, together with several squawking penguins, which were bundled into the boats. D'Urville had remained aboard the *Astrolabe*; he now decided to name the land they had found 'Adélie Land', to honour – and possibly appease – his distant and distraught wife.[21]

As the French ships wended their difficult way westward along the barrier, enduring fog and occasional snowstorms, d'Urville was disconcerted to see a man-o'-war, with all its sails set, loom out of the fog at speed toward the French corvettes. On 29 January 1840, in this most isolated place on Earth, Lieutenant Cadwallader Ringgold, in the American ship *Porpoise*, had chanced upon their French rival. But no meeting took place between them, not even a shouted greeting across the water.

D'Urville had been in the process of resetting the *Astrolabe*'s mainsail and gave orders for the activity to be suspended so that the American vessel could get close. However, when the *Porpoise* showed no sign of taking in its sail or otherwise reducing its speed, d'Urville instructed that the mainsail of the *Astrolabe* be set so that he might at least keep alongside the faster ship for a time. This move was interpreted by the Americans as indicating that the French had no wish to communicate and wanted to keep their discoveries secret, or so Wilkes later wrote in his account of the voyage. In fact, Wilkes had been instructed by the navy secretary to keep strictly secret any information 'referring to discoveries, or any circumstances connected with the progress of your enterprise'.

For d'Urville, the *Porpoise*'s apparent refusal to slow down was consistent with the accounts he had received of the Americans' behaviour in Sydney. Later, he rejected allegations that it had been the French who had behaved secretively, noting that the time had long passed 'when navigators, in the interests of trade, believe themselves obliged to conceal their routes and their discoveries carefully to avoid the competition of our rival nations'. The French, he said, were motivated by a desire to 'enlarge the extent of our store of geographic knowledge', rather than by a desire simply to beat their rivals to new territory.[22] Yet the discovery and possible claiming of new territory had of course remained on the French agenda, as they had shown by their self-conscious claiming of Adélie Land.

For the Americans, scientific inquiry had given way to the more practical concerns of commerce. In order to ensure political support for an Antarctic expedition, Jeremiah Reynolds had been forced to emphasise the benefits for American whalers and merchantmen of knowing the precise location of shoals and reefs that might otherwise endanger their vessels. Wilkes' instructions had noted that the 'primary object of the Expedition is the promotion of the great interests of commerce and navigation.' The intention to 'extend the bounds of science, and promote the acquisition of knowledge' was secondary.

Nevertheless, whereas d'Urville's instructions had only envisaged one attempt on the Antarctic, the American instructions had envisaged two. Like d'Urville, Wilkes was ordered to begin his exploration by taking his smaller vessels 'to explore the southern Antarctic' by following the path taken by Weddell. Then he was to head into the Pacific, visiting Fiji and other islands before fetching up in Sydney, from where he was to make 'a second attempt to penetrate within the Antarctic region, south of Van Diemen's Land, and as far west as longitude 45°E, or to Enderby's Land'. After that, he was to head for the northern Pacific coast of the United States, then to Japan, before returning home by way of Singapore. It was an expedition concerned primarily with creating an informal economic empire rather than a formal territorial one. At each place he visited, Wilkes was told to respect the rights of the peoples he might encounter, since the expedition was 'not for conquest, but discovery'.[23]

The expedition left Norfolk, Virginia, in mid-August 1838, which meant it had plenty of time to reach Orange Harbor in Tierra del Fuego, from where Wilkes would launch his voyage towards the South Pole. He was meant to return from this southerly foray by the latter half of February 1839, thereby avoiding any danger of his ill-prepared ships being trapped by the ice. However, the six ships did not reach Orange Harbor until mid-February, which meant that any thought of following Weddell's path was out of the question. Instead, Wilkes left the larger *Vincennes* to survey Orange Harbor while he went aboard the smaller *Porpoise* to survey the south-east coast of Palmer's Land, accompanied by the schooner *Sea Gull*.

At the same time, he instructed Lieutenant William Hudson to take the other small ships, the *Peacock* and the *Flying-Fish*, on a voyage south-westward, to the southernmost point Cook had reached – about 71° S, 105° W – and then to return by way of the western extremity of 'Graham's or Palmer's Land, (its proper American name)'. Assuming that Palmer's Land was a large island rather than the peninsula of a continent, Wilkes ordered that the two ships go along the southern coast of Palmer's Land. If his assumption was correct, this would be 'a very important discovery', he wrote.[24]

Hudson's two ships managed to get to the point where Cook had abandoned his voyage south, but the lateness of the season saw them confronted and almost captured by the freezing of the sea. Rather than continuing south-east, Hudson called off the quest and headed for Valparaíso, justifying his abandonment by noting the great danger in which he would otherwise have placed the lives of his men, one of whom had already slipped to his death from the height of the icy yardarm.

Wilkes, too, was confronted by hostile elements while trying to survey the south-east coast of Palmer's Land and step onto its shore. With the deck of the *Porpoise* covered in ice, and with the sailors' clothes woefully inadequate for the conditions, Wilkes was beset by impenetrable fog and blinding snowstorms, looming icebergs and masses of floe ice, as well as the occasional fierce gale. After just nine days at sea, Wilkes turned his ships about and headed back.[25] Their failure had been even more short-lived and miserable than d'Urville's.

The dangers were not imaginary, with the *Sea Gull* later being lost without trace in a gale during its voyage to Valparaíso. Unsure of its fate, Wilkes continued the expedition with his diminished fleet of four vessels, while the storeship *Relief* returned home. It bore several disaffected officers who had fallen out with the ill-tempered and insecure Wilkes, who had become more despotic and increasingly isolated the longer the voyage continued.

By appointing the relatively lowly Lieutenant Wilkes as commander over officers who had been above him on the promotion list, the government had guaranteed trouble on deck once the ships set sail. To try to enforce subordination among his officers, Wilkes had made the desperate decision to display from his ship the pennant of a captain, rather than of a lieutenant, and to add a captain's epaulets to his uniform, as if he really were one. The deception provoked puzzlement among his officers, who had received no official notice of any promotion. It would prove to be a useless ruse.

Almost to a man, the officers, sailors and scientists of the expedition continued to withhold their respect from Wilkes.[26]

After spending more than six months visiting various islands in the Pacific, the expedition sailed into Sydney on 29 November 1839. After offloading the scientists, who would have little to do amongst the ice, the ill-assorted ships left Sydney on 26 December, with three convict stowaways hidden in the hold of the *Vincennes*, presumably unaware of their dangerous destination.[27] As the ships ploughed their way through the Southern Ocean, a young officer on the *Peacock*, William Reynolds, relished the thought of finding 'a Continent, the Existence of which has been so much disputed', and which would allow the United States to 'reap the fame of having at last Contributed Something to the general Knowledge of the World'. His hopes seemed likely to be disappointed when a solid barrier of ice was reached and no passage was found to the supposed Antarctic sea beyond.

Along with Henry Eld, a fellow officer, Reynolds climbed to the masthead on 16 January 1839 to obtain a better view. Convinced that they were looking at more than just ice, the pair returned aloft with a spyglass. They were surprised to see what they took to be mountains in the distance, their peaks disappearing into the clouds. Eld described in his journal how the two men 'almost at one accord . . . pronounced it the Southern Continent' But there had been a number of reports of land being sighted that had subsequently been shown not to be the case, and their excited report was ignored by the ship's commander, William Hudson, who cautiously headed the ship away.

Three days later, back among the ice, Reynolds saw something 'very much resembling high craggy land'. Even Hudson seemed convinced, but attempts to get closer proved futile and doubts began to surface; the 'land' was dismissed as an iceberg.[28] And so it went on, with several more sightings being dismissed.

On 23 January, more signs of land appeared, including a penguin that was captured from an iceberg and taken aboard the *Peacock*. The bird was considered by all to be 'a Most Beautiful Creation', with the crew being amused by its antics before it was killed and skinned for science and its flesh prepared for the delectation of the officers. Small pebbles found within its stomach were sold by the cook to eager buyers among those sailors keen to have 'South Pole stones'. The existence of the pebbles was seized upon by Hudson as solid evidence that land was nearby. He was now convinced that the ice barrier was attached to a continent. He might have been able to confirm his suspicion if the *Peacock*'s rudder had not been badly damaged in a collision with the ice. Although makeshift repairs were made, it was too dangerous for them to continue. Instead, Hudson headed for Sydney to have a replacement rudder installed. 'And so ended our attempt South!' wrote Reynolds.[29]

Wilkes was a worse sailor than Hudson, and more cautious. Back on board the *Vincennes* after his foray on the *Porpoise*, he kept the larger ship a good distance from the ice barrier. Although his officers reported from the masthead that they could see the appearance of land on the horizon, Wilkes could not be induced to risk his vessel in the drift ice and icebergs that lay between it and the barrier. The sightings kept coming during the latter part of January, although there was never unanimity among the officers as to what they had seen. The frequent gales and snowstorms interrupted their attempts to stay within sight of the barrier.

From mid-January, the American ships had been sailing along the ice barrier in zigzag fashion because of the winds and weather. Originally reaching the continent at about 160° E, they had sailed some 1300 kilometres and reached 112° E by 12 February 1839, when Wilkes climbed the mainmast to see a snow-covered mountain range rising in the distance above the ice barrier. After so many sightings of land over the previous fortnight, Wilkes wrote in his journal how the sighting of the mountains 'settles the question of our having discovered, the *Antarctic Continent*'. It was only now that he and his officers celebrated in his cabin with champagne. Nine days later, after passing his original goal of 105° E, Wilkes announced to the assembled crew that they were returning to Sydney.[30]

As Wilkes headed north, Ringgold and the *Porpoise* were still several days' sailing behind him, having become separated during a three-day gale. The officers on the *Porpoise* had not had the good fortune to make any confirmed sightings of the continent, although they believed that it was likely hidden somewhere beyond the barrier. They did not realise that the ice barrier, some 200 feet high, was attached to the continent and formed its coastline. Ringgold and his officers noticed rocks in an iceberg, which they could have taken as confirmation of the existence of nearby land, but the iceberg was believed instead to have drifted all the way from the distant Kerguelen Islands.

On 30 January, at 135° E, the *Porpoise* chanced upon d'Urville's two ships, initially believing them to be the *Vincennes* and the *Peacock*. Then it was thought they were the two British ships of James Clark Ross. Only when the French flags were raised was the truth realised. Then followed the misunderstanding as the American and French ships sailed past each other without any attempt at communication. Ringgold continued on his westerly track until 14 February, when he had reached about 105° E, the limit of his instructions. He then ordered the ship to head for the expedition's rendezvous point in New Zealand's Bay of Islands. Ringgold believed that they had to find a way through the barrier if the supposed continent was to be found, and he had not been able to find such a passage. As a result, he and his officers concluded, there was nothing 'to warrant the belief that land exists anywhere in our vicinity'. The officers on the schooner *Flying-Fish* came to a similar conclusion when their foreshortened voyage ended abruptly at 143° E. Its sickly crew had beseeched the captain to do so, arguing that the journey would otherwise 'soon terminate in DEATH'.[31]

While the *Porpoise* and the *Flying-Fish* headed for the Bay of Islands, where the scientists were awaiting them, the *Peacock* went to Sydney for repairs to its rudder and hull. Wilkes also took the *Vincennes* back to Sydney, arriving there on 11 March 1840. The three convict stowaways were handed in and flogged for their escape; the youngest died during the ordeal.

Wilkes learned that d'Urville had arrived in Hobart and was telling all and sundry that the French had discovered the continent on the evening of 19 January. Putting aside his instructions to maintain secrecy, he met in his cabin with the US consul and drew up a statement for the Sydney press, which announced that the American search for a southern continent had been 'completely successful', with land having first been sighted on the *morning* of 19 January.

In fact, although there had been an unconfirmed sighting by an officer on the *Peacock* as early as 16 January, and although Ringgold later claimed to have seen a distant mountain that same day from the *Porpoise*, there was no record in any of the ships' logs of land being definitely sighted before 30 January, when Wilkes saw rocks on an elevated area a few kilometres from the *Vincennes* and mountains beyond. On that day, he had declared in his journal: 'Antarctic Land discovered beyond cavil.'[32]

Despite his talk of an 'Antarctic Continent', Wilkes had not discovered Antarctica; that honour had already been won by Bellingshausen twenty years before. However, Wilkes had done much more than simply bestow on it the name 'Antarctica'. By sailing more than 1300 kilometres along its barrier, he had shown the existence of a large land mass that might well be part of a polar continent.

Although one of the scientists now assured Jeremiah Reynolds in New York that 'his expectations respecting the Southern Continent have been realized', the original promoter of the expedition was far from impressed by the news.[33] It was all very well to find land and to argue that it was part of a continent, but Reynolds had envisaged the expedition claiming such a continent for the United States. He was mortified that Wilkes had coasted so far along the Antarctic coastline without once 'planting the Stripes and Stars high on the mountain top'.[34] Reynolds could not comprehend the difficulty of landing ashore when confronted by the sheer face of the ice barrier.

After all, the French had stepped onto solid land in the Antarctic, albeit on an islet. Moreover, d'Urville had done what Wilkes had seemed disinterested in doing. He had claimed the nearby coastline for France by performing traditional rites of possession, and he had named the place after his wife. As a result, French ownership would be clear to the world, and d'Urville's own association with the place would be forever memorialised. Wilkes had been more concerned with securing for himself and his nation the glory of the place's discovery. By maximising the extent of the discovery in calling it a continent, Wilkes thereby maximised the glory.

In fact, D'Urville wanted both the glory of discovery and its possession. His encounter with the *Porpoise* on 29 January made him realise that both would be imperilled if the Americans were the first to return to civilisation with news of their voyage. Just three days after the chance meeting, d'Urville turned his ships about and headed for Hobart, despite conceding that 'it would have been possible to push further west and to chart a longer stretch of the ice barrier, perhaps even to encounter land there'.[35]

Reaching Hobart on 17 February 1840, d'Urville immediately wrote a long report to the French navy minister. He enclosed it, along with charts of the voyage, in a dispatch that he sent aboard an English ship leaving for Europe the following day. He also provided an account of his voyage to the local newspapers. While waiting to translate it, one newspaper noted that d'Urville seemed to 'have discovered a large continent to the Southward, but we suspect it is the same land seen by Captain Biscoe'. This brought an immediate retort from d'Urville's secretary, who pointed out that Biscoe's discovery – Enderby Land – was 2700 kilometres distant from d'Urville's Adélie Land. The French navigator was not going to have the credit for his discovery usurped by a British sealer.

D'Urville had suspected that the American ships might follow him to Hobart but there was no sign of their sails coming up the Derwent estuary. His inquiries for news of the Americans proved fruitless, since they had not yet arrived in Sydney. More frustration would come in New Zealand, where d'Urville arrived to discover that the *Porpoise* had preceded him, leaving behind a plaque that made no mention of any American discoveries. D'Urville responded with a plaque of his own, reporting his own visit and proclaiming the French 'discovery of Adélie Land'.[36]

Meanwhile, Wilkes had done what he could in Sydney to ensure his own accomplishments were recognised by the world before he disappeared from view for two more years of exploration around the Pacific.

Wilkes knew that it was not only the French who might snatch his glory. There was also the expedition of the famous British explorer James Clarke Ross, who was reported to be on his way to the Antarctic. Having located the North Magnetic Pole in 1831, Ross was set on doing likewise in the south. Both Wilkes and d'Urville had taken magnetic readings during their voyages in an effort to locate the South Magnetic Pole, but neither had managed to reach it. If Ross proved successful, his expedition could well overshadow that of Wilkes.

In order to forestall such a possibility, when the *Vincennes* joined the other American ships in New Zealand's Bay of Islands Wilkes wrote to Ross in Hobart, advising him of the American discoveries and enclosing a chart showing where the Americans had gone. Although it was a breach of his instructions, Wilkes clearly felt compelled to notify Ross of the discoveries, thereby precluding him from later proclaiming them as his own. There was also much advice for Ross about the nature of the winds, currents and ice conditions in that part of the Antarctic, and a prediction by Wilkes as to where the South Magnetic Pole was likely to be located.[37]

Ross was grateful for the information, although he interpreted the inclusion of the chart as an inducement to have him head for the same stretch of coast. He refused to take the bait. As he later explained, it was demeaning for an explorer from a country such as England, which had always '*led* the way of discovery in the southern as well as the northern regions . . . to follow in the footsteps of the expedition of any other nations'. Instead, he resolved to set his two ships on a course that would take him to parts of the Antarctic coastline unseen by either Wilkes or d'Urville.

Rather than heading south from Hobart, Ross went across the Tasman Sea to Enderby Island, south of New Zealand, where he recorded magnetic observations and found the plaques left by d'Urville and Ringgold, together with a bottle containing a water-stained note written by Ringgold that gave more detail about the movements of the *Porpoise* but made no mention of finding a continent. Ross ascribed this omission either to the American obsession with secrecy or to Ringgold having taken a more northerly route than Wilkes.[38]

The two naval ships of the British expedition, the *Erebus* and the *Terror*, were the best equipped vessels to have ventured to the Antarctic. Although each was only about half the size of the *Vincennes*, they were mortar ships specially designed for bombarding shore fortifications, which meant that their timbers had been strengthened to withstand the recoil of their guns. They had been further strengthened for the polar voyage. Now they were headed for the testing conditions of the gale-prone Antarctic seas.

Before his departure from London, Ross had met with Balleny and learnt of his discovery of the Balleny Islands, just to the east of the discoveries by Wilkes and d'Urville. Balleny had also reported finding an open sea near those islands, which might allow Ross to sail much further south than Wilkes and d'Urville. Although the expedition had been proposed by the British Association for the Advancement of Science and the Royal Society to investigate terrestrial magnetism, the Admiralty had included instructions relating to geographical discovery. If Ross found 'any great extent of land', he was to chart its coastline, and he was also to confirm the positions of the already discovered Graham Land and Enderby Land.[39]

Wilkes had reported to Ross that the magnetic pole was probably located at about 70° S, 140° E, and that he had been blocked by the ice barrier from reaching it. Balleny's discovery of an open sea at about 170° E raised the prospect that Ross could perhaps approach the magnetic pole from a more easterly meridian. That was where he headed in December 1840, roughly following the 170° meridian southward, only to encounter a coastline with an extensive mountain range. It would turn out to be the western entrance of the Ross Sea.

Although disappointed at this apparent setback to his southerly heading, Ross took solace from having 'restored to England the honour of the discovery of the southernmost known land', which had hitherto been held by Bellingshausen's more northerly discoveries. Naming the closest point of land 'Cape Adare' in honour of one of his aristocratic supporters, and the mountain range 'the Admiralty Range', Ross attempted to land on the shore of what he called 'Victoria Land', named after the young English queen. When a landing proved impossible, Ross instead went ashore on the stony beach of a nearby island.

With the weather worsening and an army of penguins protesting their invasion, Ross ordered that a hasty ceremony be performed to take 'possession of these newly-discovered lands, in the name of our Most Gracious Sovereign, Queen Victoria'. The British flag was raised to the cheers of the men, who then 'drank to the health, long life, and happiness' of the queen. Taking whatever rocks and penguins they could fit in their rowboats, Ross headed back to the safety of the ships. Following James Cook and many other British explorers, Ross named the place 'Possession Island'.[40]

Finding that he could still proceed southwards, Ross carefully took his ships into the partly frozen waters of the sea that opened before him; it would later come to bear his name. Hoping that he might still find a way towards the South Magnetic Pole, he gradually realised that it could not be reached by ship. He had to be content with claiming possession of another island, which he named after Sir John Franklin. On it he discovered two massive volcanoes, one of which was 'emitting flame and smoke in great profusion'. Ross did not realise that the volcanoes, which he named after his two ships, were on an island that was attached by ice to the mainland.

More British names were scattered onto other snow-covered geographic features, before Ross was finally halted by an ice shelf some 200 feet high, which stretched across the southern reaches of the Ross Sea. He had reached 78° S, much further south than Weddell or any other explorer had managed to go. The sailors were rewarded with a double ration of rum, while the blacksmith on the *Erebus* correctly surmised that from there to the South Pole 'must be one Solid continent of Ice and Snow'.

Ross considered whether the well-supplied ships could winter in some sheltered spot and then make an overland approach the next summer to the South Magnetic Pole, where he hoped to plant the British flag, just as he had done in the Arctic. However, the lack of a suitable protected anchorage forced him instead to return through the encroaching winter ice to Hobart. It was only now that he deigned to follow the track of Wilkes. Heading west past the Balleny Islands, Ross was bemused as his ships sailed over what Wilkes had marked on his chart as the coastline of the continent. Ross was 'compelled to infer' that the land claimed to have been seen by Wilkes 'has no real existence'.[41]

The later publication of Ross's expedition report touched off a fierce dispute with Wilkes, whose reputation by then was being assailed by his own officers. Wilkes suggested that it was the sighting of land by Balleny that had prompted him to extend further east the chart of the Antarctic coastline that he had sent to Ross, which had given Ross the mistaken impression that Wilkes had sighted the entire coastline. This failed to convince Ross, who responded by expressing doubts about the rest of Wilkes' supposed discoveries.

To emphasise those doubts, Ross refused to include on the published chart of his own discoveries any of the geographic features that Wilkes claimed to have found in the Antarctic. Only those of d'Urville, Balleny and Biscoe were included on the new map, while the misleading chart that Wilkes had sent him in Hobart was included only in an appendix. By omitting Wilkes' discoveries from his 'South Polar Chart', Ross ensured that the coastline he had discovered was by far the largest discovery depicted.[42]

After spending much of the winter in Hobart and Sydney, Ross returned to the Antarctic in December 1841, taking up where he had left off in the Ross Sea before heading to the Falkland Islands. The following summer, he tried to replicate Weddell's feat of sailing south into the ice-free sea that promised a passage to the South Pole. However, it was early March 1843 when Ross made his attempt, which was too late in the season to venture so far south.

After nudging his ships through forty-three kilometres of loose pack ice, reaching 71° 30' S and 14° 51' W, the thickening pack ice and an approaching gale forced Ross to call a halt. Before turning north, he and his officers signed a document detailing their feat, which was then consigned to a cask and thrown overboard, so that their deed might still be known even if the ships met with disaster.[43]

It proved to be the last of his southern voyages. After four years at sea, Ross returned to London in September 1843, having failed in his ambition to reach the South Magnetic Pole. However, he had succeeded in taking magnetic observations that would assist future navigators, and he had discovered an ice-free sea with a coastline that would allow future explorers easy access to the continent's interior.

Ross also returned with a new appreciation of the Antarctic. Whereas Cook had memorably described the 'inexpressibly horrid aspect of the country', Ross described how the members of his expedition had 'gazed with feelings of indescribable delight upon a scene of grandeur and magnificence beyond anything they had ever before seen or could have conceived'.[44]

Together, d'Urville, Wilkes and Ross had added a few thousand kilometres of coastline to maps of the southern polar region, but there was still no agreement as to whether the stretches of coastline connected to make a single, large continent.

Wilkes had suggested that they did, and had given it the name 'Antarctica'. He would laud his voyage as having 'discovered not a range of detached islands, but a vast Antarctic continent.'[45] D'Urville was more cautious. Although he thought it likely that 'land does surround most of the south polar circle', this could only be confirmed if an explorer were 'lucky enough and daring enough to break through the accumulation of pack ice that usually encircles it'.[46] Ross was even less inclined to believe that Wilkes was right. Although he was convinced that the coastline he had discovered was connected with the nearby coastlines discovered by Balleny, Wilkes and d'Urville, he was not convinced that they were connected to the much more distant coastlines of Kemp Land and Enderby Land. Ross thought it more likely that the widely separated coastlines formed 'a chain of islands' rather than 'a great southern continent'.

This belief had important implications for the area's ownership. If the land was composed of large islands, they properly belonged to their separate discoverers, whether English, French or American. If they were a single continent, Ross argued, neither the Americans nor the French had any claim whatever to the land they had discovered, since the discovery of the continent would rightfully belong to the British sealers – Biscoe in 1831 and Balleny in 1839 – rather than to Wilkes or d'Urville.[47] It would take another century before the existence of the southern continent was proved beyond doubt.

CHAPTER 5

'Where an almost virgin field is offered'

1843–1895

After three years at sea, and debilitated by gout, Dumont d'Urville was exhausted when he returned to France in November 1840. For two months he stayed within the bosom of his diminished family at their Toulon home, restoring his strength and commiserating with his wife, Adélie, over the death of their young child. Eventually, he was drawn to Paris as the honours of his grateful nation were heaped upon his frail frame. He was promoted to rear-admiral, admitted to the *Légion d'Honneur* and awarded a gold medal by the *Société de Géographie*.

Among his achievements, d'Urville had discovered a new stretch of coastline in the Antarctic, which he had claimed for his king and named for his wife. With the support of the government, d'Urville began work on a multi-volume report of his expedition, which would enshrine his achievements and reinforce the territorial claim that he had made. He was partway through this massive work when he took his wife and son on a Sunday excursion to see the royal festivities at Versailles in May 1842. The day ended in disaster when the crowded steam train in which they were travelling ran off the rails, causing the first three carriages to land amidst the burning coal of the over-turned engines. Along with more than fifty others, d'Urville and his family were trapped in the wreckage and burned to death.[1]

A month after d'Urville's terrible demise, Charles Wilkes directed the *Vincennes* back into Virginia's naval dockyard, completing a voyage that had been even longer and more dramatic than d'Urville's. There was no official reception awaiting the American explorer as he stepped ashore alone. There was just 'a cold insulting silence' from the administration of President John Tyler, noted Wilkes, while one of the principal scientists, Titian Peale, recalled how they were 'received with a *cold shoulder*'. Peale had hoped that his work with the expedition would secure him a position at the new Smithsonian museum in Washington, where the expedition's scientific material had been deposited, but he was passed over for the post.

The officers and scientists waited in vain for the honours and promotions that they believed they deserved. Peale complained that he and his fellow scientists had 'returned poorer than when we started; and we have been much mortified in being deprived of the honors hoped for, in the non-publication of reports – an injustice to us, and our country'. There was a similar lack of regard by Congress, with the House of Representatives refusing to pass a motion of commendation and the Senate declining to honour Wilkes and his officers with an invitation to its chamber. Although Congress ordered that Wilkes' report of the expedition was to be published – with expensive illustrations on a scale that matched d'Urville's multi-volume work – it only authorised the printing of 100 copies. Wilkes was permitted to have another 150 copies printed at his own expense.[2]

At the time, the president and Congress were at loggerheads, and the return of a mostly scientific expedition was unable to seize either political or public attention. Moreover, while there might have been glory to be won in the Antarctic, Wilkes had not done so. His attempt to follow Weddell's track towards the South Pole had begun too late in the season and had ultimately been abandoned, while his later attempt on the South Pole had been thwarted by the ice barrier, along which he had sailed but upon which he had not landed. He had bestowed the name 'Antarctica' on the supposed continent, but he had not made any territorial claim on behalf of the American nation.

Consequently, there had been no waving of the Stars and Stripes, which might have excited patriotic feelings among the public. The news of his fractious command had also preceded his return, and his disgruntled officers would heap more opprobrium on his proud head as they began to submit further complaints to the navy department. The charges by his officers, and his counter-charges against them, were played out in a series of courts martial. One of the most serious charges against Wilkes was that he had lied when he tried to outdo d'Urville's discovery of land on the evening of 19 January 1840 by claiming that he had done so hours earlier that same day.

The charges by Wilkes against his officers were dealt with first, resulting in a mixture of acquittals and minor punishments. The charges against Wilkes were more serious and cast a shadow over the whole expedition. While he was exonerated on some charges, and others were dismissed on technical grounds, he was found guilty and reprimanded for excessive floggings of his men. On the crucial charge of lying about the discovery of Antarctic territory, the overbearing lieutenant found that none of his officers were willing to bear witness to him having seen land from the *Vincennes* on 19 January. (In fact, it would later be shown that there was no land at the location where Wilkes had claimed to have seen it.) Just one sailor claimed to have heard Wilkes make such a declaration on deck that day.

Wilkes' reputation was in tatters, although national honour was somewhat retrieved when Reynolds and Eld testified that they had seen land from the topmast of the *Peacock* on 16 January. The captain of the *Peacock*, William Hudson, who had dismissed the sighting and ordered it to be recorded in the ship's log as an iceberg, now testified that he believed he had been mistaken and that it was land that they had seen. This did not exonerate Wilkes of lying about his sighting there days later, but the court was unable to find him guilty. If he swore that he had seen land, how could they judge to the contrary?[3] Still, there was no happy ending to the sorry saga, and the reputation of the expedition was sullied ever after. The testimony at the court-martial did, however, enable the United States to claim that the sighting of land from the *Peacock* had preceded by three days the sighting of land by the French.

None of this was of any account to James Clark Ross, who was determined to assert the primacy of British explorers over both the Americans and the French. In his account of his voyage, Ross argued that the British sealers Biscoe and Balleny had discovered the Antarctic coastline well before both Wilkes and d'Urville, which therefore negated any right of these later arrivals to be regarded as the discoverers of the land mass lying to the south of Australia.

Moreover, Ross used the misleading chart that Wilkes had sent him before his own voyage south to question the supposed achievements of the American navigator. He told the Admiralty hydrographer Francis Beaufort that Wilkes had made a 'great mistake' with his careless charting, which was 'sufficient . . . to throw great doubt over all he has done and I have no doubt that many other of his Mountain Ranges will prove to be delusive appearances by which an unpractised eye in Icy Regions is so likely to be deceived'.

When calling at New Zealand's Bay of Islands in August 1841, Ross had made a point of showing Wilkes' chart to the captain of an American naval vessel, explaining how his own ships had sailed over locations that Wilkes had marked as being mountainous land. The American officer was no friend of Wilkes and had spread the story around when passing through Honolulu. It had then been relayed to newspapers in the United States, causing Wilkes and his expedition to be lampooned long before they had arrived home.[4]

Wilkes tried to rebut the accusations, but the stain on his reputation remained, even though England's Royal Geographical Society awarded him its founder's medal in 1847. He had given a name to the continent, but the world remained mostly unsure whether there really was a continent there. In 1928, a leading British historian of the Antarctic, J. Gordon Hayes, was dismissive of the American's achievements:

> Out of at least eight new lands, which Wilkes claimed to have discovered, six have no existence, the seventh is improbable and only one is a possibility . . . The only land claimed by Wilkes, that has been verified, was discovered by d'Urville nine days before Wilkes saw it.[5]

Ross's reputation was not greatly enhanced by his Antarctic expedition. Although he was knighted and received medals from the geographical societies of both London and Paris, he did not receive the public acclamation that had greeted his discovery of the North Magnetic Pole. The account of his voyage took four years to publish, had a small print run and was written in a way that did not excite the public's interest. Yet he was convinced that he had made important discoveries and had blazed a trail that others would soon follow.[6]

It was not the newly discovered land that was important, which he mistakenly regarded as just one of several large islands in a polar sea, but the abundant marine life that he had seen in the surrounding seas. On his voyage south from New Zealand, Ross reported, a 'great many whales were seen'; he and his men 'might have killed any number we pleased'. Most of the whales, wrote Ross, were 'of unusually large size, and would doubtless yield a great quantity of oil, and were so tame that our ships sailing close past did not seem to disturb them'. When he reached the Ross Sea he saw even more.

Ross reported that 'wherever you turned your eyes, their blasts were to be seen'. He thought most were humpback whales, with a smaller number of the more sought-after sperm whales. The whales had 'enjoyed a life of tranquillity and security', but Ross predicted that they would now 'be made to contribute to the wealth of our country'.[7]

Later, while surveying islands south of the Falklands, Ross saw 'a very great number of the largest-sized black whales, so tame that they allowed the ship sometimes almost to touch them before they would get out of the way; so that any number of ships might procure a cargo of oil in a short time'.[8] Ross clearly expected that this would be an alluring vision for whalers, who were always on the hunt for fresh whaling grounds.

If Ross was right, Britain was well placed to reap the benefit. Its navigators had claimed ownership of many of the sub-Antarctic islands that had previously hosted extensive seal colonies and which could now become sites for shore stations for the whaling fleets. The South Shetlands, the South Orkneys, South Georgia and the Falklands all provided possibilities in this regard, as did the new-found Victoria Land, which Ross had recently claimed for Britain.

But such developments did not happen. There was a hiatus of half a century before the wildlife of the Antarctic was again disturbed by significant human intrusion. Despite the abundance of whales reported by Ross to live in Antarctic waters, there were still ample whales in the North Atlantic and North Pacific. Moreover, the whales in the northern hemisphere were easier to catch, being the slow-moving bowhead whales, which were restricted to the Arctic and grew to lengths of twenty metres. The bowheads had a thick layer of blubber, which caused them to float when killed rather than sink to the bottom of the sea, as many other species of whale were prone to do. Their large percentage of blubber, which could be boiled down for oil, made them particularly profitable for whalers, as did the length of their baleens, through which they filtered their food and which were used for a large variety of products, from mattresses to dress hoops.

Bowheads were part of the family of so-called 'right whales', whose main member in the southern hemisphere was the southern right whale. It is doubtless that many of the whales seen by Ross and other explorers were southern right whales, which resorted to Antarctic waters in the summer to feed on krill before heading towards the equator to breed during the winter. Their predilection for breeding in shallow bays in temperate climes, where they were relatively easy to kill and haul ashore for processing, meant that there was little incentive for whalers to confront the greater difficulties and dangers of hunting and killing them in Antarctic waters.

Some whalers and sealers did venture to the Antarctic during the middle and latter parts of the nineteenth century, but invariably they returned disappointed. One such voyager was Mercator Cooper, an American who left New York in August 1851 for the Southern Ocean. Attracted by Ross's description of Victoria Land, he reached there in January 1853 and stepped onto its ice shelf on 26 January, thereby making the first documented landing on that part of the continent. There were penguins aplenty but no valuable fur seals, and he left without further ado.[9]

Polar explorers also failed to follow in Ross's wake. Their focus was on the Arctic and the obsession with finding a northwest passage that might provide an easy, ice-free route between the North Atlantic and the North Pacific, thus connecting the consumers of Asia with the factories of Europe. Britain was determined to be the first nation to do so.

Ross's two ships, the *Erebus* and the *Terror*, which had proved their worth in the Antarctic, were sent by the British government in 1845 on just such an expedition. Ross was offered the command but declined. He was exhausted from his years in the Antarctic, and he had his expedition report to write and a wife to placate. The command went instead to Sir John Franklin, the elderly Arctic explorer and lieutenant-governor in Hobart who had hosted the visits of both d'Urville and Ross. It was an unfortunate appointment. The ships left the Thames in May 1845, never to return.

Franklin had sufficient stores to last four years, and so no alarm was raised until 1848, when Ross was sent with two ships to mount a search that proved fruitless. Many more expeditions followed over the succeeding decades, both British and American, as the mystery of Franklin's disappearance deepened. The successive searches, and the sad story of Franklin's grieving widow, captivated the attention of the world. Eventually, some remains of the missing men were found and an account of the tragedy was pieced together. It told a dreadful tale of death from hunger and disease aboard the trapped ships. The local Inuit people suggested that the survivors who had tried to escape from their icy imprisonment had been driven to cannibalism.[10]

With the unresolved details of Arctic geography beckoning polar explorers from relatively close at hand, there was less impetus to answer the many remaining questions about Antarctic geography. There was also much colonial activity in Africa and Asia during the nineteenth century, as Britain, France, Germany and other European countries carved up those continents between them, opening up new areas of exploration and geographic discovery, and new fields for scientific research. The coastlines discovered in the Antarctic by d'Urville, Wilkes and Ross, apparently barren of life and largely devoid of accessible geology, could not compete with the life forms and geology to be found in these other places.

It was only when the science of oceanography was developed that some fleeting scientific attention was again directed towards the far south. After rich marine life was discovered in the deep ocean off the coast of Scotland in the late 1860s, where no life was thought to exist, Britain's Royal Society combined with the Royal Navy to send a scientific expedition to explore the depths of the world's oceans. In 1872, six scientists were commissioned to join the corvette *Challenger* and take detailed observations of currents and water temperatures every 320 kilometres of the voyage, and to dredge the sea floor for rocks and new life forms.

Powered by sail, and with an auxiliary steam engine for working among the ice, the *Challenger* reached the Antarctic, south of the Kerguelen Islands and west of where Wilkes had left off his exploration. By dredging the sea floor for the debris dropped there by melting icebergs, the naturalist John Murray found that the rocks were similar to those of other continents, which led him to postulate the likely existence of 'a mass of continental land quite similar in structure to other continents'.[11] Of course, whether it was a single large continent, as Wilkes maintained, or several large islands, as Ross argued, still could not be confirmed.

At the same time, a German whaling captain, Eduard Dallmann, was commissioned by the German Polar Navigation Society to take the steam-driven whaling ship *Grönland* to look for right whales and seals in the waters around Graham Land, and to confirm the accuracy of the existing charts of the region. The society was funded by the wealthy German ship-owner Albert Rosenthal; its aim was to increase German participation in whaling and sealing and in the exploration of polar seas.

When Dallmann reached the South Shetlands in November 1873, he found that there was already a British party killing seals, which by now had repopulated the islands' shores. After leaving a plaque on King George Island to record his visit, he went westward along the Antarctic Peninsula, charting Anvers Island and discovering a strait along its south-east coast, which he named 'Bismarck Strait' after the German chancellor. Dallmann's discoveries corrected the existing charts and added detail, but were not of great importance and were only published in German.

The commercial results were even less important. Dallmann found none of the slow-moving right whales he had been sent to kill, only the faster-moving rorqual whales, such as fin, sei and blue whales. He tried to recoup his losses by hunting for seals on the beaches of the South Orkneys and managed to obtain a fair cargo of skins and seal oil, although only a small proportion were from the valuable – and now rare – fur seal. It was a disappointing result for Rosenthal, and Dallmann thereafter concentrated his activities in the Arctic and New Guinea.[12] The Antarctic had gained another reprieve, but it would not last much longer.

European scientific organisations designated 1882–83 as the 'First International Polar Year', and year-long observations were taken at stations established at both ends of the globe. Most were in the Arctic but two stations were established in the far south: a French station at Tierra del Fuego, and a German station on the island of South Georgia.[13] Both were outside the Antarctic Circle, but their activities renewed international interest in the Antarctic.

Some of this interest came from Australia, where the German-born scientist Baron Ferdinand von Mueller was Victoria's government botanist. With most of the great questions concerning Australian geography now answered, Mueller told a meeting of the Victorian Geographical Society in April 1884 that the Antarctic would now provide 'some of the grandest results for geographic science'. Australia was looking outward and would soon colonise part of New Guinea, while Mueller wanted it also to annex the Auckland Islands, as well as Macquarie and Campbell Islands, south of New Zealand, arguing that they were 'naturally Australian possessions'. It was hoped that the society might soon see 'some adventurous explorer with a steam vessel at his command attempting a summer's dash into our antarctic regions, where an almost virgin field is offered'.[14]

Although there was no immediate response in Australia, Mueller's challenge prompted both German and British scientists to echo his call. One was the German scientist Georg von Neumayer, who had been the government astronomer in Victoria in the late 1850s before returning to Germany in 1864. Neumayer, who had been appointed as the hydrographer of the German navy, noted in October 1885 that no one had ever spent a winter in the Antarctic. There was a pressing need, he argued, for an expedition to 'pass a winter there, in order to compare the conditions and phenomena with our Arctic knowledge'. He believed that a sledge party might even be able to get all the way to the South Pole. In Britain, the Association for the Advancement of Science established a sub-committee in September 1885 to encourage research in the Antarctic. This, in turn, gave fresh impetus to the Australian proponents of Antarctic exploration.[15]

In June 1886, the Royal Society in Victoria joined with the local geographical society to establish an Antarctic Exploration Committee. Its aim was to promote geographic discovery, as well as 'extended investigations into climatology, terrestrial magnetism, geology and natural history' and into the 'accessibility and the utilitarian resources of that part of the globe'. As befitting a gold-rich colony of relatively recent creation, practical questions were to the fore. There was the possible commercial benefit from whales and seals, and the benefit to Australian meteorology from studying the Antarctic, from where much of southern Australia's weather was believed to originate. Even at this early stage of Antarctic research, there was an expectation that it might shed light on whether 'climatic change is in progress'.

There was also the prestige that an Antarctic expedition would bring to a colony whose capital, Melbourne, had grown to compare in size and wealth with some of the larger cities of Europe. As one of the expedition's supporters argued in 1888, an Antarctic expedition would 'secure to this colony universal attention, and the approbation of the entire civilized world'. And if Australia did not do it, then the rising German Empire surely would, 'to our mortification and disgrace'.

But there was a limit to what even a wealthy Australian colony could do, and a realisation that Britain would have to take the lead in funding and organising any expedition, while Australia would provide some of the scientists. When Britain declined to help fund an Australian expedition, or to send its own, the Australian interest died away.[16] It was left to the whalers to take the lead.

The whaling industry had been in a state of decline since the 1860s, as the use of whale oil for lighting was replaced by gas and kerosene, and for lubrication of machinery by petroleum oils. The whalers were kept afloat by new uses that were found for baleen. Female fashions, for instance, dictated the wearing of tight-fitting corsets that used the flexible whalebone. Fluctuations in the price of baleen became as important as, and sometimes more important than, the changing price of whale oil in determining whether a voyage returned a profit.

Yet even the demand for baleen could not prevent the gradual extinction of the American whaling fleet during the latter half of the nineteenth century, along with much of the British fleet. More than thirty American boats were lost to the Arctic ice in 1873, and the American Civil War saw others lost. There were still whalers operating in the Arctic from Dundee in eastern Scotland, where whale oil was used to soften jute. It was also used for cheap soaps and candles. Even greater quantities of oil were imported into Dundee from Norwegian whalers, who gradually became the dominant force in world whaling, as British and American capital was largely shifted to other enterprises. With the price of whale oil slumping in the 1880s, there was even less reason to mount a speculative whaling voyage to those far distant seas.[17] But that was about to change.

Several important developments occurred during the last decades of the nineteenth century that would have profound effects on the Antarctic. One was the invention in the late 1860s of a grenade-tipped harpoon gun with a flexible head, introduced by the Norwegian Svend Foyn. It killed fast-moving rorqual whales quickly, and secured them to the ship with a steam-powered winch, thus reducing the chances of them diving or sinking to the depths. A steam-powered compressor was then used to fill the whales with air so that they would float. American whalers had experimented since the 1850s with cannon or rocket-fired harpoons or lances, but had met with indifferent results. They usually shot and lost many more whales than they captured. With Foyn's harpoon gun mounted on the bow of a small steamship, it became much easier to hunt the rorquals.

This did not produce an immediate rush to the Antarctic, as there were plenty of rorquals in the North Atlantic and Arctic whose numbers would have to be severely reduced before whalers began hunting further afield. It was only when that occurred in the late 1880s that attention began to turn again to the Antarctic, although even then efforts were concentrated on the hunt for the more lucrative and easily caught right whales rather than rorquals.

The southern summer of 1892–93 saw whaling ships from Scotland and Norway head for the Antarctic in search of the right whales that Ross and other explorers had reported were there in abundance. A Scottish pamphlet printed in 1874 had called on Scots to create an Antarctic whaling industry, but it made little sense when whales were still relatively abundant in the North Atlantic. That had all changed by 1891, when whale stocks in the Arctic had declined; the pamphlet was reprinted for a more receptive audience.

Attracted by Ross' descriptions of whales off Graham Land, and by the suggestions of the Antarctic Exploration Committee in Melbourne, a Dundee whaling company dispatched four of its whaling ships to the western Weddell Sea in September 1892. Rather than being fast, modern steamships capable of chasing and killing rorquals, they were old barque-rigged sailing ships with auxiliary engines. The expedition also had a scientific purpose, with the Royal Geographical Society and the Meteorological Office both providing instruments for weather observations and geographical discoveries. In charge of these was a young doctor and amateur naturalist, William Bruce, who would become a passionate advocate for scientific investigation of the Antarctic.[18]

News of the Dundee expedition provoked calls in Norway for its whalers to mount their own. The Norwegians had come to dominate the northern whaling industry and had experienced men and suitable ships. One of the centres of Norwegian whaling was the port of Sandefjord, near Oslo, where the whaling company owned by Christen Christensen was located. He had offered to supply four ships for the proposed Melbourne expedition, and when the Australians had failed to secure finance had decided instead to mount his own expedition. The same week that the Dundee ships headed south, Christensen sent the double-masted sealing vessel *Jason* off in pursuit. It was effectively a joint German–Norwegian expedition, since the ships and crews were Norwegian and the controlling company was financed largely by German capital.

However, just as the Dundee expedition had been sent south with equipment designed to catch the slower right whales, so too had the

Jason. In charge of the vessel was a young sealer, Carl Larsen, who had much experience in the Arctic and who expected to reap an easy harvest of right whales. Instead, both the Scots and the Norwegians found there were plenty of blue, fin and humpback whales, which they were not equipped to kill, and no right whales at all. Cargoes of seal oil and skins had to suffice, although their value was not enough to recoup the cost of their nine-month voyages.

Although Christensen was persuaded to try again the following year, this time sending four ships intending to catch only seals, again the venture proved unprofitable. The Dundee expedition was similarly unsuccessful, although it returned with some scientific specimens and observations and made some minor geographical discoveries.[19]

The now venerable Svend Foyn thought that he had the answer to finding riches in the Antarctic. He argued that his Norwegian and Scottish rivals had been looking for right whales in the wrong places. Pointing to Ross's sighting of whales in the Ross Sea, Foyn suggested that it was there that the whalers would find right whales.

He had been approached by a Norwegian friend who had returned from Melbourne with news of the Australian proposal for an Antarctic expedition. The eighty-four-year-old Foyn put his informant, Henrik Bull, in nominal charge of an expedition on the renamed *Antarctic*, a former Arctic sealing ship, which left Norway in September 1893 with Leonard Kristensen as captain. After stopping in the Kerguelen Islands for water, Bull stayed long enough to kill about 1600 elephant seals for their skin and oil. He noted how the large, lumbering animals 'look on with quiet curiosity and interest at the preparations for their own execution'.

Yet the killing was wasted. The ninety-five tons of oil was sold in Melbourne for a disappointing result, while the skins had to be sent to London and earned even less. Moreover, the delay caused by the hunting meant that the meandering expedition now had to wait until the following summer to make the onward voyage to the Antarctic. Some of the time was spent whaling off New Zealand, but harpoon problems meant that only one right whale was actually killed and processed. Several others were shot and lost.

Although the expedition had been feted in Melbourne, some disquiet was expressed at the Norwegians mounting an expedition to a part of the Antarctic which was regarded as being rightfully British, because of its relative proximity to the British colonies of

Australia and New Zealand and the claim of ownership made by Ross. Bull pushed on regardless, with his multi-national crew – 'a mixture of Swedes, Danes, Poles, and Englishmen'. Also among the crew was a Norwegian-born resident of Melbourne, Carsten Borchgrevink, who would go on to have a distinguished record of Antarctic exploration. In mid-January 1895 the *Antarctic* finally reached the Ross Sea, where Foyn's hopes of finding right whales were not borne out. There were plenty of fast-moving blue and fin whales but the men were unable to catch them.[20] Financially, the expedition was another disaster, although it was successful on other grounds.

After exploring part of the Ross Sea without result, and having landed on Ross's Possession Island, Bull decided to attempt a landing on the continent itself. On 24 January 1895, with the *Antarctic* anchored in calm seas off Cape Adare in Victoria Land, Bull, Kristensen, Borchgrevink and four of the crew clambered into one of the ship's boats and set out for the precipitous coastline. It would become a matter of fierce dispute as to who was first to step ashore. Kristensen, Borchgrevink and one of the crew all claimed that honour, oblivious to the fact that the American sealer Mercator Cooper had done so in 1853. Bull made no claim for himself, being content to observe the 'strange and pleasurable' feeling of being among 'the first men who had set foot on the real Antarctic mainland'.

Their landing on the narrow beach was contested by the inhabitants, it being the site of a massive colony of Adélie penguins, some of which 'bravely attacked' the boots of the interlopers. A drawing of the scene suggests that at least two seals were killed during their two-hour sojourn ashore, while the penguins had to be driven away with sticks.

Bull and Kristensen had named some of the islands and other geographical features they had seen in the Ross Sea, although they were conscious that they had probably already been named by Ross. Believing their landing on the mainland to be the first, they erected a pole, on top of which they had fixed a box painted with the Norwegian colours, together with the date of their visit and the name of their ship. It was done as evidence of their feat, rather than as a claim of possession to a land that Ross had long ago discovered and claimed for Britain.[21]

The expedition had done what d'Urville, Wilkes and Ross had all been unable to do. With little effort, the seven men had stepped ashore onto the mainland and thereby opened the possibility of future expeditions exploring by land. As Bull later argued in his book about the expedition, they had:

> . . . proved that landing on Antarctica proper is not so difficult as it was hitherto considered, and that a wintering-party have every chance of spending a safe and pleasant twelvemonth at Cape Adare, with a fair chance of penetrating to, or nearly to, the magnetic pole by the aid of sledges and Norwegian ski-es.[22]

There were additional reasons for exploring on land. Borchgrevink had discovered the existence of lichen on Possession Island, which overturned the accepted view that the Antarctic was too cold for vegetation. The discovery would add to the growing scientific interest in the Antarctic, which Bull helped to encourage by pointing to the 'millions of unexplored square miles [that] offer problems of the most fascinating character to the meteorologist, geologist, and geographer', as well as to the botanist, biologist and zoologist. That was little consolation to Foyn, who had lost a small fortune on the venture. He would have been pleased by Bull's landing on the Antarctic shore, but he died before Bull could telegraph him the news.[23]

The failure of so many whaling voyages might have been expected to dissuade any others from venturing there. However, they had not failed through lack of whales. The problem was simply that they had gone hunting for a species of whale that was no longer in great numbers in the Antarctic. Bull argued that the lack of southern right whales did not mean that it was impossible to make a profit from Antarctic whaling. After all, they had sighted numerous rorquals during their expedition. They just did not have the fast steamships required to chase and kill them, or the factory ships or shore stations to efficiently process them.

The Norwegians had developed the means of doing so in the Arctic, and Bull confidently predicted if these methods could be brought to the Antarctic and used to hunt rorquals, they would bring 'great wealth to whoever sets about their capture'. The Norwegians in the Arctic mostly towed their catches to nearby shore stations, but there were no suitable places for such bases in the Ross Sea.

Even this was not an insurmountable problem, argued Bull, suggesting that two ships be sent on any future whaling expedition: one a small steamer for hunting the whales, and the other a larger ship for processing and storing the oil, and for holding fuel and supplies.[24]

The stage was set for the return of the whalers, this time steaming south in the hunt for the mostly fast-moving rorquals. And the whalers would be joined in the Antarctic by a new rush of explorers and scientists.

CHAPTER 6

'National honor and duty'

1895–1906

Standing on the pitching deck of the Dundee whaler as it returned home in 1893, the young Scottish doctor William Bruce had much to ponder. He had gone to the Antarctic in the hope that he could pursue his interest in natural history, but the whalers' vain hunt for right whales had taken precedence over science and Bruce had been forced to make do with whatever observations he could take at sea. Nevertheless, he had been captivated by the environment and was convinced that many scientific discoveries would be made there. He told a friend that 'the taste' he'd had of the Antarctic had made him 'ravenous'.

This most passionate Scottish nationalist called for a government-financed, national expedition to be sent, with scientific research as its priority. It would 'show that the Britain of to-day is not behind the Britain of our fathers', and would thereby allay the concerns of those who feared that Britain was being overtaken by the rising empires of Europe and North America. If the British government would not do it, Bruce was convinced that he could organise a Scottish expedition of his own. Prestige would come before profits. It would be the honour that came from scientific discovery, rather than from financial success or from feats of manliness, such as a race to the South Pole.[1]

This view put him at odds with the leading English advocate of Antarctic exploration, Clements Markham, who had the conquest of the South Pole firmly in his sights. Markham had been born to a religious family in Yorkshire and had joined the Royal Navy at the age of fourteen. Sailing the world, from South America to the Arctic, he sought to understand all that he encountered. When in South America, he felt impelled to learn Spanish and he read voraciously about the history of the Incas. When he went to the Arctic in 1850 to search in vain for Sir John Franklin's long-lost expedition, the young Markham returned to write a justificatory book about the much-criticised search.

The navy could not contain such a restless and forthright adventurer. He established a geographical department within the India Office but was forced to resign in 1877 after he went without permission on a naval expedition to the Arctic. By then, he was the secretary of both the Royal Geographical Society, which promoted exploratory expeditions, and the Hakluyt Society, which published historic accounts of discovery, many of them translated from Spanish by Markham. In 1893, the sixty-three-year-old adventurer had become the president of both societies, which gave him the perfect platform from which to campaign for an Antarctic expedition.[2]

In Markham's view, the 'real objects' of an Antarctic expedition were finding new lands and the opportunities that would provide for 'young naval officers to acquire valuable experiences and to perform deeds of derring doe'. And he had identified a young naval officer, Robert Scott, as one of several candidates who might lead such an expedition.[3]

To assist his campaign, Markham turned to the esteemed Scottish oceanographer from the *Challenger* expedition, Sir John Murray, whom he asked to lecture at the Royal Geographical Society on the need for England to renew its interest in the Antarctic. William Bruce was among the audience in November 1893 when the venerable oceanographer called on Britain to secure its 'power and progress' by unravelling 'the many riddles' of the oceans. Arguing that there was an enormous Antarctic continent waiting to be discovered, Murray asked whether 'the last great piece of maritime exploration' was to be 'undertaken by Britons' or by 'those who may be destined to succeed or supplant us on the ocean'. He could not promise that there would be any commercial advantage, but he did argue that 'the results of a well-organized expedition would be of capital importance to British science'. There was also the prestige that would accrue to a nation that was prepared to support an expedition for no other purpose than the furtherance of human knowledge. Britain had done so with the *Challenger* expedition, said Murray, and it now led the world in oceanography, whereas its lacklustre support for other branches of science had seen it 'outstripped by foreigners'.[4]

For Markham, science was just the means that enabled him to mount an expedition. He had already convinced the Royal Geographical Society to appoint a committee to plan the best way 'of achieving the objects of Antarctic exploration'. As Markham assured the audience gathered for Murray's lecture, he was committed to the cause of Antarctic exploration and would 'never swerve until it is completed'. It was not only for geographical research and science, said Markham, but because he was 'an Englishman' who regarded the expedition as a means to encourage 'that spirit of maritime enterprise which has ever distinguished the people of this country'.

It was stirring stuff. Roused by the rhetoric as much as by the scientific challenge, the audience was supportive. After several had risen to express their approval and offer suggestions, Markham asked Bruce to tell of his experiences on the whaling expedition. The Scotsman confessed that it had not been successful from either a commercial or a scientific viewpoint. Nevertheless, he agreed completely with Murray's proposal for 'another great Antarctic expedition', this time one with 'a national character' that would maintain Britain's leading reputation in Antarctic research. Bruce offered to join it and be among the first to spend a winter on land in the Antarctic.[5]

Markham's campaign still faced the disinterest of a British government that could see little advantage in the Antarctic and had no wish to add those frozen wastes to its bloated empire. Although a succession of British explorers from Cook onwards had named and claimed parts of the Antarctic Peninsula and its nearby islands, no British government had ever followed up those claims with an official assertion of ownership. That left the way open for other countries to make their own claims.

The Argentine government began to show interest in 1892, when a Buenos Aires company requested fishing rights off Graham Land and the South Shetland, South Orkney and South Sandwich islands. The company claimed that 'no act of sovereignty had been performed there' and argued that the geographic position of those places made them the rightful property of Argentina, which should 'take possession of them and execute acts of sovereignty and occupation'.

When this proposal was reported in Britain, government officials searched through dusty files for evidence of their claims. Although reports were found of explorers raising the British flag on those frozen, fog-prone shores, bureaucrats could find no evidence of the government backing those claims. This meant that any British title was tenuous at best. The Colonial Office showed some interest in forestalling the Argentinians, noting that the islands 'abounded in seals', yet the Admiralty could not see any strategic reason for annexing them and the Foreign Office thought doing so was 'quite undesirable'.[6] Argentina had also failed to see any compelling reason to assert its own sovereignty over the islands, and the matter was allowed to lapse.

The lack of official British interest in holding onto the sub-Antarctic islands did not bode well for Markham's campaign, which was also hampered by the depressed economic conditions of the mid-1890s. Struggling to get his Antarctic expedition onto the government's agenda, Markham turned to the international scientific community for support. He had been encouraged by the news of Henrik Bull's voyage in the *Antarctic* and the landing at Cape Adare, which showed that even a small expedition might land men ashore. If government funding was not forthcoming, perhaps private funding could be raised for an expedition on a smaller scale. If men could be landed from the Ross Sea, they might be able to strike out for the South Magnetic Pole – or even the South Pole itself.

The Norwegian-born Carsten Borchgrevink was among those who had landed at Cape Adare, and he was eager to lead an expedition of his own. Unable to raise funds in Australia, he rushed to Europe so that he could be the first to provide a personal account of the group's feat, and use his presence to seek British support for his own expedition. Borchgrevink arrived in time to address the International Geographical Congress, which met in July 1895 at the recently built Imperial Institute in London's South Kensington. Under Markham's chairmanship, the delegates agreed that the Antarctic was the place that most required explorers' attention. They called for the dispatch of Antarctic expeditions 'before the close of the century'.[7]

There was a rush to respond. As Markham well knew, there was already support among scientists in Germany, where the long-time proponent of Antarctic exploration Georg Neumayer had proposed a German expedition to a congress of geographers in Bremen in April 1895. With the support of the Arctic explorer and professor of geography at the University of Berlin Erich von Drygalski, a committee was established under the chairmanship of Neumayer. Its report recommended that a German expedition be sent to fill in more of the blank spaces of the Antarctic map and to undertake 'the study of meteorology, of terrestrial magnetism, of the shape of the globe, of zoology, botany and geology, and finally of the investigation of Antarctic ice'. As befitting a rising empire, the Germans did not want to explore areas that had been mapped by other nations but planned instead to head for an area that had 'not yet been searchingly examined, and [where] new results cannot fail to be secured'.[8] The interests of scientists and the emperor might thereby coincide, and the government might be forthcoming with funds.

While Drygalski and Markham were struggling to obtain sufficient funds, Belgium put larger nations to shame by announcing its own expedition, which would be led by a young naval lieutenant, Adrien de Gerlache, and supported by the Brussels Geographical Society and funds from a wealthy patron. However, it received little support from the Belgian government and had to look to other countries for experienced crew members and scientists. Some would go on to have distinguished polar careers, such as the twenty-five-year-old Norwegian Roald Amundsen and the thirty-two-year-old Frederick Cook, an American doctor who had been the surgeon on the 1891 Arctic expedition of American explorer Robert Peary. Cook had subsequently tried unsuccessfully to organise an American expedition to the Antarctic.[9] Also aboard Gerlache's multinational expedition were scientists from Poland and Romania.

As Cook's experience indicated, there was now little American interest in the Antarctic. The American Arctic explorer General Adolphus Greely suggested that there was more interest in the Arctic because of the relative ease and economy of voyaging there, and the 'comparative paucity of results to be obtained from explorations of the Antarctic circle'. Moreover, he argued, the Antarctic was a place of 'freezing temperatures' and 'blinding snow-squalls' where few living things could subsist, which made it a much harsher place for explorers to survive.[10]

The American state of Alaska lay partly within the Arctic Circle. It attracted much attention in the late 1890s, when it became the scene for a frenzied gold rush. At the same time, the great trading opportunities of the Pacific were the focus of considerable American attention, particularly after the Spanish–American war of 1898 brought the Philippines and Cuba under American control.[11] Compared to the South Pole, there was the promise of profit aplenty in both those places, and much to occupy the attention of American generals, admirals and diplomats.

Profit was not at the forefront of de Gerlache's mind when he planned his expedition to the eastern coast of the Antarctic Peninsula. Leaving in August 1897 in a former Norwegian whaler, renamed the *Belgica*, de Gerlache did not reach the peninsula until late January 1898, as summer was coming to an end. The lateness of the season threw his plans into disarray. Instead of heading to its iced-up eastern coast, de Gerlache began exploring its western coastline, discovering a number of islands and the 320-kilometre channel that would later bear his name. Frederick Cook described the scene, noting that the:

> . . . scores of new islands which dot the virgin waters are inhabited by countless millions of penguins and cormorants, while great numbers of seals are in evidence on every accessible rock or ledge of ice. In the waters are huge numbers of finback whales which, with the seals, will in the near future offer a new industry.[12]

The exploration came to an abrupt end within six weeks when the ship was caught by the remorseless grip of the spreading ice of the Bellingshausen Sea. It remained drifting in the current for the next thirteen months.[13]

De Gerlache's men had not been provided with proper winter clothing or sufficient stores to see them through such an extended stay. As the encroaching dark and pervading cold wore away at their physical and mental health, the indomitable Cook could still find 'many pleasures for the eye and the intellect in the flashing aurora australis, in the play of intense silvery moonlight over the mountainous areas of ice, and in the fascinating clearness of the starlight over the endless expanse of driven snows'.

On a more practical level, Cook and Amundsen had killed and stored sufficient penguins and seals as food to last the winter, with Cook correctly believing, at a time when the cause of scurvy remained in dispute, that fresh meat was essential in order to keep the disease at bay. A novel aspect of Cook's treatment for scurvy was to have the men sit naked by an open fire for an hour each day. The ever-present threat of darkness-induced depression, or even insanity, among the crew was reduced by regular rounds of work and entertainment. Despite Cook's precautions, one scientist who refused to eat life-giving penguin meat died, and two of the crew were driven mad by their dreadful situation.[14]

The party's fate was almost sealed when the ice refused to release the ship the following summer. Only after they had spent more than a month using ice saws to cut through to an open basin was the ship finally freed, when on 14 March 1899 a channel fortuitously opened to the sea. Instead of proceeding with his planned exploration, de Gerlache promptly returned to Belgium.[15]

The voyage had been the first to winter, however unwillingly, below the Antarctic Circle, which gave confidence to those planning future expeditions. The months in the ice had also given the Belgian scientists a rich scientific haul, and the results of their work were subsequently published in ten volumes.[16] But the expedition had not been all about science. Cook concluded that there was money to be made in the Antarctic, excitedly describing it as a 'penguin El Dorado' and urging that 'the penguin world [should be put] into the field of man's conquest'. He called for 'red-blooded men' to establish a 'new empire' centred on the South Shetlands, with penguins and seals providing the food for a fur industry worked by 'a few healthy families of wild Eskimos, and a breeding stock of white bears, dogs, foxes and some other arctic fur bearers'.[17]

The prospect of profits raised the inevitable question of ownership. As Cook noted in his account of the *Belgica* expedition, anyone who was considering investing in the Antarctic would first need to know 'to whom do these lands belong'. In Cook's view, the vast, ice-covered expanses of the Antarctic 'belong to nobody; at least, there are no valid claims filed, except for those which accrue from the right of discovery'. Yet those rights of discovery could be asserted by several countries, including the United States, Britain, France, Russia, Norway and now Belgium. But they had mostly been established decades before, without any subsequent action being taken, and had weakened over time.

With a great deal of legal force, Cook argued that 'any one who now takes the trouble to occupy any portion of it would undoubtedly become the owner'. Extolling the economic possibilities of fur-farming, Cook predicted that 'these wild wastes' would soon 'form an island empire of thrifty fur-farmers'. Which nation, asked Cook, would step forward to 'guard the interests of this coming race of hardy pioneers'?[18] He later urged the United States to press its claims to the ownership of these unoccupied territories, since 'God is with those that help themselves'.[19]

Cook did what he could to reinforce any future American claim by giving American names to several geographic features, thereby creating an aura of American possession and priority of discovery. While de Gerlache named four large islands after Belgian towns, Cook named the whole group of associated islands the 'Palmer Archipelago' after the American sealer Nathaniel Palmer. Cook also gave American names to several islands, while his fellow officers bestowed their own national names on other features.[20] Such naming did little to advance any of the tentative claims of ownership that had been made during the nineteenth century. Governments would have to take much more definite action for any of these claims to be recognised, but British and European governments were still prevaricating over sending expeditions to the Antarctic.

The Belgians were followed by another private expedition, this time British. Both American and European newspapers had financed Arctic expeditions and published dramatic reports of icy adventures to boost sales of their papers. In 1898 a British newspaper owner, Sir George Newnes, agreed to finance an Antarctic expedition by the pushy Borchgrevink. Having stepped ashore at Cape Adare in 1895, he now wanted to build a base there before heading south across the ice. It was a plan designed to capture the public imagination, in the same way that attempts to reach the North Pole had done.

With £40,000 from Newnes, the thirty-four-year-old Borchgrevink purchased a former Norwegian whaling ship, which was renamed the *Southern Cross*, and assembled an experienced crew and several scientists. They included the Belgian-born physicist Louis Bernacchi, who had migrated to Hobart as a child. He had originally hoped to join the ill-fated *Belgica*, but when that plan had collapsed he travelled to London to offer his services to Borchgrevink. Although many of the crew and one of the scientists were from Norway, the expedition was dubbed by Newnes as 'the British Antarctic Expedition'.[21] It would be the first Antarctic expedition to leave in a blaze of publicity, which was essential to its profit-making purpose.

Before setting out from London in August 1898, Borchgrevink did his best to stimulate public interest by raising the possibility of finding native people in the Antarctic. Even if there were no people, he wrote, there were millions of penguins that were 'so fat that . . . if you dropped a wick down one of their throats and lighted it you would have a living lamp'. The scientifically minded Bernacchi must have squirmed at such statements. He had been advised by his father to stay at his scientific post in Melbourne and 'not seek after Cheap Notoriety'. But the 'vast possibilities' for 'scientific research and geographical discoveries' caused him to ignore his father's advice.

With more than seventy sledge dogs barking and defecating on the deck of the *Southern Cross*, Newnes celebrated the expedition's imminent departure by holding a farewell lunch. The Scottish geographer and librarian of the Royal Geographical Society, Hugh Robert Mill, told the diners that the venture 'reflected the greatest credit on the human race as a whole', since it was 'a real disgrace . . . that there should be any part of this ridiculously small earth of ours upon which no one had ever set foot on or had even tried to tread'.

Markham was notable by his absence. He had been maddened by Borchgrevink's success in raising funds and had poured scorn on the expedition and its leader. While he had convinced learned societies to remain aloof from the expedition, the general public was suitably excited. As the ship pulled into the Thames, thousands of people lined the river banks to cheer it off, while pleasure boats accompanied it downstream. It was 'striking proof of the popularity of the Expedition', Bernacchi wrote.[22] Newnes would have been pleased at the sight, which promised a good return on his investment.

There would be little in the way of geographic discoveries, since Borchgrevink was intent on returning to the familiar Cape Adare, although there was some excitement en route when the captain of the *Southern Cross* thought he saw new land in the distance, which he promptly named 'Newnes Land'. Bernacchi eventually convinced him that it was one of the Balleny Islands. Disappointed, the captain continued to steer the specially strengthened ship through the jostling ice floes. An emperor penguin was captured on one of the floes and later killed and stuffed. Later, when three other penguins were sighted on another floe, the stuffed penguin was put onto the ice to entice the others closer, but they wisely kept their distance, looking on with 'an expression of infinite sadness' before slowly waddling to the edge of the floe and disappearing beneath the water.[23]

When the ship arrived at Cape Adare on 17 February 1899, the men erected what Borchgrevink described as 'the pioneer camp', two prefabricated huts made of Norwegian pine. They were the first man-made structures and the first human settlement to be established on the Antarctic continent. The huts were designed to house ten of the men during the coming winter, while the *Southern Cross* retreated to New Zealand.[24]

On 2 March 1899, as the ship prepared to leave, Borchgrevink hoisted a massive British flag – given by the Duke of York – and told the assembled officers and men that he was 'hoisting the first flag on the great Antarctic Continent'.[25] In fact, the Norwegian colours, albeit painted on a box, had been erected at the same place five years before, with Borchgrevink looking on. But his account of the British colours would satisfy his British readers, with the supposed primacy of its display giving added significance to the event. Bernacchi took a photograph of the scene, the first photograph to be taken on the continent. He later described the 'picturesque and impressive sight', with 'the men grouped around the flagpole on this little strip of land surrounded on nearly all sides by grim, high peaks of snow'. As the ship steamed away and Bernacchi focussed his camera for another photograph, the men on shore 'fired a volley from their rifles, answered by guns from the ship'.[26]

The raising of the flag was not accompanied by a claiming ceremony on behalf of Britain. That would have been inappropriate, given the mixed group of British, Norwegian and Finnish men. Anyway, Borchgrevink had no authority from the British government to do so. Nor was a ceremony performed during the year that the party spent ashore, although small British flags provided by Newnes were scattered across the landscape to give a semblance of British ownership. The party occupied themselves with their scientific observations, collecting rocks and biological specimens, and using the dogs and sledges to make short forays into the hinterland.

Surveying the surroundings of their 'pioneer settlement' from a nearby mountaintop, Bernacchi described in his diary how it was 'unexpressibly desolate', with 'snow peaks rising beyond one another until by distance they dwindled away to insignificance. The silence and immobility of the scene was impressive. Not the slightest animation or vitality anywhere.'[27] For Bernacchi, there was no economic use to which this desolate place could be put. In a subsequent book, he described the Antarctic as being 'enveloped in an atmosphere of universal death'.[28]

In many ways, the expedition was a disappointment. It made no geographic discoveries of any great consequence, nor any other achievements of historic significance other than being the first party to survive a winter onshore. Borchgrevink wanted to achieve something more. When the *Southern Cross* returned to take them home in February 1900, he took the ship south into the Ross Sea. When it reached the edge of the ice shelf, a party was landed, making them the first to have landed on the Ross Ice Barrier, and set out across the ice with sledge and dogs for a token distance, reaching 78° 50' S. After this brief symbolic foray, Borchgrevink was able to declare that he had gone further south than Ross's 78° S, and indeed further south than anyone else to that time.

But it was hardly a feat fit for headlines. It was nowhere near the coveted South Pole, or even near the South Magnetic Pole, which Ross had wanted to reach, although it did open the way for other expeditions to achieve those goals. The expedition was notable for having had the first person to be buried on the continent. The unfortunate man was a Norwegian zoologist, Nicolai Hansen. As he died a lingering death from beriberi, caused by thiamine deficiency, he told his companions that he wanted to be buried on the bleak ridge overlooking Cape Adare. They regretted their ready agreement to do this when it took two days to excavate a shallow grave in the rock and ice. Finally, Hansen was interred, his body wrapped in the Norwegian flag and the grave topped with a wooden cross and brass plate.[29]

Reaching New Zealand on 31 March 1900, Borchgrevink told journalists of his winter in the Antarctic. However, much more dramatic events were hogging the headlines of newspapers throughout the British Empire. The outbreak of the Boer War in 1899 had shifted the public's gaze from the Antarctic to South Africa. Borchgrevink later complained that they had returned to London at a time when the public 'only wanted books about Transvaal and the Great Boer War'.[30]

Moreover, there did not seem to be any profit to be made from a return visit to Antarctica. Bernacchi even dismissed the idea of whaling being profitable, wrongly claiming that the whales were almost extinct. Although he conceded that the conquest of the South Pole would attract future expeditions, Bernacchi argued that the Antarctic was only important for science, which required 'a steady, continuous, laborious, and systematic exploration of the whole Southern Region with all the appliances of the modern investigator'.[31] Such a high-minded purpose was unlikely to attract people such as Newnes to sink their money into another expedition.

But money was forthcoming for expeditions pitched to the baser emotions of imperial competition and territorial acquisition, with four more expeditions going south soon after Borchgrevink's.

German and British expeditions left within days of each other in 1901. The Germans had been late starters in the race to acquire imperial territory around the world and had to be content with seizing lands that other empires had not bothered to grab for themselves, from arid south-west Africa to jungle-clad north-east New Guinea. Yet not even they rushed to add the icy Antarctic to Germany's scattered territories, nor was the allure of scientific discovery sufficient to stir the Berlin politicians' interest.

The German explorer Karl Fricker was so frustrated by the continued inaction that he published a book in 1898 warning his fellow citizens that they were in danger of being beaten to the Antarctic by Belgium and Sweden. How could Germany 'retain its designation of the "Nation of Thinkers and Investigators"', asked Fricker, if it allowed others to take the lead in proving 'the existence or non-existence of an Antarctic continent'? He wanted German science to 'have her share in the solution of this last and greatest problem of geography'. And if the government would not contribute, he wrote, all Germans with an interest in science and exploration should 'aid in the realization of this aspiration'.[32]

With Germany's newspapers reporting the preparations for expeditions by other nations, its scientific organisations agreed in February 1898 to support a proposal by Drygalski for a privately funded expedition. It was a matter of 'national honor and duty', argued Drygalski, invoking sentiments that impelled the German government to offer its support. Following a joint meeting of the Berlin Geographical Society and the German Colonial Society in January 1899, the government finally agreed to finance the expedition. The rising German navy was particularly keen to learn more about the oceans that it wanted to dominate. With ample funding, a three-masted barquentine, the *Gauss*, was built with room for a crew of thirty-two, including five naval officers and five scientists. Geographic discovery and scientific investigation were the expedition's public aims, while prestige for the burgeoning German empire was the reward that was confidently expected by Kaiser Wilhelm II and the expedition's supporters in the Reichstag.[33]

Similarly, the British expedition was initiated only with the support of the Royal Geographical Society, which agreed with Markham's proposal of June 1898 that it should commit £5000 to a public appeal. It was another nine months before a private benefactor agreed to contribute £25,000, which inspired further contributions and made the expedition a viable proposition. Markham's prolonged campaign had finally been successful.

Officers began to be recruited, with Markham choosing the men who were to be what he called 'the Antarctic heroes'. With the massive donation in hand, Markham was able to pressure the government, which until then had offered only to contribute scientific instruments. Markham used his trump card, declaring that there was 'a duel in progress between England and Germany as scientific nations – an international race to the South Pole'. Thus, the idea of a race was born between the fading empire and its rising rival. British mettle would be pitched against German, acting out in the Antarctic the great imperial rivalry.

The idea of a race helped convince the Prince of Wales to become the expedition's patron, and prompted the government finally to commit £45,000 and provide naval officers and sailors.[34] The government's support came after a meeting between Markham and the chancellor of the exchequer, Arthur Balfour, who agreed that it was not acceptable for people of the 'scientific age' to remain in 'total ignorance' of the Antarctic. He was assured by Markham that scientific cooperation with Germany would ensure that there 'cannot be any territorial rivalry between any of the countries engaged in Antarctic exploration'.[35] This was a forlorn hope, given that Markham himself was fomenting the idea of a race.

In planning for the expedition, Markham tried to have Britain's primacy in the Antarctic recognised by the division of the area into quadrants to which he attached British names, calling them the Victoria, Ross, Weddell and Enderby Quadrants. Their boundaries were set along the 90° lines of longitude. Markham thereby paid no regard to the exploration efforts of other nations and effectively raised a British flag over the whole Antarctic. He announced the nomenclature in September 1899 to a bemused audience at the International Geographical Congress in Berlin.

His talk was also a diatribe against the use of dogs in polar exploration, arguing that their use was 'very cruel' and that the achievements of expeditions with dogs could not be 'compared with what men have achieved without dogs'. British explorers had hauled sledges in the Arctic, and he could see no reason why they should not do likewise in the Antarctic. He wanted the expedition to be a test of British manhood, to reassure the country after the desultory fighting of British soldiers in the Boer War.

Two days after the Berlin congress, Markham met with Drygalski and agreed that the Germans would go to the Enderby and Weddell Quadrants, south of the Kerguelen Islands, while the British would explore the Victoria and Ross Quadrants, between Australia and South America. Markham assured the Germans that all four quadrants 'present equal opportunities for penetrating into the unknown, and for making discoveries of the greatest value to science'. Despite the scientific cooperation, there was an inevitable rivalry between the expeditions, which carried the hopes and expectations of their respective empires.[36]

Markham hoped to preserve English naval supremacy by providing a proving ground for the heroism of young officers such as Robert Scott, who would be tested in the icy conditions and judged as much by their feats of courage and endurance as by their geographic discoveries.[37] Markham had supreme confidence in his young acolyte, lauding him as 'an admirable organizer' and 'a born leader of men' who had 'the instincts of a perfect gentleman'.

Being well-bred was important to Markham, who sketched out the lineage of his chosen officers. He also designed the flags that would adorn their sledges and make them easy to identify from a distance. The common element of the flags was the English Cross of St George, which was also prominent on the flag of the expedition's expensive and purpose-built ship, the *Discovery*. Markham was following the tradition of the historic knights of the age of chivalry, with each officer's flag intended to indicate that he was 'first and foremost an Englishman'.[38] For Markham, dispatching the expedition was akin to sending an army of English knights into battle, with science a secondary consideration. When the Royal Society tried to have a geologist and experienced explorer, John Gregory, appointed leader of the expedition over Scott, Markham made sure that his chosen naval officer remained leader on both ship and shore. It was a victory of adventure over science. Among the subordinate scientists would be Louis Bernacchi, who had arrived back from the Borchgrevink expedition in time to take responsibility for magnetism observations, while a biologist and a geologist rounded out the small scientific party.

Markham ensured that William Bruce would not be aboard the *Discovery*. As soon as the expedition had been announced in early 1899, Bruce had dashed off a letter to Markham offering his services and proposing a meeting. Markham took more than a month to reply, and in the end the meeting never happened. It was nearly a year before Markham sent a message to Bruce, suggesting that he apply to be a scientific assistant. This was a gross insult to Bruce, who probably had more experience than any other applicant. Yet he complied, at the same time notifying Markham that he was close to raising sufficient funds to mount an expedition of his own, which he described as 'a second British ship to explore in the Antarctic Regions'.

Bruce appeared to be keen to cooperate with Markham on a joint British enterprise, although Markham regarded his words as a threat to his own funding and railed against the 'mischievous rivalry'. Before receiving this criticism, Bruce informed Markham that 'the sending of a second ship is now assured' and that it would constitute a 'Scottish Expedition', which he wanted to make 'complementary to . . . the German and British Expeditions' by concentrating on the Weddell Quadrant.[39] The fight was now on between the English and the Scots, with Murray and other Scottish scientists and the Royal Scottish Geographical Society lining up with Bruce.

Markham's fears for his funding were unjustified. With government backing, his preparations were unimpeded by Bruce's activities. In late July 1901, Markham's long campaign finally reached fruition. He was aboard the *Discovery* at London's East India Dock as the ship was readied for its voyage. Amidst the chaos of eager spectators and tearful relatives, bags and crates were heaved aboard, including heavy gas bottles for the hydrogen balloon that would later take Scott aloft. Two pianos were also carefully taken aboard, one for the officers and one for the sailors. The provisions for entertainment during the long winters ahead did not end there. Junior officer Ernest Shackleton had practiced conjuring and been provided with a typewriter, a make-up box and dresses for shipboard dramas. The bishop of London went aboard in his robes to remind the assembled men 'never to forget that God is always with them'. Then they were off, with Markham staying aboard for the short voyage to Cowes, where King Edward inspected the ship, telling Scott that his 'labours will be valuable not only to your country, but to the whole civilized world'. As Markham took his leave of the ship, he noted that the young men he had so carefully chosen were 'on a glorious enterprise; fighting no mortal foe, but the more terrible powers of nature . . . Truly they form the vanguard of England's chivalry.'[40]

The focus of the expedition was to be the Ross Sea, from where Scott intended to strike out for either the South Pole or the South Magnetic Pole. The ship would press as far south as possible, leaving stone cairns along the coast in which Scott would deposit records of his passing for the subsequent relief ship. When the *Discovery* could go no further, the party would go ashore to erect prefabricated huts – provided by the Asbestos Company – in which most of the scientific observations were to be taken. The men would spend the winter months ensconced in their ice-bound ship. At the end of the first winter, they would make sledge trips into the interior. Markham made clear that the 'whole force of the expedition must be concentrated on a great scheme of inland exploration'.[41] As it turned out, Scott's experience had hardly prepared him for the tasks that Markham had set him.

It began well enough, with the voyage to New Zealand taking them past Macquarie Island, where penguins were captured and eaten to accustom the men to the taste.[42] Heading south from New Zealand, there was a sense of trepidation about what they might experience. Scott's steward, Reginald Ford, wrote to his sister that they were all 'looking forward to our first introduction to that dread monster [the ice] whose fastnesses we are going to invade, and we hope, to conquer'.[43] By 9 January 1902, the *Discovery* had reached Cape Adare and proceeded to follow the coastline south.

When it finally reached the Ross Ice Barrier, the ship skirted east along the forbidding cliff of ice, looking for the mountains that Ross had seen. At the eastern end of the ice shelf, with mountains looming in the distance, Scott went aloft in the tethered balloon to get a better view of what he dubbed 'Edward VII Land'. Shackleton followed in a flight of his own, taking photographs when the balloon reached the limit of its nearly 200-metre rope. But there was only ice stretching into the distance. Scott then took the *Discovery* back to the western end of the ice shelf and established his base at Hut Point on Ross Island, which was connected by ice to the adjacent land mass.

There they endured the long winter darkness, entertaining themselves with amateur theatrics. In one comic play Scott acted as a housemaid, while twelve sailors gave a 'nigger minstrel performance'. All these diversions were reported in a monthly newspaper, the *South Polar Times*, which Shackleton produced with his typewriter.[44] Among other activities, the officers and scientists debated whether Antarctica was a continent. They resolved the question by six to five in favour.[45]

When the sun finally emerged, sledge parties flying the Cross of St George headed off in several directions across the ice. Scott, Shackleton and one of the expedition doctors, a devout Christian, Edward Wilson, headed south in November 1902, hoping to reach all the way to the South Pole. Starting out with nineteen dogs, they failed even to get off the huge Ross Ice Barrier to the mountainous land beyond. They travelled about 440 kilometres and reached just beyond 82° S, which was further south than ever before, but it was still about 800 kilometres short of the South Pole.

Even that effort nearly ended in disaster, when the dogs sickened from their tainted food and died one by one, and the men weakened from hunger and became stricken with scurvy. Shackleton became so ill that he was coughing up blood, suffered chest pains and was unable to help pull the sledge. The dogs, meanwhile, had become so weak and few in number that they were allowed to walk along behind the sledge until they were killed for food with Wilson's scalpel.

In their desperate situation, relations between Scott and Shackleton soured. They were never to be repaired. When they reached their furthest point south – 82° 15' S – Scott pointedly pushed on with Wilson for another kilometre or so, leaving Shackleton behind with the surviving dogs so that he would not share in the honour. The outbreak of scurvy was a poor reflection on Scott's leadership; he was slow to concede the protective effects of fresh seal meat.

With their food almost gone, the three men barely made it back to Hut Point alive. When in January 1903 the scheduled relief ship arrived, it left supplies that would allow Scott and the ice-bound *Discovery* to remain there another year, while it took away those men considered by Scott as unsuitable to remain. To Shackleton's great chagrin, he was one of those sent home, although he was hailed as a hero in London.

During the second year, Scott led a two-month sledge journey that went more than 550 kilometres south-west and onto the continent itself, reaching into the heart of Victoria Land. Scott wanted to do more, but that would require him remaining for a third year, which was not an option.[46]

With funds running short, and with it no certainty that the *Discovery* would be able to break free of the ice, Markham organised two ships to bring Scott's party home. One was the *Morning* and the other a Dundee whaler, the *Terra Nova*. If the *Discovery* had to be abandoned, these two ships would have sufficient capacity to accommodate Scott and his party, along with all the scientific collections, instruments and stores that were worth saving. It seemed on 5 January 1904, when the two relief ships arrived, that they might have to do just that: the *Discovery* was still stuck fast in the ice. It took another six weeks and the use of explosives before the ice relaxed its grip.[47]

Bernacchi, who had taken over the editing of the *South Polar Times* from the departed Shackleton, was taking his second leave of the Antarctic. He had held great hopes that the English and German expeditions would finally be able to confirm whether or not the great masses of land that had been found in the Antarctic comprised 'a vast continent, or an archipelago of islands smothered under an overload of frozen snow'. Yet he was forced to concede that they had not explored sufficiently to know the truth.[48] All the sledging across Victoria Land had done nothing more than confirm what Bernacchi already knew: that it was a land of great extent. Its precise boundaries remained unknown.

As for the Antarctic's ownership, Scott had paid little attention to claiming a territory that had no obvious value. Nevertheless, his voyage of discovery, the two years spent at Hut Point and the exploration of the interior all added weight to any claim that Britain might make. Markham lauded Scott's 'story of heroic perseverance', which had uncovered 'a new and hitherto unknown world'. Markham implied that these discoveries would be followed by ownership, writing that:

. . . Britannia's flag has thrown
Her shadow on the ice, and hailed the land her own.[49]

For others, though, the expedition had been about discovery and the glory that accrued from it, rather than adding worthless wastes of indeterminate size to Britain's empire. Reginald Ford, the purser on the *Discovery*, later told those in Britain who wondered about spending so much money on an enterprise without any tangible benefit that science and national glory were sufficient justification. It would be 'a very bad day for England', said Ford, 'when she thought of nothing but the possession of land or wealth or power'.[50]

Despite the limited achievements of the costly expedition, and the questions about its organisation, Scott was received with considerable acclaim on his return to Britain. He had an audience with the king at Balmoral, where he lectured the monarch for two hours, before returning to London for a public lecture at the packed Albert Hall on 7 November 1904. The sledge flags that the men had taken to the Antarctic were arrayed on stage like knightly regalia as Scott told the 7000-strong audience of their feats, which were dramatically illustrated with 150 slides of their two years in the Antarctic.

The United States' ambassador to Britain used the occasion to present Scott with a medal from the Philadelphia Geographical Society and to suggest that he be allowed to 'complete the map of the world by planting the Union Jack upon the South Pole', while America's Arctic explorer, Robert Peary, should 'plant the Stars and Stripes upon the North Pole'. This sharing of discoveries, declared the ambassador, would leave the world 'in the warm and fraternal embrace of the Anglo-Saxon race'.[51] But Britain and the United States were not the only contenders for the poles.

The German expedition had left just five days after Scott in August 1901. Drygalski had agreed to explore south of the Kerguelen Islands because he expected that it had better prospects of geographical discoveries. There remained a serious dispute as to whether there was a coastline between about 50° E and 110° E, or whether there was open sea all the way across the Antarctic to the Weddell Sea. Drygalski was prepared for either eventuality.

The *Gauss* reached the edge of the previously unseen ice barrier at about 90° E in February 1902, which suggested that there was such a coastline all the way west to Enderby Land, rather than an open sea. To confirm it, the *Gauss* would have to survey the barrier for hundreds of kilometres. But within a few weeks the ship had become trapped by the ice about ninety kilometres from the coastline, with no hope of escape until the following summer.

The scientists spent the following eleven months making meteorological and other observations, writing by the light of penguin oil, and organising relatively short dog-sledge trips into what Drygalski dubbed 'Wilhelm II Land', situated between about 85° E and 95° E. There, he found an extinct volcano, which he named 'Gaussberg'. On one of these sledge trips, Drygalski built a cairn into which he deposited a bottle containing a document 'detailing the history of the expedition so far'. The German flag was then raised beside it, both to signal their accomplishment and to act as a claim of ownership of the place, although, as Drygalski later noted, the document 'will probably never be seen again'. Like Scott, the Germans used a balloon, tethered nearly 500 metres above the ship, to obtain an elevated view of the ice-covered land, which sloped inexorably upwards and southwards from the barrier.[52]

The scientific results of the German expedition, which were later published in twenty volumes, should have produced enough prestige for any empire. Yet the German emperor wanted more. He had wanted to raise his flag on a larger swathe of new territory. However, when the *Gauss* was eventually freed in February 1903, the ice prevented the ship from getting sufficiently close to the coastline to continue mapping it.

With conditions only set to worsen with the approaching winter, Drygalski decided to head to Cape Town. There, he cabled for permission to await the following summer and make another attempt at extending the territorial limits of Wilhelm II Land. While in Cape Town, Drygalski was disappointed to read of critics who attacked his failure 'to reach a record high latitude'. Sadly for Drygalski, the German emperor was among these critics and refused his request to head south for another summer's work. As he headed home, Drygalski comforted himself with the thought that he had 'achieved all that could have been achieved, and that we were bringing a wealth of certain knowledge about the Antarctic with us'.[53]

Drygalski's fellow geographers and scientists were more appreciative of his achievements, warmly congratulating him when he subsequently addressed the Royal Geographic Society in London. With Markham absent, the evening was a celebration of international cooperation in the Antarctic. The chairman of the meeting, Sir Thomas Holdich, welcomed the collaboration, which, he envisaged, should allow the remaining mysteries of the Antarctic to be revealed 'more quickly, more accurately, [and] more satisfactorily'.

Drygalski agreed that the Antarctic was 'too large to be satisfactorily dealt with by one expedition'. Moreover, his team's scientific observations would be more valuable when compared with observations made elsewhere. Although Sir John Murray gave the Germans a backhanded compliment for having 'proved by their work that this continent exists where we predicted it would be found',

Holdich thought there was still some doubt whether the Antarctic was 'one great continuous land'.[54] Drygalski had certainly added to the evidence that it was a single continent, but he too was cautious in his conclusions. He was content to have discovered and named a relatively small stretch of coastline, which allowed Germany to establish a tentative claim to its ownership. Much more would need to be done if that claim were to be made definite.

The British and German expeditions had been accompanied south by a Swedish one. Sweden had made its mark in polar exploration when Adolf Nordenskiöld had sailed around Europe's Arctic coastline to the Pacific in 1880. The young Otto Nordenskjöld had been inspired by his uncle's feat and led a Swedish expedition to Tierra del Fuego in 1895. Now he was off south again, enlisting the services of Henrik Bull's *Antarctic*, with the whaler Carl Larsen as captain. The focus of this private Swedish expedition was Snow Hill Island, near the eastern tip of the Antarctic Peninsula, and it was there that Nordenskjöld was landed with five companions in February 1902. They remained throughout the winter in a prefabricated hut, while the *Antarctic* retreated to ice-free islands.

When the ship returned the following summer to collect Nordenskjöld's party, the ice was too thick to penetrate. Three men went ashore to walk to Snow Hill Island, while Larsen searched for a way through. Both parties met with ill luck. After making their way across the ice, the land party was thwarted by a stretch of open water that separated them from Snow Hill Island. They returned to where they had been landed so that Larsen could pick them up, but he was having troubles of his own. The *Antarctic* had been caught by ice and sunk, with its twenty-man crew and their cat finding shelter on a nearby island.

The three separated parties had to spend the winter of 1903 surviving as best they could, living in makeshift shelters and eating a monotonous diet mainly of penguin meat. With summer approaching, the three-man land party made a second attempt, this time successfully, to reach Snow Hill Island, where a rescue party on an Argentine corvette found them a few weeks later. Larsen and some of his men then stumbled into the camp after enduring a hazardous journey by small boat and on foot. The remainder of the crew was then rescued and the whole party taken to Buenos Aires.

The expedition's limited scientific results were later published in six volumes, the most important finds being fossils that proved the ancient existence of a giant continent.[55] There had been no official Swedish support for the expedition, and there would be no further Swedish activity in the Antarctic for nearly fifty years.

With national prestige to be gained, it might have been thought that France would also be in the race. Although a French expedition eventually was mounted, leaving Le Havre in August 1903, it wallowed in the wake of its European rivals and was on a smaller scale than most of them. The fact that it went at all was due to the enthusiasm of its wealthy commander, Jean-Baptiste Charcot, who financed much of it from his inherited wealth. The son of a famous doctor, Charcot had abandoned his own medical career for the demanding life of a polar explorer. He later lamented the 'extremely limited' official support that he had received and expressed a hope that France would one day 'take her part with the other great nations in the peaceful struggle against the unknown'.[56]

French eyes were elsewhere. Exploration was concentrated in its colonies, particularly in Africa. D'Urville's claiming of Adélie Land in 1840 had left little impression on the French psyche. Charcot might have excited more interest had he pitched his expedition in terms of national rivalry and honour, as the British and Germans had done, but his interest was purely scientific. He had no time for national rivalry, declaring that the poles had 'no Frenchmen, no Germans, no English, no Danes; there are only people of the Pole, real men'.[57]

Charcot wanted to make his mark through cooperative scientific investigation of a small region, rather than by making a dash to the South Pole or searching for large stretches of new coastline. As he later wrote, it was better to thoroughly explore 'a narrow corner' than sail 'listlessly up and down the seas, exhausting our efforts in haphazard researches which might prove more satisfactory to our vanity, but would assuredly have been far less useful to science'. He would do this by continuing the work of the Belgian and Swedish expeditions along the north-west coast of the Antarctic Peninsula and its associated islands.

His small purpose-built ship, the *Français*, carried twenty officers and crew and six scientists to the South Shetlands and the nearby peninsula. They spent the winter of 1904 ensconced on the ship and in a prefabricated hut on Wandel Island. Observations were taken during the winter and specimens collected from land and sea, but there was little to capture the public imagination until stories began to circulate in France that the ship had foundered and the men perished. The fears for their fate boosted the public interest when Charcot eventually returned safe and well in early 1905. He had made no attempt to lay claim to any Antarctic territory, which had in any case already been discovered by others. Glory would have to come from the eighteen volumes of scientific reports that Charcot went on to publish.[58]

Science and national glory were the motivating forces of William Bruce's Scottish expedition. He made this clear by changing its name from 'the Scottish Antarctic Expedition' to 'the Scottish *National* Antarctic Expedition'. With support from the wealthy owners of a Scottish textile manufacturer, James and Andrew Coats, and token assistance from the British government, Bruce purchased a barque-rigged Norwegian whaler with an auxiliary steam engine, which was refitted and installed with laboratories. Renamed the *Scotia* – after the ancient Scottish nation-kingdom – the 400-ton vessel housed twenty-seven crew members and seven scientists and assistants. Bruce planned to winter ashore for three years, 'as near to the South Pole as practicable', while the ship would carry out deep-sea research in the ocean south of South America. The expedition was farewelled from Edinburgh at a dinner hosted by the venerable Sir John Murray in October 1902. The Scottish origins and non-government nature of the expedition were celebrated, with the *Scotsman* arguing that the expenditure was 'a good national investment'.[59]

With kilts and bagpipes aboard, the *Scotia* reached the South Orkneys in February 1903. It headed east towards the South Sandwich Islands, before turning south into the eastern reaches of the Weddell Sea. Like other explorers who had tried to emulate Weddell's feat of finding open water and a possible passage to the South Pole in that sea, Bruce pushed through the pack ice to about 70° S, 15° W, only to find impenetrable ice beyond. He had long before decided that he would not allow the *Scotia* to be trapped in the Weddell Sea for the winter, which would prevent him from continuing his all-important oceanographic research, so he retreated north to the South Orkneys and anchored in a sheltered bay of Laurie Island.

Although Laurie Bay, at 60° S, was far outside the Antarctic Circle, it was there that Bruce decided to build his land station for meteorological and other observations. It was a more permanent structure than that of any other expedition. Rather than a prefabricated wooden building, Bruce used dog sledges to gather large rocks for a solid stone building with walls up to five feet thick. Taking more than six months to complete, it was designed to last centuries. To announce his expedition's presence to the world, Bruce built a massive stone cairn, which he topped with a flagpole that flew both the ancient Royal Standard of Scotland and the Cross of St Andrew. Throughout the long building process, Bruce's party used the ship as their base; it soon became ice-bound during that particularly cold winter.[60]

The icing of the bay ended Bruce's hopes of continuing his oceanographic research before the next summer, although he did what work he could by cutting holes in the ice and dropping a dredge to the seafloor below, and by netting various marine specimens. He explored and surveyed the island, giving Scottish names to prominent features, including the name of the ship's engineer, who had died of a heart ailment and was buried on shore. Whenever the weather allowed it, the scientists and their helpers roamed the shore, killing penguins, seals and birds for the expedition's specimen collection, as well as for the cooking pot. On one day in October 1903, the botanist Robert Rudmose Brown recorded that twenty-three penguins were killed by members of the crew who had become 'quite keen on penguin meat'. Brown noted that it was 'very difficult to restrain the men from killing indiscriminately'. One only had to 'turn away for a moment and they'll batter into pulp the nearest living thing they can lay hands on'.

Bruce had tried to enforce rules about which animals could be killed and the best way of doing so to prevent their scientific value being destroyed. Bludgeoning their heads was not approved, since Bruce wanted to collect skulls and skeletons as well as organs. He preferred to strangle penguins, noting that it was 'the quickest and the most satisfactory way', since there was little 'chance of blood getting on to the feathers' and it was 'the least painful death'. Bruce was a keen photographer of the wildlife and the spectacular scenery. He had brought to the island both still cameras and a cinematograph, the first such movie camera to be taken to the Antarctic. He had also taken a phonograph to record the sounds of the birds and animals. Newborn Weddell seal pups were captured and taken back to the ship so that their pitiable cries, which Bruce likened to those of a human infant, could be recorded before they were killed and preserved.[61]

On 27 November 1903, Bruce left meteorologist Robert Mossman and five others at the shore station and sailed to Buenos Aires, where the *Scotia* would go into dry dock for repairs. He was also seeking further funds so that he could remain in the Antarctic for another year. Bruce realised that public attention and the satisfaction of his supporters would depend on the expedition reaching a high southern latitude, which he planned to do in 1904 – so long as he could combine it with oceanographic research. He did not want to race the English expedition to be furthest south, noting that he would 'not sacrifice oceanography and other scientific research for the sake of getting one degree – or mile – further than somebody else'.

His beseeching letters to Edinburgh soon brought the desired result, with £6500 being sent by James Coats. Support also came from Argentine companies in the form of coal and other stores, while the Argentine government agreed to take over the shore station on Laurie Island and retain it as a permanent meteorological station after Britain had declined to do so. In return, Bruce agreed to take three Argentinians to staff the station, while Mossman would remain in command there for another year as an employee of the Argentine government.[62]

After taking stores to Laurie Island and dropping off the Argentinians, Bruce sailed the *Scotia* southwards. Mossman bid him farewell from the shore, where the Argentine flag joined the Union Jack on the flagpole, even though there was no official British involvement other than its tentative title to the ownership of the island. Bruce headed back into the Weddell Sea, this time managing to get further south than the previous year, reaching 74° S. More importantly, the ship finally came in sight of what Bruce described as an 'ice face' with a 'gradually rising ice-sheet behind it'. It was actually the Antarctic continent, although Bruce could say no more than that it was a land mass of some extent, which he presumed was connected to Enderby Land and which he named 'Coats Land' in honour of his benefactors.

The slaughter of wildlife and the collection of specimens continued apace whenever Bruce and his party could safely get onto the ice. On 10 March 1904, Bruce shot, skinned and dissected a large Weddell seal. Then, after dinner, he 'spent a considerable time, as it was sunny, photographing the piper, the ship and [an] Emperor penguin'. Laboratory assistant Gilbert Kerr, who had become 'a proficient skinner' of penguins, was dressed in his kilt and played his bagpipes as Bruce photographed the penguin, which was apparently standing calmly alongside him. In reality, Kerr was standing on a tether that was tied to the foot of the unfortunate penguin, which was then killed and dissected. And so it went on, along 240 kilometres of the ice face, before Bruce quit the forsaken place on 12 March 1904.[63]

The occasion of the Scottish expedition's departure from Antarctica was marked with a suitable ceremony. The *Scotia* was surrounded by ice at the time, so Bruce had all hands get onto the ice for a photograph in front of the ship, which was dressed with the 'Royal Scottish Standard on the foremost, the bargee and blue ensign from the mizzen, the Union Jack and the silk Saint Andrew's cross made by my wife, ahead of the ship'. Back on board, they found that the ice still would not let go, so Bruce tried to force the issue with explosives. He even had all the men on the ice, 'shoving with their backs against the ship's side'. Finally, he tried getting 'all hands running at given signals from one side of the ice to the other'. It was all to no avail.

Later that day, the ice released the ship of its own accord and they were able to head for home. A small group of captured Emperor penguins accompanied them, although they did not get far. There were no fresh fish to feed them and they soon sickened, but not before Bruce walked them out on deck during an increasingly rough sea and 'cinematographed them'. Their eventual fate was not recorded.[64]

Bruce's presence, and the proposal for Argentina to take over the shore station, led to renewed calls for Argentina to claim sovereignty over all the South Orkney Islands. When British officials in Buenos Aires alerted London, the British government showed no more interest in the South Orkneys than it had in the 1890s. The Admiralty advised that the islands were 'desolate' and mostly 'ice-bound', and that they had never been formally claimed by Britain; 'nor does it appear that they would ever be of any value'. The Colonial Office agreed, and the Foreign Office instructed its ambassador in Buenos Aires not to raise any objection to Argentina running the meteorological and magnetic observatory.

With Britain seemingly uninterested in owning the islands, Argentina proceeded to lay the basis for a claim of its own. It not only took over the meteorological station, but also designated one of the Argentinian party as a postmaster and the stone house as an Argentine post office.[65] Thus, whenever this official banged his cancellation stamp onto a letter affixed with an Argentine stamp, it constituted an effective exercise of Argentina's authority on an island that was now deemed to be Argentine territory. What was more, the first batch of such letters were sent off in the *Scotia* and passed on to British postal authorities in Cape Town, who thereby implicitly acknowledged Argentine authority in the South Orkneys.

Or so the Argentinians argued. The British lack of interest would soon change when wealth was discovered in the Antarctic. The question of ownership would come to dominate the history of Antarctica.

CHAPTER 7

'Die like gentlemen'

1907–1912

A dramatically different world greeted the French explorer Jean-Baptiste Charcot in late December 1908, as he steered his small ship towards the looming bulk of Deception Island. The empty wilderness through which he had sailed on his previous expedition, just four years before, was now a scene of frantic and bloodied industry.

At the entrance to the sunken caldera that provided the island's deep harbour, Charcot came across two whaling boats, one towing a freshly killed whale. As the carcass wallowed past, the other boat led Charcot's new ship, the cheekily named *Pourquoi-Pas*, safely through the harbour's mouth. Although Charcot had been informed of the whalers' presence – he had even arranged to purchase a supply of coal from their stores – he was taken aback by the sight that unfolded before him as his ship slowly followed the whaling boat into the sheltered anchorage.

Charcot found 'a veritable flotilla of boats, all at work as though in some busy Norwegian port'. It was nearly a century since sealers had first laid waste to the seal colonies of the South Shetlands and South Georgia. Now those islands were again the scene of furious activity.[1] Once more, there was big money to be made in the Antarctic. Instead of temporary sojourners, as the sealers had been, the whaling stations were like Norwegian villages and had an air of permanence. The presence of the settlements would finally bring the question of ownership to the fore. A new era had begun.

The Antarctic whalers were led by Carl Larsen, the captain of the ill-fated *Antarctic*, the ship used by Nordenskiöld's Swedish expedition until it was crushed by the ice and sank in 1903. When the crew were rescued and taken to Buenos Aires, Larsen had regaled Argentinians with stories of South Georgia and its potential as a base for hunting rorquals. A company was formed in February 1904 to do just that, and Larsen returned to South Georgia with three ships in December that year to establish a base at a place he named 'Grytviken'. It was located in a small, protected cove on the island's north coast and surrounded by a picturesque panorama of snow-covered mountains.

Crucially for the whalers, the cove had safe anchorages for their ships, flat land for their buildings and sloping beaches where whales could be dragged ashore and dismembered. They used the accounts and maps of explorers such as Charcot to guide them through the treacherous waters to the places where whales had been observed in large numbers. That first summer, 183 whales were killed and processed. Larsen's success quickly attracted other companies to the island, as well as to the nearby South Shetlands. By 1910, more than 6000 whales had been killed and processed on South Georgia by six shore stations and seven factory ships. The money, the ships and the men mostly came from Norway, although Argentine, Chilean and British companies were also involved, often with Norwegian participation as managers, employees or part-owners.[2]

Improved harpoons and other shipboard equipment meant that a whale would not be lost if a harpoon broke off, or if a dying whale dived. The introduction of anchored factory ships gave the whalers greater flexibility, allowing them to move their operations to wherever the whales were most abundant and where there was a harbour in which a factory ship could be based. Smaller, steam-powered whale catchers would then hunt the whales in nearby waters and tow the carcasses to the factory ship, where the whales would be tied alongside and their blubber stripped off. Then the oil would be removed by the new and more productive method of steam boiling in closed containers.

The whalers not only had new methods of killing and processing, but there were also new uses for their whale oil. It was in demand from makers of cheap soaps and candles, and had begun to be used in the making of nitroglycerine, both for explosives and as a heart medicine.[3] The demand for whale oil would have been even stronger had its use as a foodstuff not been prevented by its strong taste and smell, while the market for whale meat as a foodstuff had to await better methods of shipboard refrigeration to allow its transport to markets in the northern hemisphere. Until then, there was still some profit to be had from the meat and bones in the production of fertilisers, although shore stations were usually required for this processing to take place.[4]

Some concerned observers worried that whales would be hunted to the brink of extinction, as they had been in the Arctic. While governments, and even some whaling companies, wanted the killing to be controlled so that Antarctic whaling could become a sustainable industry, the nascent conservation movement began to agitate for marine sanctuaries that would protect the species. Swiss scientist Paul Sarasin was one of the movement's leaders, arguing in 1909 against the use of factory ships and warning of the devastation they were likely to cause to 'the most marvellous mammals on earth'. He called on whalers to dispense with 'the old idea of destroying rare and wonderful creatures' in pursuit of 'fat dividends', and embrace instead the 'new idea' of becoming 'the protector of nature and her creatures'. In 1910, Sarasin became chairman of a Provisional Commission for the Protection of Nature. He used that position to increase his agitation on behalf of marine mammals, convincing the Society of German Scientists and Physicians in 1912 to call on the German government to support 'the creation of natural reserves for whales and seals through international agreements'.[5] However, the profits to be had from the killing of whales ensured that these early calls for conservation went unheeded. For governments, controlling the Antarctic and reaping revenue was more important than stopping the unbridled killing.

The establishment of shore stations on South Georgia and Deception Island had changed Britain's view of the Antarctic. Previously dismissed as worthless by London, the snow-swept territories were quickly reappraised by officials in the Colonial Office, which administered the nearby Falkland Islands. Whereas Larsen had established a shore station at Grytviken in the confident belief that the island had no owner, the British government now advised him otherwise. In fact, the governor of the Falkland Islands had already offered a mining and pastoral lease over the entire island to a Falkland Islands company that wished to use it for sheep farming. The shepherds were surprised to find when they arrived that Larsen was already there with his whaling boats. They were anchored off a small settlement, which was flying the Argentine flag because of Larsen's Buenos Aires-based company.

Alarmed by this challenge to its ownership, Britain sent a frigate in February 1906 to assert its sovereignty. Until then, Britain had done little about following up its tentative claim to the island. Now, under the shadow of the British guns, Larsen sensibly sought a businesslike solution. He would not contest British ownership if he could lease the land on which his station was situated, and the British governor agreed, leasing five hundred acres to Larsen for twenty-one years at £250 per year.[6]

By just the second year of operations, Larsen was producing a handsome profit for his backers and himself. When Norwegian companies learnt of Larsen's success they turned their sights southward, but they were wary of falling foul of the British government by landing on islands, or fishing in waters, claimed by Britain. So the Norwegian minister in London asked the Foreign Office in May 1906 whether the South Shetland Islands were claimed by Britain or free to all. After some archival investigation by British officials, and after first ensuring that Argentina would not protest, the Norwegians were told that the South Shetlands, South Georgia, the South Orkneys and the ill-defined 'Graham Land' were all owned by Britain. This meant that whales could only be caught in those waters with permission from the governor of the Falkland Islands.

Britain claimed that its ownership rested upon acts of possession performed in 1829 by Captain Foster of the *Chanticleer*, and in 1843 by Sir John Ross.[7] They seem to have forgotten the earlier acts of possession performed by Captain Cook. Privately, the British officials conceded that their claim of ownership was relatively weak since they had 'never formally taken possession of it'.[8] That is, they had not followed up the historic flag-raising with an official announcement by the government, nor had they actually occupied the land.

Both Chile and Argentina wanted these islands for themselves. Argentina had long disputed the British ownership of the Falkland Islands, and had gradually added the South Shetlands, the South Orkneys and their adjacent islands and lands to its list of territorial grievances with Britain. Taking over the meteorological station on Laurie Island provided Buenos Aires with an opportunity to press its case, and in December 1906 the Argentine government issued a decree authorising the payment of salaries to meteorological observers in what it called the 'Southern Argentine lands'.

Britain quickly reminded Buenos Aires that it was British territory, with London taking comfort from the fact that it had supposedly invited Argentina to take over the station, which 'made the

British claim to the islands all the stronger'. Although the Argentine flag was being flown over the station, British officials argued that it did not threaten British sovereignty since no claiming ceremony had been performed by the Argentinians on Laurie Island. The Argentinian foreign minister could only express surprise at Britain claiming an island that it had not attempted to occupy, especially since it had invited another nation to do so.[9] Neither nation wanted to take the matter further in 1906. Britain did not value the islands sufficiently to do so, while Argentina presumably believed that time, and the gradual strengthening of their hold, would eventually make the territory theirs.

For its part, Chile had been encouraging people to settle and develop the sparsely populated southernmost parts of its country, and it saw the new whaling industry as one means of doing so. When the Norwegian Adolf Andresen – of the Chilean ship *Magallanes* – successfully harpooned a humpback whale near the Magellan Strait in 1903 – the first to be killed in such seas – he quickly formed a company with other expatriate Europeans in Chile's southern outpost of Punta Arenas to exploit the large whale stocks of the Antarctic. The governor of the southern Chilean province duly gave the company authority in 1906 to establish a shore station on Deception Island and to use a factory ship, both there and elsewhere in the part of the Antarctic that Chile considered to be its territory.

Another Chilean whaling company was created in 1906 by the Norwegian H. C. Korsholm, who then teamed up in 1908 with the Norwegian whaler Lars Christensen to form yet another company. It would hunt whales in the waters around the South Shetlands, South Georgia and the Antarctic Peninsula in the summer and then follow the whales northwards along the Chilean coast in the winter.[10]

The increasing whaling activity finally convinced British officials to confirm their ownership of the sub-Antarctic islands. Although Larsen and others on South Georgia had implicitly acknowledged British sovereignty by agreeing – under pressure of the frigate's presence – to pay rent, it was clear that British sovereignty needed to rest on more than a few acts of flag-raising in the distant past. When Norway continued to ask Britain to provide a legal basis for its claim to South Georgia and other islands, British officials decided to put the question beyond doubt. On 21 July 1908, the king issued a proclamation known as 'letters patent', which proclaimed British ownership of the Sandwich Islands, the South Orkneys, the South

Shetlands, South Georgia and 'the territory known as Graham's Land'. These territories would all be administered by the Falkland Islands governor as part of a newly created entity called 'the Falkland Islands Dependencies'.[11] Britain followed this by establishing an administrative post next to Grytviken on South Georgia. Although the largely Norwegian settlement of Grytviken had grown to seventeen buildings with about 160 inhabitants, the presence of the British officials provided physical proof of Britain's ownership and effectively prevented other nations from establishing an official presence of their own.[12]

To the relief of British officials, the letters patent did not provoke a protest from the United States or any of the European nations that might have been able to assert a superior claim, based upon their own acts of discovery, to one or more of the relevant places. However, it did lead to a 'violent press campaign' in Buenos Aires, which became so heated that one British diplomat suggested that Britain cede the South Orkneys to Argentina as a 'gift', arguing that they were 'useless' to Britain. Although the Admiralty was open to the idea, not seeing any naval use for the islands, the Colonial Office objected to losing control of islands that had become valuable through whaling. British diplomats in Buenos Aires continued to seek a resolution to the dispute, fearing that it would harm the relationship between the two nations. They even suggested in 1911 that the islands be exchanged for a parcel of land in Buenos Aires on which a new British legation could be built. Nothing came of it. Although an agreement was drawn up, the new Argentine government took umbrage in 1914 at paying for something that was considered part of Argentina. So the dispute over sovereignty continued.[13]

On the islands themselves, a symbiotic relationship quickly developed between whalers and explorers. While the whalers provided supplies of coal and other stores, as well as a place of recuperation and repair, the new wave of explorers alerted the whalers to suitable anchorages and places where whales were abundant. One of the first of these explorers was Charcot, who returned in 1908 for a more intensive look at the western coast of the Antarctic Peninsula.

He was the epitome of a scientist-explorer. Denied government funding for his first expedition, Charcot had largely financed it himself. His ship, the *Français*, had narrowly survived its experience among the ice and had limped back to Buenos Aires, where it was sold to the Argentine government to supply their station on

Laurie Island. Now supported by French government funding, Charcot commanded the lavishly equipped *Pourquoi-Pas*, which had eight scientists, a library of 3000 books and a generous supply of French wine. Although he described his expedition as being part of the 'great effort . . . for the conquest of the Antarctic', Charcot was interested in the acquisition of knowledge rather than territories. His second voyage saw him chart 2000 kilometres of Antarctic coastline over two summers; he returned home with sufficient data and specimens to fill twenty-eight volumes. He had no interest in claiming places on behalf of France, and his major acts of naming commemorated his wife and father rather than his nation. He still hoped that his expedition would be of benefit to France, if only by showing that it could do as well as other nations in the Antarctic. He would leave it to others to make 'the final attack on the South Pole itself'.[14]

With several expeditions trying to reach the North Pole, including rival American expeditions led by Robert Peary and Frederick Cook, a sledge journey to the South Pole was an adventure that was certain to capture the attention of the world and make a rich person of the expedition's leader. Scott had resumed his naval career and seemed to be out of contention, but Shackleton was footloose after having failed to find a lucrative career outside of exploring. In February 1907 he announced that he would lead a new British expedition to the Antarctic. Shackleton had rushed to release the news when he heard that a Belgian expedition was about to be announced. He feared the Belgians would head for McMurdo Sound in the Ross Sea, where he and Scott had been based in 1902. In fact, the Belgian expedition did not eventuate.[15]

Shackleton wanted to use Scott's old base at Hut Point as a launching place from which he might conquer both the South Pole and the South Magnetic Pole. He believed that his sledge journey with Scott and Wilson in 1902 had given him valuable knowledge of how he might do this. Although that journey had been blocked by mountains and the men beset by scurvy before getting even halfway to the South Pole, Shackleton was convinced that horses would provide a surer means than dogs of pulling sledges across the ice and snow. They would also provide more food than a dog when they had fulfilled their purpose. Both Shackleton and Scott had been repulsed by having to butcher their dogs in 1902. This time, Shackleton planned to take a pistol to deal with the horses when their job was done, and he also intended to take one of the newfangled automobiles to see whether it might dispense with the need for animals altogether.

Scott was angered when he read of Shackleton's plan. Not only was Shackleton trying to pre-empt him by reaching the South Pole first, but he intended to use Scott's old base. Although Scott was serving on a naval ship in the Mediterranean at the time, he had been quietly developing a plan of his own to be first to the South Pole. In consultation with the Royal Geographical Society, he too was proposing to use his abandoned hut as a base.

Shackleton's announcement was both a serious breach of etiquette and an infringement of what Scott considered to be his ownership of that part of the Antarctic. Because he had led the first expedition there, Scott told Shackleton, 'anyone who has had to do with exploration will regard the region primarily as mine'. That was the unwritten rule of the gentleman-explorer, he suggested.

Not wanting to be thought less of a gentleman than Scott, and conscious of his rank as a former merchant seaman, Shackleton reluctantly agreed to shift to the eastern side of the Ross Sea, known as King Edward VII Land, hoping he could establish a base at the bay where he had followed Scott up in the balloon. Whatever happened, Shackleton solemnly pledged, he would stay away from McMurdo Sound, although he refused to leave the whole Ross Sea for Scott, arguing that Scott's 'rights end at the base he asked for, or within reasonable distance of that base' and that he had no 'right to King Edward the Seventh's Land'. And so the matter rested, with the two men agreeing to launch their attempts at the pole from opposite sides of the Ross Sea.[16]

Shackleton was desperate to succeed. He was seen off by the king and queen in August 1907 and presented with a Union Jack to raise when he reached the South Pole. But his funding was so tight that he had to make do with the *Nimrod*, a forty-year-old Dundee sealing ship of just 300 tons, whose limited coal-carrying capacity would severely restrict his options. Indeed, Shackleton was so strapped for cash that he was fortunate to get the *Nimrod* to sea before his creditors seized it for unpaid debts.[17] Shackleton paid lip-service to science, telling the Royal Geographical Society that he did 'not intend to sacrifice scientific utility of the expedition to a mere record-breaking journey', but he conceded at the same time that one of his 'great efforts will be to reach the southern geographical pole'.[18]

Despite his talk of science, Shackleton took only two scientists with him, a biologist and a geologist. It was only when the *Nimrod* arrived in Australia that local scientists were belatedly recruited for the expedition, as a way of securing much-needed money from the Australian government. Australians had been discussing the idea of an Antarctic expedition since the 1880s but had never actually stumped up the money. Australia, like the United States, had lost touch with its whaling past and no longer had the practical expertise or people with capital prepared to finance a speculative voyage of exploration. Neither were they as interested as their European counterparts in funding scientific ventures that offered no immediate financial return. The young Louis Bernacchi had complained in 1897 that the pursuit of science had 'no prestige for the majority' of Australians, to whom 'the accumulation of money is the all-absorbing object'.[19]

The arrival of Shackleton changed all that. When he appealed to the Australian government to supplement his meagre budget, at a time when he did not even have the money to pay his crew, the government and opposition rose as one to approve a grant of £5000. The well-connected professor of geology at Sydney University, Dr T. W. Edgeworth David, helped secure the grant by telling Prime Minister Alfred Deakin that Australia 'cannot afford to neglect our nearest neighbor, our white sister'.[20] Along with David, a young geology lecturer at Adelaide University, Douglas Mawson, was recruited by Shackleton as a physicist. The presence of David and Mawson would help answer the naysayers who questioned the sense of spending so much money on a mere dash to the pole.

Although Shackleton assured Deakin that he hoped to gather 'scientific material', his interest in science was scant. He planned to offload the scientific results to Australian scientists and museums to work up and publish. It was the dash to the pole that most motivated him. On its success would depend his fame and his bank balance; Shackleton told his wife that reaching the South Pole would ensure 'there will be ample money . . . for us to live our lives as we wish'.[21]

New Zealand helped the impecunious explorer with a government grant of £1000 and gifts in kind, including a number of sheep. The money helped finance last-minute changes to the ship and ensured that the crew's wages could be paid for the onward voyage.[22] The New Zealand government also provided Shackleton with a hundred sheets of one-penny stamps that were overprinted with 'King Edward VII Land Post Office'.[23] This caused some concern in Australia, where a senator questioned why the government had given £5000 to Shackleton's 'speculative advertising venture', while New Zealand, for a grant of just £1000, had 'secured a world-wide advertisement for that country by the sale of New Zealand postage stamps, impressed with words and letters indicating the connexion of that country with an alleged proprietorship of the South Pole'.[24]

The senator was right to be concerned. Just as the Argentinians had used postage stamps and sworn in a member of the meteorological observatory as a postmaster to establish its claim to the island, so Shackleton was solemnly sworn in by the New Zealand governor as postmaster of King Edward VII Land. He also took with him a rubber stamp with which to cancel the stamps; it bore the words 'British Antarctic Expedition'.[25] Shackleton hoped that he could sell the stamps at a considerable profit to philatelists, while the exercise of his authority as postmaster in the Ross Sea would reinforce the inchoate British claim to the region.[26]

The voyage from New Zealand did not begin well. The *Nimrod* was so overloaded with stores and equipment that five of the fifteen long-haired Manchurian ponies that Shackleton intended to take had to be left behind. There was also too little space for the coal that was required for the ship to steam all the way to Antarctica. The New Zealand government and a sympathetic steamship company saved the situation by providing a steamer to tow the *Nimrod* all the way to the edge of the ice.

Looking on as the *Nimrod* left the port of Lyttelton were 50,000 New Zealanders, taking advantage of the New Year's Day holiday to cram the wharves and wave from the steamers that would accompany the two boats out of the harbour. Sentimental songs about departure and patriotic airs were sung by all and sundry. And when the ropes tying the *Nimrod* to civilisation were dropped, there was a roar of 'effective cheers that can only come from British throats'. The ship's second officer, Arthur Harboard, watched the Union Jack flutter from the bow, the sight making him feel 'proud that we are British, though why I cannot tell'.[27]

The chaos of the expedition's departure was matched by the stormy Southern Ocean, which threw 'mountainous seas' at the *Nimrod*, the like of which Harboard had never seen. Waves crashed onto the crowded deck, threatening to 'take motor car, sledges, boats and pony stalls over the side'. One horse died after falling on its back during the tempest.[28]

When Shackleton arrived in the Ross Sea, a fresh obstacle complicated his plans: he found that large parts of the ice barrier had broken off and disappeared since he had been there with Scott, destroying the so-called 'Balloon Bight' in which he had planned to spend the winter, and from where he hoped to launch his bid for the South Pole. Although he soon found another bay in the barrier, which he named the 'Bay of Whales' because of the abundant mammals in its protected waters, he decided against using it for fear that that part of its barrier might also break away once his base had been established on the ice. The *Nimrod*'s limited coal supplies left him in the awful predicament of having to break his word to Scott, because McMurdo Sound was now the only safe place for him to go from which to make a bid for the South Pole.[29]

Shackleton set up his base at Cape Royds in McMurdo Sound, the sheltered fifty-kilometre-long body of water at the south-west corner of the Ross Sea between Ross Island and the barrier. Although it was on Ross Island, it was about thirty-two kilometres from Scott's old base at Hut Point. This meant that, even if he was not strictly adhering to his agreement with Scott, he could still claim to be staying away from Scott's abandoned base. Tortured by what he had been forced to do, Shackleton tried to justify his action to his much-suffering wife, noting that he 'had a great public trust which I could not betray' and a 'duty to the country and King since I was given the flag for the Pole'.[30]

Such an explanation would not have satisfied Scott, who was furious when he read of Shackleton's apparent betrayal of their agreement. He angrily typed up multiple copies of Shackleton's letters in which the agreement had been reached, then posted them to fellow explorers and people of influence. Scott told Bernacchi that he could now 'have nothing more to do with [Shackleton] when he returns[,] whatever he does'. Moreover, Scott declared that he would 'find it impossible not to doubt any result he claims. I am sure [Shackleton] is prepared to lie rather than admit failure and I take it he will lie artistically. The whole thing is sickeningly vulgar.'[31] In a similar vein, Scott told his future wife, Kathleen Bruce, of the 'terrible vulgarity' that Shackleton had 'introduced to the Southern field of enterprise', which had been 'so clean and wholesome' till then.[32]

As the ship was being tied securely to the shore, a 'regular regiment' of small Adélie penguins came alongside it, not suspecting that some of them would soon be killed and stuffed, or butchered and eaten by both men and dogs. Like many instances of first contact, relations between newcomers and the indigenous inhabitants were marked at first by friendship and curiosity, with David suggesting that the penguins 'had come to give us a civic welcome'. Harboard described in his diary how '[w]e talked to them, and they gabbled back at us, as though they didn't understand, but would like to'.

The following day, two of the larger Emperor penguins waddled across the ice towards the bow of the ship and stood as though 'on sentry duty'. One of the men went onto the ice 'and made a most polite bow, which the penguins each returned, though in a most frigid manner'. This brief interlude would soon come to an end, as the matter-of-fact killing commenced in the interest of science and sustenance.

One seal's gruesome end was graphically described by Harboard: an officer 'shoved a sword bayonet into the thing's side and stirred it all around, leaving it in the seal's side. The poor unfortunate creature writhed about in agony for a quarter of an hour, and then died.' Penguins fared no better, with a dignified-looking Emperor penguin being dragged aboard the ship to be skinned, then its innards were examined and bottled for science. The curiosity of penguins was used against them. One sailor danced about to attract their attention, luring them closer until he could grab an unsuspecting bird by the neck and carry it aboard to be skinned and stuffed.[33]

After the canine slaughter during his previous time with Scott, Shackleton was more protective of his dogs. He had decided against relying on them to pull the sledges and would depend instead on the ponies and a motorcar, which he hoped would be able to speed its way across the ice. However, when the car was lifted onto the shore and its engine cranked into life, it 'went a few feet, and then stopped dead, pulsating violently until [the mechanic] soothed it with a series of hammerings and screwings'.[34] It did not auger well for the greater test to which the car would soon be put.

The ponies had been reduced to just eight in number after two had died en route. They would certainly provide more food when their exhausted frames could pull the sledges no longer, but they also required a great deal of food to keep them going. Dogs required less, and their food could be sourced from the abundant seals and penguins. Unlike horses, dogs were also willing pullers of the sledges. Their dead bodies could even be used to feed the other dogs or the explorers. They could also add greatly to their numbers by having pups. The ponies continued to die when they ate grit blown from the nearby volcanoes. By August 1908, as Shackleton began to establish food dumps for his journey to the pole, there were only four ponies left. Although he had brought some dogs with him, he had no experienced dog handler and the animals were never used. Man-hauling was the inevitable consequence of Shackleton's unfortunate choices.

The first party to set out comprised David, Mawson and Alistair Mackay, a Scottish Highlander and former Boer War soldier who was one of the expedition's doctors. The three headed west in early October for the South Magnetic Pole, dragging their sledge behind them. If they reached their goal, the feat would provide something that could be celebrated in the event that Shackleton did not make it to the South Pole. They were also told to look for valuable mineral deposits.

Shackleton and three companions left on their 1200-kilometre journey towards the pole three weeks later, accompanied by six other men who would lay down the food depots for Shackleton's return journey. After taking a formal photograph of the group holding the Union Jack given to Shackleton by Queen Alexandra, the flag was stowed away until he could 'plant [it] on the last spot of the world that counts as worth the striving for'. The group headed off into the white Antarctic fastness. Four sledges were pulled by the surviving ponies, while the remaining sledge was pulled by the motorcar, with the six men of the support party seated in it. They had barely settled down when the vehicle was brought to a halt by the drift snow; they were forced to dismount and harness themselves to the sledge. The long trudge south had begun.[35]

Scott and Shackleton had failed to get off the Ross Ice Barrier in 1902. Their progress had been painfully slow, and their passage south had been blocked by the imposing bulk of the Transantarctic Mountains. Six years later, Shackleton and his three companions made better time. They chanced upon a way through the mountains in the form of a huge glacier, some fifty kilometres wide and 160 kilometres long. Still, ascending it was no easy task. There was only one pony left alive by the time they began to climb the glacier, and it soon fell to its death down one of the many crevasses, leaving the four men to drag the two sledges for the nearly 640 kilometres that remained to the South Pole.

Their hopes of reaching the pole were raised once they reached the surface of the polar plateau, which covered the continent's interior and sloped up towards the pole. Ever the gambler, Shackleton decided to jettison most of their stores and make a dash for his distant goal. It was not as easy as he imagined. The changing surface of the icecap and the constant ascent wore away at their energy and their temper, with one of the men, the hard-drinking Yorkshireman Frank Wild, railing against the 'dreary God forsaken spot'. Moreover, their food intake was half the amount required to sustain them during such heavy work in freezing temperatures.[36]

Christmas Day 1908 should have been decision day, the time when Shackleton conceded the impossibility of completing two months' journey on just one month's food. Ensconced in the team's tent as he enjoyed a celebratory meal – complete with cigars and crème de menthe – Shackleton convinced himself otherwise and pushed on, ever upwards. Although he was still 400 kilometres from the pole, he could not accept that he had pioneered a trail that another explorer would complete.

The struggle only became harder as the party passed 3000 metres above sea level, a height where altitude sickness begins to take effect. With their body temperatures dangerously low and starvation sapping their strength, Shackleton finally decided on 4 January 1909 that the South Pole was beyond his reach. He agreed with his companions that they should make a last dash to get within a symbolic 100 miles (160 kilometres) of the pole. To go any further would seal their doom.

Five days later, when he estimated that they had reached 88° 23' S, Shackleton called a halt. There had been days of cloudy skies, with no chance of getting an accurate fix on their position with a sextant or theodolite, but Shackleton was satisfied that they were now just ninety-seven miles (155 kilometres) from the South Pole.[37] Writers have since disputed his calculations, suggesting that Shackleton fudged the figures during those final few days so that he could say that he had gotten within 100 miles of the South Pole.[38] Whatever the truth, getting closer than any other party to either the South or North Poles was a monumental achievement, made more so by his serious misjudgements, which had to be surmounted by steely determination and a willingness to take huge risks.

Instead of the South Pole, Shackleton had reached what he called 'Furthest South', and he quickly marked the occasion by raising the silken Union Jack given to him by the queen, with each of the four men taking turns to photograph his companions beneath it. Despite the urgency of starting the 1160-kilometre trek back to Cape Royds, Shackleton took the time to perform a brief claiming ceremony. With the flag flying from its bamboo pole, Shackleton 'took possession of the plateau in the name of His Majesty'. The claim was cemented by Shackleton's naming of the surrounding area as 'King Edward VII Plateau'. He left behind, in a brass cylinder, a sheet of the specially printed expedition stamps, along with some other, unspecified documents. While the queen's flag was packed away for the return journey, a second Union Jack was left to fly in the 'icy gale'. The men took a moment to look forlornly through their binoculars towards their unreachable goal, only to 'see nothing but the dead white snow plain'.[39]

Thus, as Hugh Robert Mill noted in his biography of Shackleton, 'the Plateau was formally annexed to the British Empire'. Although the cylinder would become lost beneath the snow – and would move, very gradually, with the shifting ice towards the faraway coast – it represented yet another British claim to part of the Antarctic continent.[40] A week later, David, Mawson and Mackay did likewise on a spot they calculated to be the South Magnetic Pole, but which almost certainly was some distance from it. David raised a bamboo flagpole planted in a mound of snow, while a camera was set up to photograph the scene. 'We then bared our heads,' wrote David, 'and hoisted the Union Jack at 3.30 P.M.' He then intoned the words given to him by Shackleton: 'I hereby take possession of this area now containing the Magnetic Pole for the British Empire.'[41]

Although he had fallen short of the South Pole, Shackleton was hailed as a hero. The British government was so impressed by 'the great value of the discoveries' that it relieved Shackleton of his remaining debts by granting him £20,000. Newspapers, book publishers and lecture agents, to whom Shackleton had been contracted, added to the windfall. With the help of a New Zealand journalist, he had completed a book during the voyage back to London, which was quickly published in two volumes as *The Heart of the Antarctic* – which, of course, implied that he really had conquered the continent. A worldwide lecture tour followed, during which the now knighted explorer was bestowed with all manner of prestigious medals from learned societies.

Scott could have ruined these celebrations by publicising Shackleton's broken promise, but he kept his anger and his reservations about Shackleton's achievement to himself. He was there to meet the returning explorer when he arrived in London on 14 June 1909 and attended various dinners and lectures at which his former junior officer was feted.[42] Scott could afford to smile, albeit through gritted teeth. The plans for his own expedition were well advanced; they were finally announced to the public on 13 September. Although the 'main object' of his expedition was to 'reach the South Pole, and to secure for the British Empire the honour of that achievement', Scott was careful to pay full regard to science and thereby appease those who questioned the sense of spending so much on a venture to complete the ninety-seven miles that Shackleton had failed to cover. Science now had to be at the forefront of any expedition.[43] As a result, ten scientists were signed on to Scott's second expedition, more than had ever gone south before.[44]

Despite this, in Scott's view and in the public mind, it was very much a race to the South Pole. The scene was set just days before Scott's announcement, when the American explorers Robert Peary and Frederick Cook arrived separately in northern Norway, each claiming to have reached the North Pole. Cook and Peary had been sponsored by rival newspapers – the *New York Herald* and the *New York Times*, respectively – and their almost simultaneous arrival sparked a furious dispute between the pair, as each explorer accused the other of fabricating his achievement.

The daily distances that Cook claimed to have travelled were not credible, argued his critics, particularly as Cook did not have a sledge meter that would have provided an accurate record. Although Cook would be widely regarded as having perpetrated a hoax, opinion later turned against Peary as well. For the present, though, there was a frenzy of public interest as representatives from newspapers, publishers and lecture agents rushed to Norway to sign exclusive deals with the rival claimants.[45]

In one urgent letter from a British publisher, Cook was told that his 'magnificent achievement . . . sent a thrill through the whole civilized world', which was 'on tenterhooks to hear the detailed story'. A London literary agent assured Cook that he would be able to secure at least $US40,000* for the newspaper, magazine and book rights, so long as the story was 'full of human, popular interest', while lecture rights were likely to earn 'an amount almost impossible to estimate'. One lecture agent cabled with an offer of $2000 a week for Cook to appear on vaudeville, while a menswear shop in Jersey City asked Cook to name his price for exhibiting the clothes he had worn at the North Pole.[46]

With such a mad scramble for the stories of Cook and Peary, the South Pole beckoned to explorers as exploration's last major prize. Scott was determined to win it, but he had made little preparation for another expedition, other than trying to develop a motorised sledge. Despite this, the return of Peary and Cook impelled him to announce his plans. Scott's instincts proved right, as Peary quickly announced that he was going to the South Pole himself, although this never eventuated. The German explorer Lieutenant Wilhelm Filchner made a similar declaration from Berlin, while a retired Japanese army officer, Lieutenant Nobu Shirase, did likewise from Tokyo.[47]

The one explorer who kept a studious silence was the Norwegian Roald Amundsen, who had made history in 1906 by being the first to discover a north-west passage in the Arctic, beating the British to their coveted prize. He'd learned much from the Inuit about travelling and living on the ice, particularly about the use of dogs and the dietary benefits of seal meat. He had intended to follow that success with an attempt on the North Pole, but now realised that he had no hope of getting funding for a goal that was already claimed by others. First he would have to 'awaken the interest of the masses' with a spectacular feat that would ensure funding for an Arctic expedition. Cook would later claim that he had encouraged Amundsen to race Scott to the South Pole, showing him the incredible offers he was receiving from newspapers, publishers and lecture agents. With such riches on offer, Amundsen turned his attention there, while keeping his ambition secret from the world in general and Scott in particular.[48]

Scott wanted the Ross Sea to himself and convinced Filchner to base his expedition on the opposite side of the Antarctic, where the Germans could attempt to strike out for the South Pole from the Weddell Sea. The English press had raised a howl of protest at

---

* All dollar amounts that appear throughout this book are in US dollars, unless otherwise stated.

Filchner for daring to organise an expedition at the same time as Scott, as if the Antarctic could only accommodate the activities of one explorer at a time. Anxious to appease the English, Filchner had rushed to London to meet with Scott, and the two men had agreed they would head for the South Pole from opposite directions and cooperate in their scientific observations.

Filchner also tried to allay English concerns by eschewing the name 'South Pole Expedition' and adopting instead the name 'Antarctic Expedition', so as to make clear 'that this enterprise was not concerned with reaching the Pole, but was primarily aimed at solving the problem of the relationship between West and East Antarctica'. He wanted to 'verify the theory that the antarctic continent consists of two islands divided by frozen straits extending across the antarctic region from Weddell Sea to Ross Sea'.[49] After Filchner announced that he planned to cross the continent, Scott also talked of crossing the continent and rejoining his ship on the Weddell Sea. That way, he would match Filchner and not simply be following in Shackleton's footsteps by completing the last ninety-seven miles to the pole.

The Scottish explorer William Bruce also announced a planned crossing of the Antarctic from the Weddell Sea by way of the South Pole, but the funds for this expedition would not be forthcoming. Although Scott and Shackleton would receive government funding, Bruce's Scottish expedition would be refused, prompting the *Scotsman* to describe it as 'an insult to Scottish geographical research and Scotland generally'. While Bruce might not have 'added . . . to British territory' during his 1901 expedition, wrote the *Glasgow Herald*, 'he has definitely extended the territory of knowledge'.[50] But no amount of complaining from across the border would convince the British Treasury to loosen its purse-strings for Bruce.

Science would play a large part in Scott's new expedition. Appointing his close friend Edward Wilson as scientific leader, the party of ten scientists would include four other Cambridge graduates as geologists and biologists, as well as a distinguished meteorologist. Wilson assured his father that he and Scott 'want the Scientific work to make the bagging of the Pole merely an item in the results'. It was designed, wrote Wilson, 'so that no one can say it has only been a Pole hunt, tho' that of course is a *sine qua non*. We *must* get to the Pole.' Even the venerable and still influential Sir Clements Markham wanted this expedition to focus on exploration rather than simply make a dash for the pole.[51]

Douglas Mawson was one of the scientists whom Scott wanted to take with him, but Mawson would only go if Scott appointed him chief scientist. Scott tried to entice him with the title of chief geologist instead, but the Australian refused. Anyway, Mawson wanted to explore the 3200 kilometres of coastline west of Cape Adare rather than go on a pole-hunting exercise, and Scott was unwilling to endanger his plans by indulging him. So Mawson announced that he would mount an expedition of his own, only to have Shackleton suggest that he would lead another expedition and Mawson could be his chief scientist. It was a good way for Shackleton to needle Scott. He told his former commander in February 1910 that he was 'preparing a purely Scientific Expedition' that would leave in 1911 to explore the coast west of Cape Adare.[52]

The multi-volume scientific publications from the French and German expeditions had set a benchmark that the British could not ignore. Moreover, the prospective scientific results of Scott's expedition could be used to justify the £20,000 that the government was contributing. Not that the popular press and their readers cared. They were anxious to have a race to the South Pole and to read of the triumph of English courage and endurance over their continental rivals. For all his talk about science, Scott was happy to oblige. After all, it was the attainment of the South Pole that would ensure his place in the history books and his promotion in the navy.

For Scott, who was newly married and had only just shifted out of his mother's house, the expedition was also an opportunity to prove his masculinity and that of his nation. On 31 May 1910, at the send-off lunch for Scott's ship, the former Dundee whaler *Terra Nova*, the president of the Royal Geographical Society told the assembled guests that Scott would 'prove once again that the manhood of the nation is not dead and that the characteristics of our ancestors, who won this great empire, still flourish amongst us'.[53] It was an added burden for Scott to carry, and it would prove overwhelming.

Scott thought that he was competing only against the Germans and the Japanese, and believed that his previous experience and base on McMurdo Sound would ensure he would be first to the pole. He had not calculated on Amundsen, who had kept up the pretence of heading to the Arctic, even to the extent of accepting instruments from Scott so that the two expeditions could coordinate their observations at opposite ends of the Earth. But Amundsen was planning to head for the Arctic – by way of San Francisco – only after making his attempt on the South Pole, hoping that his success in the south would provide the finance that he lacked for his northern expedition. Expecting that his feat would bring glory to the new nation of Norway, Amundsen chose the long summer twilight of 7 June 1910 – five years to the day since its independence from Sweden – to take leave of his homeland in the famous three-masted schooner, *Fram*.[54] There were no scientific pretensions about this Antarctic mission, just a carefully planned dash for the pole using skis and dog sledges.

Oblivious to Amundsen's scheme, Scott left London by train on 16 July 1910 to board a fast mail boat that would allow him to catch up with the slower *Terra Nova* by the time it reached South Africa. Farewelling him from the station were Shackleton and Filchner, with Scott calling out to Filchner, 'See you at the South Pole.'[55] It was only when he reached Melbourne on the *Terra Nova* that Scott got some inkling of Amundsen's plan, receiving a telegram from the Norwegian that said simply 'Beg leave to inform you *Fram* proceeding Antarctic.' This was simply a courtesy by Amundsen, who had of course informed the Norwegian press that he was now to 'take part in the fight for the South Pole.' Naturally, he had expected that the news would be flashed around the world to Scott. However, the British press had largely ignored the news, which meant that there was nothing in the Australian newspapers to provide Scott with further details. Only after he went on to New Zealand at the end of October was he told by a reporter that Amundsen was intent on racing him to the pole rather than exploring elsewhere in the Antarctic.[56]

It was also in New Zealand that Scott received news from Mawson that he was continuing with plans to mount his own scientific expedition, after Shackleton had confirmed that his would not proceed.[57] Now, Scott had to face not only the rivalry of Amundsen, and possibly Filchner, in the race to the pole, but also the risk that his achievement would be diminished if Mawson explored previously unseen territory.

Scott could no longer ignore the possibility that he was heading for a tragedy rather than a triumph. His overloaded vessel developed a serious leak during a storm in the Southern Ocean and was barely saved from being swamped.[58] Failure became more certain when Scott's party reached McMurdo Sound on 4 January 1911. He sent a group on the *Terra Nova* to explore King Edward VII Land, but they soon encountered the *Fram* anchored in the Bay of Whales. Amundsen was already settled in his base, dubbed 'Framheim', and he left his prefabricated hut to meet the unexpected visitors. In their brief discussion, each group was cagey about its plans.

The English party rushed back to report their worrying find to Scott. The geologist Raymond Priestley noted in his diary that the news made Scott 'as uneasy as ourselves, and the world will watch with interest a race for the Pole next year'. The sighting of Amundsen, who had a small party of men and more than a hundred dogs, put Scott on notice. Although Wilson thought that Amundsen's dogs might be defeated by the 'monotony and the hard travelling surface' of the Ross Ice Barrier, he still feared that the lightly equipped Norwegians might reach the pole with their dogs and skis before the heavily laden British party with their ponies.[59]

Scott was despondent at the news, writing in his diary that 'Amundsen's plan is a very serious menace to ours', since the Norwegian was nearly 100 kilometres closer to the pole. Still, Scott characteristically kept a stiff upper lip and decided to 'proceed exactly as though this had not happened. To go forward and do our best for the honour of the country without fear or panic.'[60] In Scott's view, the stage was now set and he would play out his part till the end.

Anxious not to be beaten by Scott, Amundsen courted disaster by setting out for the pole on 8 September 1911. It was much too early and the Norwegians were beaten back by the intense cold, with temperatures reaching as low as minus 56° Celsius. They left again on 15 October and covered more than thirty kilometres a day as they raced across the Ross Ice Barrier to their first supply depot. Once Amundsen reached the limit of the ice, he had to find his own passage through a gap in the Transantarctic Mountains, up a crevasse-ridden glacier and onto the 10,000-foot-high polar plateau. By the time this was achieved, Amundsen had fed most of his exhausted dogs to his eighteen surviving dogs, as he had planned. All the while, he was naming significant geographical features with the names of his Norwegian supporters and fellow explorers.

With clinical precision, Amundsen and his four companions pushed on towards the pole. When they reached Shackleton's 'furthest south' point, they erected the Norwegian flag on ski sticks attached to the leading sledge to show that, henceforth to the pole, they were blazing a new trail on behalf of their young nation. 'No other moment of the whole trip affected me thus,' wrote Amundsen, as 'tears forced their way to my eyes; by no effort of will could I keep them back. It was the flag yonder that conquered me and my will.' When they finally neared the South Pole on 15 December 1911, one of his companions noted how they had 'attained the goal of our desires . . . and the great thing is that we are here as the first men, no English flag waves, but a 3 coloured Norwegian'.[61]

Amundsen later described how he and his four companions symbolically grasped the makeshift flagpole and 'lifted the fluttering flag on high and planted it together as the very first at the Geographic South Pole'. As they did so, Amundsen declared: 'So we plant you, dear flag, on the South Pole, and give the plain on which it lies the name King Haakon VII's Plateau.' Photographs were then taken of the historic scene, and an exhausted dog was killed with a blow to the skull so that it could be eaten by its fellows; at the end, just its teeth and the tuft of its tail were left. Only then did Amundsen make laborious calculations of their position, finding that they were still more than eight kilometres distant from the pole.

Not wanting to repeat the Cook/Peary controversy, Amundsen established a new camp, which he named 'Polheim', and sent his companions several kilometres in different directions, leaving markers to show Scott that they had indeed covered the South Pole with their ski tracks. Still not satisfied, and with the weather holding, Amundsen decided to travel the final eight kilometres to the point where he calculated the South Pole was situated. More observations were taken, which showed that they were still 'not on the absolute Pole'.

Amundsen realised that his party could keep circling for days without finding the exact spot. So he called a halt, satisfied that they had got 'as close to it as we could hope to get with our instruments'. A tent was left behind, with a Norwegian flag flying atop it. Amundsen also left a letter telling of their discoveries for Scott to forward to King Haakon, in case the Norwegians did not make it back alive. Then they were off, determined to be first to tell their tale and reap the rewards. So blessed was Amundsen's expedition, and so well organised was its leader, that the party arrived back at Framheim fatter than when they had begun. Eleven of their dogs were still alive to pull their sledges.[62]

Of course, Shackleton had already named the plateau after the English king; Norway and England would later squabble over which country had the greater claim to its ownership. Scott could have settled the matter by getting there first, but he was more than 480 kilometres away when Amundsen reached the South Pole. Scott's three motorised sledges, which had caterpillar tracks, might have been the saviour of his expedition. They could haul tons of supplies, and Scott had hoped they would crawl their way relatively quickly across the ice. However, one sledge had been lost when it was carelessly unloaded from the *Terra Nova* onto ice that was insufficiently thick. The heavy machine had crashed through into the depths.

Scott's two remaining machines were used to establish food depots along the route he and his ponies would take. The motorised sledges began their depot-laying on 24 October, nine days after Amundsen's lightly loaded party had set off for the pole. It was another week before Scott and the rest of his five-man party set off, accompanied by another depot-laying party and eight sledges drawn by ponies. The ill-fated explorer soon found that he had left behind the Union Jack given to him by the queen mother to display at the pole. Ironically, it was a Norwegian member of his party who was instructed to fetch it; he used skis to quickly cover the distance of twenty-seven kilometres. Having spurned skis himself, Scott trudged on with the ponies, which struggled whenever they encountered soft snow. The motor sledges, too, proved a disappointment and had to be abandoned after just eighty kilometres.[63] As for the ponies, they were shot as planned, one by one, as they became too exhausted to go on.

Before long, Scott and his companions were hauling the sledges themselves. It was madness, celebrated by Markham and embraced by Scott as proof of English manliness. Not all the party members agreed. While the evangelical Christian and deeply racist marine Henry Bowers relished getting to the pole by 'the traditional British sledging method', the cavalry officer Lawrence Oates, who had paid £1000 to join the expedition and had been detailed to manage the horses, was bitter about what he called 'wretched man-hauling'.[64]

The extra effort required by man-hauling meant that Scott and his four companions were slowly starving. Their inadequate rations left them short of vital vitamins, and the duration of their journey made them vulnerable to scurvy. Scott's poor planning and execution had them approaching the pole as the summer was coming to an end, forcing them to endure much colder temperatures and worse weather than Amundsen had, and making their safe return much more difficult.

It was not until 16 January 1912, by which time Amundsen was almost back at his base, that Scott came across a black marker flag left by the Norwegians and saw in the snow the tracks – from sledges, skis and dogs – left by their rivals. The English were not quite at the pole but it was clear that the Norwegians had preceded them. The diary of the devout Wilson betrayed little emotion at their defeat, simply noting that Amundsen 'can claim prior right to the Pole itself. He has beaten us in so far as he made a race of it. We have done what we came for all the same and as our programme was made out.'[65]

Scott was less restrained: 'Great God! this is an awful place and terrible enough for us to have labored to it without the reward of priority.' All his hopes and ambitions were shattered, although he still thought that he might yet achieve something if he was able to return quickly and 'get the news through first'. Before leaving, they found Amundsen's tent and stood at what they took to be the South Pole, where they built a cairn of snow and raised the Union Jack. They took the obligatory photographs, which would now be of less value to the world's press. Ironically, neither Scott nor Amundsen had stood at the South Pole: both had missed it by a kilometre or two, due to the difficulties of taking accurate sightings at the apex of the Earth.[66]

As Scott and his four companions struggled back across the plateau, weighed down by scurvy, frostbite and a crippling sense of failure, Scott stopped to collect nearly fourteen kilograms of rocks. It cost valuable time and added an unnecessary weight to the sledges, which their weakening bodies had to drag in the face of the deteriorating weather. Gathering the geological specimens helped to seal their doom, but it was done to embellish their scientific credentials and thereby distinguish their expedition from Amundsen's. Scott was telling the world that his expedition, and the likely sacrifice of their lives, had not been done as a mere race to the South Pole. If they died, it would be in the cause of science, rather than in the pursuit of a pointless adventure.

They began dying, one by one. The first to go was Edgar Evans, whose strong frame belied his sad end. Weak and befuddled by scurvy, he sank to his hands and knees in the snow, unable to go on. Put on a sledge, he died in the tent that night, 17 February, most probably from the combined effects of scurvy, hypothermia and starvation. A month later, it was the turn of Lawrence Oates, as his frostbitten feet turned gangrenous, adding to the toll taken on his body and mind by hunger and vitamin deficiencies. He pleaded to be left in his sleeping bag in the snow, but was encouraged to press on in the hope they would meet rescuers with dog sledges laden with food. Instead, there was only silent emptiness, which offered no hope of Oates bridging the final 200 kilometres or so that separated them from their salvation. The following morning, Oates left the tent, never to return. According to Scott's account, probably invented for posterity, Oates told his three companions as they huddled in their sleeping bags that he was 'just going outside and may be some time'.

A few days later, Scott convinced his companions to remain in their tent and await their own end, rather than press on and probably die in their tracks. The tent offered more hope that their bodies and their records would be found. Scott would have the death of a tragic martyr, rather than return humiliated by failure and crippled by frostbite and possible gangrene. It took at least nine days for the three men to die. With the wind howling outside, Scott scribbled away with his pencil, writing a bundle of letters and messages that absolved himself of blame and self-consciously created a heroic portrait of himself and his men.

In one letter, Scott claimed that their deaths would show 'that Englishmen can still die with a bold spirit, fighting it out to the end', which 'makes an example for Englishmen of the future'. In another, Scott wrote of how they would 'die like gentlemen', which would 'show that the Spirit of pluck and power to endure has not passed out of our race'. Months later, when their bodies were eventually found, they were left where they lay, with just a cairn of snow and ice erected over them. Back at Scott's base a cross was placed on a nearby hill, inscribed with words from Alfred Tennyson's 'Ulysses': 'To strive, to seek, to find, and not to yield.'[67]

While Scott's increasingly desperate journey came to its tragic conclusion, Amundsen was packing up his base and loading his dogs and supplies onto the *Fram* for the stormy passage across the Southern Ocean to Hobart. It was more than a month before Amundsen was able to get ashore in Tasmania, from where he sent a coded cable on 7 March 1912 to his brother in Norway announcing his success. 'The South Pole has become ours,' Amundsen later wrote in a letter to one of his Norwegian supporters, as he headed for the northern hemisphere to revel in the plaudits of the world.

Shackleton was quick to tell journalists that he had preceded Amundsen to the polar plateau, and that his British name for it therefore had precedence over Amundsen's Norwegian name. That was 'absurd', replied Amundsen, since Shackleton had no 'right to name a territory he had never seen'. Some other English and American observers were similarly stinting in their praise, believing that Scott had somehow been unfairly robbed of his prize. In Scott's absence, and with no knowledge yet of his fate, these churlish responses were little more than murmurings.[68] Yet they scraped the lustre off Amundsen's prize, causing him later to blast the British as 'a race of very bad losers' and to resign in protest from the Royal Geographical Society.[69]

While the British had to concede that Amundsen had been first to reach the South Pole, the question of the ownership of the plateau had just begun. Punctilious British officials later pointed out to their Norwegian counterparts that Shackleton had reached the plateau long before Amundsen had named and claimed it for Norway. More importantly, it was the tragic manner of Scott's demise, and the stirring nature of his last messages, that imbued the British with the deepest sense of ownership over the South Pole. To the chagrin of both Shackleton and Amundsen, Scott's death had captured public attention in a way that their deeds could not.

The bumbling incompetence of Scott and his expedition was realised by some at the time. Shackleton was one of those who wondered aloud how such a well-equipped expedition could be defeated by a blizzard, implying that there were other reasons for the failure. These were never fully explored until Roland Huntford's searing exposé in his 1979 book *Scott and Amundsen*. Back in the anxious pre-war years, the English empire needed Scott as a hero. It embraced his self-constructed myth with an almost religious fervour.[70] In the manner of his death, the failed explorer had forced the Antarctic into the British imagination, which would make it that much easier for British leaders to bring the Antarctic securely within the British Empire.

CHAPTER 8

'In the name of the King and the British Empire'

1912–1918

Scott and Amundsen had viewed the crevasse-ridden path to the South Pole as a road to fame and fortune. Scott wanted to get there first so that he could dispel the dispiriting talk of the English as a declining race. He also wanted wealth to support his widowed mother, and his new wife and son, and he expected the achievement would lead to his promotion to admiral in the Royal Navy. For his part, Amundsen thought that winning the race to the pole would bring glory to the young nation of Norway, produce much-needed finance for his planned drift across the Arctic and convince his Norwegian lover to leave her husband for him.

For both men, the Antarctic was simply a means by which they could achieve dreams and ambitions located elsewhere. They had no more interest in owning the ice-choked continent than in owning the moon. Douglas Mawson was different. He recognised that much greater wealth might lie concealed in the Antarctic and its surrounding waters than was available via newspaper and book deals. He became the first explorer to make the claiming of Antarctica his primary purpose.

Mawson had been born in Yorkshire in 1882 but had migrated with his family just two years later to Australia. His father was a farmer who had sought prosperity working the land outside Sydney, only to see his ventures fail. He began working as an accountant in inner Sydney, while his wife supplemented their income by taking in boarders. The threat of financial insecurity impressed itself upon the young Mawson and would permeate his life. Although he gained a good public education and became a geology lecturer at Adelaide University, he was forever pursuing fortune-making schemes. His father, too, never lost the gleam in his own eye that had brought him to Australia. He would later unsuccessfully seek his fortune developing a rubber plantation in New Guinea.

As a geologist, Mawson was often trying to find a rich deposit of gold or some other precious metal, or patenting new methods of processing minerals. While on Shackleton's expedition in 1907–09, he realised that the Antarctic might have rich mineral deposits and he became determined to find them. Additional impetus for his fortune-finding came when he fell in love with the Dutch-born daughter of a wealthy mine manager; Mawson felt impelled to somehow match her father's financial standing.[1]

When Shackleton abandoned his plans to lead a second Antarctic expedition, Mawson went ahead with his own. In January 1911, he took his plans to a meeting of the Australasian Association for the Advancement of Science in Sydney, appealing to the curiosity and nationalism of his fellow scientists. Leaning over the lectern, the lanky geologist asked them whether they were 'content to allow distant countries to poach on their inherited preserves', thereby suggesting that the Antarctic coastline closest to Australia rightfully belonged to Australia. He went on to ask how Australians could 'remain heedless of this land of great potentialities lying at our doors'. There was little talk by Mawson about selflessly adding to the store of human knowledge, and more about self-interestedly uncovering a new source of human profit. He also mentioned the nation-building potential if Australia's young men were able to achieve greatness in the Antarctic. As he later declared, the expedition would bring Australia to the attention of the world and wrap the nation in 'the prestige [that comes from] being strong enough to investigate and claim new territory'. And Australia had to act before 'foreign nations . . . step in and secure this most valuable portion of the Antarctic continent for themselves'.[2]

The scientists acclaimed his plans, voted £1000 to support the expedition and established a committee to oversee the scientific program and seek further funding. Mawson needed much more money – at least £40,000 – if his expedition was to eventuate. He hoped that wealthy Australians would contribute, which would ensure that it was a private expedition controlled by him rather than a government expedition controlled by learned societies or bureaucrats. A cartoon in Sydney's *Daily Telegraph* called on its rich readers to 'be a sportsman and back this young man against the foreigners'. Several wealthy Australians were quick to do so, including the tobacco manufacturer and newspaper proprietor Hugh Denison, who was also a staunch imperialist.

To elicit more private donations, Mawson promised major donors a share in the ownership of any mineral resources. However, private donors were not coming forward in sufficient numbers, or offering sufficient amounts, to fund the expedition. Mawson realised that he would have to look to governments for the bulk of the budget. He went to Melbourne to meet the Australian defence minister, Senator George Pearce, to press his case for federal government funding.[3]

Pearce later told reporters that Mawson had noted the 'great scientific importance of the expedition, but had dwelt more strongly on its commercial side'. Mawson told Pearce that 'the prospects of mineral discoveries were good, and that there were other commercial possibilities in the way of sealing and fishing enterprises'. The proximity of the Antarctic to Australia and the practicability of its permanent settlement were also emphasised, which raised the dangerous implication of what might happen if an enemy nation ever took possession of the place. Pearce was assured that Australia could forestall such a possibility by taking possession first.

Australia had some cause to be concerned. The increasing naval rivalry between Britain and Germany had evoked widespread fears of a war. Japan was seen as an even greater threat to Australia. It had recently defeated Russia's European fleet and was set on a policy of territorial expansion. With a Japanese expedition already on its way south, and with Filchner's German expedition soon to depart for the Antarctic, Mawson played up Australian fears about those two nations as he sought official funding for his own expedition. Pearce promised to put the request to Prime Minister Andrew Fisher.[4]

Before receiving a formal response, Mawson sailed for England on 26 January to seek further funding in London, to order clothing, sledges and other supplies, and to find a suitable ship. He asked the Royal Geographical Society for £1000, telling a meeting of its members that the long stretch of coastline that he wanted to explore had rarely been seen and only once been landed upon – and that was by d'Urville more than seventy years ago, albeit on an offshore islet. Consequently, declared Mawson, his expedition 'should have no difficulty in achieving great geographical successes'. He was also acutely conscious of the 'scientific data . . . waiting to be collected' and had 'ardently sought for an opportunity to reap the harvest'.

He would not only explore the coastline and collect specimens and observations, but was also seeking the 'authority to raise the Union Jack and take possession of this land for the British Empire'. This authority was everything. Anyone could raise a flag, but Mawson saw clearly that the legal effect of taking possession would be all the greater if it was backed by an official imprimatur. That had to come from Britain rather than Australia, which was still very much a dependent dominion within the British Empire. But the British government refused to give Mawson its blessing. Leaving London on 21 June 1911, he decided to go ahead and act on his own authority, in the hope that it would be endorsed after the event. Shackleton certainly thought this was worth doing. He had been in the audience at the Royal Geographical Society and had opined, after Mawson's talk, that the Australian's proposal 'may not have the glamour of the Pole around it, but it is work that will stand for ever if successfully accomplished'.[5]

The Royal Geographical Society proved sympathetic, although it only granted Mawson £500. Other appeals for money from private British donors proved mostly fruitless, but with Shackleton's help he convinced a British press baron to appeal for donations from the readers of the *Daily Mail*. Money and goods to the value of £12,000 flowed in, allowing Mawson to purchase a ship, another ice-proven Dundee whaling ship, the rather elderly *Aurora*, and to enlist the experienced polar sailor John King Davis as its captain.

Mawson also decided to take an aircraft with him; he would be the first explorer to do so. This was at the suggestion of Scott's wife, Kathleen, with whom Mawson stayed for a time. She thought an aircraft would stimulate public interest, and might also be used to raise money in Australia by making demonstration flights.

Despite his wish for a private expedition, much of Mawson's funding came from governments: £2000 from the British government, £18,500 from four Australian state governments and £5000 from the federal government. The latter donation was a quarter of what he had requested. Like so many explorers, Mawson would leave for the Antarctic deeply in debt to those who had made loans rather than donations, and to those suppliers who had provided goods on credit.[6]

The aircraft never made it to the Antarctic – at least, not as an aircraft. During a demonstration flight in Adelaide, it crashed to the ground and was wrecked beyond repair. Mawson decided to take it without wings, hoping it might serve as a motorised sledge.[7] The patched-up wreck was dubbed by Mawson an 'air-tractor sledge', so that its use might still excite public interest.[8] Although denied the aircraft that might have allowed him to quickly survey large swathes of land, Mawson still had two other innovations to grab newspaper space from the pole-chasing Scott and Amundsen expeditions, whose fate was then unknown.

One was the use of radio, which would allow instant reports of his activities and achievements to be printed in the world's newspapers within hours – or, at most, a day or so. There would be a radio at his main base and another at a base he would establish on Macquarie Island, which was necessary to relay the messages across the Southern Ocean to Australia. The *Aurora* would also have a radio, but only to receive messages rather than to send them; that way, Mawson could retain control of all outgoing communications from the Antarctic. As a member of the *Aurora* crew later noted, Mawson wanted 'no information whatever as to what we are doing, where we are, or where we are going, to leek [sic] out before we get back again to civilisation'. While Amundsen had to battle the tempestuous seas of the Southern Ocean for more than a month to get news of his triumph to Hobart, Mawson could theoretically do it in an instant. The second innovation was Mawson's decision to use the newly invented means of taking colour photographs. The young Australian photographer Frank Hurley was given the job of bringing the Antarctic to life for distant audiences.[9]

There were no misconceptions about the purpose of Mawson's expedition. While he prepared to leave for the south, the Adelaide *Register* observed that Mawson had convinced 'Parliaments, scientific and learned bodies, and the people generally, to see eye to eye with himself regarded the practicability and desirableness of Australia becoming, in a sense, the suzerain of a vast area of the Antarctic continent'.[10]

The *Aurora* sailed right into a gale when it left Hobart on 2 December 1911, its deck crowded with assorted crates and chained-up dogs. Several years' supply of cheese was packed into a cabin, and two tons of butter was lashed to the roof of the deckhouse. So crowded was the small ship that another vessel was chartered to take most of the men and some of the supplies as far as Macquarie Island, where a meteorological and wireless base was to be established. From there, Mawson headed south for the Antarctic, where he intended to establish three bases, strung out across 3200 kilometres of coastline.

He had hoped that the most easterly one would be at the much-visited Cape Adare, where there was already a hut and an ice-free shoreline, and from where another bid might be made to reach the South Magnetic Pole. However, Mawson had made the mistake of telling Scott of his plans. Scott checkmated the Australian by sending part of his group to occupy Cape Adare.[11] A very angry Mawson was forced to sail much further west along the unsurveyed coastline to look for a suitable landing place of his own.

It was during this coastal voyage that Mawson cast doubt on Wilkes' claims to have discovered the Antarctic continent. Where Wilkes claimed to have sailed over open sea, Mawson encountered the ice barrier that indicated the edge of the continent. Percival Gray, the *Aurora*'s second officer, looked on as Mawson and the ship's captain, John King Davis, excitedly compared their position with Wilkes' charts. It was just as Scott had previously suggested, wrote Gray, and Wilkes was now 'practically proved to be a liar'. Gray noted in his diary how 'Mawson and Davis are in fine humours, as this is apparently a very important discovery'.[12] If Wilkes could be proved wrong, it would weaken the American claim to the continent Wilkes had named and supposedly discovered, while strengthening Mawson's hand in claiming the coastline for the British Empire. Strangely, though, Mawson acknowledged Wilkes' voyage by using the name 'Wilkes Land' for much of the coastline that he was intent on claiming. The name had been used by American mapmakers in the wake of Wilkes' voyage, although British officials were now seeking to have it expunged from their maps. Mawson's use of the name would be a source of some frustration to them.

Making a claim on the extensive coastline would require Mawson to find a landing place for his base somewhere along the seemingly interminable barrier ice. Wilkes and d'Urville had been unable to do this, but Mawson managed it on 8 January 1912, after five days' sailing. It was a rocky shore on the headland of a natural harbour that he named 'Commonwealth Bay', after the recently federated Commonwealth of Australia, while he named the headland 'Cape Denison', after his influential donor Hugh Denison. Although calm on the day of their arrival, the place was often beset by hurricane-force winds coming off the icecap. These would complicate Mawson's planned activities.

Instead of two further bases, the shortage of coal on the *Aurora* convinced Mawson to establish just one more. While he busied himself at Cape Denison, eight men – led by the now experienced explorer Frank Wild – were taken 2400 kilometres further west on the *Aurora*, fruitlessly scanning the coast for another landing place. Eventually, they decided to land on an ice shelf that extended out from the continent into the surrounding pack ice. They named it the Shackleton Shelf. It was hardly an ideal situation, but there was no alternative. Moreover, they had reached the eastern edge of Kaiser Wilhelm Land, where Filchner had been based and which provided the western limit of the territory that Mawson wanted to claim for Britain. With Wild and his companions safely ashore in the west, there were now eighteen men under Mawson's command at Cape Denison.[13]

With these two bases, Mawson had covered much of the Antarctic coastline that lay to the south of Australia. It was mostly unsurveyed coastline situated between the British-discovered Cape Adare and the German-discovered Gaussberg. On 25 February 1912, once his huts were built and scientific equipment set up, Mawson assembled the men on the adjoining rocky outcrop and thanked them for their work. Then the Union Jack was hoisted atop the main hut as Mawson 'took possession of the land in the name of the King and the British Empire'.[14]

Although Wilkes and d'Urville had sailed along part of this coastline during the 1840s, neither the Americans nor the French had actually landed on the continent itself, and their governments had done nothing subsequently to cement the claims of their explorers. Nevertheless, Mawson acknowledged the work of d'Urville by referring to the coastline on which his base was situated as 'Adélie Land'. That acknowledgement, like that of 'Wilkes Land', would later complicate Australia's claim to the territory.

By his own intensive exploration of the area's coastline and immediate interior, Mawson now intended to establish a claim for the British Empire, based upon discovery, which would outweigh any claims that France or the United States might make. Mawson planned a sledge journey from Cape Denison all the way east to Oates Land, where he knew he might meet up with a party from Scott's expedition at Cape Adare. Others of Mawson's party would strike out west from Cape Denison, while the parties on the Shackleton Shelf would head both west and east so that as much of the long coastline between Cape Adare and Gaussberg would have been surveyed by British explorers.

Mawson was keeping largely to the coastline because that was where he expected to discover any recoverable mineral deposits, and where any whale or seal fishery might be based. The only inland journey that he wanted to make was to the South Magnetic Pole. He acknowledged that the attempt he had made with Shackleton's expedition had failed to find the shifting pole's precise location. He would have no greater luck this time, with the sledge journey to the magnetic pole falling short by eighty kilometres due to shortage of food. Other parties explored the ice shelf and the glacier tongues to the east of Cape Denison, finding deposits of coal but little else. At the furthest reach of each party, and at other notable points, the British and Australian flags were raised and three cheers given for the king. Mawson intended to be the one to go furthest east, taking two companions with three sledges and sixteen dogs. While each of the parties would face various hardships and dangers, it was Mawson who would confront the greatest challenge.

Mawson's trek involved nearly five weeks of hard slogging across 560 kilometres of twisting coastline, which rose and fell several thousand feet at a time as the group crossed each promontory. Disaster came on 14 December 1912, when Mawson and his two companions, the Swiss skier Xavier Mertz and the former English soldier Belgrave Ninnis, encountered an area of snow-covered crevasses. Although forewarned by Mertz and Mawson, the unsuspecting Ninnis was suddenly swallowed by a large crevasse. Also falling into its depths was the strongest team of dogs, which was pulling a sledge carrying the party's tent, much of their food and all the dog food. The whole lot fell hundreds of feet down the sheer-walled crevasse. Snow shoes or skies might well have prevented Ninnis from collapsing the snow bridge, which opened a hole that the dogs and sledge had no way of avoiding.

Exploration was now at an end. Mertz's and Mawson's very survival was at stake. As Mawson wrote in his diary, they had lost their 'sleeping bags, a week and a half food, the spare tent without poles, & our private bags & cooker & kerosene'. Their only hope was to head back immediately, relying on the dogs for food to cover the 480 kilometres or so. 'May God help us,' Mawson wrote. The dogs posed perhaps the greatest danger of all to both men, who would suffer serious complications from eating their livers, which caused them to ingest excess vitamin A.[15]

At the time, with food running low, they had been close to turning back anyway. Mawson had intended to mark the occasion by raising the Union Jack at the 'furthest east'. It was not until they had gone back more than thirty kilometres that Mertz reminded him of the ceremony he had failed to conduct. So it was belatedly done where they were, the day after Ninnis's death.

Mawson chose a shorter return route that would take them further from the coast and its crevasses and difficult topography. The downside was that there would be no penguins or seals to supplement their diet. By 23 December, after eating an evening meal of dog bone stew, Mawson complained that his hunger was preventing him from sleeping. Two days later, it was dog stew for Christmas dinner; on another day, dog brain for breakfast, from the last of their dogs. Even the paws were utilised, although they took much longer to produce a palatable stew. Still it was not sufficient.[16]

Three hundred and twenty kilometres of travel, often across soft snow, saw their diet-deprived bodies continue to weaken and suffer from frostbite. The end for Mertz came slowly during the first week of January 1913, which was spent mostly in their tiny tent, interspersed with several bouts of fitful progress that failed to take them more than a few kilometres. Mertz was starving and could not go on. His clothing was continually wet from the soft snow and condensation in the tent, his skin was peeling off in sheets because of the excess vitamin A, and he was suffering from dysentery.

On 6 January, after a trek of just three kilometres, Mertz 'refused to go further'. They needed to cover about sixteen kilometres each day, Mawson wrote, or 'we are doomed'. He could have pushed on by himself, but he felt unable to leave Mertz. While life beckoned him forward, the spectre of death held him with its grip. 'If only I could get on,' wrote Mawson. 'But I must stop with Xavier, and he does not appear to be improving – both our chances are going now.' The following day, Mertz was delirious, raving and thrashing about, forcing Mawson to hold him down. Within hours, he was dead.[17]

With Mertz gone, there was more food for Mawson. In fact, he would have to battle rumours for the rest of his life that Mertz's body had provided some of the food that would sustain him for the remainder of his trek. In the absence of any more dogs, he may have been tempted to do so, but there really was no need since the remaining rations no longer had to be shared.[18] After waiting out a blizzard and burying Mertz in a mausoleum of ice blocks, Mawson pressed on with a renewed determination to get his story out to the world.

And what a story it was, with the remaining 160 kilometres of the trek adding triumph to the tragedy. Ten days after Mertz's death, Mawson described in his diary how he was sinking up to his thighs in the soft snow of a steep slope. When he tried to seek a firmer surface, he found himself 'dangling on end of rope in crevasse', with only the weight of the sledge above keeping him from falling to his certain death. Despite his 'whole body . . . rotting from want of proper nourishment – frost-bitten fingertips festering, mucous membrane of nose gone, saliva glands of mouth refusing duty, skin coming off whole body', Mawson described how he 'made a great struggle, half getting out, then slipping back again several times, but at last just did it'. Exhausted, Mawson set up his improvised tent for the night.

The following day, he fell into another crevasse that saw him sink only to his knees. Things became relatively easier thereafter, and he made relatively quick progress with a following wind on the mostly downward slope. Salvation came on 29 January. Having just two pounds of food left, Mawson came across a cairn of food and supplies left by a rescue party earlier that same day in the hope that he would find it. A further store of food, little more than forty kilometres away, ensured that he would survive his epic journey.[19]

It was not until 8 February that Mawson reached the safety of the hut, only to find that the *Aurora* had come to evacuate the base and had sailed away with most of the men just a few hours before. Although he was able to radio Captain Davis, stormy seas prevented the ship getting close to shore. With the eight men of the western base facing a dire situation if they were not picked up before the winter set in, Davis took the *Aurora* off to their rescue. Shortage of coal and the spreading pack ice would prevent the ship's return to pick up Mawson.

Davis left confident in the knowledge that Mawson would survive until the following summer with the six men and ample stores. It was a terrible situation for Mawson, who had been anxious to tell the world of his accomplishments. Instead, he was stranded at Cape Denison, where he learned from his companions that Amundsen had conquered the South Pole. Mawson could only imagine the public reaction to this momentous news, and he worried about how he was going to make a splash of his own. There was no immediate news of Scott's fate, just that he had not returned in time to leave with his relief ship and was staying another winter in the Antarctic. This was reassuring for Mawson, for it meant that they would be emerging from the ice at about the same time. Meanwhile, Mawson had one important advantage over Scott: he could use his radio throughout the coming year to bring his name and works to the attention of the world.

One of the first things Mawson did was to notify the king of the 'large area of newly discovered land' between Victoria Land and Adélie Land, over which the teams from Cape Denison had sledged during the previous summer, and which Mawson now proposed to call 'King George V Land'. Later, he affixed the name 'Queen Mary Land' to the land around Wild's base, further west. The name would effectively prevent the name of the adjoining Kaiser Wilhelm Land from being extended eastward into the area that Mawson wanted to be the exclusive preserve of the British Empire.

A three-man party from Wild's base had trekked westward as far as Drygalski's Gaussberg, the extinct volcano where the Germans had left two stone cairns to mark their presence. On Christmas Day 1912, Wild's men had done likewise, leaving a cairn of their own with a record of their 480-kilometre journey. Several hundred kilometres to the east, Wild had taken another party on a trek in the other direction. They had celebrated that same Christmas with plum pudding and shots of spirits at a place Wild named 'Possession Nunataks' – a *nunatak* being an exposed rocky outcrop. The pudding and alcohol, recalled Wild, produced 'quite a festive feeling'. It was in this after-dinner atmosphere that Wild raised the British and Australian flags on the rocks and 'formally took possession of the land in the name of the Expedition, for King George V, and the Australian Commonwealth'.[20]

The building of the cairn would reinforce the sense that Gaussberg was the eastern limit of Kaiser Wilhelm Land, while the acts of flag-raising – and the mapping and naming of Queen Mary Land and King George V Land, joining as they did to Victoria Land and King Edward VII Land – would reinforce the British claim to that part of the Antarctic. Bringing back rocks and other scientific specimens, and later writing up the results for international consumption, was also part of this claiming process, demonstrating that the claimant nation knew the region better than its rivals.

It was not sufficient to photograph or film the wildlife; they had to be captured, killed, eviscerated and stuffed. A sailor on the *Aurora* described how he assisted the taxidermist to capture penguins. Men would stand still on the ice until the curious creatures milled about their legs, whereupon the men would each grab a penguin by the flippers. They would:

> . . . sit on his back and ride him till he got tired, then one holds while the other gets a pithing needle, shoves his beek [sic] in the snow, then puts the needle in from the back of the skull bone and works the point about in his brain, being careful not to prick his eyes, as if you do, the eyes bulge out and stretch the skin, spoiling it.

Eleven were quickly captured and killed, both for scientific study and for the delight of museum visitors.[21]

Names on maps, photographs and films of claiming ceremonies, and penguin organs in jars of formaldehyde together aided the construction of a multi-layered title of ownership of the quadrant. But it would remain an inchoate claim until the British or Australian government gave legal authority to Mawson's private claim, and then buttressed it by performing acts of administration over the territory. It would be even better if the territory was actually occupied, although no one could yet envisage how a permanent settlement could be established in the Antarctic. During the dark winter months at Cape Denison, Mawson had other things on his mind as he slowly recovered from his ordeal and considered how best to reap a reward from his expedition.

The radio communication with Macquarie Island was fitful at best. This was not helped by Mawson's radio operator gradually going insane. But the radio was working sufficiently in mid-February 1913 for Mawson to learn of Scott's sad fate. There would be no race back between Mawson and Scott to secure the plaudits of the English-speaking world. Instead, Mawson was faced with having to compete with a tale of tragedy and courage that he could not equal.

While the first radio message just gave Mawson the bare details of Scott's demise, further messages gradually brought all 'the tragic details' to their isolated hut. Anxious not to have his own story buried by Scott's, and needing to earn funds for his prolonged stay in the south, Mawson immediately sent 'a fuller account of our own calamity', which brought 'many kind messages of sympathy and congratulation' from around the world.[22]

As his health slowly improved, Mawson set about planning an account of his expedition. This would not only fulfil his pre-existing publishing contract, but would also help with his pressing need for funds and satisfy his desire to establish the pre-eminence of his scientific expedition over the mere 'adventures' of his Norwegian and English rivals. Mawson worked hard to heighten the sense of drama of his expedition. For instance, while his diary has him returning to the hut after the deaths of Ninnis and Mertz and seeing no sign of the lately departed *Aurora*, his book has him dramatically seeing 'a speck on the north-west horizon' that 'looked like a distant ship; it might well have been the *Aurora*'.[23]

Similarly, the account in Mawson's book of his fall into the crevasse differs in some important respects from the account in his diary and from the initial accounts he provided to newspapers. The diary has him falling to the unspecified length of his rope, and making 'a great struggle, half getting out, then slipping back again several times'.[24] His initial comments to journalists on his return to Adelaide in February 1914, however, made no mention of him falling down a crevasse. Mawson told them that he 'would rather not say too much' about his ordeal, other than to report that he:

... was 30 days absolutely alone, and I had a most marvellous escape. In the end I was reduced to the last stages of starvation. I was tramping alone through the deep snow when I noticed something black in front of me. It was a bit of food that had been dropped by the search party sent to ascertain my whereabouts. It was by the luckiest accident that I saw it ... I reckon I had on that occasion the closest shave I ever want to experience ...

He was similarly reticent to provide details of the sledge journey during a reception laid on for him at Adelaide's Conservatorium of Music, attended by the governor-general, Lord Denman.[25] It was only when Mawson reached Melbourne and attended a dinner in his honour at the Oriental Hotel that he was more forthcoming, telling an audience of well-fed worthies that he had not expected to survive on the meagre rations, 'and every day it was getting less'. He went on to describe how he once 'fell down a crevasse; and . . . by some extraordinary slice of good luck that crevasse was not the end of me; I did not go very far down, and I managed to work my way out'.[26] The days of starvation were still central to Mawson's story, rather than his fall, or falls, down a crevasse.

In the exclusive account that Mawson cabled to the London *Daily Mail*, the newspaper that had helped him raise much-needed funds in Britain, he described how he felt after the death of Mertz, when his

> own condition afforded little hope, but I decided to push on . . . Several times I fell into crevasses to the length of my sledge pole and was scarcely able to crawl out. My skin and nails came off owing to the intense cold. The discovery of a food cache finally enabled me to reach the hut.[27]

Mawson had certainly made an epic solo journey – it had lasted thirty-two days – but there was still no dramatic climax that would allow him to maximise the returns from his book and lecture deals. Having now seen the public reaction to Scott's expedition, and having gauged the press and public reaction in Australia to his own expedition, Mawson went by ship to London in April 1914 to provide his publisher with the manuscript of his book and to embark on a lecture tour. He had already sketched out some chapters of the book while detained during that last winter at Cape Denison, being helped with the writing by the expedition medico Archibald McLean. He now paid for McLean to accompany him and his new wife on the voyage to London. It was during these months at sea that McLean helped Mawson devise a more satisfying and triumphant climax to the story of the expedition.[28]

The resulting book described for the first time how Mawson had fallen down a crevasse, claiming that he fell not to the length of his sledge pole but to the length of his knotted sledge rope, which he said was fourteen feet long. His diary had described how he had climbed to the surface, only to slip back down again 'several times'. It would be incredible – in his starved and weakened condition, with frostbitten fingers, bleeding gums, skin sloughed from the soles of his feet and his clothes weighed down with snow – to have been able to climb up *fourteen feet* of rope to the surface, only to slip back 'several times'. Presumably realising this, Mawson described how he climbed the fourteen feet, only to reach the surface and slip back just once to the end of the rope, before successfully climbing out. Still, the feat defies credulity.[29]

Mawson later embellished the story by telling a lecture audience in Chicago that it had taken 'a struggle of four and half hours' for him to emerge from the crevasse.[30] When a modern-day adventurer, Tim Jarvis, tried in 2007 to replicate Mawson's climb out of a crevasse, he was unable to do so. That was despite having a support crew, being in a better physical condition and experiencing a journey that had not emulated Mawson's in its harshness.[31]

Whatever the truth of the events that occurred during Mawson's monumental journey across the ice and snow, the strength of the story that eventually captured the popular imagination in Britain and Australia buttressed the sense of connection between the people of the British Empire and the Antarctic continent. The *Daily Mail* thought that 'nothing in the whole story of Antarctic exploration can be compared with [Mawson's] solitary journey across an unutterably savage waste'.[32] Mawson had a financial interest in creating such a connection, which he hoped would relieve his expedition of about £8000 of unpaid bills. But he also hoped that such a connection would strengthen the territorial claim that the British Empire could make to the part of the Antarctic lying to the south of Australia.

Although the British government had denied him official authority to make such a claim, Mawson had performed perfunctory claiming ceremonies at seven locations. He had also flown the British and Australian flags from his hut, sledges and tents, and had named the territory that his teams had 'opened up' after the new British king and queen. It was clear that he had tried to make his expedition look as official as possible. And when he had returned to Adelaide in February 1914, he had called on the Australian government to

> make some claim upon the Antarctic regions. Just as Canada had issued an edict that all the lands north of Canada to the Pole belonged to Canada, so Australia might say that all lands south of the Commonwealth belonged to it. It would be a grand thing to have one country stretching from the equator to the Pole.

But Australia was still taking its lead from Britain, and London was refusing to agree to Mawson's suggestion that the territories he had discovered and claimed should now be formally annexed.[33]

The outbreak of the First World War in August 1914 upset many of Mawson's plans. The publication of his book was delayed indefinitely, as was his British lecture tour and the showing of the expedition film. A European lecture tour was out of the question. Some of Scott's men had already done the British lecture circuit in 1913, which Mawson realised would limit the attention that he was likely to receive. His hopes of getting the expedition out of debt and of providing money to fund the publication of its scientific reports were now in tatters.

He tried to recoup something from this mess by going to the United States in early 1915, where his book was being published and where a lecture tour was organised. But neither proved to be as lucrative as he had hoped. Indeed, after an exhausting tour across America and Canada, Mawson spent a month in New York lecturing to small audiences that produced no profit at all.

When the British edition of the book appeared later in 1915, it sold slowly and was eventually remaindered. The returns from the film of the expedition also proved disappointing. Although the various projects helped to pay off the expedition's remaining debts, there was no fortune to be made.[34] Despite these disappointments, Mawson remained optimistic about the possible rewards that might be reaped from the Antarctic in other ways, whether through whaling and sealing or through mining the coal and minerals that had been found there.

To Mawson's chagrin, Scott's failure had overshadowed his own success at exploring a far greater expanse of the Antarctic than anyone previously. He had also exceeded by far the achievements of the Japanese and German expeditions.

After leaving Germany in May 1911, Filchner's hopes of crossing the continent by sledge were dashed when his ship, the *Deutschland*, was caught in the ice of the Weddell Sea in February 1912. An earlier attempt to establish a base on an iceberg connected to the barrier was thwarted when the ice broke away, taking men and animals and huts out to sea; only with some difficulty were they rescued. When Filchner tried to find a more suitable landing place further along the coast, the *Deutschland* was caught by the pack ice, forcing him to wait out the winter with little more than oceanographic and meteorological research to occupy the time of his scientists. While his Manchurian ponies and Greenland dogs remained cooped up uselessly on deck, penguins and strips of seal blubber were passed down below to be fed into the ship's auxiliary boiler to save on coal.

It was not a happy ship. Filchner had a bitter falling-out with the captain, Richard Vahsel, who had been second officer on Drygalski's ill-fated expedition and who undermined Filchner at every turn. Filchner, who suffered severely from haemorrhoids, later implied that Vahsel had placed faeces in his cabin and had made fun of the time he spent in the toilet. The apparently syphilitic Vahsel did not survive the expedition, dying from his disease just prior to the ship's release from the ice in October 1912. A bay on the eastern side of the Weddell Sea was named after him.[35]

It was a disappointed Filchner who left for home by way of Buenos Aires, hoping to raise funds for a second year of exploration. However, his achievements during that first year had not been sufficient to give anyone confidence that a second approach from the Weddell Sea would be any more profitable. Anyway, the feat of Amundsen and the fate of Scott had captured the public imagination in a way that Filchner could not.

As with Drygalski's expedition, there was little from Filchner's expedition that the German Empire could flaunt to the world. Having landed only briefly on the Antarctic continent, Filchner had had no opportunity to spread German names across the forbidding landscape, or to claim new territories. Anyway, Filchner seems to have been little interested in such matters. He was more interested in scientific cooperation than territorial competition.

But his supporters had to be satisfied. When he reached Buenos Aires, he announced that he had 'discovered a new country', which he named 'Prinzregent Luitpold Land', while the ice barrier was named in honour of the German emperor, Wilhelm II. Several minor geographic features were also given German names. The Germans had twice made the mistake of allowing themselves to be pushed by the English away from areas that had relatively easy access, only to find themselves frozen in the pack ice far from land. After such discouraging results, there was little appetite in Germany for any further expeditions to the far south. Filchner would never go back, opting instead to concentrate on further work in Tibet, where he had first made his name as an explorer.[36]

The Japanese expedition of Lieutenant Nobu Shirase had begun well but ended up similarly dogged by ill luck. Like Amundsen, Shirase had focused on the Arctic until Peary's claim of having reached the North Pole ended his northern ambitions. Turning his sights south, Shirase planned to strike out for the South Pole, pitching himself against Scott and any other European or American explorers who might join the race. It was a time when Japan was emerging from centuries of self-imposed isolation and wanted to emulate the empires of Europe. Its navy had recently defeated the best ships of the Russian Empire, its army had routed the Russians in Manchuria, and the ancient kingdom of Korea had become a Japanese colony. The pursuit of prestige for the burgeoning Japanese Empire was foremost among Shirase's aims when he petitioned the parliament for funds for an expedition to 'expand the nation's territories and become a rich and powerful nation'. Although the parliament approved the funds, the government refused to ratify its decision and release the grant.

Undeterred, Shirase turned to a former prime minister, the one-legged Count Shigenobu Okuma, to act as patron of the expedition. It was an inspired move by the forty-eight-year-old explorer, who soon had an influential committee of supporters and backing from the *Asahi* newspaper group, which organised a successful campaign of public subscriptions. After some practice in the Arctic, and with a motley assemblage of scientists and two native Ainu men from Hokkaido, Shirase and his companions were farewelled from Yokohama by a crowd of 50,000 at the end of November 1910.

When he went aboard the expedition's smelly, three-masted fishing boat, the *Kainan-maru* – or 'Southern Pioneer' – Shirase carried a copper casket containing the names of all those who had contributed money; it was to be buried when Shirase reached the South Pole. The expedition had already met with some ridicule in Japan, and the news of Shirase's departure did not cause much apprehension among his rivals. One report from Tokyo predicted that his poorly prepared expedition was 'foredoomed to failure'.[37]

The expedition was already in trouble when it arrived in Wellington on 8 February 1911. Fourteen of its twenty-six dogs had died from disease, which left insufficient dogs for the planned march to the South Pole. Worse was to come. The *Kainan-maru* did not reach the Ross Sea until 10 March. By then, Scott and Amundsen were already ashore, establishing their camps and laying down supply depots for their attempts on the pole the following summer. At least Shirase had beaten the Germans and the Australians; Filchner was still preparing to leave Germany, while Mawson was in London raising funds.

However, his late arrival left him poorly placed to compete with Scott and Amundsen.

Shirase's position only got worse, as the spreading winter ice blocked access to the southern reaches of the Ross Sea and his dogs continued to die. Conceding defeat, he turned his ship about and sailed across the stormy Southern Ocean to Sydney. After passing through the heads of Sydney Harbour on 1 May, the Japanese initially received a chilly reception from customs officers, who were charged with enforcing the racially exclusive provisions of the 'white Australia policy'. Ever since the Japanese defeat of Russia, there had been widespread fears in Australia of a Japanese invasion. Some thought that Shirase might be more intent on exploring Sydney's defences than the distant Antarctic. The *Cairns Post* noted that the 'most careful provision was made to prevent [the Japanese] learning anything about the forts at Sydney Heads, should childish curiosity lead them that way'. But the suspicions gradually abated and the Japanese were permitted to establish themselves in bushland on the shore of the harbour.[38]

The Japanese took advantage of their stay in Sydney to consult with the Antarctic explorer and geology professor Edgeworth David. Shirase and his companions later attended a public meeting to raise money for the Mawson expedition as the professor's honoured guests. With their own money fast depleting, the *Kainan-maru*'s captain went to Tokyo to raise funds and seek further instructions. Count Okuma and the committee decided that they could not 'permit failure to sully the honour of Japanese men', so more funds were raised, dogs purchased and extra men sent to join the expedition. Okuma cabled Shirase: 'Go forth. Set sail anew. Though you perish in the attempt, do not return until you have achieved your aims.'

The captain returned to the Antarctic in mid-November with another scientist, Masakichi Ikeda, a cinematographer and a pack of twenty-nine dogs. Whatever else he managed to achieve, Shirase could be confident that the cinematographer would show Japanese audiences, and perhaps the wider world, the stirring sight of the Rising Sun Flag fluttering above the ice. It would not be fluttering at the South Pole; there was little hope of that now. Although Australian newspaper reports claimed that Shirase and his men had taken an oath to reach the South Pole or take their own lives, Shirase told a curious reporter in Sydney that he had no intention of 'making for the South Pole.' He claimed that the expedition was purely scientific. As Ikeda explained, by the time they reached the Antarctic, the glory of conquering the pole would likely have been taken by Amundsen or Scott and there 'would be no use' in the Japanese 'going further south than the near Antarctic regions'. In the event, that was precisely what they did.[39]

The *Kainan-maru* raised anchor on 18 November 1911, with boatloads of well-wishers gathered to wave them farewell. Professor David was on board with Shirase as the ship sailed down the harbour. Before he left in a launch, he was given a Samurai sword in appreciation for his 'many kindnesses and courtesies'. Meanwhile, Scott and Amundsen were heading on their separate tracks towards the pole, and Mawson was preparing to leave Hobart on the *Aurora*.

Shirase's timely departure ensured that, this time, his ship was less troubled by ice when it reached the Ross Sea. He was able to land the base party on the Ross Ice Barrier in January 1912, next to Amundsen's base at the Bay of Whales. By then, Amundsen was returning from his successful trek to the pole. Shirase had the *Kainan-maru* sail further east to explore King Edward VII Land, while the base party remained at the Bay of Whales taking meteorological observations. Shirase himself, along with four companions, including the two Ainu dog drivers, took the dog sledges on a dash southwards to establish a Japanese base 'furthest south'.[40]

Not having laid down any food depots, Shirase's so-called 'Dash Patrol' could only go as far as the food on his lightweight sledges allowed. On 28 January 1912, after eight days, he finally called a halt. He had traversed about 275 kilometres and reached 80° 5' S. Although only about a quarter of the way to the pole, and still not off the Ross Ice Barrier, it was one of the fastest recorded sledge journeys by an Antarctic expedition, which was mostly due to the experience of the Ainu dog-drivers.

Although Shirase would later tell reporters that they had 'confined [their] attention to scientific exploration', they were much more interested than Filchner in territorial acquisition. When they reached their 'furthest south', Shirase buried his copper casket and 'raised a bamboo pole from the top of which the national Sun flag was flown, revolved by a red-painted triangular weather vane of tin. The men then paraded before the Sun flag and raised a threefold *Banzai* for the Emperor.' Photographs were taken and ownership of the surrounding region was claimed for Japan, under the name

'Yamato Setsugen'. This combined a poetical name for Japan with the word for 'snowplain', even though the area was a floating ice shelf, over which a troupe of other explorers had already tramped. According to the expedition report, 'for as long as the Earth may last' the Yamato Setsugen was now 'the territory of Japan'. Although the continent was presently uninhabited, the report envisaged a time when 'the smoke of home fires will surely rise into the air, and there will be a whole town built here with carriages plying to and fro'.[41]

The two-man Japanese party that had landed on the coast of King Edward VII Land also made an implicit claim on that place, by heading sixteen kilometres inland towards the Alexandra Range and erecting 'a memorial board recording the visit', not realising that men from Amundsen's expedition had done likewise just six weeks previously. The Japanese had Scott in mind. They were conscious that the English explorer had seen and named King Edward VII Land although he had not been able to land upon it. Ignorant of the Norwegian party's presence in King Edward VII Land, the Japanese believed that they were the first to 'explore an area in which no man had been able to land since the very dawn of time'.

Returning to the Bay of Whales, the *Kainan-maru* retrieved Shirase and the base party, leaving behind their tent as a memorial of their stay. They also had to abandon twenty dogs when bad weather forced the ship to make a hasty departure. Although they had not achieved their original aim of being first to reach the South Pole, Shirase and his companions could return to Japan content that they had successfully completed Japan's first exploratory expedition; they had 'created an opportunity for Japan to take its place as a nation on the stage of world affairs'.

As a public mark of their success, Shirase and several of his companions were invited to the Imperial Palace in Tokyo, where they showed the expedition's fifteen-minute film to the Imperial Family. Afterwards, it was exhibited to the public at a sumo wrestling arena. The emperor made a belated, token contribution to the expedition's funds, but still Shirase had to spend the next five years lecturing to pay off the expedition's debts. He even had to sell his house to pay the crew's wages.[42] The British Foreign Office would later concede that the symbolic actions and activities of the Shirase expedition had laid the basis for a 'possible Japanese claim to territory'. Not that the Foreign Office thought it would have any trouble rebutting such a claim.[43]

The Japanese realised that it was not sufficient only to have their feat recognised in Japan; the prestige of their empire and the preservation of their territorial claim required that it be acknowledged by other nations. After his return to Japan, Ikeda wrote to the Royal Geographical Society on 18 August 1912 with details of an inlet in the ice barrier and two peaks in the Alexander Mountains, none of which had been named by Scott. Accordingly, Ikeda had given them Japanese names. He asked the society to use the names on any future maps so they would be 'universal'. Two days later, Ikeda had second thoughts and dashed off a postcard asking the society to await a fuller report before publicising the expedition's achievements. A month later he wrote again, confirming that the 'opinions[sic] of our scientific party is now settled' and the three names should be used, along with the name 'Waseda Sea' for the waters beyond 160° W.

Even those modest requests were too much for the elderly Markham, who urged that the society do no more than publish 'a short paragraph saying that the Japs report they have sighted King Edward VII land and reached 150°W in Captain Scott's track'. He was concerned that the Japanese were detracting from Scott's expedition and undermining British pre-eminence in the Antarctic. 'These cursed gad flies,' wrote Markham, 'are lowering the whole plane of polar exploration into a scramble for self advertising, and plastering names about where they are not wanted.' He warned the society against giving them any encouragement, which he said would be 'most unwise and improper'.

As a result of Markham's intervention, the Japanese names never appeared on any British maps and the expedition received no more than the briefest mention in the society's journal. When Ikeda later sent a manuscript for publication in England, the secretary of the Royal Geographical Society helped to ensure that London publishers rejected it. Although the expedition's official report was published in Japanese in 1913, it would be a century before it was translated and published in English. Shirase's personal account still awaits an English publication.[44]

While these rival expeditions competed to be first to reach the South Pole, or to lay claim to other parts of the Antarctic, most Americans remained aloof, ignoring Frederick Cook's repeated calls in the early 1900s for the United States to stake its own claim on the continent. Ironically, it was Scott who inspired calls for an official

American expedition, when he reported in 1902 that he had sailed over areas that the American Wilkes expedition had reported as land. This provocative claim caused some influential Americans to demand that the US Navy rebut Scott's insult to their reputation by sending a ship to retrace Wilkes' voyage.

Prominent among these was the sometime lawyer, keen mountain climber and amateur painter Edwin Swift Balch. His call in 1903 for the United States to re-explore the coast of Wilkes Land received support from both Wilkes' daughter and the Arctic explorer Robert Peary. The American Geographical Society joined the campaign in 1906, only to be told by the navy that no suitable vessel was available. The American Philosophical Society tried to broaden the campaign in April 1909 by calling on all scientific and geographical societies to pressure the government into sending a vessel 'to thoroughly explore and survey the coast of Wilkes Land, and other parts of Antarctica'. That same month, the society published a paper by Balch, who had researched the early history of American sealers in the Antarctic. He concluded that 'America's record in the Antarctic' was 'the most brilliant of any nation'. Despite that record, Balch complained, Americans were now allowing other nations to dominate Antarctic exploration and reap the resulting glory, with Markham and Scott 'eager to wipe out all American discoveries from the map'.[45]

It was apparently due to pressure from Balch that Peary announced in 1908 that he would 'promote and organize a National American Antarctic Expedition, to secure for this country its share of the honors and valuable scientific information still awaiting the explorer in that region'.[46] As the campaign for the United States to re-explore Wilkes Land gathered support, council members of the American Geographical Society agreed to contribute $10 each to assemble and release some of the unpublished scientific results of the Wilkes expedition.[47] It was a way of bringing the largely forgotten Wilkes back into the public spotlight. But the society met with a negative reaction when it told the secretary of the navy that it was 'incumbent on the Navy to do something to sustain the reputation of its officer'.[48] There were still 'no suitable vessels and no officers experienced in ice work'; besides, the possibility of Peary leading a private expedition to the Antarctic effectively meant that the navy did not have to take any action of its own.[49]

Despite all the activity of Scott's second expedition and Mawson's opening up of a massive new area, there was still no push by the US government to counter the territorial claims that the British Empire was starting to make across the Antarctic. Even if the United States did not send an expedition of its own, Balch was anxious that the American Geographical Society should at least defend American names on Antarctic maps against the push by the English to remove them and thereby 'obliterate . . . all American discoveries.' In an article for the society's *Bulletin*, Balch argued that the naming of geographic features should reflect 'loyalty to humanity and to science, and not spring from servile obedience to national prejudices and national greed'. In Balch's view, precedence in naming should be given to the actual discoverers, which meant that the names scattered by Wilkes on the Antarctic coastline 'must stand for all time', while Markham's English names for the Antarctic quadrants – Weddell, Ross, Victoria and Enderby – should be replaced by his own politically neutral suggestion: East and West Antarctica.[50]

Americans could take some comfort from a legal argument by Balch's young brother, the jurist Thomas Willing Balch, who poured scorn on Britain's use of letters patent in 1908 to create the so-called 'Falkland Islands Dependencies', which encompassed the South Shetland, South Orkney and South Sandwich Islands and Graham Land. Buttressing the calls by his older brother, Balch argued that such a move could not be made legally valid by Britain 'simply saying that they are hers'. Neither could the activities of Shackleton's private expedition give rise to a territorial claim in the absence of territorial occupation. A claim could only be sustained, wrote Balch, if someone authorised by the British government took 'formal possession . . . and something were promptly done to follow it up by making as much use of the place as circumstances would permit'.[51] This legal argument would come to underlie the official American attitude to other nations' Antarctic claims: that they could be ignored unless they were followed by effective occupation.

The general American disinterest in the Antarctic did not prevent proposals being made for American expeditions. Although Peary had abandoned the idea of organising his own expedition, two of his companions on the North Pole voyage – the wealthy big-game hunter Harry Whitney and the captain of Peary's ship, Robert Bartlett – proposed a voyage to the Weddell Sea. However, this also failed to eventuate.[52] Scott and Amundsen seemed to have sewn up the South Pole, the feat that would most capture public interest, which made it more difficult to raise funds for other Antarctic ventures. Moreover, Mawson had explored much of the so-called 'Wilkes Land', casting doubt on the reported discoveries of Wilkes but also leaving little for a new American expedition to explore.

While no American expeditions were forthcoming, Shackleton began preparing in early 1913 to mount yet another British expedition. It had to be a feat that would capture public attention and provide him with his long-sought fortune. The only such feat that was left, Shackleton confided to his wife, was a crossing of the continent from the Weddell Sea to the Ross Sea. Filchner and Scott had failed to make the crossing, and Shackleton resolved that he would achieve it.[53]

Scott had met with opposition from scientists and geographers over his dash to the pole. Some hoped that such stunts had now come to an end. In his 1912 survey of Antarctic exploration, the Scottish geographer Hugh Robert Mill welcomed the reaching of the South Pole, expecting that it would mean that there was 'no further occasion for sensational "dashes" and acrimonious discussions between rival claimants'. In place of these adventurers, wrote Mill, would go 'explorers of a more scientific . . . disposition'.[54]

The sort of explorer Mill had in mind was his Scottish colleague William Bruce, who had written his own survey of polar exploration in 1911. He too had dismissed those who pursued the 'boyish Pole hunt' as explorers who were not serious, although he conceded that a crossing of the continent could provide important scientific results. While scientific objectives were now a requirement for government funding, Bruce could only bemoan the fact that the public still wanted 'pure sensationalism' rather than science.[55]

Shackleton had a keen appreciation of what the public wanted and was eager to provide it. Having secured a promise of £10,000 from the British government, Shackleton went public with his plans in late December 1913, announcing that the 'Imperial Transantarctic Expedition' would cross the continent, 'carrying out, for the British Flag, the greatest Polar journey ever attempted'. After Amundsen's defeat of Scott, he hoped, this would re-establish Britain as the pre-eminent Antarctic power – and Shackleton as the pre-eminent polar explorer.[56]

In his fundraising appeal, Shackleton held out the prospect of making both geographic and scientific discoveries, thereby carefully combining the English public's demand for spectacle with a more serious-minded scientific purpose that would satisfy those who demanded a practical return for their contributions. But crossing the continent was foremost in his scheme. As he told the Royal Geographical Society, he had 'put the crossing of the continent as the great object of this expedition, and there is not one individual . . . who does not wish the British flag to be the first national flag ever carried across the frozen waste'. They were going not as disinterested scientists but as 'agents of the British nation'.[57]

Shackleton reminded potential donors that the flying of the flag would cement the British claim to the large swathe of Antarctic territory that had been brought within the empire by the creation of the Falkland Islands Dependencies, which included the western coastline of the Weddell Sea. With Filchner's German expedition having failed to get ashore there, Shackleton conjured up the prospect of his own Weddell Sea party opening up 'vast stretches of unknown land', with the 'whole of the area southward to the Pole [being] British territory'.[58]

With a dreadful European war just months away, flag-waving patriotism was rampant, and there was nothing better than beating the drum of empire to get governments and private donors onside. Just as British battleships had become bigger than ever, so Shackleton's venture would be on a grandiose scale. There would be two ships: the newly constructed *Endurance*, built by the Norwegian whaler Lars Christensen for tourist trips to the Arctic that had never eventuated, and Mawson's old ship, the *Aurora*.

Shackleton planned to have the *Endurance* put fourteen members of the expedition ashore at Vahsel Bay in the Weddell Sea, where Filchner had been thwarted. Shackleton planned to set out from here with five companions on the 2400-kilometre transcontinental sledge journey, while the other eight set out in different directions to explore the immediate region.[59] On the other side of the continent, the *Aurora* would land six men on the shores of the Ross Sea, who would lay down food depots along the final part of Shackleton's planned route. Shackleton envisaged his own triumphant return to England in April 1915, with the majority of the expedition returning a year later.[60]

England was sufficiently excited by the vision to provide him with the wherewithal to set off. On 5 August 1914 the King presented him with the traditional Union Jack to be raised over any new territory he might cross. But some had serious doubts about the wisdom of the immensely ambitious enterprise. One astute observer claimed that 'nine Polar men out of every ten look upon it as the most costly, useless (from a scientific point of view) and trust-to-Providence journey yet undertaken'. The elderly Markham dismissed the expedition out of hand, privately suggesting that it was 'designed solely for self-advertisement'.[61]

The mad adventure almost never began, after war with Germany broke out on the same day that the king presented Shackleton with the British flag. On hearing the news, Shackleton offered to turn the ships and their crews over to the Admiralty but was ordered by the up-and-coming First Lord of the Admiralty, Winston Churchill, who had earlier described the expedition as 'a sterile quest', to proceed regardless. There was no place for Shackleton in his navy.[62]

It turned out that there was no place for Shackleton in the Antarctic either. Having sailed off for what he called his 'white warfare', he found that the unpredictable ice conditions of the Weddell Sea had ruined his plans, just as they had for Filchner and others.[63] Although Shackleton had been informed when he reached the whaling port of Grytviken, on the northern coast of South Georgia, that the ice in the Weddell Sea was particularly bad that year, he had pressed on regardless. Pushing the ship through hundreds of kilometres of pack ice, he finally came within sight of Vahsel Bay in late January 1915, only to have the ice tighten its grip around the ship and force it on a slow drift northwards. Each day took them further away from their intended destination.

By October 1915, the pressure on the hull of the *Endurance* was so great that the ship was pushed over at an angle, its timbers cracked and leaks developed. Shackleton and his men abandoned the ship to live in tents on the northward-floating ice, and then, after the ship sank and the ice began to break up in April 1916, took to three small boats to sail to desolate and isolated Elephant Island, off the tip of the Antarctic Peninsula. Leaving most of his men huddled beneath two of the upturned boats on the island's rocky shore, Shackleton and five companions went on a desperate 1300-kilometre voyage to get help from the whalers of South Georgia. They landed on the southern shore of the island and made their way across the snow-covered mountains that lay between them and the whaling ports on the northern coast. Help for the men on Elephant Island had to wait until the winter ice receded; they finally were rescued on 30 August 1916.

The men of the Ross Sea party, who knew nothing of Shackleton's plight, had faced great hardships of their own. After laying down food depots for Shackleton, one man died from scurvy and two others died in a blizzard while trying to cross thin sea ice. Shackleton finally managed to organise a relief expedition for the survivors.

Shackleton's epic journey and the saving of his men, while doing much to rescue his reputation, could not save the expedition. He had not carried the Union Jack across the continent, and his plan to buttress the British claim to the unknown lands of the Falkland Islands Dependencies had gone unfulfilled. Nevertheless, his voyage to South Georgia and the weeks he spent with the whalers had confirmed for Shackleton that Britain was sitting on a virtual goldmine. Whales abounded in Antarctic waters and there were great profits to be made. Shackleton calculated that a whaling company could count on a return of ten to twenty per cent a year.[64]

The war made these profits even greater, as the world's increasing hunger for fats went unsatisfied. The development of hydrogenated whale oil allowed it to be used to make margarine that did not have a tainted taste. More importantly, the glycerine from whale oil was used in the manufacture of explosives. This gave the Antarctic a new economic and strategic significance that the British government could not ignore. By the end of the war, Britain was determined to bring the entire continent within its burgeoning empire.

CHAPTER 9

'Extending and asserting British control'

1919–1926

The diminutive Leo Amery was the man who wanted it all. A forty-five-year-old former journalist, he was the politician who put the whole Antarctic squarely on Britain's political agenda. As a junior minister at the Colonial Office and a staunch enthusiast of empire, Amery had been a member of the British delegation at the Paris Peace Conference in 1919, where the colonies of the vanquished empires were carved up among the victors.

Almost as an afterthought, Germany was forced to relinquish any rights it might care to claim over those parts of the Antarctic that had been discovered by German explorers. It was the least of the concessions made in those months of tense negotiations, with Germany being stripped of its empire, its borderlands, its navy and much of its industrial apparatus. The empty and icy wastes of the distant Antarctic meant little to the disheartened German delegation, but Amery recognised its potential strategic and economic value. In a secret memo, he urged his colleagues to seize the moment and move 'quietly to assert our claim to the whole continent'.[1]

The post-war world had seen the hunt for whales in the Antarctic take on a new intensity. The Atlantic was safe again from submarines, and the market for whale oil continued to promise good returns. As the mainly Norwegian-owned whale catchers returned to scour the iceberg-infested ocean for signs of their quarry, Amery convinced his colleagues to adopt a secret strategy that would vastly expand Britain's territorial claim in the Antarctic. Britain already controlled the Falkland Islands and had extended its control southward to bring the sub-Antarctic island groups and the Antarctic Peninsula within the ambit of its authority. Now Amery wanted to grab the remaining millions of square kilometres of ice-bound fastness, most of it still unseen by man, and bring it within the ambit of the British Empire. It was the beginning of a decades-long struggle for supremacy in the Southern Ocean.

179

For Amery, the attraction of Antarctica lay in the wealth of its surrounding waters, where thousands of oil-rich whales congregated each summer, and in the mineral resources of the continent, where deposits of coal had already been discovered. With these in mind, he argued that Britain should make its move while the war-weary world was distracted by the discussions in Europe and the problems of post-war recovery. He blithely dismissed the 'vague French claims', which were based upon Dumont d'Urville's raising of the French tricolour off Adélie Land in 1840, and what he called the 'shadowy' American claim, based upon the United States Exploring Expedition of Charles Wilkes that same year. Although Wilkes had been the first to recognise the continental extent of Antarctica, British officials had long disparaged his supposed territorial discoveries.

Their scorn had seemed justified when other explorers reported having sailed over locations where Wilkes claimed that land existed. Mawson had been one who had done this, but he had nevertheless continued to refer to a large swathe of the Antarctic coastline south of Australia as 'Wilkes Land'. Yet this did not give the United States any right to the land, argued Amery, since 'no American has actually seen the land in question, still less set foot on it and I don't think there is any evidence, except in our own imaginations, that the Americans ever would claim it'.[2] Amery ignored altogether the claims made by Norway, Belgium, Argentina and Chile.

Britain might have been able to seize Antarctica had its government moved quickly and decisively in 1919. But it too was distracted by the many other pressing post-war issues that were competing for the country's depleted resources. There was the subjugation of Germany, the takeover of German and Turkish colonies, the ongoing war in Soviet Russia and the risk of political upheaval at home. The Antarctic did not bulk sufficiently large in Britain's strategic or economic calculations.

Aware of this reality, Amery wanted his colleagues to commit themselves in principle to controlling the whole continent, and to begin by moving to 'assert our effective authority' over the Ross Sea area, south of New Zealand. This was where whales had been reported to be in abundance. One of Ross Sea's inlets was even called the Bay of Whales. Amery advised that the Ross Sea was 'the best known and in some ways most accessible part' of the continent. It was also 'the scenes of Shackleton's and Scott's expeditions', which would enhance Britain's claim to the area.[3] Of course, it was also the scene of Norway's triumphant assault on the South Pole, an inconvenient fact that Amery neglected to mention. Shackleton had, after all, been first to discover the South Pole plateau, although he'd failed to reach the pole itself.

As Amery embarked on his ambitious program of territorial aggrandisement, Shackleton was planning to return on a fourth expedition to Antarctica, where he wanted to explore the 3200 kilometres of uncharted coastline of west Antarctica. Deep in debt, as always, the inveterate schemer had originally planned to lead a Canadian expedition to the Arctic, after Canada became concerned that its isolated Arctic islands might be claimed by the United States or Denmark. When the Canadian government was slow to back Shackleton's plan, the impatient explorer convinced a private benefactor to finance it and then had him agree that the expedition should go south instead.

Shackleton had bought a small Norwegian sealing ship for the Arctic expedition, driven by sails and an unreliable auxiliary engine. Now it would have to go much further and face more testing seas. Shackleton planned to take a two-seater seaplane to scout a safe passage through the shifting ice, to look for lost islands and to take dramatic photographs of the landscape.[4] Scott and Shackleton had taken to the air in a tethered balloon in 1902 and Mawson had taken a wingless aircraft to the Antarctic in 1911. Now there was the prospect of an explorer using an aircraft to explore and map large swathes of ice-bound territory that would otherwise take months or years to cover.

The possible use of aircraft raised interesting questions about the claiming of new territory, which traditionally had been done by stepping onto newly discovered land and raising a flag, leaving a cairn of stones or some other marker, or erecting a building. Diplomats and lawyers would have to decide if territory could be claimed without anyone actually standing upon the ground and performing a ceremony of possession. They would also have to decide if the explorer could claim only the territory that his aircraft passed over, or whether all the territory that he could see in any direction was able to be claimed. Despite the potential of aircraft to assist Amery's plan to bring Antarctica under British control, the heavily indebted and hard-drinking Shackleton was denied government help, apart from the loan of some equipment from the

Admiralty. He was forced to make economies by having his fifteen expeditioners crew the ship as well as perform their scientific and other roles.[5]

Another British expedition, led by John Lachlan Cope, was being organised for 1921–22. Cope was an explorer of even more dubious reputation than Shackleton, and his plans were even more ambitious. He had signed on as a surgeon and biologist with the Ross Sea party of Shackleton's ill-fated expedition in 1914, during which he 'suffered from constant boils' and displayed 'childish outbursts of temper'. By the end, he was complaining of 'shitting nanny-goats turds' and was regarded by his companions as 'quite irrational'.[6] The latter quality was still very much in evidence when he announced, in January 1920, that he would 'circumnavigate the Antarctic continent' and 'explore the interior by means of aeroplanes', flying across it by way of the South Pole.

It was to be an elaborate expedition of about fifty men, costing a massive £100,000 or more, and would last up to six years. The name of the expedition – 'the British Imperial Antarctic Expedition' – certainly promised great things. According to Cope, it would be the largest and longest expedition ever sent to the Antarctic, with twelve aircraft charting and photographing the unknown interior. He even talked of establishing permanent bases there. As one writer has recently observed, Cope's plan for permanent bases 'would have put Britain in a position to annex three-quarters of the entire continent – the last and greatest land grab in history'.[7] However, it was all hokum.

While Shackleton and Cope were planning their expeditions, British naval officials were poring over historical reports of voyages that could allow Britain to extend its claim over the entire continent. The Admiralty's hydrographer, Admiral Sir Frederick Learmonth, produced a lengthy report on all the claims that nations might mount to different parts of the Antarctic, dividing them into those that were 'indisputable' and those that were open to challenge. Not surprisingly, the report largely reinforced Amery's view of the superiority of Britain's claim to most of the Antarctic continent.

It pointed out that the British naval captain Edward Bransfield had been the first to discover any part of Antarctica in 1820, although he had not realised it was a continent. As for the United States Exploring Expedition of 1840, Wilkes and his men were dismissed as 'absolute novices in Polar work', whose discoveries had mostly been proved to be non-existent. Of all the other nations, only France was considered still to have claims that could be classed as 'indisputable', and these were just to Adélie Land, a narrow sliver of land south of Australia that had been claimed by d'Urville in 1840, and to Charcot Land, on the western side of the Antarctic Peninsula, which had been discovered and charted by Jean-Baptiste Charcot in 1909.[8] It would later be realised that Charcot Land was an island rather than part of the continent.

The Admiralty report gave comfort to Amery but also raised some important questions about the claiming of new territories – questions that the Admiralty was unable to answer. For instance, even if Bransfield was acknowledged as the first person to discover part of the Antarctic coastline, should that give Britain the right to claim the entire continent, given that Bransfield had been oblivious to the fact that it was a continent? Or should the United States have that right, since Wilkes had been the first to realise that Antarctica was a continent and to give it that name? It could even be argued that none of these early explorers should have any claim to territories that they had merely sighted from their vessels, often far from shore, when later explorers had actually clambered onto the continent itself. Some had gone even further, exploring the hinterland, raising their flag and performing some recognisable claiming ceremony.

These were matters for nations to negotiate or for an international court to adjudicate. The Admiralty was content to arm the Colonial Office with material that would ward off any challenges from rival nations. At the same time, it re-examined its charts of the Antarctic so that it could expunge any questionable discoveries and foreign names that might undermine Britain's claims.[9]

Amery used the Admiralty report to enlist the support of Australia and New Zealand in his secret plan to claim the entire continent. There were clear benefits in having the two British dominions share the cost of exploration and administration. Britain's claim to the Ross Sea area would also be strengthened by having Australia and New Zealand as fellow claimants, based upon their proximity and their history of exploration in that area. Their southern ports were also the best jumping-off points to that part of the Antarctic. So Amery told them of his desire to bring 'the whole of the Antarctic . . . within the British Empire'. He would achieve this by a 'consistent policy . . . of extending and asserting British control with the object of ultimately making it complete'. Amery pointed to the economic possibilities of the continent and even predicted that the Antarctic seas might become important trade routes. He also played on Australian and New Zealand fears, warning that Antarctica might provide secret bases for hostile airplanes and submarines, and advised that British control would allow better regulation of companies that wished to exploit the area's marine resources. This issue was likely to find sympathy in Australia, where there had been a press campaign against the 'wanton butchery' of penguins and elephant seals.[10]

However, the Australian prime minister, Billy Hughes, was more concerned with the development of the Australian continent and its new territory in New Guinea, and could not see how Antarctica might offer economic benefits or pose a threat to Australia.[11] It was only after pressure from Britain that Hughes finally asked Australia's Antarctic explorers to give their views.[12] They were unanimous in wanting Australia to control the Antarctic quadrant that lay immediately west of the Ross Sea. Professor David claimed that the region had a massive coalfield that was capable of yielding billions of tons of coal, while Mawson emphasised the profits to be had from whaling.[13] Fearing that Hughes would ignore their recommendations, Mawson told a journalist in January 1921 that the government 'should not neglect its duty' to accept responsibility for the Australian quadrant. According to Mawson, Australia had a right to the territory because of its 'work of exploration' and the 'international axiom' that 'uninhabited Polar regions should be controlled by the nearest civilized nation'.[14]

Mawson made his comments as dominion representatives were meeting with Amery in London. They could not agree on how the empire should proceed with Amery's plan to seize the Antarctic gradually. While Australia and New Zealand wanted to control their own areas, Amery wanted to keep open the possibility of Britain sharing in their administration. More importantly, the meeting could not decide how the empire should assert its claim, 'whether it was necessary to send a ship specially to the Antarctic to raise the flag, or whether approval of the raising of the flag in earlier years would be sufficient'. There was also the unresolved question of what legal acts had to be undertaken before British authority could exist over the Ross Sea.[15] More fundamentally, how could a nation claim title to a territory that was so inhospitable that it was seemingly incapable of occupation? For centuries, nations had gained sovereignty over uninhabited places by 'effective occupation', but even temporary settlements in the Antarctic were fraught with difficulties.

The officials decided that 'effective title' could still be created by the act of 'discovery and exploration'. In the case of the Ross Sea area, they suggested that British title could be claimed immediately, since its discovery and exploration had been done mainly by British expeditions.[16] The Australian Sector, on the other hand, was more complicated because it included the French-claimed Adélie Land. Although the French had 'done nothing to keep any claim alive' since d'Urville's fleeting visit in 1840, the Colonial Office warned that the French 'are very touchy on such questions'.

Moreover, the British government had complicated the question in 1911 by asking France whether it claimed that part of the continent known as 'Wilkes Land', which had only recently been given that name by Mawson and which went all the way from 52° E to 160° E. It was the coastline along which Wilkes had sailed at the same time as d'Urville, but he had not formally claimed it for the United States. Because d'Urville had actually stepped onto an offshore islet and raised the French flag, Britain had carelessly suggested that d'Urville's claim potentially extended over all the coastline that Wilkes had supposedly seen, rather than the much more limited coastline that d'Urville had actually seen. Not surprisingly, the French government had seized upon this suggestion, informing the British Foreign Office in April 1912 that 'these lands were taken possession of in the name of France in 1840 and that [France] has no intention of renouncing its rights over them'.[17]

The French reply left Britain in a dilemma. France had confirmed that it still regarded itself as the rightful owner of what it called 'these lands', making reference to an article from 1840 in the *Sydney Herald*, which had reported d'Urville's discovery. However, France had not defined the exact geographic extent of the territory that it was claiming. When British officials quickly examined their newspaper archive, they found that the *Sydney Herald* had reported d'Urville's discovery as extending from 136° E to 147° E. Although this was much less than the extent of Wilkes Land, it was still greater than the area that Britain believed d'Urville's voyage entitled France to claim. More worryingly, France had not explicitly confirmed that its claim was limited to the lines of longitude mentioned in the article.

Britain left the question unresolved in 1912.[18] By the early 1920s, this uncertainty was proving to be a major impediment to Britain's desire to claim the Ross Sea area. Indeed, the British were so wary of the French reaction to their claiming of the Ross Sea that they decided to delay any decision until the dominion prime ministers gathered in London for the imperial conference of June 1921.[19] But that conference also failed to reach a decision, despite pressure from the new colonial secretary, Winston Churchill.[20] Other urgent issues had dominated the discussions, from the Anglo–Japanese alliance to the continuing question of German war reparations. Moreover, some of the impetus for British action had dissipated in April 1921, when Amery lost his responsibility for the Antarctic after becoming First Lord of the Admiralty.

There might have been more interest in the Antarctic if the Shackleton and Cope expeditions had discovered new land or otherwise led to exciting newspaper headlines. However, both were dismal failures. Cope's expedition had been first to leave Britain, but its prospects were dealt a deadly blow when the Royal Geographical Society refused to approve its plans or Cope's leadership.[21] Without such support, Cope's cause was hopeless. Instead of his elaborate expedition of fifty men, it was a sad group of just four men who made their own way to the South Shetlands in December 1920. They only managed to get there through the generosity of the wealthy Norwegian whaler Lars Christensen, whose ship took them as far as the whaling station on Deception Island. Yet the scheming Cope told the *New York Times* that his plans were even more fabulous than before, involving five ships, 120 men, a budget of $750,000 and an adventure 'more thrilling' than any conceived in fiction by Jules Verne.[22] In fact, on the day this account was published, Cope was trying to cadge an onward passage on a whaling ship from Deception Island to the nearby Antarctic Peninsula.[23]

Cope's pathetic party comprised an experienced Australian explorer, Hubert Wilkins, a nineteen-year-old geologist, Thomas Bagshawe, and a twenty-two-year-old surveyor from the naval reserve, Michael Lester. Cope also had a handful of huskies, but he had none of the vaunted ships or aircraft and had to rely on the goodwill of a whaler to take them to Hope Bay on the eastern tip of the Antarctic Peninsula. When a landing there proved impossible because of the ice, on 12 January 1921 they were dumped at Paradise Harbour on the west coast, where a beached and derelict barge boat gave them some shelter. From there, they hoped to cross the peninsula to their intended destination. When that proved impossible because of the difficult terrain, the bickering party faced the prospect of spending a year living in the cramped quarters of the boat.

Cope and Wilkins decamped and went their separate ways after getting passage on a passing whaler. Cope tried unsuccessfully to raise further funds, while Wilkins headed for the United States, from where he hoped to organise an expedition of his own. Lester and Bagshawe spent the following year expanding their living quarters at Paradise Harbour and collecting meteorological and other data before they too returned home, courtesy of a Norwegian whaler.[24] The expedition had been a farce. It provided no headlines to stimulate British interest or activity in the Antarctic, and failed to reinforce Britain's claim to other parts of the continent.

Shackleton might have been expected to do better. There was certainly a lot of favourable publicity at the start, after Shackleton invited Boy Scouts to join the expedition and around 1700 applied.[25] The expedition was lauded as an inspiration to boys everywhere, and a photograph of the two successful boys with Shackleton appeared on the cover of the magazine *Young Britain*. As Shackleton's ship, the *Quest*, was readied for departure on 17 September 1921, a large throng of people lined the Thames to watch the two scouts hoist yet another Union Jack given by the king to be raised on any territory that Shackleton might discover.[26] Also on board was Wilkins, who, on Shackleton's invitation, had rushed to London to join the *Quest*.

The voyage was dogged by difficulties, beginning with an unscheduled stop in Lisbon to repair the engine. A further month was spent in Rio de Janeiro so the engine could be given a complete overhaul. The delay forced Shackleton to cancel his plans to call at Cape Town to pick up cargo that had been sent ahead. Instead, the ship would head straight for the Antarctic before the summer exploring season closed. Without the stores that were left behind at Cape Town, it would not be possible to fly the aircraft. Both Cope and Shackleton had lost the chance to be first to use this novel means of claiming territory.

Shackleton's plans were now in complete disarray. The forty-seven-year-old explorer had graver things on his mind, having suffered a heart attack during the stressful weeks in Rio. Treating the pain of his condition with champagne, Shackleton decided to head straight for the Grytviken whaling station on South Georgia. He was desperate to salvage something from the summer; he had already sent Wilkins ahead by steamship to South Georgia to collect whatever he could in the way of natural specimens.

Finally at anchor off the world's southernmost township of Grytviken, where the pervading stink of the rotting whales clashed with the natural beauty of the place, Shackleton suffered a second heart attack, this time fatal. Still dressed in his blue and white pyjamas, his body was placed in a plain coffin, which was 'covered with tar and draped with a stained Union Jack' and then taken to the settlement's Norwegian church. There it remained until a ship was ready to take his remains, and the news of his death, to South America and on to England. Shackleton's shattered deputy, Frank Wild, took to drinking as he sailed the *Quest* on what would be an abbreviated voyage. The ship was caught by pack ice before heading back to South Georgia by way of Elephant Island, the scene of Shackleton's great trial of 1916. Meanwhile, Shackleton's body had been shipped as far as Uruguay before his long-suffering widow instructed from London that it should be returned for burial to the region that had made his reputation.[27]

On 5 March 1922, a few weeks before the *Quest* returned to South Georgia, Shackleton's much-travelled remains were finally carried by Norwegian whalers to the cemetery at Grytviken, where he was buried with a brief ceremony. A few local British officials, stationed there to assert British sovereignty, attended the burial. When Wild and his companions arrived back on 6 April, they visited the simple grave with its small wooden cross and decided to leave a more visible memorial, erecting a cairn of rocks topped by a large cross and marked with a brass plate to 'Sir Ernest Shackleton, Explorer'. The sight of the cairn would greet Norwegian whalers each time they sailed into the harbour. Along with Shackleton's grave, it would serve as an implicit and enduring reinforcement of Britain's claim to the area, which was part of the disputed Falkland Islands Dependencies.[28]

For all the hoopla of the Cope and Shackleton expeditions, the cairn was practically their only legacy. It was not much comfort for Britain's Antarctic enthusiasts and their secret scheme to extend Britain's control over the continent. Nevertheless, the Admiralty report of 1919 had shown just how much of Antarctica was potentially Britain's to claim. Three years later, though, as Wild's dejected party arrived back in England, there was still no decision on how Britain should achieve its ambitious scheme. It was only after a Norwegian whaling company asked London's permission in June 1922 to hunt whales in the Ross Sea that Britain was finally impelled to act.

Whaling at South Georgia and the South Shetlands had involved a mixture of shore stations and factory ships moored in sheltered inlets. These worked in tandem with small, steam-powered whale-catchers, which scoured the surrounding waters, a keen-eyed harpooner on their bow to look for surfacing whales. Once their quarry was caught and killed, the whales were inflated with compressed air, and their quickly putrefying bodies were towed by the tail to the shore stations or factory ships. In the case of the factory ships, the smaller whales would be lifted onto the deck for processing, while the larger ones would be tied alongside and the blubber flensed off in great strips, which were then hoisted on deck. There it was cut into smaller portions and packed into massive boilers, where steam reduced it to oil. The whaling companies had enjoyed bumper seasons and strong prices. Now, one of them wanted to use the same methods in the Ross Sea, where the Bay of Whales held out the prospect of being a profitable killing field. It was the first move by a whaling company to explore the potential of the Antarctic coastline.

Most prominent among the companies operating South Georgia's several whaling stations was the company headed by Carl Larsen and financed by investors from Norway, Britain and Argentina. Larsen had first recognised the potential of these seas in 1894; with a licence from the British government, he had established a land station at Grytviken ten years later. Now he wanted to exploit the potential of the Ross Sea. Britain was in a quandary, since Larsen was implicitly acknowledging British authority in an area where no such authority had been formally asserted. Undaunted, Churchill urged the immediate granting of a licence, noting that the Norwegian's 'acknowledgment of Sovereignty would be valuable support of British claims'.[29] The New Zealand government agreed to confer with British officials on the exact terms of the licence and on how the empire's authority should be extended to the Ross Sea.[30]

It was finally decided in early 1923 that the king should issue an 'order in council', rather than publish letters patent, as had been done in the case of the Falkland Islands Dependencies. This was an important distinction. Letters patent were generally used when a new territory was being annexed. Britain was careful not to do this in the case of the Ross Sea, since it would suggest that it had not previously had title over the area. In contrast, the order in council would allow Britain to perform 'acts of ownership' that would reinforce the idea that it had long enjoyed 'an inchoate title' over the territory, based upon discovery. In other words, it would demonstrate to the world that British sovereignty already existed over the Ross Sea area. Britain simply had to strengthen the area's pre-existing status as a British possession by undertaking acts of administration. So an order in council was published on 30 July 1923, declaring that 'the coasts of the Ross Sea, with the islands and territories adjacent thereto, between the 160th degree of East Longitude and the 150th degree of West Longitude . . . are a British settlement'.[31]

In keeping with the Falkland Islands Dependencies, the new territory was dubbed 'the Ross Dependency' and its administration placed under the control of New Zealand's governor-general, Lord Jellicoe, who had been Britain's naval chief during the First World War. New Zealand's attorney-general, Sir Francis Bell, who had been instrumental in negotiating the outcome, told journalists that Jellicoe would follow instructions from the Colonial Office, although he expected that any such instructions would be drawn up in consultation with the New Zealand government, which was taking over 'the Ross territory . . . on behalf of the Empire as a whole, and not specially in the interests of the Dominion'.[32] This would present a more palatable picture of the continent being divided between several countries, even though all of them were members of the British Empire.

The peremptory British takeover of the Ross Sea caused outrage in Paris. The French government had made it clear in 1912 that it regarded itself as the rightful owner of the vaguely defined 'Adélie or Wilkes Land'.[33] In response to Britain's order in council, Paris moved to put its own claim beyond doubt. Just as d'Urville had consciously followed British precedent by raising the French flag to claim Adélie Land, so the French government now followed the recent British precedent by issuing a decree on 27 March 1924 that simply asserted French control, rather than going to the trouble of sending an expedition to demonstrate French control by acts of exploration, mapping, naming or scientific endeavour.

In November 1924, France followed up its decree with an announcement that its Antarctic territories would be administered as part of its Madagascar colony. The colonial minister, Édouard Daladier, explained to the French president that successive French governments had not done anything about 'the sovereign rights long since acquired by France' because they had no knowledge of 'the economic value of these uninhabited lands'. Now that its ignorance had been dispelled about the wealth to be won there, France was determined to retain its Antarctic territories, while still remaining remarkably reluctant to define their precise territorial extent.[34]

The British government was in a bind. While it could lightly dismiss the claims of Norway or Argentina, it could not wave away the claims of its powerful neighbour and wartime ally. However, it was determined to limit the French claim to the 240 kilometres of coastline that d'Urville had actually sailed along. Britain feared that France wanted to take much more. At least, that might be the implication of the French use of the words 'Adélie or Wilkes Land'. As Admiral Learmonth warned, if the French wanted to claim 'the whole extent of territory *claimed to have been discovered* by Wilkes, such a claim . . . might conceivably lead to a claim to the ownership of the entire Antarctic continent'. Even if the French were only using the term 'Wilkes Land' as a synonym for 'Adélie Land', Learmonth feared that this might create 'a lever for putting forward a claim' to the entire continent, which would undermine the 'consistent policy pursued by this country with reference to the Antarctic regions'.[35] Britain was not about to let France have more than a tiny slice of the continent.

While Britain might concede a narrowly defined Adélie Land to the French, the Australian government was not so sanguine, since that would remove a slice from the Australian quadrant, which the dominion wanted for itself. This quadrant was the region that Britain next wanted to annex after the Ross Sea, and which Australia planned to administer on behalf of the British Empire. The Cambridge-educated Australian prime minister, Stanley Bruce, urged Britain to 'assert rights over these regions at the earliest opportunity', and later noted that 'Australia's interest in this part of Antarctic is very great'.[36]

Mawson dismissed the French claim completely, telling journalists that d'Urville 'did not go ashore at Adelie [sic] Land, but simply sighted it and coasted along for two days, whereas [Mawson's] Australasian Antarctic Expedition spent three years exploring

Adelie [sic] and other Antarctic lands'.[37] This was not a compelling argument in London. Amery had returned to the Colonial Office in November 1924, this time as colonial secretary, and he was conscious that Britain's claim to much of the Falkland Islands Dependencies was based upon similarly fleeting acts of discovery.[38] As a way out of its bind, the Admiralty suggested that Britain negotiate with France to swap Adélie Land for the sub-Antarctic Heard and MacDonald Islands.[39] That way, Britain might still get the complete Australian quadrant, and the whole continent might yet belong to the British Empire. But the offer was never put to France, as it was thought it would be rejected.

France was not the only nation the British had to consider. There was also the United States, as some Americans were becoming concerned that territory discovered by Wilkes was about to be seized by Britain or France. They did not realise that Mawson had named the territory 'Wilkes Land' to honour Wilkes' voyage rather than to suggest that Wilkes had discovered or even seen that territory. Not that the United States government was about to claim it. In reply to a letter from a concerned American citizen in 1924, the US secretary of state, Charles Hughes, denied that any 'valid claim of sovereignty' had been created by the Wilkes expedition. Even if Wilkes had discovered and formally taken possession of Antarctic territory, Hughes argued that it could only be regarded as American territory if the discovery was 'followed by an actual settlement of the discovered country'.[40]

Of course, this argument also meant that Washington was refusing to recognise the sovereignty of any country in the Antarctic until it had actually settled the territory. Although the United States did little to promote this view in London, Oslo or elsewhere, it remained on the backburner at the US State Department for possible use at a later time.

In the mid-1920s, the United States was much more concerned with the Arctic than the Antarctic. It was in the Arctic that a frenetic burst of exploration was taking place, as those nations bordering the Arctic Ocean sought to extend their domain northwards. With the use of aircraft and airships, explorers were racing to uncover the remaining secrets of the Arctic Circle. Some wanted the celebrity and wealth that was likely to accrue from being first to fly to the North Pole. But many were convinced that there was a greater prize to be had.

The Arctic was believed to hide the last undiscovered land mass on Earth. It was this that aroused the interest of nations as well as adventurers.[41] If such a continent could be found, it was likely to be much more valuable, both economically and strategically, than the more isolated and much colder Antarctica. Apart from possible mineral deposits, much of its value would come from providing landing places for the air routes that were expected eventually to crisscross the Arctic, providing the shortest connection between northern Europe and North America and Asia.

The competition came to a head in the northern summer of 1925, with an excited report in the *New York Times* describing the 'air race' that was about to begin in the Arctic between three national expeditions. There was a large measure of journalistic licence in describing it as a 'race', since the expeditions were leaving from separate starting points and each had a different objective in view.

The first expedition was American, led by Donald MacMillan and sponsored by the National Geographic Society. It was also supported by the US Navy, which sent the soon-to-be-famous aviator Richard E. Byrd to fly one of its three seaplanes. In accordance with American government policy, MacMillan and Byrd were instructed not to make a formal claim over any land they might discover. But neither were they to acknowledge in any way the existing claims of Canada over islands in the Arctic. The second expedition was led by the veteran Norwegian explorer Roald Amundsen, and included Lincoln Ellsworth, the forty-year-old son of a wealthy American coalmine owner, and a Norwegian pilot, Hjalmar Riiser-Larsen. The Norwegian government had instructed Amundsen to carry Norwegian flags on his two aircraft 'and to claim new lands in the name of Norway'. The third expedition was the British Arctic Expedition, led by the young Icelander Grettir Algarsson. It would use a vessel and a small airship.

Although the newspaper headlines suggested that the goal of the three expeditions was to fly over the North Pole, one of MacMillan's former colleagues, the US Navy officer Fitzhugh Green, wrote excitedly in the magazine *Popular Science* that the pole was 'just an *excuse. Three nations are racing for the last undiscovered continent on the surface of the globe!*' Green called it the 'most sensational sporting event in human history'. In fact, none of the expeditions reached the North Pole, nor did any of them discover a new land mass.[42] But so long as the apparition of an undiscovered continent continued to beguile the nations of the northern hemisphere, and to consume the funds and energy of polar explorers, Britain might yet be able to extend its domain over the Antarctic continent.

However, the great wealth to be had from whaling ensured that Norway followed France in challenging Britain's Antarctic ambitions. If Oslo recognised Britain's claim to the Ross Sea, and then perhaps to the Australian quadrant, Norwegian whalers intending to operate in those areas would be burdened with the same British fees and duties they were forced to pay in the Falkland Islands Dependencies. Consequently, Norway disputed Britain's right to claim all the Ross Sea area. For one thing, it argued, Britain could not claim any yet-to-be-discovered islands in the Ross Sea. It also disputed Britain's right to claim waters in the Ross Sea that were beyond the three-mile territorial limit. This posed a particular problem in the Antarctic, where the actual shoreline was often impossible to discern; in the Ross Sea, much of it lay under a thick layer of ice. As for the hinterland, Norway pointed out that Amundsen had been the first to reach the South Pole from the Ross Sea, and he had formally claimed the South Pole plateau 'in the name of the King of Norway'. Norway also demanded that Britain exclude the territory on either side of Amundsen's route to the pole.[43]

With its whaling fleet operating in the Ross Sea each summer, Norway was the best placed of all the aspiring Antarctic nations to establish a shore station and effectively occupy the territory that Amundsen had claimed. Britain would not let that happen. It simply denied the validity of Amundsen's prior act of discovery. The Admiralty pointed out that Shackleton, although he had not quite reached the South Pole, had taken possession of the South Pole plateau three years earlier than Amundsen. It went on to deprecate Amundsen's historic achievement, arguing that he had merely 'penetrated a few miles further than Shackleton'. While there was some basis for this argument, Britain was on much weaker legal ground regarding its attempt to claim the international waters of the Ross Sea and any possible undiscovered islands. But it refused to engage with Oslo on these issues. With the confidence that comes from controlling the world's largest empire, Amery recommended that Britain simply 'resist any pretensions on the part of the Norwegian Government to any part of the . . . Ross Dependency'.[44]

At the same time, the Australian government continued to pressure Britain to resist the French claim to Adélie Land.[45] Prime

Minister Bruce was being pressured in turn by the Australian National Research Council, which wanted Australia to make a much wider claim of its own. If the French claim was allowed, the council warned, that would permit the United States to do likewise for the part of Wilkes Land that lay to the west of Adélie Land. This would further reduce 'the territory that should be Australia's by right of its geographical position and its exploration work'.

As the Norwegians had, the council argued that it was 'continuous occupation or exploitation' that gave rise to a recognisable claim under international law. In this respect, Mawson had done much more than d'Urville. He had made Adélie Land his main base and 'added a thousand miles of coastline to the map, collected physical and biological scientific information over a wide field', and had claimed possession by raising both the British and Australian flags. The latter act reflected the conflicting Australian identity of the time. Although still attached to the British Empire, Australia had imperial aspirations of its own, with the council noting the alluring prospect of Australia controlling territory 'from the Equator [New Guinea] to the Pole'.[46]

A delegation from the council, including Mawson, met with Bruce in July 1925 to press their case, pointing to what they called the 'broad principle' that 'empty lands should be administered by the nearest civilised power interested in them'. Describing the Australian Sector as 'the birth-right of Australia', Mawson told Bruce that Australia knew the place better than any other nation because of the 'immense quantities of facts' that he had brought back. These could be found in his popular record of the expedition, *Home of the Blizzard*, a copy of which he presented to Bruce, as well as in the volumes of scientific reports that would soon be published. Bruce told the deputation that 'the matter had to be treated very carefully', however, since the French were 'apt to get a little hysterical' if Australia challenged their claim to Adélie Land.[47]

This was the reason Britain had remained reluctant to annex the still vaguely defined Adélie Land. Nor would it accept the Australian suggestion to stop France from extending its claim from the coastline to the South Pole, along the lines of the sector principle used by Canada in the Arctic and by Britain in the Antarctic. Nor did Britain support the Australian argument that the closest civilised nations should control the different sectors of the Antarctic, since such an argument could be used by Argentina to reinforce its claim to the Falkland Islands and the Antarctic Peninsula. The Australian argument about discovery and exploration was also regarded with some coolness in London, since other European nations had done much exploration in the Falkland Islands Dependencies, as well as in other areas of the Antarctic that Britain wanted to incorporate into its empire.[48] Britain certainly wanted to secure control of the Australian quadrant, but it had to be careful about the possible implications elsewhere of the arguments it used to justify the annexation.

Although Amery wanted to press on and annex the large Australian quadrant, minus Adélie Land, he remained hamstrung by the fact that the French had never defined the territorial limits of Adélie Land. Britain could not ask the French directly for fear that they might define Adélie Land very widely. Foreign Secretary Austen Chamberlain suggested that Britain should simply annex the whole Australian quadrant and wait for the expected French protest. Britain would then have an excuse to ask France to define and justify the limits of Adélie Land, which would allow Britain to adjust the limits of the Australian quadrant accordingly.

Armed with Chamberlain's advice, Amery asked the Admiralty for 'the geographical limits of the maximum area' that Britain could now 'reasonably' annex in Antarctica. In response, the Admiralty cautioned that Britain should claim only those parts that 'had been discovered by British [Empire] explorers'. These comprised large, discontinuous stretches of the coastline, beginning at the Weddell Sea and moving eastward to include Coats Land, Enderby Land, Kemp Land, Queen Mary Land, Wilkes Land, King George V Land and Oates Land'. In the Admiralty's view, France's Adélie Land should be restricted to a small sliver of territory from 137° E to 142° E. When these large areas were added to the Ross Dependency and the Falkland Islands Dependencies, more than half of the continent would still remain unclaimed by anyone. Indeed, most of it still remained unseen by anyone.[49]

This was hardly what Amery had envisaged in 1919, and he remained determined to have the whole continent, except for Adélie Land. Rather than accepting the Admiralty's advice, Amery suggested that Britain annex all the territory, other than Adélie Land, from the western boundary of the Ross Dependency to the western boundary of Coats Land – that is, from 160° E to 20° W. This was much larger than the quadrant that Australia wanted to claim, which stretched from 160° E to 90° E. Amery was advocating that Britain ignore completely the claims that other nations, such as Norway, Argentina, Chile, Japan, Belgium and the United States, might care to make. In his view, the key was getting the French to limit the extent of Adélie Land to the coastline that d'Urville had actually seen. If the French restricted their claim, the Admiralty recommended, then Britain should annex the rest of that region.[50]

The Foreign Office agreed in November 1925 that Amery could proceed with his land grab, on the understanding that it 'may have to be . . . modified in the event of any other foreign government successfully contesting some part of it', such as the United States in regard to Wilkes Land. As for the legal basis of Britain's annexa-tion, the Foreign Office argued that it came from Britain's acts of discovery, with sovereignty then being 'acquired by occupation'. In London's view, occupation did not mean having people actually living there but arose from the performance of two symbolic acts. The first was 'a formal claim of annexation or some public act which implies a definite claim to sovereignty'. The second was to establish 'an administration over the territory', as New Zealand had done for the Ross Dependency. Before getting the king to issue an order in council for Australia to do likewise for the Australian quadrant, the Foreign Office suggested that the government should decide on the method of administration, so that both acts could be done together.[51] But they put off any final decision until the imperial conference in 1926, when all the dominion prime ministers would be in London.[52]

In the meantime, the Norwegian whalers were pressing ahead with their plans to expand their operations from the Falkland Islands Dependencies to other areas of the Antarctic, which poten-tially threatened Britain's territorial ambitions in those areas. At least Carl Larsen's company had acknowledged British sovereignty in the Ross Sea, when it had asked in 1922 for a licence to hunt whales there. Now Larsen bought a steel cargo steamer that had formerly plied the Britain–India route, which he converted into a factory ship and renamed the *Sir James Clark Ross*, in honour of the British explorer.

The ship had the latest German-designed boilers and bulk storage tanks for whale oil, while its bow was protected by a sheath of African hardwood. The ship had many other modifications and carried supplies and equipment to guard against disaster, including a powerful radio transmitter, a searchlight to guide it through the ice, and timber for huts in the event that the ship was crushed and sank and the crew had to shelter ashore. The huts could also be used to establish a Norwegian claim to sovereignty over the territory on which they were erected. Accompanied by five small whale-catchers, the *Sir James Clark Ross* would be the largest vessel ever to operate in Antarctic waters, and the first steel vessel to do so.[53] The continent that had been the exclusive preserve of occasional exploratory expeditions was finally opening for business.

George Hooper was one of those who clambered aboard the *Sir James Clark Ross* when it reached Hobart in November 1923. The New Zealand government's nautical adviser, Hooper had been hurriedly sworn in as administrator, magistrate and justice of the peace of the Ross Dependency. By rushing to Hobart to join the Norwegian fleet and report on its operations, Hooper showed that the British Empire was exercising its sovereignty over the region. By providing Hooper with passage on the ship, the Norwegians were again implicitly acknowledging British sovereignty. With Hooper ensconced in his cabin, the *Sir James Clark Ross* steamed slowly down the Derwent River, with the whale-catchers being towed in a line behind it to save fuel. Also aboard the ship, as it rolled with the prevailing westerly swell of the Southern Ocean, was a twenty-year-old Australian, Alan Villiers, an aspiring writer. He had signed on to the *Sir James Clark Ross* after convincing the editor of the Hobart *Mercury* to publish his reports.

The first voyage did not go according to plan. The Bay of Whales was strangely devoid of whales, and one of the catchers became separated from the fleet and was feared lost. This forced Larsen to mount a long search for the missing boat and to leave a cairn of supplies on the shore, topped with a Norwegian flag. After this, most of the whales they encountered were large blue whales that had to be flensed alongside the factory ship. This was dangerous in the open sea, where a carcass being heaved by the waves could toss the men working on it into the freezing waters. So three of the bloated whales were towed through the fog to the relative shelter of Discovery Inlet, which had been formed by the curling shape of a glacier that was pushing its way out from the ice barrier.

Although Villiers noted how 'awe-inspiring it all is', Discovery Inlet was not the sort of protected anchorage that Larsen had hoped to find.[54] Its deep waters made it difficult for a ship to anchor, while the prevailing southerly winds could erupt into blizzards and force a sheltering vessel against the curving cliff of ice. The only way to escape was to head for the open sea, which meant having to stop work on the tethered whales for days at a time. Even normal winds could make the inlet too choppy for the flensing to proceed. At one time, Villiers counted thirty-two blue whales that were rotting in the cold waters as they waited to be processed.[55]

With these drawbacks, there was no profit to be had that first year. The storage tanks, which were capable of holding 60,000 barrels of oil, were less than one-third full when the ship left for New Zealand in March 1924. Nor was there much revenue for New Zealand, since duty was only payable when the catch exceeded 20,000 barrels. So the dominion was paid only the £200 annual fee, which was not much return for Hooper's time and expenses. But Larsen would be back.

While the whale-catchers wintered in New Zealand, the factory ship went to Norway for further modifications.[56] The elderly Larsen returned aboard it the following season, only to die of a heart attack in Antarctica in December 1924, just as the company was about to earn its first profit from the new venture. The whaling pioneer would not see his factory ship return at the end of the season with 31,500 barrels of oil, a figure that vindicated his vision in exploring the possibilities of the Ross Sea. The company continued without him, and the *Sir James Clark Ross* returned the following season to take 38,000 barrels of oil – worth £250,000 – along with a collection of young Emperor penguins for the Auckland Zoo. A New Zealand newspaper predicted that the growing profits would doubtless cause other companies 'to seriously consider the Ross Sea as a suitable location for an extension of their activities'.[57] Ominously for the British Empire, whaling companies were about to implement a revolutionary change that, within a few decades, would spell doom for the large population of blue whales.

From late 1925, a new type of factory ship appeared in the Antarctic.[58] Sloping ramps were installed at the rear of the existing factory ships so that the heavy blue whales that predominated in the Antarctic could be winched straight onto the flensing deck. Instead of being limited to one of the two inlets along the Ross Ice Barrier, the converted factory ships could remain at sea and process whales even in relatively rough seas, thereby reducing both their fuel costs and the problem of putrefaction, which had a bad effect on oil quality. More importantly, the new factory ships could remain beyond the three-mile territorial limit and therefore potentially avoid paying licence fees and duty.

By 1926, one Norwegian company had completed a successful season using a factory ship that operated completely in international waters. A second Norwegian company was in the process of being formed to do so in the Ross Sea. And a third Norwegian company was threatening to do likewise unless Britain granted it a licence. Companies now only applied for a licence if they wanted protection against their valuable ships and cargo being seized on some pretext by British officials.[59]

The new factory ships meant that the whole Antarctic coastline was open to the whalers' operations. Fleets of Norwegian whaling ships would soon be charting coastlines that no explorers had seen, providing Norway with the basis for territorial claims. In a desperate attempt to stop this dangerous development from threatening Britain's growing control over Antarctica – and the revenue of its Falkland Islands Dependencies – Amery instructed Britain's officials there to stop whalers from taking on the supplies they needed to operate in international waters. He also urged New Zealand to deny its facilities to any unlicensed Norwegian company.[60]

While Amery tried to hold back the tide of Norwegian whalers, news of the profitable operations in the Ross Sea spurred Australia's interest in the adjacent Australian quadrant.[61] But there remained serious disagreements within the British bureaucracy about how the remainder of the continent should be claimed. While Amery wanted to claim most of the continent, regardless of whether its coastline had even been discovered, the Foreign Office and Admiralty wanted to restrict any claim to those areas that had been discovered by British or Australian expeditions.[62] In the event, Amery's more ambitious plan was overruled. The advice prepared by British officials for dominion prime ministers at the 1926 imperial conference recommended that only territory discovered by British explorers should be claimed. This meant that Australia could still claim sovereignty over its quadrant, apart from Adélie Land, but that Amery would have to put aside his grander scheme to incorporate the whole continent within the empire, at least for the time being.[63]

When the imperial conference convened in London in November 1926, Amery chaired a committee of British and dominion representatives to discuss 'the potential importance of [Antarctica] to the

British Empire'. Bruce was content to leave Antarctic policy in the hands of the British government; in fact, he only bothered to attend the last of the three committee meetings. In his absence, the second meeting was addressed by Sir Cecil Hurst, the legal adviser to the Foreign Office, who warned that Britain could only pursue Amery's plan of getting title to the Antarctic by basing it upon 'either actual occupation or effective control'. Hurst recommended that future assertions of sovereignty should include formal acts 'on the spot'. Although that had not been done when Britain had claimed the Falkland Islands Dependencies and the Ross Dependency, Hurst 'considered that the absence of opposition in those cases was a piece of good fortune which might not recur'. He warned that Australia should send 'periodical expeditions' to the so-called 'Australian quadrant' if it wanted to secure control of the region, to which it otherwise had an uncertain legal title.[64]

As a result of the discussions, the conference was assured that Britain could claim all the territory that its explorers had discovered. In Britain's view, this comprised all the known territory of the Antarctic except for Adélie Land. But the empire would have to progress its claims gradually and not attempt to claim unexplored areas, which might provoke opposition from countries with potential claims of their own. If such countries protested at the British action or appealed to international law, delegates were warned that 'it might become impossible to pursue the British policy of acquiring the Antarctic region'. However, if Britain were to 'proceed cautiously, and steadily follow up and develop the valid claims they now possess', it might be hoped that 'foreign Powers will acquiesce, and that practically complete British domination may in time be established'.[65] It was clear that Amery's scheme to control the Antarctic remained very much on the imperial agenda, although whether it would ever be achieved remained a moot point.

The first step in establishing the British claims was taken with the publication of the conference report, which informed the world of the seven areas to which Britain believed it had title. The second step would come with the dispatch of an expedition that was to take formal possession of those territories for which a claiming ceremony had not previously been performed. And the third step would be to issue 'Letters Patent annexing the area and making provision for its government'. There were already plans to expand both the western boundary of the Falkland Islands Dependencies and the eastern boundary of the Ross Dependency to include the intervening area, which presently was unclaimed by anyone. This was where the enterprising Norwegian whaler and explorer Lars Christensen was seeking British permission to hunt for whales. As had been done for Larsen in the Ross Sea, the conference decided that Christensen should be given a licence, as that would allow Britain to perform 'a useful assertion of authority in this region'.[66]

Seven years after Amery had first formulated the British plan to take over the Antarctic, it had finally been rubber-stamped by all the representatives of the empire. As the dominion leaders took their leave from London, Amery wrote in his diary of how the 'process of incorporating the Antarctic in the British Empire . . . is now going to make a substantial further stride'. At the same time, he wondered whether the ice-covered continent, as opposed to its surrounding waters, would ever be of any value – other than perhaps 'for the purpose of all round winter sports'.[67]

Amery's self-congratulatory musings show no sign that he had any sense that his ambitious plan was already under threat. Yet even as he farewelled the dominion prime ministers, the rival nations that Amery had so blithely ignored were busily preparing their own schemes to secure control of the world's last continent and its bountiful seas.

CHAPTER 10

'To safeguard this country's territorial rights'

1926–1928

When the prime ministers posed for photographs after the imperial conference in November 1926, they were confident that the Antarctic continent would soon be part of their British world. But Colonial Secretary Leopold Amery's secret plan to secure all of the Antarctic for the British Empire was already under threat.

Firstly, the French were adamant that Britain could not have Adélie Land. That still left the bulk of the continent available, of which the British Empire had already laid claim to two sizeable wedges: the Falkland Islands Dependencies and the Ross Dependency, which amounted to about one-third of the continent's area. However, two other threats loomed on the horizon. The most immediate was the post-war whaling boom, which had brought fleets of whaling vessels to hunt in Antarctic waters. It was this that had made the Antarctic a desirable territory for Britain to control, but it had also caused other whaling nations to want the Antarctic for themselves. The other threat to Amery's plan came from aircraft, which would bring a renewed rush of exploration every bit as frantic as the pre-war race between Scott and Amundsen. Americans would be in the forefront of this airborne phalanx, which would prompt the United States to make its own grab for Antarctic territory.

It must have been frustrating for Amery. It was seven years since the ardent imperialist had proposed to his colleagues that Antarctica be annexed and made a part of the British Empire. Creating the Ross Dependency and placing it under New Zealand administration, was just a first step, which brought under British control a sea rich in whales. Even that proved contentious when the Norwegian government, in the wake of the 1926 imperial conference, questioned Britain's right to include the Ross Ice Barrier within its annexed territory. After all, this great body of ice was now known to rest on water rather than on land, and was therefore mostly more than three miles from the actual coastline, which lay somewhere far beneath the snow and ice. At the time, three miles from land was the internationally accepted sea boundary of a nation's territory.

If Britain accepted the Norwegian argument, practically all of the Ross Sea, including the Bay of Whales, would lie beyond the three-mile limit in international waters. Moreover, the Norwegians contested Britain's right to claim Edward VII Land, pointing out that Scott had merely seen it from the deck of his ship in 1902 – he had not stepped ashore or made a formal claim to the land on behalf of Britain. Norway's claim was much stronger, they claimed, because in December 1911 a three-man group from Amundsen's expedition had actually traversed the land, occupied it and 'formally took possession of it in the name of the King of Norway', at the same time that Amundsen was doing likewise on the polar plateau.[1]

Britain could not allow this argument to go unanswered. Its officials pointed out that the Norwegian party's exploration of King Edward VII Land was limited to about forty kilometres, and that the 'occupation' had been 'no more than a fortnight's camping in tents'. Moreover, the Norwegians had referred to Scott as their 'respected precurser', and in fact had named the only exposed land they saw during their short traverse as 'Scott's Nunataks'. There was no indication in the English edition of the expedition's account to show that they had claimed possession of King Edward VII Land or had been given authority by Amundsen to do so. Because of these factors, argued the Foreign Office, the Norwegian activity could not override the British claim, which was based upon Scott's 'prior discovery'.

As for whether Britain exercised sovereignty over the Ross Sea, that would partly depend upon the position of the coastline, which was not easy to define in the Antarctic. In papers prepared for the 1926 imperial conference, officials had argued that a seemingly permanent ice barrier should be regarded as the coastline, even though it was resting on water rather than land. London put this argument to Oslo in August 1927, noting that where a barrier – such as the Ross Ice Barrier, now known as the Ross Ice Shelf – was 'to all intents and purposes, a permanent extension of the land proper, there is good reason for treating the Barrier as though it were terra firma'. Since this was not an accepted legal opinion, the British also suggested that in at least some places the floating barrier was resting on land.[2] One way or another, the Norwegians had to be dissuaded from challenging British sovereignty over the Ross Dependency. By keeping the coastline vague, the exact position of the three-mile limit in the Ross Sea was also kept imprecise, which was meant to make it difficult for Norwegian whalers to operate in the Ross Sea without first having obtained a licence from New Zealand.

Things might have been difficult if New Zealand was actually 'administering' the Ross Dependency by having bases ashore or even just by having a ship patrol the waters during the summer months, when whalers were active. Instead, its administration of the territory had consisted only of sending an officer of its marine department on board one of the licensed Norwegian factory ships, the *Sir James Clark Ross*. No New Zealand official had ever stepped ashore on the Ross Dependency. Moreover, at the end of the 1926 season, the marine department officer reported that the *Sir James Clark Ross* had operated almost wholly in international waters and had only once resorted to Discovery Inlet on the Ross Ice Barrier, which was only within New Zealand's territorial waters if the ice barrier was regarded as coastline. This meant that the whaling company was paying for a license that it did not really need, and which carried conditions that restricted the type of whales that could be caught and forced its men to process whole carcasses rather than just strip the blubber and discard the rest.

While two Norwegian companies had paid for licenses, the captains of their ships were dismayed during the 1926–27 summer to see an unlicensed Norwegian factory ship, the *Nielson-Alonso*, steam with its whale-catchers into the Ross Sea, where it proceeded to kill whales, strip the blubber and leave the carcasses. That gave the interlopers a real advantage over their licensed rivals. Unlicensed whalers could kill and process more whales, as they did not have to spend time processing the less valuable parts.[3] And there was nothing that the New Zealand official could do about it.

New Zealand had been collecting £2500 from each factory ship operating in the Ross Sea as a license fee, as well as a royalty based on the amount of oil that it processed. All that revenue was now at risk, both because whalers had little need to obtain a license if they restricted their activity to international waters and because the unrestricted entry of unlicensed whalers could soon see whales hunted 'to the point of extermination'. Such an eventuality seemed more likely when the *Nielson-Alonso* arrived at Hobart in March 1927, after completing its summer hunt in the Ross Sea. Captain

R. N. Gjertsen proudly told reporters of having killed 456 whales, the blubber of which had been processed to produce 36,700 barrels of oil. Moreover, he had been able to keep working in bad weather and to haul whales weighing as much as 100 tons aboard the ship's rear slipway. There had been no need to pay for a license, Gjertsen said, because he had been operating only in international waters.

For Gjertsen, the ownership of the Antarctic meant nothing, as he would always be operating beyond its territorial waters. So he could quite unconcernedly suggest that Australia claim some of the continent, for its possible mineral resources, while there was still some land left to claim. The New Zealand government was so concerned by these developments that it urged Britain to seek an international agreement to regulate Antarctic whaling, so that it did not go the way of Arctic whaling. However, neither Britain nor Norway, which together controlled most of the whaling in the Antarctic, wanted to call an international conference that would only see other nations demand a piece of the very lucrative industry.[4]

Although Gjertsen was unconcerned about claiming any part of the continent, one of his Norwegian colleagues certainly had that in mind. After it became more difficult to find whales around South Georgia and the South Shetlands, Lars Christensen began to send his ships further afield. If he could find new whaling grounds and establish bases outside of the British-controlled Falkland Islands and Ross Dependencies, he could avoid paying license fees and royalties to the British. In January 1927, he sent the whale-catcher *Odd I* from Deception Island to the Bellingshausen Sea to look for whales. Encountering Peter I Island, a lonely speck of land on the edge of the pack ice that was discovered by Bellingshausen, the Norwegians were disappointed to find that there were no whales in the vicinity and no suitable harbour in which a factory ship could anchor. Indeed, wrote one Norwegian, 'this island looks quite dead'.

Unable to get ashore, they nevertheless sprinkled Norwegian names on its prominent features, calling its mist-covered mountain 'Lars Christensen Peak', a cape after his wife, and a bay after the whaling port of Sandefjord. Undaunted by this unpromising reconnoitre, Christensen sent a wooden sealing vessel, the *Norvegia*, from Sandefjord in September 1927 to explore the possibilities of Bouvet Island, which had first been seen by the French in 1739 and which had later been looked for in vain by Captain James Cook.

A British sealer, George Norris, had landed on the island in 1825. Not realising it was Bouvet Island, he had claimed it for Britain and named it 'Liverpool Island'. He named an adjacent island – which was probably an overturned iceberg – 'Thompson Island'. Norris's claim was never followed up by the British government, nor were the islands ever marked on maps as British possessions. The Norwegian whalers hoped that the forty-nine square kilometre Bouvet Island, which was situated south-west of South Africa and on a similar latitude to South Georgia, might provide a valuable base for Norwegian whalers, as the much bigger British-controlled South Georgia had.[5]

Goaded into action by the 1926 imperial conference, which had revealed the scope of Britain's territorial ambitions and its push to control Antarctic whaling, Christensen was determined to stake a territorial claim on behalf of Norway and retain Norwegian control of whaling. For Christensen, it was not just to protect his profits. He regarded whaling as part of Norway's 'ancient inheritance', believing that it provided 'spiritual capital' for the 'Norwegian race'. He also believed that the polar regions were the Norwegians' natural home, that over the centuries they had become inured to the ice and cold of the Arctic reaches that had come within their dominion. So too with the even colder Antarctic, where 'nobody else has ever worked so long'. Christensen's own father, Christen Christensen, had been a modern pioneer with his dispatch of the *Jason* to the Antarctic in 1892.[6] Lars aimed to secure his father's legacy by working in tandem with the Norwegian foreign office to secure part of the Antarctic continent for Norway. Having recently lost its tentative hold on East Greenland to Denmark, the Norwegians wanted to ensure that Britain would not similarly exclude them from the Antarctic.

Armed with advice from the retired Norwegian shipping broker and whaling historian Bjarne Aagaard and the venerable Arctic explorer Fridtjof Nansen, Christensen was well aware of what had to be done to ensure recognition for a territorial claim. The first thing was to have authority from his government to make such a claim, which was duly given on 31 August 1927. It empowered the captain of the *Norvegia* 'to occupy on behalf of Norway all land which had not previously come under the dominion of other Powers'. This was why Christensen was focusing on Peter I and Bouvet Islands, as both lay outside of the Falkland Islands Dependencies. But his ambitions were much wider.

As he explained in his 1935 account, *Such Is the Antarctic*, Christensen had already decided 'to bring under the sovereignty of Norway all the land between 60°E and 20°W'. This represented a huge wedge of the Antarctic continent, stretching from the eastern shore of the Weddell Sea to the eastern edge of Enderby Land. It was nearly a quarter of the continent. If the claim was successful, it would end Amery's plan to claim the whole land mass for the British Empire. The region was chosen because even the latest English map of the Antarctic had no names anywhere between 20° W and 50° E. It was therefore open to the Norwegians to attach their own names to it. At the same time, Christensen instructed the *Norvegia*'s captain, Harald Horntvedt, to abstain scrupulously from naming any geographic features within the Falkland Islands Dependencies, which might appear to threaten Britain's hold on that region.[7] He was clearly hoping that, in return, Britain would allow Norway free reign in those parts of the Antarctic not yet claimed by any other nation. So that it was not seen as a selfish land grab by a whaling company, Christensen sent two scientists who would invest the voyage with the semblance of being a science-driven expedition.[8]

The presence of the scientists did not allay the concerns of the British Admiralty when news of the expedition's departure reached London in November 1927. The navy's hydrographer, Admiral Henry Douglas, dismissed the 'professedly scientific' purpose of the expedition and warned that its real aim was to claim part of the Antarctic coastline, in order to free Norway's whalers from having to obtain license fees from Britain or New Zealand. He pointed to the expedition's plan to examine 'approximately half the known, and unknown, coastline of the Antarctic Continent', noting that any new land that was found was likely to be claimed on behalf of Norway. This would cause problems for Britain, wrote Douglas, since most of the coastline Christensen was planning to examine was 'British by discovery', even if that discovery was sometimes of the most uncertain kind, by sealers more than a century before. He urged that the Foreign Office take immediate measures 'to safeguard this country's territorial rights'.[9]

Oblivious to the alarm bells ringing in London, the *Norvegia* arrived at Bouvet Island on 1 December 1927, and Horntvedt promptly claimed it for Norway by raising his country's flag and making the required declaration in the name of the king. Christensen had planned to establish a meteorological station on the volcanic island, which would have been useful for the Norwegian whaling fleets and would have allowed Norway to put its claim beyond doubt by actually occupying the ice-covered place. When that proved impossible, they built a hut that they stocked with food and medical supplies; it would serve as a shelter for shipwrecked sailors. The erection of a hut was a traditional Norwegian means of asserting ownership of new lands. Most lately it had been used during Norway's unsuccessful attempt to wrest ownership of East Greenland from Denmark. Apart from the symbolism of the hut, the Norwegians also spent a month surveying the island, collecting specimens of its life forms and rocks and killing any fur seals they could find on its rocky shores. Horntvedt had planned to go ashore on Enderby Land but was forced to retreat to South Georgia for repairs after striking a rock. He radioed Oslo with news of his claim, although the government decided to await his written report before announcing the news.[10]

Ironically, it was another Norwegian whaling company that nearly scuppered Christensen's careful plans by asking Britain for a license to hunt for seals and whales in the waters of Bouvet and Thompson Islands. Because Norris had landed on an island roughly in that position, naming it 'Liverpool Island' and claiming it for Britain, the government duly gave permission on 17 January 1928 and pocketed the license fee. When this news became public, the Norwegians immediately announced that they had already claimed Bouvet Island for themselves and had begun hunting there for whales and seals. It rejected Britain's claim to the island, which was based on a fleeting visit by a British seafarer more than a century ago. They also pointed out that the supposed 'Thompson Island' did not exist.[11]

The British press couldn't decide how to react. Some papers erupted with barely suppressed amusement at their own government's apparent stupidity, while others expressed righteous outrage at the Norwegian intrusion. It was certainly 'a shrewd stroke of business', as the *Daily News* archly observed, for the Colonial Office to lease 'one island that does not exist and another that belongs to somebody else'.[12] Although Foreign Secretary Sir Austen Chamberlain tried to defend his government's decision to lease the island, Norway's pre-eminent Antarctic historian, Bjarne Aagaard, wondered in a letter to the London *Times* how Britain could claim ownership of Bouvet Island when Norris had not even landed on it. Even if Liverpool Island and Bouvet Island were one and the same, the Norwegians argued that any claim the British might have made to Liverpool/Bouvet island had long since lapsed because their sovereignty had 'not been effectively maintained' over the subsequent century.[13]

Norway was now on notice about Britain's determination to defend its supposed ownership of even the most miserable speck of land in the South Atlantic if there was the prospect of a profit to be made from it. Christensen was just as determined to establish Norway's hold on the Antarctic, for reasons of profit and patriotism. He duly announced in March 1928 that he would send the *Norvegia* back to Bouvet Island later that year to establish a meteorological and radio station.[14]

This put Britain in a fix. While it might concede Bouvet Island to Norway, Christensen had made clear that his main territorial ambitions lay on the Antarctic continent itself. This raised the possibility that Norway, with its many whaling vessels in Antarctic waters, might take the two-thirds of the continent that Britain had not yet claimed. London was particularly concerned about the Australian quadrant, which was next in line to be formally claimed. This could have been done back in 1911–12, when Mawson's expedition had explored and claimed large parts of it, without having Britain's authority to do so. His calls over succeeding years for Britain or Australia to formalise his private claims by having the king issue an order in council annexing that part of the Antarctic had gone unanswered. When the issue had finally surfaced at the 1926 imperial conference, British legal advisers had warned that another expedition needed to be sent to survey the coastline and raise the flag at as many places as possible before Britain could annex the Australian quadrant. That would take time to organise.

In the meantime, the Norwegians had to be prevented from intruding into the Australian quadrant or the unclaimed region between the Ross Dependency and the Falkland Islands Dependencies. It would be even better if Norway would agree to recognise those places as British, but that was considered unlikely. London dallied with the idea of doing a deal with Oslo. Perhaps it could swap the unclaimed and largely unexplored region between Enderby Land and Coats Land in return for Norway recognising British sovereignty to the remainder of the Antarctic, other than Adélie Land. This would give Norway about thirty per cent of the continent, but that would exclude the areas traversed by Amundsen's expedition and claimed by him on behalf of Norway. All those areas would be included in the seventy per cent or so of the continent that Britain wanted for itself. It was less than the entire continent that Amery had originally wanted, but it encompassed the best whaling waters, the easiest points of access by sea, and the areas most likely to have mineral deposits. The British officials hoped that if Norway explored and claimed the remaining thirty per cent, that might 'soften the blow for public opinion in Norway', which was still smarting after having so recently lost East Greenland to Denmark.

But there were problems with this approach. The Norwegians had opposed the idea of sectors in the Arctic, which had enabled Canada to claim any lands north of its coastline all the way to the North Pole. Norway could hardly now agree to this method in the Antarctic. At the same time, Britain's attachment to the sector principle meant that it could not recognise just the coastline and immediate hinterland that Norway might want to claim. Being limited in its ability to do a deal with Oslo, the British government decided that it should not push for Norwegian recognition of British claims but should simply try to forestall 'active Norwegian opposition' to those claims.[15]

The strategy met with some early success. In November 1928, the British government agreed to recognise Norway's claim to Bouvet Island, while at the same time reminding Norway of all the areas listed by the 1926 imperial conference that were British by right of discovery. To the relief of the British, the Norwegians agreed not to occupy any of those areas.[16] Helping make sure that Norway's territorial claims were contained within that thirty per cent, a young Australian official in London, Richard Casey, encouraged a British whaling company to claim as much of the coastline as possible between Enderby Land and Queen Mary Land – roughly between 60° E and 90° E. The British company's licence already required it to 'hoist and maintain the British flag over any and every establishment that they may erect or maintain in the lands or territorial waters of the said area', with Casey asking that the company go further and assert British sovereignty 'at as many points as possible between Enderby Land and Queen Mary land'.[17] Britain might thereby create a solid eastern boundary at 60° E against possible Norwegian encroachments, which would keep the Australian quadrant free for annexation by the British Empire.

The *Norvegia* was already on its second voyage to Bouvet Island when news of the British recognition was received. This time, it was supported by one of Christensen's factory ships, *Thorshammer*, which carried equipment and men for a meteorological and radio station, only to be again unsuccessful for want of a suitable site. As for the hut that had been erected the previous year, they found it had been blown away in a gale. The newly claimed territory was not proving to be much of an asset to Norway, and an attempt to find the non-existent 'Thompson Island' ended fruitlessly after an eight-day search by the *Norvegia*. At least the Norwegians knew that Peter I Island existed. The vessel headed there in February 1929, to 'occupy' it for Norway by raising the flag and erecting a small hut.[18] Norway could now claim ownership of the two widely separated islands, but a Norwegian claim to part of the continent itself would have to wait for future expeditions. Meanwhile, Britain was facing an even more serious challenge to its remaining Antarctic ambitions.

It had been nearly ninety years since the United States had sent the 1840 Wilkes expedition on its extended voyage to the Pacific, during which it made brief and controversial forays to the Antarctic. American interest in the South Pole had been almost non-existent since that time. From the early 1900s, a small band of geographers, scientists and descendants of early American sealers and explorers had been arguing the case for America's pre-eminent historical position in the Antarctic and agitating for another American expedition. But they had not managed to excite either public or official enthusiasm.

That all changed in the late 1920s, with the advent of more reliable aircraft and the possibilities they created for polar exploration. Although the American government remained unwilling to sponsor an expedition, private benefactors now had compelling reasons to do so. Aircraft manufacturers wanted to prove the safety and reliability of their machines in the harshest conditions imaginable, and newspaper proprietors wanted to use tales of American adventurers to boost sales. And they had a ready-made American hero to do so.

Richard Byrd was a man on the make. He was the second of three sons born to a well-connected Virginian family that had fallen on relatively hard times, partly through one of his ancestors having an addiction to gambling and alcohol and having backed the British in the War of Independence. From a young age, Byrd was determined to make a name for himself and help restore the fortunes of his family. Short in stature and frail as a child, he had built up his physique with a determined routine of exercise and sought his father's approval by engaging in risk-taking adventures with his brothers. His alcoholic and politically minded father served as a lawyer and public official, while his formidable mother was a Virginian 'blue-blood' with 'a mind as sharp as a steel trap'. It seems that it was his mother – whose photograph he later would keep on his dresser, surrounded by fresh roses – who sent him as a fourteen-year-old on a voyage to the Philippines and back via Europe, opening his eyes to a wide world of adventure and danger. Byrd later exaggerated the story by saying that he was only eleven or twelve years old and that he'd been unaccompanied. It was perhaps this trip that ensured Byrd would eschew the careers in Virginian politics and business chosen by his brothers and seek his fortune elsewhere. At the age of nineteen he went to the naval academy at Annapolis to train as a naval officer. Although he suffered a permanent injury to his leg while doing gymnastics, he was soon serving aboard a battleship in the Caribbean, where he had his first flight in an aeroplane. Byrd was hooked.[19]

In the air, Byrd was not so hampered by his physical infirmity, and aerial feats promised promotion and possible fame and fortune. When the United States went to war in 1916, Byrd applied successfully to be trained as a naval pilot. Although he did not serve in Europe, he received plenty of flying experience, along with plenty of political experience in Washington. His brother Harry was a rising power in the Democratic Party and Richard was used by the US Navy to lobby for its appropriations. One of his close friends in Washington was the young Franklin D. Roosevelt, with whom he went moose-hunting in Canada.

It was in aerial exploration that Byrd had decided to make his name. In 1924 he was to join a naval airship that planned to fly across the Arctic, with a possible landing at the North Pole. But the venture was abandoned before it began when the airship was damaged. The following year, Byrd convinced the navy to lend him three planes for another expedition that would explore the Arctic between Alaska and the North Pole, during which he would claim any land that he found for the United States. It was a time of frenetic activity in the Arctic. Denmark and Norway were still contesting the ownership of East Greenland and Canada had claimed any undiscovered islands to the north of its coastline. Canada established police posts in its frozen north and moved Inuit people there to buttress its legal claim with an effective claim based upon occupation. Russia was doing likewise north of Siberia, after the Canadian explorer Vilhjalmur Stefansson had established a party of Inuit and Europeans on Wrangel Island in the hope that a 'quiet occupation' would allow Canadian ownership to be established before any protest was raised by Russia. Stefansson promoted the island as a landing place for a future polar air route. The survivors of Stefansson's ill-fated group were soon evicted by the Russians, who made clear that all Arctic islands off their coastline were Soviet-owned.[20]

There was also a race to reach the North Pole by air. It was a contest that attracted an immense amount of public interest, with an Italian airship being pitched against a Norwegian expedition that planned to use two large Dornier Wal seaplanes. The latter expedition was led by Amundsen and financed by the wealthy American adventurer Lincoln Ellsworth. Both expeditions planned to leave for the North Pole from Spitsbergen, off the northern coast of Norway, with fame and fortune being assured for the winner.

Byrd had a chance to join the race, flying north from Greenland or Ellesmere Island, but he was forced by the US Navy to attach his three small seaplanes to the expedition being organised by Donald MacMillan under the auspices of the commercially driven National Geographic Society. Whereas Byrd wanted to make a trans-polar flight, MacMillan intended to discover the large piece of land that was believed to exist in the Arctic north of Baffin Island. Both men were destined to be disappointed, but the expedition did bring Byrd to the notice of the American public. As for the expedition of Amundsen and Ellsworth, it nearly ended in disaster when one of their aircraft was damaged landing on the ice; the remaining plane barely managed to get aloft with all the men and returned safely to Spitsbergen in June 1925.[21]

The summer of 1926 saw a renewed flurry of activity in the Arctic. Amundsen and Ellsworth returned with an Italian airship, which was named *Norge* by Amundsen and piloted by the Italian Umberto Nobile. Amundsen and Ellsworth hoped that the airship might be able to achieve what their two aircraft had not. Rather than simply making for the North Pole and then returning to Spitsbergen, the airship would fly on across the Arctic to Alaska, passing over the previously unseen region where undiscovered land might lie. Amundsen wanted any such land for Norway.

Just days before the airship was due to leave on its historic flight in May 1926, an American ship arrived in Spitsbergen carrying Byrd and a fifty-man expedition with two aircraft. Byrd was determined to beat the unwieldy 'Amundsen–Ellsworth–Nobile Transpolar Flight' to the pole, and thereby prove the superiority of aircraft over airships and the 'consequent awakening of the public to the vast possibilities of the airplane'. At one time, his plans included establishing a base on the northern tip of Greenland, to where he would fly from Spitsbergen before embarking on the 650-kilometre flight to the North Pole. Such an approach would allow him to fly over a huge unexplored area, where land might be located. If he discovered any, Byrd told the readers of the *New York Times*, which devoted the entire front page of its Sunday edition to his announcement, he would 'descend on it, if possible, and hoist the American flag'.

However, coming from the other direction was the Australian explorer Hubert Wilkins, who was planning to fly from Alaska to the North Pole, hoping that he might be the first to the North Pole and the first to 'claim for the United States any lands that may be found'. Wilkins was sponsored by the Detroit Aviation Society, a group of public-spirited businessmen in the home of the burgeoning American car industry; they also wanted to dominate aircraft manufacturing. Henry Ford's son Edsel was a leading aviation enthusiast and a supporter of both Wilkins and Byrd, hoping that they would join forces. But Byrd wanted any glory to be his alone.[22]

The whirring newsreel cameras of the press representatives captured the preparations of the rival camps as they readied their respective craft in the late spring of 1926. With the shadow of the *Norge* looming over him, and the distant threat from Wilkins in Alaska, Byrd cut back his ambitious plans to cross the Arctic via the North Pole. He decided simply to make a dash for the pole from Spitsbergen and return. Being the first to reach the North Pole by air was glory enough. And there was not a moment to lose, if he was to beat the secretive Amundsen.

On 8 May, the day after the *Norge* nudged its nose towards the recently erected mooring mast at Spitsbergen and Wilkins radioed his own readiness to leave Alaska for the pole, Byrd and his pilot, Floyd Bennett, clambered into their heavily laden tri-motor plane, the *Josephine Ford*, before lifting it ponderously aloft to the cheers of the American party and the anxious looks of the Norwegians. Less than sixteen hours later, they were back, and Byrd claimed triumphantly to have reached the North Pole. He was met by the lanky Amundsen, who quietly embraced his American rival while being determined to go one better.

On 11 May, Amundsen climbed into the gondola of the *Norge* as it prepared to depart on its epic journey to Alaska. It passed over the North Pole just after midnight on 12 May. To mark the occasion, Amundsen dropped a Norwegian flag onto the frozen ocean, while Ellsworth dropped an American flag and Nobile an Italian one, before the airship headed on to Alaska.[23] As for Wilkins, he had still not left Alaska due to fog. He abandoned his plans once he learnt of his rivals' success.

Just as the Cook and Peary expeditions to the North Pole had caused controversy, with each disputing the other's claim to have reached their goal, so too doubts were immediately raised by querulous European newspapers as to whether Byrd had really reached the pole before turning back. Some even suggested that he had simply flown out of sight and then circled for the required amount of time before returning. Others questioned whether the flight had been long enough to cover the distance to the pole, and whether Byrd's navigational skills were sufficient to allow him to know when and if he had actually reached it.

Byrd's backers were adamant that he was right. Just as it had supported Peary in his claim to have reached the North Pole by sledge, the National Geographic Society proved to be a stalwart supporter of Byrd's claim to have reached the pole by air. The American Geographical Society was similarly protective of Byrd's reputation and carefully kept the records of his flight away from any of his likely critics.[24] However, the doubts would never be completely resolved and would dog Byrd's reputation throughout his life and long after his death. For the moment, however, Byrd revelled in the glory that came on his return to New York on 22 June 1926, being feted with a tickertape parade down Broadway before going to Washington, where he received the Congressional Medal of Honor from President Calvin Coolidge.[25]

The following year, Byrd flew across the Atlantic with three companions in another tri-motor Fokker, dubbed the *America*, eventually landing off a Normandy beach after being unable to find the landing field in cloud-covered Paris. As Byrd and his companions waded ashore, the aircraft was left to be ignominiously swamped by the incoming tide.[26] Several months beforehand, Byrd had confided to the geographer Isaiah Bowman, head of the American Geographical Society in New York, that he hoped a successful flight would 'do something for international relations. I am thinking particularly of England and France.'[27] He also hoped it would keep him in the public spotlight, now that he was in what he called 'the hero business'.

It certainly did that. The four aviators were greeted by crowds in the streets of Paris and 'made citizens of three French cities'. Unlike the North Pole flight, there were no records to be won. Charles Lindbergh had preceded Byrd to Europe by more than a month. Having flown single-handed all the way to Paris, Lindbergh had received the laurels and prize that Byrd had hoped to win. Although Byrd and his companions received another tickertape parade on their return to New York, and a luncheon at the White House, he needed to do something more to elevate his heroic status.[28] The Antarctic now beckoned him with the glittering promise of glory and riches, particularly if he could claim to be the first aviator to fly over both the North and South Poles.

Byrd had been mulling over the idea of an Antarctic flight well before he had flown across the Atlantic. In February 1926, he had negotiated an exclusive newspaper contract for an Antarctic expedition that was still two years away.[29] Although he also dallied with ideas of crossing the Pacific between California and Hawaii, or crossing the Arabian desert, his focus kept returning to the Antarctic. That would be a dramatic way to increase public confidence in modern aircraft, and to establish himself as a great scientific explorer rather than just a cowboy flyer eager to outrace his rivals. 'Aviation cannot claim mastery of the globe,' Byrd wrote in 1928, 'until the South Pole and its vast surrounding mystery be opened up by airplane.'[30]

Byrd's serious side was encouraged by Isaiah Bowman, who repeatedly pointed Byrd towards the Antarctic. The American Geographical Society was publishing an edited collection by leading polar explorers, giving accounts of their experiences and explaining what remained to be done in both the Arctic and Antarctic. It was designed to give the American public 'the means . . . to evaluate between expeditions that may be not unrightfully termed "sporting events" and those which add to the sum total of human knowledge'. It was the latter that would stand for all time, Bowman told

Byrd, urging him to write a chapter on polar aviation and thereby have his name 'associated with a group of serious scholars who are interested in the actual scientific problems which . . . are the things that keep polar expeditions alive in the long run'.

Anxious to have the support of the American Geographical Society, with its academic credentials and well-heeled members, Byrd assured Bowman that he was 'interested in the scientific end of the Arctic far more than anything else and if I am ever fortunate enough to get to the Antarctic continent I believe that we can gather a great deal of scientific data [and] hope to take with us a number of scientists'.[31]

In early June 1927, as Byrd was waiting to leave on his Atlantic flight, Bowman reminded him to 'keep in mind the suggestion of doing that Antarctic flight and then flying to London to tell about it. The English would be crazy about a man who would continue the traditions of Shackleton and Scott.' Byrd did not take much convincing. He was already set on going to the South Pole, so that he could claim to be the first person to have flown over both poles. But that would not be the expedition's only objective. Byrd planned to take a team of scientists so that the venture could not be portrayed by his critics just as a publicly funded sporting contest.

In his 1928 book about his flying experiences, *Skyward*, Byrd set out his plans for the Antarctic. In doing so, he was careful to emphasise that 'the primary object of the expedition is scientific' and that there would be 'plenty of work for the dozen specialists we will take with us'. At the same time, he conceded that 'although the primary object of the expedition is scientific, it will be most gratifying if we succeed in planting the American flag at the South Pole – at the bottom of the world'.[32] He knew that would embellish his fame and set him apart from his fellow prize-seekers. Soon after Byrd had landed in France, Bowman cabled to congratulate him on his Atlantic flight and his 'fine Antarctic plan'.[33]

Other aviators also had the South Pole in their sights. One was the Argentinian engineer Antonio Pauly. His plan for a flight to the South Pole was part of a larger scheme to reinforce Argentina's territorial claims in the Antarctic, which overlapped with that of Chile and with Britain's Falkland Islands Dependencies. With such a nationalist agenda, he received ready support from the Argentine Geographical Institute and the Argentine government. The expedition was sponsored by the Buenos Aires newspaper *La Prensa*, with Pauly's reports and spectacular photographs expected to boost its sales and excite greater public interest in Argentina's distant territorial claim.

Pauly knew that claim would be much stronger if the news of his expedition could also be splashed across the pages of newspapers elsewhere. Doing so would also boost his expedition's budget. He tried to sell publication rights to American newspapers and to gain the support of the American Geographical Society, confiding to Bowman in September 1926 that he wanted 'to land at the pole itself to hoist up the Argentine flag and to look for the documents left there by the ill-fated Capt. Scott'.[34] Although Pauly was unable to get his expedition ready for the summer of 1926–27, Bowman and Byrd were on notice that at least one other aviator would probably be heading for the South Pole at the same time as Byrd. As early as April 1927, American newspaper articles about future flights noted that both Pauly and Byrd were planning flights in the Antarctic.[35]

When Byrd returned from Europe in July 1927 he immediately began planning his Antarctic expedition, doing the rounds of his benefactors for more money and asking Bowman for advice on which scientists he should take and 'the exact area of the unexplored part of the Antarctic continent'. Bowman put the staff and resources of the American Geographical Society, which had some of America's best mapmaking experts, at Byrd's disposal and offered him an office in which to do his research work.[36] Despite the assistance, the scale of the expedition, which Byrd estimated would cost more than $250,000, quickly convinced him to postpone it until the summer of 1928 so as to ensure 'very thorough preparation'. That was all to the good, wrote Bowman as he enclosed yet another map of the Antarctic, noting that Hubert Wilkins was 'always too hurried with his preparations'. There was little time for planning in 1927, with Byrd spending months writing an account of his Atlantic and North Pole flights, published as *Skyward*, and shuffling across the United States by train on a lucrative lecture tour. During that hectic schedule of 'one-night stands', he was forced to use mail, cable and telephone to make all his arrangements.[37]

Although the National Geographic Society also threw its support and money behind Byrd, it was to its rival American Geographical Society, with its commitment to 'scientific rather than popular objects', that he continued to look for advice. Bowman remained anxious to help, drawing up an Antarctic map marked with wind directions and speeds, details of crucial importance to an aviator. He assured Byrd that he had 'the best chance of anyone in the world today of putting through a big Antarctic expedition', and that he himself was 'more interested in this than in any other part of the world from the standpoint of airplane exploration'. In return for the society's help, Bowman hoped that Byrd would allow him to publish the resulting maps of the expedition along with an article by Byrd in the society's journal. When Ellsworth called by on 10 April 1928 and paid Bowman $1000 to produce up-to-date maps of both polar regions, Bowman assured Byrd that they would work on them slowly so that Byrd's forthcoming activities in the Antarctic would appear on the map. 'In other words,' wrote Bowman, 'we shall leave a hole in the map and expect you to bring back material to fill it!'[38]

Byrd was certainly keen to make his mark on the map. In *Skyward* he wrote eagerly of having 'a chance to take off the maps for the ages to come, a part of that great blank white space at the bottom of the world'.[39] But he could not be sure that he would be first in the field and that the names he bestowed on the landscape, rather than those of a competitor, would be the ones to endure. The support of the two important US mapmaking bodies, the National Geographic Society and the American Geographical Society, would certainly help in that regard. Byrd could also take comfort from the news that Pauly had dropped out of the race after his aircraft was damaged during a flight to Rio de Janeiro. But a new rival had arrived on the scene: Hubert Wilkins had now switched his attention from the Arctic to the Antarctic.

Wilkins' attempt to fly from Alaska across the Arctic to Norway had been thwarted in 1926 by fog along the Arctic coast, and in 1927 by mechanical problems. But he returned in the summer of 1928, and this time successfully made it across in a single-engine monoplane from Barrow to Spitsbergen. He was on the lookout for land, much to the consternation of British and Canadian officials, who feared that the American-financed explorer would claim any new-found land for the United States. However, there was no land left to be found, with Wilkins merely able to confirm the earlier observations of Amundsen and Ellsworth.

Nevertheless, his flight of more than twenty hours was the first by an aircraft across the Arctic from America to Europe, and

Wilkins earned the plaudits of both continents. There was a knighthood from the British king and an official dinner in London in June 1928 hosted by Colonial Secretary Leo Amery, the politician who had been pushing for Britain to claim all of the Antarctic. He now likened Wilkins' flights in the Arctic to Vasco Balboa's sighting of the Pacific in 1513. For his part, Wilkins told the dinner guests that his task in the Arctic was done. He wanted now to go to the Antarctic to find suitable sites for a ring of meteorological stations that might allow long-range weather forecasting, which would benefit the farmers of the southern continents.[40]

The Australian aviator had been planning this scheme for the past four years and wanted to begin by flying from King Edward VII Land to Graham Land. In London in 1926, Richard Casey had introduced him to Admiralty officials, in the hope that they would help, but they had thought his plan was 'madness'. Nevertheless, Casey had become a friend and supporter of Wilkins, regarding him as 'a serious adventurer, a bit of a mystic, and a very stout-hearted fellow'.

Now that Wilkins had completed his Arctic flights, Casey again introduced him to British officials and wealthy benefactors, hoping that the Australian would not have to rely on American money for his Antarctic expedition. If he could get British or Australian funding, wrote Casey, it would 'add something to our claims for extended Antarctic suzerainty'. But there was little British money for Wilkins, especially since Mawson was also in London seeking funds for his own expedition and denigrating Wilkins for his lack of scientific focus.[41] And the same day that Wilkins was being feted by Amery in London, a British polar explorer, Commander Douglas Jeffery, who had been on Shackleton's last expedition, announced from New York that he was organising his own expedition and also planned to fly from Graham Land to King Edward VII Land. Fortunately for Wilkins and Byrd, Jeffery's expedition never eventuated after he fell out with his prospective pilot and was arrested for issuing a fraudulent cheque.[42] The contest would be between Byrd and Wilkins.

The United States gave Wilkins a warm welcome when he travelled on to New York, with a tickertape parade down Broadway and a reception hosted by the mayor. And there was money aplenty when newspaper and radio magnate William Randolph Hearst sensed the possibility of a race to the South Pole and stumped up the funds to make it happen, with the promise of a large bonus if Wilkins got there first.

Although Bowman tried his best to dispel 'the foolish rumours that there will be any race between them to the South Pole', that was inevitably how it was portrayed by editors who had newspapers to sell. The 'Wilkins–Hearst Antarctic Expedition' had the advantage over Byrd and his *New York Times* backers of having a small and nimble organisation of just five men and two single-engine aircraft, the same planes that Wilkins had used so successfully during his Arctic flight. Byrd was using two ships that had to be restored at great expense. They would take to Antarctica his fifty-strong party, along with three aircraft, ninety-five dogs, building materials and supplies for up to a two-year stay, and all the paraphernalia of a scientific expedition. Wilkins simply wanted to make his flight from Graham Land to the Ross Sea, and possibly the pole; he would then go home with photographs and charts of the previously unseen land. His ostensible purpose was still to discover suitable sites for his meteorological stations. He also hoped to determine whether Graham Land was attached to the rest of Antarctica or whether, as some believed, it was separated by one or more frozen straits.[43]

The British now faced the prospect of two American-financed expeditions exploring the region between King Edward VII Land and Graham Land, which comprised all the unclaimed area between the Ross Dependency and the Falkland Islands Dependencies. This was territory that Britain wanted for itself. And there were reports in the American press that the State Department was about to claim both Wilkes Land, which Australia regarded as its rightful possession, and what America called 'the Palmer Peninsula', but which was otherwise known as Graham Land and part of Britain's Falkland Islands Dependencies. New Zealand was also concerned that the Byrd expedition, which was going to the Ross Sea by way of New Zealand, might infringe the sovereignty of the Ross Dependency, which it administered on behalf of the British Empire.

However, Britain feared that any move on its part to prevent Byrd from establishing his base on what it claimed as its territory might provoke the United States into annexing the parts of the Antarctic that Wilkes or the early American sealers had discovered. Moreover, if it tried to pre-empt the Byrd expedition by issuing letters patent to annex the Australian quadrant or other parts of the continent, that might be taken as a challenge by the United States and 'provoke action on the part of that expedition which otherwise they would be unlikely to take'. So Britain did nothing, hoping that its silence about sovereignty and delay in annexing further parts of the continent would cause the United States to refrain from asserting any sovereignty of its own.[44]

Although Wilkins was an Australian, the British could not be sure that he would not be raising the Stars and Stripes wherever he landed, or even dropping American flags onto the ice, as Ellsworth had done at the North Pole. He might even declare the land claimed for the United States by the simple expedient of flying across it. This prospect raised interesting legal questions. While the legal ramifications of exploration by aircraft would have to await the determination of a suitable international tribunal, the panicked British officials moved to limit the damage that Wilkins might cause by trying to enlist him to their cause.

Richard Casey, who had become friendly with Wilkins, casually asked him in August 1928 whether he planned 'to drop British or Australian flags along the coastline from Edward VII Land to Graham Land'. Casey described such a move as being 'a nice gesture' that might prove valuable in the future, particularly if Wilkins 'made a record of the exact position of the flags and if possible photographed them from the air'. He did not think Byrd intended to do so, since his expedition was apparently scientific; it didn't appear that 'the Americans have any Antarctic aspirations'. At the same time, Casey could not exclude that possibility and worried that it would 'add very considerable complications to the Antarctic complex if Byrd were to scatter American flags about'.[45]

By the time Wilkins reached the Falkland Islands, courtesy of a Norwegian factory ship on 29 October 1928, Casey's casual suggestion for him to drop Union Jacks onto the ice had become an appeal to Wilkins' patriotism. When Wilkins stepped ashore at Port Stanley, the acting governor of the Falklands handed him a cable from Casey formally asking him to claim any new land on behalf of the empire.

Although competing territorial claims would complicate Wilkins' aim of creating a cooperative ring of meteorological stations around Antarctica, he put aside his internationalist inclinations to declare himself also a 'Britisher' who was willing to help 'the cause of Empire by dropping or planting British flags in the manner suggested'. He was duly handed a pile of Union Jacks and given authority by the acting governor to claim any 'new' land over which he flew, while keeping his activities – and his authorisation – secret from the world.[46]

Wilkins was not well served by the weather. He had been relying on the enclosed bay of Deception Island being covered with thick ice, so it might serve as a runway for his two aircraft. But the weather was unusually warm that year and he was forced to resort to a rough runway that he and his Norwegian whaler friends managed to create on land. This meant he had to use wheels rather than skis or floats on his aircraft, making it impossible for him to land at his intended destination of the Ross Sea, or indeed anywhere but back at the improvised runway on Deception Island. His flight would also be briefer than he had planned, since the runway was too short for the aircraft to get airborne with full tanks of fuel.

Nevertheless, he was able to take off on 20 December 1928, the first aircraft flight in the Antarctic. With sufficient fuel aboard his aircraft to take him the 3200 kilometres he had hoped for, Wilkins settled for the lesser goal of investigating whether Graham Land was connected to the rest of Antarctica. It was still a very long flight of more than twenty hours, over unfamiliar territory and through uncertain weather conditions. The view from the air led Wilkins to believe – mistakenly – that there was at least one channel, and probably more, separating Graham Land from the remainder of Antarctica, making it an archipelago rather than part of the continent.

He sketched rough maps as he went, and photographed and named many of the prominent features. However, as he couldn't land and get a proper fix on his position, his maps were almost useless. Nevertheless, one apparent channel was named after Casey, and what he wrongly took to be a strait was named for Stefansson. The name of his principal benefactor was reserved for the massive plateau that stretched into the distance at the limit of his flight, which thereafter became known as 'Hearst Land'. As Wilkins prepared to turn around at about 71° S, 64° W, he opened a hatch in the floor and 'dutifully dropped a Union Jack and a written claim to British sovereignty'.[47]

The flight had been much more limited than either Wilkins or Hearst had wanted. It was historically important as the first aircraft flight in the Antarctic, and it had proved the usefulness of aircraft for exploration. But Wilkins had not reached the end of the Antarctic Peninsula and had not ventured outside the territory already claimed by Britain as part of the Falkland Islands Dependencies. Dropping the Union Jack where he had did not add anything to Britain's existing territory. The great expanse of territory that lay along the route that Wilkins had intended to take to the Ross Sea remained unseen and unclaimed, and he had made no attempt to be the first to fly to the South Pole. Hearst would have to be satisfied with Wilkins' account of the flight, which was illustrated with spectacular photographs from the air, and with the naming of Hearst Land. As for the flag-dropping, Wilkins reported to British officials what he had done, while keeping it secret from the world. He left his aircraft for the winter at Deception Island, intending to return the following summer to complete his expedition by flying to the Ross Sea and claiming all the 'new' territory that he might pass over along the way.

With Wilkins claiming territory on behalf of Britain, it was only Byrd who continued to cause concern in London, Canberra and Wellington. He was intending to base himself on the Ross Ice Barrier, which meant his activities threatened to undermine New Zealand's hold on the Ross Dependency, Australia's desire to annex the Australia quadrant and Britain's ambition to annex the territory east of the Ross Dependency. British officials tried to reassure themselves and their counterparts in the dominions that Byrd's expedition was 'of a purely scientific character'. But they could not be sure. Byrd certainly had the capacity to do a lot more exploring than Wilkins. It was the largest and most expensive expedition ever sent to the Antarctic, with a budget of about $700,000, although not all had been raised by the time Byrd departed for the south in October 1928.[48]

There was a flurry of worried cables between Wellington and London when Byrd's two small ships, the wooden barque *City of New York* and the steel-hulled freighter *Eleanor Bolling*, arrived in New Zealand, accompanied by two much larger Norwegian factory ships, the *C. L. Larsen* and the *Sir James Clark Ross*. Byrd tried to allay the concerns of New Zealand journalists and officials by declaring that his expedition was purely scientific and that he was carrying a Union Jack, which he planned to hoist at the South Pole in honour of Scott and Shackleton. Ever suspicious of the ambitions of others, Amery asked the New Zealand government to discover, without alerting Byrd, whether he was also carrying the Stars and Stripes. If the American flag was raised at the South Pole, or on any other part of the continent claimed by Britain, it could be interpreted as an assertion of American sovereignty.

But the New Zealand officials could not shed any light on whether Byrd was carrying a cache of American flags. They could only repeat what he had told a public meeting, that the objects of his expedition were 'purely scientific', and he had a party of scientists to prove it.[49] This was hardly sufficient reassurance for the nervous British and New Zealand governments. The Foreign Office in London tried a different tack, sending a note to the US State Department that ostensibly welcomed Byrd's expedition while notifying the Americans that his base was going to be located on British territory. The note went on to mention the conclusions of the 1926 imperial conference, which set out all those parts of the continent that Britain believed were British by right of discovery and exploration. Britain hoped that its note would elicit an acknowledgement from Washington about British sovereignty, but there was only silence.[50]

The British had pinned their hopes on Wilkins being able to scatter Union Jacks across the ice-clad territories that Britain had already claimed, or that it wanted to claim in the future. But Wilkins had only made one long flight, and it had come nowhere near the unexplored lands that Britain had wanted him to claim. The news of that flight reached Byrd as he was establishing his base, which he dubbed 'Little America', close to Amundsen's old base of Framheim on the Ross Ice Barrier. Byrd sent a message to Wilkins offering to put his facilities at the service of the Australian, if he should want to fly from there to the South Pole, but he was confident that the prize was beyond Wilkins' reach.

So it turned out to be, when further news was received that Wilkins had ended his flying for that season. Until Wilkins' return the following summer, the field was wide open for Byrd. He busily laid the groundwork for a series of flights and sledge trips that would expose a massive area of the continent to human eyes for the first time. Despite his assurances in New Zealand, Byrd most certainly intended to claim any new land for the United States.

CHAPTER 11

'This bloody flag-raising business'

1929–1930

By late 1929, the Antarctic continent was coming under sustained assault from several directions. Richard Byrd had spent the winter huddled beneath the ice at Little America and was about to launch a program of exploration that would take his men by dog sledge and aircraft into the unknown reaches of the continent. He feared that he might be beaten to the prize of the South Pole when he received news that Wilkins was on his way south again, intending to resume where he had left off the previous year. Out at sea, the Norwegian whaler Lars Christensen also had his sights fixed on Antarctica. Having already claimed Bouvet and Peter I Islands for Norway, he sent the *Norvegia* to claim parts of the continent itself. Lastly, there was the Australian explorer Douglas Mawson, who was intent on seeing off both the Americans and the Norwegians by charting the coastline of the so-called 'Australian quadrant'. Once that was done, it could be formally annexed on behalf of the British Empire.

Byrd had assured the New Zealanders that his was a purely scientific expedition. But scientific activities did not preclude him from claiming territory on behalf of the United States. In fact, science had become almost a necessary condition for claiming territory. After all, claiming a place was not just about seeing a place for the first time, or raising a flag over it; it was also about mapping and naming and, more generally, knowing its geographic and natural features. Moreover, by cloaking his expedition with science, Byrd gave it the sort of serious purpose that Wilkins' expedition largely lacked, allowing him to attract the greater funding that he needed from both private benefactors and government sources.

His winning ways and higher public profile also ensured that he had a much higher media profile than Wilkins, and much more lucrative media deals. The *New York Times* bought the newspaper rights to his articles and sent a reporter along with the expedition, while *National Geographic* bought the magazine rights. Paramount Pictures bought the film rights, Putnam the book rights, and a speakers' agency the lecture rights. There were also the rights to radio broadcasts, which for the first time would be made direct from Antarctica.

With all these deals in place, few Americans would remain untouched by the Byrd 'circus', although some would resent the success and Barnum-like ways of the Virginian blue-blood. Nevertheless, as a result of all the media attention, Antarctica would come to occupy a place in the popular American consciousness that it had not enjoyed since Reynolds' activities in the 1820s and 1830s. With this attention would come a growing sense of American entitlement to those parts of the continent explored by Byrd and his companions.

On the eve of Byrd's departure from New York, the director of the American Geographical Society, Isaiah Bowman, assured Byrd that the expedition's return would receive 'as much rejoicing . . . as awaited [Sir Francis] Drake when he came home with a shipload of plunder after ravaging the Spanish coast'.[1] The 'plunder' that this politically connected geographer mostly had in mind was geographic discoveries, and the prospect of claiming parts of Antarctica for the United States.[2]

While Byrd was always keen to win personal glory, he was ambivalent about claiming new land, which he feared could only promote territorial rivalry and create conditions conducive to another terrible war. Like Wilkins and some other Antarctic explorers, he had internationalist sympathies and would devote part of his life to fostering peaceful relations between nations. Indeed, one of his reasons for encouraging the development of aviation was based on his belief that aircraft would bring nations closer together and break down the prejudices and suspicions that could lead to war.

Despite fears in London and Wellington, Byrd was not going to provoke a dispute with Britain or New Zealand by claiming any part of the Ross Dependency, which went from 150° E to 160° W. Nor was he looking towards the Australian quadrant, whose coastline Charles Wilkes had partially discovered and charted nearly a century before. Byrd's eyes were elsewhere, directed towards the 'no man's land' to the east of the Ross Dependency, which Britain aspired to own but had not yet claimed. And Byrd wasted no time in staking an American claim to that region.

Within weeks of his arrival in December 1928, as a veritable village of huts and hangars and igloos was being created at Little America, Byrd sent aircraft on reconnaissance flights into those previously unseen eastern lands. Although much of their activity would necessarily be within the Ross Dependency, where Little America was located and across which the flight to the South Pole would take place, it was the region beyond the Ross Dependency's eastern boundary that most interested Byrd. On 27 January 1929, the aircraft dubbed *Stars and Stripes* sighted a new range of mountains looming up from the ice, with just a scattering of snow on its rocky peaks. Byrd named it the Rockefeller Range after one of his most generous benefactors, the oil magnate John D. Rockefeller, and sent his deputy, geologist Laurence Gould, on a flight to take a closer look. In fact, the Rockefeller Range was not a line of mountains and would eventually be renamed as the Rockefeller Plateau.

Gould landed to examine the rocks and used his theodolite to take an accurate fix on what turned out to be relatively low hills so that they could be properly mapped. In a report to the navy secretary, Byrd noted how it was the first time that 'aviation has discovered a new land, surveyed and landed on it for scientific investigation'. All told, they had 'seen at least 20,000 square miles . . . of hitherto unknown Antarctic areas'. Byrd named the region Marie Byrd Land after his wife and, because it was outside the Ross Dependency, claimed it on behalf of the United States.[3]

But was seeing this area from an aircraft, which was flying at 160 kilometres an hour and a kilometre or more above the ice, sufficient to claim it for the United States? Byrd could not be sure, so he sent an aircraft aloft with a movie camera designed for mapmaking so that he could have 'permanent, authentic, and complete records of what the human eye only had time to scan'.[4] Meanwhile, one of Byrd's big planes had been destroyed in a storm, so the remaining planes were secured for the winter while he and his men prepared for his historic flight to the South Pole.

While newspaper proprietors promoted his flight to the pole as a race with Wilkins, Byrd did not regard the Australian as a serious threat. As he confided to Bowman, Wilkins was 'a high type gentleman' who would not try to steal a march on him, as Amundsen had done to Scott. Moreover, the Australian would not be 'in any position to fly to the pole . . . without extraordinary and unwarranted hazzards

[sic]', since he would not have store depots laid down in case of the aircraft being forced to land.[5] Nor did Wilkins have the additional aircraft and men to mount a rescue mission, if one became necessary. In fact, the real rivalry between the two men would not be about racing to the South Pole but rather being first to claim the territory between the Ross Dependency and the Falkland Islands Dependencies. By flying from Deception Island to Little America, Wilkins would be flying right across all that unclaimed land and might snatch it for Britain while Byrd was preparing for his South Pole flight.

After Wilkins' first attempt in the summer of 1928, during which he claimed land on behalf of Britain, Wilkins wrote an article for the Hearst newspapers in which he questioned the validity of what he had just been doing. To the chagrin of his friend Richard Casey, he also ridiculed to his American readers 'the idea of anyone claiming territory by having flown over it'. When Wilkins went on to London in May 1929 to seek additional funding from the British government for the coming exploration season, Casey got his friend back on message before helping him.[6] Apart from the government funds, Casey secured for Wilkins the use of the British research ship *William Scoresby*. He also convinced the government to give Wilkins a commission from the king that authorised him 'to take formal possession of any territories now unknown which he might discover between the Ross Sea and the Falkland Island Dependencies'.[7]

Unlike Hearst, the British had no interest in Wilkins racing Byrd to the South Pole. Their contribution to his expedition was intended to ensure he beat Byrd to the unclaimed territory east of the Ross Dependency. As Casey confided to the Australian prime minister, Stanley Bruce, in April 1929, the 'most useful role [for Wilkins] in the coming Antarctic season is to try and complete his contemplated flight from Graham Land to the Ross Sea – and to do so before Byrd can do it in the reverse direction'. Likening Wilkins to a 'tin-opener', Casey told Bruce not to expect scientific results but to 'look on him merely as an individual who can do a good deal to keep our end up in the way of straight discovery'. The assistance of the *William Scoresby* was designed to give Wilkins the measure of safety that he had lacked the previous year, allowing him to establish a takeoff point much further south than Deception Island and thus increasing his chances of being able to complete the 3000-kilometre flight to the Ross Sea.[8]

Both Byrd and Wilkins tried to keep their plans secret from each other, with Byrd warning his manager in New York that Wilkins was 'going to make every effort to beat us to it' and should not be given 'any information as to when we start flying'. At the same time, he pestered Bowman to find out from Wilkins whether he planned to fly to the South Pole. Bunkered down in the isolation of the Antarctic winter, Byrd was worried that if Wilkins thought Byrd was going to start flying early in the summer, Wilkins would 'naturally hurry the more and make it very difficult for us'.

Byrd need not have worried. Once again, Wilkins was dogged by ill luck as bad weather prevented him from making anything other than several short flights. Despite the support of the *William Scoresby*, all were confined to the Antarctic Peninsula, well within the boundaries of the Falkland Islands Dependencies. As a result, Wilkins made no significant new discoveries and was again limited to reinforcing the existing claim to the British territory, which he did by dropping three Union Jacks by parachute at the furthest extent of his flights, along with a document taking possession of the surrounding territory in the name of the king. On the flight that took him furthest south – to 73° S and 101° W – Wilkins was forced to drop his flag 'on the pack-ice, far from land'.[9]

Although time would show Byrd that he had been panicking over nothing, he could not be sure in November 1929 that Wilkins' small aircraft would not suddenly appear out of the eastern sky at Little America, quickly land, refuel and take off again for the South Pole. Although he wrote privately of doing his 'utmost to uphold the prestige of the United States',[10] Byrd was still portraying his flight as a mainly scientific exercise. Its purpose was not a race to the pole, he said, but would 'explore and make an aerial survey . . . between our base and the Pole'.

With a camera filming one side on the way to the pole and the other side on their return, Byrd planned to create a map of a strip of land about 1250 kilometres long and more than 300 kilometres wide. Without ground control points to get an accurate fix on geographic features, Byrd conceded that he 'could not hope to get a very accurate survey' but maintained nonetheless that the strip map 'would be of much scientific value'.[11] It was territory that had been walked over by the Norwegians and British and claimed by both those nations. But Byrd would be able to see much more of it from the air, and he would return with both a map and aerial photographs of the landscape. Although he would not explicitly contest the Norwegian and British claims by making a claim on behalf of the United States, he would perform acts that the American government, if it so desired, could use to sustain such a claim.

Byrd had intended that the pilot who had flown him on his North Pole flight would also take him to the South Pole, but Floyd Bennett had died of pneumonia in April 1928. As his replacement, Byrd chose the Norwegian-born Bernt Balchen, the pilot who had landed Byrd's trans-Atlantic flight in the French surf. To create the symbolism of the same two men flying over both poles, Byrd named the tri-motor aircraft in which he would make the attempt the *Floyd Bennett*, and he took on the flight a stone from Bennett's grave.

In fact, however, there were more than two men aboard when the aircraft finally lifted off from Little America in the late afternoon of 28 November 1929 for the 1300-kilometre flight. Apart from Byrd and Balchen, there were two cameramen: one from Paramount to capture the event for cinema audiences, and another to work the aerial survey camera. The extra weight of the additional cameraman and his heavy equipment would increase the 'chance of failure', wrote Byrd, but 'it was worth the risk to secure photographs of every mile of our route, both to the east and to the west'. The presence of the cameramen would also dispel any doubts that might arise about the authenticity of his achievement. In the bowels of the aircraft there were also a dog team and sled, along with food and other supplies to be used in case of a forced landing.[12] Some of these supplies were ditched overboard as the plane struggled to get sufficiently high to make it between the mountain peaks and above the 3400-metre-high polar plateau.

As navigator, it was up to Byrd to calculate when they had reached the South Pole, and he announced the milestone soon after midnight. He had talked in New Zealand of landing at the pole and hoisting the British flag to honour Scott but he made no attempt to do so. Having lost one of his two large planes, there would be no suitable aircraft to rescue him if the landing went awry. With threatening clouds rolling towards them, Byrd simply opened the trapdoor in the floor of the plane and dropped a small American flag, in which was wrapped the stone from Bennett's grave. As it fell to the snow about 800 metres below, the four men 'saluted our country's flag and the spirit of our gallant comrade'.

Byrd then radioed the news to Little America and onward to the listening public of America. The British flag returned with Byrd to Little America, along with a Norwegian flag carried in honour of Amundsen. Dropping them along with the American flag would have reinforced the British and Norwegian claims to the Antarctic, and Byrd was not about to do that. He would later write of the amount of territory he had sighted from his plane, noting that he had 'covered 160,000 square miles'. Indeed, Byrd had deliberately taken a more easterly route on his return to Little America so that he could 'bring within range' of his mapping camera 'as much new territory as was possible'. At the end of it all, he exulted: 'Well, it's done. We have seen the Pole and the American flag has been advanced to the South Pole.'[13]

The world knew of Byrd's achievement even before he had completed his nearly sixteen-hour flight. Having been radioed onward to the New York Times office in Times Square, the news was broadcast to thousands of excited people crowding the surrounding streets.[14] As the Floyd Bennett landed in a flurry of snow, congratulatory messages were already arriving over the radio. From New York came a radiogram from the editor of the New York Times, Arthur Sulzberger, who combined his congratulations for Byrd's 'successful mission' with urgent advice from Bowman that 'it is highly desirable that you complete a flight across Rockefeller Mountains to the coast [to the] east of one hundred and fiftieth meridian'.

This meant that the five flights that Byrd and others had made earlier in the year to the interior of the newly named Marie Byrd Land – each of which had been cut short by ice or bad weather – needed to be reinforced with a long flight that would tie it to a stretch of hitherto unclaimed coastline. There was a difficulty, advised Bowman, 'in establishing [a valid] claim except where [the] section of land has in a sense been cut loose from the unexplored and unclaimed by means of a coastal connection'. Bowman also sent his own message to Byrd, urging him to be 'sure to carry out suggestion conveyed in Sulzberger's message and tie flights to new coast'. Byrd did not have to be told twice; he assured Sulzberger that he 'had every intention of making a number of flights over to the eastward' and was well aware of 'what our mutual friend has stated'.[15]

On 5 December 1929, Byrd took off with three companions and headed for the Rockefeller Plateau, from where he pointed the plane towards the coast. Along the way, he discovered a substantial mountain range, which he named after his other major benefactor, Edsel Ford. This was where he wanted to be, flying beyond 'the eastern boundary of the British claims' and entering 'an area which had been unseen before, unknown and unclaimed'. They were more than 1200 metres high and lurching along at a hundred and sixty kilometres an hour, and the new land was unfolding before their eyes at a rate that would have been unimaginable to Scott. Not only were aircraft 'doing what surface craft had for many years been failing to do', wrote Byrd, but 'every foot of this area was being recorded precisely and in its full perspective' by his cameraman.

With Bowman's advice clearly in mind, Byrd noted how the photographer was careful 'to keep the coast line in his photographs', which was 'a most important consideration in the discovery and mapping of a new area'. With the coastline indicating sea level, the height of any mountains in the photographs could be better estimated and the resulting maps made that much more accurate. Byrd was conscious of the mistakes made by his predecessors in the Antarctic, who had been misled by atmospheric conditions into claiming the discovery of lands or islands that later proved to be non-existent. Having all the advantages of modern technology, he was 'determined to claim discovery only of those things which could be and were recorded by the unforgetting and unassailable memory of the camera'.[16]

'Magnificent!' exclaimed Bowman. Byrd had done 'exactly the right thing'. By tying the 'Rockefeller Mountains' to about 400 kilometres of previously uncharted coastline, Byrd had given the United States the right to make a valid claim to about 90,000 square kilometres of territory that 'lies entirely outside the Ross Dependency claimed by Great Britain'.[17] If he had not connected the inland region to the coast, Britain would have been free to chart the coastline and use the sector principle to claim all the territory, including the Rockefeller Plateau, between the coast and the South Pole.

Although Byrd had made it difficult for Britain to claim the massive wedge of largely unexplored territory between the Ross Dependency and the Falkland Islands Dependencies, a formal claim by the United States government was still required before Britain could be properly checkmated in that part of the continent. And there was no sign of that happening any time soon. Nevertheless, Bowman ensured that the American Geographical Society awarded Byrd its prestigious Livingstone Medal, maintaining that it was only granted 'after careful consideration of the purely scientific value of the work'. At the same time, the society noted that Byrd's flight on 5 December, which had 'established a sound basis for an independent territorial claim', had been done 'at the direct suggestion of the society'.[18]

While photographing and naming the new land were important steps in securing it for the United States, Byrd knew that the American claim would be all the stronger if some of his party could actually walk on that land, rather than just fly above its surface. The American Geographical Society's polar expert and cartographer, W. L. G. Joerg, declared at the time that there was a distinction between seeing an Antarctic territory and exploring it; he argued that 'the most important part of exploration must be done on the ground'.[19] Since Gould was already leading a geological party exploring the Queen Maud Mountains, at the southern extremity of the Ross Ice Barrier, Byrd instructed him to work his dog sledges further eastward into the newly discovered land.

On 20 December 1929, Gould radioed Byrd at Little America, saying he had done as instructed and was now camped at 85° 27' S, 147° 30' W. Climbing the nearest mountain, Gould and his five companions made a cairn of rocks, in which he placed a page from his notebook reporting their feat in having reached beyond the 150th meridian. No longer being within the Ross Dependency, Gould was able to 'claim this land as part of Marie Byrd Land, a dependency or possession of the United States of America'. They are the 'first men to set foot on American land in the Antarctic', wrote Byrd. It was that act that made the land securely 'American', in Byrd's view. As he noted at the time, it allowed the area all the way to the South Pole to be 'claimed for the United States'.[20]

Yet Byrd was careful to eschew such ambitions when the ice-scarred *City of New York* arrived back at Dunedin in March 1930. Questioned by journalists, he said that he was 'not the least concerned with claiming the land for America' and was 'merely [continuing] the work begun by British pioneers'. Although he had named Marie Byrd Land after his wife, Byrd said that the territory was 'not American' but 'belongs to the world'.[21]

That was not the prevailing view in the United States, where the excitement generated by the expedition had engendered a sense of ownership, which had been helped along by Byrd giving American names to geographic features, and calling his base 'Little

America' and one of his aircraft the *Stars and Stripes*. The base had the appearance of a frontier village. Its various buildings included an administration building, a storehouse, a machinery shop, bunk-houses, a photographic laboratory, a mess hall for the men, an electricity generator hut, radio towers, a taxidermy station and even a 'seal slaughter house'.[22] Many were connected by tunnels under the snow and ice, so as to allow access during blizzards.

Although the base had been located in an area claimed by Britain, and despite the fact that seven of Byrd's men were Norwegian and there were others who came from outside the United States, the Stars and Stripes was flown atop Little America's mess hall as soon as it had been constructed. Although it was taken down with the coming of winter, as soon as the sun returned in August 1929 the flag was returned to its proud position; it would remain there until the base was abandoned.[23] The sense of American ownership was also enhanced by the radio reports from Little America, which were regularly broadcast nationwide, and the newspaper reports of their activities that were splashed across the nation's front pages. It all combined to strengthen the connection between Americans and that far-off land.

As a consequence, there were calls on the government to annex all Antarctic territories that had been discovered by Americans, from Nathaniel Palmer onwards. However, congressional motions and newspaper editorials to that effect failed to convince the government to take action. With the stock market crash of October 1929 causing mounting unemployment, the government of President Herbert Hoover had more pressing issues to address, although officials in the State Department did discuss the possibility of extending the Monroe Doctrine to the Antarctic as a means of warding off British and European claims.[24]

This would have been a disappointment to the growing number of Americans interested in Antarctica. Mostly, their interest had begun well before Byrd's media-driven arrival on the continent. In the early 1900s, Edwin Balch and Frederick Cook had encouraged the descendants of sealers such as Palmer to search the attics of their Stonington homes for any logbooks or other documents that might prove the primacy of American discovery in the Antarctic.[25] As these documents were gradually revealed to the world, they were written up by Balch and others.[26]

More popular interest in the saga of the sealers came with the publication in 1922 of a biography of Palmer by the maritime historian and journalist John Randolph Spears, who relied on Palmer's niece, Elizabeth Loper, for material concerning her uncle. Spears was smitten by Loper's first-hand description of Palmer. He told her he was 'glad to learn that Palmer Land was discovered by an American who was great in every sense of the word instead of some little runt of a man who accidentally was in the place'.

By the time he had completed the first draft of his book, Spears had become convinced that Palmer was America's unsung hero of the Antarctic. He intended to prove it by publishing relevant entries from the log of Palmer's sloop, the appropriately named *Hero*. Barely containing his excitement, Spears dashed off a letter to Loper imploring her to send him a copy of the log, noting that 'the English tried to rob Cap Nat of his honors, but *the publication of the simple statements of the Hero's log will end all controversy*', making it the 'most important' thing he had ever written.

But the scrappy and spasmodic entries in the log did not provide the conclusive evidence that Spears had expected to find. In particular, there was no explicit mention by Palmer of having found a new continent. Undaunted, Spears ascribed the gaps to Palmer's young age, telling Loper that it was not surprising for 'a boy of 21 to get tired of writing up each day's work in detail. The weather was most uncomfortable and he was tired. He was hunting *seals* – not for undiscovered continents!' Spears nevertheless dismissed British and Russian claims and called on Americans to celebrate Palmer as the real discoverer of Antarctica.[27]

Spears' argument won the ready agreement of Colonel Lawrence Martin, chief of the maps division at the Library of Congress in Washington. The politically minded geographer had become an expert on glaciation in Alaska before working with military intelligence during the First World War. He later served with Bowman as an adviser on national boundaries at the Paris Peace Conference. Questions of territorial sovereignty came to occupy much of his subsequent work, and Martin had a particular interest in the Antarctic.[28]

As Byrd was preparing for his 1928 expedition, the bearded and bespectacled Martin was securing the evidence that might allow the United States to make territorial claims. In September 1927, he had gone to Stonington to get the *Hero*'s log and other documents from Loper so that he could mount an exhibition at the Library of Congress featuring the logbook, along with 'maps showing the land discovered by Captain Palmer in 1821'. He promised Loper that her loan of the material would be acknowledged in the library's annual report, along with a statement that 'the Antarctic Continent was discovered by Captain Nathaniel B. Palmer'.[29] Nevertheless, it was another thing for the government to honour the American discoveries, from Palmer to Byrd, by formally annexing those lands.

While the State Department saw no sense of urgency in making territorial claims, Byrd's activities propelled the British and Australian governments into action. They were motivated also by pressure from the Hudson's Bay Company, which wanted to exploit the marine resources of the Australian quadrant once its ownership had been clarified by an official act of claiming.[30] This came as a relief to Mawson, who had been frustrated by the Australian failure to follow up his 1911 expedition with the formal annexation of all the territory he had explored and claimed on behalf of the British Empire. He had hoped that it could be done by simply issuing letters patent, as had been done in the case of the Falkland Islands Dependencies and the Ross Dependency. Although the 1926 imperial conference had approved Amery's plan for the gradual takeover of the whole Antarctic continent, British legal advisers had warned that further acts of exploration and claiming were required before the Australian quadrant could be formally annexed.

When the question was referred by the Australian government to its National Research Council in March 1927, a committee that included Mawson and John King Davis pointed to the danger of being pre-empted by the Norwegians or the Americans and urged the government to take immediate action to establish the necessary legal basis for the quadrant's annexation by Britain. With hundreds of whale-catchers scouring Antarctic waters each summer, the committee advised that there was money to be made from licensing their activities and controlling the killing in ways that would make whaling a 'perpetual industry' for Australians. All they had to do was send Mawson back on another expedition to 'establish British domination in the Australian Sector of the Antarctic and to enable possession to be taken' of unclaimed areas. However, the Australian government recoiled at the cost and suggested instead that it be claimed by the publication of an order in council. It was only when Britain rejected this as not achieving the desired legal validity, by which time Byrd had established himself in the Ross Dependency, that Australia reluctantly accepted the necessity of sending Mawson on another expedition.[31]

With permanent bases still considered impossible, there were limited ways in which nations could take possession of places with such a forbidding climate. For a clear legal title to be established, discovery was meant to be followed by occupation, which usually meant permanent settlements. But the 1920s dispute between Denmark and Norway over the ownership of East Greenland had seen a more limited definition of 'occupation' deployed to support their separate claims. According to these arguments, 'occupation' might encompass just flag-raising, exploration, scientific investigation, administration and merely temporary occupation.[32] Although Mawson had done some flag-raising and exploration, mainly on land, during his 1911 expedition, the claims that he had made back then had not been ratified by either the British or Australian governments. Further acts of flag-raising, along with exploration and charting of the coastline, were deemed necessary before the Australian quadrant could be formally annexed by Australia and incorporated within the British Empire.

So these were the activities that Mawson was directed to do by the Australian government after a meeting at the home of Prime Minister Bruce on 6 December 1928, which was attended by Attorney-General John Latham, Minister for Defence George Pearce and Mawson himself. In the wake of this meeting, the British government was told that Australia would send an expedition 'to carry out exploration and scientific work, together with flag-planting between Oates Land and Enderby Land', on condition that Britain bore part of the cost by providing Scott's old ship, the *Discovery*, free of charge for Mawson's use.[33]

The *Discovery* had been used for some years for scientific voyages to investigate Antarctic marine life, particularly whales, so that they would not be fished to extinction. Initially, there was resistance by British Treasury officials, who argued that the threat of the United States or Norway annexing the Australian quadrant had been averted by Byrd concentrating his exploration elsewhere and by Norway acknowledging Britain's claim to that region by right of discovery. They also argued that Australia should pay for the expedition, since it would reap the benefits of any annexed territory.

However, Amery convinced the chancellor of the exchequer that the danger came not just from the United States and Norway. The profits from whaling were attracting other nations, such as France and Germany, to the Antarctic. Germany had also flown a zeppelin to the Arctic.[34] Although Germany had been compelled to surrender its Antarctic claims in 1919 at the Paris Peace Conference, there was nothing to prevent a resurgent Germany from returning to the location of its pre-war expeditions to the Australian quadrant to establish new claims to the place. That fear seems to have been sufficient for the British Treasury to waive its objections and agree that the *Discovery* would be given to Mawson for two consecutive summers of exploration, beginning in late 1929.

With the United States and Norway already exploring in the Antarctic, and other nations thought to be planning their own expeditions, Britain wanted to keep its activities and intentions relatively secret from the world. As with Byrd's expedition, most of the public justification for Mawson's venture concerned its scientific objectives. Privately, though, officials concentrated on questions of sovereignty. As Casey advised Bruce in June 1929, the 'broad objects of the Expedition [were] the strengthening of our claims to the whole area from the Ross Sea to Enderby Land . . . by frequent landings'. Although the scientific activities were 'most admirable', Casey wrote, they were 'really a means of bolstering up our claims to the area'.[35] And the claims in turn were just a means of reaping the revenue that was expected to come from whaling, whether by licensing the existing Norwegian whalers or establishing new Australian whaling companies.

Although he was the scientific leader of the expedition, Mawson was less interested in its scientific than its economic possibilities. He had assured Bruce in January 1929 that his expedition would 'report on the economic future of the Territory' and that the cost to the government would be recouped 'within 2 or 3 years from royalties on whale oil'. Moreover, Mawson hoped to profit from whaling himself. He had already been approached by Australian businessmen wanting to establish whaling companies, and he suggested to Bruce that he would join such enterprises once the forthcoming expedition was completed.[36]

Despite all the secrecy, the plans of Mawson's expedition revealed its true objectives. Unlike Byrd's expedition, it would spend little time ashore. There would be no dogs or sledges. Nor would there be long flights like those undertaken by both Byrd and Wilkins. Rather, it would be a largely ship-borne expedition, using a small aircraft with floats to survey some 4000 kilometres of largely uncharted coastline and investigate the resources of its offshore depths. Mawson had described these seas as being so 'teeming with life' that they were 'the pastures of the future'.[37] Wherever there was a suitable landing place, Mawson was to go ashore and conduct a claiming ceremony. The charting, the investigations and the claiming ceremonies were all seen as necessary preconditions for the formal annexation of the whole quadrant. But little of this could be revealed to the world.

Although the Australian, British and New Zealand governments were all supporting the expedition, Mawson was relying on private benefactors to make up the sizeable budget shortfall he faced; he also needed media companies to buy newspaper and other rights. Those deals and donations would be put at risk if the expedition was seen as being a government one. So Mawson emphasised its scientific credentials, noting that it was being done under the auspices of the 'Australian National Scientific Council for oceanographic and other scientific work in the Antarctic'.[38] Bruce adopted Mawson's suggestion and established a mainly scientific committee to organise the expedition, and announced to the parliament that its aims were 'mostly of a scientific nature'.[39] After all, what's not to like about science?

When the organising committee met, it became clear that science was far from the top priority. These were listed as being 'firstly, political; secondly, economic and commercial; thirdly, scientific'.[40] The choice of route provided a further indication of the real priorities of the expedition. Rather than heading south from Hobart and then sailing westward along the Antarctic coast, it was decided to head south from Cape Town so that Mawson could begin his survey in Enderby Land, at the western extremity of the Australian quadrant. He would then proceed eastward along the coast before ending in Australia. The Australians feared that the Norwegians were also interested in Enderby Land, which had remained unseen since its discovery by Biscoe in 1831.

In fact, Lars Christensen was planning to send the *Norvegia* back to the Antarctic in the summer of 1929–30, hoping to discover whether the elusive Enderby Land had suitable sites on which he might base his whaling operations. If he could claim it for Norway, he could avoid paying British license fees.

Time was of the essence for both Mawson and Christensen. As the head of Australia's department of external affairs, Dr Walter Henderson, told Mawson, the 'British title to this region was not very strong at present'. It had to be reinforced by Mawson's expedition 'before any other parties could get there'.[41]

When Mawson joined the *Discovery* at Cape Town in October 1930, he carried a commission from the king that authorised him to take possession of any lands he discovered that were not already claimed by another power. He was to take possession by planting 'the British flag wherever [he found] it practicable to do so'. When hoisting the flag, he was ordered to 'read the proclamation of annexation . . . attach a copy of the Proclamation to the flagstaff, and place a second copy of the proclamation in a tin at the foot of the flagstaff'.[42] This was similar to ceremonies that British explorers had done ever since England had first started amassing an empire in the late sixteenth century, and not unlike the ceremonies that Christopher Columbus had done even earlier in the West Indies.

Apart from Adélie Land, the narrow sliver of territory claimed by France, the great stretch of coastline to which Mawson was heading seemed to be his for the taking. However, alarm bells went off when he received a cable from Casey warning him that the crew of the *Norvegia* had left Norway on 23 August aboard one of Christensen's ships, the *Thor I*, while another of his ships was taking the polar explorers Hjalmar Riiser-Larsen and Finn Lützow-Helm and their aircraft.[43] They would all join the *Norvegia*, which had remained at Christensen's South Georgia whaling station since its previous voyage.

Although the objective of the Norwegians' new voyage was not stipulated – except that they would replace the depot on Bouvet Island – Mawson was under no illusions about their other goals. Back in July 1928, he had privately warned the Australian government that 'the Norwegians were preparing an expedition to seize Enderby land in the ensuing summer, and that their ship would continue year by year to explore the Antarctic and would take possession of the lands visited'[44]. The whole idea of sending the *Discovery* was to pre-empt the Norwegians, yet now it looked as though the Norwegians might reach the Antarctic first. The same day that the *Discovery* arrived at Cape Town, the Norwegian aviator Captain Finn Lützow-Holm also arrived there from Europe.

When the South African and British press realised that the two expeditions were making for the same part of the Antarctic, headlines talked of a race between Britain and Norway to claim undiscovered land. As he read these alarming reports, Mawson's fears of being beaten by the Norwegians increased. The public veneer of scientific cooperation was now stripped away and their private race made very public. The reports claimed that the Norwegians were intent on establishing new whaling bases and were planning to annex territory by dropping flags from aircraft, as Wilkins and Byrd had done.[45] This not only raised the possibility that the Norwegians might pre-empt Mawson's flag-raising along that coastline, but also threatened Mawson's hopes of establishing an Australian whaling industry there. His expedition seemed set for failure even before it began.

Desperate to ward off the Norwegians, Mawson sent a cable to London asking the government to find out from Norway what its expedition was planning; in return, Mawson would divulge his own plans to the Norwegians. Before he received a reply, a cable arrived from the London *Daily News* asking Mawson to comment on the reports of a race between the two expeditions to claim land.[46] In a fit of pique, Mawson stoked the controversy by replying with an indignant cable in which he portrayed his own expedition as disinterested scientists conducting investigations 'for the benefit of the world at large', while the Norwegians were 'not deeply interested in science' and simply wanted 'to extend their whaling industry' and 'hoist their country's flag in unknown parts of Antarctica'. Moreover, argued Mawson, that part of Antarctica was properly 'the heritage and concern of New Zealand, Australia and South Africa'. The *Daily News* joined in, blasting the Norwegians for pursuing whales to the verge of extinction while Mawson was concerned with studying 'the life and habits of the whale from the point of view of preserving the mammal'.[47] When the newspaper hit the streets of London, it caused immediate alarm in the Foreign Office and outrage from Norwegian diplomats.

The British government had accepted Norway's earlier assurances that it would respect the British claim to those parts of the Antarctic listed by the 1926 imperial conference as being British by right of discovery. This did not mean that Norwegian whalers would not claim parts of those areas, only that the Norwegian government would not buttress any such unofficial claims by annexing those territories. Britain had not sought explicit assurances from Norway concerning the activities of the *Norvegia*, for fear that broaching the subject with Oslo could cause the Norwegians to change their view and dispute the tenuous British claims. Now that Mawson had caused 'great indignation' in the Norwegian press, the British government was forced to disown his comments and provide a 'frank statement' of the expedition's plans to the Norwegian foreign minister.[48] Norway was informed that Mawson would be exploring the area between Enderby Land and the Ross Sea, and that the Australian government intended to 'establish British sovereignty formally over this sector'.[49]

Casey, who had been appalled by Mawson's ham-fisted statement, cabled to Cape Town imploring Mawson not to exacerbate the issue with any further public statements and assuring him that Norway had declared its expedition to be 'solely and absolutely scientific'.[50] In fact, the Norwegians had also told London that Riiser-Larsen had been authorised to claim any new land he discovered in the name of the king of Norway, while respecting those British areas listed in the report of the 1926 imperial conference.

The problem was that Christensen was not as respectful as the Norwegian government. To assuage the anger in Oslo, Britain's envoy assured the Norwegian government that Britain did not want the whole continent, pointing to the area between Enderby Land and Coats Land as being unclaimed by anyone and therefore open to the Norwegians. He also told the Norwegians that everywhere else, apart from Adélie Land, had an 'unimpeachable' British claim, which had been, or was being, translated 'into concrete sovereign possession'.[51]

It was a rather chastened Mawson who stood on the deck of the *Discovery* with his eleven fellow scientists, all dressed in grey trousers and blue blazers, as the ship pulled away from the Cape Town dock to the cheers of the crowd on 19 October 1929.[52] Having stopped at the Kerguelen Islands to take on coal left for him by a South African whaling company, Mawson headed south by way of Heard Island to chart the coastline that stretched some 2000 kilometres between Wilhelm II Land and Enderby Land. Australia's Antarctic ambitions had grown greatly since 1914, when Mawson had called for Britain to annex the area between 160° E and 90° E. The 1926 imperial conference, when South Africa had disavowed any interest in the so-called 'African quadrant' of Antarctica, had seen Australia stretch its proposed claim to encompass all the territory between 160° E and 45° E.[53]

The western third of this territory, to which Mawson was now headed, was an area that had lain mostly undiscovered since Biscoe's sighting in 1831 of the coastline that he named Enderby Land, after the British whaling company. It also lay just beyond the area that Mawson and his companions had explored in the Australasian Antarctic Expedition of 1911–12. With Britain's title to the area so tenuous, it was vital for Mawson to survey and claim that sector before the Norwegians did so. However, he was already too late.

On 7 December 1929, Riiser-Larsen had, in Christensen's words, 're-discovered Enderby Land' after sighting it in the distance from their small seaplane, which had been lent to the expedition by the Norwegian navy. Steaming along the edge of the pack ice, using seal blubber to supplement the overloaded ship's supply of coal, Riiser-Larsen and Lützow-Holm were the first people in a century to come within sight of Biscoe's Enderby Land. On 22 December their ship reached Cape Ann, the Enderby Land promontory named by Biscoe. Unable to get through the ice to make a landing onshore, Riiser-Larsen and Lützow-Holm took off again in their seaplane, carrying a tent and rifle in the hope that they would be able to land on the continent and claim it for Norway.

However, their heavily laden aircraft could not get sufficient altitude to make it onto the continent, forcing them to land on the water and then power their plane onto the sea ice, from where they tried to reach the continent on skis. When a sheer twenty-metre-high ice cliff made that impossible, and with fog threatening their return to the ship, they decided instead to climb an offshore rocky outcrop. Although they were not on the continent itself, at least it was solid land.

Acutely conscious of being 'the very first human beings who had ever visited this spot', they set up a flagpole from which they flew a silken flag that had been presented to Riiser-Larsen by the king and queen for an earlier expedition to the Arctic. After photographing and filming the scene, and having left a tablet at the base of the pole noting the name of their ship and the date of their visit, he replaced that historic flag with one given to him by Christensen's wife. Satisfied, Riiser-Larsen flew back to the *Norvegia*, declaring that 'now Enderby is Norwegian'. He radioed the news to Oslo, where the press reported excitedly that the pair had 'taken possession of this land for Norway in the . . . internationally recognized form'.[54]

At the time, Mawson was still more than a thousand kilometres to the east. His pilot, Stuart Campbell, was struggling to get the engine of the expedition's Gipsy Moth to work, and Mawson filled in time by going off in his motor launch to take pot-shots at any wildlife within shooting distance. A hapless Emperor penguin was one such casualty. Mawson noted with amazement how it had been shot through the chest, shoulder and head but was still alive when it was lifted onto the *Discovery* an hour and a half later.[55]

It was not until 31 December that conditions became suitable for the first flight by the two-person biplane. After taking off from the water, it rose to 1500 metres, from where Campbell could see new land some eighty kilometres away, confirming the 'appearance of land' that Mawson had seen from the ship five days earlier. Mawson promptly named it 'Mac. Robertson Land' after his private benefactor, the Melbourne chocolate manufacturer Sir MacPherson Robertson, who was commonly known by the name of his chocolates, as 'MacRobertson'. But there was no attempt to reach it by plane or to drop a flag upon its surface. Although naming it would help to bring it within the British world, a more formal claiming ceremony was required before it could be annexed. And that would require Mawson stepping ashore and raising the flag, rather than having Campbell simply drop one onto the ice.[56]

The forty-seven-year-old Mawson had other things on his mind, with almost daily disputes between himself and the *Discovery*'s captain, John King Davis, over the running of the ship. The two experienced explorers had been put in an impossible position. Mawson had been made commander of the expedition and the ship, while the irascible Davis had been given the authority to countermand Mawson's orders if he considered the safety of the ship was at stake, which he often did. Not surprisingly, Mawson's diary is dominated by long diatribes about Davis, who had captained the *Aurora* on Mawson's 1911 expedition but had had a desk job for the last decade as Australia's director of navigation. Mawson was so outraged by Davis's behaviour that he considered him to be almost insane. The captain's temper was not helped by his being kept in the dark about the expedition's objectives. Mawson had waited until 2 January 1930 before showing Davis the instructions he had received from Bruce, who had since been tossed from office.

That same day, after newspapers in Oslo had carried reports of Riiser-Larsen's claiming of Enderby Land, Casey had radioed the worrying news to Mawson. The claim had prompted a British protest to the Norwegian prime minister, who had assured the

British minister that the *Norvegia* expedition was 'a purely private venture' and that Riiser-Larsen's claim would not be supported by the government. Nevertheless, it lent a new sense of urgency to Mawson's mission and finally prompted Davis to increase the speed of the ship and push on towards Enderby Land.[57]

The end of hostilities between Mawson and Davis was short-lived. The following day, the two men had a raging argument over lunch, during which Davis declared that 'the Norwegians had every right to try and anticipate us at Enderby Land' and that the British and Australians 'had been most disgracefully secret' about their plans. Mawson's argument that the *Discovery* expedition was 'a scientific expedition' was dismissed out of hand by Davis, who rightly pointed out that it was 'all eyewash, we were out to grab land'. He went on to argue that if they were really scientists, they should have remained in Australia, 'where there was a much better field for scientific work'. It was not until one of the scientists deliberately turned up the volume of the gramophone that the argument was brought to an uneasy end.[58] But it did not end the disputes between Mawson and Davis concerning the purpose of the expedition.

Convinced that the Norwegians were intent on seizing all unclaimed territories in the Antarctic, Mawson pressed on with his plans to find somewhere he could step ashore and proclaim Australian ownership. As the *Discovery* waited offshore for the weather to clear on 9 January, and as photographer Frank Hurley prepared a suitably impressive proclamation, a cable was received from Canberra indicating that the *Norvegia* expedition had not claimed the area between Coats Land and Enderby Land, as previously reported. Instead, they had discovered and claimed 100 kilometres of coastline between Kemp Land and Enderby Land. Mawson noted with dismay that this was 'just where we now are'. It was all 'most exasperating', wrote Mawson in his diary, 'for they have evidently made a direct voyage here to raise their flag, and they knew this was in our itinerary'. While the Norwegians had done this, Mawson had spent time on oceanographic research and consequently arrived too late. The behaviour of the Norwegians was 'not helpful to science', complained Mawson, because it would mean that future expeditions would have to abandon their scientific work and 'just rush to [the] most likely points of the coast to make landing and raise flags'.[59]

Mawson was desperate to get ashore to raise the flag and read out his proclamation, but he did not want to land where the Norwegians had been and thereby cede primacy to his rivals. Mawson wanted Davis to take the ship to an untouched side of the short stretch of coastline claimed by the Norwegians. But Davis considered the weather was still too dangerous, fearing that the ship might be driven ashore or trapped by the pack ice for a year or more, as others had been before. He would not risk his ship for what he called 'that bloody rubbishing business of raising the flag ashore'. With Davis continuing to complain that 'this bloody flag-raising business' was 'all tosh', Mawson instructed him to head further west to prevent them being 'forestalled in everything' by the Norwegians.[60]

Finally, on 13 January 1930, the seas were sufficiently calm and clear of ice for the *Discovery* to be eased towards a small rocky island. Mawson took his party of scientists ashore in a launch, and they quickly made their way through a bustling penguin rookery to the island's 250-metre summit, from where they could see more than a hundred grounded icebergs. On this spectacular site, a flagpole was erected using a cairn of rocks, underneath which was buried a canister with the required proclamation, duly signed by Mawson and Davis. A wooden sign was then attached to the flagpole 'on which Hurley had beautifully carved, "The British Flag was hoisted and British Sovereignty asserted on 13th Jan., 1930"'.

With the men formed in a hollow square in front of the pole, the flag was raised and Mawson prepared to read the proclamation, which unfortunately now lay deep beneath the rocks. He had to rely on his memory and help from Hurley to recite the required words, which he did precisely at noon, asserting in the name of the king 'the full sovereignty of the territory of Enderby Land, Kemp Land, MacRobertson Land' and all off-lying islands between 73° E and 47° E. Then came three cheers for the king and a singing of 'God Save the King'. Without even stepping onto the continent, Mawson had claimed a massive wedge of territory comprising more than 1000 kilometres of coastline. Hurley took a commemorative photograph of the historic scene.

The ceremony done, the men made their way back to the ship, where the impatient Davis was pacing the deck, anxious to get away from what Mawson would later call 'Proclamation Island'. Mawson wanted to push on further westward to 40° E, which was just past the western limit of the land he had been instructed to claim and where he feared the 'Norwegians may be busy'.[61]

The following evening, Mawson discovered just how busy the Norwegians had been when the heavily laden *Norvegia* was sighted at about 49° E. A meeting with Riiser-Larsen took place in Mawson's cabin. Ostensibly adopting the friendly attitude of two explorers meeting in the wilderness, it was nevertheless with wariness that the two men exchanged information about their activities. Both were conscious that what they said and did could have diplomatic repercussions. The British government had already protested to the Norwegians about Riiser-Larsen's claiming of Enderby Land on 22 December and Christensen had instructed him on 10 January not to claim any more land east of 45° E. Riiser-Larsen now admitted to Mawson that he had been told not to do anything that 'would be resented by Great Britain', which Mawson wrongly presumed to mean that the Norwegian flag had not been raised on Enderby Land or Kemp Land.

Curiously, Mawson's diary suggests that he did not ask Riiser-Larsen to confirm this, although the Norwegian later claimed that he had 'explained in detail exactly what we had done, and what we intended doing during the remainder of the season'. Mawson may not have wanted to know. Making his own claim would have been complicated by the knowledge that the Norwegians had preceded him.

For his part, Mawson told Riiser-Larsen that he had mapped the coast all the way from 73° E to their current position. He deliberately exaggerated the extent of his work 'in order to turn the Norwegians westwards'. During their hour-long exchange, he also told Riiser-Larsen of his dismay on learning in Cape Town that the *Norvegia* expedition might overlap his own, which was 'intending a full scientific programme' in what he called 'the British area of Enderby-Kemp Land'. Riiser-Larsen riposted that the Norwegian plans 'had been made public as far back as 1927', and they 'were not invading other people's territories'. Mawson again suggested that the *Norvegia* henceforth remain west of 40° E, while Mawson would restrict his activities to the eastern side of that line of longitude. But the Norwegian refused to give any such commitment.

As Riiser-Larsen pulled away in his boat, the men of the *Discovery* lined the rails and gave three cheers for their departing rival, only to watch in dismay as the *Norvegia* headed east along the coveted coastline of Enderby and Kemp Lands. The *Discovery* continued its westerly course to the limit of the Australian quadrant.[62]

While the two men had been meeting, a coded message had been received from Australia instructing Mawson to raise the flag on the continent itself. Mawson was told to head west as far as 45° E and, if possible, to 40° E. But Davis had had enough. He regarded their job as complete and was concerned that there would soon be insufficient coal to get them home. He was also sick of what he called 'this flag waving business'. In a long diatribe on 16 January, he told Mawson that the expedition's work was 'nothing but a cinema show', and Mawson and his scientists 'nothing but a lot of flag raising humbugs'. Mawson carefully recorded all the comments in his diary as evidence of 'how utterly imbecile [Davis] is. He is not mentally balanced.'

Mawson was not going to head for home just yet. He worried about what the Norwegians might be doing and he had been reminded by a radio message from Canberra that the 'flag should be hoisted as often as possible on lands seen', noting that so far Mawson had only raised it once. And that had been done on an island rather than the mainland. Mawson was determined not to leave the Antarctic until he had raised the flag on the shore of Enderby Land and managed to take aerial photographs of its mountains. As well as claiming territory for the empire, he had lucrative media commitments to fulfil, which required him to return with spectacular photographs. He also needed to kill some seals to provide samples of oil and skin for the Hudson's Bay Company.[63]

After passing 45° E, Mawson abandoned plans to go any further west and headed back east in pursuit of the *Norvegia*, all the while looking for somewhere suitable to land. Although the *Norvegia* continued eastward after leaving the *Discovery*, Riiser-Larsen reversed course after Christensen instructed him by radio to 'refrain from occupying any more land east of 45° E'. In doing so, the whaling magnate was not relinquishing the claim that Riiser-Larsen had made to Enderby Land on 22 December, the resolution of which he was happy to leave to later adjudication by 'international experts'.[64]

By 25 January, the *Discovery* had returned to Proclamation Island and Mawson was able to get the aircraft aloft so that Hurley could take both photographs and cinema film and so that Campbell could look for somewhere to land on the continent. After Hurley's flight, Mawson went up in the plane with a flag and the required proclamation. As Campbell piloted them across the ice-splattered water towards the continental coastline, Mawson attached the flag to a short mast and passed it forward to Campbell. When they were well over land, Campbell cut the engine and dropped the flag over the side from a height of nearly 1000 metres as Mawson read out the proclamation. Mawson was confident that this ensured the 'claiming once more [of] all the land discovered, and this time including the newly discovered slice at our furthest west' – in other words, all the land along which they had sailed up to the western limit of the Australian quadrant at 45° E.

To confirm the claim, Campbell circled back over their drop point and 'spotted the flag lying on the ice surface and drew my attention to it'. That was the most that could be done. Davis resolutely refused to attempt a landing ashore for a proper claiming ceremony, fearing that hidden rocks would endanger the ship, and insisted that they head for home while there was still sufficient coal for the engine. Mawson reluctantly agreed to do so. He carefully kept the news of his retreat secret from the Norwegians so that they would not return to explore the abandoned coastline.[65]

Riiser-Larsen's attention was elsewhere. The Norwegians had taken the British hint and abandoned their original plan to be just the fifth expedition to circumnavigate the continent. Instead of continuing eastward, the Norvegia turned west to explore the vast unclaimed coastline between Enderby Land and Coats Land. Although hampered by the ship's ice-damaged bow, and by an unusually wide belt of ice that kept them far from the coast between Enderby Land and Coats Land, they were able to discover and chart a stretch of coastline on the western edge of Enderby Land, which Riiser-Larsen named 'Queen Maud Land', and more coastline on the eastern edge of the Weddell Sea, which he named 'Crown Princess Martha Land'. Because he could not get close enough to the shore, or even reach it safely by aircraft, the great expanse of coastline between those two places remained a mystery.

Nevertheless, Riiser-Larsen's voyage had charted nearly 1000 kilometres of coastline, finding new bays and seas that were rich in whales. Sketches, maps and photographs were all carefully compiled, both to reinforce the Norwegian claim to the several stretches of coastline and to be of practical assistance to Christensen's whaling fleet. At the beginning of March 1930, Christensen instructed Riiser-Larsen to take the Norvegia to Cape Town for repairs and to wait out the winter.[66]

It had been a frenetic two years. Aircraft had transformed exploration in the Antarctic. Wilkins had been first in the air and had returned with spectacular photographs of the landscape. His apparent discovery of channels cutting across the Antarctic Peninsula, dividing the continent into two land masses, would later prove to be wrong. More disappointingly for the British government, Wilkins' flight had been cut short before he had reached the unclaimed territory lying between the Ross Dependency and the Falkland Islands Dependencies, which Britain had wanted to make its own.

With a wary eye on Wilkins, Byrd had mounted the largest ever Antarctic expedition, and had returned in triumph with the coveted prize of being first to have flown over the South Pole. More importantly, after ninety years of American disinterest in the Antarctic, he had placed Antarctica firmly on the national agenda of the United States. He had also made the first tentative steps towards claiming a section of the continent for the United States, flying across part of the territory that Wilkins had been unable to reach.

Norway also had returned in force with the largest whaling fleet the world had ever seen, complete with aircraft for whale-spotting and territorial acquisition. Britain was on notice that its dream of controlling the entire continent could not be realised. The carve-up of Antarctica by the rival powers had begun in earnest.

CHAPTER 12

'What a bloody farce'

1931–1933

The successful use of aircraft in the Antarctic created a sense of human mastery of the continent. While reading newspapers at their breakfast tables, people from Berlin to Buenos Aires could behold the camera-captured stillness of crevasse-ridden glaciers twisting their way between snow-covered mountains. The veil that had hidden Antarctica's secrets could now be swept away by planes that crisscrossed the continent, with regular newspaper updates showing more and more of the map being filled in.

Aircraft also accelerated the race to control the continent. Just when competition for the Antarctic had begun in earnest, the New York stock market collapse of October 1929 and the subsequent economic depression restricted the funding that governments and private benefactors would give to speculative ventures. After two unsuccessful summers in the Antarctic, Australian aviator Hubert Wilkins declared that he would give up polar aviation for good. America's polar hero Richard Byrd wanted to go back after being feted by the American public, but he was forced to postpone a second expedition to Little America due to lack of funding. Only the Norwegian whaler Lars Christensen and the Australian geologist Sir Douglas Mawson returned in the summer of 1930–31 to resume their rivalry.

The Norwegians had the advantage, not only in the solo voyage by the small expedition ship *Norvegia*, but also in the carefully coordinated investigations by much of Christensen's whaling fleet. The nimble whale catchers were often able to get much closer to the coastline than the more ponderous factory ships, and Christensen instructed them to chart any new land that they might encounter during their hunt. The factory ships carried coal and other supplies, and could transport aircraft, which allowed the *Norvegia* to make much longer voyages than Mawson could contemplate.

For the summer of 1930–31, Christensen wanted the *Norvegia* to circumnavigate the entire continent, which would be only the fifth time that the feat had been achieved, and the first for ninety years. Leading the expedition was the former Norwegian army officer and polar topographer Gunnar Isachsen, who joined the *Norvegia* in Cape Town in September 1930. His instructions were to circle the Antarctic, looking for islands whose existence or location was doubtful and which might provide bases for whaling, to investigate the number and distribution of whales and to reinforce and extend Norway's existing territorial claims.[1] The captain of the *Norvegia*, Nils Larsen, was given instructions on the 'method of procedure' for claiming any land that had 'not previously been occupied by any other nation'.[2]

The sixty-one-year-old Isachsen was well suited to the task of leading the expedition, having been involved with exploration and mapping in the Arctic for more than thirty years before becoming the Norwegian Maritime Museum's director. Most recently, he had served as a Norwegian government inspector on the Antarctic whaling fleet, which meant that he was heading for familiar seas when the *Norvegia* left Cape Town in October 1930.

After spending more than two months searching for islands that, it turned out, did not exist, Isachsen headed for Peter I Island. The island had been discovered by Bellingshausen's Russian expedition in 1821 and claimed for Norway in 1929, when the *Norvegia* had landed a party who erected a hut for shipwrecked mariners. This act had both an obvious practical purpose and a symbolic meaning for Norwegians. It was a physical sign of Norwegian administration and occasional Norwegian occupation, and therefore – in Norwegian eyes – laid the basis for a territorial claim. Isachsen had instructions to reinforce the claim by erecting yet another hut and a depot of stores, but he was prevented by the kilometres of ice surrounding the island.

Isachsen was forced to press on with his voyage in order to meet up with Christensen and Riiser-Larsen, who were on board the tanker ship *Thorshavn*. Once that rendezvous was achieved on 9 February at 33° 53' E, Isachsen handed over control of the *Norvegia* to Riiser-Larsen, and he and Christensen returned to Cape Town on the *Thorshavn* with a cargo of whale oil. Before they left, a small seaplane was transferred to the *Norvegia* to expedite the discovery and claiming of new land.[3]

Having been thwarted the previous year in having his claim to Enderby Land recognised by the Norwegian government, Riiser-Larsen wasted no time in exploring and claiming the nearby coast-line, which lay within the sector that was as yet unclaimed and to which Britain had indicated Norway should direct its territorial ambitions. The previous year, Riiser-Larsen had risked his life to stand upon the continent and raise the Norwegian flag. Following the examples of Byrd and Mawson, he had since decided that it was sufficient to see land from an aircraft in order to be able to claim it.

Although this contention had not been tested in any international court, both Riiser-Larsen and Christensen argued that there were numerous historical precedents of explorers claiming land from the deck of a ship offshore, from which position they could have had little sense of its topography or extent. At least from the vantage point of an aircraft the location and size of a territory could be more precisely determined, and much more accurate charts could be created.[4] Others argued that it was necessary to actually step onto a land in order to claim it. As a Scottish newspaper observed in the wake of Byrd's flight to the South Pole, the American aviator had looked upon the Antarctic in the same way 'as we all have seen the moon'; the United States could no more gain legal title to the Antarctic by Byrd looking upon it from a great height than any person could gain legal title to the moon merely by having seen it from afar.[5]

The Norwegians were content to follow the precedent set by their powerful rivals, Britain and the United States. On 17 February 1931, Riiser-Larsen and the *Norvegia*'s captain, Nils Larsen, climbed to a height of more than 1100 metres in their seaplane, from where they saw a landscape of snow and ice stretching into the mist-draped distance. As soon as they passed over what they took to be 'the edge of the inland ice', Riiser-Larsen 'dropped the flag and documents, taking possession of the land for Norway'. Once back on the *Norvegia*, he radioed the news to Oslo, asking permission of King Haakon VII to name the land after the monarch's grand-daughter, Princess Ragnhild. Permission was promptly given.[6]

A few days later, the *Norvegia* met up with the factory ship *Antarctic*, whose captain reported that he had been mapping Queen Maud Land and Enderby Land. It was just one of several Norwegian whaling ships that had been mapping the coastline and bestowing Norwegian names upon its geographic features, both to improve the safety of their navigation and to buttress the Norwegian claim to the sector lying between the eastern boundary of the Falkland Islands Dependencies and the western boundary of the sector that Australia was intent on claiming. As that Antarctic summer drew to a close, the *Norvegia* and its sister ships returned to the north with details of their sightings.

When the *Norvegia* steamed slowly into the whaling port of Sandefjord on 15 May 1931, there were great festivities to honour the four-year exploration, with Christensen handing out silver medals to the crew. Nils Larsen was awarded a medal from the Norwegian Geographical Society, while Christensen was made a commander of the second class of the Order of St Olav. During the speeches, the name for the newly discovered territory was announced as 'Lars Christensen Land'. It was among the sightings that were subsequently traced on two new hydrographical charts published at Christensen's instigation by the Whalers' Mutual Insurance Association. The *Norvegia* also brought back results from its meteorological, hydrological and other observations, which were later published at Christensen's expense by the Norwegian Academy of Sciences.[7]

All this helped to cement the unofficial Norwegian claim to the African quadrant, with Christensen's maps showing that his whalers had mapped the principal features of the Antarctic coastline all the way from 20° W to 100° E. Much of what had been blank or conjectured on Antarctic maps was now filled in, and Christensen invited people to compare his maps with the much less detailed British maps that had been published in 1926.[8]

Christensen had not relinquished his hopes that Norway might lay claim to the Australian quadrant too. As he argued in his account of the Norwegian expeditions, Norway had 'great and real interests to safeguard in the lands that we have discovered'. Christensen had a special reason for wanting to do so. It would not only extend the area in which his whalers would be able to operate free of British licences, but a large part of the sector was named after himself.

Isachsen wrote a report for the American Geographical Society's *Geographical Review* in which he listed the many discoveries by Norwegian whale-catchers along the coastline of what they now called Lars Christensen Land. Located between 75° E and 60° E, this was practically identical to Mac. Robertson Land, the sector that had been named, claimed and inaccurately mapped by Mawson a year earlier. Mawson had not been the first to see the coast, having arrived some weeks after the Norwegians. Now they had preceded him for a second time.

While Isachsen brought that fact to the attention of American geographers, Christensen did so for a wider audience in a book that was first published in Norwegian before being translated into English in 1935. Titled *Such Is the Antarctic*, Christensen told the world about the series of *Norvegia* expeditions and the associated discoveries of his whaling ships, including three voyages that he and his wife had made aboard the *Thorshavn*. Describing the coastline between Lars Christensen Land and Queen Maud Land as a 'maiden area' that had not been visited for a century, the wealthy whaler recounted how it had 'become, in the course of two years, a happy hunting-ground for the Norwegian whaling industry'.[9]

Conscious that the Norwegian government had agreed not to formally claim any land within areas that Britain had marked out for itself, Christensen wanted nevertheless to place on the public record the priority of the Norwegian discoveries. Although he acknowledged Mawson's work, he made clear that Mawson's names for the geographic features of Lars Christensen (or Mac. Robertson) Land had prior Norwegian names, with the Norwegians often using the names of Christensen's ships and their officers. For instance, the Norwegian name of 'Thorshavn Bay' had been overlaid by Mawson with the rather grander name of 'Mackenzie Sea'.

The Norwegians had also mapped and named other regions within the sector that Mawson was intent on claiming. Just west of Lars Christensen Land, they explored and charted Kemp Land, Enderby Land and Queen Maud Land. Isachsen made clear that they had made careful calculations of their location each time, by taking 'many observations on the sun as well as on the stars', and had made similarly careful calculations of the position and height of any mountain peaks that came within sight of their ships. The Norwegian maps of that coastline were, consequently, much more accurate than those of Mawson, which might become an important consideration if Norway ever considered claiming that sector.[10] As far as Christensen was concerned, the voyages of the *Norvegia* and the discoveries of his other whaling ships marked the time when 'the Norwegian mainland in the south came into being'.[11]

Mawson was determined that the 'Norwegian mainland in the south' would not intrude into the Australian quadrant. His first voyage had gone some way towards doing this, before it had been cut short when the *Discovery* had run low on coal and its captain, John King Davis, had been panicked into returning early to Australia. Although Britain had loaned the *Discovery* for two years, the all-important funding for a second year from the Australian government had not yet been guaranteed.

Mawson did what he could to convince the new Labor government of James Scullin, emphasising the amount of territory that he had claimed, the oceanographic and meteorological research that had been conducted, and the rich whale fishery he had discovered off Enderby Land. The whale fishery alone, he argued, would return millions of pounds within the next few years. Mawson was supported by Macpherson Robertson, who had laid on a welcoming dinner after the first voyage during which he spoke of the Antarctic's 'great economic and Imperial importance to Australia and Great Britain'. Robertson promised to contribute £6000 for a second voyage if the government agreed to match the amount.[12]

The British government also urged Australia to fund a second voyage, noting that the first expedition had 'succeeded in occupying and making a detailed survey of a long stretch of coast-line', thereby preparing 'the way for a formal assumption of sovereignty and the vesting' in the Australian government of its administration. Although Australia had dallied with the idea of not proceeding with a second voyage, the sight of four Norwegian factory ships and tankers calling into Australian ports with full cargos of whale oil – on their way back to Norway – helped to change its mind.

On 10 May 1930, Scullin informed the British government of Australia's decision and outlined Mawson's plans for the second voyage.[13] With the Depression lengthening the unemployment lines, the prospect of creating a local whaling industry and taxing the Norwegian whalers made the cost of another voyage seem relatively trifling. Now that Norway had agreed not to claim any more territory within the Australian quadrant, it also made sense for Mawson to be sent south for a second year so it could finally be annexed and brought within the British Empire.

While Mawson was finalising his preparations for the second voyage, delegates were assembling in London for another imperial conference at which the question of British territorial claims in the Antarctic would be reviewed. Britain's hopes of controlling the whole continent had had to be revised when France let it be known that it would not let go of Adélie Land. Meanwhile, South

Africa advised that it had no interest in administering the African quadrant on behalf of the empire. British officials now conceded that the Norwegian discoveries of new land in that sector, and their charting of the coastline, gave it the strongest claims to sovereignty there.

That left the sector between the Ross Dependency and the Falkland Islands Dependencies, as well as the Australian quadrant. Despite Byrd's aerial forays into the former, Britain had not relinquished its hopes of bringing it under its control. That had been why Britain had supported Wilkins' proposed flight over that sector to the Ross Sea in 1929. Although bad weather had prevented Wilkins from venturing any further than the Antarctic Peninsula, Britain believed that Byrd's limited activities had not established an unassailable claim by the United States to the region. Once Mawson's voyages had been completed and the Australian quadrant had been brought within the empire, British officials argued, 'there still remains a vast stretch of coastline lying between longitude 80°W and 140°W, which has never been explored, either from the sea or from the air'. That was where future British exploration should be concentrated. Firstly, though, Mawson had to complete his mission.[14]

For his second voyage, Mawson intended to cover as much coastline as possible from the Ross Sea to Mac. Robertson Land, although the British government wanted him just to concentrate on consolidating their claim to the sector west of Adélie Land, from 130° E to 75° E.[15] After the debacle of the previous year, when Mawson had only managed to conduct one flag-raising ceremony on an offshore island, he planned to go onto the continent itself as often as possible, in order to firmly cement in place a British territorial claim.

There was no question in his mind that he had the right to do so. In a newspaper article prior to leaving, Mawson made clear that he was going to be exploring land that was British by right of discovery, based upon the visit of British sealer John Balleny in 1839 and the work of Mawson's own expedition in 1911–12.[16] However, 'discovery and formal acts of annexation' were insufficient to provide a valid title of ownership. It also required 'occupation', although international legal rulings suggested that 'occupation' had a special meaning in polar regions, where it was considered impossible for people to survive. Rather than requiring permanent settlements, a title based upon occupation would exist when a nation could show that it was exercising a suitable 'degree of control' over the area.[17] In the Antarctic, this might be done merely by occasional visits and the regulation of whaling in nearby seas. British and Australian officials believed that by returning and visiting the place, and by raising the flag, Mawson's British, Australian and New Zealand Antarctic Research Expedition – known as 'BANZARE' – would be effectively fulfilling the legal condition regarding 'occupation'.

Funds for the tight-strapped expedition were sought from newspapers in Australia, Britain and the United States, although Mawson found, to his chagrin, that editors were not as excited as he hoped by his plans. Sailing along the Antarctic coastline and occasionally scrambling ashore to raise a flag were not activities that were likely to grip the imagination of readers who had been raised on stories of Scott and Amundsen, and of the younger Mawson himself. Where was the daring and the danger this time? The London *Times* and America's Hearst Corporation both declined to buy the rights to Mawson's second expedition, despite having supported his first. Although Casey was able to find an alternative British news service that was willing to buy the rights, Mawson was forced to write to American geographer Isaiah Bowman for advice regarding a replacement press organisation in the United States. He was fortunate to secure the support of the *New York Times*, albeit at a much reduced rate.[18] Even Australian newspaper editors were unimpressed at the prospect of a second voyage; they were particularly annoyed at being charged for the second voyage after the reports from the first voyage had been distributed free of charge in Australia.

Privately, Mawson berated the press for taking 'an extraordinarily narrow view', predicting that when his reports started being received 'more of them will wish to have it'. The government official in charge of the expedition conceded that the 'absence of untoward incidents may detract to a certain extent from their news value', but he believed 'a certain percentage of readers' would be interested in the daily doings of the scientific staff on the *Discovery* as they hauled up another net of marine creatures or released yet another weather balloon into the Antarctic sky.[19]

It was not just about money for the expedition. Publicising the expedition's activities was an important prelude and justification for the annexation that would come later. With the press reluctant to take his stories, Mawson had to rely even more on the ability of his accomplished photographer, Frank Hurley, to bring the expedition to the attention of the world through his dramatic pictures and cinema film.

Hurley was even then putting together a film of the first voyage, which would incorporate a lot of footage of the Antarctic wildlife along with shots of the science and the claiming of territory. Called *Southward Ho!*, the government-sponsored film was meant to provide much-needed revenue for the expedition, while also engendering a sense of ownership of the Antarctic in the minds of British and Australian audiences. But it was threatened by the arrival in Australia of the Paramount film of Byrd's expedition. With Hurley's film not due for release in Sydney cinemas until August 1930, the government had its film censor keep the American film from Australian audiences until *Southward Ho!* had completed its run, free from competition. The delay helped maximise ticket sales of Hurley's film and emphasised Mawson's achievements over those of his American rival.[20]

Hurley's film would still have been playing in some Australian cinemas when the *Discovery* left Hobart on 22 November 1930. As a missing crew member leaped on board, clad only in his underwear after a last night ashore, the ship was cheered on its way by a large crowd of well-wishers waving handkerchiefs.[21] The irascible and ageing Davis had been replaced as captain by the *Discovery*'s former chief officer, Kenneth Mackenzie, while the problem of providing sufficient coal to steam hundreds of miles along the ice-prone coast would be solved by drawing on supplies from Norwegian factory ships operating in the same seas.

After calling briefly at Macquarie Island, which was now unoccupied after the mass slaughter of penguins and elephant seals was banned, Mawson headed for the Balleny Islands, off the western entrance to the Ross Sea, where he was due to take on 100 tons of coal from the Norwegian factory ship *Sir James Clark Ross*. The two ships met on 15 December 1930, using the inflated carcass of a dead whale and long strips of blubber as fenders between the vessels, so that bags of coal could be slung across to the deck of the *Discovery*. As Mawson and Mackenzie dined with the Norwegian officers on whortleberries and Swedish punch, the Australian aviator Stuart Campbell was preoccupied by the 'gargantuan scale' of the slaughter and the industrialised processing of the kill. With numerous carcasses bobbing in the water alongside the *Sir James Clark Ross*, and with up to four whales being processed at one time on the ship's huge flensing deck, it was 'literally one mass of blood and guts'. Campbell watched with some horror as the whalers worked in 'rivers of blood 2 to 3 inches deep and fully 20ft. wide'. Such was their success that year that oil of inferior quality from decomposing whales was dumped over the side to make room for the more valuable oil from freshly killed whales. Even 800 tons of fuel oil was jettisoned to make room.[22]

With the coal safely stowed, the *Discovery* wallowed its way westward, making regular stops for Mawson to plumb the depths of the ocean for marine life and signs of a continental shelf. Mawson wanted to land on the coastline of what he had earlier named King George V Land, the scene of his disastrous sledge journey with Ninnis and Mertz. At the limit of that journey, he and Mertz had raised the British flag, but they'd no authority to claim the newly discovered territory for Britain. Now that Mawson did have the authority, he was determined to exercise it.

As the *Discovery* probed the northern edge of the pack ice for a way through to the coast, Mawson described in his diary how on 26 December they were blocked by 'large rafts of even floe of fair thickness, evidently broken out of coast off King George V Land and not long at sea. Too heavy to push through.' The disappointed explorer reported by radio to Casey that it was 'probably impossible to hoist flag at King George V Land as defined by myself in 1911 expedition'. Instead, he proposed to push on to Commonwealth Bay, where he had based his 1911 expedition. Although that was not within King George V Land, as he had previously defined it, Mawson suggested that he stretch its western boundary to encompass Commonwealth Bay. That would allow him to land at his old base and 'hoist the flag at Commonwealth Bay taking over King George V Land'.[23] So the ship continued to heave itself westward through the sizeable swells.

On 28 December, as the *Discovery* skirted the edge of the pack ice and the sun arced low across a cloudless sky, Campbell came on deck to see the horizon dotted with 'majestic icebergs and small floes glinting in the light or standing out as purple shadows against the golden heavens'. He likened it to 'standing on the rim of the world looking across into eternity'. But the tranquillity was disturbed by more Norwegian whalers towing their dead quarry to the massive maw of the factory ship *Kosmos*, which had the dubious distinction of having processed forty-five whales in a twenty-four-hour period. As the Norwegians provided Mawson with fifty more tons of coal, Campbell wondered how long the unrestricted slaughter of whales could continue. Some sense of the scale of the slaughter was seen as the coal was being transferred to the *Discovery* and a tanker arrived to offload 60,000 barrels of oil from the *Kosmos*. The transfer allowed the factory ship to remain until its capacity of 120,000 barrels was reached. With that much whale oil being worth about $1.5 million, it would not be long, thought Campbell, before the whales followed 'the fur seal to extinction, never to return'.[24]

Mawson would also have been conscious of this risk and doubtless been concerned as to how it might undermine the value of Australia's territorial ambitions and his own fortune-seeking ambitions in the whaling industry. However, the disappearing whale stocks did not divert him from his mission of claiming the Australian quadrant, starting with King George V Land. He began doing this as soon as he reached his old base at Cape Denison on 4 January 1931. Watching through binoculars as the *Discovery* edged its way carefully into Commonwealth Bay, Mawson saw with satisfaction that the main hut where he had waited out the winter after the deaths of Mertz and Ninnis was still standing. Nearby was the poignant memorial cross. Campbell noted how Mawson was 'very excited at getting back to the old spot . . . and was shouting frantic instructions to all'.

The hut's roof had almost collapsed, and snow and ice had worked their way inside, compelling Mawson and his party to scramble their way in through the skylight, whereupon they looked with wonder on the 'great masses of delicate ice crystals hung in festoons'.[25] While magnetic readings were made and two decades of ice movement measured, the old hut was reoccupied for the two days of their visit to give some semblance of Australia being in actual occupation of the millions of square kilometres that it was intent on claiming. If the issue was ever challenged in an international court, this might provide evidence for the Australian case.

While marooned at Cape Denison in 1913, Mawson had sought permission to name the surrounding area 'King George V Land'. Now he lost no time in formally claiming the area, vesting sovereignty in the British king and 'His heirs and Successors forever'. The territory comprised the sector between 142° E and 160° E, included all the offshore islands and extended all the way to the South Pole. It therefore enclosed the previously unclaimed sector between the Ross Dependency and Adélie Land.

Mawson had precise instructions as to how the claiming ceremony had to be performed. One requirement was to have his party form a hollow square in front of the flagpole – but the terrain made this 'utterly impossible', wrote Campbell. So they formed a circle instead, as Mawson, 'slightly embarrassed, read the Proclamation', which was signed by Mawson and witnessed by Mackenzie. A copy of this was placed in a sealed container and buried beneath the cairn of rocks that secured the flagpole. With his tripod balanced on the rock-strewn slope below the ridge, Hurley photographed the Union Jack being raised triumphantly as the men gave three cheers and sang 'God Save the King'. Then they did it all again for the cinematograph.

When the film of the expedition was released, Australian and British audiences would see the claiming ceremony for themselves and gain their own sense of ownership over the world's last wilderness. Some, though, would doubtless share Campbell's derisive view of the carefully staged event: he described with a mocking tone in his diary how 'thousands of square miles of virgin ice clad land was claimed on behalf of His Majesty, King George the Fifth, by his beloved servant, Douglas Mawson (what a bloody farce)'. The aviator found the ceremony more than a little ludicrous, wondering whether their failure to form a hollow square would 'arouse international complications'.[26]

This was not altogether a groundless fear, particularly when they learnt from the Norwegian factory ship *Falk* on 6 February that Riiser-Larsen in the *Norvegia* had discovered new land in the vicinity of 76° E, which was where Mawson was headed. The news 'takes the wind out of our sails to a certain extent', wrote Campbell, although there was 'still a chance for us a bit further to the east'. As the *Falk* took on coal from a Swedish cargo ship, some of the men on the *Discovery* were even more dismayed 'to see a woman leaning over the bridge'. Although Campbell thought it was one woman on the Swedish ship, Harold Fletcher recalled seeing two women 'looking over the rail of the *Falk*; one with bare arms and the other in a thin dress'. Whether one or two, the Antarctic's place as an exclusive male preserve had clearly ended. In fact, it had ended the previous year, when Christensen had taken his wife with him on the *Thorshavn*. Campbell now wryly observed how the ownership of 'man's last place of exclusive retirement [has] gone'.[27]

Campbell's colleagues would have been even more dismayed had the plans of the *Discovery*'s former captain, J. R. Stenhouse, come to fruition. In early 1930, he had announced a twelve-month round-the-world cruise aboard a trans-Atlantic liner, which would dip down to the 'Great White South' to allow its British and American passengers 'to join in a two day's dash in dog sleighs over the Antarctic continent' and stay in the abandoned huts of Scott, Shackleton and Amundsen. It was expected that the cruise would particularly 'appeal to women, as the Antarctic is the only remaining part of the earth on which they have not set foot'. Originally scheduled to depart in December 1930, it was postponed to the following year and changed to a three-month cruise. But the prospective passengers, hard hit by the Depression, never appeared.[28]

Nor did Mawson's nemesis, Hjalmar Riiser-Larsen, appear on the horizon as the *Discovery* continued its westward voyage. There were just the smudges of smoke from some of the hundreds of whaling ships that were in the Antarctic that year. A passing Norwegian whaler reported to Mawson that Riiser-Larsen was now much further westward, exploring Enderby Land.[29] With heavy pack ice preventing the *Discovery* from approaching the coast, Mawson was uncertain about what he should do. He had wanted to visit the hut of his so-called 'western base' during the 1911 expedition, but the 100 kilometres or so of intervening ice prevented him from doing so. Mawson cabled to Casey for instructions, unsure whether he should press on all the way to Queen Mary Land before conducting another flag-raising ceremony – although there would be no guarantee that he could get through the ice to make a landing there either. It is not clear whether Casey replied to Mawson's cable, as he had relinquished his post in London and was returning to Australia to forge a career in politics.

Whether or not he received a reply, Mawson seems to have decided to claim land as often as he could, so long as it did not unduly disturb his scientific program. When land was sighted from the aircraft on 11 February, Campbell dropped a flag from on high to claim it for the empire, while Mawson broke out champagne and cigars at supper to celebrate their success. Continuing their westward voyage, a further stretch of coastline was sighted two days later, which Mawson was also determined to claim.

Faced with an ice barrier with rocky islets at sea level, he decided to raise the flag as best he could. Approaching the ice barrier in their motor launch at 66° 58' E, the swell made it too dangerous to attempt a landing. So the launch was edged carefully towards one of the islets, where Mawson read the required proclamation and touched the rocky shore with his oar. He then placed the proclamation in a copper cylinder and threw it amongst the boulders onshore. He tossed a wooden plate with a copper inscription after it, only to see it bounce back off the rocks into the sea. A flag and pole were also hurled at the shore but they too fell back into the surging sea.[30]

Although Hurley photographed their efforts, it was not the sort of ceremony envisaged in Mawson's official instructions, and he could hardly claim to have raised the flag on the territory he was purporting to claim for the empire. So a few hours later, he again set off in the *Discovery*'s launch, this time heading towards a rocky red monolith about 300 metres high, which seemed to promise a landing site. It was on a stretch of the coast that Mawson had named Mac. Robertson Land the previous year, but he had been unable then to land upon it. Now, Campbell leaped into the shallow water with the launch's rope, and Mawson, Hurley and several others followed in quick succession. They were not alone, since a place that allowed landing by humans was invariably also suited to penguins and seals. A cacophony of nesting penguins was arrayed up the slopes, while a variety of other birds circled above and a mass of somnolent seals lolled on the narrow, rocky beaches.

Wasting no time, they 'erected flag and repeated taking possession', this time in the customary way, as Mawson later scribbled in his diary. While Hurley captured the scene for posterity, and as Mawson and Campbell collected samples of seaweed and rocks, others made a 'haul of old and young birds – Antarctic Petrel, Snow Petrels, fulmar'. And so, wrote Campbell, 'we established our first valid claim to the newly named "MacRobertson Land" ', with the monolith being named after Prime Minister Scullin. That evening at supper, more cigars were brought out to celebrate their latest territorial acquisition.[31]

A week later, Mawson reached the end of his westward voyage at 61° E. He had almost skirted his way around the entire sector of the Antarctic that Australia was anxious to annex, and for the last ten days he had repeated the voyage he had made the previous year, this time closer to the coast. After reaching the eastern edge of Enderby Land on 18 February 1931, it was time to head for home, but not before Mawson went ashore one more time. The cautious Mackenzie was nervous about taking the *Discovery* too close to the shore, which was protected by a rampart of rocky islets and promised the danger of hidden shoals. Mawson was more concerned by the possibility that the launch might break down during the ten-kilometre trip to the shore and that the *Discovery* might be prevented by a change in the weather from picking them up.

Refusing at first to go closer, the captain only relented when he realised how far the ship still was from the shore; he then carefully nudged his charge into the bay. After using the launch to explore one of the islands – during which time a small Weddell seal was killed for its meat and skin, and a number of Emperor and Adélie penguins were similarly dispatched – Mawson stepped onto the continent for what would be the final time in his life so that he could complete the claiming of what Australians had come to call the 'Commonwealth Sector'. Campbell recorded in his diary how they again 'raised the Flag and went through the usual formalities of possession and opened a bottle of Champagne, poured a little on the ground and had a toast all round. We then had a half hour to spare whilst Hurley climbed up one of the rocky hills to take some photographs.'[32] It is not clear whether Mawson thought that pouring champagne on the ground would add some symbolic significance to the ceremony.

As the *Discovery* headed north, with its sails full and its funnel belching black smoke, Mawson looked wistfully upon the icy shore and rocky mountains that were disappearing astern. This voyage had been very different to his earlier expeditions. There had been no sledging journeys into the unknown, where Mawson and his companions could be tested to the limit of human endurance, just the regular routine of scientific investigation offshore, interspersed with occasional fleeting visits to the land. It was not much to excite a depressed public hungry for uplifting tales of heroism.

In a wireless message for the press as the *Discovery* headed for Hobart, Mawson listed the achievements of his latest voyage as being mostly scientific. Only at the end did he disclose that on 'several occasions during the cruise the flag was flown on these friendly lands', with it being done 'with special ceremony at Cape Denison, Scullin Monolith and Cape Bruce'.[33] Some of the names bestowed by Mawson on geographic features recognised prominent British and Australian politicians, as well as the members of the BANZARE expedition itself. Leo Amery, the British politician who had initiated the Antarctic land grab back in 1919, was acknowledged by having a prominent cape named after him – as thanks for his 'assistance and help in connection with the organisation and despatch' of the expedition.[34] Only time would tell whether the claiming, naming and mapping, along with the two voyages themselves, would be recognised by other nations as being adequate activities to establish a valid title to the massive wedge of territory – comprising forty-two per cent of the entire continent – that Mawson had claimed during his two voyages.

The British government and its representative in Oslo, Charles Wingfield, had been keeping abreast of the activities of both Mawson and the Norwegians, but were unsure how best to keep the Norwegians at bay. They thought that the 'gentlemen's agreement' they had reached with the Norwegian government would see the activities of its explorers restricted to areas that Britain was not interested in claiming. But the Norwegian whalers had continued to explore and sometimes claim areas that lay within the Australian Sector, leaving the British in a bind.

Wingfield advised London in March 1931 that it would be counterproductive to protest 'against mere acts of exploration carried out in the course of a private whaling expedition'. Instead, he recommended, Oslo should be formally advised of Mawson's work and how he had been authorised to confirm 'by definite acts of annexation' the British claims to all the territory between the Ross Dependency and Enderby Land, with the exception of Adélie Land. To pre-empt the Norwegians' objections to Mawson claiming such an extensive territory by merely the raising of flags, they should be told that this had been merely the 'climax' of Mawson's explorations. Wingfield advised that this would be the best way of reminding the Norwegians that 'none of this sector is open to annexation by any other power'. But the British government scotched the idea, since Mawson had done so little to strengthen Britain's existing claims. This did not matter, wrote Wingfield, since the Norwegian whalers were not returning to the Antarctic during the coming season, and the *Norvegia* expeditions, and 'the constant possibility involved of the "occupation" of land by them', had also come to an end for the time being.[35]

To try to get wider recognition of his work, Mawson planned to publish the scientific results in multiple volumes. But the expedition was in debt and he had to appeal to the British government for assistance. The interdepartmental Polar Committee in London agreed that publication should occur as soon as possible, although it doubted 'whether the publication of the records could have any material effect on strengthening the Australian claim in the Antarctic'. And the British government declined to provide any money of its own. The cash-strapped Australian government was hardly better placed to help. Finally, it agreed in 1935 to provide £1000 for five years to publish just 500 copies of the scientific series.[36] The New South Wales government would later provide further funding, in return for Mawson giving its institutions most of the expedition's records and specimens.

These funding problems meant that more than forty years would go by before Mawson's final volume was published. Moreover, the reports would be read only by a few of his fellow scientists. As the Polar Committee observed, their publication was something that had to be done, mainly for prestige purposes, but it could not be expected to convince other nations or an international tribunal of the validity of Britain's territorial claim. Nor would these volumes give the people of the British Empire a sense of ownership over those parts of the Antarctic that Mawson had claimed.

The burden of popularising the expedition's achievements fell to Hurley. His film *Siege of the South* promised to tell 'in story, sound and song an epic of man's glorious struggle with nature in the frozen south'. The poster for the government-sponsored film showed the sun rising over the ice barrier as six men hauled a small boat ashore through the rocks and broken ice. Territorial acquisition rather than science was the prevailing theme, with the poster proclaiming: 'British courage wins a continent for the empire.'

The film itself continued this theme, with the 'friendly' penguins being depicted as willing participants in their dispossession. The script has Mawson and his party arriving at Cape Denison, watched by the 'citizens of King George V Land', who 'greet us with squawks of welcome'. Then they were received by the penguin 'Mayor and his councillors [who were] waiting to confer on us the freedom of the land'. Subsequent scenes have shots of landings further westward, when they are seen approaching 'the wilderness of rock and ice upon which no human foot has ever trod' and later landing 'on the foreshore of a well-sheltered boat harbour that has waited since creation for man's coming'.

Mawson then 'hurries off to find a site on which to raise the flag', and 'the ceremony of taking possession is performed'. As the men pull away in their launch:

> . . . the sight of our flag fluttering from the cairn fills us with satisfaction, and it is with gratification we realize that the expedition has added to the chart over 800 miles of new Antarctic coast line, and collected such a wealth of scientific data as to make the record of the B.A.N.Z.A.R.E. Expedition pre-eminent in polar history.

The curtain closes with the reading of a 'congratulatory telegram from the king' and an 'orchestral playing of God Save the King'.[37] With no mention of Riiser-Larsen, or of any other explorers and whalers who had seen parts of the same coastline, audiences were left with the firm impression that an Australian claim was irrefutable.

It was an impression that the Australian government was keen to promote. In July 1931, Prime Minister Scullin told the new British dominions secretary, Jimmy Thomas, that Mawson had now 'discovered or revisited' most of the sector between 160° E and 45° E, and that 'British sovereignty has been formally proclaimed on five occasions extending over the whole area', except for Adélie Land. No other country had a stronger claim to the sector, argued Scullin, since any discoveries by other nations had occurred so long ago or, in the case of Norway, had been seen off by Mawson.

In fact, as the Australian polar explorer Phillip Law would later concede, Mawson had been preceded in several cases by the Norwegians in his discovery of new land, and had not been very assiduous in mapping the coastline along which the *Discovery* had sailed. Wealth was to be won from the Antarctic in the surrounding seas, and it was these Mawson was most interested in investigating. Often he had kept far out so sea, using the ship's depth sounder to trace the line of the continental shelf and its nets to haul in krill, rather than staying closer to shore to trace the coastline. As a result, large parts of the coastline remained a hypothetical dotted line after he had completed his work.

Law complained that Mawson's mapping results were 'extremely disappointing' and compared poorly with the 'detailed mapping carried out a few years later by the Norwegians'.[38] This was not just a matter of practical assistance with navigation. There was an unspoken competition between nations with territorial ambitions in the Antarctic, with each trying to have their national names dominate the landscape.

The Hydrographic Office of the Admiralty had long had a virtual monopoly on the publication of maritime charts and books of navigation advice – known as *Pilots* – for different parts of the world. This monopoly reflected the worldwide supremacy of Britain's navy, merchant marine and empire. But it was not until the late 1920s that the Admiralty decided to publish a *Pilot* especially for the Antarctic, to advise mariners about the challenges of sailing in Antarctic seas. Until then, only part of the Antarctic had been covered and published in the *South America Pilot*.

The new publication raised immediate problems for the British authorities, who wanted it to be the standard reference work for mariners of all nations. Officials knew that protests would emerge if it used the *Antarctic Pilot* to assert British sovereignty over the disputed regions of the Antarctic, or if it privileged British names over the names of other nations. While Mawson's first voyage was being planned, Richard Casey became so concerned that the publication of the *Antarctic Pilot* would provoke a rush of exploration and rival claims that he argued strongly for it to be delayed until Mawson had completed his voyages and Britain had annexed the Australian quadrant. If Britain were to refuse, then Casey urged 'that all mention of sovereignty over the areas and all historical references should be scrupulously avoided'.

In fact, the Admiralty had been so careful to avoid offence that it had acknowledged French sovereignty over Adélie Land and other places while making no mention of British sovereignty over 'certain territories and islands which were indisputably British'. To Casey's relief, the British officials agreed to publish the first *Antarctic Pilot* in 1930, and that no reference would be made to 'sovereignty, administration or discovery'. Only when Mawson had completed his work and the Australian claim had been secured would a revised *Antarctic Pilot* be issued with all the disputatious references included.[39]

Yet the 1930 edition could not avoid controversy altogether, since any choice of names had implications for sovereignty. Its use of the British name 'Graham Land' for the Antarctic Peninsula, which was part of the British claim to the Falkland Islands Dependencies, thereby strengthened that claim, while at the same time diminishing the American claim, which was based upon the discoveries of early sealers such as Nathaniel Palmer. While the *Antarctic Pilot* noted that most of the Antarctic coastline remained 'very little explored, and largely unknown', it included a brief history of discoveries in the Antarctic, and it was generally the British finds that were privileged. American geographers, in particular, would have been dismayed to see that there was no mention by name of Palmer or other American explorers of the early nineteenth century.[40]

The publication of the *Antarctic Pilot* could not be delayed for long if Britain was to retain its position as mapmaker for the world's mariners. Norwegian whalers had already started to make maps of their own when they found that British ones were not sufficiently comprehensive or accurate for the use of their fleets, which were beginning to work in areas of the Antarctic where British explorers had not ventured. The Whalers' Mutual Insurance Association of Norway compiled their own maps, which were edited by the staff of Lars Christensen's Whaling Museum in Sandefjord.[41] These maps were not only useful but were also the only sure way of ensuring that Norwegian names and discoveries were adequately acknowledged. As Christensen complained in his account of Riiser-Larsen's voyage in the *Norvegia*, Mawson had sailed along the coastline in the wake of the *Norvegia* and had given British names to geographic features that Riiser-Larsen had named just days or weeks earlier. Christensen was particularly chagrined by Mawson's claimed discovery of 'Mac. Robertson Land', part of which had been discovered earlier by Riiser-Larsen and named 'Lars Christensen Land'. In an attempt to defend the Norwegian names, and the 'great and real interests' they represented, Christensen produced a map of all the Antarctic coastline between 20° W and 100° E.[42]

The Norwegian maps were not sufficient to prevent Lars Christensen Land from being included in the vast sector annexed by Australia in 1933. Although Christensen could not convince his government to resist the British and Australian takeover of territory that Norwegians had been first to discover, he could at least take solace that some Norwegian names would be perpetuated on British as well as Norwegian maps. 'In the long run,' wrote Christensen, 'it is of far greater importance than may appear at first sight,' for it acknowledged the priority of Norwegian discovery. The Norwegians would continue to 'cling closely to these Norwegian names on the chart, where, indeed, they have every right to stand'.[43] Although he did not say so, Christensen may well have surmised that the presence of the names, along with the activities of Norwegian whalers, might one day lead to Norway's sovereignty being recognised by an international court.

In fact, some of the Norwegian names had been placed on the maps by Mawson, who acknowledged the work of Riiser-Larsen by naming a tall mountain after him and an ice-covered dome after Lars Christensen. During his 1911 expedition, Mawson had made the mistake of naming a large section of coastline in honour of the American Charles Wilkes. He had also stretched the limits of Adélie Land far beyond the 240 kilometres of coastline that Dumont d'Urville had actually seen. Mawson's gentlemanly genuflection towards his predecessors had annoyed British officials, complicating their attempts to confine – or dismiss altogether – the potential territorial claims of other nations.

During his 1929–31 voyages, which had been driven by political rather than scientific objectives, Mawson had been more conscious of the implications of his naming. He made amends for his early actions by using only British names for the new lands that he claimed to have discovered. Whereas the ill-defined Wilkes Land and Adélie Land had formerly sprawled across a large part of the Australian quadrant, they were now strictly confined, with Mawson adding 'BANZARE Land', 'Sabrina Land', 'Princess Elizabeth Land' and 'Mac. Robertson Land'. He also stretched the limits of Enderby Land. On British and Australian maps, at least, the sector that Australia wanted to annex was now dominated by British names.[44]

With several rival maps of the Antarctic seeking to be regarded as the standard work, calls began to emerge for the naming of geographic features to be done according to agreed international principles. When Mawson's report of his expeditions was read to a meeting of the Royal Geographical Society in March 1932, the British geographer and historian Hugh Robert Mill criticised the tendency of explorers to scatter as many names as possible on the landscape so as to crowd out the names of their rivals. He suggested that explorers should have to submit names to an international scientific body, which would lay out general principles on the naming of places and adjudicate any disputes. He was particularly concerned that names should 'fall pleasantly on the ear like Enderby Land, Mount Erebus and Cape Goodenough', which were all good

English names and 'not like certain cacophonous ejaculations which have been cast forth during some recent explorations'.[45] Of course, names that fell pleasantly on an English ear might well jar when heard by a Norwegian. Clearly, there was no easy answer to the problem of deciding on internationally acceptable names in the Antarctic, particularly as the outcome could be crucial in deciding wider questions of sovereignty. Even Mill, who had purported to be nonpartisan, could not help but be Anglo-centric in his comments.

The expeditions of Byrd and Mawson, and the activities of the whalers, saw hundreds of names applied to maps of the Antarctic; sometimes there was more than one name for the same geographic feature. In other places, names were applied to features of no consequence, simply in order to have as many names as possible of a certain nationality, or to have as many expedition members and supporters as possible memorialised. When the secretary of the Royal Geographical Society, Arthur Hinks, took up Mill's suggestion and proposed general principles to guide cartographers and explorers in their naming of places, national considerations still came to the fore.

A memorandum by Hinks was discussed by the British government's Polar Committee in October 1933, with the Admiralty's hydrographer, Captain Edgell, complaining to his colleagues about the large number of names Byrd had used on a map of his expedition's work that was published by the American Geographical Society. The names were either on territory already claimed by Britain – the Ross Dependency – or in the area to the east of the Ross Dependency, which Britain wanted to claim. Rather than accepting the names, when Edgell compiled a new Admiralty chart he omitted about seventy-five per cent of the American names, in order to ensure there were opportunities for British names to be applied in those areas by subsequent explorers.

Hinks suggested that the British position might also be strengthened by a stipulation that the final decision on naming should rest not with the explorer but with the 'administrative authority over the areas concerned'. In other words, Britain would have the authority to decide on names throughout the two-thirds of the continent that it had annexed. Explorers were also to be told that they should avoid using names that were not British. Moreover, names announced by radio from the Antarctic – as Byrd had done – would not be accepted. It was publication that was important to the British, preferably in a respectable geographical journal rather than a mere newspaper.[46] Despite these attempts at rational resolution, there would be decades of dispute about names and naming between the rival territorial claimants.

While Norway had refrained from formally claiming the territories its whalers had discovered and named, Britain had no qualms about pressing ahead with its long-term ambition of controlling most of the continent. In February 1933, Britain added a huge swathe of territory to its existing Antarctic holdings when the king issued an order in council that annexed the sector that lay between 45° E and 160° E, other than Adélie Land. The administration of the sector was vested in the Australian government on behalf of the British Empire.

A few months later, legislation was introduced in the Australian parliament to create the 'Australian Antarctic Territory'. In opening the debate on 26 May, Attorney-General John Latham of the United Australia Party provided members of parliament with maps of the territory, on which were marked the major geographic features, some of which had names that the Norwegians had given them. The government was conscious of the exploration work that had been done by Riiser-Larsen and other Norwegians, and of the protests that were likely to come from Oslo when the territory explored and claimed by their whalers was snatched away by Australia. Keeping some of the Norwegian names – thereby acknowledging 'the association of these intrepid Norwegian sailors with this area' – was a means of appeasing Norwegian anger while at the same time declaring that the discovery of the sector was largely due to Australian enterprise.

Albert Green, a Labor representative for the rich goldmining district of Kalgoorlie, in Western Australia, offered cross-party support, agreeing that 'the land has come to us, not by right of conquest, but by right of discovery'. Richard Casey was there to lend his support, having returned from London and been elected to parliament. Having been closely involved in organising support for both Wilkins and Mawson, he now declared that the takeover of the sector was not a sudden land grab but 'the culminating point of twenty years of continuous and concerted effort on the part of Australians to consolidate their interests in the Antarctic'. At the same time, he was careful to assure the Norwegians that their interests would not suffer because of the British annexation.[47] In reality,

Australia was out to undermine the Norwegian dominance of the whaling industry.

Albert Green was one of several MPs who argued that the takeover of the territory would encourage Australians to re-engage with the whaling industry. It would 'develop in them that bold and adventurous maritime spirit which has for so many centuries characterized the people of Great Britain'. Latham was more conscious of Norwegian sensitivities and consequently more circumspect about lauding the riches to be gained from whaling. Although he acknowledged its 'considerable actual and potential economic importance', he concentrated mainly on the possibility of gold and other mineral discoveries, as well as the value of seasonal weather forecasts that Antarctic weather stations might provide for Australia.

Latham also spoke of the need to bring the unbridled killing of whales under control before their stocks were 'totally destroyed'. He pointed to the massive increase in the whale slaughter: in the summer of 1919–20 some 11,369 whales had been killed, while in the summer of 1930–31 more than 40,000 whales were slaughtered; the price of whale oil had plummeted from £80 to just £13 a ton. With forty-three factory ships, six shore stations, 232 whale-catchers and ten transport ships operating that year, the frenzied killing of whales had to be curbed so the industry could become sustainable. Although an international whaling convention had been agreed to by the League of Nations in 1931, it was not yet in force and would in any case need interested nations to enforce its provisions.[48]

There were only a few voices raised in opposition. The maverick Labor MP Dr William Maloney feared that Asian nations, some of which had already described Australia as 'a vacant land', would be emboldened to make an even 'stronger claim to this country if we add to our territory an area equal to that of Western Australia'. Rather than Australia administering the sector, Maloney suggested that the League of Nations should take control so that the people of Asia would have no justification to accuse Australia of 'greed for additional territory'. This would have been a good way of avoiding future territorial disputes, but the claimant nations in the Antarctic, let alone the Australian parliament, were not yet ready to consider such a suggestion. When the bill reached the Senate, one senator questioned how the mere fact of Australian administration could prevent the extermination of whales. Instead, he predicted, the annexation would complicate Australia's relations with other nations, particularly the United States and Norway.

Despite these prescient arguments, Latham's promise that the territorial takeover would not cost Australia a penny – at least in the short term – was sufficient to convince the parliament of its merits.[49] Australia, which already had territory in New Guinea, now had an empire that stretched from the equator to the South Pole, although it would take another three years before the creation of the Australian Antarctic Territory was formally promulgated on 24 August 1936.[50] As some had warned, its creation only intensified the rivalry in the Antarctic.

Although Britain and Norway had implicitly agreed to claim separate sectors, Christensen still wanted to control the entire coast-line that he and his whalers had explored. There was a pressing financial imperative for him to do so. As he openly admitted, all his actions had been 'based on one special motive: we were out to get whales'. And with international moves to regulate the killing of whales, Christensen asserted his 'right to carry on whaling', particularly in those areas that his ships had explored, which included the newly created Australian Antarctic Territory.

He complained that the Australian move 'supersedes those natural rights which we have won for ourselves through the whaling industry'. While it was 'perfectly natural' for Australia and New Zealand to desire the ownership of the Antarctic coastline that lay closest to their shores, Norway was 'more closely bound up with it', both in a commercial and a practical sense. With Lars Christensen Land having been 'entirely engulfed' by the Australian Antarctic Territory, Christensen bemoaned the fact that there was 'not much left to us of all our discoveries'. By this, he meant not just his own discoveries but the discoveries of his fellow countrymen, going back to Roald Amundsen, Henrik Bull and Carl Larsen.

Rather than accepting just the sector to which Britain wanted to restrict Norway, Christensen called on the Norwegian govern-ment to claim all of what he called 'the Norwegian mainland', which included the sector from 50° E to 15° W (from Coats Land to Enderby Land), the sector from 60° E to 75° E (Lars Christensen Land/Mac. Robertson Land) and the sector near Peter I Land from 80° W to 100° W (Ellsworth Land). Together, these sectors comprised more than one-third of the continent.[51]

The competition between Mawson and Christensen, and between their respective countries, was a precursor to a much more intensive struggle for supremacy in the Antarctic. The whalers had swamped the world's whale oil market in 1931, causing whaling companies to keep their fleets at home and to permanently close some of their shore stations. But they returned to the Antarctic as the glut of whale oil was gradually run down and prices began to recover.

This time, it was not just the Norwegians and British who were turning their attention southward. As international relations deteriorated during the 1930s and the threat of another world war loomed large, Germany and Japan began to look to the Antarctic to secure vital supplies of animal fats for food, and glycerine for explosives. The United States government also began to take a much closer interest, mainly due to the strategic importance of the Drake Passage, which provided a vital maritime link between the Atlantic and Pacific Oceans.

The British dream of having the Antarctic and its riches all to itself was becoming more distant than ever, as the competition for control of the region took a new and more dangerous turn.

English explorer
Captain James
Cook proved
that the fabled
Great South Land
did not exist.
(National Library
of Australia)

The first explorer to
sight the Antarctic
continent was
Captain Gottlieb
von Bellingshausen.
(Bridgeman Art Library)

Edmund Fanning's *Voyages Round the World* shows sealers killing their helpless prey. (Alexander Turnbull Library, ref. no. PUBL-0138-354)

Clambering onto a rocky islet, sailors from d'Urville's expedition take possession of Adélie Land in the name of France. (National Library of Australia)

James Clark Ross reaches the farthest south in the *Erebus* and the *Terror* only to be confronted by the ice barrier that will later bear his name. A whale can be seen blowing in the foreground. (Linda Hall Library of Science, Engineering & Technology)

C.E.Borchgrevink

The beginning of the so-called "Heroic Age"? Carsten Borchgrevink poses in this studio shot for popular consumption. (State Library of Victoria)

A massive Union Jack given to Borchgrevink by the Duke of York is raised next to the hut at Cape Adare. Hundreds of smaller flags were given by patron George Newnes to be spread across the surrounding region. (Norwegian Polar Institute)

An aerial photograph taken from a tethered balloon shows Erich von Drygalski's ice-bound ship, *Gauss*. (National Oceanic and Atmospheric Administration/Department of Commerce)

Scott and his disappointed companions fly the British flag at the South Pole. Despite their defeat by Amundsen, the British government still claimed ownership of the polar plateau. (Mawson Centre, South Australia Museum)

Australian explorer Douglas Mawson poses on the stern of the *Aurora*. He was the first explorer to make claiming Antarctica the primary purpose of an expedition. (Mawson Centre, South Australia Museum)

When Mawson's plan to explore by air was thwarted, he converted the crashed plane into an "air tractor" so that it might still excite public interest. (New South Wales State Library)

Photographer Frank Hurley, shown here during Mawson's first expedition, accompanied three expeditions to the Antarctic. His photographs and films popularized the Antarctic and helped the British and Australians develop a sense of ownership over it. (New South Wales State Library)

Members of the Japanese
expedition photographed
aboard the *Kainan Maru*.
(Alexander Turnbull Library, ref.
no. PAColl-6304-44)

Ernest Shackleton found fame
despite a succession of failures.
Lucrative lecture tours helped
to pay the bills, but Shackleton
and other explorers were often
left deeply in debt by their
expeditions. (US Navy Military-
Sealift Command)

A tickertape parade along New York's Broadway greeted Admiral Richard E. Byrd on his return from the Antarctic. (Library of Congress; Washington, D.C.)

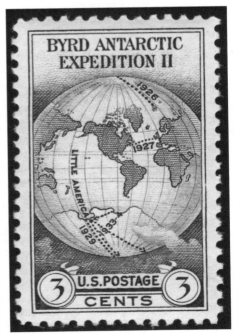

Stamps such as this, and the naming of "Little America," were used to establish a sense of American ownership over Antarctica. (Smithsonian National Postal Museum)

After the Norvegia expedition reached Enderby Land in December 1929, Finn Lützow-Helm went ashore to fly a silk flag provided by the Norwegian king and queen. On returning home, he declared that "Enderby [Land] is Norwegian." (Norwegian Polar Institute)

Douglas Mawson and Campbell Stuart are lifted from the *Discovery* in their Gypsy Moth plane to make a flight over Enderby Land. Aircraft allowed large areas of the Antarctic to be explored quickly and claimed from the air. (National Library of Australia)

In February 1935, Caroline Mikkelsen, the first woman in Antarctica, watches the Norwegian flag being raised to claim Ingrid Christensen Land. (Norwegian Polar Institute)

A large crowd gathers on the Hobart dock to gawk at the Norwegian-registered *Wyatt Earp*. While American explorer Lincoln Ellsworth claimed part of Antarctica for the United States, his Australian deputy Hubert Wilkins did likewise on behalf of Australia. (Photo courtesy Australian Antarctic Division)

Lincoln Ellsworth (left) and Hubert Wilkins pose with pilot Bernt Balchen in the early 1930s prior to attempting a flight across Antarctica. (Ohio State University)

A Nazi flag is displayed on the Antarctic ice to claim Neuschwabenland for Germany. (Scientific Committee on Antarctic Research, Scott Polar Research Institute)

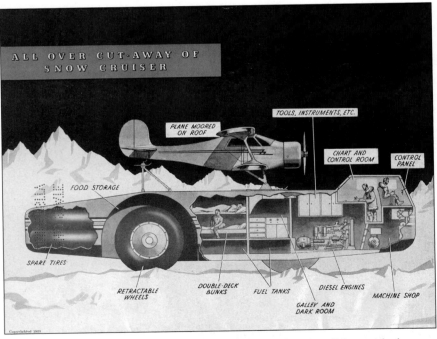

Byrd's ill-fated snow cruiser was meant to provide his expedition with the capacity to explore and claim the entire continent for the United States. (Schreiber, *The Snow Cruiser* [Chicago, Armour Institute of Technology, c 1939])

New Zealand found that its sovereignty had been effectively expunged by the huge American base at McMurdo Sound. (US Antarctic Program Photo Library)

These hapless penguins were stuffed and used as bowling pins in a makeshift bowling alley at the McMurdo base. (US Antarctic Program Photo Library)

The Australian post office on Heard Island. Post offices were used by several nations as a means of exercising authority over territory. (National Archives of Australia: A1200, L10025)

The icebreaker *USS Staten Island* carves a channel through McMurdo Sound. (US Antarctic Program Photo Library)

A Russian Orthodox church erected in 2002 on the hill overlooking the Russian base on King George Island. The building could be used to reinforce any claim that Russia might care to make to the island, where several other nations also have bases. (University of North Carolina Wilmington)

Anything goes in Antarctica. From mountain climbing to marathons, amateur athletes combine their favourite sport with adventure. (© Michael Walsh/Capella)

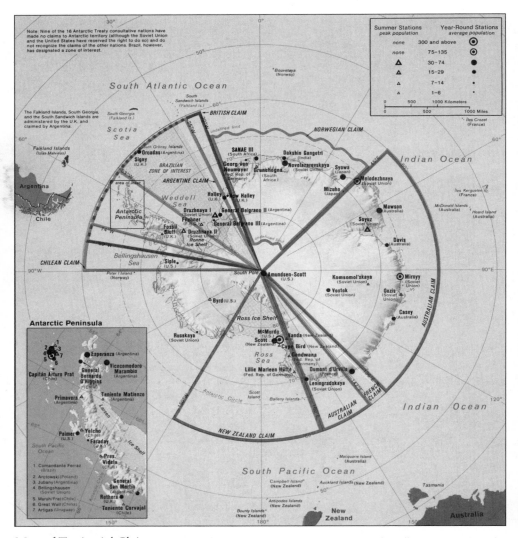

Map of Territorial Claims. (Library of Congress; Washington, D.C.: Central Intelligence Agency, 1986)

CHAPTER 13

'The last unclaimed territory in the world'

1934–1936

The effects of human activity had long been felt in the Antarctic, carried there by the winds and deposited in layers on the ice. For centuries, the effects were imperceptible and inconsequential. Sealers in the early nineteenth century could still look with wonder on what appeared to be an untouched wilderness when they splashed ashore onto the Antarctic's offshore islands, and then quickly wiped out much of the wildlife. A century later, hundreds of whaling ships went south to harpoon whales in their tens of thousands. The annual return of the factory ships and their tankers, laden down with ever greater cargoes of oil, prompted dire predictions that whales would be exterminated. The calls for the slaughter to abate went largely unanswered as other nations took up their own harpoons. By the mid-1930s, there was a renewed frenzy of killing in Antarctic seas as whalers returned in even greater numbers, accompanied by explorers who regarded the Antarctic as their own. Foremost among these was the American Richard Byrd.

Byrd had returned from Antarctica in June 1930, receiving the usual popular ballyhoo in the streets of New York, Boston and Washington. President Hoover had presented him with the gold medal of the American Geographical Society, then Byrd was taken up the Hudson River by destroyer to Albany, where he was given another medal by his old friend and state governor Franklin Delano Roosevelt, who was already positioning himself for the coming presidential race. There was also a celebratory, men-only dinner with 200 of his benefactors and supporters, at New York's Biltmore Hotel, where Byrd's expedition headquarters had been located. Adolph Ochs, the publisher of the *New York Times*, told the tuxedoed diners that Byrd was 'the hero of the American boy, on a par with the greatest of ancient heroes'.

And Byrd was able to talk directly to boys across the nation when he did a radio talk and three lectures to schoolchildren on NBC radio. The lectures were sponsored by the Tidewater Oil Company, which had provided fuel for his expedition.[1] American children were also taken by their parents to see the travelling Antarctic exhibition organised aboard the expedition ship *City of New York*, and to see the 100-metre-wide cyclorama of Little America that was constructed at Coney Island. It even had a model radio mast emitting a blue spark, and a model of the *Floyd Bennett* suspended in front of mock glaciers. According to a spokesman for Byrd, the story of the expedition had 'become one of the most popular topics of discussion in current events classes, in Sunday schools, young people's clubs and high schools'.[2]

All the tickertape and the patriotic headlines provided a welcome distraction from the depression that was tightening its grip on the nation, and on Byrd himself. Despite the media attention, his lectures were not drawing the usual audiences; some had to be cancelled for want of numbers. People had become tight with their pennies, let alone their dollars. Byrd confided to his lecture agent in December 1931 that at least half of his friends were 'in terrible straits and in one way or another I have come to their assistance'.[3] Not that he had a great ability to help after the stock market crash destroyed $180,000 of his savings.[4] The expedition remained $100,000 in debt, while the financial returns from the Paramount film had been disappointing.[5] Ever the trooper, Byrd pressed ahead with his lectures, often in half-filled halls, and completed his book-length account of the expedition, which was titled *Little America*. But it too had disappointing sales.

Some thought Byrd had achieved all there was to be achieved at both the North and South Poles, and that the only remaining challenge was to explore the newly discovered planet Pluto. But Byrd was adamant that there was 'much exploration yet to be accomplished in the world', predicting that 'some hitherto unsuspected sources of power' might be developed in the Antarctic.[6] That might have been an alluring prospect in prosperous times, but during the Depression people were much more hard-headed. It was difficult for Byrd to see where funds for a new expedition might be sought.

For a time in 1931, he was preoccupied with politics. The presidential race raised the possibility that his brother Harry, the influential governor of Virginia, might capture the Democratic nomination. Despite his friendship with Roosevelt, Byrd encouraged Harry to try for the nomination, offering to draw on his own powerful friendships and organisational links to help him.[7] However, as Roosevelt's political steamroller gathered momentum, Byrd began to hedge his bets by assuring Eleanor Roosevelt how much he and Harry were devoted to FDR, and suggesting to Harry that he might settle instead on being Roosevelt's vice president or treasury secretary.[8] Having his brother in either position would be helpful to Byrd in achieving his aim of returning to the Antarctic.

That had been Byrd's goal ever since his arrival in New York, when he had talked of the great areas of the Antarctic that were still waiting to be explored. He had only explored about 325,000 square kilometres of a continent that was about as big as the United States and Mexico combined, and which would later be measured at just over 14 million square kilometres. That comparison was deliberately designed by Byrd to make it easy for American audiences to comprehend the scale of the Antarctic. He also drew upon familiar metaphors that were designed to appeal particularly to Americans, when he told a nationwide radio audience that the Antarctic was 'the world's last frontier'.[9] The idea of the frontier, ever moving westward, had played an important part in the nation's foundation story and was one of the central motifs in American identity. By pointing to a new frontier, with the snow-covered settlement of Little America and his pioneering expedition at its core, Byrd was trying, whether consciously or not, to enlist the public in a project to make the Antarctic part of the ongoing foundation story of the modern American nation. Yet while the original American frontier remained powerful in the public imagination, the attraction of the Antarctic was not so clear.

Whereas the British and Norwegians had incorporated Antarctic exploration into their national stories, and had lucrative whaling industries to ensure their continuing participation in such exploration, the Americans had long ago lost their whaling industry. Indeed, until Byrd's expedition they had abandoned any interest in Antarctic exploration. While the Norwegians and British were more interested in the surrounding seas and their rich resources than in the apparent wasteland of the frozen land mass, Byrd's focus was very much on the continent. As an aviator, it was necessarily there that his heroic feats had to be played out. But how was he to interest the American public, and his business and government supporters, in financing a new expedition, when his previous one had already 'conquered' the South Pole by aircraft?

Byrd pointed to the great geographical question that remained to be answered: whether the Antarctic was one land mass or two lands divided by a sea or channel that connected the Ross and Weddell Seas. Wilkins had suggested the latter after his flight in 1928, but it remained to be confirmed. There was also the possibility that riches might be concealed beneath the ice. It was a traditional ploy of explorers over the centuries to hold out the allure of great wealth, if only they were given the means to discover it. Byrd told reporters in New York of the geological findings made by Gould, which indicated 'great coal deposits of commercial significance'.[10] Gould, who had become besotted by the Antarctic and was desperate to return, did likewise when accepting his American Geographical Society medal during a ceremony at New York's Explorers' Club, assuring the audience that there 'must be a coal field covering some hundreds of thousands of square miles in the Antarctic'.[11]

In February 1931, as Mawson was frantically raising the Union Jack wherever he could, Byrd's lecture tour took him to Detroit and the National Education Convention. There, a massed choir of 850 schoolchildren entertained the thousands of delegates before Byrd was presented with bound volumes of tributes from the nation's schoolchildren. The convention president told the delegates, and the much larger radio audience, that the children regarded Byrd as greater than Columbus, with his polar expeditions having 'enthralled their very souls'. Dr Gilbert Grosvenor of the National Geographic Society, one of Byrd's principal supporters, described how Byrd had 'carried the American flag 1,500 miles further south than it had ever penetrated before' and had established a village lit by electricity and lived in it for fourteen months.[12] Grosvenor's description of Byrd's exploration and occupation precisely met the conditions required by international law for sovereignty over new lands to be recognised. And there were Americans prepared to support Byrd in extending that sovereignty even further than his previous expedition had done.

While in Detroit, Byrd lunched with Edsel Ford, the car magnate and his long-time financial supporter. He had provided Byrd with aircraft for some of his historic flights, along with a Ford 'snowmobile' that had broken down soon after being landed on the ice during the 1928–30 expedition. It was following his lunch with

Ford that Byrd, with renewed determination, pressed ahead to make practical preparations for another expedition. As the train took him on to Nashville for more lectures, and with his coffers apparently replenished, he wrote to Bowman for advice on where he might get a ship that was 'large enough to house and transport the whole expedition' so that he would not again have to rely on two smaller and inadequate ships. He also wanted to know the exact places where Mawson and Riiser-Larsen had discovered land during their previous year's expeditions.[13]

Bowman was unable to provide advice on a suitable ship, but he did send Byrd all the material relating to the discoveries of his rivals.[14] As a politically minded geographer, Bowman was more interested in getting Byrd to complete his own discoveries of the previous year by having them quickly immortalised in maps and articles. In particular, he pressed Byrd to provide an article for the American Geographical Society's journal about the flight that had been made – at Bowman's own suggestion – along the coast of Marie Byrd Land. 'That in many ways is a flight of special importance,' wrote Bowman, since it would establish an American claim to that whole area.

He also sent Byrd copies of a new map of the Ross Sea region, which included names that had been proposed by Gould during his ground expedition along the base of the Queen Maud Mountains. Bowman urged Byrd to 'systematically complete the naming of all of the many features still unnamed' so that the American Geographical Society could then 'reissue the map as the definitive edition of that region' and send it to the '80 geographical societies of the world and other institutions and individuals with geographical interests'.[15] Bowman had prepared an edition of the map in 1928, in the wake of Wilkins' flight. About 15,000 copies, along with an explanatory booklet, were sent to schools and colleges across America. He estimated that five to ten million people would examine the maps. The cost of the exercise had been paid for by Hearst, whose name was immortalised in Antarctica's Hearst Land. As news of Byrd's flights had been received, the *Detroit News* noted how recipients of the maps could see them 'as a living thing, coast lines and relief changing with each new radio report'.[16] What Americans would also see was the gradual spread of the Stars and Stripes across the continent.

By February 1932, a year after Byrd's lunch in Detroit with Edsel Ford, he was able to announce to a dinner of the Explorers' Club in New York that he had a ship lined up for his next expedition. Thirty-five tons of supplies were being stored at Boston's naval yard. He also had a program that combined a semblance of science with a feat designed to capture the public imagination and ensure funding from media companies. He planned to establish an outlying base near the Queen Maud Mountains, where he would spend a lonely winter making scientific observations, while the remainder of his team would reoccupy Little America.

This would mimic a feat that had been achieved the previous year by a British expedition to Greenland led by Henry 'Gino' Watkins. It had investigated weather conditions for a possible polar air route and had established a base atop the Greenland icecap, where an observer had spent five months alone taking regular meteorological observations. Its success had excited much public interest, which Byrd was now keen to emulate. Byrd said that he wanted to confirm whether or not there was a channel connecting the Ross and Weddell Seas, and also to explore more of Marie Byrd Land. But he could not yet confirm when he would leave on his next expedition, suggesting that he would first have to publish the scientific results of his first expedition.[17]

The idea of spending a lonely vigil in the Antarctic interior was not part of the program that Bowman had recommended. The geographer was keen to build on the achievements of the previous expedition by exploring and claiming Marie Byrd Land for the United States. In particular, he urged that a flight be made across territory that 'lies in the unclaimed sector between 80° and 150°W' so that 'the land within it could be claimed for the United States'. Byrd's previous expedition had barely penetrated the western edge of the enormous slice of unclaimed territory that lay between the Ross Dependency and the Falkland Islands Dependencies. Moreover, his previous flights had suffered for want of ground control points. Spectacular aerial photographs had helped to sell newspapers, but the task of compiling accurate maps from the photographs was impossible without such control points that would help to fix the location and height of geographical features. And Bowman was acutely aware that accurate maps were a desideratum for a strong territorial claim.[18]

After making his Antarctic announcement in February 1932, Byrd was distracted by a more pressing mission, as political debates raged in the United States about how to drag the country from depression and balance the government's budget. With his public profile and powerful business and political connections, Byrd was enlisted by business interests to argue the case for government spending cuts after Congress had called for a $2 billion bonus for war veterans. Controversially, though, he focused only on slashing benefits for veterans. In July, Byrd was made the temporary chairman of a newly formed lobby group, the National Economy League, and announced that he was postponing his Antarctic expedition indefinitely. Instead of going south, he would remain and 'lead the fight against governmental extravagance just as he would have felt impelled to remain in case of war'. He told Bowman that he would stay 'until this job is finished'. With the presidential election campaign in full swing, the National Economy League's arguments came to dominate the campaign, as Byrd called for twenty million Americans to join 'a peaceful army of constructive protest'. He ended up recruiting 60,000 members. By October, he was giving three or four talks a day as he fought to 'save this country from disaster from radicalism', enthusing to Bowman that he was 'thinking of nothing else – morning, noon and night'.[19]

Even after his friend Franklin Roosevelt was elected president in November 1932, Byrd continued his single-minded and controversial campaign against government support for veterans. The campaign was affecting his popularity, however, and he found that the door of the White House was shut to him; Roosevelt feared upsetting the veterans. Drunk on demagoguery, or just plain drunk, Byrd wrote to his brother Harry in January 1933 that 'Franklin can go to blazes. If he wants to see me from now on, he will have to send for me.' Byrd saw himself as being on a crusade of national salvation from which there could be no retreat. The thrill of the tickertape parade had been replaced by the heady addiction of partisan adulation and the wielding of political power.[20]

There is no telling where this might have led, had Byrd's more astute brother not suddenly changed tack and urged him to abandon his tub-thumping. Harry Byrd had entertained ideas of capturing the Democratic presidential nomination but was forced to be content with watching Roosevelt capture both the nomination and the presidency. After stepping down as governor of Virginia, Byrd became a senator in March 1933. In that position, it was important for him to have a good relationship with the president and his fellow Democrats, and not have his brother endanger his political position by calling for cuts to veteran benefits. So he called on Byrd to abandon his pension-cutting campaign and swing the National Economy League in behind Roosevelt. He also warned his brother that people were 'saying that you are representing the big interests of the country, and that Ford and Rockefeller financed your past expeditions and have promised to finance future ones, and you are doing this service in return for what they have done for you'. The choice was clear: Byrd could be a popular hero or a partisan political figure. He could not be both.[21]

Harry's sage advice caused Byrd to beat a hasty retreat. Not wanting to admit his error, Byrd told Bowman in April 1933 that he was planning to resign as chairman of the National Economy League, but only because its objectives 'have been realized one hundred percent'. After campaigning across the country for nine months, he was turning his back on domestic politics and was now 'head over heels' in preparing for his second Antarctic expedition. It was the politics of the Antarctic that now consumed him. Byrd told Bowman that he would be visiting Roosevelt to 'see what he thinks of the Antarctic'. He was also 'extremely anxious' to talk with Bowman 'about some of the unknown areas down there', and wanted particularly to discover whether there was 'a connection between Marie Byrd Land and the rest of the continent', towards the Weddell Sea and the South Pole.

But that was not what most interested Bowman. The geographer still wanted Byrd to concentrate instead on continuing his exploration of the unknown lands east of the Ross Dependency. Bowman reminded Byrd of their previous agreement on making 'a flight that continues your so-called easterly flight still farther eastward'. Filling in the blank space on the map that lay between Marie Byrd Land and Hearst Land would be 'a discovery of the first importance'. Again he stressed the importance of Byrd linking these lands to the coastline, since the Antarctic coast was the starting point of all territorial claims under the sector system, which allowed nations to claim all the land from a discovered coastline to the South Pole.[22]

As he pressed on with his preparations for an early October departure, Byrd was faced with competition from a more nimble American expedition led by the millionaire explorer Lincoln Ellsworth, who had teamed up with Byrd's former aviator Bernt Balchen. There were also two British expeditions being planned, with each seeking government funding and the support of the Royal Geographical Society.

The first proposal was from a young lieutenant of the Royal Naval Volunteer Reserve, J. H. Martin, who was questioned by the secret interdepartmental Polar Committee on 5 October 1933. Martin told the committee, which was chaired by Sir Harry Batterbee of the Dominions Office, that he wanted to go south in 1934 'to claim for the British Empire land hitherto unclaimed or to substantiate existing British claims'. Since the government had effectively ceded the wedge of territory west of 45° E to the Norwegians, the only unclaimed territory was that which lay between the Ross Dependency and the Falkland Islands Dependencies – the same territory Byrd was intent on claiming. The prospect of British and American expeditions competing for the same territory alarmed the Foreign Office, which believed that 'enough Antarctic territory had for the present been claimed as British, and it might be better to consolidate control in areas already claimed'. With more than two-thirds of the continent now claimed by the British Empire, it was feared that a further British claim that shut the Americans out of the Pacific quadrant might provoke Washington into challenging the existing British claims. The committee suggested that Martin focus instead on the Australian sector and complete the work begun by Mawson. But the budding explorer was adamant that he wanted to explore the blank, unclaimed spaces east of the Ross Dependency, where greater glory waited to be won.[23]

Martin's relative inexperience saw him passed over for funding in favour of the Australian polar explorer and pilot, John Rymill, who had been on Gino Watkins' second expedition to Greenland, during which Watkins had disappeared from his kayak while hunting for seals. The lanky and dyslexic Rymill had taken over command and now wanted to lead a small expedition, originally planned by Watkins, in exploring the southernmost parts of the Falkland Islands Dependencies. With a grant of just £10,000 from the Colonial Office, the 'British Graham Land Expedition' would reinforce the existing British claim rather than intrude into territory that Byrd wanted for the United States.

Using a small Breton fishing boat, the *Penola*, and with Martin signing on as first mate, the three-year expedition set out in 1934 to make an intensive geographic and geological survey of Graham Land, and study its marine and bird life. Living largely off seal meat – some 550 seals were killed during the expedition – the nine men of Rymill's land-based party included a biologist, a geologist and glaciologist, and the ornithologist Brian Roberts, who would later play an important role in buttressing Britain's Antarctic claims. Although Rymill took a small biplane for reconnaissance purposes, most of the exploring was done with dog sledges.[24]

Tormented during the first year by poor weather and mechanical problems with the *Penola*, Rymill had more luck the second year. The team left their base on Marguerite Bay and picked their way carefully through uncharted seas towards the southern reaches of Graham Land. Only now was it discovered that Bellingshausen's Alexander I Land was actually an island; it was separated from Graham Land by a 400-kilometre frozen strait. Rymill's painstaking survey also disproved the existence of a channel connecting the Weddell and Ross Seas. It was yet more proof that Antarctica was a single continent, and that Graham Land was part of a large peninsula and not an archipelago.

More discoveries might have been made if a sledge journey across the mountainous spine of Graham Land to the Weddell Sea had not been brought to an early end when Rymill ran low on food. Nevertheless, his expedition had brought greater definition to the map of Graham Land, solved some of its major puzzles and attached countless British names to its geographic features. It was a good return for the paltry amount of money that Britain had spent on the expedition, which had reinforced Britain's claim to the Falkland Islands Dependencies while staying carefully clear of the territory further west.[25]

Nevertheless, there still would be a race between Byrd and his rivals, as it appeared that Byrd's laborious preparations and weighty expedition might be overshadowed by the wealthy Ellsworth and his experienced polar pilot. Ellsworth had inherited great wealth and lavish homes in Italy and Switzerland from his coalmining father, but his closest connection was with the American West and the Ohio home of his pioneer grandparents, from whom he had inherited his 'love of the open frontier'. After growing up in Chicago under the strict tutelage of his widowed father, he had left university in 1899 'to become an axeman in the very first survey party sent out to explore a transcontinental route for a railway across Canada', as he later told a journalist. This was a time when there were still immigrants 'making their way in the wilderness by means of covered wagons'. Ellsworth wistfully recalled how he 'lived a wild, free life, blazing the way for civilization. Before us went the prospector; behind us followed the settler. The story is always the same. First discovery, then exploration, then exploitation.' For Ellsworth, the Antarctic represented one of the world's last frontiers, an untamed place where men could be men and women would be absent. As he told the *Boy's Life* magazine, exploration was 'a school for manliness'.[26]

Having been weak as a child, Ellsworth became obsessed with physical fitness. When not living in New York, he kept to a rigid routine of walking precisely eighteen miles a day. When he was in New York he would maintain his fitness by sparring with a professional wrestler for an hour a day. His heroes included the Western lawman Wyatt Earp, who had helped bring order to the American frontier and whose memorabilia Ellsworth collected. According to Ellsworth, Earp 'represented the exact combination of breeding and human experience which laid the foundation of the Western empire'. Now Ellsworth would help lay the foundation for a possible American empire in the south.

Another of his heroes was the empire-building president Teddy Roosevelt, whose largely confected book *Ranch Life and the Hunting Trail*, first published in 1896, had entranced Ellsworth during his childhood. And finally there was Roald Amundsen, who had accompanied Ellsworth and Riiser-Larsen on his 1925 Arctic expedition by aircraft and in 1926 by airship. Amundsen had disappeared without trace in 1928, during an Arctic rescue flight. Ellsworth, who had attended the memorial service for Scott in 1913 in London, described how exploration had been Amundsen's 'work, his ambition, his calling, his recreation, his life, his death', and how the Norwegian regarded trailblazing through unknown lands 'as a romantic epic'. This was how Ellsworth approached the organisation of his Antarctic expedition.[27]

For Ellsworth, it was all about geographic discovery. He had the means to buy a purpose-built aircraft, a Northrop all-metal, low-winged monoplane that he named the *Polar Star*, and to recruit the best pilots to fly it. There would be little science involved in Ellsworth's expedition, which was centred on a single trans-Antarctic flight from the Weddell Sea to Byrd's abandoned base on the Ross Sea. The only science would be some meteorological observations and geology conducted by the support party, led by

Byrd's former deputy Laurence Gould, who would wait at Little America for Ellsworth to complete his continental crossing. The expedition could thereby be portrayed as playing America's part in the program of the Second International Polar Year, scheduled for 1932–33.

Whereas Byrd had flown to the South Pole and back from the Ross Sea in 1928, Ellsworth would fly clear across the continent. It was perhaps the last remaining Antarctic feat guaranteed to achieve headlines and fame. Like Byrd, he had advice and assistance from the American Geographical Society's Isaiah Bowman. It was Bowman who sent a cable on Ellsworth's behalf to the Norwegian whaler Lars Christensen in May 1931, proposing that it be a joint American–Norwegian effort and that Christensen charter him the *Norvegia* and allow the experienced Lützow-Holm or Riiser-Larsen to pilot his plane. Ellsworth was even prepared to call it the 'Ellsworth American Norwegian Antarctic Expedition'. But the Norwegian whalers were not going south in 1931–32, due to the Depression-induced glut of whale oil in the market, and there was no guarantee that they would return the following year. Riiser-Larsen had suggested to Ellsworth that he take Eskimo men and women and their dogs, but that hardly accorded with Ellsworth's heroic and racialised vision of a 'romantic epic'.[28]

It was not until April 1932 that Ellsworth finally announced his plan for a 4600-kilometre flight across Antarctica, which he scheduled for the summer of 1933–34. Bernt Balchen would be his pilot, while the hard-up Hubert Wilkins would organise the expedition and write up its achievements. After scouting around for a suitable vessel, he settled on a small wooden fishing vessel, which he renamed the *Wyatt Earp*. He even visited Earp's widow in California before leaving for the Antarctic, and was given Earp's gold wedding ring to wear.[29] In a joint announcement with Bowman, Ellsworth portrayed the flight as being the 'last great adventure in South Polar exploration' and 'purely a voyage of discovery'.

The American Geographical Society provided a map of the continent, which showed the small amount of known land and the much greater amount of what it called 'conjectured land'. With topography, the 'Ellsworth Trans-Antarctic Flight Expedition' would 'determine the geographical features along the line of flight through the great snow continent, a mass of land . . . which has never been seen by man'. Its achievements were designed to be dramatically splashed across double-page spreads of America's Sunday newspapers, rather than detailed drily in the little-read pages of academic journals. An editorial in the *New York Times* heightened the drama by couching the expedition in the military terms that were often applied to the Antarctic, telling its readers that it would 'not want for the sinews of war in the siege of the glacial continent'.[30]

In September 1933 Ellsworth travelled comfortably to New Zealand by steamer to await the arrival of the *Wyatt Earp*. He was met with a message from Bowman, who was looking forward 'intensely' to news of Ellsworth's activities and 'eagerly' anticipating 'a glorious story'. Bowman was advising both Byrd and Ellsworth, and kept each of them informed of the other's plans. He assured Ellsworth that his staff were 'standing by to give you any help in the way of maps that you may require'.[31]

Yet Bowman was doing much more besides. He would ensure that news of the Ellsworth expedition's achievements was distributed to relevant organisations and newspapers around the world. In a circular translated into four languages and sent to hundreds of newspapers from Buenos Aires to Beijing in January 1934, on the eve of Ellsworth's first flight, Bowman described how mapping would be done 'by means of two Zeiss hand cameras for horizontal and oblique exposures and a new type of aerial camera operated by a clock which will take a vertical picture every ten seconds'; this would 'provide a continuous strip record of the route traversed'. A newly devised and simplified method of taking frequent astronomical positions during the flight, it was hoped, would overcome problems that had previously been encountered when making maps from aerial photographs.[32] Given Bowman's expertise in the politics of asserting territorial claims, the circular was clearly intended to do more than just inform the world of Ellsworth's activities. Along with the subsequent newspaper reports and resulting maps, it would show that the United States knew that particular Antarctic territory better than any other nation, and therefore had a greater claim to it.

Ellsworth had also been advised by the State Department, which had given him a form of words and actions to use when claiming newly discovered land. His departure for the Ross Sea had aroused concern in both London and Wellington, where officials feared that he would infringe British sovereignty over the Ross Dependency. The British could not be sure whether Ellsworth's expedition had any official American support, and they were apprehensive about asking Washington for clarification. In an implicit declaration of British sovereignty, a message was sent to Ellsworth making him welcome to operate in the Ross Dependency and offering any facilities that he might require. Ellsworth's failure to apply to New Zealand for a license to operate his radio equipment and his aircraft in the Ross Dependency was remarked upon, but the American explorer was not required to redress the situation.

Ellsworth had requested permission from the governor of the Falkland Islands to use a harbour in the South Shetlands as a base, with the governor taking the opportunity to authorise Ellsworth's flights in the Falkland Islands and in the Falkland Islands Dependencies. Only belatedly did the State Department realise the implications of the governor's action. It made clear to the British Foreign Office in April 1935 that the American acceptance of the authority to operate an aircraft in the Falkland Islands Dependencies 'cannot in any way be implied to have any bearing on the question as to what country or countries may validly claim ownership of or title to the various territories embraced within the term "dependencies" '. Not wanting to spark a dispute, the British declined to reply.[33]

When Ellsworth was about to take off on his first test flight on 9 January, he broadcast a radio message to the world's press announcing that he had 'permission of the State Department, [to] drop the Stars and Stripes, and, so far as that act will suffice, claim the area we discover up to the 120th meridian [120° W] for the U.S.A.'.[34] But it all came to nothing. The *Polar Star* had landed on the Ross Ice Barrier after its first flight and been left for the night too close to where the *Wyatt Earp* was tied up in the Bay of Whales. During the night, the edge of the ice shelf calved off, leaving the aircraft precariously situated on a small floe of ice, from which it was only rescued fortuitously and with a great deal of effort by the ship's crew. The aircraft had sustained such serious damage to its wing and its skis that it could not be flown without being mended at its factory in California, while the ice-damaged *Wyatt Earp* would also need to have repairs. Undaunted, Ellsworth decided to try again the following summer. Because the flying weather in the Ross Sea was better in October and November, while the Ross Sea was unapproachable by ship until January, he decided to base himself on an island in the Weddell Sea and fly across Antarctica to Little America, where he would await the arrival of the *Wyatt Earp*.[35]

Ellsworth had no better luck the following summer. Rejoining the *Wyatt Earp* in Dunedin with Wilkins and Balchen, he set off in September 1934 on the 6000-kilometre voyage to Deception Island. He hoped the island's harbour would have a layer of ice which might act as a runway for his aircraft, but found to his disappointment that it was ice-free. A heavy snowfall then raised hopes that an airfield might be created on the snow-covered land, only for the plane's engine to suffer a mishap that required replacement parts to be fetched by ship from Chile. By the time the *Wyatt Earp* returned, most of the snow had gone and a takeoff on skis became impossible. The plane was loaded back onto the ship so that Ellsworth could search for a more suitable site for an airfield.

Eventually, one was found in early December on Snow Hill Island, where a crevasse-free glacier offered a perfect airfield for a ski-equipped aircraft. There followed weeks of waiting for fine weather, with Ellsworth becoming increasingly frustrated by the prospect of another summer wasted. Wilkins was frustrated not only by the weather but even more by the pessimism of the ageing Ellsworth. At the end of December, the Australian radioed to Bowman that Ellsworth was so discouraged by having to wait for the weather to improve that he was packing to go home. There were still weeks of potentially good flying weather, complained Wilkins, and he wanted to see out the season and possibly the following summer as well. He asked Bowman about the possibility of taking over the expedition's leadership from Ellsworth, but he would need Ellsworth's agreement and a further $10,000 to $20,000 in funds.[36]

Before Wilkins could do anything, the weather cleared sufficiently for Ellsworth and Balchen to make a flight on 3 January 1935. As they took off into the unknown, Ellsworth radioed his newspaper supporters that 'conditions look good as far as we can see and we expect to do much to clear up the great problem of unexplored Antarctica'. But he was again disappointed when Balchen took fright at the weather ahead and turned the aircraft around after flying only about 300 kilometres. An angry Ellsworth was left to lament another wasted summer. Nevertheless, he still tried to claim it as a success, since the brief reconnaissance had seen 'another section of the unknown . . . wrested from Antarctica and added to the map of human knowledge'. The apparent finds included 'five islands, three deep fjords [one of which he named after his father] and several conspicuous mountain peaks not marked on the latest official charts'.

Privately, Ellsworth admitted to Bowman that he was 'awfully sorry not to have achieved what I set out to do' but it was 'better to have tried and failed than not to have tried at all'. The following week, the bad weather forced him to abandon any further flights for that season. With the aircraft packed away, he concentrated on trying to get the *Wyatt Earp* freed from the ice that had covered the waters around Snow Hill Island. It was not until 18 January that what Ellsworth called 'the guiding hand of Providence and faith in bold adventure' saw the vessel finally freed, allowing the party to explore the northern parts of Graham Land for fossils.[37] It would provide some concrete return from two frustrating seasons in the Antarctic.

By the end of February 1935, Ellsworth had returned to his comfortable digs at New York's Metropolitan Club, where he settled down to write magazine articles, compile a book about his expedition and plan the following season's work.[38] It also allowed him to make a personal report to Roosevelt during a teatime visit to the White House. The president questioned him closely about the results of his first two seasons, asking whether he 'intended to return and carry out his plans for a flight across vast unexplored territory in the Antarctic'. Ellsworth told Roosevelt that he was still unsure whether he would return for a third attempt at crossing the continent. He soon found the Antarctic drawing him back.

Balchen had decided that he would not go back, preferring instead to explore the career opportunities opening up in civil aviation in Europe.[39] So Ellsworth enlisted two Canadian pilots who were used to taking off from fields of ice and snow. This time, he took the *Wyatt Earp* to Dundee Island, at the tip of the Antarctic Peninsula, where flat, snow-covered landing fields beckoned. From there, Ellsworth planned to make the 3700-kilometre flight to Byrd's empty base at Little America, where he would survive on whatever he could carry in the plane and whatever stores Byrd had left behind, while awaiting the arrival of the *Wyatt Earp*.[40]

After two thwarted attempts, Ellsworth eventually set off with Canadian pilot Herbert Hollick-Kenyon on 23 November 1935, taking Earp's cartridge belt and holster along for good luck on what was expected to be a fourteen-hour flight. Unlike Byrd's flight to the South Pole, which had merely traced Amundsen's track, Ellsworth's flight would cover the length of the Antarctic Peninsula before heading across a large swathe of previously unseen land to

Little America. With the words 'Ellsworth Trans-Antarctic Flight' daubed in large letters down the length of the aircraft, Ellsworth was ostensibly crossing the continent, although the route he had chosen would allow critics to argue that he had merely fringed part of it. Had he left instead from, say, Enderby Land and passed over the South Pole to Little America, he would have been flying a similar distance and there could have been no quibbles about his achievement. However, for Ellsworth, the flight was also about discovering and claiming new land.[41] And there was new land aplenty once he had got beyond the peninsula.

Flying over the region that Wilkins had named 'Hearst Land', Ellsworth discovered a high mountain range with peaks that rose nearly 4000 metres above sea level. With his penchant for mysticism, Ellsworth named it 'the Eternity Range', and called its three highest peaks 'Faith', 'Hope' and 'Charity' as he snapped away at them with his Leica camera. A smaller group of mountains was named 'the Sentinel Range' and its highest mountain after Ellsworth's wife, Mary Louise Ulmer. All the way, he kept in radio contact with Wilkins on the *Wyatt Earp* at Dundee Island, who had been left with detailed instructions to follow in the event of a mishap to the aircraft. But just after passing the halfway mark to Little America, problems with the radio caused communication to be cut. After being repeatedly thwarted during his previous attempts, Ellsworth pressed on regardless, while Wilkins began to implement their prearranged rescue operation.[42]

After fourteen hours in the air, and with little indication of their speed, neither Ellsworth not Hollick-Kenyon had any idea of their position as they flew across a high and featureless plateau. Concerned about their fuel level, Kenyon landed on the hard-packed snow so they could get a fix on their location. Using his sextant, which he did not know was faulty, Ellsworth decided they were at 79° 12' S, 104° 10' W, which put them just over 1000 kilometres short of Little America. That made their fuel position rather precarious, but Ellsworth's attention was elsewhere as he realised that they were standing on a part of the continent that had never been seen or claimed before. He was overwhelmed, later describing how it made him feel 'a very meek and reverent person. To think that I, of all those who had dreamed this dream, should be permitted its realization!' He fetched the American flag that had been brought for precisely this purpose and raised it to claim the sector that lay between 80° W and 120° W, naming it 'James W. Ellsworth Land' after his father. With their tent set up alongside the aircraft, a meal of bacon and oatmeal was prepared while Ellsworth rechecked their position. Finally, they took off after nineteen hours on the ice.[43]

Bad weather forced the plane down again after just thirty minutes, and there they stayed for the next three days as both men struggled in the overcast conditions to get an accurate fix on their position with the faulty sextant. Still unaware that the instrument was faulty, they took off again on a flight which lasted just fifty minutes before bad weather again forced them to land. This time, they were stuck in their tent for a week. They finally solved the problem with the sextant and, during a sunny interval on 1 December, got the first accurate fix on their position. They were still more than 800 kilometres from Little America.

After a four-hour flight, Ellsworth and Hollick-Kenyon landed on the Ross Ice Barrier, just 200 kilometres from their destination, in order to get another fix on their position. After a night's sleep they were off again, confident there was sufficient fuel to get them there. Twenty-five kilometres short of Little America, the engine went dead from lack of fuel and they landed for the last time. Although they knew they were close to Byrd's abandoned base, there was no way of knowing in which direction the buried buildings were situated. Ten days later, after a haphazard trudge over 160 kilometres with their sledge, they chanced upon signs of the base poking above the snow.[44]

It had been more than three weeks since the world had heard from Ellsworth, and newspaper headlines were predicting his doom. While Wilkins sailed the *Wyatt Earp* towards Little America, stopping along the coast to check the various places where Ellsworth had suggested he might seek refuge, an international rescue was mounted using the steel-hulled British research vessel *Discovery II* and two aircraft of the Royal Australian Air Force. It was an aircraft from the *Discovery II* that was first to reach Little America and put an end to the world's suspense and to Ellsworth and Kenyon's isolation. Wilkins arrived several days later in the *Wyatt Earp*. The expense of the joint British, Australian and New Zealand rescue was justified by officials who alluded to the way in which it would reinforce the British claim to the Ross Dependency. Since Little America was located in the Ross Dependency, the dispatch of the *Discovery II* was seen as an implicit exercise of British sovereignty.

The Foreign Office would later claim that 'British administration of the Ross Dependency had been effectively exercised' and that they had fulfilled 'their moral responsibility for the safety of visitors to the region'.[45]

Britain and its dominions had been nervous about American intentions in the Antarctic. And that nervousness had been heightened by the location of Little America and the possibility that it would lead to an American claim, based on both discovery and occupation. The British had been reassured by Byrd having kept his territorial claims scrupulously to the area east of the Ross Dependency. Having been instructed by the State Department, Ellsworth did likewise. On his return to the United States, he announced that he had claimed only the territory between 80° W and 120° W, which had previously been undiscovered and unclaimed.

Like Byrd, he was met with popular acclaim. There were the usual lunches and dinners, while the US Congress awarded him a gold medal 'for claiming on behalf of the United States approximately three hundred and fifty thousand square miles of land in Antarctica . . . representing the last unclaimed territory in the world'. Unlike Byrd, however, the wealthy Ellsworth had no need or inclination to hit the lecture circuit to recoup the costs of the expedition. And the claiming of the land was less important to Ellsworth than its naming after his father. What really lingered in Ellsworth's mind was 'the memory of the great silent, purple-tinted, ice-bound world over which we flew and where, in touch with the vastness of the unknown, it is not difficult to sense the magnitude of the universe and the nearness of its creator'.[46]

Clearly concerned by the challenge from Ellsworth, as he had been by his earlier rivalry with Wilkins, Byrd assured Bowman in July 1933 that his expedition would be the more notable because it was driven by science. It would be easy, he wrote, to 'go down, make a few flights, and come back, and that is what the public would like best, but I am damned if I am going down there without getting some scientific information'. There would be a government meteorologist, courtesy of Roosevelt, a geologist, a physicist, a biologist and a radio engineer. There would also be a geographer, a surveyor and an aerial surveyor for the mapping that was to be central to the expedition. However, complained Byrd, the serious side of the expedition meant 'more men, more food, and more equipment'. With a seventy-man expedition heading for a two-year stay, he would again be taking two ships, one of which was the 10,000-ton freighter *Pacific Fir*, while the other was the 1700-ton SS *Bear*, a former Dundee sealer that had later been used in Alaska by the US Coast Guard. The more elaborate preparations meant much more money was needed from his supporters than Ellsworth had required. And scientific credentials were essential to Byrd's fundraising efforts.[47]

Byrd's benefactors wanted to know that their contributions were being used to uncover Antarctica's multitude of scientific mysteries, with Bowman providing Byrd with the required reference. He also continued to provide Byrd with strategic advice about where he should explore. Byrd's own plans were very vague. Just weeks before his planned departure, he informed Bowman that he expected 'to fly over the unknown, on a line, from South America to Little America; and across the South Pole, several hundred miles beyond, perhaps'. There would also be 'other flights towards the Weddell Sea in several directions', with the expedition doing 'ten times as much flying as before'. Still he wanted Bowman to advise 'as to what flights it would be valuable for me to make, or any other work you would like to see done'.

There was no question in Bowman's mind that the best work Byrd could do would be to extend his previous flights east of the Ross Dependency, flying over the 'unclaimed sector between 80° and 150°W' so that all 'the land within it could be claimed for the United States'. That claim would be all the stronger if Byrd used the most 'rigorous photo-surveying methods' so that more accurate maps could be made than had been possible during the previous expedition.[48] More importantly, there were increasing indications that the United States government was prepared to reinforce Byrd's private territorial claims with an official claim.

Byrd's formerly warm relations with Roosevelt were restored now that the explorer was concentrating on exploration rather than politics. The president's interest in the Antarctic was apparently piqued by the prospect of the United States establishing its own claim to the continent, although there was a limit to what Roosevelt could do to assist Byrd without the explicit approval of Congress. But after a drive with Senator Harry Byrd through Virginia's Shenandoah Forest, the president agreed that Byrd could take a meteorologist and that US stamps would be issued to commemorate the coming expedition. An expedition member would be sworn in as US Postmaster at Little America.

After a meeting with Roosevelt in early September, Byrd was provided with his letter of endorsement, which noted their close friendship and Roosevelt's intention 'to keep in close touch with your new expedition'. Byrd was assured that his expedition had 'the full support of the United States government' and that he could 'call on the government in case of need or emergency'. As a keen philatelist, Roosevelt requested in return that Byrd send him a letter from the Little America post office for his stamp collection.

Byrd would later claim that Roosevelt had wanted him to do much more, suggesting that he embark on 'a comprehensive aerial mapping and claims project' that would see large parts of the continent come under the Stars and Stripes. However, the lack of suitable planes prevented such a project from being mounted. Buoyed by their meeting, and armed with the president's letter, Byrd flew to New York, where he told reporters of his dream of 'discovering and claiming for this country a new continent', describing Antarctica as 'earth's last unconquered outpost'.[49]

With Roosevelt's support, the conquest of Antarctica became Byrd's new aim, and science slipped down his agenda. Amidst the frenzy of the final preparations, there was no longer any time for consultations with Bowman. Instead, Byrd just sent him a copy of his scientific program, admitting that it was 'a bit incomplete' but claiming that he was 'deadly in earnest' about science and planned to 'do infinitely better than we did last time'. Bowman was encouraged by Byrd's outline, predicting that it should result in 'a tremendous amount of plunder, photographic and otherwise'. But the value of the territorial plunder, wrote Bowman, would depend on Byrd bringing back ground control points to go with his aerial photographs so that accurate maps of his discoveries could be produced. Much to the frustration of the mapmakers of the American Geographical Society, the last Byrd expedition – like that of Wilkins before him – had brought back thousands of photographs but few of the ground control points that were required if they were to locate geographical features on a map.[50]

News of Byrd's second expedition to the Ross Dependency caused alarm in London and Wellington. Although it was ostensibly administered by New Zealand, no New Zealand official had ever stepped ashore there. Now the Americans were set on spending another two years at Little America, during which time New Zealand's sovereignty would be seriously challenged. Byrd would again be flying aircraft and operating radio transmitters without any regard for the relevant New Zealand regulations. Neither would he be asking permission to establish his base in the Ross Dependency. This was in accord with American policy not to recognise territorial claims in the Antarctic.

But it was the establishment of an official United States post office at Little America that most concerned British and New Zealand officials, particularly when two of the expedition members were sworn in as postal officials by the American postmaster general and Roosevelt campaign manager James Farley, in a well-publicised ceremony in Washington. This gave Byrd's second expedition an official imprimatur that the first had lacked. The United States also issued two commemorative stamps, which displayed a globe on which Little America was prominently marked. The implicit challenge to British and New Zealand sovereignty could not go unremarked.[51]

While the New Zealand government sent a goodwill message to Byrd offering to provide him with facilities, Britain's ambassador in Washington informed the State Department in January 1934 that the establishment of an American post office and the use of the commemorative stamps in the Ross Dependency would infringe 'British sovereignty and New Zealand administrative rights in the Dependency'. Britain wanted this reaffirmation of its claim of sovereignty to be on the record, although at the same time it did not want to create a diplomatic spat. So the ambassador let it be known, as he handed over the letter, that no reply was needed.

The United States might have let it pass without comment in the 1920s, but Byrd's expeditions had created a groundswell of popular feeling in favour of America claiming the territory that its citizens had explored, named and mapped. So Secretary of State Cordell Hull made a point of acknowledging the note, while making clear that he reserved 'all rights which the United States or its citizens may have with respect to this matter'.[52] In other words, the United States did not recognise the British claims to any part of the Antarctic, but neither was it making any formal claims of its own. Yet it reserved the right to do so at any time.

Byrd maintained the American pretence of disinterest by portraying his expedition as being an endeavour primarily driven by science. He dismissed the idea that there was any economic advantage in the Antarctic. There were only whales, wrote Byrd, and their numbers were being savagely depleted. As for the potential of coal or other minerals, 'they might as well be on the moon'. With the continent itself of no economic importance, Byrd argued, it had become 'the common domain, the particular sphere of influence, of world science'.

Included under the rubric of science was geography, and it was geographic exploration that dominated Byrd's planning for the expedition as he assembled a variety of vehicles and aircraft for mounting a virtual military campaign on Marie Byrd Land, which held 'the most substantial American gains on the continent'. He had two snowmobiles, courtesy of Edsel Ford, a tractor capable of carrying more than 9000 kilograms, which Byrd described as 'a snow dreadnought', three trucks with caterpillar tracks provided by the French car manufacturer André Citroën, as well as the usual sledges and dogs. At sea, Byrd had the use of two ships, while in the air he had three aircraft and a newfangled helicopter. After getting ashore and re-establishing himself at Little America and waiting out the winter, he planned to 'press the attack into the interior' during the summer of 1934–35.[53]

The two ships of the expedition, the wooden-hulled *Bear of Oakland* and the steel freighter *Jacob Ruppert*, sailed into the Bay of Whales in January 1934. Just days earlier, a disconsolate Lincoln Ellsworth had left the Bay of Whales in the *Wyatt Earp* after his aircraft and ship were damaged by the shifting ice. While Ellsworth was away having them repaired, Byrd would have the Antarctic to himself. He quickly put his inexperienced deputy, Dr Tom Poulter, in charge of restoring the ice-encrusted base to working order, constructing ten new buildings and organising a massive seal kill to provide food for both men and dogs.

Although Little America was mostly covered by ice and snow, its buildings connected by tunnels through the ice and reached from the outside by trapdoors, Byrd tried to portray the place, with its fifty-six inhabitants, as akin to a frontier settlement of the American West. In his book about the expedition, Byrd would include a panoramic shot of Little America, which he captioned as 'Frontier Settlement', while another was captioned as 'Main Street, Little America'.[54] But the real frontier that first winter was 160 kilometres away, where Byrd erected the isolated outpost, known as 'Advance Base', in which he planned to spend the winter alone.

The rationale for the base was ostensibly to observe the winter weather far from the coast. Such a feat had never been done before.

Meteorology had always been prominent amongst the sciences in the Antarctic, with theories suggesting that the weather of Antarctica affected all the continents of the southern hemisphere, as winds spilled from the polar plateau onto the Southern Ocean. Now Byrd would go further, making meteorology appear to be the pre-eminent feature of his expedition. It would silence the critics who had dismissed his expeditions as expensive adventures designed for personal glory.

Behind the cover of science, he could engage in both glory-hunting and territorial acquisition. As a writer in *Vanity Fair* remarked in 1930, Byrd used science as a path to glory, for science could be used as a justification for just about anything in the Antarctic. Not that science was impelling him to take up his lonely vigil. Byrd candidly conceded later that he had not gone there just for science, but because he was 'interested in the experience, for its own sake'. Moreover, as his biographer Lisle Rose observed, the dramatic act 'would undercut any similar action by Ellsworth'.[55] On his other ventures, Byrd had shared the fame and glory with his pilots or other companions. This time, it would be his alone. It would be one man against nature, battling both the external elements and his internal demons.

Back in 1932, Byrd had talked of establishing his forward base at the foot of the Queen Maud Mountains, about 800 kilometres from Little America.[56] In the event, delays forced him to establish the underground base on the Ross Ice Barrier just 160 kilometres south of Little America. There, Byrd was left to begin his vigil on 28 March 1934. Alone at last, he immediately set to rereading the diary that Scott had kept during his failed attempt on the South Pole. Byrd's deputy on his previous expedition, Laurence Gould, thought the whole exercise was inane, asking Bernt Balchen whether there was 'anything more silly and cheap than his present attempt to be heroic'.[57] It almost cost Byrd his life. Buried beneath the ice, he began to suffer the slow effects of carbon-monoxide poisoning from a faulty heater.

Meanwhile, Poulter was observing meteors in the winter sky. Beset by the ill-discipline and heavy drinking of his subordinates, he was keen to get away from his responsibilities as acting leader. When Poulter suggested by radio to Byrd in June that he might take simultaneous observations from Advance Base, he began to suspect there might be a problem with his isolated leader. Concerned by Byrd's responses, he organised a rescue mission. It took weeks of preparation before they could set off, only to have the tracked vehicle break down and have to return. Another was hastily prepared. It pushed through the gloom and past the intervening crevasses towards Byrd, finally reaching Advance Base on 11 August. It was another two months before an aircraft could get into the air and bring Byrd back to Little America.[58]

As Byrd slowly recovered from his carbon monoxide poisoning, he took charge of the coming summer offensive that would use all the available aircraft, vehicles and sledges to solve one of the major remaining mysteries of the Antarctic: was it one continent or two? For decades, there had been suggestions that there was a strait connecting the Ross Sea with the Weddell Sea. Such a strait, wrote Byrd, 'held out the promise of a great potential waterway connecting the Atlantic and Pacific oceans across the bottom of the globe'. Byrd hoped to settle the matter. While his lonely vigil at Advance Base had tested him as a man – and, he hoped, would attract immense public interest – it was the exploration of Marie Byrd Land and beyond that most interested Byrd. It was 'geographical discovery', he later wrote, that 'had drawn me back to Antarctica'.

Despite the concerns of his doctor, Byrd flew off on 15 November on the first exploratory flight of the summer, following a triangular route southeast off the Ross Ice Barrier and onto the plateau of Marie Byrd Land, then turning due north to make contact with the Edsel Ford Range, before finally turning for home. The flight took nearly seven hours, and 'surveyed, within our range of vision, approximately 50,000 square miles of unknown Antarctica – a very satisfactory beginning of the flight programme'. Bowman had wanted him to connect Marie Byrd Land with its coastline so that the United States would have a stronger territorial claim, but Byrd had been prevented from doing so by the intervening Edsel Ford Range. Byrd remained at Little America for the next flight, which was similarly unsuccessful in reaching the coast. He listened on the radio as his subordinates flew across 'a region which I looked upon as peculiarly my own'. Byrd made another flight on 23 November that surveyed the eastern edge of the Ross Ice Barrier, finding that it was all ice-covered land with no gaps for the theoretical strait. Yet he was still unable to declare without 'a shadow of doubt' that Antarctica was one continent.[59]

While the aircraft made their exploratory flights, photographing as they went, scientific parties spread out south and east from Little America by dog sledge and tracked vehicle. Paul Siple, the former Boy Scout who had won a competition to accompany Byrd on his previous expedition, was sent on a 1300-kilometre foray by sledge into Marie Byrd Land. The trek took two and a half months, and was the 'first scientific penetration into this newest American geographical claim'; upon returning, Siple suggested that the mountains of Marie Byrd Land might be rich in minerals, particularly coal. The Australian geographer and polar explorer Griffith Taylor had earlier speculated that the Antarctic might 'possess the greatest coal reserves in the world', and the reports from Byrd's expedition suggested that he might be right.[60]

This was the sort of thing that was likely to excite the interest of the American public, which so far had been largely unmoved by Byrd's reports. Bowman was so concerned at the relative lack of public interest that he suggested to Byrd's wife in December 1934 that the next statement by the expedition's New York office should have a 'full general summary of the scientific work that has been accomplished', in the hope that it 'might greatly stimulate public interest'. It might also answer some of the criticisms about the expedition's cost and the absence of any achievement that could compare with Byrd's flight to the South Pole. Whatever was done, wrote Bowman, the American public had to be 'prepared for a certain amount of letdown from the highly dramatic achievements of the past'.[61]

The public wanted the derring-do of men pitting themselves against the elements, not the humdrummery of scientists taking weather observations. Waiting out the dark winter down a hole just 160 kilometres from Little America could hardly compete with the stirring stories of Scott and Amundsen, or even of Byrd flying to the South Pole. His second expedition certainly had scientific achievements across a range of fields, but there was little to capture the public imagination. Byrd had promised Bowman that his second expedition would 'do ten times as much flying as before', but he had come nowhere close to doing so.[62] His plan to beat Ellsworth by flying across the continent from the Weddell Sea to the Ross Sea had not even been attempted, and the flights that had been made had not gone much further eastward than the first expedition. As a result, Byrd had failed to establish an American claim to the sector lying between the Ross Dependency and the Falkland

Islands Dependencies. But his reoccupation of Little America, and his further exploration of the Ross Ice Barrier and the Queen Maud Mountains, had reinforced the potential American claim to the Ross Dependency.

That was reinforced even further when postmaster general Farley announced in October 1934 that he was sending one of his officials, Charles Anderson, to take charge of the post office at Little America; the expedition member operating the post office had gone insane during his winter under the ice. The bags of mail that had been taken south with the expedition in 1933, with the intention of having them immediately postmarked and returned, had been lost under a snowfall and were not discovered till midwinter, at a time when there was a desperate hunt for any liquor that had not been destroyed by Poulter. Even though the aim was ostensibly to provide a better service for American stamp collectors, whose letters Anderson would take to the base for cancellation, the move represented a serious escalation by the United States in its implicit challenge to British sovereignty.

Britain's ambassador asked unofficially for an explanation, noting that the action might be 'construed as an assertion of sovereignty'. Rather than calming the situation, the question opened the way for Secretary of State Cordell Hull to challenge the basis of British sovereignty over the Ross Dependency. After explaining that Anderson was only going to the Ross Sea to take 'charge of handling mails at that place', Hull went on to point out that 'mere discovery' of part of a place, as Britain had done in the Ross Sea, was insufficient for a nation to be recognised under international law as its owner; discovery had to be accompanied by 'occupancy and use'.[63]

With Hull having issued a 'definite challenge to British sovereignty', officials in London scrambled to devise a solution that would allow Anderson to operate the post office without infringing British sovereignty. They considered asking for an assurance that Anderson's presence was not 'an official exercise of United States postal functions', or maybe having a New Zealand postal official accompany him. Then again, they thought, maybe they should demand that New Zealand stamps be used alongside the American ones, or they might demand that the United States ask New Zealand's permission to use US stamps in the dependency. Each of these possible solutions carried a danger of escalating the issue.

Fortunately for London, the issue was solved when Anderson assured postal officials when he arrived in New Zealand on his way to the Ross Sea that he had no 'intention actually to open a Post Office at Little America'. He predicted that problems with oiling his cancelling machine in the bitter cold of the Antarctic would force him to use it only on the ship and therefore not on New Zealand territory. With New Zealand's agreement, Britain decided it was best to treat Anderson's visit as being 'devoid of political significance'.[64] In fact, when the relief ships arrived to remove Byrd's expedition in January 1935, the *Little America Times* reported that Anderson did go ashore, and that he 'exercised a sort of national sovereignty, by selling stamps and postmarking U.S. mail'. Anderson spent sixteen days working frantically in the world's most unusual post office, twenty feet under the ice, where he processed more than 70,000 letters.[65]

While British officials were prepared to turn a blind eye to Anderson's activities, Hull's statement was a different matter. A couple of weeks before Anderson arrived at Little America, the British ambassador handed Hull a note that challenged the American argument that 'the British claim to sovereignty over the Ross Dependency is based on discovery alone'. Although New Zealand's prime minister, George Forbes, had advised London that its whaling licenses had never been exercised in the territorial waters of the Ross Dependency, and that New Zealand officials had never set foot on its shores, the ambassador told the State Department that New Zealand had exercised administrative and governmental powers over the Ross Dependency ever since it had been placed under its control in 1923. Keen to calm the situation, the note advised that New Zealand had no objection to Anderson's visit, on the understanding that his activities would be limited to the expedition's vessel and that the stamps had been issued merely as 'a matter of philatelic interest'. However, if his visit had been 'designed as an assertion of United States sovereignty over any part of the Ross Dependency . . . they would have been compelled to make a protest'.

With the United States feeling itself on ever stronger legal ground after the activities of Byrd, should it ever want to make a claim to the territory, Hull had his own reasons for not escalating the issue and perhaps provoking Britain or New Zealand into actually occupying the Ross Dependency themselves. So he told the ambassador that 'no useful purpose would be served by a discussion at this time' and repeated the usual American mantra about the United States reserving 'all rights which this country or its citizens may have with respect to the matter'.[66] Privately, British legal advisers still believed that their empire's claim to the Ross Dependency rested on solid legal ground created by the decision of the Permanent Court of International Justice, which had ruled that polar territories only required discovery to be 'followed by periodical visits and the exercise of administrative functions'.[67]

Byrd's second visit to the Ross Dependency came to an end on 5 February 1935, when the *Bear of Oakland* and the *Jacob Ruppert* finally took their leave of the Bay of Whales after several frantic days of loading stores and equipment, which had been hurriedly dismantled and transported the few kilometres from Little America. Back on board went the aircraft, including the plane that had taken Byrd to the South Pole, which had been stored beneath the snow ever since. Also on board went two of the three Citroën tracked vehicles, along with the dogs and four cows that had been lent to the expedition by a New Zealand farmer.[68] Packed carefully away were the aerial photographs and sledging reports that would allow geographers to add additional detail, including many more American names, to the existing maps of the continent.

The first port of call for Byrd and his men was Dunedin, where New Zealand journalists and officials were anxious to know whether the Americans had done anything to challenge British sovereignty over the Ross Dependency. Conscious of Britain's concern, Byrd assured its governor-general in New Zealand 'that the United States had no ambitions regarding any land discovered by his recent Antarctic expedition'. This left the British with the impression that Byrd had made no territorial claims.[69]

After criticism in the American press, Byrd was quickly forced to correct that impression. He told New Zealand journalists that what he'd meant to say was that 'there was no possibility of America asserting rights over land within the Ross Dependency, which has always been recognized as British territory'. He was prepared to recognise British sovereignty, even though the Ross Dependency was the site of Little America, and his two expeditions had seen more of it than anyone else. The only territory he was claiming, said Byrd, was that which lay beyond the eastern boundary of the Ross Dependency, which had 'never been seen by representatives of any other nation but the United States'. Moreover, it was 'of no practical value', with the territory being 'of interest only from a scientific point of view'.[70] Byrd was telling the British what they wanted to hear. He had a different message for his American audience.

On his triumphant return to the United States on 10 May 1935, Byrd was met at the dock by President Roosevelt and representatives from both congressional houses, with Congress having passed a resolution praising his 'successful and heroic exploration of Antarctic lands'. At a reception organised by the National Geographic Society in Washington's Constitution Hall, Byrd told the assembled guests that he had 'discovered and taken possession of . . . a land area as large as the combined Atlantic seaboard States from Maine to Georgia'. There could be no dispute about America's rightful title to the territory, he argued, because it was a no-man's land that lay 'beyond the British claims'. He also claimed to have settled the question of whether the Antarctic was one continent or two by showing that there was no channel connecting the Ross and Weddell Seas.[71]

Byrd later sent his thanks to Bowman for helping him to 'map and take possession of thousands of square miles of new territory for the United States', enclosing with his note 'an autographed piece of insulation from the wall of the Advance Meteorological Base', where he had almost died and which was 'the southernmost habitation ever occupied by man'.[72] His supporters lauded his achievements. The chief of IBM, Thomas Watson, who had had an escarpment named after him, hosted a testimonial dinner for Byrd in the grand ballroom of New York's Waldorf Astoria, telling the diners – all men – how Byrd had 'added hundreds of thousands of square miles to the territory of this, his country'.[73]

It was all academic, though, until the United States government made Byrd's claim official. And there were no signs that it would do so, despite a call from the influential Columbia University law professor Charles Hyde, who had formerly been a legal adviser at the State Department under Charles Hughes, the politician who had established America's policy on Antarctic claims. In accordance with that policy, Hyde warned that 'the mere act of claiming possessions for the United States by planting flags constitutes a flimsy claim that might easily disappear'. To reinforce Byrd's flag-planting, Hyde called on Congress to immediately declare to 'the world that there is a region in the Antarctic which belongs to Uncle Sam'.[74]

Of course, under the policy established by Hughes, the United States would have to go on and occupy the territory if it really wanted to have its claim recognised. And it might not restrict its claim just to Marie Byrd Land. Even though Byrd had eschewed any intention to claim the territory around Little America, a State Department official confided to a correspondent in January 1936 that while Little America was within Britain's Ross Dependency, no British explorer had 'set foot on Antarctica at any point within 300 miles of Little America'. Moreover, Byrd's failure to claim Little America 'does not preclude the United States from making a claim to that area if it should decide to do so'.[75]

Taken together, Ellsworth's epic flight and Byrd's second expedition had renewed American focus on the Antarctic. From the radio hut beneath the ice at Little America, Byrd had on 1 February 1934 made the first radio broadcast direct to living rooms across the United States. It would be followed by many weekly radio broadcasts, sponsored by a breakfast cereal company. According to a later State Department study, the brief broadcasts helped to make Marie Byrd Land appear 'in the popular mind peculiarly American'.

There were also newspaper and magazine articles, books, films and lectures, which enthralled millions of Americans with their tales of Antarctic adventure and accomplishment. Despite the ongoing Depression, Byrd lectured about his second Antarctic expedition to more than a million people, reaping nearly $200,000 in the process. He was not eager to return, announcing instead that he wanted to devote the remainder of his life to reducing international tensions and fostering friendship between the United States and the rest of the world.[76] It was a noble impulse, but he would find that the rising international tensions could not be so easily allayed. Indeed, they would extend all the way to the Antarctic.

CHAPTER 14

'We must do something to justify our claims'

1937–1938

Most winters, the Antarctic was the only continent without human inhabitants. For decades there had been a general conviction that the occupation of Antarctica was impossible. By the late 1930s that view began to change. The Arctic explorer Vilhjalmur Stefansson propagated the idea that the North Pole was a 'friendly' place where intrepid explorers with a rifle and a tent could live off the local wildlife.[1] In the Antarctic, Norwegian and other whalers established permanent settlements in the South Shetlands and South Georgia, while Argentina had maintained a permanent meteorological station on Laurie Island since 1904. The arrival of women helped to soften the popular image of the South Pole as a place where only men went to test their manliness. There was even talk that it might become a tourist destination, where women might go to ski and men to climb mountains. Nations that had long accepted that the continent was uninhabitable began to consider ways in which permanent settlements might be possible. They came to realise that only by actual occupation could their claims of ownership be placed beyond challenge. The Antarctic would never be the same again.

When British and dominion leaders gathered for their regular imperial conference in mid-1937, defence questions dominated their deliberations. The waning empire was faced with threats from a resurgent Germany and a rising Japan. The Antarctic figured in these threats, since both Germany and Japan were now sending whaling fleets to the Southern Ocean.[2] Eleven years earlier, the imperial conference had set itself the task of bringing the entire Antarctic within the ambit of the empire; over the following years, it had annexed the Australian Antarctic Territory, the Ross Dependency and the Falkland Islands Dependencies, comprising about two-thirds of the continent. In the process, it had been forced to concede that part of the continent could be set aside for France and Norway. Although France remained reluctant to agree with Britain on the precise boundaries of Adélie Land, and Norwegian whalers were still discovering and claiming areas within the sectors that Britain had annexed, the British position in the Antarctic seemed relatively strong.[3] But the fast-growing whaling fleets of Germany and Japan were eroding the British and Norwegian dominance of the industry, and the United States was starting to assert its own territorial aspirations.

In the light of these challenges, and the American and Norwegian argument that actual occupation was required to give a valid legal title to newly discovered territory,[4] the British Empire began to consider ways in which such occupation might be achieved. One possibility was to establish meteorological bases on territory that was considered vulnerable to a competing claim. The imperial conference proposed that this be done in Enderby Land, at the western extremity of the Australian Antarctic Territory, and also in the Ross Dependency, as a counter to Byrd's base, Little America. But there was little sense of urgency in London, since British officials considered that 'no nation would seriously attempt the settlement of the Antarctic Continent on a large scale for very many years, if ever'. Nevertheless, there was a conviction that British title needed to be strengthened.[5]

Australia was particularly concerned that it had not done sufficient to ensure its sovereignty over the Australian Antarctic Territory, particularly in view of the exploration by Norwegian whaler Lars Christensen. In late December 1936, the portly Christensen had left from Cape Town aboard his tanker *Thorshavn*, which was taking fuel oil to the Antarctic for his twenty-five-strong whaling fleet. Decorated with bunting, the brightly painted ship carried a Stinson seaplane for exploration and a small party of pleasure-seekers, including Christensen's wife, his youngest daughter and two other women. The whaling magnate told journalists that he planned to 'supervise the mapping and re-mapping of the 3,000 miles of Antarctic coast-line from 100 degrees East to about 10 degrees West', which would include a large part of the Australian Antarctic Territory.

After reaching the ice and transferring the fuel oil to his whalers, taking on whale oil in return, the aircraft and its pilot and mechanic were loaded aboard one of the whale-catchers, along with

Christensen and the four women. On 29 January, the women stepped onto the continent, the first females ever to have done so. A flag was raised and a depot established at what the Norwegian had named 'Klarius Mikkelsen Mountain' – Mawson's Scullin Monolith. Over several days in early February 1937, the Christensens flew over the territories that had been named after them, while a photographer took hundreds of photographs for mapping purposes, as well as motion-picture film for the edification of cinema audiences. On 5 February, after flying over the coastline at about 38° E, Ingrid Christensen threw out a weighted pole to which was attached a Norwegian flag, watching as the pole spiralled down to land in the snow far below. It was a new way of raising a flag. Christensen made clear upon his return to Cape Town that he had not formally claimed any territory on behalf of Norway, as he had no authority from the government.[6] But he had made it easier for Norway to annex the territory, should it ever decide to do so.

In the wake of Christensen's voyage, and after reports of increasing activity by Japan and Nazi Germany, the Australian official John Cumpston suggested that American explorer Lincoln Ellsworth be commissioned to make his forthcoming flight from Enderby Land to the Ross Sea 'on behalf of the Commonwealth Government'. The proposed flight would pass over the interior of the territory whose coastline Christensen's whalers had done so much to explore and map. If the flight was successful, wrote Cumpston, it 'would give us an indisputable title to the hinterland for the time being and would enable us to combat both French and Norwegian claims'.[7] It is not clear how an American explorer could reinforce an Australian claim, especially just by flying over it. Anyway, it was British policy to concentrate on claiming the coastline and using the sector principle to include the territory behind it all the way to the South Pole. Legal advisers to the British government did not accept the idea that it could claim the hinterland separate from the coastline. Australia would have been pressured to comply with that policy. As a result, Cumpston's suggestion was doomed from the start and was not adopted.

Australia had already been pressured by Britain into accepting French control of the ill-defined Adélie Land, which divided the Australian Antarctic Territory into two unequal parts, despite Mawson being adamant that his own exploration and claim on that part of the Antarctic coast in March 1912 should give Australia precedence over the French. Whereas French explorer Dumont d'Urville had not stepped upon the mainland, or even realised he was sailing along a coastline of continental extent, Mawson's own expedition, he argued, had helped to prove that Antarctica was a continent. Moreover, his claiming ceremonies had been done with due solemnity and on the mainland itself. Not only had Mawson raised a flag that had been donated for that purpose by the staunchly imperialist British Empire League, but the ceremonies 'were most formal affairs with suitable speeches, etc'. If the French claim was to be recognised at all, Australia argued, it should only apply to the small stretch of coastline of about 240 kilometres that d'Urville had actually seen from his ship, while the hinterland should be controlled by Australia. However, Britain's reliance on the sector principle for its own claims meant that it had to accept that France would consequently control the sector from the Adélie Land coast all the way to the South Pole.[8]

The most that Australia could do in the short term to reinforce its claim on the Australian Antarctic Territory was to send a meteorologist, Allan Cornish, aboard a cruise by the British research ship *Discovery II*, in order to show that it was effectively administering its newly annexed territory. Cornish joined the ship when it docked in Fremantle, from where it headed south to the Antarctic and then back north to Dunedin. Ostensibly on board as a scientist, Cornish was instructed to report on any possible sites for meteorological bases, the latest whaling methods being used in Antarctic waters, any concentrations of whaling ships, and any radio reports that might be overheard by the ship 'of landings, or other activities by foreigners in the Australian Antarctic Territory'. Cornish was also provided with a secret memorandum, which explained how the imperial conference had decided that 'the present British title to the Continent was not sufficiently secure' and that increased whaling activity in Antarctic waters could allow 'some other nation . . . to establish a title to a portion at least of the Continent, which may prove to be stronger than the present British title'.[9]

The voyage of the *Discovery II* during the summer of 1937–38 did little to buttress Australia's claim. It was an oceanographic voyage that did not allow for landings, claiming ceremonies or mapping of the continent from the air. What Australia needed was more landings on the continent and more mapping of its coastline and hinterland. That would require another sort of expedition entirely, one along the lines of John Rymill's Graham Land expedition of 1934, which had shown what could be done in the way of exploration and mapping with limited funds and a small number of keen personnel serving in an honorary capacity. In the wake of the *Discovery II* voyage, the Australian government discussed the possibility of recruiting Rymill to lead an expedition to the western portion of the Australian Antarctic Territory, which might 'definitely implement Australia's title to sovereignty over all that territory'. The veteran Antarctic explorer John King Davis told journalists that such an expedition to complete the mapping of the Australian Antarctic Territory was essential. 'We claim this land,' noted Davis, 'and we must do something to justify our claims.'[10]

With Lars Christensen active in the area, and American explorer Lincoln Ellsworth planning to head in its direction, there were calls for Australia to mount another expedition to place the possession of its territory beyond doubt. The United States and Britain had recently disputed the ownership of several uninhabited Pacific Islands because Britain had not actually occupied them. The United States was keen to control the islands so that they could become part of a proposed American trans-Pacific air route, and it used the logbooks of its nineteenth-century whalers to show that the islands had been discovered, mapped and named by American mariners. To ensure they now remained American, the US Department of the Interior sent one of its officials, Richard Black, to Honolulu to supervise their occupation. Black knew something about claiming territories, after having participated in Byrd's second expedition to the Antarctic.[11] His actions in the Pacific, where occupation became the basis for claiming sovereignty, was feared by Britain, New Zealand and Australia as setting a possible precedent for their similarly unoccupied territories in the Antarctic.

Australia's pre-eminent Antarctic explorer, Sir Douglas Mawson, urged the establishment of a permanent meteorological base to avert such a possibility, while another Antarctic explorer, Raymond Priestley – who had become Melbourne University's vice-chancellor – suggested instead that Rymill be enlisted to mount a two-year expedition that would concentrate on exploration and mapping. Priestley had chaired one of the lectures Rymill was giving around Australia and had become a fervent supporter of the young explorer. Australia must realise that it had a possibly valuable possession in the Antarctic, declared Priestley, and it 'must either throw it away or occupy it'.

With pressure from both Mawson and Priestley, as well as Richard Casey, who was now the Australian treasurer, the minister for external affairs, Billy Hughes, urged his cabinet colleagues in June 1938 to send another expedition that would fill in the remaining gaps in the map of the Australian territory's coastline. According to Hughes, it would be another act of effective occupation by Australia. It would add to the government's existing support for the publication of Mawson's scientific results, its sending of Cornish on the *Discovery II* and its preparation of a new map of the Antarctic that would be 'the most comprehensive of its kind'. However, the only suitable ship for such an Australian expedition was the *Discovery II*, and it would not be available until late 1939.[12]

While Australia dallied with the idea of one day sending another expedition to the Antarctic, the Southern Ocean was alive with hundreds of whaling ships. Whales were taking on a new importance, both to feed consumers with margarine and other fats, and to fuel growing military machines with a vital raw material for explosives. Japan was also using them as a source of meat. By the summer of 1938–39, there were nearly 13,000 people engaged in the dangerous business of hunting and processing whales in the Antarctic. While one or two explorers might still be able to create headlines by mounting daring expeditions to the distant and apparently empty continent, they would now encounter more than thirty factory ships arrayed around its icy shores. As these massive ships digested the bodies of the countless whales fed into the sloping maws of their flensing decks, nearly 300 whale-catchers rushed around nearby waters, with highly paid harpooners scanning the waves for signs of their prey. Five factory ships and more than fifty whale-catchers sailed under the swastika flag of Nazi Germany, and a growing number flew the flag of the Rising Sun.[13] While the Union Jack still flew from the stern of some whalers, the Stars and Stripes was nowhere to be seen.

The American whaling industry had withered away in the nineteenth century, and there had been no official American presence in the Antarctic since the Wilkes expedition of the 1840s. While other nations sent their explorers to plant their nation's flags on the ice, the United States had left it to well-heeled private adventurers, such as Ellsworth and Byrd. Increasingly during the 1930s, the American government had begun to give quiet support to their explorers' territorial acquisitions, advising them as to the proper forms that should be followed, while publicly asserting that the United States did not recognise the claims of other nations and made none of its own. It also encouraged archival research into the activities of the American whalers and sealers of the early nineteenth century, whose dusty logbooks were retrieved from the attics of New England homes and lodged in Washington's Library of Congress. They became part of the armoury that was deployed to argue that it was Americans, rather than the British or Russians, who had been first to discover the Antarctic continent.

When the logbook of the American sealer Nathaniel Palmer was loaned to the Library of Congress by his proud descendants, it was seized upon by zealous geographers as finally providing conclusive documentary proof that Palmer had been first to sight the Antarctic continent when he sailed his small boat, the *Hero*, off its shores in November 1820. As the Library of Congress cartographer Colonel Lawrence Martin declared in November 1937, Palmer's logbook provided 'irrefutable evidence' of the primacy of American discovery.[14]

Very much a political geographer, Martin had worked with the State Department and taught at various universities before becoming chief of the division of maps of the Library of Congress in 1924. The donation of Palmer's logbook and papers to the Library of Congress brought Martin into close contact with the Palmer family, which made him an ardent supporter of the family's campaign to have their forebear recognised as the discoverer of Antarctica.

He told the family that he wanted 'to help restore to [Palmer] the credit he justly deserves'. Martin planned to do so by buying their logbooks for preservation in the Library of Congress and by touting Palmer's achievements in 'lectures and publications'.[15] This was not just about preserving history. Martin's earlier work for the State Department, as well as the constant press discussion in the 1930s about the territorial rights accruing to the United States from the activities of Byrd, made him acutely conscious of the standing that America would enjoy if it could claim that its citizens were the first to sight Antarctica.

Martin gave a lecture to Philadelphia's venerable American Philosophical Society in November 1937, citing the logbook of the *Hero* as proof that Palmer had discovered the Antarctic. At the same time, he dismissed the British claim that its naval officer Edward Bransfield had discovered the Antarctic nine months earlier, noting that Bransfield had left no surviving logbook that proved such a discovery. The following July, Martin went off to Europe to spread the word at the International Geographical Congress in Amsterdam. He wrote to Palmer's descendants, saying that his paper would 'give adequate credit to your great uncle, as it will be printed in English, French, Dutch, and other languages', thereby ensuring that the 'announcement will have the wide-spread circulation which you and I know Captain Nathaniel B. Palmer's achievement deserves'. On his return to the United States, Martin continued his campaign with a lecture to the National Academy of Sciences.[16]

The argument became more heated when a combative geologist and geographer at the University of Michigan, William Herbert Hobbs, joined the fray. Palmer could only be the discoverer of Antarctica if Bransfield's rival claim was somehow refuted. Hobbs was the ideal person to take on this challenge. An ardent patriot, Hobbs courted controversy and was unrestrained in his language. He had been a fervent supporter of Peary's claim to be the discoverer of the North Pole, and a vehement denigrator of Peary's rival, Frederick Cook, whom he described as 'the foremost imposter of the age'.[17] Hobbs would later oppose a congressional move to award its medal of honour to Peary's black American companion.[18] During the First World War, Hobbs had been a passionate proponent of American involvement, leading a fanatical campaign at the University of Michigan that saw six members of the German department sacked for their allegedly unpatriotic views. His interest in the polar regions had seen him publish papers on glaciology and lead three university expeditions to Greenland in the late 1920s, during which he had established a radio station to warn of Atlantic storms. Now retired and in his mid-seventies, Hobbs had lost none of his ardour and hunger for controversy, although he had developed a little more judgement with age.[19]

In September 1937, Martin had given Hobbs a letter of introduction to Palmer's descendants, assuring them that they would enjoy knowing the 'scholarly and delightful gentleman'.[20] Hobbs not only met with the descendants but also made a diligent search for all available maps, logbooks and other records relating to Palmer and the Stonington sealers. This took him to the libraries and museums of the old American whaling ports, and across the Atlantic to England and Europe, where he critically examined the maps of the British discoverers and lectured to audiences on Palmer's achievement.[21]

Back in the United States, Hobbs began his campaign to privilege American discoveries by blasting the British mariner James Weddell as 'a fake explorer of the Antarctic', disputing Weddell's claim to have reached 74° S in the sea that came to bear his name.[22] Then he turned his attention to Palmer and Bransfield, writing a long paper for the American Philosophical Society that was published in January 1939. Dismissing out of hand the contemporary charts and articles that showed Bransfield had sighted Antarctica in January 1820, Hobbs accused British officials and writers of conducting a campaign of misrepresentation and forgery over the previous century.[23]

Hobbs' vituperative article received widespread press coverage in the United States.[24] Its author tried to ensure that it was noticed elsewhere, too, sending copies to fellow geographers around the world. The paper sparked a flurry of replies from Hobbs' British counterparts, who described him as 'scurrilous' and 'fraudulent'. Even some American geographers thought he was a 'scrapper' with 'a very definite anti-British complex', although Byrd described him as 'one of the world's greatest authorities on the Antarctic'. The academically minded Bowman was simply embarrassed by Hobbs, describing him as 'a strange mixture of a man with scientific interests which seem to me to be almost invariably under the control of a conclusion already arrived at or an emotion that is out of hand'.[25]

A frantic search was made for other logbooks that might support American claims. Finding these early logbooks, and establishing America's right to be the discoverer of Antarctica, was only one step towards cementing an official claim to the continent. Any such claim would be supported by the private expeditions of more recent American explorers, such as Byrd and Ellsworth. But history had shown, and international legal opinion had long argued, that territorial claims could only be established with finality when the claimant actually occupied the territory. For more than a century, the peculiar difficulties of living in the Antarctic had seemed to preclude that course from being pursued. This view gradually changed in the late 1930s, as the deteriorating international situation imbued the Antarctic with a new-found strategic and commercial significance, and as technological advances made it easier to live in the Antarctic.

Ever since the First World War, Britain had wanted to have Antarctica for itself, and it had enlisted its southern dominions – Australia, New Zealand and South Africa – to buttress its claim.

But Britain's war-weakened state, and the lack of any compelling commercial or strategic advantage, had made it difficult to mobilise political support in pursuit of that aim. Other nations began to take up the slack. Norway's whaling fleet had a big presence in the Antarctic seas, and its whalers had established informal claims to parts of the continent. The Japanese whalers were relative newcomers to the Antarctic, but the nation had some claim to Antarctic territory based upon the Shirase expedition of 1911–12. They would be joined in the Antarctic by a German expedition, due to be dispatched there in December 1938 by Field Marshal Hermann Göring. This would be the first step of the Nazi government's plan to establish a territorial claim of its own, as it built up its fast-growing whaling fleet in an effort to end its dependence on Norwegian-caught whale oil.

Even before news of the German plans reached Washington, the American government was planning to respond in a way that would establish the primacy of its own claim to the Antarctic. The Byrd and Ellsworth expeditions of the 1920s and 1930s had seen large swathes of the continent photographed from the air, and its features named and mapped. When the explorers had returned, the *New York Times* and the Hearst newspapers, backers of the rival expeditions, had given whole pages to dramatic descriptions of the territory that had been flown over and which now could be claimed as belonging to the United States. Even more dramatically, live radio reports had brought the Antarctic activities of Byrd crackling into the living rooms of millions of Americans. Although the government had refrained from officially confirming those claims, the pressure on Washington to do so was growing.

Some of the impetus came from Byrd himself, who pressed the State Department in June 1937 to make a formal claim for the Antarctic regions he had discovered and mapped.[26] At the time, Byrd was increasingly restless, although he was still suffering the effects of carbon-monoxide poisoning from his last stint in the Antarctic. For a time, he immersed himself again in political agitation, becoming involved with powerful and conservative businessmen who wanted to keep the United States out of any future war with Germany. Prominent among them was the president of IBM, Tom Watson, who sympathised with the Nazi regime and developed close business ties with it. Partly at the behest of Watson, Byrd used his public profile to make calls for peace, arguing for a plebiscite to be held before America could go to war, an idea that was roundly rejected by Roosevelt.

Once again, Byrd found himself excluded from Roosevelt's close circle. Although the door to Secretary of State Cordell Hull's office remained open, Byrd was surprised to find that when he went there to discuss his contentious peace plans, Hull wanted to talk mainly about the Antarctic and the status of American claims. Byrd reported to his brother Harry that Hull and his officials were 'much interested in the Antarctic situation' and apparently eager to outmanoeuvre the continuing British attempts to lay claim to most of the continent. Byrd strongly urged the State Department to 'claim the areas east of the 150th meridian that we discovered and mapped', assuring them that doing so would not cause problems with the British, since they had not 'been in that part of Antarctica'.[27] Having sniffed the political wind, Byrd quickly decided to abandon his peace campaign and organise yet another expedition to the Antarctic.

While Byrd was suggesting to the State Department that it annex Marie Byrd Land, the Department of the Interior was also investigating how America's territorial claims in the Antarctic might be strengthened. It was its role to administer territories that the State Department had decided to annex. In October 1937, the head of the department's Division of Territories and Island Possessions, Ernest Gruening, asked Richard Black to present plans for an official expedition.[28]

By the time Black presented his proposal in May 1938, the race to claim the Antarctic continent had accelerated. American newspapers were reporting the territorial ambitions of other nations, and there were increasing calls in Congress for the government to annex the areas that Ellsworth and Byrd had discovered and explored. Black's proposal called for a small expedition to be sent to the coastline east of the Ross Sea. This so-called 'Pacific quadrant' lay between New Zealand's Ross Dependency and the sectors claimed by Britain, Chile and Argentina, and had been the focus of the previous Byrd and Ellsworth expeditions. Although explorers of other nations had also been to the area over the years, Black argued that 'practically all exploration within these boundaries has been done by American citizens'. He suggested that a small ship, either financed by American businesses or provided by the government, should drop off a few men on the coastline, who could then use dog sledges to chart as much land as possible before being picked up further along the coast. Black envisaged that he would lead the expedition, in association with another former Byrd expeditioner, Finn Ronne.[29]

But Black and Ronne had left their run too late. Not only had Byrd announced his own expedition to the Antarctic, with plans to return to Little America, but Ellsworth and Wilkins were also planning an expedition. In May 1938, as Black was sending his proposal to Washington, Ellsworth used an article in the *New York Times* to announce his plans to explore 'the Enderby Quadrant of the Antarctic continent', the relatively unknown region in the western part of the Australian Antarctic Territory. Ellsworth had vowed he would never go south again. But he could not resist the pull of the Antarctic and was possessed by 'the thrill of starting once again for the unknown'. If the weather conditions were clear, he hoped to fly from Enderby Land clear across the continent to Little America. It would answer the naysayers who had suggested that the Ellsworth Trans-Antarctic Flight of 1935 had not been truly trans-Antarctic. If a flight from Enderby Land to Little America was impossible, he intended to explore the hinterland of Enderby Land, 'mapping by camera as much of the unknown areas as possible' and also mapping 'the coast line more completely than has ever been done in the past, and possibly find suitable spots for future weather observatories'. This son of a coal magnate wanted to confirm the existence of 'important oil and mineral deposits', noting the likelihood of there being 'rich wealth inland', given that the Australian explorer Douglas Mawson had found indications of silver, copper and other minerals along the Enderby coast.[30]

Although the mooted flight from Enderby Land was likely to excite much public interest, Ellsworth's first choice had been to explore the coastline of the land he had named after his father, east of the Ross Dependency, which would make the American claim on James W. Ellsworth Land that much more secure. Yet that would not have been the sort of expedition to make headlines in the United States, and it was Wilkins who convinced the wealthy explorer to tackle Enderby Land instead.[31] It is unclear why Ellsworth agreed to the change of plan, since, as he freely acknowledged, Enderby Land was 'already claimed by Australia' and he therefore would 'be unable to claim any new territory for the United States'. The coastline had also been extensively explored by Norwegian whalers and some Norwegian names had been applied to its coastal features.

But a focus on Enderby Land did open up the prospect of making a trans-Antarctic flight, and of discovering new stretches of land that he would be free to name in memory of his father. After all, as Ellsworth told the *New York Times*, that quadrant of Antarctica contained 'the largest unknown territory anywhere in the world'.[32]

Once again, science was not high on Ellsworth's list of priorities. Geographic discovery was foremost, and he asked the State Department 'which part of Antarctica he should explore in order best to serve American interests'. He was fobbed off by its officials, who questioned how he could make claims on behalf of the United States as a private citizen when his pilot was Canadian, his crew was mainly Norwegian and his deputy was Australian.[33] Moreover, any discovery would be done in the manner of a dilettante rather than a diligent explorer. Instead of taking a proper aerial mapping camera, which might help the American Geographical Society's cartographic section compile fairly accurate maps, Ellsworth insisted on taking his usual Leica camera, which was only good at taking small snapshots that were blurred when blown up for mapping purposes.[34] There would also be no ground control points to allow cartographers to pinpoint the precise location of the mountains and other features that Ellsworth photographed. Once again, Ellsworth left the organisation of the expedition to Wilkins, while he went off to the beach at Bournemouth in England to tramp his prescribed eighteen miles each day on the sand. Then, while en route to join the *Wyatt Earp* at Cape Town, he flew with his wife to Nairobi to further build up his fitness with a bout of African mountaineering.[35]

Once the *Wyatt Earp* had been readied and departed for Cape Town, Wilkins went aboard a more comfortable passenger liner that would take him to South Africa by way of Australia. Although he was going as Ellsworth's deputy on an American-funded expedition, Wilkins wrote to Richard Casey offering to do what he could 'in the interest of Australia while I am down there'.[36] He reconciled any conflict of interest by noting that he was an 'adviser' to Ellsworth rather than a 'member' of the expedition, and was therefore 'free [to] conduct independent actions while in [the] Antarctic'.

Wilkins had been told by Norwegians that Mawson's claiming ceremony on Proclamation Island in 1930 had given Australia no title to the nearby Antarctic coastline. Bearing those discussions in mind, Wilkins urged that 'the Commonwealth miss no opportunity to strengthen the claim'. However, when he reached Sydney on 5 September 1938, Wilkins found that the Australian government did not want him to raise the flag or read proclamations on territory already claimed by Mawson. After meetings with the secretary of the Department of External Affairs, William Hodgson, and his minister, Billy Hughes, Wilkins was told that any such action could 'lead to an international belief that we ourselves doubt the validity of the Australian title to the territory'.[37]

During his discussions with Hodgson, Wilkins was told of all that Mawson had done to assert British sovereignty, the details of which had not been reported. He was also provided with a draft map of the Antarctic that Australian officials were busily compiling in such a way that the work of Mawson would be privileged, and that of the Norwegian whalers diminished. The Australians particularly wanted to define Lars Christensen Land out of existence, arguing that there was no unnamed space between Mac. Robertson Land and Princess Elizabeth Land into which it could fit. So that the Norwegians were not too piqued by the omission, it was decided to retain Lars Christensen's name on the map, relegating it to a small stretch of coastline rather than to the much greater region to which it had originally been applied. Similar moves were made with respect to King Leopold and Queen Astrid Coast and Ingrid Christensen Coast.

The information from Hodgson allayed Wilkins' concerns about the strength of the British claim. Nevertheless, he was still provided with a general authority by the Australian government 'to enter upon, explore and report on the Australian Antarctic Territory'. Whether or not Wilkins did anything with this authority, his appointment 'to carry out work' would show that Australia was taking action to get international recognition of its claim by performing 'additional acts of sovereignty over the Territory'.[38]

Britain thought that it might be a good idea for Australia to welcome the Ellsworth expedition and offer it any facilities that it might require, as New Zealand had done for both Byrd and Ellsworth. Of course, Australia had no facilities in the Australian Antarctic Territory, and the *Wyatt Earp* was leaving from Cape Town rather than Hobart, but an offer would be symbolic rather than practical. It was an opportunity for Australia to tell the world of its territorial claim. However, the Australian government decided that such an offer would only irritate the American government. It might also irritate Ellsworth, which the Australian government was also anxious to avoid.

The less said about territorial claims the better, decided the government, which was also hoping that Ellsworth might 'perform valuable work so far as the Commonwealth is concerned by filling in gaps, confirming doubtful areas and counteracting the activities of the Norwegians'. Anyway, the purpose of the proposed invitation was to make an implicit statement about Australian ownership while hopefully receiving in return an acknowledgement of that ownership by other nations. While the United States government had steadfastly refused to make any such acknowledgement, Wilkins assured the Australian government that he would have Ellsworth write a letter recognising Australian sovereignty and send it to Canberra prior to the *Wyatt Earp* leaving Cape Town. But the promised letter was never sent. As Wilkins soon discovered, Ellsworth had been secretly enlisted by the American government to make a claim on Enderby Land.[39]

Although State Department officials had fobbed off Ellsworth when he asked for advice about which part of the Antarctic he should explore and claim, they now had a change of heart, perhaps because of reports from Australia about Wilkins' plans for territorial acquisition on behalf of Australia. The United States did not accept the British view that administering an Antarctic territory from afar and occasionally visiting it was legally equivalent to occupying it. Since the Americans did not regard Australia as having occupied any part of the Australian Antarctic Territory, they believed that its sovereignty remained open to other nations to claim. With Washington having decided to make an eventual Antarctic claim of its own, Secretary of State Hull instructed his consul in Cape Town to explain to Ellsworth how to claim any unexplored territory for the United States.

Just before the *Wyatt Earp* left Cape Town on 29 October 1938, the consul rushed to the wharf with a memorandum detailing the procedure that Ellsworth should follow to ensure his claim would be recognised. He was instructed 'to assert claims in the name of the United States . . . to all territory he may explore, photograph, or map which has hitherto been undiscovered and unexplored, regardless of whether or not it lies within a sector or sphere of influence already claimed by any other country'. The State Department suggested that he do so by 'dropping notes or personal proclamations, attached to parachutes, containing assertions of claims, and subsequently making public the text of such claims, together with approximate latitude and longitude of the points concerned'. When announcing his claims, Ellsworth should keep secret the fact that the American government had advance knowledge and approved of his activities.[40] He was also instructed to keep the memorandum secret from Wilkins. Despite having disavowed any intention to claim any Australian territory on behalf of the United States, Ellsworth now agreed to do so.

But he would again be dogged by bad luck. It took more than two months for the *Wyatt Earp* to reach the edge of the ice, only for Ellsworth to find that he was still almost 1300 kilometres from the continent, which compelled him to spend another forty-five days trying to force a way through the ice. By then it was too late for him to make his planned flight across the continent.[41]

Following the consul's instructions, Ellsworth prepared a copper cylinder that would hold the proclamation he planned to drop from his aircraft onto the Antarctic continent. Although he had been told to keep Wilkins in the dark, the elderly explorer took him into his confidence as the ship wallowed its way towards the ice. Ellsworth later described how the ship 'twists and screws around in all sorts of gyrations so that we had hardly left Capetown heading South when I was thrown into the engine room, dislocating my arm and breaking a tooth'.[42]

Anxious to justify his plans, the injured Ellsworth recalled for Wilkins the British proclamation that he himself had dropped from his aircraft when he had reached the limit of his flight over the Antarctic Peninsula in December 1928. Ellsworth confided that he only planned to do likewise over Wilkes Land. He conceded that, unlike Wilkins in 1928, he did not have any official authority to claim territory on behalf of his government, but his talk with the consul and his reading of the State Department documents made him 'feel that he should make a claim'. So began an extraordinary competition between the two men, as each sought to lay claim to the same territory on behalf of their respective countries.[43]

Wilkins got an early advantage by convincing Ellsworth to make for the nearby Ingrid Christensen Coast – about 77° E – where he predicted it would be easier to launch the aircraft, rather than heading further east to Wilkes Land. An inchoate American title to Wilkes Land arguably existed by virtue of Wilkes' exploration in the 1840s and would be strengthened if Ellsworth dropped his proclamation upon it. Although Wilkins pointed out that Ingrid Christensen Coast had been seen and claimed by Mawson and thus was part of the recently created Australian Antarctic Territory, Ellsworth was adamant that he would claim 240 kilometres to each side of his flight path and all the way to the South Pole on behalf of the United States. Wilkins then convinced him to 'limit his claim to the new area actually seen and explored during the flight'. That would leave Mawson's sighting of the coastline alone. If the Arctic's sector principle was accepted for the Antarctic, it would mean that Mawson's claim to the Australian sector took precedence over Ellsworth's claim to a haphazard strip of territory.[44]

While Ellsworth pressed ahead with his flight preparations, Wilkins continued to do what he could to outsmart his expedition leader by going ashore and making claims on behalf of Australia. Taking the Canadian pilot J. H. Lymburner as a witness, Wilkins landed on a small island on 8 January 1939. Climbing beyond a penguin rookery, Wilkins raised the Australian flag above the bemused birds, before depositing 'the flag and a record of the visit in a small aluminum container' that was placed at the foot of a rock and covered with stones. Wilkins later reported to the Australian government that he had chosen the islands because they showed signs of mineral deposits. Indeed, he had collected several boxes of rocks to take back with him. Soon after, Wilkins went ashore again, this time onto the continent itself near the western end of the Vestfold Mountains. More rock samples were collected, and, with Lymburner, Wilkins repeated the flag-raising and deposited another flag and a record of their visit. When Ellsworth went aloft on 11 January, Wilkins went ashore for a final time and did it all again, depositing a document that recorded them 'having set foot on the Antarctic mainland in several places and upon several of the islands . . . having flown the flag of Australia, [I] leave it with this record'. Wilkins was not claiming the territory, since that had been done by Mawson and the subsequent British order in council, but he was reasserting the existing Australian sovereignty.[45]

While Wilkins and Lymburner were collecting rocks for their cairn, Ellsworth was being flown southward with his copper tube and the proclamation whose words Wilkins had helped to craft. In the end, rather than his planned series of flights reaching 800 kilometres inland, Ellsworth had only been able to make one major flight, which travelled just 460 kilometres southward. As the aircraft turned back towards the ship, Ellsworth opened the door so that he could drop out the tube with its American flag and a signed record of the flight, which allowed him to 'claim for my country, so far as this act allows', the area extending 240 kilometres to each side of the flight path and another 240 kilometres beyond the turning point. 'Serene in its solitude,' wrote Ellsworth, 'no human eye sees nor human tongue speaks its beauty.' Now it was his. It was a small fraction of what he had hoped to explore and claim. Nevertheless, Ellsworth later told reporters that the area was 'almost the size of Nebraska', and that he had named it 'American Highland'. He might have gone on to explore more but was forced to cut short the expedition on 13 January, when three of the ship's crew were injured while chopping ice to make fresh water. The chief officer's knee was so badly crushed that the *Wyatt Earp* had to head straight to Hobart for him to obtain treatment.[46]

Wilkins' relations with Ellsworth had become strained. An expedition with two ageing prima donnas, each eager for publicity, was always going to be a fraught exercise. Even as Ellsworth's aircraft was being packed aboard the *Wyatt Earp* for the voyage to Hobart, Wilkins was looking ahead to his next Antarctic expedition. He wanted the Australian government to purchase the *Wyatt Earp* and commission him to go back south.

In a cable on 12 January 1939, Wilkins warned Canberra of Ellsworth's actions and proposed that he lead an expedition to reinforce Australian sovereignty over the territory that Ellsworth was secretly claiming. To make the claim more solid than Ellsworth's, Wilkins proposed to stay throughout the winter. It was meant to be a confidential message to the Australian government, but because of Ellsworth's commercial arrangement with the *New York Times* the cable was routed through New York, from where a copy was sent to the State Department in Washington. American officials were now on notice about the plans being considered in Australia that would undo Ellsworth's work and shut the United States out of much of the Antarctic. Their concern would have turned to alarm when they read, soon after, that Ellsworth had sailed the *Wyatt Earp* to Australia and was negotiating to sell his ship and its aircraft to the Australian government. The State Department saw the Australian interest in the *Wyatt Earp* in the context of Britain's ambition to control the entire continent.[47]

As it happened, just as the *Wyatt Earp* was chugging its way along the Derwent River towards Hobart on 4 February 1939, ships of the Australian navy were also visiting Tasmania, along with government ministers who were preparing for a cabinet meeting in the Tasmanian capital. Mawson had been consulted about the *Wyatt Earp* and was keen for Australia to purchase it.[48] He had radioed Ellsworth from Adelaide, urging him to hold the ship in Hobart until it could be inspected. Mawson particularly wanted Treasurer Casey to look at it, along with any naval officers who might attest to its seaworthiness. But Mawson did not want the ship for Wilkins' proposed expedition; he had a grander scheme in mind.

Rather than just sending Wilkins south for a year, Mawson wanted to establish an 'Antarctic Club', with members from universities and museums who would man at least one permanent land station for scientific research. He did not want the government to fund this base, but he did want it to buy the *Wyatt Earp* as a supply ship, since there was no other ice-strengthened vessel in Australia. Mawson recognised that the demands of national defence and the lingering effects of the Depression precluded the government from supporting another extensive voyage like his 1929–31 expedition. But if the ship could be used to transport men and materials to the Antarctic for a permanent base staffed by unpaid volunteers, then 'very valuable scientific work' could be done, and 'permanent occupation of Australian Antarctic territory [could be] achieved at a minimum of expense'.[49] It would be colonisation by scientists.

Although the Australian government had earlier rejected suggestions that it purchase the *Wyatt Earp*, ministers now quickly agreed to do so. The deal was helped when Ellsworth dropped the price to just £4000, which Casey thought was 'remarkably low'. In announcing the purchase, Casey assured Australians that the ship would allow the exploitation of whaling and minerals in the Antarctic and also, by the establishment of a meteorological base, allow for long-range weather forecasting in Australia.[50] This was a big issue at the time, as a long drought had culminated in widespread fires across the east coast, causing much death and devastation, only to be followed by widespread flooding. The fundraising for the fire victims had undermined Mawson's efforts to gain money for an Antarctic base, so he was mightily relieved when the government bought the *Wyatt Earp*.

When the ship sailed on to Sydney, Mawson met with Ellsworth and Wilkins and inspected the vessel and its aircraft. He told journalists that the acquisition should be used to transport men and materials for a permanent scientific station at the South Magnetic Pole.[51] That plan was soon imperilled when the government decided instead to place the ship under the control of the navy, which wanted to use it for the storage and transport of explosives. Mawson had to be content with the government's agreement that it would be made 'available for polar work when required'. That gave Mawson the means to approach Australian universities, which agreed to support his idea of the Antarctic Club and provide scientific personnel to man a permanent base in Antarctica, beginning in 1940.[52]

Australia's willingness to buy the *Wyatt Earp* was not just because the twenty-year-old ship appeared to be a bargain. The government was conscious of the challenge that Ellsworth's expedition had posed to Australia's sovereignty, and saw the ship as a means of fighting back.[53] Ellsworth had trumpeted his achievement in having 'claimed the inland area I explored . . . for my country'. He had also dismissed talk of the Antarctic as a 'white and worthless continent', arguing that it would one day be found to be 'as rich in minerals and oil as the United States'. It was now up to 'governments and lawyers', wrote Ellsworth, 'to consider and rule upon the support and permanency of such a claim', which amounted to more than 200,000 square kilometres from his last expedition and an additional 900,000 square kilometres from the expedition in 1935. He assured Australian journalists that he had not claimed any of the coastline seen by Mawson, only the hinterland over which he had flown.[54]

Australian officials were aghast. Before his expedition, Ellsworth had told journalists that he would not be making any territorial claims. Then Wilkins had promised that Ellsworth would acknowledge Australia's ownership of the Australian Antarctic Territory before he left Cape Town. Now he had done the exact opposite.

Ellsworth's challenge could not go unanswered. Newspapers were quietly briefed that the dominion already claimed sovereignty over the territory that Ellsworth purported to claim, while an Australian diplomat in Washington approached the State Department to see whether it intended to make a formal claim based on Ellsworth's discoveries. To Australia's chagrin, the Americans continued to keep everyone guessing, refusing to comment until they had received Ellsworth's report.[55]

Ellsworth returned by steamer to the United States, where he told reporters of his plan for another expedition in 1941. Next time he intended to spend the winter camped at the South Pole, not just 160 kilometres from Little America, as Byrd had done. Rather disingenuously, Ellsworth declared that he was 'only interested in trail blazing – not claiming land' and that it was 'time for the government to take charge to make maps and look for minerals'. As for the contest for territory, he suggested that an 'international commission' be established 'to settle overlapping claims in the Antarctic'.[56]

Such a commission had been talked about for several years but nothing had come of it. However, so long as it remained in prospect, nations were anxious that their claims should be as strong as possible in the eyes of the international community. That way, if an international conference on the Antarctic was held, their particular land claims were more likely to be upheld. This appeared to be reason enough for the United States to reinforce the activities of its private explorers with an officially sponsored expedition. There were even more compelling reasons.

While Ellsworth had been dropping an American flag and statement of claim on the so-called 'American Highland', Alfred Ritscher and the aircraft of the *Schwabenland* had been operating just to the west of the *Wyatt Earp*, dropping their swastikas on the so-called 'Neue Schwabenland', so as 'to secure for Germany her share in the approaching division of the Antarctic among the world powers'.[57]

Meanwhile, there were reports of the Japanese government being pressured to assert its 'right to certain snow-covered territory in the Antarctic', which had been explored in 1912 by the now eighty-year-old Nobu Shirase. He had raised the Japanese flag and left a copper case containing the names of the expedition supporters and members and the achievement of his Dash Patrol in reaching 80° S. Although there were calls in Japan for 'the Rising Sun [to] be unfurled over the South Pole', Shirase had not got beyond the Ross Ice Barrier in his fruitless race with Scott and Amundsen, before being brought to a halt by blizzards.[58] So the basis for a Japanese claim on the South Pole was non-existent.

Nevertheless, the American reports of the public clamour in Tokyo, combined with the growing Japanese whaling fleet in the Antarctic, added to the pressure on the US government to respond with moves of its own. The colonisation of the Antarctic was about to begin.

CHAPTER 15

'To people the land'

1939–1941

As the beginning of 1939 saw the world sliding inexorably toward the abyss of another widespread war, officials in Washington and Canberra were beginning to put the colonisation of the Antarctic on their national agendas. While Sir Douglas Mawson was urging his government to support a permanent base in the Australian Antarctic Territory, there were proposals in Washington for the United States to do likewise, but on a much larger scale.

For the past decade, President Roosevelt had taken a close interest in the Antarctic activities of his explorer friend, Richard Byrd. He was keen to establish a basis for the formal annexation by the United States of those parts of the continent that had been discovered or explored by Americans. Although there had long been calls for this in Congress and elsewhere, the increasing Antarctic activities of Nazi Germany and Japan finally provided the compelling strategic reason for the United States to have an Antarctic presence of its own. The last continent to be occupied by humans was about to enter a dramatic new era.

The Interior Department official and former Byrd expeditioner Richard Black had in May 1938 proposed a limited American expedition to the region east of the Ross Dependency. However, the rising crescendo of activities by rival claimants to the continent prompted Roosevelt to propose, in early 1939, a much grander scheme. Rather than a small, possibly private expedition, Roosevelt wanted it to be organised jointly by the Departments of State, War, the Navy and the Interior.

Whereas Black had recommended landing a few men with a dog sledge, later suggesting that the expedition might also include an old aircraft, Roosevelt wanted two ships to establish bases on opposite sides of the continent. One party would be based at Byrd's Little America and the other on the Enderby coast, to the south of

South Africa, where American explorer Lincoln Ellsworth was then operating. Roosevelt proposed that the two bases could be evacuated each winter and reoccupied the following summer.

To Roosevelt, this occupation would have seemed as close to permanent as the Antarctic would allow. He was certainly aware that issuing executive orders and doing occasional surveys of the coastline and flights over the interior, as the British had done, would not suffice to ensure 'international recognition of American jurisdiction'. Anxious to press on with the expedition, Roosevelt instructed the State Department to consult with Byrd and Ellsworth about the likely annual cost of his plan.[1]

At the time, Ellsworth was still in the Antarctic, which meant that Byrd was in the box seat to receive any government funding that might be in the offing. When State Department official Hugh Cumming went with the department's geographer, Samuel Boggs, to Byrd's Boston home in January 1939 bearing a letter from Roosevelt, the explorer was quick to seize the opportunity. Rather than just advising the officials on the likely cost, Byrd offered to abandon the private expedition he was planning and lead a government one instead. He proposed that the old converted whaling vessel that he had bought for his expedition, the *Bear of Oakland*, could be taken over by the government at minimal cost.

By the time Black arrived in Washington from Honolulu to advise the Department of the Interior about his limited expedition, it had already been ditched in favour of the president's arrangement, with the high-profile Byrd nominated as leader.[2] Replacing the relatively unknown Black and Ronne had the added advantage for Roosevelt of diverting Byrd from his unhelpful meddling in foreign policy and immersing him instead in polar exploration.

On 17 February 1939, Black and other officials gathered in Byrd's suite at Washington's stately Willard Hotel for a week-long discussion of how Roosevelt's scheme might be implemented. With Byrd now back in Roosevelt's favour, the officials readily agreed that he should 'act as overseer of all plans', which were intended to be a response to the territorial claims of other nations and to 'consolidate' the territorial claims that had been created by the recent exploratory work of Byrd and Ellsworth, along with the much earlier discoveries of Wilkes and Palmer. Although the State Department seems to have had some concern about the legal basis of the American claims to parts of the Antarctic claimed by other nations, the US Coast Guard was keen to be involved, offering one of its cutters, the *Northland*, for the expedition. The meeting agreed that the vessel should be moved from California to Boston for refitting, with the transfer to be done for the ostensible purpose of patrolling the North Atlantic. Journalists would be kept in the dark until a statement was needed to 'allay conjecture by the press as to the complete mission'. Congress would also be kept in the dark for the time being. It would not be asked for funds for the initial expenses, which would be sourced instead from one of the departments. The money would be said to be for another purpose.[3]

At the end of the conference, it was clear that the officials had taken Roosevelt's plan a further step. Instead of two bases being established on opposite sides of the continent, only to be vacated during the winter months, it was proposed that they be permanently occupied settlements. In his report for the Department of the Interior on 21 February, Black noted accordingly that the aim of the expedition was 'United States Government colonization in the Antarctic'. American policy in regard to 'the claiming of new territory', he wrote, had always argued that a recognised claim could only be achieved by 'actual occupation and residence'. This had presented difficulties, which would now be overcome by the government maintaining 'permanent bases at suitable points on the coast of the Antarctic continent, relieving their personnel yearly and developing a far-reaching program of exploration and scientific research'.[4] American authority would also be asserted by appointing a postmaster to each of the bases, with the establishment of a United States Post Office being designed to 'materially aid in the later presentation of territorial claims'.[5]

The officials envisaged that American scientists would be the settlers of Antarctica. According to the official plan, geographers would be in the lead, drawing upon physiography, surveying, cartography and aerial reconnaissance to compile detailed maps of the continent. Then there would be the geologists, who would investigate the possible oil, mineral and other resources that would help to justify the settlements' expenses to the many doubters. There would also be meteorologists, physicists and biologists. Not all would be government scientists: it was intended that 'explorers and men of science who wish to work out special scientific problems would be welcomed and offered full facilities of the stations'.

As for their location, the existing facilities at Little America on the Ross Ice Barrier were given first consideration, even though it was within New Zealand's Ross Dependency. Perhaps because of this, and the 'added advantage of placing a station on continental ice', Black wrote that the first base should be established 'somewhere to the east of Little America and closer to the area of field operations which are considered of greatest interest to the American Government, namely, the long unknown coast in the Pacific Quadrant'.[6] It would be closer to the strategically important Strait of Magellan and the Drake Passage, linking the Atlantic and Pacific Oceans.

The second base would be located on the other side of the continent, where Ellsworth had recently been exploring. Doing so might provide the basis for an American attempt to claim the whole continent, and might counter German plans to establish bases in those regions. It might also open up the possibility of Byrd making an historic, headline-grabbing flight across the continent from one base to the other, as Ellsworth had hoped to do.

An interesting addition to the plan was a proposed third base, which was to be established on Heard Island in the Southern Ocean, to the south-west of Australia. The ownership of this windswept and unoccupied island was a matter of some dispute. It had been named after an American sealer who had discovered it in 1853, with the island having been occupied for some years by American sealers as they ravaged its seal population. British mariners had also been there, while Australia considered that the island belonged rightfully to it, partly because Australia was the closest inhabited country.[7]

The British claim to have sighted the island first was dismissed by Paul Siple, who now was a thirty-year-old geographer at Clark University and, along with Black, one of the two deputies on the prospective expedition. Siple assured Gruening that Heard Island had been discovered, occupied and mapped by Americans. As for the British claim, Siple suspected that 'some British cartographer just painted the island red and everyone else has accepted it because America has not objected'.[8]

Black suggested that a base on Heard Island might provide 'a semi-permanent meteorological and general scientific station' and 'a training station and breeding ground for a superior type of sled dog'. More likely, it was added by Byrd as a weather station for a flight that he had wanted to make across Antarctica and on to

Australia, in an attempt to prove the feasibility of new trans-polar air routes that would connect the southern continents.[9] In the event, the United States did not proceed with its plans for Heard Island, after the Coast Guard vessel was diverted to patrol duties in the Atlantic. It may also have been due to Siple's advice that there were no safe landing places for aircraft on the island, nor was there a safe anchorage for either ships or flying boats.[10]

It was fortunate for Byrd and Roosevelt that their efforts to obtain congressional approval in March 1939 coincided with news of German activities in the Antarctic. The German expedition had an advantage over its competitors. It was using the catapult ship *Schwabenland*, which had been used by Lufthansa to establish a faster airmail route across the South Atlantic, connecting Berlin and the major South American capitals. Stationed in the mid-Atlantic, the *Schwabenland* allowed aircraft to be lifted aboard, refuelled and then catapulted back into the air to complete their onward passage. Letters would thereby reach their destination in a few days. When used in the Antarctic, it was hoped that the catapult mechanism would allow aircraft to be launched at times when ice conditions or rough seas would otherwise prevent it, thereby increasing the area that could be flown over, photographed, mapped and claimed by Germany. However, although the *Schwabenland* had the advantage of the catapult, it was not designed for operating in the Antarctic.

So rushed was the expedition, under the command of the polar explorer and aviator Alfred Ritscher, that instead of installing additional bulkheads to guard against the steel-hulled ship being holed by the ice and sinking, the Germans had simply filled the hold with thousands of empty casks in the hope that they might keep the vessel afloat in such an eventuality. The expedition also had no ground transport, such as tractors or dog sledges, which made it unable to obtain more than a few ground control points for the aerial photographs that were to be taken. Anyway, even if Ritscher had brought tractors and dogs, he arrived too late in the summer to organise extensive ground expeditions. As a result, Ritscher later conceded, the expedition maps were produced 'without the absolute exactitude which can only be obtained by means of triangulation', which required ground parties using theodolites to survey the territory.[11]

In his official report, Ritscher glossed over the expedition's shortcomings. He noted that its purpose had been 'to secure for Germany her share in the approaching division of the Antarctic among the world powers' and to assert 'Germany's right to continue and develop her whaling industry'. It had done so by embracing 'the most modern methods of science', particularly in its use of aircraft, rather than the 'previously complicated methods of polar expeditions with dogs and sleds'. The superiority of its methods, Germany argued, gave it a claim superior to that of Norway or any other nation to that part of the Antarctic that lay south of Africa.

Not content with flying over the interior and photographing it, the Germans had left permanent marks of their presence with specially designed aluminium shafts. These were one and a half metres long, with steel points on one end and three stabilising planes on the other, one of which was decorated with the German swastika. Prior to the expedition's departure, they had been tested on glaciers in the European Alps, where most had landed correctly with their tips penetrating the ice. In the Antarctic, they were dropped from the two seaplanes every twenty to thirty kilometres; the swastikas on the ice were intended 'to establish a right to the territory so marked out'.[12]

Although the flags were dropped from the aircraft, having them land upright on the ice meant that the Germans could argue they were effectively *raising* their flag on the territory that they were claiming. This subtle distinction from the actions of the Americans and the British, who were content to have their markers drop from aircraft and lie on the ice, might make a difference to the outcome of any subsequent legal argument.

The Germans were certainly keen for the whole world to know of its expedition's accomplishments, and of the nation's determination to defend the territorial claim its men had made. In March 1939, the German news agency reported that Ritscher had flown over and dropped swastikas upon the territory claimed by Norway, and that the German government intended to 'secure the fruits of the expedition for Germany'. The Nazi government dismissed Norway's assertion that the area was Norwegian by right of discovery. Now that it had been 'discovered and investigated in detail by the German expedition', Berlin announced, its 'empire stands behind the work of these men with the whole weight of political world power'.[13]

Just a few days after these reports appeared, officials from the Departments of Interior and State, including Black and Gruening, testified before a Senate subcommittee in an attempt to obtain funding for an American expedition. It proved easier than expected, with an initial $10,000 being recommended, and the senators indicating that they were likely to approve the further $340,000 that was required. In fact, even before meeting with the subcommittee, work had begun to install equipment on the expedition vessels so that they could meet the challenges of Antarctic seas.[14] It was an irregular way to proceed, but time was pressing. It would usually take Byrd eighteen months or more to organise supplies and personnel for a year-long expedition; now he had only six months before his departure in October 1939. In addition, planning the expedition was complicated by the requirement to establish permanent bases.

There were more delays as the Senate's formal approval of the $10,000 took several weeks to be confirmed. Although Senator Harry Byrd assured his brother on 6 April that he was looking after the 'appropriation for the colonization of the Antarctic' and did not anticipate any problems getting it through Congress, it was still a frustrating delay for Byrd and his planned expedition.[15] At the same time, Roosevelt was taken ill with sinus trouble and left Washington for a few days to recuperate. He was gone before officials were able to have him to sign a vital memorandum instructing the various departments to cooperate in organising the expedition. When he returned, the politically savvy Roosevelt ordered that nothing should be done until the $10,000 was formally made available by Congress. He did not want the enthusiasm of Byrd, Black and other likeminded officials to get ahead of the congressional process in a way that might call the expedition into question.

There had been plans for Byrd to take over a warehouse at the Boston naval yard, for personnel to be appointed and for supplies to be stockpiled. These plans were now put on hold.[16] As were the plans for the scientific program that was being organised to help justify the whole enterprise. Alton Wade, professor of geology at the University of Miami, had been put in charge of the scientific program. He had preliminary talks with more than thirty scientists about what scientific activities should be carried out at the different bases. However, nothing conclusive could be organised before the expedition had been formally approved and the location of the bases decided.[17]

Any doubts in the White House, or among the few senators privy to the expedition, were dissipated in April by the return to Germany of Ritscher and the *Schwabenland*. The previous month, Roosevelt had asked the State Department's geographer, Samuel Boggs, for a map 'showing in colored crayon the claims and recent activities of various nations in the Antarctic'.[18] Now the entire world could read of Germany's territorial ambitions. While German newsreel footage showed penguins cautiously waddling their way down the gangway to the Hamburg dockside before being whisked off to the Berlin zoo, newspapers reported the serious purpose of the expedition. Germany had 'staked out her first colony outside Europe and is proposing to take possession of about 230,000 square miles of Antarctic territory'.

The Germans argued that their claim was strengthened by not being a random stretch of territory but 'a geologically complete part of the land, bounded on the east and west by an expanse of ice which rises rather abruptly polewards'. Dismissing the rival Norwegian claim as 'purely theoretical', an influential German newspaper argued that it was 'only actual survey and seriously planned utilization of the territory [that would] provide certain rights to this Antarctic sector'. It noted that the territory was now 'unmistakably marked by Reich flags on the south, east and west and the expedition likewise raised the Great German colors on the most important coastal points'.[19]

The implication that Germany was planning to return to 'seriously utilize' the territory would not have been lost on Roosevelt. If the United States was to pre-empt the Germans, as well as the anticipated Australian expedition, he would have to move fast. However, Roosevelt's plan almost came unstuck when the press heard of it and began questioning Hull and Gruening, who were meeting in Washington on 18 April with the recently returned Ellsworth. It was perhaps as a result of his meeting with Hull that Ellsworth cabled to Australia offering to buy back his expedition ship, the Wyatt Earp, only to receive no response.[20] The Australian government was still keeping open the option of sending an expedition in Ellsworth's ship.

Meanwhile, the American government was keeping the world guessing about its own plans. Instead of conceding the existence of a plan that had received the support of the Senate subcommittee, Gruening left journalists with the impression that the government was still merely considering a proposal for an expedition, which was intended only to survey 'lands discovered by Americans, preliminary to a determination of what, if any, this country may claim as permanent possessions'. The press was told that the United States was responding to a challenge being mounted by Great Britain, Norway and Germany, which were racing to claim territory that had been discovered by citizens of the United States. There was no mention of permanent bases being established or anything about the American colonisation of Antarctica. Black noted with relief that Gruening had 'cleverly minimized the whole thing', with his vagueness having 'killed the story effectively'.[21]

With the press misled, the officials quietly proceeded with their plans. Gruening told a meeting at the State Department on 27 April of the 'proposed colonization projects for Antarctica and Heard Island'. With Byrd in attendance, the meeting agreed that the expedition should establish three bases on the Antarctic mainland, on the understanding that the weather or ice conditions would probably make one or more of the three impossible to achieve. Despite the deteriorating European situation and the increasing likelihood of war, the officials were determined to press ahead with their Antarctic plans. Indeed, they justified it by pointing to the 'present unsettled world situation and the probability that these areas will prove of considerable importance in the future development of aviation'.[22] It seems that it was still Byrd's intention to prove the aviation possibilities of the Antarctic by flying across the continent, and perhaps onward to Australia by way of the disputed Heard Island.

The American plans on land were becoming even more ambitious, with a massive 'snow cruiser' being offered for the use of the expedition. The innovative vehicle was designed to have a range of 8000 kilometres and be capable of sustaining its crew for up to a year or more in its commodious interior. Ever since Scott went to the Antarctic in 1910, explorers had been trying to adapt ground transport for use in the continent's difficult conditions. Byrd had considerable success with tracked vehicles on his second expedition, but his deputy, Dr Thomas Poulter, had been concerned by the difficulties he had faced when using the vehicles to rescue Byrd from Advance Base. Poulter had spent the subsequent years trying to design a more reliable form of transport that might be driven regardless of weather conditions and act as a secure refuge for its occupants.

Working at the Armour Institute of Technology in Chicago, Poulter and his team designed a massive behemoth, fifty-five feet long and twenty feet wide. Based on the size of a railway carriage, two diesel engines gave the machine a maximum speed of about fifty kilometres per hour, while the four huge wheels could be moved individually and lifted clear of crevasses or other obstructions. On top of the vehicle would be a small aircraft with a range of 480 kilometres, which could be easily offloaded down the sloping back onto a ramp of snow. The plane was meant to act in concert with the snow cruiser, directing its driver to the quickest and safest route across the icecap and photographing the region from above.

When Poulter heard of the proposed expedition, he went to Washington on 29 April to offer the services of his snow cruiser. Although the vehicle was still on the drawing board and the expedition was meant to leave for the Antarctic in six months, Byrd and government officials commissioned Poulter to produce one, which would then be loaned to the expedition. If it worked as promised, its advantages were clear. The *Schwabenland*'s catapult mechanism had given the German aircraft greater mobility, which supposedly had improved the Germans' claim to the disputed territory. The snow cruiser, it was hoped, would do that much and more for the United States. Whereas the range of the German aircraft – and consequently, their ability to penetrate far into the interior – had been circumscribed by their inability to fly at sufficient height above the icecap, which rose to 3000 metres or more towards the centre of the continent, the snow cruiser would allow a small party of Americans to travel at will across the continent and base themselves at the South Pole during the winter. With bases around the coast and the snow cruiser at the South Pole, the United States had a chance to checkmate its rivals. But nothing could be finalised until Congress had approved the expedition's budget.

In mid-May, Byrd complained that he had to finance the fitting of diesel engines into the *Bear of Oakland*, as well as everyday items such as stamps and stationery.[23] Although various departments helped surreptitiously with supplies and personnel, Byrd was desperate for Congress to approve the $340,000. Only then would he be sure that his expenditure had not been wasted. At the time, he was also preoccupied with his latest commercial venture, 'Admiral Byrd's Penguin Island', which had opened in the amusement area of New York's World Fair. Complete with the requisite penguins and exhibits from his expeditions, Byrd provided added authenticity by appearing there himself as often as he could; one writer described in the *New Yorker* the 'woebegone Admiral Byrd seated among a few equally woebegone Antarctic penguins'. But even his presence failed to draw crowds in numbers that would make Penguin Island the success that Byrd needed it to be.[24]

In late May, Byrd reminded Roosevelt of the urgent need for the money to be approved if the expedition was to proceed during the coming southern summer. Roosevelt had so much else on his mind. He was trying to convince Congress to repeal the 1937 neutrality legislation that prevented the United States from selling armaments to Britain and France, and he was about to host a four-day visit by the British king and queen, every detail of which was absorbing his close attention.[25] Because of these distractions, Congress was left wondering about the strength of Roosevelt's support for the Antarctic venture.

The case for the expedition was not helped when the State Department suddenly passed responsibility for its passage through Congress to the Department of the Interior. When the House Appropriations Committee took evidence from officials on 2 June, Byrd was accompanied by senior officials from Interior, including First Assistant Secretary Ebert Burlow, while the State Department sent only one very junior official. This was not calculated to convince the committee of the pressing need to send an expedition that year.

The committee might also have been alarmed when the scope of Roosevelt's scheme was finally revealed in a press release from the secretary of the interior, Harold Ickes, who disclosed that it would be a 'continuing project over a period of three or four years'.[26] With more than ten million Americans still unemployed and a possible war in the offing, government expenditure was a sensitive issue. Now the government was being asked to fund a costly expedition that was portrayed by critics as being for the enrichment and aggrandisement of Richard Byrd.

Roosevelt might have been able to stiffen the committee's wavering resolve, but he was busy entertaining the visiting British royals from 7 June to 11 June. Byrd was there too, and had a long talk with the king and the president about 'the coming expedition'. Byrd later reported to his brother Harry that they were 'both much interested'.[27]

While the great and the powerful hobnobbed on the White House lawn, and later picnicked at Roosevelt's Hudson River retreat, disturbing new reports arrived from the American embassy in Berlin. They confirmed the German intention to establish a base in the Antarctic, from which they could organise their whaling activities and assert their claim to the territory that Ritscher's expedition had explored. An article by a senior Nazi technocrat – Göring's deputy, Dr Helmuth Wohlthat, who had been responsible for organising the expedition – argued that 'none of the nations claiming sovereign rights in the Antarctic has even approximately as full knowledge regarding the territory claimed or as precise maps and charts as Germany possesses'. While Wohlthat conceded that an official German claim would have to await the evaluation of Ritscher's results, he pointed out that 'the acquisition of unclaimed land' requires 'the intention to occupy it, i.e. to people the land and administer and rule it'.[28] And no nation had yet done that on the continent itself.

The article was seized upon by a senior official at the Department of the Interior, Ebert Burlew, in an attempt to swing the congressional vote. On 12 June, he sent a translated copy to congressman Clifford Woodrum of the House Appropriations Committee, warning that the Germans were likely to take the 'first opportunity' to 'make an official move into the Pacific sector [of the Antarctic], which is the area nearest to the American Continents and in the Western Hemisphere'.[29] They would therefore be challenging America's Monroe Doctrine, which had long forbidden the entry of European powers into the Americas.

The committee was unimpressed and voted narrowly against approving the additional funding. The vote suddenly threw all the expedition's preparations into disarray. Byrd called on Congress to regard the Monroe Doctrine as including the Antarctic, announcing that he would go south anyway, in a private capacity. The State Department also renewed its interest in the expedition, with its officials meeting with the committee in an attempt to have it reverse its decision, arguing that it had become a matter of 'national policy' to forestall other countries from establishing themselves in the Pacific Quadrant. When the committee again rejected the funding request, Gruening feared that it was too late to mount the expedition that year. For one thing, fur clothing and sleeping bags had to be ordered from Inuit craftsmen and would take months to make.[30]

Before Gruening could postpone the expedition, Byrd and officials of the State Department mounted a last-ditch attempt to pressure the committee to approve the funding for the current year. The committee was assured that Roosevelt had a 'very deep interest' in the expedition, and that the latest information confirmed that 'Germany is on the verge of sending an expedition this year'; there were also signs that Australia was about to send an expedition.[31] On 30 June 1939, as Congress rushed to finalise its business before the 4 July holiday weekend, the funding was finally pushed through both houses and sent to the president for signature.[32] Since the Department of the Interior had responsibility for the expedition and administering the bases, it was Gruening who sent out urgent messages calling Byrd and the relevant departmental representatives to a conference in Washington on 5 July. He blamed the delays on the State Department blowing hot and cold on the expedition, with Gruening still doubtful whether an expedition could be organised that year. He was worried that rushing things might result in a disaster that would be blamed on him.[33]

So the first issue that Gruening raised at the conference was the difficulty of organising the expedition within such a tight timeframe, particularly if it involved three vessels and four bases. He was also upset at the irregular way in which the project was being progressed, complaining to Ickes that he had 'never had any authoritative instructions concerning this project' and had to rely upon verbal assurances from Byrd that Roosevelt 'wanted the expedition to go through'. To Gruening's chagrin, Byrd rushed into the meeting two and a half hours late, telling the officials that 'there was no question in his mind that the expedition could be carried through successfully even at this late date', although he did concede that one or two bases should be dropped from the scheme to save costs.

Still Gruening was not convinced that it could be organised in time, even after the State Department representative declared that it was 'vital that there not be another year's delay'. When it seemed that Gruening was going to recommend against the expedition going ahead, he was called to a meeting at the White House, where he was surprised to see Byrd and representatives of the State Department and the US Navy, who made clear to him that there was 'no doubt in the President's mind that the expedition can be carried out this year'.[34] Byrd had played the presidential card and got his way.

The press was informed of the expanded scope of the expedition. The *New York Times* reported on 7 July that officials were considering plans 'to establish semi-permanent colonies as a basis for pressing formal claim to vast stretches of insular and continental masses for the United States'. The plan was portrayed as a logical extension of the earlier American claims to Canton and Enderbury Islands in the Pacific, whose colonisation Richard Black had supervised. That same day, after meeting with Byrd, Gruening and the Coast Guard's Rear Admiral Russell Waesche at the White House, Roosevelt announced that he had appointed Byrd as the expedition leader and that all relevant departments had been asked to assist the work of the expedition. The three visitors then posed for photographers with a large globe of the world, as Byrd pointed out the territory he intended to occupy.[35] It was all being done, the press was told, to prevent Germany from extending its claims into that part of the Antarctic lying within what was called the Western Hemisphere and 'to substantiate American claims to territory within the sphere of influence of the Monroe Doctrine'. Byrd said that he would be taking three ships and would 'establish three permanent bases west of the 180° Meridian [that would] put this country's earlier claims to the area beyond any question of international law'.[36] Actual occupation would do what flags and maps and names could only partly do.

The American expedition was not just about buttressing historical claims. It was also very much about extending them, and perhaps laying the groundwork for a much greater claim. The key lay in the capabilities of the snow cruiser. As Poulter told a congressional committee, the aircraft carried aboard the cruiser could make 'short flights at 300-mile intervals' and thereby 'explore about 5,000,000 square miles of unknown territory during a single Antarctic Summer'.[37] That was an extraordinary assertion, since it would mean that the cruiser and its aircraft could travel over the entire continent. It is difficult to see how that could be achieved, given the cruiser's top speed of forty-eight kilometres per hour and the many problems of travelling on the icecap. Yet Poulter clearly thought highly of the capability of the snow cruiser, which would carry thousands of stamped envelopes embossed with the words 'The Snow Cruiser Reaches the South Pole'. The combination of the snow cruiser crisscrossing the continent and providing a winter base at the South Pole, of permanent American bases being established around the coastline, and of Byrd making the first flight across Antarctica would lay the most solid basis yet for an American claim to the entire continent.

As photographers at the White House jostled to get the best photograph of the three men, Byrd told the journalists that the expedition was intended to reinforce earlier American claims in the Antarctic and pre-empt any further move by Germany to reinforce its own Antarctic credentials. Aviation was also a consideration. Byrd noted that the United States had lost its chance to claim part or all of Greenland, which would have provided American-controlled landing grounds for an air route to Europe. The Antarctic had similar snow-covered landing grounds, which might provide an essential link in a strategic air route between the Americas and Asia in the event of other air routes being cut by war. And there was the distant possibility Antarctica had mineral resources to be exploited, with Byrd assuring journalists that there was sufficient coal in the Antarctic to keep the United States supplied for forty or fifty years.[38]

Any hesitation that Roosevelt might have harboured about his plans would have been dissipated by the generally enthusiastic press reaction to the news. The *Washington Post* thought that the United States must 'take a leading part in exploring and mapping that area' because 'Great Britain, Germany, Norway and other countries have shown a desire to secure claims on Antarctic territory'. The *New York Times* agreed, noting that the US moves would 'ward off Germany'. Although the re-establishment of a base at Little America would infringe Britain's claim to the Ross Dependency, the paper argued, it would not be a problem since Britain did not have a strong title to the territory and international law made clear that 'merely to claim land does not establish title to it'. For sovereignty to be established, the territory must be 'permanently colonized'.[39] And Byrd was the person to do it.

Six months after Roosevelt had given the State Department instructions to draw up plans for the establishment of permanent bases, he was finally able to tell Byrd how 'deeply happy' he was to appoint him to 'command the first American Expedition for the actual occupation of a portion of the Antarctic Continent'. The expedition would be run by an interdepartmental committee headed by Gruening, along with Coast Guard commandant Rear Admiral Russell Waesche, the US Navy's Captain Charles Hartigan and the State Department's Antarctic specialist Hugh Cumming. The purpose, wrote Roosevelt, was to 'prove (a) that human beings can permanently occupy a portion of the Continent winter and summer [and] (b) that it is well worth a small annual appropriation to maintain such permanent bases because of their growing value for four purposes – national defense of the Western Hemisphere, radio, meteorology and minerals'. After establishing the base, Byrd was to return to Washington so that he could 'explain to the Congress and the public all the reasons for continuation'. Funds could then be secured for the following year and beyond.[40]

It was only after appointing Byrd that Roosevelt turned his attention to devising a name for the expedition. State Department officials had proposed that the name should have some association with the Wilkes expedition of a century before, so as to create an historical connection between the two. It would implicitly suggest that the territorial claims of the new expedition, based upon occupation, were built upon the much earlier discoveries of Wilkes. Taking up this suggestion, Gruening had initially thought of calling it the 'US Antarctic Expedition', the 'US Antarctic Exploring Expedition' or the 'US Government Antarctic Expedition'.[41] However, in a later memorandum to the White House, Gruening 'hoped that something suggestive of permanency might be introduced into the title'. Roosevelt agreed, latching on to another of Gruening's suggested names and instructing that it be called 'The U.S. Antarctic Service', since it has 'an annotation [sic] of permanency'.[42] The American colonisation of Antarctica could now begin.

With the Antarctic summer season just a few months away, there was no time for delay. Prudence might have dictated that the expedition should be held over until the succeeding summer, but the United States wanted to pre-empt attempts by other nations to establish bases in Antarctica. It also wanted to be ready for any international conference on Antarctic sovereignty. However, as Byrd battled in Boston to ready the expedition for an October departure, the ostensible reasons for sending it began to disappear. The likelihood of the German government sending another expedition to the Antarctic became less with each passing day, as Europe lurched towards war. The possibility of an Australian expedition had also diminished. Wilkins had returned to New York, from where he told the Australian government in July 1939 that, in the light of moves by the United States and Argentina, it was 'even more necessary than before for the Australian Commonwealth to maintain her rights in the Antarctic by establishing permanent occupation not only by scientific observers but by appointing one of the occupants as an official representative of the Government'.[43] But the Australians were increasingly distracted by the looming war in Europe. The

Australian government decided on 3 August 1939 to abandon plans for an Antarctic expedition.[44]

However, the announcement of the American expedition had so alarmed Argentina that it decided to assert its own territorial claims more vigorously.[45] To add to Byrd's troubles, the expedition began to spark domestic criticism in the United States, with one critic describing Byrd as 'the greatest American showman, up to and including Barnum', and lambasting the expedition as 'a crisis in asininity beyond the wildest winged imagination'. Another critic called for the government 'to keep Byrd home and let Hitler have Antarctica in the devout hope that he would go there to cool off'.[46] Lastly, Byrd began to complain that he was being forced to mount a million-dollar expedition with a budget of just $350,000, and that there might not be sufficient funds to return the expedition at the end of its first year.[47] Gruening agreed that the expedition was facing 'financial disaster' and warned Byrd that the Department of the Interior would not allow him to go over budget.[48]

In an attempt to solve his financial crisis, Byrd visited Roosevelt again and had him write another letter to the relevant government departments urging them to cooperate with the expedition, so that some of the expense could be transferred to their budgets. Byrd estimated that the navy had already contributed more than $250,000 in goods and services, but that he had still been forced to stump up about $200,000 himself in materials and money to cover the shortfall, or have it donated by 'patriotic citizens'. Apart from two planes provided by the navy, Byrd had managed to have a seaplane loaned by its manufacturer. Such was the need to cut costs that Byrd suggested that the expedition artist be asked to act in an honorary capacity and have his paints and canvasses donated.[49] As for the expedition cameraman, he had to supply his own cameras and film and was paid a token one dollar a year.[50]

Due to all the delays, it was not until 22 November that Byrd's former whaling ship, built of English oak in 1874 and now designated as the USS *Bear*, finally left Boston. Initially, it headed for Panama, before going on to Little America, which the *New York Times* described as a 'complete village' awaiting their arrival. A few days later, the Interior Department's icebreaker, the USMS *North Star*, left Philadelphia, following the *Bear* as far as Panama. It then steamed to Dunedin before heading south to search out a suitable site on the Ross Ice Barrier for the western base.

In the hold of the *North Star* were six tanks, loaned by the Department of War for testing on the ice, while chained across the deck was Poulter's huge snow cruiser, which had to have part of its rear section removed so that it would not hang over the water. The cruiser had been hurriedly constructed at the Pullman coach-works in Chicago, and created a sensation when it was rushed the thousand miles or so to the Boston docks, with police forcing cars off the road to allow the lumbering giant to pass. Even so, it ran off the road into a creek and was only with some difficulty extricated. It was hardly a propitious or sufficient test run for what was to confront the cruiser in Antarctica, but there was no time to test it on snow and ice.[51]

The cruiser was so large that the navy had wanted to leave it behind, with concerns that the heavy vehicle might threaten the ship's stability. But Byrd insisted that it must be included, citing contractual arrangements that had been made with its owner, the Armour Institute of Technology, which had in turn done a lucrative deal with a philately company for the cruiser to carry thousands of first day covers to the South Pole. Although this deal would complicate the government's plan to establish post offices at the two bases, and thereby provide 'evidence of occupation', the State Department had agreed not to press the issue.[52] After all, the evidence of occupation that had been created in the past by temporary post offices would not be so necessary this time, as they would be greatly outweighed by the permanent bases that were to be established.

It was hoped that the snow cruiser would buttress the presence of the bases by providing a connection between them while at the same time acting as a moveable, self-supporting base of its own, which might extend the American claim into areas that their rivals may have only flown over or briefly sledged across. As the *New York Times* noted on the expedition's departure, the paper's readers might one day learn 'that the snow cruiser has connected West Base with East Base; or has rolled along that coast which no man has ever surely seen . . . or, perhaps, made of itself a laboratory base, for a period of months, at the Pole itself'.[53]

Establishing a territorial claim was paramount in the American activities. There had been a belated conference at Washington's National Academy of Science in late July to discuss a scientific program for the expedition. Presided over by Isaiah Bowman, who by now was president of John Hopkins University, the thirty-two participants included Byrd, Poulter, Black and Alton Wade, as well as the State Department geographer Samuel Boggs, the American Geographical Society's representative, Charles Hitchcock, and the chief of the maps and charts division at the National Archives, W. L. G. Joerg. Although they discussed programs for meteorology, geology, terrestrial magnetism, seismology and oceanography, it was geography that was uppermost in the discussions, with the conference poring over plans for 'the mapping of a region some 5,000,000 [square] miles in extent, 3,000,000 [square] miles of which is still to be explored'.[54] Wade was given the task of compiling a program that would coordinate the activities of scientists at both bases, but he never managed to complete it. It was an indication of how science was a cover for territorial acquisition that the expedition departed without its scientific program having been agreed. Neither Byrd nor anyone else seemed to notice its absence.

Despite Byrd's suggestions that the expedition was only interested in areas unclaimed by other nations, the talk at the conference of mapping Antarctica's entire area was further confirmation that America's territorial ambition was potentially continental in scope. Mindful of the sensitivities of other nations, Roosevelt issued Byrd with official instructions that were much more circumscribed. Such was the rush to get away that the instructions only reached Byrd when he flew into Panama to join the *North Star*.

Byrd was told to establish one of the two bases, to be known as 'East Base', either on Charcot Island or on the shores of Marguerite Bay. Both sites were just within the boundaries of the British Falkland Islands Dependencies, and also fell within the overlapping Chilean and Argentine claims. The second base, to be known as 'West Base', was to be established on the eastern shore of the Ross Sea, which could place it just outside the boundary of New Zealand's Ross Dependency. If he was unable to establish it there, Byrd was told to try in the vicinity of his former Little America base, on the western shore of the Ross Sea, which was well within the Ross Dependency.[55]

According to Roosevelt, the 'principal objective' of the expedition was 'the delineation of the continental coast line between the meridians 72° W and 148° W, and the consolidation of the geographical features of Hearst Land, James W. Ellsworth Land, and Marie Byrd Land'. Byrd was to use 'long range aerial flights, equipped with mapping cameras, [to] consolidate these areas'.

A secondary objective was to chart the 'unknown west coast of the Weddell Sea between Cape Eielson and Luitpold Coast', and 'investigate by air the area in the vicinity of the South Magnetic Pole and the unknown areas between the Weddell Sea and the South Pole'.[56] The resulting maps would show to the world that the United States had ventured further than others, and that, consequently, it knew the continent more intimately and precisely than others. Germany had based its territorial claim on the supposed superiority of its Antarctic knowledge; the United States would do likewise.

Roosevelt reminded Byrd that the United States had never recognised the territorial claims of other nations in the Antarctic. He instructed that the members of the expedition do nothing that might compromise that policy – by, for instance, asking permission of the New Zealand government to establish a base in the Ross Dependency. While the United States had also never officially made territorial claims of its own in the Antarctic, Byrd was told that the expedition members were to lay the basis for doing so by 'dropping written claims from airplanes, depositing such writings in cairns, et cetera, which might assist in supporting a sovereignty claim by the United States Government'. It was all to be done in secret, with notes being made 'of the circumstances surrounding each such act', until the State Department decided to publicly and formally assert a claim.

Such a claim would be supported by Roosevelt's instruction for the expedition leaders and scientists to 'maintain journals of the progress of the Service, and enter thereon events, observations, and remarks'. There would be no lucrative newspaper or other deals for the expeditioners, who were required to hand Byrd all their material, including private diaries, before the returning vessels docked in the United States. Moreover, there would be only one history of the expedition, and it would be written by Byrd, 'under the supervision of the Executive Committee'.[57]

It was also in Panama that Byrd was handed a telegram from the State Department that specified the official wording to be used when making a territorial claim. From these instructions, Black made multiple copies of a form, which were given to the leaders of the expedition bases and snow cruiser. They were told of the 'necessity for secrecy' and reminded that 'a record should be kept on duplicate sheets each time a form is deposited in a cairn or dropped from an airplane'.[58] In the time-honoured fashion, the explorers were to note when and where they had 'raised the flag of the United States of America' to 'claim this territory in the name of the United States of America'. Just as Columbus had claimed some islands in the Caribbean by sailing past while making the required declaration of Spanish sovereignty, so Byrd and his men would sometimes fly across the Antarctic, symbolically displaying the American flag in their noisy aircraft cabins while dropping a copy of the suitably inscribed claim onto the ice below. No announcement of any claim was to be made by Byrd without specific authorisation by the US secretary of state.[59]

The advisory committee of scientists appointed by the July conference was never consulted by Wade. As a result, when a congressional committee asked in January 1940 for a copy of the scientific program, there was nothing to give them. The secretary of the expedition's executive committee, Commander Robert English, had presumed that the National Academy of Science had drawn up the program. He was surprised to discover that its involvement had ended with the initial conference. With Byrd and Wade now in the Antarctic, English radioed Byrd, frantically asking whether there was a copy of the scientific program at the expedition's offices that he might give to the congressional committee, only to be told by Byrd that there was no written program anywhere. Byrd blamed Wade for the neglect, claiming that he had instructed the geologist to write one but that Wade had been 'too preoccupied with the snow cruiser in Chicago'.

With the scientists now in Antarctica, and no overall program to coordinate their activities, English was forced to quickly compile a program to satisfy the demand of the congressional committee. He based it upon his notes of the July conference and 'his study of the scientific records of other Antarctic expeditions'. English sent a copy of this to the expeditioners, although it was not accepted by Byrd or the scientists.[60] Nevertheless, it allowed the government to claim that the expedition had a comprehensive scientific program covering 'many scientific fields' and 'drawn up with the cooperation of the National Academy of Sciences'.[61]

It was an extraordinary situation for an expedition that purportedly had a serious scientific purpose to have no program to guide its activities. On one level, it could be taken as confirmation of those critics who regarded Byrd as being more showman than serious explorer, with science always having been simply a means to an end.

On another level, it was perhaps a reflection of Byrd's physical and mental decline after his testing experience alone on the ice in 1934, and his history of alcohol abuse. More fundamentally, though, it was further confirmation that scientific inquiry often served as a screen for the more prosaic objective of territorial acquisition. It was useful for justifying the expense of an expedition and, later, for helping to reinforce a territorial claim.

The expedition was hampered from the time its two ships arrived at their initial destination at the Bay of Whales in January 1940. The unloading of the snow cruiser almost ended in disaster when it broke through the wooden ramp leading to the ice shelf, against which the *North Star* was moored. Byrd was riding on its roof and was nearly thrown off. The situation was only saved when Poulter hit the accelerator, causing the cruiser to lurch forward onto the ice.[62] Worse was to come. The vehicle was meant to be able to climb slopes of up to thirty-seven degrees, and to have sufficient supplies to keep its four-man crew in the field for up to a year. However, Byrd found that it was practically immovable on the ice and snow, even after two additional tyres were fitted. Nicknamed 'Bouncing Betty', the ungainly vehicle was simply too heavy, even when unloaded, and its innovative engine system, individually driven wheels and massive tyres were unable to gain traction on the snow. It was only when it was driven in reverse that any distance could be covered, and then at such a slow speed as to be useless. After much experimentation, Wade was forced to consign the cruiser and its on-board laboratory to a stationary existence at West Base, although a press release in March 1940 was still lauding its capabilities and the great distances it was expected to travel.[63]

With its limited funding, having lost one of its three ships and with the cruiser useless, the expedition was forced to rely on more traditional means of transport – dog sledges – as well as on the two tanks and two artillery tractors that had been lent by the army for testing on the ice. There were also two Curtiss Condor aircraft with skis that would have to play a major role in surveying and mapping the Pacific sector, which would now be the only focus of the expedition's attention. With Paul Siple left in charge of West Base, and Wade still grappling with the ill-fated snow cruiser, Byrd took the *Bear* off into the ice pack in search of a suitable site for East Base. He used a break in the weather in late February to make three flights in the loaned Barkley Grow seaplane along the previously uncharted coastline of Marie Byrd Land, during which he named what he called the 'Franklin Roosevelt Sea'. Although he would later trumpet his fly-by discoveries, they did not amount to much and, without ground control points, could not result in accurate maps being produced, which were a precondition for his earlier territorial claim to the region to be reinforced.[64]

In March 1940, Byrd and Black eventually settled on a site for East Base after flying over a small island in Marguerite Bay, where they saw the abandoned hut and other facilities built there in 1936 by John Rymill and the British Graham Land Expedition.[65] Although Rymill had named it 'Barry Island' and it lay within Britain's Falkland Islands Dependencies, Black proposed that it be called 'Stonington Island', after the home port of American sealer Nathaniel Palmer. Black was consciously connecting the present expedition with Palmer's activities of 120 years before, in accordance with the suggestions of Colonel Martin and the United States Board of Geographical Names.

Once the name 'Stonington Island' had received official approval, Black proposed to go on and attach the names of Palmer's crew to geographical features in the vicinity.[66] In American eyes, Nathaniel Palmer was the discoverer of Antarctica. What was Graham Land to the British was Palmer Land to the Americans. With West Base in New Zealand's Ross Dependency and East Base in Britain's Falkland Islands Dependencies, the expedition concentrated its attention on surveying the largely unclaimed area between the two.

American hopes of traversing the continent, of establishing a base in the African Sector – as well as a temporary one at the South Pole – and of laying the basis for a claim on the continent as a whole had all been dashed. These setbacks might have been expected to push Byrd and his colleagues to make a greater effort to compensate for these losses. But it seems to have had the opposite effect. Instead of remaining in Antarctica, Byrd returned to Washington in May 1940 to report on the expedition and direct its operations from afar.[67]

On his return, Byrd told reporters that the achievements of the expedition had been much greater than he had anticipated, with the 'discovery and charting of 900 miles of unknown coastline', but he also conceded that there was little strategic or commercial value to the discovery, although 'it might later be used as a stop on an airplane route to Asia'.[68] Byrd had a more difficult time convincing the members of the executive committee about the achievements of the expedition, with the committee noting the paucity of operations and the continuing absence of a clear and coordinated scientific program.

Commander English complained that 'the only operations undertaken at the West Base were several aircraft flights, and at the East Base one short depot-laying flight and one reconnaissance flight', which meant that the expedition was unlikely to achieve the objectives that Roosevelt had set it for the coming spring. As for the scientific work, English noted that 'a detailed program has not been drawn up and placed into effect at both bases'. Indeed, the committee still had no confirmation 'that any scientific program is being undertaken at the East Base, or that such studies as might be made will coincide with those being pursued at West Base'.[69]

Byrd tried to limit the criticism by arguing that it was not a matter for the committee, only to have English remind him that it was very much their responsibility, since the committee was in charge of 'the Direction and Coordination of the Antarctic Service'. Not only had the base leaders 'lost sight of their objectives', he argued, they had also lost several vital months of preparation. When Byrd again prevaricated and suggested that he consult with Black, Wade and Siple, English warned that that would only lead to more delays. Time was running out and 'further delay would materially detract from the scientific accomplishments of the Antarctic Service'. The committee agreed with English, instructing him to 'prepare dispatches to the bases directing appropriate action'.[70] Byrd was finding that a government expedition was a very different beast to a private one.

Byrd had to consider not only the executive committee but also Congress. Although the Senate had authorised $250,000 for the expedition to continue for another year, the House of Representatives had struck out the amount. Indeed, there was not even money to fund the relief of the present expedition. Byrd told journalists that it would be 'tough on those poor devils down there', while Roosevelt told congressmen that reasons of 'continental defense' made it 'imperative that we keep a clearer title to this area than that claimed by any other non-American country'.[71] Byrd made his own appeal to the House Appropriations Committee, telling it that even an evacuation of the bases would cost an estimated $170,000.[72] Still the committee would not be moved.

The Department of the Interior was also tired of the Antarctic commitment, which was intruding on its other responsibilities, particularly in Alaska. Moreover, the department found that it had responsibility for the budget of the Antarctic Service but had 'no authority whatever over the administration of the projects'. As Harold Ickes, the department's secretary, complained to Roosevelt in May 1940, the Antarctic Service was dominated by the navy department. Not only was Rear Admiral Byrd the commanding officer, but the chairman and the secretary of the executive committee were naval officers, the communications and publicity were being managed by the navy, about half the expedition members were from the armed services, and the civilian administration of the expedition was run from the Navy Building in Washington. Ickes urged Roosevelt to relieve the Department of the Interior of what had become an onerous responsibility.[73]

Byrd had also had enough. He had been personally attacked by one congressman, who had accused him of profiting from the government expedition. More importantly, with German troops in Paris and with London seeming set to fall, Byrd was more interested in helping in the struggle against Germany than in leading the Antarctic Service. Although he regaled journalists with stories about the achievements of the expedition, he advised Roosevelt during several private discussions that the Antarctic Service should be wound up because of the war in Europe.

Yet Roosevelt remained committed to his vision of colonising the continent. According to Byrd, Roosevelt told him that 'the south polar undertaking should be continued because of diplomatic "swapping" which might be brought about when a peace treaty is eventually arrived at after the termination of hostilities in Europe'.[74] It is not clear precisely what Roosevelt had in mind, but it seems he intended by swapping territory to reinforce, rather than reduce, the American hold on the most strategically important parts of Antarctica.

Unable to convince Congress to authorise another year in the Antarctic, and with a presidential election in November 1940 and the German army running rampant through Western Europe, Roosevelt had more pressing political issues on which he needed to spend his political capital.

Moreover, there was little public support for – or even interest in – the expedition. In great contrast to Byrd's privately run expeditions, this one had been largely ignored by the press, whose attention was concentrated on the dramatic events in Europe and on the war preparations at home. Byrd might have been able to generate greater public interest, but he had lost interest himself and wanted only to devote himself to supporting Roosevelt's war efforts.

With German troops in Paris, and the British army trapped on the beaches of Dunkirk, the Antarctic seemed more remote than ever. It was the gunfire-swept battlefield, rather than the windswept icecap, that would become the arena for manly heroics. While Roosevelt had failed to colonise the Antarctic, he had signalled to the world the extent of America's territorial ambitions there. And the world would respond in kind.

CHAPTER 16

'A matter of great importance'

1941–1945

The creation of the United States Antarctic Service in 1939 marked one of the most significant milestones in Antarctic history. For the first time, the continent was to have permanent settlements. However, the developing war in Europe, and the prospect of war with Japan, prompted the US Congress to force the closure of the two American bases. It brought to a sudden end President Roosevelt's ambitious attempt to colonise the continent.

The war also saw the whalers largely leave the Southern Ocean, as a result of their capture or sinking by enemy action, or because it had become too hazardous to make the long voyage. Without explorers or whalers, and with the war largely restricted to north of the equator, it might have been expected that the Antarctic would become once again a sanctuary for its wildlife. However, Roosevelt's dispatch of the Byrd expedition, and the talk of establishing perman-ent bases, had ignited concerns among America's Antarctic rivals. Rather than abating, the competition for territory was about to intensify and take on a dangerous new edge.

The order to close the two American bases did not mean the end of the United States Antarctic Service. There was an assump-tion among officials in Washington that it was merely a hiatus, after which there would be a return to the Antarctic and a reoc-cupation of the bases.[1] Roosevelt remained as committed as ever to the United States claiming as much of the continent as possible. He was also personally attracted by the appeal of exploration. He relished the idea when the Explorers Club offered to make him an associate life member in recognition of his support for the Byrd expedition, noting that he was 'glad to be numbered' as one of the modern equivalents of 'those tireless travelers who used to be romantically called "gentleman adventurers"'.[2]

Knowing Roosevelt's views, Byrd wanted to leave much of the food and equipment in the Antarctic, confident that there would be a 'resumption of the expedition upon the passing of the existing national emergency'. He convinced the US Navy to leave the two aircraft that it had loaned to the expedition, while the Armour Institute of Technology agreed that the ill-fated snow cruiser could also remain, provided that it was returned whenever another expedition was sent south. Instructions to remove as much food and other supplies as possible were only issued after it was realised that there might be political problems if material was left on the assumption that the expedition would be resumed, when Congress had given no such authorisation.[3]

For the Americans in the Antarctic, there was still the summer of 1940–41 during which they could complete their scientific observations and lay claim to as much territory as possible. By dog sledge and aircraft, they spread out from the two bases, photographing the landscape and calculating ground control points for the maps that would be made from their efforts. The seriousness of this part of the expedition was shown by the presence of cadastral engineer Leonard Berlin of the Interior Department's General Land Office, who led a party from West Base across 340 kilometres of ice and snow to the slopes of Mt Grace McKinley, a peak that had been sighted from the air by Byrd on one of his earlier expeditions and which would now be precisely located for mapping purposes.

Using the regulation brass cap that the Land Office employed to mark boundaries and locations in the United States, Berlin informed its commissioner by radiogram that he would set the cap in a prominent position at the 'exact time that I claim this area on behalf of the Antarctic Service for the United States'. As with other modern claiming ceremonies, photographs recorded the event for posterity and possible legal purposes. Berlin realised he was making history and sent off a press release to announce his claim to the world. He was quickly reminded of Roosevelt's instruction that no publicity was to be issued without the prior authority of the secretary of state.[4] While the claiming was to be done surreptitiously, the claims had to be scrupulously recorded on the mimeographed forms that Black had produced on board the *North Star*.

The blanket of secrecy that was thrown over the expedition's claiming activities was due to the continuing uncertainty in Washington as to whether to proceed with the formal annexation of Antarctic territory. Despite all the talk of potential coal and oil deposits, the value of the Antarctic remained a matter of debate. American annexation would also threaten Washington's relationships with countries such as Britain and Argentina.

Britain had already expressed its concern in August 1940 at the raising of the American flag by Black over East Base. Its ambassador told the State Department that he hoped the flag-raising 'had no political significance'.[5] The State Department made no reply, and the ambassador did not press for one. Britain was content to have its communication remain as a matter of record, in the hope that it might somehow deter the Americans from claiming territory within the Falkland Islands Dependencies. As for the Argentinians, their government reacted to the American activities by asserting their own territorial claims, and by preparing to expand their own presence in the Antarctic from their long-time meteorological base on Laurie Island. This went ahead despite the American withdrawal from the Antarctic in March 1941.

The evacuation was not straightforward. The *Bear* and the *North Star* first went to fetch the men from West Base – known as 'Little America III' – in January 1941. It was done in such a hurry that most of the food was left ashore, which left the *North Star* dangerously low on supplies for its now increased complement. The ships still had much to do. However, when they arrived off Marguerite Bay in mid-February to pick up Richard Black and the other twenty-five men from East Base, they found that the bay was still blocked by ice. They waited a month for an easterly wind to break up the ice sufficiently for them to push their way in. But the right winds never came, and it looked as if the men might have to remain at East Base for another year. Even if the ships could get into the bay, there was a real risk that the vessels might be trapped by the ice. The only possibility of escape was in the Curtiss Condor aircraft, and at least two perilous and crowded flights would be required.[6]

On 20 March 1941, with the Antarctic winter approaching, Byrd met with the executive committee at the Navy Building in Washington. He was concerned that using the obsolete Condor in the deteriorating weather conditions might end in disaster, yet he was desperate that the men be evacuated. Congress had not authorised any money for them to remain another year, and the two expedition ships were required by their respective departments for war purposes. Byrd decided to lead the rescue himself.

He told the committee that it was 'his duty' to fly by Pan American Airways to Punta Arenas, Chile, where two US Navy seaplanes from Panama should meet him. Byrd and the planes would then be taken aboard the *North Star*, which would steam as far south as the ice would allow. The seaplanes then would be launched to relieve the base.

This was Byrd at his heroic best, and the committee was not going to deny him another of his moments in the headlines. However, the committee also left the captain of the *Bear,* Lieutenant Commander Richard Cruzen, free to act in any way he thought necessary prior to Byrd's arrival – which he did. Cruzen took the *Bear* to an anchorage off Mikkelsen Island, about 180 kilometres from East Base. Black and half the marooned men were packed into the Condor and flown to the island, from where they were taken by whaleboat to the waiting *Bear*. The process was repeated for the rest of the party. By 25 March the small ship was heading for Punta Arenas to meet up with the *North Star*.[7] So ended, for the time being, the American colonisation of Antarctica. It finished not with a fanfare but a flurry of desperate activity that was hardly noticed by a world at war.

The withdrawal of the American expedition from its two bases left the abandoned huts to the mercy of the Antarctic winds and the weight of the winter snow. But it did not end America's efforts to proceed with its Antarctic claims. When he had clambered aboard the Condor aircraft, Black had to leave all his personal possessions behind. Yet he was careful to take with him the claim forms that had been dutifully filled in by the pilots and leaders of the land parties, recording the locations where they had conducted claiming ceremonies, the dimensions of the areas they had claimed and, in the case of land parties, where they had deposited the records so that they might later be retrieved.

As the *North Star* and the *Bear* steamed their way back to the United States in April 1941, Black gathered together the forms – eighteen in all – which he would present to his superiors in the Department of the Interior. They would later be sent to the State Department for safekeeping.[8] If the United States decided to annex territory based upon the work of its short-lived Antarctic Service, these forms might be vital in establishing the legitimacy of the American title. Although Byrd told journalists that the United States could now annex more than two million square kilometres of the continent, there was no move to do so.[9] For the time being, the eighteen forms remained in a State Department filing cabinet, while Black and several of his companions worked at other ways of reinforcing America's territorial title.

Publicising the achievements of the expedition was one way they could do this. But it had been difficult to get publicity for a peaceful expedition when the world was being wracked by war. It was not helped by the press releases being issued by government bureaucrats, rather than by Byrd or his publicity-minded assistants, who had always ensured widespread exposure for his previous expeditions.[10] And when the expedition was over, there was no popular account published about the expedition, nor were there lecture tours by Byrd and his companions. As a government expedition, no one could make a personal profit from it.

An official narrative of the expedition was meant to be published, but it was dogged by delays and disputes between the participants. In the interim, the secretary of the executive committee, Commander Robert English, wrote a brief outline of its main activities, based upon radio reports received in Washington. Published in the *Geographical Review* in July 1941, it was a matter-of-fact report devoid of drama or personalities – and it was careful to conceal from the world the territorial claiming that had been so central to the expedition.[11]

Recognition of the American title would be more likely if the United States could show that it knew the areas better than its rival claimants. As other nations had done, the Americans needed to compile their scientific observations and publish the results. However, the refusal by Congress to provide additional funding for the Antarctic Service left it unable to pay the scientists to prepare their results for publication. The Bureau of the Budget refused to commit any new funds until after 30 June 1941, when the Antarctic Service's present funding was set to expire and it would be clear whether there was any unspent money. With Congress looking unlikely to approve any additional funding, the Department of the Interior was asked to place seven of the expedition staff on its payroll to ensure that there would be 'a permanent record of the accomplishments of the expedition'. Three of the seven proposed staff were cartographers, while others were scientists or base leaders writing narratives of the expedition. Without such a commitment, the department was warned, the $521,000 spent on the expedition 'might be largely wasted'.[12]

The preponderance of cartographers, under the leadership of Dr Paul Siple, reflected the expedition's concentration on exploration and mapping. The mapmakers had to make sense of all the aerial photographs and convert them into maps that would serve America's territorial interests. That meant splattering the frozen landscape with American names.

Some names, such as Stonington Island, created associations between the territory and the Connecticut port from which American sealers had sailed in the early decades of the nineteenth century. While the port was memorialised as the name for the island, which in fact had an existing English name, lesser geographical features were named after various crew members of the early sealing boats. As Black noted in a radiogram from East Base in December 1940, it was all done at the behest of Colonel Martin and the US Board of Geographical Names.[13]

Other names acknowledged particular supporters of the expedition, including the crusading geographer William Hobbs, who would have an extensive coastline north-east of Little America named after him. In a letter to Hobbs, Byrd explained that he had shifted the name of brewery owner Jacob Ruppert, a generous and recently deceased supporter, in order to accommodate Hobbs. Ruppert's name would be applied to a cape instead. Byrd told Hobbs that he had thought of using his name for one of 'two beautiful glaciers coming down from your coastline', but 'thought it was a much bigger honor to have the coast line with your name on it'.[14]

The United States was keen to outdo the 1939 Australian map of Antarctica, the most recent and most comprehensive map of the continent, which had incorporated the latest discoveries and privileged British names. It had been distributed around the world in an attempt to have it and its names accepted internationally. Fifty copies of the map, along with an accompanying handbook and index, were sent to Australia House in London, where the Australian representative was instructed to bring it to 'the notice of the English press and the English teaching profession', as it 'has greatly strengthened Australia's claim to the Australian Antarctic Territory'. Copies were also distributed to relevant institutions in the United States and to other claimant nations.[15]

Realising the political danger of this, there was a rush in Washington to produce an American equivalent that would serve the practical needs of navigators in Antarctic seas and the political needs of the State Department in claiming territory for the United States. It would not be easy. The charts prepared under Black's supervision at East Base were judged by an assistant of Byrd's to be 'totally inadequate' as the basis upon which to compile a map, while the charts done by Ronne were regarded as 'the best of the lot'.[16] By August 1942, the Antarctic Service still had ten staff, with Siple being the most senior and Wade acting as assistant field representative. There were three cartographers and a cartographic assistant. However, the demands of the war were making it difficult to hold onto them, with even Siple, now a US Army captain, being diverted into work for the War Department while promising to continue the Antarctic Service's cartographic work.[17]

It was not only Australia's map that the United States wanted to overshadow. There was also the British *Antarctic Pilot*, which had been first published in 1930 and was required reading for navigators heading for Antarctic waters. There would have been copies aboard the *Bear* and the *North Star*, but it was humiliating for an official American expedition to be dependent on the navigational aids of its principal Antarctic rival. As soon as the expedition had returned with its charts of newly discovered coasts, there was an urgent push to produce an American equivalent.

Commander English took charge of the task, guided by advice from Hobbs, Martin, Boggs and Joerg. Known as *Sailing Directions for Antarctica, 1943*, the guide was issued by the US Navy's Hydrographic Office in May 1943. Still, it would be a brave navigator who relied on the publication for finding a safe passage to an anchorage on the Antarctic coast. As its compiler, English was careful to warn potential users that they must exercise 'great care', since little of the coastline had been properly surveyed. Providing navigational advice was only one part of the publication's purpose. Like the *Antarctic Pilot*, it was concerned with putting forward a particular view of Antarctic history. Not surprisingly, it was a view that favoured American activities over those of British and other explorers, with Palmer and Wilkes lauded as the continent's discoverers. It also enshrined American names on its geography.[18]

In 1930, the *Antarctic Pilot* had eschewed explicit mention of sovereignty for fear that it would upset the Americans and Norwegians, in particular. The British government had wanted to wait until Mawson's voyages of 1929–31 had completed their survey of the Australian sector's coastline, after which it had intended to publish an updated edition with the additional coast-line marked in, along with a statement about the sovereignty of the three Antarctic sectors claimed by Britain and its dominions. However, this new edition had not appeared by the time that *Sailing Directions for Antarctica* was published. Not surprisingly, the American publication raised the hackles of officials when it reached the Foreign Office.

The former polar scientist and now head of the Foreign Office's Antarctic research section, Brian Roberts, dismissed it as being 'obviously inspired by political motives', saying it was 'highly inaccurate, especially in matters relating to priority of discovery and exploration'. He also noted how the Americans had made 'numerous changes in place-names within British territory'. Roberts would have been concerned that replacing British names with American ones was intended to lay the basis for a future American territorial claim. As such, he warned, there was now an 'urgent need for a new edition of the *Antarctic Pilot*', along with an 'up-to-date large-scale map of the Falkland Islands Dependencies' and the 'publication of official lists of accepted place-names in British Antarctic Territories'. The latter was important, wrote Roberts, since 'many Antarctic place-names are of political significance as well as of historical and practical interest'.[19] Together, the three publications would go far to establish the case for British sovereignty in the Antarctic.

Meanwhile, the Americans were struggling to produce the official narrative of the 1939–40 expedition. Byrd had convinced the executive committee to appoint a journalist, Roger Hawthorne, as expedition historian. Hawthorne had accompanied Byrd on one of the Antarctic flights and had a mountain named after him. However, Black and Siple demanded that, as commanders of East Base and West Base respectively, they be allowed to write the narratives of their separate bases. Byrd eventually agreed, as long as Hawthorne could 'correlate the two base narratives and write the story of the voyages and other activities'. Byrd knew that if the overall narrative was restricted to the activities of the bases, he would hardly make an appearance since he had spent little time ashore. With Hawthorne's input he might ensure the usual starring role for himself.

However, Siple's work with the War Department and his super-vision of the cartography left him little time to write his narrative, while Black was sent off to Honolulu by the navy before he had started his. Although Black was permitted to take copies of the base records with him, the Japanese attack on Pearl Harbour soon put paid to his good intentions. Even had the narratives been written, no money had been appropriated for their publication.[20] In April 1945, an inquirer was informed that 'the history and narrative of the Antarctic Expedition will be completed and published by the Government after the war'.[21] It remains unwritten.

There were also problems with the films and paintings that were supposed to be produced by expedition members. The artist Leland Curtis had promised to produce two oil paintings for the Department of the Interior, with its secretary, Howard Ickes, to decide where they would be displayed. However, there were repeated delays in their production, and their political impact would have been slight. As for the films, the photographer, Ennis Helm, who had provided his own cameras and film, unsurprisingly felt a sense of ownership of the resulting production. The executive committee had instructed that the film was to be handed over by 15 March 1941, only to learn that Helm was incarcerated in the Oklahoma State Penitentiary and the film had been hidden away. From his prison cell, Helm offered to sell the film for a substantial sum. Byrd refused to negotiate, confident that Helm would be forced to drop his price.[22] However, delay meant death at the box office. In any case, the film that Helm had put together lacked a compelling story and would have to compete with dramatic newsreel footage from the war.

The publication of the scientific results faced similar problems. The tetchy Wade was in charge of getting the scientists to complete their reports but had proved himself to be incompetent. He had not drawn up a scientific program for the expedition before it went south, while his relationship with the executive committee had become vexed when he was in the Antarctic. At the end of the expedition, the frustrated committee had pursued the scientists for their reports, only to find that several had been drawn into the war effort before they had written up their results.[23]

With no funds from Congress to finance their publication, the National Academy of Sciences passed responsibility for the publication to the American Philosophical Society, which had a long association with Antarctic exploration. The society had already organised a symposium on the expedition in November 1941, at which twelve scientific papers were presented detailing some preliminary results. The Japanese attack on Pearl Harbour just two weeks later caused delays in their publication in the society's journal. It would also have been just a partial record of the expedition's results, which encompassed much more than the twelve papers.

Rather than having the papers appear in piecemeal fashion, the opportunity was taken to collect another fifteen papers and additional reports and publish them in one volume. This was finally done in a special 400-page edition of the *Proceedings of the American Philosophical Society* in July 1945.[24] Compared with other expeditions, the publication of these results was relatively expeditious. However, although there were important papers by Siple, Black and Ronne on the expedition's geographical discoveries, their publication did little to lift the expedition from its position of obscurity. The expedition continues to have the distinction of being one of the most important expeditions in the history of Antarctica and one of the least known.

While the United States Antarctic Service had been putting American furred boots on the snow, Antarctic enthusiasts back home continued to prosecute the case for American priority in discovery. As ever, William Hobbs was the loudest and most vituperative of those arguing for the primacy of American discovery. And the centenary of the Wilkes expedition gave him an ideal platform. The American Philosophical Society held a two-day symposium in Philadelphia on 23–24 February 1940, during which Hobbs presented a paper on the discovery of Wilkes Land. He was particularly concerned to have Wilkes acknowledged as the first explorer to confirm that Antarctica was a continent.[25]

This was a considerable exaggeration. Wilkes had certainly suggested the name 'Antarctica', but his brief voyage along a small part of the Antarctic coastline had hardly *proved* the existence of a continent. He could suggest that the existence of a continent was likely, and he could propose a name for it, but he could not claim to be its discoverer.

No matter. While Hobbs argued that Wilkes was the first to discover Antarctica, Colonel Martin was concerned with having Palmer similarly acknowledged. He repeated his now familiar argument about Palmer in an article for the *Geographical Review* in October 1940, in which he declared that Palmer 'recorded the first sighting of Antarctica' on an unspecified day in November 1820. Martin drew on sealers' logbooks and other records in the Library of Congress, together with a contentious article by Hobbs, to make a seemingly conclusive argument about Palmer's discovery of Antarctica.[26] The advocacy by Martin and Hobbs seems to have been designed to invest the concomitant American push into Antarctica with a greater sense of moral legitimacy.

Hobbs and Martin were joined by the familiar coterie of political geographers. They included State Department geographer Samuel Boggs, National Archives cartographer Dr W. L. G. Joerg, and John Hopkins University president Isaiah Bowman. While some of these men might have flinched at the more extreme statements that Hobbs was prone to make, they were united in wanting to highlight the historical roots and recent achievements of American contact with Antarctica in order to strengthen any territorial claims that the United States might decide to make.

Another participant was the US Navy's Captain Harold Saunders, who presented a paper on Byrd's flight to the South Pole and the exploration of Marie Byrd Land. Saunders had been a geographer on Byrd's first two Antarctic expeditions and was involved in the subsequent compilation of the expedition maps. He would come to have an even more crucial role in America's claiming and naming activities after the war.[27]

Britain could not afford to let Hobbs and Martin go unanswered. The American articles provoked a strong rejoinder from the leading British geographer – and long-time secretary of the Royal Geographical Society – Arthur Hinks, who was then working closely with the Admiralty and other British departments.[28] Hobbs and Hinks were both angry old men. Hinks was handicapped in his response by not having access to Palmer's logbook so that he could check the accuracy of the claims made by Hobbs and Martin. He was also frustrated by Martin's tardy publication of the papers that he presented to various conferences. For instance, it was only as Hinks was going into print with an article in the British *Geographical Journal* of October 1940 that Martin sent him photographs of some pages of the Palmer logbook.

Although Hinks questioned some of Martin's conclusions, and wondered whether the Palmer logbook was really the original or perhaps a later transcription, he conceded that the book was 'fair evidence' that Palmer had seen the Antarctic continent on 18 November 1820. But that did not make Palmer the first to have done so, he argued, since Bransfield and Smith 'had already seen the same land on 30 January 1820'. This assertion had already been rejected by Hobbs, who had accused the Admiralty of falsifying the maps to give Bransfield primacy over Palmer. More importantly, Martin had implicitly supported Hobbs' inflammatory accusation. It was one thing for a retired professor to make such an accusation, but it was quite another thing for a senior official at the Library of Congress to do so. Hinks was so outraged that he demanded Martin justify his rejection of the British evidence.[29]

In case Martin chose to ignore the British article, Hinks wrote another article along similar lines for the American *Geographical Review*, of which Martin was a contributing editor. Picking apart Martin's argument, Hinks revealed for an American audience the several grievous errors in Martin's evidence, and the gaps in the historical record that Martin tried to cover with unsupported assertions. At the end of the article, Martin was given an opportunity to reply to the points raised by Hinks, but he claimed that there was insufficient space in which to do so.

Instead, Martin promised that a full reply would be provided in a book that he was completing. It would not be fair to Bransfield, Palmer or Hinks, he argued, to reply other than at such length.[30] But the promised book never appeared during the eleven years that remained of Martin's life. Nor has it appeared since. In 1955 there appeared instead an extensive American study by a scholar of the Stonington sealers, Edouard Stackpole, who acknowledged Bransfield's voyage as being the first recorded sighting of the continent. At the same time, Stackpole concluded than an unnamed American sealer on a ship captained by John Davis was the first to step ashore onto the continent.[31]

Apparently undaunted by Hinks' apparent victory, Martin made a new attempt to enhance the moral legitimacy of America's Antarctic claims. In 1943, he told the American Scientific Congress in Washington that America's scientific engagement with the Antarctic stretched back to the 1820s. He particularly lauded the work of the largely forgotten James Eights on the Reynolds expedition of 1828–30. Martin noted that Eights had discovered boulders in icebergs around the South Shetlands, which he had suggested must have originated from lands further west. Although Eights had reasoned that they probably came from a chain of undiscovered islands, Martin argued that the nonexistence of such an island chain meant that Eights had actually 'forecast the existence of an important portion of the Antarctic coast'.

To cement Eights' place in Antarctic history, and to strengthen America's claim on a strategically important part of the continent that Eights had probably never seen, the US Board on Geographical Names agreed in 1943 to call what was thought to be part of the Antarctic Peninsula the 'Eights Peninsula'. It was later found that it had already been named by Byrd as 'Thurston Peninsula'. When Thurston Peninsula was subsequently found to be an island, and renamed as such, Eights' name was shifted to part of the adjacent Antarctic Peninsula, which was called the 'Eights Coast'.[32]

While British and American geographers continued their debates, other nations had their own claims to prosecute, and were just as concerned as the British by the surge in American activity. In the late 1930s, the Argentinians and Chileans, not having pressed their Antarctic claims much over the previous three decades, became determined to do so. Washington's citation of the Monroe Doctrine as justification for its expedition particularly alarmed the South Americans. They realised it might be used to justify the United States' ousting of Britain from Antarctica and its annexation of what Americans called the Palmer Peninsula for themselves. There was also an expectation that the international polar conference planned for Norway in October 1940 would lead to the carve-up of the Antarctic between its several existing claimants. Neither Argentina, Chile nor the United States was widely acknowledged as being a claimant. This had helped to prompt the creation of the United States Antarctic Service, and it similarly inspired the Argentinians and Chileans to reassert their own claims to the Antarctic and its nearby islands.

In the wake of Byrd's expedition being formally approved by Congress in mid-1939, the Argentine government established an interdepartmental commission tasked with preparing evidence for the Norwegian conference. Its duty was to show the strength of Argentina's claim to the sector of the Antarctic lying between 20° W and 68° W.[33] The *Buenos Aires Herald* described the American expedition as 'a political challenge to all nations claiming territory in the Antarctic region'.[34] Argentina was convinced it had a strong case, pointing to international legal opinion that stipulated a requirement for occupation before a legal title to territory could be recognised. Argentina had had a permanent meteorological base on Laurie Island in the South Orkneys since 1904, making it the only nation that had been in continual occupation of what could be described as an Antarctic territory.[35]

Although the German invasion of Norway ended plans for the polar conference, Argentina was not diverted from pressing ahead with its territorial claim. Nor did the evacuation of the American bases in 1940 lead Buenos Aires to reconsider its stance. Indeed, the work of the interdepartmental commission and the trend of events in the Antarctic convinced Argentina to push ahead with a permanent Antarctic organisation, along the lines of the US Antarctic Service, which would be 'responsible for the consideration and handling of all questions connected with the defence and development of Argentine interests in the Antarctic'. It was called the National Antarctic Committee and was controlled by the Ministry of Foreign Affairs. The chairman of the three-person committee was the Foreign Ministry's Isidoro Ruiz Moreno, while the other two members represented the Argentine Navy and Argentine Meteorological Bureau.[36]

The problem with the Argentine claim was that it overlapped not only Britain's Falkland Islands Dependencies but also the territory that Byrd had indicated the United States might claim. There was no way that Argentina could assert its claim by force of arms against Britain or the United States, and it did not believe such a course was necessary. Convinced that it had a strong legal case – based upon occupation, proximity and the sector being 'a prolongation of the American Continent' – Argentina suggested to the British government in September 1940 that an international conference be held to discuss the conflicting claims. This was not a suggestion that Britain was willing to consider, since it was well aware that some of its territorial claims were legally dubious, compared with Argentina's. But the issue would not go away. Indeed, the situation became even more complicated in November 1940, when Chile informed Britain that it 'had issued a decree laying claim to all Antarctic territory' between 53° E and 90° W, which again overlapped with the Falkland Islands Dependencies as well as with Argentina's claim. While Britain stood by its own claim, it was concerned to learn that Chile and Argentina were planning a conference of their own to reconcile their competing claims.[37]

The British were even more concerned when the subsequent conference of Chilean and Argentinian legal advisers led to an agreement between the two governments in March 1941 to pursue jointly the 'indubitable sovereign rights of Chile and Argentina in the Antarctic Zone'. Emboldened by the agreement, and doubtless annoyed by the continued British refusal to countenance the Argentine claims, Buenos Aires announced in mid-July, as German forces stormed into Russia, that it would begin to staff its meteorological base on Laurie Island with naval wireless operators rather than civilian scientists.

The British naval attaché at the embassy in Argentina warned London that this was being done both to strengthen the Argentine claim to the South Orkneys and to test British resolve, since 'such an act would not normally be tolerated by another owner'. But the British Navy was otherwise occupied by the war with Germany and Italy.

A few months later, the emboldened Argentinians went a step further, announcing the establishment of an Argentine post office on Laurie Island to be staffed by the base's radio telegrapher. Letters from the post office would carry Argentine stamps postmarked 'Islas Orcadas del Sud: Argentina'. The British ambassador in Buenos Aires warned Foreign Secretary Anthony Eden that this was intended as 'a definite exercise of sovereignty', which was designed to appeal to young and nationalist-minded Argentinians, who had been encouraged by the semi-official newspaper La Prensa to regard that part of the Antarctic and the Falkland Islands as their own.[38] In more normal times, the British government might have responded with a strong protest or even by the dispatch of a warship. These were not normal times. The ambassador's dispatch was received in London at about the same time that Japan was launching its war in the Pacific.

Britain was unsure how to react to the Argentine challenge. In the early 1900s, its officials had seen no value in retaining the South Orkneys and had offered to give the island chain to Argentina in return for a block of land in Buenos Aires on which to build a new British embassy. But the offer had lapsed and the islands had become valuable with the growth in Antarctic whaling. By 1925, Britain decided that it had to hold on to all its island possessions in the Antarctic and stretching north to the Falklands, since the loss of one island chain to Argentina might see the whole British position in the Antarctic collapse like a house of cards. By the early 1940s, officials wanted to retain the islands for strategic and economic reasons, although mainly to deny them to other nations rather than for their intrinsic worth.

The British officials noted the comments of Byrd, who had lauded the possibility of establishing an American naval base on the

Antarctic Peninsula to control the vital seaway between the Atlantic and Pacific Oceans. This had long been controlled by Britain, and it was not keen to cede control to the United States. Nor did it want Argentina to gain a foothold there, which might be a precursor to it dislodging Britain from the contested Falkland Islands. At the same time, Britain did not want to cause a rupture with the Argentinians, whose foodstuffs were essential for the British war effort. Anyway, there was no spare British naval ship that could be sent to the South Orkneys. The officials decided that such action would have to await the end of the war.[39]

In the absence of a British response, Argentina shifted its gaze from the South Orkneys to the South Shetlands. In late January 1942, it sent the transport ship *Primero de Mayo* to Deception Island. A British warship had visited the island in early 1941 to destroy a store of fuel oil abandoned at the unoccupied whaling station. For nearly a year, only the recovering wildlife had been in residence. Now an Argentinian officer went ashore to formally claim the island by 'hoisting an Argentine flag, depositing the Act of Possession in a chest on the island and painting the national colours of the Argentine Republic on the walls and roof of certain installations'. With no whalers or British officials in residence, there were only penguins and seals to watch the Argentinian sailors painting their flag onto the seaward-facing walls of the boiling-down works. Then the island was left once more to its wildlife, as the *Primero de Mayo* sailed south-west to erect an Argentine flag and a light beacon on one of the nearby Melchior Islands.

Rumours of the claims were not reported in the Buenos Aires press until March, and no official notice was sent to the British government. At the same time, a new map of Argentina's territorial claim in Antarctica was published in Buenos Aires.[40] Argentina might have hoped that Britain would not notice these transgressions, or be too preoccupied to react, since its forces were by then being seriously beset on two fronts, with the Germans threatening the British garrison in Egypt and the Japanese having just taken Singapore. Indeed, such was the glacial pace of the British diplomatic reaction to developments in the Antarctic that it was the end of June 1942 before Foreign Secretary Anthony Eden reacted to the establishment of the Argentine post office on Laurie Island. He informed Buenos Aires that Britain would not recognise any mail originating there. At the same time, he asked for confirmation of the newspaper reports concerning the naval officer's action in claiming Deception Island.[41]

Britain was hamstrung. Fulminate as they might in the Foreign Office, the officials could not afford to risk a breach with the Argentinians. But nor could they sit and watch as British sovereignty over the Falkland Islands Dependencies was whittled away by increasingly bold Argentinian actions. The officials prepared a protest note but it was never delivered. A diplomatic protest would hardly suffice, it was realised, since it would be unlikely to make Argentina desist from actions that were popular on the streets of Buenos Aires. Nor would the dispatch of a naval ship on a symbolic visit to the islands have the required effect, since it was hardly likely to make the Argentinians pack up and leave.

British legal advisers warned the government that its sovereignty was being progressively weakened and might disappear altogether unless more decisive action was taken. In the case of the South Shetlands, the Foreign Office confided that the British title was 'extremely weak'. Although officials were divided on the potential economic and strategic value of Britain's Antarctic territories, they were agreed on 'the importance of strongly resisting any attempt on the part of foreign governments to contest the British title'.[42] Still nothing was done. It was not until January 1943, when London learnt that Argentina was preparing to send the *Primero de Mayo* to perform further claiming ceremonies on the South Orkneys and the South Shetlands, that the British government finally decided to take decisive action to thwart the Argentine ambitions.

An armed merchant cruiser based in the Falkland Islands, HMS *Carnarvon Castle*, was sent to the disputed islands. Leaving Port Stanley on 25 January 1943, the converted passenger ship headed first to Deception Island, where its sailors splashed ashore intent on removing marks of Argentine ownership from the island's dilapidated buildings. A Union Jack was raised and a record of the ship's visit was left. Then the Argentine colours were painted over and other traces of the Argentine visit 'obliterated', while a notice was pinned to a prominent place on one of the buildings indicating that the owner's lease had lapsed and the buildings were now the possession of the British government. Then the ship was gone, steaming off to Signy Island in the South Orkneys, where flagpoles were erected to fly the Union Jack and a record of the visit was deposited in a cairn of rocks.

Nearby was Laurie Island, with its Argentine meteorological station and staff of naval officers, and it was here the ship was next to visit. The British were concerned by the possible Argentinian reaction to the arrival of the *Carnarvon Castle*, and its captain was specially instructed 'not to make a demonstration of force if the Argentinians showed any disposition to resist a landing'. So careful was the captain when he went ashore on 9 February 1943 that he pointedly ignored the Argentine flag flying above the station on the supposedly British island. He also did not talk at all to the Argentinians about the vexed question of British sovereignty. Instead, he explained his ship's presence as being merely a patrol to discover whether or not various island anchorages were being used by German ships. And so the visit passed with good feelings all round.[43]

The flag-waving cruise of the *Carnarvon Castle* left the Argentinians securely in occupation of Laurie Island and free to continue their assertions of sovereignty throughout the Falkland Islands Dependencies. Britain remained just as determined to stop them. While the *Carnarvon Castle* was steaming towards Deception Island, the British war cabinet met to consider its next move. Its members decided that they would initiate an occupation of their own. Churchill approved the dispatch of an expedition in the summer of 1943–44 that would assert British sovereignty over the Falkland Islands Dependencies by establishing two permanent bases. There would be a small base of about four men on Deception Island, while the main base of about eleven men would be at Hope Bay in 'Grahamland', on the very tip of the Antarctic Peninsula.[44]

This indicated a dramatic change in British policy, which had hitherto argued that actual occupation was not required in polar regions to achieve valid title to a territory. Only acts of discovery and exploration were needed, followed by acts of administration. The Argentinians and the Americans had effectively rebutted the British argument by repeatedly arguing that occupation was necessary, and by showing that permanent bases in the Antarctic were possible. It was only a matter of time before Britain was forced to acknowledge that reality and to respond in kind. That time had now come.

It was not a moment too soon. In the wake of the *Carnarvon Castle*'s visit to Deception Island, the British government protested to Buenos Aires about the display of Argentine colours at the abandoned whaling settlement, declaring that it was determined to defend its title to the island. But the Argentinians maintained their claim and protested at the removal of their national emblems. The glacial pace of Antarctic diplomacy had been replaced by a frenzied tit-for-tat, with British intelligence reporting that the *Primero de Mayo* had left Argentina for the Antarctica on 4 February with two Chilean naval officers aboard as observers. While the *Carnarvon Castle* was visiting the South Shetlands and South Orkneys to assert British sovereignty, the *Primero de Mayo* was on a long cruise of its own to assert Argentine sovereignty. The presence of the Chilean officers was to reassure Chile that, despite their overlapping territorial claims, Argentina's ambitions in the Antarctic posed no threat to it.

However, the Argentinians tried to keep secret from the Chileans the acts of sovereignty they performed at the several places they visited on the Antarctic Peninsula and in the South Shetlands. Among these was the hastily abandoned East Base of the United States Antarctic Service at Marguerite Bay, where American supplies and personal possessions were pillaged. When the Chileans were not watching, Argentinian officers concealed cylinders containing proclamations that claimed all the Antarctic between 25° W and 68° W. The last port of call for the *Primero de Mayo* was Deception Island, where the Argentinian sailors painted over the Union Jack. Then, just before the ship sailed and when they thought the Chileans were not watching, they painted back the colours of their own flag. However, it was noticed by the Chileans, who duly reported it to a British intelligence officer in Santiago.[45]

The British then implemented the decision of their war cabinet with 'Operation Tabarin', which involved establishing permanent bases in the Falkland Islands Dependencies as a counter to the Argentine activities. Although the move had been authorised by the war cabinet in January 1943, it was not until December that the troopship *Highland Monarch* left Britain with a mixed party of service personnel and scientists. It was bound initially for the Falkland Islands, where four men were put ashore on Deception Island on 6 February 1944, while ten were sent south-west to Port Lockroy on Wiencke Island, just off the west coast of the Antarctic Peninsula. The plan to have a third base at Hope Bay, on the tip of the peninsula, had to be abandoned because of heavy ice.

Lieutenant Commander James Marr of the Royal Navy Volunteer Reserve, who had been a Boy Scout on Shackleton's last expedition and a hydrologist on Mawson's 1929 voyage, was placed in command of the two bases. As an explicit act of sovereignty, he was sworn in as a magistrate for Graham Land, the South Orkneys and the South Shetlands. He was also instructed that if he encountered an Argentine or Chilean expedition, he should 'assert British sovereignty by all means short of violent force'.

The cover story for the secret operation, as far as Argentina was concerned, was that the parties were being sent to keep a watch for German raiders, while the British public was told in April 1944 that it was a resumption of Britain's pre-war scientific and survey work in Antarctica. The personnel also had a scientific program to keep them busy, which would provide Britain with a moral title to the territory that would be superior to that of the Argentinians. Meteorological and tidal observations, along with surveying, would provide practical assistance for British forces operating in the area, while studies in botany, biology and geology would allow a proper assessment of the region's potential value to Britain. The two bases were equipped with low-powered radio sets that were unlikely to be overheard by any Argentine listening stations but could be picked up in the Falkland Islands capital, Port Stanley. The parties were instructed to be circumspect in their use of the radios, since 'too much advertisement of our presence . . . will attract attention not only from our enemies but also from our anti-Imperialist friends on the American continent'.[46]

Evidence of that year's Argentine visit was seen at both Port Lockroy and on Deception Island, where the Argentinians had obliterated all signs of British ownership. That was quickly put right by Marr and his men. Once again, the Argentinian flag was painted over on the old whaling buildings and the Union Jack painted in its place. This time, however, the British were there to stay, and they quickly occupied the whaling station, thereby answering the legal arguments of the Americans and the Argentinians.

The site of the other base, Port Lockroy, was chosen because the British knew it had been a place of Argentine interest and had been visited by the *Primero de Mayo*. Although it was not well located for scientific or exploration purposes, Port Lockroy's position – roughly midway along the Antarctic Peninsula – was judged by Britain to be 'of considerable political value as a site for administrative acts'.

The first such act was to remove the proclamation and flag left there by the Argentinians. No trace would be left of the Argentine presence, with all of their proclamations and emblems removed to Port Stanley or otherwise obliterated. As the Argentinians had done, the British established post offices at their bases and issued new stamps for the Falkland Islands Dependencies in early 1944 so that postmarked mail could be sent from the bases. By the end of the first year, Marr was able to report with satisfaction that from 'the purely political standpoint', Britain's position in the Falkland Islands Dependencies 'has once again been revived'.[47] It was just the beginning of an expanded British presence.

The British government regarded the project as so important that it interrupted the production of crates for Spitfire fighters so that a British factory could build two huts for an expanded network of bases. In giving priority to the huts, Colonial Secretary Oliver Stanley noted that it was 'a matter of great importance for political reasons that this venture should be continued for a second year'. But it was all too much for Marr, who could not face a further winter in the isolation of the Antarctic. Suffering from severe depression, he was invalided home.

His departure threw Britain's plans into disarray. Although a new base was established at Hope Bay and four men took over Byrd's abandoned East Base on what the Americans called 'Stonington Island' in Marguerite Bay, the plan for a fifth base in the South Orkneys was postponed. The options of either ejecting the Argentinians from Laurie Island by force or establishing a British base alongside the Argentinian one had been rejected by British officials, for fear of provoking an irretrievable breakdown in relations with Buenos Aires. Instead, one of the specially constructed huts was erected on Coronation Island, the largest island of the South Orkneys, but it was left empty of inhabitants.[48] It would stand as a symbol of British possession and future intentions.

However, it was also a sign of Britain's limited power in the Antarctic, since Argentina remained the only nation in actual occupation of the South Orkneys. As a consequence, the Argentine claim to sovereignty over the South Orkneys was still stronger than Britain's, and its claim on Laurie Island was unassailable. Argentina also maintained its claim to Deception Island – in the face of Chilean objections and the British occupation – by publishing a map of the island, supposedly based upon work done during the visits of the

Primero de Mayo. It was a 'further provocative measure,' noted the British Foreign Office, although it dismissed the map as being based on a British chart, which had in turn been based upon an earlier French one.[49]

Chile was more circumspect in pushing forward with its territorial claim. Attempts to create a common front with Argentina were fraught with difficulties because both nations wanted much the same territory. Chile was suspicious of its neighbour, with whom it had long-running border disputes, and was angered to learn of the Argentine claim on Deception Island, which it considered Chilean. Yet the Chilean public did not share the passion that Argentinians regularly displayed about the Antarctic, or about the supposed perfidy of the British in occupying lands that were rightfully Argentinian.

This was a source of frustration for the few Antarctic enthusiasts in Chile, who were keen to have their compatriots share their ardour for the continent and its potential. One of the foremost enthusiasts was Oscar Pinochet de la Barra, whose book *La Antarctica Chilena* was published in 1944. The British Embassy in Santiago reported an upsurge of Chilean interest in the wake of the publication of the book and several newspaper articles by Pinochet.

One such article, written in November 1944, complained that the Marr expedition had, earlier that year, established British bases in the Chilean area without seeking Chilean authority. Pinochet regretted the 'complete ignorance [among Chileans] of everything connected with the Antarctic, its present value, and its immense possibilities for the future'. He urged Chile to establish a whaling industry in the Antarctic before other nations returned there at the end of the war. Pinochet also called for a scientific expedition to be sent, and urged that a permanent meteorological station be established. When Britain, the United States and Argentina returned at the end of the war to re-establish their claims within Chilean Antarctica, he wrote, they would then find Chile 'in full and effective possession of that which is ours'. Chile would be well on the way to incorporating 'those vast territories in a more effective manner, into the national economy'.[50]

As the war crashed towards its conclusion in 1945, the British government was forced to consider whether it should continue with its expanded commitment in the Antarctic. It had been easier before the war, when legal opinion and usual practice in polar regions suggested that Antarctic territories could be claimed without occupation. Now that occupation was more widely accepted as necessary for the recognition of sovereignty, Britain had to work out how it might retain control over territories that it had come to possess by little more than the stroke of a pen.

The pre-war Discovery Committee – named after the research ship that had undertaken Britain's scientific research in the Antarctic – proposed that it take over control of Operation Tabarin once the war ended. Whereas the pre-war research had been done mostly at sea by the *Discovery II*, concerning itself mainly with whaling, the interdepartmental committee suggested in November 1944 that it should base part of its post-war research at shore stations in order to 'materially strengthen the territorial position'. Doing so would also help maintain 'British pre-eminence in research and enterprise in the Southern Ocean and Antarctic'.[51] Whether Britain had really achieved such pre-eminence would likely have been disputed by Norway and the United States. What is important, though, is that Britain believed it was pre-eminent in science, and it was convinced that this gave it greater rights than others to the territories it claimed. In brief, Britain believed it 'knew' the territories in greater detail than its rivals and therefore had a superior claim to their sovereignty.

The funding of the Discovery Committee had been financed largely by the licence fees paid by whalers to the Falkland Islands administration. However, those returns had steadily reduced, as the whalers realised that they did not have to enter British waters to get a good harvest. By keeping to international waters, the whaling companies could avoid the onerous imposts altogether. As a result, while whaling was likely to resume its importance after the war, it appeared unlikely that Britain would reap much of its profits. New reasons had to be developed to justify the expense of British activity in the Antarctic.

The Discovery Committee asked the government for £250,000 to finance a five-year research program. There was, of course, the political aspect, and the government was reminded how Britain's 'title to the Falkland Islands Dependencies has benefited very much as a result of the Discovery Committee activities spread over the last twenty years'. And there was the economic aspect, since the aim of the research was to 'open the way to the general development of Antarctic and sub-Antarctic regions'. But what could be developed in such a forbidding region now that whaling had slipped from Britain's grasp?

Coal deposits had often been suggested by explorers as being one justification for their nations' involvement, but the quality of the coal and the difficulties of mining in the Antarctic made it not worth the bother. Although the committee suggested that whaling might grow in importance if whale meat could be used as food for humans, the whalers could still operate in international waters. The committee pointed instead to resources that could be exploited immediately in the territorial waters of the Falkland Islands Dependencies, such as seals, fish and seaweed, and to the likelihood that valuable minerals and oil would be found there. Oil was the great attraction.[52]

The Antarctic was possibly the least of Britain's concerns in 1945, as the war wound down and the problems of post-war reconstruction loomed large. But decisions had to be made about the future of Britain's territorial claims. The oldest of those claims on the continent dated back only to 1908, when the Falkland Islands Dependencies had been annexed. There had been little spent on them and not much more gained in return. After less than forty years in fitful control, Britain could have decided to sever its link and sail away, as it would do in other parts of its empire.

That might have happened, had Britain not established the four bases in the Falkland Islands Dependencies, which made it a matter of prestige for the waning empire not to concede to any challenges from its territorial rivals. The prospect of oil and other resources also figured in the British calculations, and officials and ministers decided in early 1945 to continue their permanent occupation.

The British would not be alone. The end of the war would see a mad scramble for polar territory, and mark the end of the Antarctic as the last continent unoccupied by humans.

CHAPTER 17

'A race to the Antarctic'

1945–1947

As the Pacific War was coming to its cataclysmic conclusion, one public-spirited resident of South Carolina wrote to President Harry Truman to suggest that scientists and engineers build 'a small, yet highly scientific and modern city' in the Antarctic. He envisioned that it would be populated by volunteer families so that it would become a 'normal city'. The continent was 'truly our last frontier', wrote this patriotic American, and it was 'our solemn duty to colonize and develop it as soon as possible'.[1]

There was no shortage of volunteers, with a man from Florida inquiring about the qualifications that were required for him to be among the 'colonists that are being sent to occupy U.S. claims in the Antarctic.' Presumably to his disappointment, the prospective settler was informed by a government official that the continent was 'not being colonized at this time'.[2] The official was only partly correct. Cities were not being planned, but several nations were racing to establish permanent bases peopled by their citizens.

President Roosevelt had led the way in 1939 with the short-lived United States Antarctic Service, under the command of his old moose-hunting friend, Richard Byrd. Two bases had been established on the coast, and an ill-fated 'snow cruiser' had been sent in a vain attempt to establish one at the South Pole, before the war forced a hurried American withdrawal. Byrd spent the rest of the war largely out of public sight, working on reports for the navy. When the Pacific War ended, Byrd was among the gaggle of senior officers gathered on the deck of USS *Missouri* in Tokyo Bay to watch General Douglas MacArthur accept the Japanese surrender.

It was while he was in Tokyo that Byrd penned a paper calling for the United States to establish bases on the Antarctic continent as a precursor to a territorial claim. He envisaged that the existing territorial claims by Britain, Australia, New Zealand, Norway, France,

Argentina and Chile would have to be resolved by an international conference, from which a 'world condominium' might be formed to control the continent. To ensure a prominent seat at any such conference table, and a powerful place within any future condominium, the United States needed to use its present military might to make its own territorial claims. 'Now is the time to act,' declared Byrd, 'while we have trained manpower and excess equipment.' Byrd's ambition was continental in scope. He wanted America to 'use aircraft carriers and long-range planes to make a complete survey of the continent', and for the United States Antarctic Service to be reinstated – with himself, presumably, as its leader.[3]

The US Navy had other reasons for going there. The end of the Second World War had left the United States and the Soviet Union as the two most powerful nations on Earth. If that rivalry ever erupted into war, it was expected the conflict would be played out in the Arctic, which provided the shortest air routes between the United States and the industrial centres of Russia. But the United States had little experience fighting in polar conditions. The US Navy's staging of fleet exercises in the Arctic in mid-1946 led to fierce Russian protests, which encouraged the navy to look to the Antarctic as an alternative testing area.

In August 1946, the navy initiated what it called the 'Antarctic Developments Project' and began secret plans to send a naval task-force south in the southern summer. Dubbed 'Operation Highjump', the Antarctic armada would comprise twelve naval ships, including an aircraft carrier, two seaplane tenders and a submarine. Also going south was the powerful Coast Guard icebreaker, the *Northwind*, and the navy's new icebreaker, the *Burton Island*, along with seventeen aircraft and six helicopters. Byrd was appointed to the operation's overall command.[4] The secrecy was all about getting a 'jump' on America's rivals, so that the United States would have the Antarctic largely to itself during the brief window of summer flying weather. But the news caused a flurry of announcements from other nations, which then began preparations to send their own expeditions south.

On board the aircraft carrier *Philippine Sea*, Byrd was back in his element. Operational control was left to Rear Admiral Richard Cruzen, who had commanded the *Bear* in 1939 and who now took charge of the assortment of warships and cargo vessels that were headed for the Bay of Whales. The expedition would establish 'Little America IV' near to where Byrd had set up his previous bases. Almost sixty years old, Byrd lagged some distance behind in the *Philippine Sea*, taking note by radio of the moves made by Cruzen's ships, as well as two other groups of naval vessels heading for different parts of the continent.

The plan was for Byrd to fly to Little America IV in one of six DC-4 transport aircraft, with movie cameras capturing his return to the scene of his earlier triumphs. Consequently, he was dismayed to read a signal from Cruzen, who was concerned about the ice conditions in the Ross Sea and wanted to end the expedition by 5 February 1947. That would leave little time to make the photographic and territorial claiming flights that were one of the expedition's main purposes. Also, warned Byrd, it would delay 'the conquering by our nation of the elements in polar regions which is so important to our national security'. With Byrd advising that the ice conditions were likely to improve, Cruzon agreed not to act until Byrd's arrival.[5] In fact, the ice was worse than Byrd had ever seen it, and the conditions would limit the aerial operations that he had planned.

There was no pretence that Operation Highjump was driven by science. When the expedition was formally announced in November 1946, the navy declared that its main purpose was to 'train members of the Navy and to test ships, aircraft and other military equipment under frigid conditions'. They were practising for a future war against the Soviet Union in which Greenland, which had similar ice conditions to Antarctica, would feature as a forward base.

The relevance of the expedition for America's territorial claims in the Antarctic lay mainly with the photographic and claiming flights, which were intended to provide the basis for maps that would surpass in detail and extent the maps of other nations. At the limit of each flight, proclamations were to be dropped onto the ice by the aircrew, who would display the Stars and Stripes as they did so. The official instructions made clear that the operation was about 'consolidating and extending United States sovereignty over the largest practicable area of the Antarctic continent' and testing 'the feasibility of establishing, maintaining and utilizing bases in the Antarctic and investigating possible base sites'.

Apart from using the new trimetrogon cameras, which took simultaneous vertical and oblique photographs of the landscape for mapping purposes, the aircraft would have airborne magnetometers that would probe beneath the surface of the ice for geological formations that might indicate the presence of oil. There was also the possibility of discovering uranium, although Byrd denied that he was engaged in a race for uranium with Britain and Russia. Nevertheless, his comments would have alarmed those countries and others when he went on to tell journalists that the Antarctic was 'the world's greatest untouched reservoir of natural resources' and that his expedition planned to 'make as complete a survey as possible of the whole area'.[6]

The news that the United States was sending the largest ever expedition to Antarctica caused immediate concern among all the existing Antarctic claimants. There was particular concern in New Zealand, since Byrd was once again planning to establish a base on New Zealand's Ross Dependency. The New Zealand press called for the government to send their own expedition so that New Zealand would be in occupation before the Americans arrived.[7] The Auckland *Truth* thought it was incumbent on New Zealand to 'race Byrd south, just as Amundsen raced Scott to the Pole'. If Byrd got there first and established a permanent base, warned the paper, New Zealand 'would be cut off from the tremendous resources of the Antarctic and its backdoor would be permanently forced open'.

Although the *New Zealand Herald* thought there was 'much to be gained by co-operation with the Americans', it wanted New Zealand to do so from a position of strength. If New Zealand had a meteorological station in the Ross Dependency, opined the paper, a 'daily broadcast . . . would leave no doubt that the Dominion is in occupation'.[8] Although some newspapers pointed to the practical problems of New Zealand trying to pre-empt the United States, or suggested that the territorial competition could be ended by having the Antarctic administered by the newly established United Nations, New Zealand did consider sending a small expedition to beat Byrd and demonstrate to the world that New Zealand was in effective occupation of the Ross Dependency.[9]

When the director of New Zealand's Department of Scientific and Industrial Research, Dr Ernest Marsden, a British-born physicist, read in his morning newspaper of Byrd's expedition, he immediately wrote to New Zealand's naval chief, stressing the importance of sending an expedition to conduct cosmic ray research. Marsden noted that there was likely to be heightened sunspot activity that year, and the work would be 'of great value in relation to atomic energy research'. His proposal received a positive response from other officials and was taken up with the government.

It was not just cosmic rays that interested Marsden. He was conscious that there was 'much at stake' for New Zealand, and was concerned by reports that Argentina and Chile were also planning expeditions. With all those nations heading for the Antarctic, Marsden was keen for New Zealand to get there first, suggesting that 'we do not advertise our plans until we are actually en route'.[10] However, when the government came to consider the proposal in December 1946, it decided that it had neither the time nor the resources to send an immediate expedition. The cabinet decided instead to plan an expedition for the following summer, when Australia might also send one.[11]

The announcement of the Byrd expedition forced Canberra, too, to hurriedly dust off its pre-war plans of establishing permanent bases in the Australian Antarctic Territory. Pressure also came from London, with the British government fearing that its own claims might be imperilled by the inaction of its dominions in relation to their claims. In October 1946, the Australian representative on the secretive interdepartmental Polar Committee reported to Canberra that British legal advice now considered that 'continuity of effective occupation' was required for a valid title. Australia certainly had not 'effectively occupied' its territory. With a conference of Antarctic powers likely to be held within eighteen months, the British government urged Australia to take 'active steps to strengthen [its] claim to disputed territory before the holding of such a conference'.[12]

The ageing explorer Douglas Mawson added to the pressure on the Australian government. Australia's territorial claim would be put at risk, warned Mawson in October 1946, unless the country took action to demonstrate its 'interest in the exploration and development of the region'. The prominent journalist Osmar White also took up cudgels in support of an Australian effort, noting that the 'Australian quadrant had been explored and charted by Australians with Australian money. Australians were the first to land on Adelie Land, where the flag was hoisted, and Australians lie buried there.'[13] Hence, implied White, their ownership of the territory was more legitimate than that of their rivals.

At the time, the Australian government was beset with the problems of post-war reconstruction, including the repatriation of service personnel and the development of a massive immigration scheme. Amidst this plethora of problems, the Antarctic might have been ignored, had it not held out the possibility of jobs being created for the fast-growing Australian population. At the federal election in September 1946, Labor prime minister Ben Chifley predicted that Australia was 'about to enter upon the greatest era in her history'; the Antarctic was expected to contribute to Australia's new 'golden age'.[14]

Various ways of securing its territory were urged upon the Australian government. From Santiago came a memo from Australian diplomat John Cumpston, who had been instrumental in preparing Australia's map of the Antarctic in 1939. He warned that Byrd's expedition 'will undoubtedly complete at least an aerial photographic survey of the Australian Antarctic territory as far to the east as Queen Mary Land', which was where America had a strong claim 'by right of prior discovery'.

To forestall Byrd from landing by helicopter and taking possession of Australia's territory, Cumpston urged that Catalina flying boats be sent south immediately to photograph the coast of Wilkes Land so that an updated edition of the Australian map could be issued 'before the U.S. are able to advance a claim based on the work of the present [Byrd] expedition'. With the 1939 map becoming obsolete, the publication of a new edition would provide 'the strongest evidence we have of the strength of our claim' and help to ensure that it was widely accepted as the standard map of the continent. It was important, argued Cumpston, that the Australia map should appear before the US Hydrographic Office was able to produce an updated map of its own. The revised Australian map, declared Cumpston, 'will be far superior to the American and should be a standard map for at least another ten years'.[15]

Although it was not possible to send flying boats on such a hazardous mission, Cumpston's call for an updated edition of the Australian map was embraced by the minister for external affairs, Dr Herbert Evatt, who instructed in February 1947 that he wanted 'the best possible map of the area [to] be prepared'. Without a photographic mission by flying boats, Australia had to gather its updated cartographic information from elsewhere. The task was given to the Department of External Affairs, which would gather the information and compile a new handbook to accompany the map, while the National Mapping Division of the Department of the Interior would draw it up. Cumpston and Mawson were asked for any information they could provide, while an appeal went out to Britain's Polar Committee and the Royal Geographical Society for the latest British maps and charts. Cumpston sent the latest Argentine and Chilean maps to Canberra, while additional information was sought from the Norwegian whaling society, the report of the 1939 German *Schwabenland* expedition and from the United States.[16] It was crucial that the Australian map remain the most authoritative in existence. But it would take more than a map to secure Australia's hold on the Antarctic.

In the wake of Chifley's re-election, officials from nine government departments gathered at the old bluestone Victoria Barracks in Melbourne in December 1946 to discuss Australia's future activities in the Antarctic. There to advise them was Mawson, who had been advocating the development of Antarctic resources for more than three decades. With the officials having been instructed to prepare recommendations that would 'ensure the development and use of the Australian Antarctic Territory and greater continuity of effective occupation', Mawson was well placed to advise them.

Chairman William Dunk of the Department of External Affairs opened the meeting by alluding to the 'intensive interest' shown by other nations in the Antarctic and the threat this posed to Australian sovereignty. Turning to Mawson, Dunk asked for 'more factual information on the resources in the territories so that consideration could be given to practical means of using them'. Mawson was more than happy to oblige. He suggested that most minerals, including uranium, were probably present in the Antarctic, and that the coal deposits could be used *in situ* to smelt other minerals, such as copper. Whaling might also provide a permanent industry for Australia, so long as international controls were implemented to prevent their extinction.[17] Mawson was averse to government-controlled expeditions and wanted any base to be a university one, which would be engaged in 'scientific exploration . . . linked with fisheries development (Mainly whaling)'.[18]

The officials gave the nod to Mawson's suggestion that a permanent base be established as soon as possible. Some even thought that two bases were necessary for purposes such as meteorology, while defence officials pointed to the strategic reasons for establishing an Australian base before a potential enemy was able to do so. But there was considerable uncertainty about where a base could or should be established.

Mawson favoured Cape Freshfield, far to the south of Sydney at about 152° E, which was where his tragic overland expedition had ended in 1913 and where he had suggested setting up a base in 1940. However, he was unsure whether Cape Freshfield was accessible by ship in summer. He advised a flyover by a four-engine bomber to show whether the site was suitable. The meeting decided instead that an Australian naval ship equipped with an aircraft should go there during the current summer on a brief reconnaissance voyage, while officials went ahead to prepare 'concrete plans for exploration and observation in [the] Antarctic'. Such was the officials' sense of urgency that within three weeks of the meeting the government authorised the dispatch of a naval ship to find an ice-free base.[19] Authorisation was one thing – finding a suitable ship was another.

The only ice-strengthened ship in the Australian navy was Ellsworth's old ship, the *Wyatt Earp*, which had been renamed the HMAS *Wongala* and used for transporting explosives. After the war, it had been decommissioned and given to the Sea Scouts in Adelaide.[20] It would need months of work in a dry dock before it was ready to face the rigours of the Southern Ocean.

On 16 January 1947, Chifley was forced to concede that Australia had no suitable ship for an immediate voyage that summer. Instead, as New Zealand had done, he appointed a committee to plan an expedition for the summer of 1947–48.[21] The change of plan was applauded by the Melbourne *Herald*, which noted that any Australian expedition should be part of 'a carefully conceived scientific project' and not a rushed response to America's 'lavishly equipped "task force"'. The paper wanted to see practical results of value to Australia in areas such as meteorology, whaling and mineral exploitation, and not just an expedition 'to stake further theoretical and controversial claims to slices of an ice-capped Polar continent'.[22]

With Australia and New Zealand hampered by the lack of suitable ships and experienced personnel, and with Norway and France distracted by more pressing post-war problems, it was left to the three remaining Antarctic claimants – Argentina, Chile and Britain – to counter the American push. Britain had already strengthened its hold on its Falkland Islands Dependencies by setting up two more bases during the summer of 1945–46, which added to the three that it had established during the war at Hope Bay, Deception Island and Port Lockroy. In July 1945, Operation

Tabarin, which controlled the bases, was renamed the 'Falkland Islands Dependencies Survey'. The new name was more appropriate to peacetime and would add to the moral legitimacy of the British claim, although its purpose remained the same. As Britain's director of naval intelligence explained to his New Zealand counterpart, 'the general purpose of the survey was to maintain effective occupation of key points in Graham Land, the South Shetlands, South Orkneys and to conduct a programme of surveying and research in those regions. The occupation of the main bases was to take precedence over all other activities.'[23] Sovereignty was everything.

With five bases, Britain's occupation of the dependencies was more complete. Four men were put ashore to establish a base at Cape Geddes on Laurie Island, despite Britain's legal adviser having suggested that, after more than forty years of occupying a meteorological station on the same island, Argentina's title was incontestable. There was a fear in London that if it gave way on Laurie Island, the whole of the South Orkneys might be open to an Argentine claim. Ten other men were landed at Neny Fjord, on what the Americans called 'Stonington Island', where the United States Antarctic Service had occupied a base from 1939 to 1941 and where it was feared that the Americans might soon return. The five bases were scattered strategically across both the Antarctic Peninsula and the two island chains that comprised the Falkland Islands Dependencies. Each base had a post office, while new Falkland Islands Dependencies stamps were issued in February 1946 to remind the world of Britain's ownership. Each also had a wireless telegraph office, from which it was intended to transmit weather forecasts for the South Atlantic as an additional reminder of British possession. The continental bases also had more dog teams to allow for exploratory sledge journeys.[24]

Any illusions that these moves would be effective by themselves in defending Britain's title were dispelled when the legal adviser to the Foreign Office warned in October 1946 of the changing legal requirements to establish a valid title. Britain had long relied largely on historic acts of discovery, but the government was now advised that international law had developed to the point where 'little or no weight now attaches to discovery'. The long-held American requirement of continuous and effective occupation, or at least of maintaining effective control, was now accepted more generally as a prerequisite for a valid title.

This left Britain and its dominions on very weak legal grounds, in so far as their title to the Falkland Islands Dependencies, the Ross Dependency and the Australian Antarctic Territory were concerned. Indeed, the British government was advised that its title to the Falkland Islands Dependencies had possibly already gone to other claimants, while the Ross Dependency and the Australian Antarctic Territory were vulnerable if the forthcoming American expedition to the Antarctic led to US bases being established in those places and Washington subsequently made a territorial claim. Only the British claim to the Falkland Islands was beyond challenge, due to their long-standing and effective occupation.[25]

The announcements of more British bases being established and of Byrd's naval task force being sent combined to convince Argentina and Chile to respond in kind. Argentina's president, Juan Perón, reacted by issuing a decree in September 1946 prohibiting the publication of maps of Argentina that 'do not show the Argentine Antarctic'.[26] The following month, he issued another decree 'declaring Argentine sovereignty over the Antarctic submarine platform and the water covering it'. A map in the Buenos Aires press indicated that the claim covered 'the Falkland Islands, South Georgia, the South Sandwich Islands, the South Orkneys, Graham Land and the entire Antarctic Sea-board'[27] – effectively, all the territories claimed by Britain. The coming summer's supply voyage for the base on Laurie Island would see further assertions of Argentine sovereignty on those British territories.

Meanwhile, Chile responded by announcing in December 1946 that it would send three naval ships to reinforce its claims. At the same time, it issued a decree asserting its right to exploit any uranium found in its Antarctic territory.[28] With instructions from the Chilean naval chief to 'extend and enlarge our territory', the frigate *Iquique* set off to establish a naval base called *Soberania* (Sovereignty), along with a seaplane anchorage, on Greenwich Island in the South Shetlands, which was renamed 'Presidente Aquirre Island'. Six naval personnel were left behind in a steel hut to act as a coastguard and to administer a post office.[29]

After visiting Deception Island, the *Iquique* returned to Greenwich Island on 6 February 1947, when the ship's commander took formal possession of the island with due ceremony. After the Chilean flag was raised and the national anthem sung, documents of possession were signed, with one copy being buried in the foundations of the building. A cross was erected as 'a symbol of peace and justice'. Chilean ski troops then completed a topographical survey of the island and raised their flag on its highest point, while a navigational light was erected on nearby Roberts Island. When the *Iquique* finally left for Chile, it took hundreds of letters postmarked as coming from '*Territorio Chileno Antarctica*'. Arriving at Punta Arenas on 26 March, the ships were met with 'speechmaking and fervent singing of the national song' by 'almost the whole population'. There was much to celebrate, since a Chilean title to the supposedly British-owned Greenwich Island, and perhaps to the entire South Shetlands, had now been established. Two special Chilean stamps were issued showing a map of 'Antártida Chilena', with its boundary set between 53° W and 90° W.[30]

During their Antarctic cruise, sailors from the *Iquique* had painted a Chilean flag on a wooden board, which they erected on the shore of tiny Gamma Island, one of the Melchior Group off the west coast of the Antarctic Peninsula. The freshly painted flag was there when an Argentine expedition arrived at the end of January 1947 to select the site for a new meteorological and wireless station. President Perón had sent three naval ships, led by the *Patagonia*, to make further assertions of sovereignty throughout the so-called 'Argentine Antarctic'. With Chilean observers on board, the Argentinians simply placed one of their own flags alongside the Chilean one, promising to protect the Chilean flag from being removed by the British.

The Argentinian ships then went on to erect a lighthouse on Doumer Island, at the entrance to Port Lockroy, where Britain's main base was located. When the ships returned to Buenos Aires in April, they were greeted by flag-waving crowds before the crews marched along festooned streets to Government House, where President Perón gave a stirring speech about how 'Argentinians have shown, once again, what they can do in defence of their rights'.[31] The threat to British Antarctica from the two South American republics became all the greater when they agreed in July 1947 to adjust their respective territorial claims so that they no longer overlapped.[32] Once that was done they could present a truly united front to Britain, and to the United States.

For a time in 1946, it seemed that there might be three US expeditions operating in the Antarctic at the same time. Apart from Byrd's, there was also one being organised under the leadership of Finn Ronne, and another being mooted by the ageing Lincoln Ellsworth. Although Ellsworth's expedition never eventuated, Ronne pressed on doggedly to win support for his proposal. The Norwegian-born explorer, who had since become an American, had a long association with the Antarctic. His father had gone south with Byrd in 1928, and he had gone himself in 1933 and again in 1939. On the latter expedition, Ronne had made a monumental sledge journey from East Base. Now he wanted to reoccupy his old quarters and take up the work that had been interrupted by the hurried evacuation in 1941. Even before the war had ended, while Byrd was otherwise occupied, Ronne had begun spruiking the expedition to potential donors and supporters. A prospectus made clear that geography and geology were at the top of his agenda. In contrast to Byrd's expedition, it was planned to have only one small ship, two aircraft and just sixteen men.[33]

Ronne had served out the war in the US Navy's Bureau of Ships. Consequently, he was confident of obtaining the navy's support. However, he first sought the backing of the American Geographical Society so that he could then declare that the expedition was being done under its auspices. It was only then that he planned to inform Byrd of his plans.[34] Although Ronne claimed to be 'on very good terms' with Byrd, his refusal to consult him was clearly a ruse to prevent the influential explorer from nipping his plans in the bud.

Once the society's council had given its support in October 1945, Ronne had its director, John Wright, ask the secretary of the navy, James Forrestal, for the loan of a wooden-hulled rescue tug that Ronne had already picked out. Forrestal was informed that the expedition would explore the Antarctic between 35° W and 80° W, and that it had already received interest from various scientific and government organisations, including the Electronic Division of the navy's Bureau of Ships.[35] Although Forrestal was favourable, the navy was unable to hand over one of its ships to an individual. So Ronne set up the American Antarctic Association as a non-profit scientific organisation, with himself as chairman. Its advisory board included the geographers Isaiah Bowman, Samuel Boggs and W. L. G. Joerg, along with geologist Laurence Gould (who had first gone to the Arctic in 1926 with his mentor, William Hobbs), Bernt Balchen and Hubert Wilkins.[36]

Even with these supporters, Ronne found it difficult to raise the meagre budget of $150,000 from the organisations that had been so generous to the pre-war expeditions. The *New York Times* wanted him to find the bulk of his money elsewhere before approaching them; the Hearst newspapers offered just $5000 instead of $45,000, and would only pay it after his return; while the National Geographic Society was unwilling to pay anything at all, saying the public interest was likely to be 'very slight'.[37] By April 1946, Ronne was almost ready to admit defeat, complaining to Gould that there was insufficient 'scientific interest in the scientific circles in this country, to justify supporting a non-profit and partially non-salaried expedition to [the] Antarctic'.

Six weeks later, about half of the funds had dribbled in and Ronne was again confident of getting away during the coming summer. He expected to receive $25,000 from the sale of the news rights and asked the American Philosophical Society for a grant of $45,000 to cover the outstanding amount, offering in return to do any scientific work that the society cared to nominate. But he was again disappointed. Ronne was forced to rely instead on obtaining contracts from the armed services for the testing of equipment in polar conditions. He was buoyed by the support both of Byrd, who had helped get congressional approval for the loan of the navy ship, and of the Smithsonian Institution, which agreed to pay the salary of his chief scientist, biologist Dr Carl Eklund, who had been on Byrd's 1939 expedition.[38] By September 1946, Ronne's expedition was being prepared for a December departure, with the hard-pressed American Geographical Society reluctantly agreeing to provide space at its headquarters for two of Ronne's people.[39]

Ronne had planned to return to the abandoned buildings of East Base and make use of the fuel, food and other goods that had been left there. However, the State Department was informed by the British government in September 1946 that much of the material had been removed by the sailors of a visiting Argentine ship, while the remainder was being prepared for return to the United States by the British expedition that was now occupying the abandoned buildings.[40] Although the Argentine government had sent some of the equipment to the United States, the loss of the supplies was a serious setback for Ronne. He would have to make up for it by taking more himself. More serious still was the news that the British were occupying the abandoned American buildings.[41]

When State Department officials asked the British Embassy whether the British would still be in occupation when Ronne arrived in March 1947, they were told that there was insufficient space in the buildings to accommodate both parties, and insufficient seals in the area that could be used as food for them and their dogs. That news did not go down well in the State Department, and the British were instructed to vacate the American buildings and leave them for Ronne and 'future American expeditions in that area'.[42]

A British emissary was sent to persuade Ronne to establish his base elsewhere. But that was not an option. Ronne needed the buildings for his accommodation. At the last minute, Chile also objected to Ronne setting up his base on territory that it regarded as Chilean. Its objections were appeased when Ronne allowed himself to be issued with Chilean visas that were valid for Chile and the Chilean Antarctic.[43]

Further problems came from the US Navy, which wanted to withdraw its contracts now that it was sending its own much grander expedition under Byrd's command. Although Ronne's shoestring budget was getting smaller and smaller, he was determined to press ahead. The navy was still providing him with the promised ship, for which fuel had been donated by an oil company, and some of the men were going as unpaid volunteers or were being paid by their home institutions. The US Army Air Force had also provided him with equipment that it wanted to be tested.[44]

Another setback came when Eklund dropped out as chief scientist; there was no time to find a replacement. Ronne promised nevertheless to provide the Smithsonian Institution with 'some information of use and interest'.[45] Ronne's other plans became that much harder to achieve when delays by the navy in refurbishing the small tug *Port of Beaumont* in Texas forced him to delay his departure until 25 January 1947, which meant they would be arriving at Marguerite Bay at the end of summer. He had planned for the ship to leave from New York, where the publicity could be maximised, but he now would have to go from Texas via Panama to Punta Arenas in Chile. Nevertheless, Ronne sent a relatively cheery message to Wright at the American Geographical Society as the ship steamed southward on 2 March, reporting that 'everything has worked out as I had scheduled it two years ago; even though there were many obstacles purposely placed in my way'.[46]

Ronne made history by taking two women with him. One was his wife, Jackie, who was on the staff of the State Department, and the other was the wife of his pilot Harry Darlington.[47] Another change was the inclusion of a Chilean observer, who was taken on board at the request of the Chilean government when the ship called at Punta Arenas. Ronne had been opposed to the Chilean presence but relented when it was made clear that the man would be paying for his passage. Ronne needed all the money he could get.[48]

Like so many leaders of private expeditions before him, Ronne left for the Antarctic weighed down by debt and the expectations of his supporters, including the United States government. Although parts of the US Navy had become half-hearted in their support once Byrd's naval expedition was announced, the Office of Naval Research recognised the potential value of Ronne's more modest venture and had pressed for it to become a government expedition. Apart from the important meteorological and cosmic ray observations that Ronne would make, and the deposits of uranium that he might find, the office pointed to the need for the United States to 'embark officially on Antarctic exploration on a large scale' so that it would be better placed to participate in any international conference on territorial claims.[49] But the expedition remained a private one, although it relied largely on government money and Ronne had been secretly appointed as a US postmaster.[50] To give the impression that it was an overwhelmingly private and scientific expedition, Ronne had called it the 'Ronne Antarctic Research Expedition'.

As the *Port of Beaumont* steamed slowly towards Stonington Island, there was no sign of any occupants, nor was there any national emblem flying above the abandoned buildings of East Base. But there was a British flag about a hundred metres away, flying above the base that had been established a year before and that presently was occupied by a small group of British scientists and soldiers. There was also a large sign on the British building declaring that it was the 'Graham Land Post Office, Marguerite Bay'. When Ronne reached the American buildings, as he later reported to the State Department, he found the doors thrown open to the elements and 'shocking evidence of complete and utter vandalism', with the 'entire place [having been] littered with rubbish in an indescribable manner'. It would take a month to make the buildings habitable.

The leader of the British base, Major Kenelm Pierce-Butler, claimed that the damage had been done by the sailors from a Chilean ship that had called there in February, and those from another Chilean ship just days earlier. When the accusation was published, it caused outrage in Chile. Oblivious to the political storm, Pierce-Butler conceded that his men had taken some of the American equipment and building materials for use at their base, and he promised to return it. Ronne insisted the British also stop using the American toilet and build one of their own. It was the start of an uneasy relationship between the two groups that lived just metres apart at the bottom of the world. The State Department counselled Ronne to 'establish and maintain amicable relations in the best traditions of both countries'.[51]

Yet their respective territorial claims made it difficult to create good relations. When Ronne hoisted the Stars and Stripes on the old flagpole of the American base on 13 March 1947, he received an immediate challenge from Pierce-Butler. Acting under instructions from London, Pierce-Butler advised Ronne by letter that he had no objection to the American flag, on condition that it did not signify an American claim to the territory. However, if it did signify a claim then he was 'bound to protest'. Ronne replied that he was neither making a claim nor recognising the British claim. Of course, Ronne knew that American claim sheets had been secreted in prominent places around Marguerite Bay by the members of the US Antarctic Service, including himself, between 1939 and 1941, although he would not admit this to Pierce-Butler. Instead, he insisted on his right to occupy the base and fly the American flag. 'As an American expedition reoccupying this base on Stonington Island,' said Ronne, 'we have reflown the American flag on the American-built flagpole at the American camp.'

Once their respective stances on sovereignty were established, and with toilet arrangements agreed, Ronne spent the remaining months of his sojourn on Stonington Island enjoying relatively amicable relations with Pierce-Butler and cooperating in their respective sledge journeys. The British commander had been instructed to maintain cordial relations with American parties, and to offer 'every material assistance' while upholding British sovereignty. In the event of a Chilean or Argentinian expedition arriving there, however, he was told to 'adopt a more formal, though courteous attitude' and 'make no offer of assistance'. He was also to emphasise the scientific aspects of his own expedition and hide 'any evidence and specimens, of any minerals of commercial significance'.[52]

Even before Ronne had left Texas for the Antarctic, the *Northwind* was pushing a passage through the unusually thick ice to the Bay of Whales. Following behind came the transport ships and submarine of Operation Highjump, ready to land hundreds of men and sufficient material to establish Little America IV. However, such were the ice conditions that one of the ships, whose hull had been damaged, had to retreat, as did the submarine.

Once ashore, the sailors and marines prepared a landing strip for the six DC-4s. The size of the aircraft meant they could barely take off from the deck of the *Philippine Sea*. They had to have jet packs attached to their wings to get them aloft. Byrd was a passenger on the first of the planes to land at Little America IV. Although there was not enough time for the planes to complete their full program of photographic flights, there was time for Byrd to fly to the South Pole on 16 February 1947, recreating for the movie cameras his aerial conquest of 1929. Although American planes were now dropping proclamations onto other parts of the Antarctic, Byrd symbolically dropped a carton containing the flags of all fifty-four members of the United Nations, along with the flag of the United Nations.[53] It was a sign of the continuing conflict between American policy-makers, and of the indecisiveness of Byrd himself, as to whether the United States should formally annex the territory it was exploring, or whether it was better to claim it on behalf of the United Nations or some 'world condominium'.

Even the proclamations made by the personnel making territorial claims had been carefully worded to allow the State Department the option of denying that any claims had been made by the United States government itself, rather than just by the individual concerned. Each proclamation noted that it was being made by a named 'member of the United States Naval Antarctic Developments Project, 1947, operating by direction of the President of the United States of America and pursuant to the instructions of the Secretary of the Navy'. The proclamations went on to declare that:

> . . . we have discovered and investigated the following land and sea areas . . . And thereby claim this territory in the name of the United States of America and in support of this claim I have displayed the flag of the United States thereon and have deposited (or dropped from airplane) this record thereof.

It was a fine legal point, but a State Department report would later argue that the proclamations were dropped from aircraft or deposited 'by individual members of the Task Force', and thus that the territorial claims were 'made by individuals as American citizens, not by the Task Force itself'.[54] Although meant to be secret, the dropping of the proclamations was reported in American newspapers in April 1947. When questioned by reporters, a State Department spokesman declared that they were not official claim forms, and that they presumably 'bore the signatures of a person in the aircraft from which they were dropped'.[55]

Apart from the proclamations, the strength of any American claim was meant to be fortified by the aerial photographs and the improved map of the continent that would result. However, the rushed nature of the expedition had not allowed the pilots to be trained in making photographic flights, and 'the camera compartments were not properly sealed against wind-blast', which meant that the photographers had to work wearing thick gloves. Because of these limitations, Cruzen reported, the photographer usually did not have sufficient time to operate the oblique cameras that photographed to each side of the plane's flight path. Although the aircraft flew over an estimated 4,000,000 square kilometres of the continent – about half of which had not been explored before – not all of the area was photographed.

There would be great problems for those trying to make maps from these photographs. Without adequate ground control points, there was no way for the mapmakers in the US Navy's Hydrographic Office to situate any newly discovered mountains on a map.[56] As far as the mapmaking was concerned, the flights had largely been a waste of time and money. However, the flights did lead to the discovery of ice-free lakes amid 'low hills of apparently bare earth', situated in the Vestfold Hills area of the Australian Antarctic Territory. The area was described by newspapers as being akin to an oasis that 'might be warm enough to support a human settlement comfortably all the year round', while the lakes were big enough for flying boats to use.[57]

When Byrd's ships returned to Wellington in early March, the six DC-4s were left on the ice, with the expectation that they would be used by another expedition the following year. However, the Americans failed to return, and both the planes and Little America IV were lost to the remorseless movement of the ice shelf, floating off into the Southern Ocean. Still, the potential American claim to the Ross Dependency remained in place, although Byrd assured reporters when he arrived back in Wellington that 'the United States had not gone into the question of territorial claims in the Antarctic, and had made none'. It was a familiar and disingenuous refrain. Byrd had made similar comments each time he had passed through New Zealand on his way to or from the Ross Dependency. With the founding of successive Little Americas and the making of more territorial claims, he was well aware that the American title to the Ross Dependency became that much stronger. Yet Byrd said that he 'could not conceive of any controversy between the United States and New Zealand over Antarctica'.[58]

Similarly, geographer Paul Siple told an Auckland press conference of his admiration for what he took to be the New Zealand attitude towards Antarctica, which concentrated 'on the valuable work which might be done there rather than on questions of national possession'.[59] That was certainly the attitude projected by the pragmatic New Zealand prime minister, Peter Fraser, who held a dinner in Wellington to welcome Byrd. During the dinner, Fraser disparaged newspaper reports that had 'tried to stage a race to the Antarctic between New Zealand and the United States'. New Zealand simply did not have the ships and 'wanted to co-operate to the fullest extent', said Fraser. Byrd replied in kind, arguing that there should be 'some kind of international organization to share scientific work in the Antarctic'.[60]

The concern in New Zealand about the United States' intentions in the Ross Dependency was partly allayed by Byrd's visit. He had provided the New Zealanders with samples of polar clothing and had suggested that, if Australia and New Zealand established bases, the United States might provide an ice-breaker to service them as well as its own bases.[61] The Americans certainly gave the impression that they would be back. Cruzen told journalists that 'intelligent defence of the poles is impossible unless [the United States] is willing to support not one but many expeditions similar to this Antarctic survey'. He noted that technological developments had placed 'both Poles within our grasp.' It would be 'unfortunate', said Cruzen, 'if we were to relinquish our hold over and the potential conquest of them'.[62]

But any misconceptions were swept away when Byrd arrived back in the United States, where reports revealed that Operation Highjump 'had an avowed purpose of laying a basis for a claim by making aerial surveys of the region and dropping insignia of sovereignty'. The *New York Herald-Tribune* predicted that Washington would 'soon make a formal claim to a vast area of Antarctica' based upon the claim sheets and American flags dropped from the aircraft of Byrd's expedition.[63] However, Byrd was unsure whether he would 'recommend official United States action toward establishing part of Antarctica as American territory'.[64] And American officials remained divided on how best to proceed, with some being concerned about the ramifications on their relationships with close allies such as Britain.

With newspapers making repeated predictions during 1947 that the United States was on the verge of annexing territory, the seven existing claimants continued to reinforce their own positions prior to the much-mooted international conference. New Zealand had a particularly shaky position. With no New Zealand expedition ever having gone to the region, and no New Zealand official ever having stepped onto its shores, it was secretly conceded that the Ross Dependency was legally a no-man's land to which the United States had the stronger claim.[65]

That did not mean that New Zealand was prepared to surrender its control. A series of papers prepared for the government in early 1947 stressed the importance to New Zealand of asserting its sovereignty. The Department of Scientific and Industrial Research pointed to the economic value of whaling and urged that a ship be converted for use as a factory ship. It noted the worldwide shortage of fats and oils, arguing the importance of whale oil for margarine and the potential of whale meat as a source of protein. The department also suggested that New Zealand should pioneer the harvesting of krill.[66] There was also the value of Antarctic weather observations for pure science – connections might be established between Antarctica's climate and New Zealand's – and the possibility that the Ross Dependency had coal, gold and uranium deposits.[67] While the New Zealand chiefs of staff believed the Falkland Islands Dependencies had to be retained to guarantee the security of the sea connection to Britain, they also thought that the Ross Dependency had 'no military significance' unless oil or uranium was found there, which might then 'warrant energetic measures to establish possession'.[68] But New Zealand was still in no position to establish an Antarctic base.

Australia was in a much better position and had much more territory to defend. It was expected that the *Wyatt Earp* and a supply vessel would be able to establish a permanent base in the Australian Antarctic Territory by early 1948. In the interim, however, its territory was vulnerable to an American claim being made. After all, the United States had a potential claim based upon the voyage of Wilkes, the recent voyage and flights of Ellsworth and the present activities of Operation Highjump. In order to avert the danger of American annexation, the Australian government went through the usual procedure of asserting its sovereignty by suggesting that the Americans seek permission if their ships or aircraft wanted to enter Australian territory. Although American policy dictated that no permission should be sought, the Australians were relieved to learn that the Americans were not planning to enter Australian territory. In fact, the aircraft of Operation Highjump did make photographic flights over Australian territory in their ambitious and ultimately failed attempt to make comprehensive maps of the entire continent.[69]

With Britain's Foreign Office urging that 'regular aerial surveys' should be done to show 'evidence of occupation', the Australians returned to the idea of sending bombers to assess the suitability of Cape Freshfield.[70] Byrd's expedition was exploring further east, and the lumbering Liberator and Lincoln bombers of the Royal Australian Air Force made several flights over the now unoccupied Macquarie Island in March 1947, both to test cold-weather clothing for Antarctic-bound flight crews and to look for possible landing places for flying boats stopping over on any future flights to Antarctica. There were also plans to reoccupy the island and use it as a meteorological station to provide weather reports for Australia. So far, so good. But the air force was reluctant to risk its aircraft and crews on a return flight to Antarctica. The aircraft would be flying blind, since they could have no inkling of the weather they might encounter and there were no emergency landing places, other than the polar icecap, if they were forced down. In such an eventuality, with no ice-strengthened ship on standby, there could be little hope of rescue.[71] The flights never ventured further south than Macquarie Island.

The practical problems of establishing an Antarctic base led to further delays. When the government set up a planning committee in April 1947, chaired by the young head of the Department of External Affairs, Dr John Burton, Mawson convinced its members that a reconnaissance voyage should be sent south during the coming summer, with a permanent base to be established at Cape Freshfield in the summer of 1948–49.

It was only in the wake of the planning committee's first meeting that the veteran Antarctic mariner Captain John King Davis was asked for his advice. As the government's director of navigation and long-time polar captain, Davis knew his ships. He was against the idea of refitting the *Wyatt Earp*, which was then being inspected in an Adelaide dry dock, and suggested that it would be cheaper to purchase a new vessel. Nor did he approve the idea of sending a steel-hulled tank-landing ship as an auxiliary to the *Wyatt Earp*. Without a suitable vessel on hand, he advised that a voyage during the current year was impossible. He was also unconvinced about the suitability of Cape Freshfield as the site for a permanent base, and was wary of the Australian National Research Council's suggestions that any Australian expedition be done in cooperation with the Americans, British and New Zealanders. Davis was concerned that Australia was rushing into a commitment and in danger of making hasty and ill-advised decisions. There was 'no call for haste in this matter,' cautioned Davis, who nominated November 1948 as the earliest time that a 'properly-equipped and planned expedition' might be sent.[72]

Mawson, though, wanted a ship sent as soon as possible. He complained to his wife about the serious delays being caused by the government's slowness in voting funds for an expedition.[73] At the second meeting of the committee, on 5 May 1947, Group Captain Stuart Campbell was chosen as the proposed expedition's leader. Campbell had been the pilot on Mawson's two voyages in 1929–31 and was well versed in the requirements for claiming territory, although he had been more than a little contemptuous of them. It was only when the navy representative raised questions about the practicability of an expedition during the coming summer, and when Mawson conceded that Cape Freshfield might not be a suitable site, that the committee decided the initial expedition with the *Wyatt Earp* should be merely for reconnaissance purposes. The Minister of External Affairs, Dr Evatt, agreed to the change of plan, while at the same time indicating 'his keen interest in the success of the undertaking' and his desire that 'everything possible be done to this end'. He even offered to ask General Douglas MacArthur, the American head of the Allied occupation forces in Japan, for the use of a Japanese factory ship.[74] Not that MacArthur was ever likely to agree. He was too concerned with obtaining whales to provide meat for the hard-pressed Japanese population, and earning revenue from the sale of whale oil.

Davis continued to raise concerns about Australia attempting to do too much too soon. His concerns, and those of the Department of Defence, seemed to have caused a rethink by External Affairs, which had charge of the expedition's organisation. In mid-July, Campbell informed Davis that the government's ambition was now only to 'endeavour if possible to establish a permanent scientific station on the Antarctic Coast sometime within the next five years'. In the first instance, Australia would concentrate on establishing parties on Macquarie and Heard Islands, while an aircraft from the *Wyatt Earp* would reconnoitre the coast around Mawson's old base at Cape Denison. It would be the first stage in a 'systematic reconnaissance of the coast of the Australian Antarctic Territory', which would be undertaken over several years until a site was found for a 'permanent scientific station on the Antarctic Continent itself'.[75] Despite Davis's reservations, the Australian government decided on 11 November 1947 that a tank-landing ship would take a party that month to occupy Heard Island, south-west of Western Australia, and then return to take another party to Macquarie Island in January 1948.

The rush to occupy Heard Island was driven partly by a fear that the Americans might get there first. It was an island whose ownership had long been disputed between Britain and the United States, based upon the respective voyages of their nineteenth-century whaling and sealing ships. Byrd had wanted it in 1939 as a landing place for cross-Antarctic flights from South America to Australia, until he realised that it had no landing places or sheltered waters for flying boats. The Foreign Office's legal adviser had confided to Britain's Polar Committee in March 1947 that any British title had probably expired during the twenty years or so since a British expedition had visited the lonely speck.

Although the island had no strategic value, Britain thought that Australia or South Africa might find it useful as a meteorological base and suggested that one of them annex it. Within days, Australia agreed to do so, while South Africa sent a warship on a clandestine voyage to annex and occupy Marion and Prince Edward Islands, further west. Australia was convinced that it was in its interests 'to secure ownership' of Heard Island and accepted that it would require 'a formal act of annexation on the spot and the maintenance of effective control thereafter'.[76]

There was a fear in Canberra that Australia might be beaten to the island by the United States expedition, or by one of the Russian whalers then operating in the Antarctic. So the objective of the Australian expedition was kept top-secret.[77] While newspapers reported the departure of the tank-landing ship from Melbourne on 15 November 1947 – under the command of Campbell, who was described as 'a rugged, athletic bachelor' – the aim of the expedition was not revealed until 5 January 1948, some days after Campbell had completed the required claiming ceremony.[78]

Having privately derided the claiming ceremonies performed by Mawson, it was ironic that Campbell now had to do the same himself. As Mawson had done, there was the usual raising of the flag and the reading of a proclamation, a copy of which was duly enclosed in a cylinder and deposited beneath a cairn of rocks at the foot of the flagpole. The carefully worded document avoided any admission about the weakness of the existing British claim and instead portrayed the Australian annexation as a continuation of the 'sovereign rights' that had been 'asserted and exercised' by the British monarch. A description of the ceremony was also written in the ship's log, while a press release told the world of the Australian accomplishment. Reports of the expedition's work emerged through further press releases, which Campbell was instructed to draft in such as way 'as to imply that the Expedition is in effective occupation of Australian territory'. A tent was designated as the island's post office, with letters carrying a special postmark to show that the place was now an Australian possession.[79]

The tank-landing ship managed to complete the landing of parties on Heard and Macquarie Islands, despite having only twenty-two hours of calm weather during the eighteen days that it had been stationed off Heard Island.[80] The ship's steel hull could not be trusted further south in the pack ice. With nothing better on hand, the task of reconnoitring the coast near Cape Denison was entrusted to Ellsworth's old ship, with its strengthened wooden hull. But it was Baltic pine rather than stout English oak. The *Wongala* had already been taken back from the Adelaide Sea Scouts and refitted under the supervision of the Australian navy, which renamed it the HMAS *Wyatt Earp* in November 1947, before it left for Melbourne to take on men and stores.[81]

The ship, which was painted a garish orange and black so it could be seen amongst the ice, made the short voyage to Melbourne through rough seas – a harbinger of things to come. Despite all the work done to it, crew members were forced to bail out water that washed over the rolling decks and down 'into the mess decks forward and . . . into the cabins and wardrooms aft'. More repairs were done in Melbourne, where the ship was visited by various government dignitaries before it departed for the Antarctic on 19 December. But its engine broke down before it had even left Port Phillip Bay.

Makeshift repairs allowed the *Wyatt Earp* to continue on through the storm-tossed waters of Bass Strait to Hobart. However, as it prepared to leave Hobart on Christmas Day, the engine broke down again and the ship crashed into the wharf. 'What an anticlimax!' exclaimed First Lieutenant W. F. Cook, who described how the gloom was only broken when the captain 'prescribed champagne cocktails and we sang with [scientific leader] Phil Law's accordion and danced and skylarked till about 3 a.m.'. They got away the next morning – farewelled by just three men, two boys and a baby – only to be swamped again by heavy seas just out of Hobart. The concerned naval authorities ordered the ship back to Melbourne for yet more repairs.[82] Australia continued to have the will but not the means to achieve its Antarctic ambitions.

In contrast, the United States had the means but continued to be wracked by indecision as to how it should proceed. It was Ronne who tried to end the uncertainty. From his cabin on board the iced-in *Port of Beaumont* during the dark of the 1947 winter, Ronne wrote a memo to Secretary of State George Marshall suggesting that America should establish a ring of four bases evenly spaced around the coastline of Antarctica, with additional temporary bases in the interior that would be occupied for several months each year. One of the primary purposes would be the mapping by air of the entire continent.

Ronne wanted one of the four bases to be at the site of his present base in Marguerite Bay, and proposed that all be manned by at least thirty personnel, including 'qualified scientists as well as men to be trained in particular fields of military pursuit'. After speaking with the personnel at the British base, Ronne warned that Britain had plans to increase its activities at each of their bases, and even to increase the number of its bases. To counter this, and to encourage Washington to have bases of its own, Ronne offered to leave his equipment behind, along with some of his men, to assist an official expedition that would assume control of the old base. If the United States was to become involved in a polar war, wrote Ronne, 'no more perfect training and testing ground for such a war could be found than the Antarctic continent'.[83]

Ronne's proposal received serious attention in the State Department and was sent to other agencies for comment. Most military officials were dismissive of Antarctica as a training ground and of its strategic importance, while those concerned with mapping argued that the aerial mapping of the continent was 'virtually impossible' because of problems with establishing adequate ground control points. When Byrd was consulted, he too expressed his opposition to the proposal, arguing that there were 'many aspects which are not sound'. He recommended instead that the United States should coordinate its activities with 'other nations having a scientific interest in Antarctica'.[84]

Cruzen was almost a lone voice among the military in agreeing with Ronne that the Antarctic was important as an alternative training ground to the Arctic, where 'political difficulties' limited the 'opportunity for military training and research'. Although Cruzen conceded that Ronne's scheme for several bases was important for 'exploration and territorial claims', he thought that one or more large bases would be more useful from a military point of view.[85] There was much more support for Ronne's proposal from scientists, who recognised the potential of the Antarctic for gathering data on meteorology and the workings of the upper atmosphere, as well as magnetism and cosmic rays.[86] It was a sign of things to come.

Although the US Army and Navy were largely dismissive of Ronne's proposal, they acknowledged that it was the prerogative of the State Department to decide whether bases were required to secure America's territorial claims. While Ronne continued his exploration of the Antarctic Peninsula by aircraft and dog sledge during 1947, both the State Department and the Central Intelligence Agency were studying how the United States might claim all the territory that its citizens had discovered or explored or claimed since the early 1800s, including the claims made during Byrd's latest expedition. In October 1947, the CIA completed a secret map of Antarctica displaying all the 'areas which the United States proposes to claim'.[87] Here at last was an official American exposition of all the areas it felt justified in claiming.

Rather than being wedges of territory from the coast to the South Pole, they were swathes of hinterland over which American planes had flown, often with little connection to the coastline, since discovery of the coastline had been done mostly by other countries. If the United States accepted the sector principle, the American claims would have been much more limited. By rejecting the sector principle the United States was intruding on the territories of the seven Antarctic claimants, whose support was required by Washington in its increasingly tense standoff, and possible future war, with the Soviet Union.

While the CIA was preparing its map of potential American claims, the State Department was trying to reconcile these issues in a way that would maximise America's advantage in the Antarctic. In a secret report of November 1947, the State Department noted the British bases that had been established to provide 'proof of effective occupation', and the largely symbolic administrative actions that Britain had taken to show the world that it was in control of the territory it was claiming.[88] With the two South American republics doing likewise and set on a collision course with Britain, and with the United States facing the prospect of being excluded from much of the Antarctic, the idea of bringing the continent under international control became more appealing to Washington.

The prospect of the Soviet Union also making territorial claims only added to the appeal of ending the continental carve-up and replacing it with an international regime marked by cooperation rather than competition. Such a regime had the added advantage for the United States, with its unequalled logistical capacity, of being able to dominate the scientific investigation and later economic exploitation of the continent. Consequently, the secret CIA map of American claims, and the similarly secret State Department report justifying the claims, were both left to gather dust.

CHAPTER 18

'For the common good of all peoples'

1948–1951

It took two American icebreakers to open a passage into ice-choked Marguerite Bay on 20 February 1948, allowing Finn Ronne and his companions to head home aboard the wooden-hulled tug *Port of Beaumont*.[1] Ronne's departure marked the last of the big private expeditions. The expense had become too great for all but governments. Private benefactors and media organisations were no longer prepared to fund expeditions that were dealing with increasingly complex science and that elicited little public interest.

Even Ronne's expedition, which had been under the auspices of the American Geographical Society, had been funded overwhelmingly by different parts of the US Department of Defense, while he had made territorial claims on behalf of the State Department. Before leaving for home, Ronne sent a radio message to Washington reporting how he had claimed all the territory that had been discovered during the expedition. He made the claims despite the joint program of geographic discovery and scientific investigation that he had organised with the leader of the nearby British base. It was, he wrote, 'the first example of international exploration in the Antarctic'.[2] And it forced Ronne to reconsider the notion of claiming territory in the Antarctic.

Ronne had begun writing a report of his expedition while working alongside the British, and had completed it during the voyage home. Writing from Chile on 14 March 1948, he informed the director of the American Geographical Society of the expedition's 'extremely rich harvest of results'.[3] Apart from meteorological and other observations, and a great collection of rocks, he had crossed the Antarctic Peninsula to the Weddell Sea and provided final proof that the peninsula was not divided from the continent by one or more channels.

Overall, he claimed to have discovered at least '650,000 square kilometres of 'new territory' and had photographed from the expedition's three aircraft a total of 165,000 square kilometres of territory. The 14,000 pictures that he had taken on his flights would be used to improve the maps of that part of the Falkland Islands Dependencies. The aerial photographs were particularly valuable because the flights had been taken in conjunction with a four-man sledge party of British and Americans, who had travelled more than a thousand miles along the Weddell Coast obtaining ground control points, which would enable mountains and bays and other features to be accurately positioned on maps.[4] These could reinforce the claim that the United States might make to the area that American cartographers called 'Palmer Land'.

The ill-defined Palmer Land had been explored by expeditions from several countries, and its sovereignty had long been a matter of dispute between the British, Chileans and Argentinians. Although his own expedition had reinforced the potential claim that the United States might make to Palmer Land, Ronne used his report to argue that the United States should 'support a policy of internationalization of the Antarctic under the United Nations'. The alternative was for the United States to lay claim to all the areas that had been discovered by its citizens. But this would result in 'something like a patch work quilt', wrote Ronne, which 'might impede the exploration and development of the Continent'. How were scientists and surveyors to operate in the Antarctic, if national borders were drawn on the ice and access was restricted by soldiers? The Antarctic was unique, argued Ronne, in being 'so completely devoid of native inhabitants, deep seated hates and jealousies, [and] economic resources in world demand'. As such, it provided an excellent opportunity 'for the United Nations to experiment in the internationalizing of disputed areas for the common good of all peoples'.[5]

When the *Port of Beaumont* arrived back in New York in April 1948, the reception was much more subdued than those which Byrd had received in the 1920s and 1930s. There were no ticker-tape parades or meetings with the president and Congress. Nor were there the grand dinners in swanky New York hotels that Byrd had enjoyed, or the lucrative lecture tours and radio talks to hundreds of thousands of Americans across the country. There was just a welcome at the US Navy wharf in Manhattan, followed by a reception and informal dinner organised by the cash-strapped American Geographical Society in the Colonial room of the Hotel McAlpin. Diners then walked to the nearby Engineering Societies' Building to hear talks by geologist Laurence Gould, now president of Carleton College, Sir Hubert Wilkins and Ronne, with maps prepared by the American Geographical Society showing where his expedition had explored and the rival territorial claims. Byrd was notably absent. In their talks, both Ronne and Gould disparaged the competition for territory and urged the creation of an international regime to govern the continent.[6]

Despite his views about the desirability of an international regime, Ronne was anxious to have American names memorialised on Palmer Land. Although he had worked in tandem with the British, Ronne wanted to have his names publicised and preserved on maps before the British were able to get their own names approved and published. While the British had been surveying the west coast of the Weddell Sea by dog sledge, Ronne had been photographing it from the air. The two groups had agreed where they each would name geographical features, but that apparent understanding was overtaken by the more compelling desire by each group to maximise the number of national names that were to be applied to maps of that most disputed of territories.

Within days of returning to New York, Ronne was off to Washington with a cartographer from the American Geographical Society, William Briesemeister. There, they met with the relevant committee of the US Board of Geographical Names so that Ronne's names could get official approval as soon as possible. Going through the names one by one, Ronne justified each in its turn, although he agreed to drop several to avoid duplication. For instance, 'Isaiah Bowman Coast' was discarded because there already was a 'Bowman Coast'. The great majority of names were approved by the committee, which was composed of Captain Harold Saunders, Dr Meredith Burrill, W. L. G. Joerg and Dr Kenneth Bertrand, all of whom were conscious of the political importance of maximising the number of American names in the Antarctic. Joerg would have been particularly pleased by Ronne naming a plateau in his honour. The names were then submitted to the Board on Geographical Names, which quickly gave them its stamp of approval. Ronne thanked them for their 'promptness of consideration'.[7]

There were so many changes to the American Geographical Society's map of Palmer Land as a result of Ronne's expedition that Briesemeister urged that an entirely new map be drawn up.[8] This was an indication of the expedition's geographical achievements, which had been made possible by the cooperation Ronne had enjoyed with the British, particularly through the loan of their trained sledge dogs. Gould also testified to the achievements of Ronne's expedition, which he thought were 'out of all proportion to its size'. In Gould's field of geology, Ronne had 'brought back the most extensive geological collection that has been brought by any Antarctic expedition'.[9]

Yet Ronne struggled to achieve any recognition. The American Philosophical Society, which had published the results of Byrd's 1939–41 expedition, declined to publish Ronne's scientific results, citing the lack of demand for the Byrd publication.[10] Popular articles that Ronne wrote for national magazines were also rejected by editors, which he began to suspect was due to Byrd's influence. That suspicion hardened when the *National Geographic*, which had a long and close association with Byrd and had published a lengthy report of his expedition, cancelled both an article and a lecture that Ronne had been commissioned to do.[11]

Ronne also struggled to find a publisher for the book he had written about the expedition. In October 1948, he appealed to the American Geographical Society's director, Dr John Wright, for help in having the manuscript considered by publisher Henry Holt. Ronne did not want the publisher asking Byrd for an assessment of the manuscript for fear that he would advise against its publication. Ronne claimed that Byrd had enjoyed 'a monopoly on the Antarctic all of his life, and I intend to continue fighting it'. Unsuccessful at Holt's, Ronne then asked Gould and others for help to find a publisher. He would eventually get the manuscript accepted, after it had been rewritten by a science fiction writer and had a preface provided by Isaiah Bowman.[12] The book included maps that privileged American names over British ones on the Weddell Sea coast, which caused considerable consternation in London when the book appeared. Published in 1949 as *Antarctic Conquest*, the sales would be disappointing, leading Ronne to conclude that 'the world, particularly the Americans, are not interested in [the] Antarctic'.[13]

As Ronne well knew, Byrd was one American who continued to be interested in the Antarctic. His expeditions had given him a personal connection to the continent, particularly to the area of the Ross Sea, where the successive Little America bases had been established. In his popular account of Operation Highjump, Byrd noted how Paul Siple, who had first gone there as a Boy Scout with Byrd and had since become a leading polar scientist, referred to his latest landing in the Antarctic as 'coming home'.[14] Byrd could almost have been writing about himself. He had a sense of ownership over the place and believed, unlike Ronne, that the United States should 'control as much of the Antarctic as possible' because America would 'use its material benefits for the good of all humanity'. He saw the Antarctic as 'a great untouched reservoir of natural resources' and envisaged a time when it would be 'practicable to procure and utilize the resources that lie buried down there at the bottom of the world'. Meanwhile, America needed to control the continent as a training ground for its forces – to prepare them for a war that would be 'fought across the top of the world'.[15]

American control of the Antarctic was not helped by the divisions between Byrd and Ronne, which were set to worsen. Although the ageing Byrd expressed support for Ronne, he was annoyed that he had not named an important geographic feature in Byrd's honour. The upstart explorer had chosen instead to name a newly discovered region 'Edith Ronne Land' after his wife, although it is now known as the 'Ronne Ice Shelf'. Ronne had even named a feature after a dog food company that had contributed food for his huskies.[16] More importantly, the two men were rivals for the patronage of the US Navy and the support of Congress for another expedition. Byrd was having trouble financing his lavish lifestyle. He now wanted to fly from one pole to the other, in an attempt to recapture the attention of the American public and potential patrons, or at least lead a follow-up naval expedition to Operation Highjump. By August 1948, just four months after his return to New York, Ronne had begun seeking support from officials for another small expedition of his own.

With a base in Gould Bay on the southern coast of the Weddell Sea, Ronne's proposed expedition would concentrate on the sector between 45° W and 10° E. Although this included Coats Land and Queen Maud Land, which had been claimed by the British and Norwegians respectively, Ronne noted that the sector remained 'unknown geographically, geologically and geophysically'. He wanted to photograph the continent east of Edith Ronne Land, and do soundings beneath the ice that might lead to the discovery of minerals. Among the first officials Ronne approached was Samuel Boggs, who lived near to Ronne's home in Chevy Chase, outside Washington. The State Department geographer was noncommittal. It was not the grand plan that Ronne had previously proposed to Secretary of State George Marshall, which had envisaged a ring of American bases and the photographing of the entire continent.[17]

Moreover, Ronne's shifting of his attention to the other side of the continent would leave the former American base at Marguerite Bay unoccupied. The British government suggested in June 1948 that it be allowed to buy the buildings so that they did not fall into 'the hands of Argentine or Chilean detachments which might visit Stonington Island during the next Antarctic season'. A British takeover would effectively end the territorial claim that the United States might assert to that part of the Antarctica, even though it was part of Britain's Falkland Islands Dependencies.

The State Department was never going to agree to the sale, both as 'a matter of utility and convenience for future American expeditions and as a matter of policy with respect to American interests in Antarctica'.[18] To protect those interests, Ronne urged Secretary of State Marshall in December 1948 that the United States reoccupy the base on a permanent basis, with a party of seven men continuing the observations that Ronne had begun the previous year. Despite his support for bringing the Antarctic under the control of the United Nations, Ronne argued that such a pre-emptive move was necessary because of 'the political situation involving the Antarctic, and because of my interest in seeing that our nation's interests are pursued in this part of the world'.[19] By that time, his recommendation had to compete with Byrd's political manoeuvring for an expedition of his own.

As the navy's pre-eminent polar adviser, Byrd wanted to lead another fleet of ships, including an aircraft carrier, to continue the work of Operation Highjump. However, he was now past sixty, suffering bouts of ill health, and his political position in Washington had been eroded. Veering ever further to the political right, Byrd was intensely critical of President Truman's policies, blasting them for turning the United States into 'a socialist nation'. He was also at the forefront of efforts by the navy to resist Truman's policy to merge the services into a Department of Defense. Sailing off to the Antarctic again on board an aircraft carrier would have been a respite from these concerns, and provide a chance to return to the spotlight. His finances could certainly have used the boost that all the publicity would have brought.

It was not to be. In mid-August 1949, just when all the planning seemed to be in place for an expedition that summer, it was cancelled. Byrd was dismayed and cast around to see who in the Truman administration he could blame.[20] But it was nothing personal: the cost–benefit analysis of another Operation Highjump simply did not stack up. Photographing the continent without hundreds of ground control points had proved to be an expensive waste of time. There was also a new aerial navigation system being developed that might allow high-altitude planes to photograph the continent in a single summer, without the need for ground control points or a cumbersome naval fleet.[21]

Ronne's expedition also encountered strong headwinds in Washington. His plan for a base on Gould Bay depended on the assistance of two icebreakers, which would force their way through the hundreds of kilometres of ice in the Weddell Sea. But the ships were committed elsewhere for the summer of 1949–50, forcing Ronne to postpone his expedition for at least a year.[22]

Both Byrd and Ronne worked away at the navy and other government departments, and cultivated their separate supporters in Congress. While Byrd could count on his brother Harry for support, Ronne had the backing of Senator Francis Case, who arranged a meeting between Ronne and the chairman of the Atomic Energy Commission to talk about exploring the Antarctic for uranium. There was a popular view that under the Antarctic ice there was 'possibly more uranium, the raw material of atomic energy, than anywhere else'. However, as Case tried to get government support for Ronne's proposed expedition, he encountered opposition from 'certain persons within the Department of State' who believed that 'the United States should not assert any claims in the Antarctic lest we offend England or some other continental powers'.[23] Still, there were some American officials who wanted the United States to lay claim to as much of the Antarctic as it could, and technological advances were providing new ways for them to do so.

While Ronne had used three small aircraft to photograph 650,000 square kilometres of the Antarctic, the flights had to be supported by regular landings and ground parties to obtain astronomical positions for mapping purposes. The wartime development of low-frequency radio navigation systems, known as LORAN, which allowed aircraft and ships to be located accurately, theoretically meant that aircraft could fly over the whole continent and photograph its surface from a great height. Since the position of the aircraft would be known with some precision at the time each photograph was taken, there would be no need for ground control points. In practice, though, there would be difficulties with radio communication due to the prevalence of electromagnetic storms in the Antarctic. Nevertheless, if LORAN stations could be established at the southern tips of South America and New Zealand, and on Antarctica itself, there was the tantalising possibility that long-range aircraft might fly from New Zealand across Antarctica to South America at a height of 40,000 feet, their cameras capturing the whole continent in far fewer flights and at much less cost than if Ronne's more intensive methods were used. At Ronne's suggestion, Boggs explored this question with the Air Force's Colonel James Tison in August 1949. They agreed that a plan should be prepared 'for producing a reconnaissance map of the entire Antarctic continent at least expense'.[24]

Boggs was enthusiastic about the idea and pursued it further with air force and naval officers. The geographer was on the Defense Department's Research and Development Board, the precursor of the National Science Foundation, which played an influential role in determining the nature and purpose of Antarctic expeditions. Boggs assured Ronne that both the air force and the board were well-disposed towards his plans, but said they were somewhat confused as to whether he was pushing for the scientific base on Gould Bay or for his earlier suggestion of an aerial survey of the entire continent. With the navy having postponed Byrd's planned naval expedition, there was an opportunity for the board to take the lead in Antarctic exploration and investigation. Boggs suggested as much, proposing that the board 'evolve a plan for scientific work in Antarctica, and particularly for the mapping which must precede making any comprehensive international scientific plan for the whole Antarctic region'.

The National Academy of Sciences had already been asked by the State Department for advice on the 'possibilities and importance of scientific research in the Antarctic' as a precursor to developing a program, possibly in coordination with other countries. The academy's committee was chaired by Bowman and had as its principal recommendation 'the production of a general map of the Antarctic Continent on a uniform scale'. Once that was done, exploration and scientific investigation could be planned in earnest. Since a program to map the entire continent would take a year or more to prepare, Boggs urged Ronne to press ahead with a limited expedition to establish a base on Gould Bay during the summer of 1949–50, and the comprehensive mapping program was planned to begin the following summer.[25]

It was all too soon for Ronne, who was unable to obtain navy icebreakers that summer. Instead, he began discussions with the board to take a scientific expedition to Gould Bay in the summer of 1950–51, with Ronne stressing that he was 'extremely anxious to maintain the highest scientific standards'.[26] This was a jab at Byrd, who had often been criticised for preferring adventure and publicity over science. It was also a sign of things to come, as science came to compete more strongly with sovereignty as the *raison d'être* for Antarctic expeditions.

Whether the driving force was science or sovereignty, the creation of accurate maps was essential, and Ronne had mapping high on his agenda. As he pointed out in an article in *Scientific Monthly*, there were still more than ten million square kilometres that remained unexplored. With 'new devices' to aid exploration, Ronne called for the army, navy and air force to pool their resources to 'undertake a comprehensive mapping program'.[27] But the armed services had other things on their mind. The outbreak of the Korean War on 25 June 1950 relegated the Antarctic almost to the bottom of America's agenda. The war also put on hold the discussions about the internationalisation of the Antarctic.

The State Department had proposed in early 1948 that the Antarctic should come under the trusteeship of the United Nations. This was intended to end the intensifying rivalry between Britain, Argentina and Chile, while allowing the United States to range over all the Antarctic without reference to the notional owners of its different sectors. The jostling for territory was threatening to escalate into armed conflict. Argentina and Chile had raised the ante in July 1947 when they increased the number of their bases and agreed that their respective Antarctic territories would no longer overlap.

In late November, eight Argentine naval ships had steamed into the sunken caldera of Deception Island, where Britain had one of its small bases, and brazenly set about establishing a base of their own.

Despite a protest from the leader of the British base in his role as resident magistrate, the Argentinians refused to budge. The British ambassador in Buenos Aires then protested about the 'continued acts of trespass' and demanded that the Argentinians either apply for permission to have a scientific base or leave forthwith. Again the Argentinians refused, with foreign affairs minister Juan Bramuglia noting that the 'military detachments which occupy those bases, on which the national flag is flown, know that they are stationed on Argentine territory'. Indeed, continued Bramuglia, the 'entire nation is conscious of this and in consequence the Government – interpreting the feeling of the whole population – rejects the request to withdraw its nationals'. A British protest to the Chilean government about their activities in the Falkland Islands Dependencies met with a similar rebuff.[28] And there was nothing that the British could do in the face of the locally strong Argentinian and Chilean forces. Worse was to come.

In early February 1948, Argentina announced that it was sending a naval taskforce of two cruisers and six destroyers for exercises in Antarctic waters. At the same time, the Chilean president, Gabriel Gonzáles Videla, disclosed that he and other senior army officers and politicians were aboard the armed troopship, *Presidente Pinto*, which was steaming with a flotilla of Chilean naval vessels towards Antarctica. Videla intended to take formal possession of Chilean Antarctica and preside over the establishment of a military base on the tip of the Antarctic Peninsula. He would name the base after Bernardo O'Higgins – Chile's equivalent to George Washington – and rename that part of the peninsula as 'Penisola O'Higgins'. It would be the first permanent base on the continent itself, and was being established despite strong British objections.

With the Chilean president raising his nation's flag on one part of the Falkland Islands Dependencies and the Argentine flotilla heading for another, the British navy rushed the powerful cruiser HMS *Nigeria* to Port Stanley. The pugnacious British foreign secretary Ernest Bevin told the House of Commons that Britain was not going to ignore 'the challenge to our authority' posed by these 'ostentatious naval and other demonstrations', while the Australian prime minister, Ben Chifley, offered to send any naval help that Britain needed. Undaunted, the Chilean president went on to visit his nation's base on Greenwich Island, from where he complained of the 'vicious and obsolete imperialisms' which 'threatened by armed violence to displace Chile and Argentina from their territories'. Although the commander of Britain's naval forces in the West Indies, Admiral William Tennant, thought a naval clash with Argentina would be 'sheer stupidity', and the Chilean president considered the idea of a naval conflict 'simply absurd', the captain of the *Nigeria* conferred with the Falkland Islands' governor, Sir Miles Clifford, about the best means of dislodging the South Americans from Deception Island.[29] Rather than seeking a confrontation, Clifford boarded the *Nigeria* for a flag-showing cruise of his dependencies, in the vain hope that it would somehow cause the South Americans to pack up and go home. However, they already regarded themselves as being home.

When the Chilean ships arrived back at Punta Arenas with Videla and his gold-braided companions on 23 February 1948, the triumphant president told a cheering crowd from the balcony of the local governor's palace how he had managed to 'defend and consolidate Chilean sovereignty in the Antarctic'. To show that the Antarctic was part of Chile, Videla announced the creation of a Department of the Antarctic, which would merge Chile's southernmost province with its Antarctic territory. Then he flew off to Santiago, where he was greeted with even more excitement as he drove in an open car through streets crowded with Chileans, who had become ardent about the Antarctic following their president's swashbuckling cruise among the ice-flecked waters.

Videla continued the nationalist symbolism by going to lay a wreath at Santiago's statue of Bernardo O'Higgins, before that night addressing the torch- and flag-waving crowds from the presidential palace. With the British embassy and Australian legation ringed by police to protect them against the popular outrage, the Australian official John Cumpston reported to Canberra how the president was 'cheered wildly during his references to the Antarctic'.[30] After their hectic summer in the Antarctic, the Chilean and Argentine governments agreed once again to defend their 'indisputable rights' to the South American Antarctic and continue their present course of prosecuting their territorial claims 'in a spirit of reciprocal co-operation'.[31] They had no interest in internationalising what they regarded as their national territories.

There had been some interest by the British in the possibility of internationalising the Antarctic. A senior Colonial Office official, J. S. Bennett, had even suggested in jest that a king penguin could be designated as an inhabitant so that the continent could be brought under the UN trusteeship system, which was meant to benefit dependent people living in trustee territories. More seriously, Bennett thought it was absurd 'for an uninhabited wilderness to be divided up among various colonial powers; and a map of the Antarctic cut up like a cake into slices of different colours is a sorry spectacle for anyone who has hopes of sanity in international affairs'.[32]

Similarly, Admiral Tennant, who had responsibility for naval forces in the Antarctic, could see little strategic interest in the continent and thought only the Falkland Islands and South Georgia were worth defending 'to the extent of going to war'. As for the rest, he suggested that it be internationalised under the control of the various claimant nations and the United States.[33] However, the British chiefs of staff still feared that losing control over the Falkland Islands Dependencies would weaken Britain's control of the Falkland Islands, which were regarded as being of vital strategic importance for controlling the South Atlantic and the sea route to the Pacific. They were also reluctant to abandon the Antarctic until the presence or otherwise of uranium deposits was confirmed, and the potential value of the continent for air routes ascertained. Accordingly, Britain's defence planners urged in August 1948 that the status quo be maintained until the strategic value of the Antarctic was clarified.[34]

Fears had emerged early in 1948 that placing the Antarctic under United Nations trusteeship would open the door to the Soviet Union, which was beginning to participate in Antarctic whaling. Britain also surmised that the trusteeship proposal would not be welcomed in Santiago or Buenos Aires, since Argentina and Chile were unlikely to relinquish their claims to the Antarctic sectors that they regarded as integral parts of their national territories.

Indeed, Chile was quick to oppose the idea of trusteeship. When the State Department suggested as an alternative that the continent could be controlled by a condominium of the seven existing claimants plus the United States, Britain dismissed the idea, fearing that it would be impossible to exclude the Soviet Union from such an arrangement.[35]

In the absence of any agreement, and to head off the risk of open conflict, British officials agreed with their South American counterparts to stop escalating the arms race in the Antarctic. The three countries agreed not to send warships south of 60° S latitude during the coming summer season, when their bases were due to be resupplied and their personnel changed over. Only warship movements that had been 'customary for a number of years' would be allowed. Importantly for Britain, it would not restrict its warship movements in the Falkland Islands and South Georgia. This would allow one or two powerful ships to be based close by, as a continuing deterrent to any untoward action by the Chileans or the Argentinians.[36]

Britain's time as an imperial power was running out. It had withdrawn from Burma and India and was rethinking its global strategic needs within the context of a possible war with Russia. While retaining control of the Falkland Islands was regarded as vital, there was much more uncertainty in London about the Falkland Islands Dependencies, where Britain's title was weaker and the strategic and economic potential was more problematic. With Chile and Argentina challenging Britain's title by sending warships and establishing their own bases in the Falkland Islands Dependencies, there was a desire in London for a solution before the growing dispute escalated out of control.

The British had tried without success to get Chile and Argentina to agree to refer the question to the International Court of Justice. Britain then suggested in March 1948 that talks be held between the United States, Britain, Argentina and Chile to settle the conflict over the Falkland Islands Dependencies. Privately, Britain was prepared to concede all the dependencies other than Deception Island and Admiralty Bay in the South Shetlands and Signy Island in the South Orkneys, which was where Britain regarded its title was 'best and our strategic and commercial interests greatest'. It was only when those talks were rejected that Britain reconsidered the American proposal for a condominium.

Such a condominium would require the support of the seven territorial claimants. However, London could not even get its fellow Commonwealth countries to agree. South Africa was willing to support a condominium provided that it did not intrude on Britain's control of the islands in the Falkland Islands Dependencies.[37] New Zealand took a different tack, describing the condominium proposal as 'a most unsatisfactory halfway house'. Its preferred option continued to be the widely rejected UN trusteeship plan.[38] Placing the continent under the control of a United Nations subagency, with New Zealand being one of the controlling powers, was better than losing the Ross Dependency altogether, in the event that the United States asserted a claim to it.[39]

With no New Zealander having been to the Ross Dependency since it was annexed in 1923, it is difficult to see how New Zealand could have argued that it had any valid title to the territory. Byrd's successive expeditions had given the United States a much stronger claim, should it ever want to exercise it. As for the future, there was no way that New Zealand could compete with the scale of resources that the United States could deploy in the Antarctic. Washington's failure to make a claim to the Ross Dependency was the only reason that New Zealand could harbour the illusion that it was in possession of the territory. This is perhaps why there was some support in New Zealand for the proposed international regime to end the territorial rivalry and develop and administer the Antarctic on behalf of, if not the whole world, then at least the several existing claimants. As Wellington's *Dominion* newspaper argued in February 1948, an international conference to settle the various territorial disputes should 'clarify the rights and responsibilities of the various countries claiming Antarctic territory' so that 'the Antarctic, with its new-found potentialities, is used for the promotion of international peace and security'.[40]

While South Africa and New Zealand had been prepared to countenance the idea, Australia was adamantly opposed to both a condominium and UN trusteeship. It had just established bases on Heard and Macquarie Islands and was hoping to have further bases on the continent itself. Making the Antarctic a UN trusteeship, or placing it under the control of a condominium, would do away with Australia's title and open the Australian Antarctic Territory to possibly hostile powers. It might also complicate the exploitation by Australia of Antarctic resources.

Accordingly, the Australians urged Britain to refuse any negotiation with Washington that 'would in any way imply that there is any doubt about the existing rights we and others have in [the] Antarctic Territory'. Of course, the Australian government was well aware that its title had become weaker in the absence of any Australian visits over the past two decades. It argued nevertheless that its title rested upon its 'continuing interest in research and development in [the] Australian Antarctic Territory'.[41] Although that would not have been the basis for any title recognisable in a court of international law, there was little else that Australia could do in the short term to reinforce its legal position.

In July 1948, the British government informed Australia that it proposed to open negotiations with the United States and other Antarctic powers to achieve a pooling of all Antarctic territory under a commission of the seven claimants and the United States. Although Britain claimed that it wanted to retain the South Shetlands and the South Orkneys, it told Australia that it was prepared even to cede their control to such a commission. The British government knew that this proposal would meet opposition in Australia but argued that 'some form of international settlement is sooner or later inevitable'.[42]

Australia remained unconvinced. While agreeing that an eight-power commission would be useful to coordinate exploration and scientific work, Australia refused to hand over its title. In contrast to the Falkland Islands Dependencies, where such a commission might resolve the dispute between the rival claimants, Australia argued that its 'title to Australian Antarctic territory is clear and has been widely recognized' and that there had been no rival claims made to it, other than the private claims of Ellsworth and Christensen. It was unaware that the American aircraft of Operation Highjump had been dropping claim forms on the icy hinterland of the Australian Antarctic Territory, and that secret maps had been compiled by the CIA showing the United States as the owner of much of the Australian territory.

Australia suggested instead that any Antarctic commission be of an advisory nature only and be used to stimulate research and development. By joining the United States and the existing seven claimants together, it might also have the advantage of deterring Russia from making a claim.[43] Although both Australia and New Zealand agreed in November 1948 that the British government could press ahead with its negotiations with the United States, these came to nothing. The United States remained hesitant about making territorial claims and was unwilling to press ahead with proposals that had met with such negative reactions from Australia, Argentina, Chile, France and Norway.[44]

Without a New Zealand expedition, it was left to the British to propose one of their own, although New Zealand was asked to provide some of its members and part of the funding. The proposal was put forward by the former Antarctic explorer Frank

Debenham, who was now head of the Scott Polar Research Institute in Cambridge. He suggested that a small party be sent to McMurdo Sound in the summer of 1950–51 to study the origin and movement of floating ice sheets. The expedition would also investigate 'possible economic assets . . . such as the fisheries and the potentialities of wind power'.

The proposal was supported by Britain's Polar Committee, partly because it would have the political benefit of reinforcing New Zealand's claim to the Ross Dependency by strengthening 'the long record of British exploration in that region'.[45] Although New Zealand prime minister Peter Fraser favoured an international regime to control the Antarctic, his government continued to hedge its bets and threw its support behind the British proposal, noting that the visit of a British expedition would help to counter the 'extensive United States scientific exploration in recent years' and strengthen New Zealand's 'territorial claims to the Ross Dependency'. However, New Zealand's Antarctic Committee was disconcerted to learn in June 1949 that the expedition would not be possible before 1951 and would require much more support from New Zealand. Interestingly, officials predicted that the government was unlikely to support such an expedition 'for political or strategic reasons alone' and would need 'cogent scientific reasons'.[46] Rather than being a cover for politically driven expeditions, this was an early sign that science could be sufficient reason in itself to mount an expedition. In this case, though, the expedition never eventuated.

Australia was little closer than New Zealand in being able to occupy any part of the Antarctic territory that it so stridently claimed as its own. Without a suitable ice-strengthened supply ship, it had to move slowly, starting with the annexation of Heard Island and the reoccupation of Macquarie Island. It was only when those tasks were completed using a tank-landing ship in January 1948 that the *Wyatt Earp* was sent south to reconnoitre a site for an eventual Australian base on the continental coastline.

The ship was not up to the task. After being called back from Hobart for yet more repairs to its engine, it finally set out from Melbourne on 8 February. It did not begin well. Expedition leader Stuart Campbell began vomiting violently after eating a 'doubtful oyster' the night before departure, and he was soon joined by many of his companions once the ship encountered the prevailing westerly swell of the Southern Ocean. The rolling ship still leaked badly, and the starboard cabins and wardroom were quickly swamped with water, staying that way till it reached the pack ice. Even then, when sailing before a following sea, the alleyway door had to be kept shut at night to keep out the seawater, which meant that the engine fumes could not be properly ventilated.

The discomforts were all for nothing. The lateness of the departure and the extent of the pack ice meant the ship could not get close to the coastline that it was meant to reconnoitre. With Commonwealth Bay choked by ice, the ship headed east, in the hope of doing 'some original survey' of a coastline that had only been seen from the air. But nothing could be done with a ship that was unable to push its way through anything but the thinnest ice, while the almost constant cloud cover prevented accurate sightings of the ship's position from being taken. As for the aircraft, it was too big to be easily employed and was able to make only two short flights The flights only confirmed that there was no way through the ice.[47]

As a naval ship, the *Wyatt Earp* was crowded by its regulation crew and could only carry two scientists, physicist Phillip Law and meteorologist Fritz Loewe. Much to the disgust of his companions, Campbell refused to change his clothes for weeks on end, consciously copying the explorers of an earlier era. It was too much for Law, who shared a cabin with him, and it doubtless helped to poison the relationship between the two men. Despite his nostalgia for the pre-war expeditions of which he had been a part, Campbell conceded that the times had moved on. Ships like the *Wyatt Earp* belonged to 'a past era of Antarctic Exploration when requirements were simple and scientific aims not very complex', whereas an expedition now required 'complicated equipment, specialized personnel and room to employ them in'.

With the voyage an abysmal failure, Campbell and many of the crew stayed up all night drinking as the ship headed across Port Phillip Bay towards Melbourne. Law awoke to find that the crew was inebriated and Campbell had fallen into the sea The ship was forced 'to turn around to retrieve him'. Fortunately, there were few onlookers at Melbourne's Station Pier when the ship tied up on 1 April and its crew staggered ashore.[48] It was an ignominious end to one of the least successful of all Antarctic voyages, which left Australia no closer to achieving its aim of establishing a permanent foothold on the continent.

In an article for the Melbourne *Herald*, Campbell tried to portray Australia's Antarctic commitment in a positive light. It was wrong to expect quick results, he argued, since long-term observations were required in order to produce meaningful meteorological results. Similar patience was needed for the biological studies into the viability of re-establishing the fur seal and sea elephant industries. Although the *Wyatt Earp* had been sent to find a suitable site for a permanent base, one could not be established without spending some years training personnel in polar work and developing equipment that could operate in the extreme cold of the Antarctic. That polar experience was now being gained by the personnel manning the bases on Heard and Macquarie Islands, and they and their successors would be the men who would 'set up the first permanent Australian settlement on the Antarctic Continent'.[49] Despite Campbell's forced optimism, Davis could not help thinking about how little had been achieved with the government's expenditure of £300,000, compared with what Rymill had done with £10,000 during the 1934 Graham Land expedition.[50] Davis would raise these concerns in official discussions about the failure of the *Wyatt Earp* voyage.

A new interdepartmental planning committee was created to devise a program for the island parties and to prepare for the eventual Antarctic base. Chaired by Campbell, it had representatives from the Bureau of Meteorology, the Mineralogical Bureau, the Fisheries Bureau, the Department of Supply, the Royal Australian Navy and the Council for Scientific and Industrial Research. Davis and Mawson attended as advisers. The committee's first meeting, in May 1948, was occupied mainly by discussions about future work on Heard Island and the possibility of using the *Wyatt Earp* for another reconnaissance voyage.

After spending so much on the first voyage and achieving so little, Davis warned that it would be politically dangerous not to send the *Wyatt Earp* back on another voyage to select a suitable mainland base. Mawson had never sailed on the ship, but he still thought the vessel might be used, along with an ice-strengthened tank-landing ship, to establish an Antarctic base, which he now thought should be sited further west on the coast of Princess Elizabeth Land or Mac. Robertson Land.[51] But there would be no more voyages by the HMAS *Wyatt Earp*. The navy refused to risk the ship and its sailors in the Antarctic ever again, and the Antarctic Committee agreed in September 1948 that the ship should be sold.[52]

An ice-breaking ship was required to supply any permanent base on the continent. However, none could be found for sale in the so-called 'sterling area', and Australia lacked sufficient American dollars to purchase a vessel from elsewhere in the world or have one specially built.[53] With the *Wyatt Earp* ruled out and no alternative vessel capable of dealing with the ice, the government reconciled itself to a delay of several years before it would become possible to mount another voyage to the continent, let alone establish a permanent base there.

Campbell was increasingly frustrated by the indecision. He told the Antarctic Committee in September 1948 that he thought the government remained interested in work being done in Australia's Antarctic territory 'from the Scientific as well as the Political angle', but the refusal of anybody to make 'a decision or even a firm recommendation had been continuing for a long time'. Not even the scientists on the committee thought that an Antarctic base could be justified on scientific grounds alone, but they were happy to draw up a scientific program if the government wanted 'effective occupation of the Sector for International and Political reasons'.

The government certainly wanted this but it was deterred by the cost, which Campbell estimated at perhaps £300,000 for the first year and up to £30,000 per year thereafter. Much of the cost would come from the purchase of a new ship, for which the government was loath to commit funds. In the absence of a firm decision about a continental base, the Australian Antarctic Territory remained as vulnerable as ever to being taken over by one of Australia's rivals. And there was little that Australia could do about it. All it could do was to maintain its presence on Heard and Macquarie Islands, in order to ensure their continued ownership and to act as training grounds for future Antarctic activities.[54] Despite all the barriers to the establishment of a base on the continent itself, Australia's commitment to cementing its Antarctic claim was undiminished.

It was decided that the Australian effort should be organised by an office under the control of the Department of External Affairs, rather than being hived off to the Council for Scientific and Industrial Research, which had little interest in the Antarctic, or to the Australian navy or air force. This decision helped to ensure that Australian activities would continue to be focused primarily on shoring up Australian sovereignty, rather than on the pursuit of scientific discovery.[55] For the present, though, it remained important to devise a scientific program for the island bases so that they could have a satisfying *raison d'être* during the several years that it would take for a mainland base to be established. While Campbell might have hoped to lead the historic expedition that would establish such a base, he was not attracted by the routine of running the island bases. He opted instead to return to his former position with the Department of Civil Aviation, in the expectation that he would resume the leadership when it came time to set up the mainland base. He was to be disappointed.

With the island bases focused on science, the organisation needed a senior scientific officer to act as assistant director. Phillip Law had been acting as scientific liaison officer while on leave from Melbourne University and was keen to take on the more senior and permanent role. However, Campbell was determined to thwart Law's ambition. 'That C[ampbell] dislikes me I have always known,' Law confided to a friend, 'just as I dislike him. We are completely incompatible. Our ideas on everything are irreconcilable.' The depth of their antagonism did not bode well for the organisation if the more qualified and scientifically minded Law was appointed to a permanent position as Campbell's deputy.

In July 1948, Campbell had argued against an extension to Law's temporary appointment. When Law went ahead in September and applied for the position of deputy, Campbell did all he could to prevent the appointment. As head of the selection committee, he was well placed to do so. Firstly, he convinced Mawson, who was also on the committee, that scientific qualifications were less important for the position than 'a wide general experience and organizing ability'.[56] However, Campbell failed to sway the committee, with the secretary of the Department of External Affairs, John Burton, arguing that it was necessary to have a scientifically trained officer to oversee the activities of the island bases and to ensure the scientific data from the islands was 'put to the best possible use'. At the same time, he assured Campbell in early December that Law would not necessarily become the permanent officer in charge of the Antarctic program or lead any future expedition to the continent.[57]

Campbell was not reassured. He knew his chances of leading any future Antarctic expedition were much slimmer if Law was given the job, while he was left to await developments in his old job at the Department of Civil Aviation. In a last-ditch attempt to retrieve the situation, just two weeks before he was due to leave his Antarctic job, Campbell sent an urgent teleprinter message to Burton advising 'most strongly' against the appointment of Law.[58] It was all in vain. Law took up his position on 1 January 1949 and Campbell's association with the Antarctic came to an end.

The diminutive and athletic Law had a taste for adventure, a strong commitment to science and a determination to do everything that was necessary to retain the Australian Antarctic Territory. In the months after his appointment, he proposed the building of an Antarctic Institute to house the expedition offices, along with a polar library and museum, which could become the 'focal centre for planning and assisting attacks on the Antarctic Continent', and would show Australians and international visitors 'the heroic achievements of our great Antarctic explorers'.[59]

Law also made a series of speeches appealing for the Australian public to support the nation's territorial claim in the Antarctic. He argued that Australia had an obligation, because of its proximity, to undertake scientific work in the Antarctic, which in turn would help to 'justify our possession'. There were benefits to be gained from such scientific work, he claimed, particularly in the field of meteorology, with its supposed ability to provide predictions about Australia's weather and climate. And there was profit to be made in the Antarctic from its 'untapped resources', particularly 'oil and uranium'. Law told the 'Carry On Club' that nuclear power stations could be established in the Antarctic to 'melt off the ice from large areas' so that these resources could be tapped. But Australia could only benefit from such developments, he warned, if it retained control of its territory. And it could only retain control by occupying it and setting men to work on 'scientific investigation'.[60]

Australia continued to be hamstrung by the lack of a ship that could smash its way through the ice and supply a base on the Antarctic continent. It had to make do with its bases on Heard and Macquarie Islands and hope that no other nation would establish a base of its own in the Australian Antarctic Territory. The difficulties of doing so were shown by a French expedition that attempted to establish a base on Adélie Land in the summer of 1948–49, only to have its ship, the *Commander Charcot*, blocked by the ice. The eleven personnel and their thirty dogs were forced to retreat to Melbourne, where the dogs were given to Australia for use on Heard and Macquarie Islands, before the ship returned to France.[61]

When the Liberal government of Robert Menzies was elected in December 1949, it was advised that the Australian title to its

Antarctic territory depended on the government undertaking 'some work of exploration or, better still, effective occupation' as soon as possible. It was readily conceded that the cost of this could not be recouped by any scientific results, but 'political reasons make it desirable for Australia to consolidate her claims'. As the Antarctic Executive Committee advised, the consolidation of these claims was 'a major and an urgent reason for establishing a continental Station'.[62]

Officials had no illusions about the tenuous nature of Australia's territorial title. While Mawson had done a lot of flag-raising during his two voyages between 1929 and 1930, Lars Christensen had done a lot more exploration of the Australian territory. Whereas the Norwegian had taken aerial photographs along about 1600 kilometres of the territory's western coastline, Australia had never taken any. Even the American Operation Highjump had taken survey photographs, albeit of dubious value, and the US Navy Hydrographer now probably had 'better information about the Territory than the Commonwealth Government'.

It was assumed that the United States was rushing to use this information to compile new maps of the Antarctic, which would be crowded with names given by American explorers and approved by the US Board of Geographical Names. The board had declared that its approval of names would be done without considering 'questions of political sovereignty'. In other words, American names were likely to replace Australian or British ones, and the 1939 Australian map of the Antarctic, which was presently being revised, was in danger of being made redundant if the American map was published first. To ensure that its map remained the best available, the Australian government was urged to gather information from the Norwegians and Americans.[63]

With even Australian Treasury officials agreeing on the need for a continental base, and the incoming Minister of External Affairs, Percy Spender, also convinced by Law's arguments, it seemed that it would be quickly achieved. The case for the base was strengthened when Russia made clear that it had territorial ambitions in the Antarctic, based upon Bellingshausen's historic voyage and the recent activities of Russian whalers.

In February 1949, the Soviet Geographical Society had met in Leningrad to discuss Bellingshausen's voyage, with delegates noting the way that the names bestowed by Bellingshausen had mostly been replaced by English names. The chairman of the society's cartographical committee complained that this showed 'utter disrespect for the remarkably precise cartographical works of the expedition and its outstanding discoveries'. Much like the Americans and British, with their dispute over 'Palmer Land' and 'Graham Land', the committee went back to the original Russian documents to prove the primacy of Bellingshausen's discoveries. This led in turn to calls for the name 'Russian Sector of the Antarctic Continent' to be given to the territories discovered by Bellingshausen, which principally lay within the Falkland Islands territories.[64] A book published in Moscow that year reprinted some original documents from the voyage in order to prove that the Russians were first to discover the continent.[65]

The Russian arguments added a compelling new element to the post-war race for control of the Antarctic. In the case of the Australian Antarctic Territory, there was now a Cold War rationale for a base that was calculated to appeal to the conservative ministers of the Australian government. The presence of a base was also essential in the event that Australia's sovereignty was tested in an international court. To strengthen its case before such a court, the government was advised, it would have to show 'evidence of occupation and continuing activity in the region'. With other Antarctic claimants already accumulating such evidence, and with the United States and Russia both likely to become claimants, the need for Australian action was 'urgent'.[66] Law pressed the government not to wait for a ship to be built but instead to charter one so that a continental base could be established by December 1951. He suggested that six to eight men be landed at a suitable place on the coastline that first summer, with a group of about sixteen men being sent to occupy the base the following year.[67] Just when it seemed certain that Law would achieve his aim, the outbreak of war in Korea on 25 June 1950 changed everything.

With Seoul falling within a week to the North Korean army, and with Australia quickly committing forces to the war, the establishment of an Antarctic base no longer seemed so urgent. There were fears that the conflict would escalate into another world war, this time between the United States and the Soviet Union. By August, Mawson was suggesting that Law's plan to charter a ship for the 1951–52 season be abandoned. He believed the world could soon be embroiled in a war that would last ten or more years, which would remove any urgency about an Australian base. Mawson even suggested that the two island bases could be abandoned until the war was won. Davis agreed, telling Law in September 1950 that the chartering of a ship no longer seemed justified and that Australia should wait until it had built a ship of its own.[68] The Australian base seemed further away than ever.

In order to defend its supposed sovereignty, Australia had been attracted by the prospect of basing an Australian whaling industry in Antarctic waters, and by the allure of discovering valuable minerals on its shores. Strategic reasons also figured in the Australian calculations. The Russians had taken control of a German factory ship and its associated whale-catchers and sent them to the Antarctic in the summer of 1946–47, manned by Norwegian crews. They were the first Russian ships in the Antarctic for more than a century, and they raised fears of a much greater Russian presence, which might then lead to the establishment of Russian bases in the Australian Antarctic Territory.

Much to the chagrin of the Australians and New Zealanders, as well as the British and Norwegians, the Japanese had also returned to the Antarctic after General Douglas MacArthur provided ships for them to resume their whaling industry, ostensibly as a temporary measure for one season. As head of the Allied occupation forces in Japan, MacArthur believed that whales would alleviate the world-wide shortage of fats and provide meat for Japanese consumption, thereby partly relieving the United States of the burden of providing food for the half-starved nation.

In that first whaling season there were two Japanese factory ships, twelve whale-catchers and seven carriers, which sailed south under the close supervision of American officers. They were the remnants of Japan's large pre-war whaling fleet, and Australia wanted them included as part of its reparations payments. Australia was keen to 'enter the Antarctic whaling industry at the earliest opportunity', and the Japanese ships would allow Australia to do so.[69] But that would depend on MacArthur, and the American general wanted the ships for his own purposes, with the whale meat being used for stock food and human consumption in Japan, although some housewives boycotted the queues when it was included among their rations. The whale oil, meanwhile, was sold on the international market. It was estimated that the first season in the Antarctic saved the American government $10 million, which would otherwise have been spent on feeding the Japanese.[70] Japanese whaling was set to continue.

By 1950–51, the Japanese sent two fleets, comprising thirty-four ships, to the Antarctic, with an additional fleet being sent the following year. The close supervision of the Japanese whalers caused them to improve their previously wasteful methods, until they had the best record amongst all the whaling nations for the 'complete utilization of the whale carcass and for the least number of violations of the Convention'.[71]

The return of Japanese whalers to the Antarctic, albeit under American control and with Australian observers aboard, was also opposed by the British chiefs of staff, who were concerned that the Japanese would 'use the opportunity to gather intelligence about the Antarctic and any ports which her whalers make use'. The British wanted to ensure that Japan could not use its whaling presence to make a territorial claim in the Antarctic, based upon the earlier work of Lieutenant Nobu Shirase's expedition. There was much discussion between British officials as to whether Japan had any existing territorial claim arising out of Shirase's raising of the Japanese flag on the Ross Ice Barrier, and whether, if it did have a claim, it should be compelled to renounce it as part of its peace treaty with the Allies. Although the discussions were inconclusive, Japan was ultimately forced via the peace treaty to renounce any rights it might have to claim part of Antarctica.[72]

The reduction of whaling during the war had allowed whale stocks to recover somewhat from the depredations of their numbers during the 1930s. However, once the war was over, there was a rush by the whalers to return. They were eager to reap the profits that were to be made from whale oil, the price of which had risen nearly fivefold since 1939. Yet it would take some years to build new ships that could replace the hundreds that had been lost during the war.

The rush was not unregulated. Whereas Japan had refused to abide by the international whaling convention prior to the war, the industry was now more effectively governed by the International Whaling Commission, which determined the length of the Antarctic whaling season and the number and size of whales that could be killed. In the summer of 1946–47, for instance, it had decided that the season would run for just four months, or less if the quota of 16,000 blue whale equivalents was reached sooner. Under this quota system, two fin whales, two and a half humpback whales or six sei whales equalled one of the larger blue whales. These regulations were circumvented somewhat by whalers operating in the tropics and killing the migratory mammals as they congregated in their breeding grounds.

The commission also decreed that only those nations that had been engaged in whaling prior to the war could participate in Antarctic whaling after the war. Apart from the Russian whaling fleet, fourteen factory ships and sixty-three whale-catchers were sent south that year by Norway, Britain, Japan and the Netherlands. In fact, half the world's whaling fleets were owned by Norway.[73] By January 1951, with the price of whale oil still four times its pre-war level, there were nineteen factory ships and 239 whale-catchers engaged in the Antarctic whale fishery.[74]

Unlike the inter-war period, the whalers had little interest in making territorial claims or exploring the continent. The factory ships simply sailed south each year, their catchers seeking out the whales whose carcasses would be dragged aboard for processing, until the signal was received that the season was over and the killing had to cease.

Away from the Antarctic Peninsula, where the British, Argentinians and Chileans continued their shadow-boxing with protests and counter-protests, there were few ships other than whalers. The post-war rush to establish bases on the continent had petered out upon the outbreak of the Korean War. With the world's attention focused upon the fighting on the Korean Peninsula, few noticed that the rivalry on the Antarctic Peninsula was about to escalate to a new and dangerous level.

CHAPTER 19

'To bolster the legitimate claims of the United States'

1952–1956

In February 1952, the British supply ship *John Biscoe* steamed slowly into Hope Bay on the tip of the Antarctic Peninsula. Ahead lay the remains of the burnt-out British base in which two men had died in November 1948. It stood as a testament to the ever-present danger of fire in the Antarctic. Britain had taken three years to muster the resources to return, only to find two supply ships lying at anchor and a scene of activity on shore. The Argentine navy had moved in and was building a base of its own.

Both Britain and Argentina regarded Hope Bay as an integral part of their territory, and each viewed the other as an interloper. With the Argentinians now the resident inhabitants, it was their turn to warn off the British. Such warnings had been given for a decade as formal assertions of sovereignty but had never been backed up with force. This time, though, as the British began shipping their stores ashore, an overenthusiastic Argentinian commander instructed that automatic guns be fired over the heads of the British landing party. The *John Biscoe* had no effective answer, and the men were forced to retreat back on board.[1] The political theatre had taken a new and dangerous turn. A war in the Antarctic had become a real possibility.

News of the Argentine action was flashed to the Falklands governor, Sir Miles Clifford, a former Royal Marine who had served as an official in different parts of Britain's empire. The gruff governor was a staunch defender of British sovereignty in far-off places, and he was not going to have the British expelled from this strategic point on the Antarctic Peninsula. After cabling the news to the Colonial Office in London, Clifford and a party of Royal Marines bustled aboard the frigate HMS *Burghead Bay*, which had recently arrived at Stanley to act as a naval guard ship.

Without waiting for a reply from London, Clifford steamed to Hope Bay, about 1400 kilometres due south. Then, under the threatening shadow of the frigate's guns, the marines went ashore to secure a landing place while the Argentinians retreated out of sight. It was all over before the government in London was able to react. A subsequent British protest to Buenos Aires brought an apology from the government of Juan Perón and the withdrawal of the Argentinian officer, but this did not end the ongoing tension between the two nations.[2]

The following summer, conflict erupted on Deception Island, on which there had been a British base since 1943 and an Argentine base since 1947, and which Chile regarded as its territory. During the resupply of the Argentine base in January 1953, the Argentine navy reinforced its country's sovereignty by transporting ten tons of soil from Argentina, ostensibly for the garrison to grow vegetables. In fact, the soil was a symbolic gesture to show that Deception Island was an integral part of Argentina. Then, in a more provocative act, an Argentinian naval party erected a hut, a tent and a flagpole on the airfield that had been constructed by explorer Hubert Wilkins in 1928, which was within a few hundred metres of the six-man British base. At the same time, Chile announced plans to build a major airfield of its own on the island, and a Chilean party countered the Argentinians by erecting a hut near the British base and by painting 'Chile' in white letters on Wilkins' airfield.

In the face of these challenges, Britain decided it must act while it still could. On 15 February, the frigate HMS *Snipe* arrived bearing the acting Falkland Islands governor, Colin Campbell, two police officers and fifteen Royal Marines. Ignoring the long-established Argentine base on the other side of the bay, they quickly confronted the two Argentinians at the new base, dismantling their hut and tent and arresting the pair and deporting them on board the *Snipe*. The unoccupied Chilean hut was also dismantled. When the British Foreign Office released news of the incident, there were protests in the Buenos Aires press and demonstrations in the streets about the 'brutal English insult to our sovereignty'.[3]

Across the Atlantic, British Foreign Secretary Anthony Eden was cheered by his supporters in the House of Commons when he declared that the action had been taken 'to dispel any doubt about [the British] attitude toward encroachments of this type on British territory'. Amid laughter, he stressed that the two Argentinians had been 'expelled not as invaders but as illegal immigrants'.

The British action did not stop the Argentinians from asserting their sovereignty. The following summer, Juan Perón sent air force planes on daily flights over Deception Island to show that 'Argentina exercised sovereignty over Antarctic skies'. He also established an air force base on Dundee Island, off the tip of the Antarctic Peninsula. Upping the ante still further, Argentinian navy minister Rear Admiral Anibal Olivieri in February 1954 went on an inspection tour of all the naval bases in 'Argentine Antarctica'. Forewarned, Britain sent the frigate HMS *St Austell Bay* to intercept the Argentine ship as it arrived off Deception Island, only to be signalled by the Argentinians, 'Welcome to Argentina.' When the ships came to anchor and a British officer went aboard the Argentine ship, he was told that 'the frigate was in Argentinian territorial waters without authorization'. Olivieri completed his tour by landing a military detachment at Hope Bay to strengthen the Argentinian naval personnel who had been set to flight by the Royal Marines in 1952.[4]

Despite Eden's bravado, Britain was in a quandary. Hard-pressed financially, it was scaling back its imperial commitments around the world and reducing the size of its armed forces. It regarded its possession of the Falkland Islands as non-negotiable but had been willing to entertain the prospect of ceding most, if not all, of the Falkland Islands Dependencies to Argentina and/or Chile. However, there was a fear in London that giving way on the Falkland Islands Dependencies would be seen in Buenos Aires as a sign of weakness, and might lead to Argentina wresting away the Falkland Islands as well.

Little was done to resolve what seemed to be an intractable problem. Every base that Britain established in the Falkland Islands Dependencies was more than matched by the Argentinians and Chileans. By the summer of 1953–54, the British had six bases, while the Argentinians had eight and the Chileans had three.[5] Britain did not have the naval force on hand to counter the South Americans. There was just one frigate based in the Falkland Islands Dependencies during the summer to provide token support for British sovereignty, and it was unable to go much further south than Deception Island for fear of the ice. Unable to dislodge its rivals, Britain had to defend its territorial title by other means. It would build more bases, do better science than its rivals, issue stamps for the Falkland Islands Dependencies and compile detailed maps covered mainly by British names.

In charge of Britain's naming work in the Antarctic was the bespectacled ornithologist, Brian Roberts, who had been on the 1934 Graham Land expedition. He had since become the Antarctic specialist at the Foreign Office, while also working at the Scott Polar Research Institute in Cambridge. During the war, he had led a small section at the Foreign Office devoted to researching the history of territorial claims in the Antarctic. It had compiled a secret report containing everything that was 'relevant to the question of claims of sovereignty', along with information on 'the nature of the different territories and their value for different purposes'. Sent to policy-makers in Britain and the dominions, it was meant to inform discussions concerning Antarctica and to provide historical background for those attending the much-mooted but never held conference on Antarctic sovereignty. Not surprisingly, the evidence was organised in such a way as to provide support for Britain's territorial claims.[6] In the late 1940s, Roberts had become secretary of a British committee that liaised with the Americans to reach agreement on Antarctic names. The rotund and pipe-smoking Roberts was zealous about protecting Britain's position in the Antarctic and had a strong belief in the power of names and maps to shore up territorial titles.

Although Roberts believed that placing British names on Antarctic maps was crucial to ensuring British possession, he realised that it was just as important to obtain international recognition of those names. Only then would British names be likely to appear on maps prepared by other nations. It might even be possible to produce a standard map of Antarctica that met general acceptance while still protecting British interests.

Since they were not territorial rivals, Britain and its Commonwealth countries were able to reach easy agreement on names in their respective territories. Norway was also ready to compromise, since its territory did not overlap with that of any other nation. The Falkland Islands Dependencies, and the Antarctic Peninsula in particular, was the most problematic area. There was little prospect of a compromise with Argentina and Chile, which were adamant about their ownership and had already replaced many British names. Britain concentrated instead on reaching agreement with nations whose explorers had been active in that region, recognising many foreign names based upon priority of discovery. Despite concern about Russian ambitions, even some of the names used by Bellingshausen in the South Shetlands were accepted. At the same time, however, Bellingshausen's names that had not survived through usage were not shifted elsewhere within the Shetlands but were allowed to disappear. It was feared that doing otherwise might weaken Britain's case for possession of the Shetlands.[7]

With little hope of reaching agreement with Argentina or Chile over the Antarctic Peninsula, Britain sought a compromise with the United States. Even that would not be easy, since the United States regarded itself, rather than Britain, as the area's true discoverer. After all, Britain's 'Graham Land' was America's 'Palmer Peninsula'. The vexed question of an overall name for the peninsula was set aside in favour of deciding names for its subsidiary features. In 1948, Roberts had been authorised by the UK Antarctic Place-Names Committee to correspond informally with his American counterpart, Captain Harold Saunders, in order to reach tentative agreement on these relatively minor names before they were submitted to their respective committees. Only after that had been done would they appear on both British and American maps, which should see them being accepted by some other nations as well.

Although both sides wanted to have the greatest scattering of their own names on the map, Roberts developed a productive relationship with Saunders. He had greater difficulties with some British officials who wanted discussions only after Britain had reached a firm view. In 1950, when Saunders and Roberts tried to arrange a meeting between members of their respective committees to reach final agreement on various names on the peninsula's east coast, the British committee was so worried about being steamrolled by the Americans that they denied the meeting official status and shifted its location from London to Cambridge. Realising that nothing definite would come from such a meeting, the Americans cancelled it. The British officials were relieved and agreed that the compilation of a gazetteer of place names in the Falkland Islands Dependencies should be accelerated.[8]

Although Roberts was frustrated by the meeting's cancellation, some of his colleagues on the committee feared that the slow process was playing into the hands of the Americans. The irascible Colonial Office representative, J. S. Bennett, mounted a furious assault on Roberts' strategy, complaining of the delays it was causing in the production of maps, and the possible weakening of Britain's title if it accepted some American names. Maps of British territory 'should carry names only of British origin', declared Bennett, who urged that the talks with Saunders 'should be discontinued' and 'names should be inserted on published maps with all possible speed'.

The Foreign Office representative explained that Roberts' approach was part of a larger strategy to cooperate with the Americans in the hope that it might help to resolve the fractious dispute with Argentina and Chile, and lead to the creation of 'some form of international regime for the Antarctic continent'. The Admiralty's Hydrographic Department also pointed to the importance of Britain's *Antarctic Pilot* and the United States' *Sailing Directions for Antarctica* having the same names on their maps. But Bennett would not be mollified, and cooperation with the Americans was suspended.[9]

In the event, Bennett was overruled and Roberts was authorised to resume his painstaking correspondence. By March 1953, he was able to report that nearly 150 published names had been rejected, mostly names given by Ronne following his return from Stonington Island in 1948. Another 172 names had been accepted, which meant that all the place name differences had been resolved as far south as 75° S.[10]

While Roberts and Saunders wrestled with Antarctic names, Britain pressed ahead with plans for an expedition to reinforce its territorial claims. Harking back to the past, it proposed to outshine its rivals with an expedition that would tackle the last great challenge. The proposal was suggested by Clifford, who was tired of being humiliated by the Argentinians and Chileans. He told the British government's Polar Committee in March 1953 that a trans-Antarctic expedition was 'the only way of competing successfully for political prestige in this area'. For some years, he had been pushing the idea of such an expedition, to be organised by the Falkland Islands Dependencies Survey.

At the same time, the forty-five-year-old scientific head of Britain's Falkland Islands Dependencies Survey, Dr Vivian Fuchs, had been planning his own dramatic crossing of Antarctica. It was the feat that Shackleton had tried but failed to achieve. Fuchs urged that Britain 'seize the opportunity' to do it soon, while its Antarctic rivals were not yet in as good a position to do 'a journey of comparable importance'. If successful, a 'trans-continental journey made wholly within territory claimed by the British Commonwealth' would 'bring world-wide prestige', declared Fuchs.[11] It would remind the world of Britain's long history of exploration, and thereby implicitly reinforce their territorial title in the Antarctic. For a nation and empire on the skids, a successful expedition would also give a boost to national morale.

Fuchs put his proposal to the Polar Committee on 15 September 1953, where officials gave it a 'ruthless examination'. There was little attempt by Fuchs to suggest that it would have much scientific value. He stressed instead its 'romantic appeal' and the effect it would have on the prestige of Britain and its Commonwealth partners. He also suggested that the establishment of British bases in Coats Land and the Ross Dependency 'would help to justify territorial claims'. Neither the Admiralty nor the Department of Civil Aviation was willing to contribute funds, while even the Foreign Office was dubious about the expedition's value.

As far as the Foreign Office was concerned, the Fuchs expedition might well have 'prestige value' but it 'would not be sufficiently permanent to reinforce the British position'. If it was going to contribute funds, the Foreign Office wanted the money spent 'at the fringe of the continent where the competition is greater'. Although Fuchs pointed out that the expedition would establish a base on the Ross Sea, where 'lack of New Zealand activity' had weakened its title to the Ross Dependency, British officials were wary about spending British money to reinforce the title to a territory under New Zealand administration.[12]

Britain was divided about the Antarctic. On the one hand, the yearly humiliation that it faced from the South Americans prompted the government to propose in August 1953 that there be 'an orderly reduction' in its Antarctic commitments until they reached a scale that the country was 'in a position permanently to meet'.[13] On the other hand, the conquest of Mount Everest by a British team in May 1953 had coincided with the coronation of the young Queen Elizabeth II, and the two events had imbued the British with the confidence that they might yet arrest their national decline. Just as Scott and Shackleton had performed acts of derring-do to convince a concerned nation that its long-held domination of the world was secure, now Fuchs was proposing to take up where Scott and Shackleton had left off.

Fuchs suggested that the expedition start either from Stonington Island on Marguerite Bay, where he had led a British base that had since closed and where an Argentine base was now located, or from Vahsel Bay on the Weddell Sea at the eastern extremity of the Falkland Islands Dependencies. Whatever the starting point, the end point would be McMurdo Sound on the Ross Sea, after the expedition had crossed parts of the Falkland Islands Dependencies, the Australian Antarctic Territory and New Zealand's Ross Dependency. Beginning at Stonington Island had the advantage of countering the Argentine base and undermining the history of American activity, but it was the longer and more expensive option. When Argentina established a base at Vahsel Bay, the advantage of that route increased accordingly. Since it was cheaper and shorter, Fuchs ultimately opted to begin from there.[14]

The planned expedition, and the public discussion it provoked, seems to have convinced the British government to reverse its earlier decision for an 'orderly reduction' in its Antarctic commitments. By August 1954, it had decided instead to defend its position and increase its presence.[15] For a decade Britain had not felt sufficiently confident to evict interlopers from its territory, nor had it regarded its Antarctic interests as sufficiently valuable to justify such action. Ever since 1949, Britain had renewed its annual agreement with Argentina and Chile not to send warships, other than on routine resupply cruises, south of 60° S.[16] That had kept the sometimes uneasy peace, but it had also allowed the Argentinians to keep boosting their presence, confident in the knowledge that they would not be seriously challenged. So desperate was Britain that it even explored the idea of designating the Falkland Islands Dependencies 'as a proving ground for work on atomic energy'. A study was made 'of all operational, technical and safety aspects of using the South Polar Regions as a Proving Ground for testing H-bombs'.[17] In the end, Britain decided that the deserts of Australia made a better testing ground than the ice of Antarctica.

The Admiralty now looked to its Falklands frigate to move beyond 'flag-waving cruises' that left 'trespassers unmolested in British territory'. As First Lord of the Admiralty Jim Thomas explained to Foreign Secretary Anthony Eden in November 1954, making such cruises only 'diminishes our prestige' and might act as 'a positive inducement to further trespass'. After giving the Argentinians so many warnings, wrote Thomas, Britain did not 'need to give them any warning before impounding a hut and deporting its occupants'. Thomas confided to Defence Minister Harold Macmillan that the Admiralty had 'always disliked the un-Navy-like job of pushing protests under the door of an Argentine hut' and wanted its frigate 'to act as a warship rather than an observation post or even a postman'. However, the Admiralty was concerned about sending it south into icy seas, where it might be trapped and have to suffer the ultimate indignity of relying for rescue on Argentina's new German-built icebreaker, the *General San Martin*.[18]

Thomas suggested that the captain of the frigate be allowed to act against the Argentinians without having to refer the matter to London. While Eden wanted the frigate to take a much more active role, he did not want the captain taking unilateral action that could see the Foreign Office having to clean up the resulting diplomatic mess. The Colonial Office was much more gung-ho. The newly appointed governor of the Falkland Islands, Raynor Arthur, called for any new Argentine bases, or any summer bases converted into permanent bases, to be forcibly dismantled by the Royal Marines. Colonial Secretary Alan Lennox-Boyd agreed 'that the frigate should be used in the way most effective to deter Argentine and Chilean aggressions', noting that Britain was facing 'an Argentinian challenge which increases in scale every season'. He wanted the Admiralty to 'take every opportunity, consistent with wise seamanship, in letting the intruders know that our frigate is about in these waters'.[19] If a more aggressive policy was implemented, armed conflict could again become a real possibility. But such an aggressive policy could not be implemented in the face of trenchant opposition from the Foreign Office.

Eden's concerns, and the failure by officials to agree on a policy for the frigate, led to a reconsideration of Britain's Antarctic policy. The cabinet decision to increase British activities in the Antarctic had come up against the practical reality of a navy that had no ice-strengthened warships or icebreakers. As the Admiralty pointed out, the cabinet had 'demanded increased activities but had made no provision for the finance or the facilities required to enable the activities to be carried out'. If the policy was to be implemented, the Admiralty suggested, Britain needed to build one settlement for each one built by the Argentinians, and construct at least two new ice-breaking supply ships. It would also have to commit sufficient warships to provide 'moral and, if need be, other support to the ships or settlements'. Having a single frigate in the Falklands, which had to be kept out of the ice, was worse than useless, since it gave an impression of British weakness that encouraged the Argentinians to expand their presence. If its title was to be protected, Britain had to 'adopt a more positive policy of exploration', for which increased naval support would be required.[20]

The Antarctic was perhaps the least of Eden's concerns in early 1955. For more than ten years, he had wanted to replace Churchill as leader of the Conservative Party. With the former wartime leader now eighty years old, Eden increased the pressure on Churchill, who finally announced his retirement in April 1955. The physical decline of Britain's long-time leader and the political machinations that led to his replacement had compounded the indecision in London about the Antarctic. More fundamentally, Britain continued to have an imperial mindset long after it had lost the economic and military power to sustain an empire. Whereas Clement Attlee's Labour government had in the late 1940s considered giving up much of the Falkland Islands Dependencies, Churchill's government was much more reluctant to concede anything.

After the dispute over the use of the frigate, the British cabinet finally tried in February 1955 to reconcile its Antarctic ambition with its means. Eden informed his colleagues that Argentina was 'forging ahead.' At least six more huts were being erected and the base at Vahsel Bay was being established. Whereas the British had no aircraft and no icebreakers, Argentina had an icebreaker and thirteen aircraft to support its operations. Moreover, Eden warned, the Argentinians were 'well equipped for survey and exploration work, and it is clear that they intend increasingly to strike out from their bases into the unexplored land mass'. He noted that Britain had ordered a new supply ship, which would allow more bases to be supported, and that it had contributed £100,000 to Fuchs' Trans-Antarctic Expedition. Yet much more needed to be done.

For one thing, Roberts had long argued that it needed to do a 'more systematic exploration and survey . . . to find out quickly what is most worth keeping'. That meant more bases and a civilian air and ground survey that would 'discover more about the mineral and other potentialities'. In turn, this would mean having 'sufficient force available in the Antarctic to support these activities'. Only the acquisition of an icebreaker and an ice-strengthened frigate would give Britain the capability 'to send an armed party . . . to show the flag at British bases or take forcible action against intruders'. The weakness of Britain's position was clear when Eden counselled his colleagues against any immediate use of force against Argentine bases. He feared that this would prompt retaliation against

British bases that were beyond the protective reach of the present frigate.[21]

In late 1955, the vulnerable frigate was finally replaced by the HMS *Protector*, a twenty-year-old net-laying warship that had been specially strengthened for the ice and carried two helicopters. Armed with this new capability, the Foreign Office suggested that 'some kind of aggressive action' be mounted either to 'overthrow one of two existing foreign bases and/or to forestall any foreign attempts to open new bases'. Although the *Protector* allowed greater scope to act 'against Argentine and Chilean intruders', the Admiralty was cautious about doing so unless it had more ships on hand. There was an added complication: the upcoming International Geophysical Year (IGY), scheduled for 1957–58, which required Britain to cooperate with other nations rather than fight with them.

So the question of aggressive action was passed to the Foreign and Colonial Offices for a report on the possible political repercussions, while the chiefs of staff examined the strategic implications. Although the Foreign Office thought it was 'undignified' for Britain to have its territory occupied by foreign powers, the chiefs of staff strongly advised against evicting the Argentinians. Britain simply did not have the means to do so without seriously weakening its forces elsewhere, and there was no strategic justification for it – so long as Britain retained control of the Falkland Islands. So the old policy continued. Britain established two new bases in the Falkland Islands Dependencies, initiated a privately chartered air survey of Graham Land and set up a base at Vahsel Bay for the Trans-Antarctic Expedition.[22] Protecting Britain's title was about to get much harder.

America had finally decided to reinforce its own rights to Antarctic territory, which included the territory claimed by Britain. Washington had repeatedly argued that only actual occupation gave a good title to Antarctic territory. Although it had held this position since 1924, the State Department was slow to act in regard to its own potential claims. Official American expeditions had twice gone to the Antarctic and established settlements at Little America and elsewhere, and had twice abandoned them. Britain, Argentina and Chile had since established permanent bases in the Antarctic, and they had been joined by France and Australia in the early 1950s. While all these bases were intended to reinforce the territorial claims of these nations, many other countries were intending to establish scientific bases as part of the activities planned by the International Council of Scientific Unions for the IGY. The prospect of non-claimant nations, particularly Russia, establishing bases lent a new urgency to the activities of claimant nations and to the deliberations of the United States. And once again it was marked by the bitter rivalry between Finn Ronne and Richard Byrd.

Ronne had been trying for more than four years to obtain government support for an expedition that would take him to the east coast of the Antarctic Peninsula. With many nations now organising IGY expeditions, Ronne proposed a way for Washington to pre-empt its rivals and for him to pre-empt the plans of Byrd. In February 1953, geographer Samuel Boggs arranged a meeting for Ronne with senior State Department officials.

Ronne told them of his plan to establish a base in Gould Bay on the Weddell Sea during the coming summer, along with outlying meteorological bases, including one at the South Pole. It would be much like his previous expedition, with a party of thirty-two staying for fourteen months to explore the interior of the continent and undertake scientific investigations approved by the National Academy of Sciences. Since they would complete their work prior to the IGY, the United States could formally annex much of the Antarctic before other nations arrived. Because the plan envisaged Ronne operating in an area claimed by both Britain and Argentina, he was anxious to have an assurance from the State Department that it had no political objections.[23]

Ronne's plan had great appeal. Although the State Department acknowledged that 'any expedition would increase tension with other interested powers', its officials were prepared to take that risk because of the benefits it would bring in 'its strengthening of United States rights in the area as a whole and its acquisition of scientific data unavailable anywhere else'. Officials were particularly attracted to the expedition area being 'little known and away from the area of earlier U.S. explorations', which would 'expand the bases for any future U.S. claims'. It would thereby satisfy those officials 'who foresee an eventual U.S. claim taking in the larger part of the Antarctic Continent'. However, it still remained a matter of contention in Washington as to whether the United States should seek to claim most of the Antarctic in the face of opposition from 'friendly powers', or whether it should limit its claims to those areas that had been intensively explored by American citizens. Although the State Department had decided in 1952 that a formal territorial claim should be made, opposition from the Defense Department meant that nothing had been done.[24]

Buoyed by the guarded approval of the State Department, Ronne proceeded to gather further support from members of Congress and the Department of Defense. However, the continuing war in Korea, together with active opposition from Byrd, ensured that the navy refused to commit any of its ships for Ronne's expedition in the summer of 1953–54. Once the war had ended, Ronne returned to the fray. He went with Senator Frank Case to the White House in February 1954 to meet with administration officials, and came away confident that he would have President Dwight D. Eisenhower's support.[25]

When nothing eventuated, he decided to pressure the president by having Case and Congressman Thor Tollefson introduce a bill in the Senate and House of Representatives in April 1954 that called for Eisenhower to provide up to $200,000 for Ronne's expedition, along with the use of two ships, four aircraft, mechanised transport and service and civilian personnel.[26] Although run by Ronne's American Antarctic Association, it would be effectively a government expedition. And Ronne had government aims to the fore. Gone was his former idealistic attachment to the internationalisation of the Antarctic. In giving evidence to the Senate Armed Services Committee in May 1954, Ronne said that he wanted nothing more than to 'make explorations into areas never yet seen by man in order to bolster the legitimate claims of the United States'.[27]

Despite support from Congress and the State Department, the Ronne expedition faced opposition from the Defense Department and the Bureau of the Budget, both for financial reasons and because of competition from Byrd's IGY expedition. When Ronne turned to Laurence Gould for support, as he had so often in the past, he found that the influential geologist and former Antarctic explorer had become chairman of the Antarctic Committee in charge of organising America's IGY contribution; he was therefore competing with Ronne for funds. With the repeated delays, Ronne began to pitch his expedition with reference to the IGY, noting to Gould how his proposed base 'could lay the ground-work for the scientific activities' of the IGY.[28] However, his participation was complicated by the poisonous relationship between himself and Byrd.

Officials in the State Department were also wary of Byrd's political influence. They did not want to see America lose its stake in the Antarctic because of a personal struggle between the two explorers. As a possible compromise, State Department officials suggested to Ronne that he abandon his proposal for a base and instead charter a Norwegian whaler to circumnavigate the continent so that ground control points could be obtained for the 80,000 aerial photographs that had been taken during Byrd's Operation Highjump.[29] But Ronne had no interest in finishing off Byrd's work, particularly when he remained confident of getting Eisenhower's approval for the Gould Bay base. Officials in Washington had other ideas.

By May 1954, American plans for the IGY were to have three bases: one at Little America, one in Marie Byrd Land and one at the South Pole. However, it was unclear which department would fund the program. The Defense Department could not see sufficient military reasons to pay for it out of its budget, which left scientists scrambling for support from elsewhere in Washington. Gould and officials from the National Science Foundation and the National Academy of Sciences asked the State Department to confirm that there were compelling scientific and political reasons to justify funding for their program. A senior State Department official readily agreed that the expenditure was justified on scientific and political grounds.

The political grounds make interesting reading. The creation of permanent bases was regarded as 'necessary if our potential claims are to be preserved', with the IGY allowing science to be used as a cover for doing so. Rather than the United States establishing bases unilaterally, which might lead to 'charges of "imperialism"', America would do so as part of the IGY.[30] In effect, it would be establishing bases in the areas it wanted to claim, but doing so at the suggestion of the international scientific community and – ostensibly – for scientific purposes.

America's Antarctic policy came before the National Security Council in June 1954, before it was considered by Eisenhower. The council's draft statement emphasised the economic resources that might be present in the Antarctic but noted that they would require further investigation. In order to secure these resources, it was considered vital that the United States make a territorial claim while part of the continent still remained unclaimed. American activities would not be restricted to the territory it claimed. The council argued that America's objectives should be to secure the whole continent for the United States and its allies and to 'exclude our most probable enemies'; to ensure 'freedom of exploration and scientific investigation' across the Antarctic for America and its allies; and to ensure 'access to natural resources which may be found to be useful'.

America's proposed territorial claim was to extend from the so-called Palmer Peninsula all the way west to Little America, which meant that it would intrude on the territories of both Britain and New Zealand. The CIA suggested that the United States might agree to recognise the claims of Argentina and Chile if, in return, the South Americans recognised the American claim from 90° W to Little America. Under this proposal, Britain would be shut out of the continent altogether. It was intended that America's IGY program would be shaped to achieve these objectives.[31] However, Eisenhower was not convinced about making a territorial claim.

For decades, there had been calls for the United States to formally claim all those areas that its citizens had discovered and explored. In more recent years, maps by the CIA and the State Department had shown where those claims might be made. But America had always refrained from actually making them, mainly for fear of upsetting its close allies. Eisenhower continued this tradition when he chaired the National Security Council on 15 July 1954; he instructed that America should 'not suddenly make claims' but should instead continue to reserve its rights. The important thing, said CIA director Allen Dulles, 'was to make sure that Russia was not invited to take part in any discussions or negotiations respecting Antarctica'. Eisenhower agreed with the exclusion of the Russians, while 'expressing strong approval of future expeditions to protect our rights in Antarctica'. The president left it to the State Department to 'figure out' how to achieve this, while also working towards an 'early resolution of conflicting claims' and the encouragement of 'international arrangements to promote the over-all reduction of international friction'.[32] Eisenhower's attitude did not augur well for Ronne's expedition.

Congress quickly fell in with the president's policy. The Senate Armed Services committee agreed two weeks later that an expedition should be sent 'at the earliest possible date . . . for the purpose of validating the territorial claims of the United States'.[33] The motion had been moved by Senator Case and supported by Harry

Byrd. But which expedition did the committee want the president to support? Although Ronne believed that he had Eisenhower's support for an expedition in the coming summer, he was concerned to hear that the Defense Department was taking control. He told Gould that he hoped that the expedition would 'not be a repetition of the Highjump show of 1947' and would be in accordance with his plan.

Byrd, however, had other ideas. He viewed Ronne's plan as a threat to his own hopes to lead one final expedition. As he told a cousin who was in the Texas oil business, there was an 'urgency' to his plans because 'of the activities of some other nations who are trying to get the oil, coal, uranium, etc. down there'. And he was not going to let Ronne disrupt his plans. Byrd drew on all his political contacts, including the chairman of the Senate Armed Services Committee, John Stennis, and officers in the navy. He also had sufficient political clout to request personal meetings with the president himself.[34] Ronne's leader at East Base in 1941, Richard Black, had advised Ronne to 'get wise' and join the IGY 'Band Wagon'. Working in the Office of Naval Research, Black knew which way the political wind was blowing. He had advised the Armed Services Committee against supporting Ronne. However, Ronne dismissed Black's advice, angrily describing him as an 'egotistical "nut" [who] would double cross his own mother for personal gain'.[35]

In this case, Black's advice was astute. Ronne's hopes of getting away to the Antarctic were dashed. Instead, the navy dispatched the icebreaker *Atka* on a reconnaissance voyage in the summer of 1954–55 to check on possible sites for IGY bases. With Gould as chairman of America's IGY Antarctic Committee, there was a happy coincidence between science and politics. As an explorer with Byrd at Little America, Gould had helped establish an American claim to Marie Byrd Land, and he was anxious for America's IGY activities to concentrate on areas that would reinforce potential American claims. In October 1954, he told Captain George Dufek, who would be the naval commander of the IGY expedition, that the scientists strongly endorsed the planned program 'at Little America, Marie Byrd Land, and the South Polar Plateau, sites which have great scientific significance both intrinsically and in terms of their role in the international network in Antarctica'. These sites, wrote Gould, should 'have the highest priority'.[36] The United States already had strong claims to the first two locations, while the South

Polar Plateau had scientific significance and could provide the key to making other claims across the continent.

The *Atka*'s first call after leaving New Zealand was at the Bay of Whales, where Dufek discovered in January 1955 that the six DC-3 aircraft left behind by Byrd had floated out to sea, along with all the tents of Little America IV. Two great icebergs had broken off the western side of the bay, leaving the oft-used location unsuitable for any future expedition. However, there was another bay about fifty kilometres to the east, which had been first discovered by Shirase and named Kainan Bay, and which was now an alternative site for what would become Little America V.

From there, the *Atka* continued eastward until it had rounded the Antarctic Peninsula and passed the forbidding ice of the Weddell Sea. It was searching for a suitable site on the sea's north-eastern shore but was unable to force its way through the ice. The Americans had to settle instead for a site on the coast of Queen Maud Land, further east, where an easy passage was found through hundreds of kilometres of ice. An American base on the Queen Maud coast could serve the expedition's scientific purposes as well as provide an alternative airbase to supply the planned South Pole base.[37]

During the course of the *Atka*'s voyage, American plans for the IGY had expanded beyond the three bases that were originally envisaged. Plans for a larger scheme were set in motion after a meeting of IGY representatives in Rome decided that five additional IGY bases should be established to fill gaps in the scientific coverage of the continent. A Russian representative was attending the Rome meeting as an observer, and the State Department became concerned that the Soviet Union would accept this international invitation and establish its own foothold in the Antarctic, which might then provide the basis for a Russian territorial claim. The United States asked Norway and New Zealand to establish bases at Peter I Island and Ross Island respectively, and urged other 'friendly powers' to fill the remaining gaps before the Soviet Union did so, but the call met with little response.[38] As a result, the United States boosted its planned bases to five: one at Kainan Bay, another in the interior of Marie Byrd Land, one at the South Pole and two on the coast of Queen Maud Land.

The first three of these bases provided Washington with the means to make a claim to the sector in which Marie Byrd Land was located, and Congressman Tollefson was determined that the

United States should do just that. On 5 January 1955, as the *Atka* continued its voyage, Tollefson moved a resolution in the House of Representatives asserting America's 'right of sovereignty over that portion of the Antarctic Continent' between 90° W and 150° W, as well as all other territories in the Antarctic where 'discoveries, explorations, and claims on behalf of the United States have been made by nationals of the United States'. According to Tollefson, America 'should share in the possible advantages, wealth, and resources of the Antarctic Continent', particularly any 'valuable minerals and oil' that might lay hidden there.[39]

While Congress was referring Tollefson's motion to the Committee on Foreign Affairs, and the *Atka* continued to crash its way through the ice, Ronne finally recast his expedition as an integral part of the IGY. All the while, he sensed the malevolent influence of his nemesis. Ronne therefore tried to keep his changed plans secret from Byrd for as long as possible. When the IGY organisers still opposed the idea of a base at Gould Bay, Ronne was able to enlist the support of the State Department, which wanted the base for political reasons. With both Britain and Argentina establishing bases nearby, the United States faced the possibility of being frozen out of the region if it did not move quickly to establish one of its own.

Although Byrd convinced senior naval officers to refuse Ronne the use of their ships, Ronne was saved by the veteran Norwegian whaler and explorer Lars Christensen, who offered to transport the expedition for free. Still, complained Ronne, the Byrd 'influence is felt'.[40]

The Gould Bay base would now allow the United States to occupy an additional swathe of the continent. Taken together, the network of American bases and the massive scale of its logistical effort would make the United States the pre-eminent Antarctic power. But it was still unclear how that pre-eminence would be translated into territorial dominance.

Although most of the existing claimants wanted to have an American presence in the Antarctic in order to ward off the Russians, they were keen to limit the United States to the continent's unclaimed sector. The Australian government, in particular, wanted to keep the Americans out of the Australian Antarctic Territory, which still remained empty of bases. With no early prospect of a continental base, the leader of the Australian National Antarctic

Research Expedition, Phillip Law, was doing all he could to reinforce Australia's tenuous title.

Law had been imbued with a much keener appreciation of Antarctic politics after accompanying the British–Norwegian–Swedish expedition to Antarctica in 1950 and returning by way of the United Kingdom, where he had long discussions with Brian Roberts at the Foreign Office. Law recalled that these talks made him aware of the 'political aspects of Antarctic work'. It was Roberts who emphasised the peril Australia would face if ever the Norwegians were to challenge Australia's possession of the western part of its territory.

Fortified by his talks with Roberts, Law returned to Australia determined to 'nullify' the work of the Norwegians by 'doing every sort of science that we could think of' and by 'developing the mapping, together with the geology that goes with this sort of field work, and the glaciology'. Roberts had stressed to Law the importance of names as a means of holding on to territory. As Law later recalled, 'when you put a name on a feature, you're saying "We got here first". So the more names you can get on features in Antarctica the better your claims are.'[41]

In Australia, Law became the sole authority to whom names had to be submitted for approval, until he passed the responsibility to a committee in October 1952. It followed the British decision to accept the names approved by the sovereign power, which meant that French and Norwegian names in their territories were applied without translation, while France and Norway did likewise with English names on their maps. At least as far as these claimant nations were concerned, their Antarctic maps would become 'substantially the same'.[42] The British decision also meant that Australia had to apply names to as many geographic features as possible within its Antarctic territory, and to decide on the names proposed by the United States for features photographed on Australian territory during Operation Highjump.

The first meeting of Australia's Committee on Antarctic Names was held in Canberra on 21 October 1952 and was chaired by Law. The committee included Mawson and the director of the National Mapping Section, Bruce Lambert, and quickly decided to complete a revision of Australia's 1939 map so that it could be published as soon as possible. Lambert had been largely responsible for the 1939 publication and was acutely aware of the power of maps to reinforce a nation's sovereignty. With American names now likely to be approved for the Australian territory, Lambert was anxious to ensure that they would be overwhelmed by Australian ones. Mawson agreed to send him any 'aerial photos of un-named features which could be fixed accurately enough to be named', while the committee decided that 'all features which had ever been surveyed or named should be listed for consideration whether they had appeared in the 1939 map or not'.[43]

The problem for the Australians was that the Americans had flown over much of the coastline and immediate hinterland of the Australian Antarctic Territory, and had produced aerial photographs that revealed in fine detail practically all of its geographical features. However, only in a few places had they landed surveyors by helicopter to obtain astronomical fixes. Law was prepared to accept American names for the major features that they had first sighted from the air but was loath to allow the Americans to 'saturate' hundreds of kilometres of coastline with their names based upon relatively brief flights. To do so would leave nothing to be named by the Australian surveyor 'who, by dangerous and laborious surface travel, later covers the same area to obtain the necessary astrofixes'.

There was also a deeper reason. The Americans had named many of the features after their explorer Charles Wilkes and his men and their ships. This, Law noted, would leave readers of the map with the impression 'that the features were discovered by Wilkes', when there was no certainty they had been, and that the United States thereby had some claim to the territory. Indeed, the subsequent American maps of the Antarctic had 'Wilkes Land' spread in large letters across most of the Australian Antarctic Territory, and Australian and British names writ small. In contrast, Australian maps had Wilkes Land writ small and Australian and British names writ large.[44]

Law suggested in late 1951 that a survey flight be made from Australia to the Antarctic as a way of reinforcing the nation's sovereignty. The pioneer aviator Captain P. G. Taylor, who had just proved the feasibility of an air route to Chile by way of Easter Island, volunteered to make a return flight to the Antarctic in the same Catalina flying boat. Apart from reinforcing its territorial rights, Law thought aircraft might provide an economical way of supplying bases. The proposal was embraced by the newly installed

External Affairs minister, Richard Casey, who had long been an enthusiastic supporter of Antarctic exploration. Casey told his cabinet colleagues in October 1951 that such a flight would go far to 'fortifying Australian claims to sovereignty' and also prepare 'the way for flights to the Australian sector after an Australian station is established on the mainland'. Flying an aircraft 2600 kilometres to land among icebergs in a place where blizzards could suddenly erupt would be a risky enterprise. However, Casey argued that the risk would be acceptable if a naval ship was stationed midway to provide weather advice.[45] Moreover, the French base in Adélie Land could provide additional weather forecasts and fuel.

The flight soon encountered problems. The French had no room on their ship for Taylor's fuel, and the United States refused to train him in the latest methods of polar navigation. Despite these setbacks, Taylor was willing to try anyway, and proposed that he take on fuel at Macquarie Island by landing on water on the lee side of the island and then using rocket-assisted take-off. The cost of the flight would only be £3400, and the cost could be recouped partly by carrying philatelic mail, which would add to the 'international publicity value for Australia in "showing the flag" for our Antarctic Territory'.

Law urged that the flight go ahead, arguing that the 'prestige value' alone would be worth the small expense. However, the navy's commitments in Korea meant that it had no cruiser available to act as a weather ship, while Prime Minister Menzies was concerned that the flight might be 'unduly hazardous'. Casey had some misgivings too and suggested that it be delayed until January 1953.[46]

Taylor was further frustrated when a fire at the French base in January 1952 destroyed its radio and weather equipment. He complained to Law that 'he had been made [to] look ridiculous in the eyes of the public and he was fed up with the government about the whole affair'. Taylor wanted to make the flight as soon as an 'opportunity presented itself', threatening to go to the press if he was 'messed around any further'. Although the French agreed to take fuel for Taylor when they resupplied their burnt-out base, the flight never went ahead.[47] It was no longer necessary.

Law had learnt of an icebreaker being built by a Danish shipping company and managed to charter the ship. It was a timely discovery, with other nations likely to establish bases on Australia's Antarctic territory during the IGY. In January 1953, the Australian cabinet finally agreed to an Antarctic base after Law convinced Casey that it could be done by reducing the number of personnel on Heard Island. As a further cost-saver and a way of finding the necessary scientists, Casey suggested that South Africa, Canada and New Zealand could be asked to contribute men and money. The participation of the other Commonwealth countries might also ensure they would side with Australia in the event of its title being challenged at a later date. This was an important consideration, because the protection of Australia's title was the rationale for the base. As Casey's cabinet submission made clear, 'other considerations are subordinate to this' since it was 'useless to talk of scientific or material wealth if the region is not ours to exploit'.[48] Not that sovereignty was foremost in the public justification for the base.

When Casey announced the establishment of the base in March, he concentrated on the practical, material benefits that were likely to accrue to Australia. Everything from uranium to coal was there in abundance, according to Casey's fevered imagination. There were also the possibilities of developing a trans-Antarctic air route and exploiting the 'great food resources' of the surrounding seas. Moreover, meteorology, and the possibility of seasonal forecasts, would be a great boon for a nation whose wealth was built on wool and wheat. Strategic factors were also noted, with Casey portraying the continent as being 'close to Australia's back door'.[49]

Australians were not like the people of Argentina or Chile, or even the United States. There had been no tickertape parades for Australia's returning explorers, and no Australian prime minister would ever emulate the Chileans by visiting the Antarctic to make a symbolic statement of possession. As a journalist found when he did a straw poll of passers-by in a Sydney street in November 1952, there was widespread ignorance of Australia's stake in Antarctica.[50] Law and Casey faced a continuous struggle to create popular interest and a sense of Australian ownership. Journalist Osmar White was one of those encouraged to spread the word. Just days after Casey's announcement, White wrote an article for the Melbourne *Herald* in which he portrayed the personnel of Australia's base as the 'first colonists' who would be occupying the 'forerunner of other permanent posts'.[51]

On 4 January 1954, Casey was on Melbourne's South Wharf to farewell the nine men who were going in the small Danish icebreaker *Kista Dan* to establish the first permanent Australian base. He told the crowd of relatives and well-wishers that the men were going 'to help consolidate our claim to a large section of the Antarctic continent and to lay the foundations of scientific research there'. In charge of the base would be surveyor Bob Dovers, whose father had been on Mawson's 1929 expedition, which had laid the legal foundation for the title to the Australian Antarctic Territory. Now Dovers was off to reinforce that title, taking with him an ice pick that his father had used back in 1929. It would provide a symbolic continuity between the past and the present. Law went on the voyage to oversee the landing and to film the experience. The official report of the departure likened the *Kista Dan* to the ships of Christopher Columbus, Francis Drake and James Cook. Describing Antarctica as a 'treasure house', the report predicted that, within twenty years, the Antarctic would 'figure in the world's commerce and conversation just as largely as uranium does now'.[52]

In choosing a site for the base, Law had convinced the committee that the western part of the territory would be best for the geophysical work that he wanted to do. It would also remove any possibility of the Norwegians going there and claiming it as their own, based upon the work of Christensen's expeditions in the 1930s. Ironically, in choosing the site, Law and Mawson had used Christensen's aerial photographs to find a safe anchorage for the *Kista Dan* adjacent to patches of bare rock on which a base might be built. Importantly, the location also had easy access to the polar plateau, which would expedite exploration and the collection of ice for fresh water. Horseshoe Bay was the best site in more than 6000 kilometres of coastline, recalled Law, and Australia owed it all to the Norwegian explorers.[53]

However, the base would not be named after the Norwegians who had done so much to explore the region but after Mawson, whose flag-raising voyages in 1929–31 had allowed Australia to annex the territory. Law went on to do some flag-raising of his own when he pressured the Danish captain to head east to two contested sites, where the Norwegian explorers and Mawson had raised their respective flags in the 1930s. One was the Scullin Monolith and the other was the Vestfold Hills, where Law went ashore and raised the Australian flag in the manner of Mawson. As with Mawson's ceremonies, it was all captured on film.

Law was not only leader of the expedition but also its official photographer, using a cine camera to create a half-hour colour documentary that blended dramatic shots of the ship battling through heavy seas, cute film of penguins cavorting in the ship's wake and a claiming ceremony that would leave audiences in no doubt about the territory's ownership. The resulting film, *Blue Ice*, was clever political propaganda that was designed both to build public support for the Antarctic effort and to inform the world of Australia's work. There was one part of the film that the government did not want the world to see, however, and Law was instructed to remove a shot that showed two men using a Geiger counter to test rocks for radioactivity. The Department of Defence decreed that it could not be shown if there was any sign of a flicker on the counter. Doubtless it feared that any possibility of uranium would only encourage other countries to compete for its possession.

Law suggested that he should show the film to audiences of influential citizens in each capital city. One of the first of these select audiences was hosted by the Lord Mayor of Melbourne, and Law suggested that Casey host a similar event for parliamentarians in Canberra. Ordinary citizens also got to see the film when the Ferguson tractor company, which had one of its tractors featured, showed it throughout rural New South Wales and Victoria. There were even greater audiences overseas, where the film was shown on television in Britain, Europe and the United States; it was even awarded a prize in Italy.[54]

The success of the film convinced Law to make an even greater public-relations effort. He pressured the government's News and Information Bureau to issue articles to overseas newspapers so that the work of the Antarctic Division would be more widely known. Yet when *Colliers* magazine asked in August 1954 to send a journalist on the next voyage of the *Kista Dan*, Law refused 'because of the difficulty of controlling such a person'. Law preferred to write the stories himself and suggested taking a cine photographer so that another film could be made. The following year he took a journalist from the News and Information Bureau who would not object to having his work censored and who had already shown that he had the Antarctic division's 'best interests at heart'.[55]

Yet Law was hard to satisfy. He was outraged when shown a draft of the commentary for the second film, *Antarctic Voyage*. Although it had been made by the Department of the Interior and written by a journalist from the News and Information Bureau, there was no mention of Law and his officers or of the Antarctic Division. Instead, it read more like a scenic travelogue, Law complained, with the Danish ship being the effective star of the film. He promptly rewrote the script to remove some references to the ship and insert mentions of himself, the base leaders and the serious nature of the expedition's work.[56] Law was similarly punctilious about the publication of an official booklet about Antarctica, calling for it to be 'far more subtle in its propaganda approach' by putting 'the accent on the scientific importance rather than the economic exploitation of Antarctica'.[57]

Casey competed with Law in writing articles for newspaper publication and would accompany them with specially drawn maps that gave a misleading view of the propinquity of Australia to its Antarctic territory. He used Australian embassies to submit them to editors around the world and was exultant when one was widely used. The purpose, according to Casey, was to have Australian ownership of its territory embraced by the Australian public and acknowledged by the world.[58] Law's aims were rather wider, and he resented Casey's efforts to control the publicity from his ministerial office.[59] Law pointed to his own record in getting good press coverage and his success in having critical articles suppressed by sympathetic editors. Moreover, the publicity was not just about politics, wrote Law, but about acknowledging the work of the personnel, who were not public servants but 'adventurers who have volunteered for a dangerous job'.[60]

At least Australia had a base established in the Antarctic before the rush of IGY activity descended on its shores. It was not clear whether New Zealand would ever have such a base. The diminutive nation had been aware since the war that its claim to the Ross Dependency would never hold up in a court of international law. The Ross Dependency was in the curious position of having been annexed by Britain and placed under the administration of New Zealand, which expected one day to become its sovereign power. But neither Britain nor New Zealand had done much to exercise sovereignty since it was first annexed in 1923. The government of Peter Fraser had refused to join the post-war scramble for Antarctica, and pushed instead for an international regime that would give New Zealand a measure of control over the continent's exploitation at a minimum cost.

With no international regime in prospect, and with other nations preparing to send expeditions, New Zealand began to reassess its position. In July 1953, the government agreed that two of its scientists could accompany the forthcoming Australian expedition to the Antarctic, provided that it did not have to contribute to the cost.[61] When Britain then announced the Trans-Antarctic Expedition, New Zealand's interest in retaining the Ross Dependency began to stir.[62]

In October 1954, Fuchs sent a confidential letter about his expedition to the English geologist and mountaineer Noel Odell, who had tried to climb Everest with George Mallory in 1924 and was now a professor in New Zealand. Fuchs was keen to learn from Odell what assistance might be anticipated from New Zealand. As Fuchs' expedition would end its journey at Ross Island on McMurdo Sound, he hoped to recruit a New Zealander as leader of the McMurdo base. Fuchs suggested that New Zealand mountaineer Edmund Hillary, who had made the first ascent of Mount Everest in May 1953, might be recruited to head the base. Such an appointment would help ensure public and government support.[63] The New Zealand government had already agreed to the importance of the expedition and the need for a base on Ross Island, but still it shrank from committing any funds. A surge in public interest soon forced the government to change its view.

There had long been a small group of New Zealanders interested in Antarctic exploration. Now they had a powerful supporter in Hillary, who attended a meeting at an Auckland home in December 1954, which agreed to form a 'Committee for the Discussion of Antarctic Matters'. The sixteen members were unanimous in wanting 'to get New Zealanders into Antarctica'. A national committee was quickly formed to bring pressure on the government. The initial plan, possibly at Hillary's suggestion, was for a base to be located in the northern part of Victoria Land near the Admiralty Range, with the prospect of climbing the mountains providing 'a draw to New Zealanders'. It was envisaged that a second party might 'capture the public imagination' by visiting Scott's base on Ross Island, before going on to recondition the cairn erected over the frozen bodies of Scott's party.[64] It was all about political symbolism rather than science.

The committee soon found itself tangled with the existing Antarctic Society, which had been formed in the 1930s and had branches in Dunedin and Wellington. The society's 'constant and unswerving aim' was to remind New Zealand of its 'territorial responsibilities in the Ross Dependency'. It could hardly claim much success in that regard. But the atmosphere was changing, with Hillary's profile and the arrival of the American icebreaker *Atka* focusing attention on the threat to New Zealand's sovereignty. The *New York Times* science journalist Walter Sullivan was on board the *Atka*, and he noted how the ship's visit had caused many New Zealanders to fear that they were about to lose the Ross Dependency 'by default'.

That was the argument used by the Antarctic Society when a deputation of its members crammed into the office of the Minister for External Affairs, Tom Macdonald, on 14 January 1955. As the recently departed *Atka* steamed its way southwards, the deputation called on the government to 'exercise acts of possession' so that New Zealand could be sure of holding on to the Ross Dependency. To keep the momentum going, a National Expedition Planning Committee was established, with Hillary's Auckland group being reconstituted as a branch of the Antarctic Society.[65]

Macdonald had already been told by his officials of the need to send an expedition. He was warned that the United States had a greater claim to the eastern part of the Ross Dependency. Moreover, Washington was hinting that it was planning a base in the western part, if New Zealand did not establish one first. To avert the possibility of the United States having a stronger claim than New Zealand to the entire Ross Dependency, the government had to show that it had 'established effective physical possession'. By having a base on Ross Island, New Zealand would restrict the Americans to the eastern part of the dependency and might even exclude the Russians altogether.[66]

These were compelling arguments, and the New Zealand cabinet decided on 18 January 1955 that it should have a base on Ross Island, which would support both the Trans-Antarctic Expedition and the IGY. However, the decision was made in the absence of Prime Minister Sidney Holland, who was in London. On his return, he announced instead that his government would contribute £50,000 to Fuchs' expedition. That decision would cause 'widespread disappointment among interested New Zealanders', predicted the Antarctic Society.[67] In the face of the negative reaction, the cabinet referred the issue to the Department of External Affairs for advice on the 'minimum action' required to maintain New Zealand's title. The government was told that it required the British government to send an expedition, and for New Zealand to be 'prominently and substantially identified' with it. It was an optimistic view, since the report also noted the necessity of permanent occupation as a precondition for sovereignty.[68]

The organisers of the IGY had asked New Zealand to man a base on the Ross Sea, but the scientific program was not regarded as sufficient to justify the expense. If a base was to be established, its primary purpose had to be 'to meet the requirements of Sovereignty and the Trans Antarctic Journey'. In April 1955, the New Zealand cabinet was urged to support New Zealand's independent participation in the Trans-Antarctic Expedition, so as to 'reinforce New Zealand title to the territory' and to 'meet the broad public demand that New Zealand show an active interest in the Antarctic'. Cabinet agreed that New Zealand should show its authority, both by making new laws for the Ross Dependency and by sending expeditions from 'time to time' to 'enter and remain for significant periods in the Dependency'. It would begin by participating in the Trans-Antarctic Expedition 'on a patently New Zealand basis, with the Base at Ross Island manned by a New Zealand party'. That would serve as 'positive evidence of New Zealand interest', while New Zealand approached Britain to have the Ross Dependency formally made part of New Zealand. In the interim, it supported the formation of the Ross Sea Committee, to which it contributed the £50,000 that had been earmarked to go to Fuchs. The government hoped that the committee might be able to raise sufficient funds from a public appeal to relieve it of any further burden.[69]

Nearly ten years of prevarication had not helped the New Zealand cause. Hillary was dismayed to find, when he went to Paris in mid-1955 for an IGY conference, that the Americans and Russians had 'ambitious plans' to establish bases during the IGY. He was particularly shocked to learn from America's Admiral Dufek that the New Zealand government had approved a proposal for a large American base at McMurdo Sound, where New Zealand had been planning a base of its own. The New Zealanders had left their run too late. Hillary was not only 'distressed at the thought of the major American Base . . . cluttering up our possible base sites' but 'also felt considerable concern at the sovereignty angle'.

Nevertheless, he and Fuchs met with Dufek to discuss how the Americans might assist the New Zealanders by transporting some of their equipment to the Antarctic.[70] This was not something that Fuchs wanted for his own expedition, which he was determined to keep separate from the Americans. He did not want to be reliant on them except in an emergency. Fuchs would not even inform the Americans of anything more than the 'broad programme and timing' of his expedition for fear they would beat him there. He also had fears about Hillary, whose fame threatened to cast Fuchs into the shade. He agreed that Hillary would be offered a 'responsible part' but made clear that there would only be 'one command'.[71]

While the Americans planned to use their McMurdo base as a supply depot for their IGY bases, New Zealand's small base would be dwarfed by the much greater American presence, and would be reliant on the Americans for transport to and from the continent.[72] Yet New Zealand somehow believed that this level of activity would secure its claim to the Ross Dependency. Even that was in doubt when the Ross Sea Committee failed to raise more than one-fifth of the £100,000 that the government had hoped it would. The public clearly wanted the government to pay for what they regarded as a national expedition.

To make up the shortfall, the government finally decided in April 1956 to purchase a ship and an aircraft for the expedition, and to provide radio equipment for the base. The ship was Britain's *John Biscoe*, which had just been replaced by a new ship of the same name. The old ship was transferred to the New Zealand Navy and renamed as the HMNZS *Endeavour*. The purchase of the ship was belated recognition that only a permanent base would suffice as the American grip on the Ross Dependency grew stronger. The United States would have not only the massive McMurdo base but also a smaller base at Point Hallett on Cape Adare, which would provide weather information. At America's suggestion, New Zealand agreed to contribute three staff to complement the nine Americans at Cape Adare. Again, New Zealand imagined that this would be sufficient to uphold its sovereignty in the area.[73]

New Zealand regarded its new-found relationship with the United States – by which the United States used New Zealand as a take-off point for its ships and aircraft and New Zealand used those same transport facilities to shift its people around the Ross Dependency – as being of 'mutual interest'. Macdonald told his colleagues that cooperation with the Americans would allow New Zealand to 'strengthen our claim to the Ross Dependency', while having 'a close and powerful ally in that part of the Antarctic'.[74] Meanwhile, New Zealand asserted its sovereignty by appointing Hillary as a magistrate and postmaster, and the captain of the *Endeavour* as deputy administrator, magistrate and justice of the peace.

The government decided that it was 'unnecessarily provocative' to also have a postmaster at Point Hallett. However, the administrator of the Ross Dependency, Captain Harold Ruegg, made a token visit to McMurdo in January 1957, where he oversaw the opening of a post office at the Ross Island base. Four Ross Dependency stamps were issued to show the world that New Zealand really was in possession of the territory; the postmaster-general was told that the purpose was to 'emphasize the sovereignty aspect'. Accordingly, the stamps depicted Ross's ship, the *Erebus*, and a laurel-wreathed Shackleton and Scott against a map of the Ross Dependency. There was also another map of the dependency – with its boundary extending all the way north to encompass New Zealand, although the distance was foreshortened – and a stamp of Queen Elizabeth, which together were to show that the Ross Dependency was British Commonwealth territory.[75]

The issuing of the stamps was just part of a flurry of activity by the seven existing Antarctic claimants in the years prior to the IGY, as they sought to shore up their separate territorial claims. Those years also saw the United States and Russia engage in similar activities in order to reinforce what they regarded as their rights in the Antarctic. Despite the increase in activity, these nations were still overshadowed in numbers by the whalers, who continued to return in their hundreds to reap their grisly harvest from the surrounding waters. By the summer of 1956–57, there were twenty factory ships and 225 whale-catchers in Antarctic waters.[76]

But the industry would soon enter a state of steep decline. The old days of the Antarctic, when it was dominated by explorers and whalers, were ending. The onset of the IGY in 1957 would see expeditions from twelve nations make a cooperative effort to establish scientific bases around the coast and across the continent's interior. Science was in the ascendant, and cooperation rather than competition was the new watchword on the ice.

CHAPTER 20

'Never again will Antarctica be deserted'

1957–1960

On 11 March 1957, Admiral Richard Byrd breathed his last. After repeatedly risking his life on perilous expeditions to the poles, the sixty-eight-year-old explorer died in his sleep in the bedroom of his Boston home. Byrd's work in the Antarctic was finished.

His last visit was in the summer of 1955–56, when he had sailed south as the notional leader of the American preparations for the IGY. Although Admiral George Dufek had occupied the larger cabin on the massive icebreaker USS *Glacier*, it was Byrd whom the newsreel cameramen wanted to film as he arrived at Little America V. His presence had helped to give legitimacy to the American effort, and to ensure public and congressional support for its considerable budget. Aged and ailing, Byrd boarded an aircraft on the ice runway in January 1956 for what would be his last, symbolic flight over the South Pole. Because of his frailty, a naval doctor accompanied him everywhere, with strict instructions not to let the old explorer die on his last expedition.

Once back in the United States, Byrd's final achievements were to get his young acolyte Paul Siple appointed as leader of the South Pole base, which Byrd had suggested be called the 'Amundsen-Scott Station'. He also ensured that his rival Finn Ronne was excluded from Antarctic decision-making. With his life ebbing away, Byrd's well-connected friends arranged for him to be awarded the Medal of Freedom, which he received in full dress uniform in the upstairs study of his home.[1] Two weeks later, the long-time ringmaster of America's Antarctic effort was dead. But the circus continued regardless.

From the mid-1950s, there was a rush of expeditions to the Antarctic, as nations sought to secure a place at the territorial carve-up before other IGY participants began arriving. The competition was most intense on the Antarctic Peninsula and its nearby island chains, where Britain, Argentina and Chile had now a combined total of twenty-one bases, while Australia and France beefed up their efforts in the Australian Sector to pre-empt any new arrivals.

They were too late. Like that of the British in the 1920s, the territorial ambitions of the United States and Russia were continental in extent, and the Cold War rivals would devote whatever resources were necessary to achieve them. Unlike the British, though, they did not want to assert sovereignty over the continent, which they knew would unleash howls of opposition from friends and foes alike. They were content to achieve their ambitions by other means.

American officials had largely abandoned the idea of claiming particular territory, in favour of securing free rein to explore and exploit the entire continent without having any recognised legal title. They would begin by establishing three strategically located bases. With Byrd's old site at the Bay of Whales now unsuitable for ships, the successor to his four Little America settlements was located some kilometres away at Kainan Bay, on the eastern edge of the Ross Sea. Little America V would not be the largest base, which was established instead on Ross Island in McMurdo Sound, as a logistical centre from which to service the American bases across the continent. The third of the preparatory bases would be at the South Pole itself.

In the American view, the key to controlling the continent was the South Pole. Whoever occupied it might claim to be in implicit possession of all Antarctica. As explorers from Shackleton to Byrd had shown, the pole had a symbolic significance in the public mind that no other place on the continent could match. And dangerous journeys by dog sledge or motorised transport were no longer needed to get there. Aircraft had proved capable of lifting huge amounts of material during the Berlin blockade, and the recent creation of a massive American airbase in Greenland had shown how they could operate from snow runways. The Antarctic icecap proved similarly suitable, with jet packs added for take-off in the rarefied atmosphere.

It was just such an aircraft that was used by Admiral Dufek when he flew to the South Pole in a modified DC-3 on 31 October 1956. The first thing he did upon landing in the bitterly cold conditions was to create a hole in the ice for a bamboo flagpole. Whereas Byrd had dropped the flags of UN members onto the ice when he flew over the South Pole during Operation Highjump in February 1947,

Dufek raised only the Stars and Stripes during the few minutes that his aircraft spent on the ice, its engines roaring to ward off the cold. The admiral lingered just long enough to insert into the flagpole a letter 'verifying that he was there', while radar deflectors were set up as a guide for the many planes that would come after him to establish a base for eighteen scientists and navy personnel, led by Siple.[2]

It took nearly a year of preparation before Dufek could make his flight. With bases at McMurdo Sound, Little America V and now the South Pole, America would go on to establish another four around the continent. One was at Gould Bay on the Weddell Sea, where Finn Ronne was finally able to achieve his desire of leading a last expedition to the Antarctic. Due to Byrd's opposition, it seemed that Ronne would have to lead a private expedition using a Norwegian whaling ship offered by Lars Christensen. However, the Defense Department brokered a compromise between Byrd and Ronne that allowed Ronne to lead an official American expedition under the aegis of the IGY.

In a meeting with General Graves Erskine and Deputy Defense Secretary Robert Anderson in May 1955, Ronne stressed the importance of beating the British and Argentinians into Gould Bay. As a former marine general, Erskine did not see the urgency, noting that if we 'wanted a permanent foothold in the Antarctic, we would probably claim it anywhere', regardless of objections from other nations. He suggested Ronne abandon his plan to accept Christensen's help and instead use a US navy ship, with Ronne going back on active service. In the event, the British and Argentinians did establish their bases on the Weddell Sea before Ronne arrived on a US icebreaker in January 1957 to establish Ellsworth Base on the Gould Bay ice shelf.[3]

The base completed the pattern of American sites across the continent. Combined with the size of the American effort and its $250-million budget, this made the United States the pre-eminent Antarctic power. Any doubts that Americans may have harboured about their rights in the Antarctic were assuaged by news stories that linked the American exploration and settlement to their earlier westward expansion across North America. The *New York Times* correspondent Walter Sullivan made the most explicit historical connections, which would only help to engender a sense of American possession. In a report about an eleven-man tractor-driven expedition to establish Byrd station in Marie Byrd Land, he wrote of the 'new type of pioneer', who 'moves across the great white prairies of this continent'. They were the 'modern equivalent of a covered wagon train', wrote Sullivan, 'constantly on guard against sudden danger – not from Indians, but from the death traps called crevasses'.

One of these crevasses had swallowed a tractor, killing its unsuspecting driver, Max Kiel, making him a casualty in the battle for Antarctica. Dufek told a memorial service that Kiel 'gave his life for science'. In this battle, the Americans were the conquerors and the penguins were sometimes depicted as the vanquished enemy. In January 1957, Sullivan described how 'a long see-saw struggle' led to sailors seizing 'a four-acre beachhead at Cape Hallett from an army of 150,000 penguins'. By January 1959, seventeen Americans had lost their lives during the ongoing battle to master the continent. Dufek consoled himself with the thought that 'it is always [thus] in the opening of a new frontier'.[4]

Not to be outdone by the Americans, the Russians established a massive logistics base of their own on the coast of the Australian Antarctic Territory, from which other bases could be established by air and by land. To counter in the public mind the American base at the South Pole, the Russians placed one of their inland bases at the so-called 'Pole of Inaccessibility'. This was the point on the continent that was furthest from any coastline, and therefore the location of what might be called the centre of the continent. Yet the remorseless movement of the ice sheet ensured that the Russian base began to move inexorably from its starting point as soon as it was established, as had happened to the American base at the South Pole. While the Russians could aspire to match the Americans in the scale of their scientific and logistical effort, the New Zealand base on Ross Island, with its handful of personnel, could never hope to equal the hive of activity at the nearby McMurdo base. There, hundreds of Americans were living and working in a blizzard-prone pastiche of a small American town, complete with a cinema and chapel.

New Zealand had set up its small base on Ross Island in a vain attempt to retrieve the territorial title that they had long ago lost to the Americans. As the New Zealanders discovered, it was too little, too late. Although the United States required New Zealand's cooperation to supply its bases by way of Christchurch, it would never acknowledge New Zealand's sovereignty over the Ross Dependency. This was brought home to New Zealand officials when Dufek and Gould casually mentioned, when visiting Wellington, the possibility of constructing an airstrip on land at Marble Point, across from the McMurdo base, rather than rely on the landing strip that had been bulldozed on the bay ice. There was no question of requesting permission from New Zealand to take over that strategic site, which had the potential to be developed into a major airfield.

The New Zealand officials were flummoxed, since the expensive development suggested the Americans were intending to remain permanently in the western part of the Ross Dependency. New Zealand was in a bind. A protest might prompt the United States to protect its McMurdo investment by annexing the area. But if New Zealand failed to object, it would weaken its title to the whole dependency.[5] Not knowing what to do, New Zealand did nothing, waiting to see whether the Americans would proceed with their plans.

In the meantime, an American aircraft made the first commercial flight to Antarctica. The four-engine propeller-driven Pan American Stratocruiser was chartered by the US Navy to take technicians and men of the constructions corps from San Francisco. After calling at Christchurch, it touched down in a flurry of snow on the ice runway at McMurdo on 15 October 1957. The sight of two female flight attendants stepping onto the ice where Scott and Shackleton had struggled for their lives was a truly modern moment. They were promptly taken on a dog-sledge race to the McMurdo mess hall, where they enjoyed a cup of coffee with men who had been starved of female company.

The flight proved the potential of Antarctica for tourism, once appropriate facilities were put in place. Indeed, a few weeks later, a group of six American congressmen, accompanied by Gould, landed at McMurdo and lauded Antarctica's potential for tourism, predicting that within five years the arrival of commercial jet aircraft would make McMurdo 'a winter sports center similar to Norway and Switzerland'. On a flight to Little America V, Dufek and Gould made sure the congressmen looked down upon Marble Point, where an ice-free airport could be developed for such thrill-seeking tourists. Gould had urged Dufek to impress them with the strategic importance of 'Marble Point as the only place yet known where an airstrip could be built'. Gould would later praise Dufek for doing 'a superb job of indoctrinating the Congressmen'. However, before any of these developments could happen, the congressmen conceded to journalists, 'questions of political sovereignty would have to be resolved'.[6]

The Pan American flight and its possible implications posed difficult legal and political problems for New Zealand. With the flight having left from Christchurch for the Ross Dependency, the token administrator of the dependency, Captain Harold Ruegg, warned Wellington that it 'raised problems of jurisdiction which need careful investigation'. New Zealand raised no objections to American military flights, but a commercial flight was a different matter, wrote Ruegg. In fact, the New Zealand government had already patched up the problem by informing Washington that it would 'regard the aircraft as being to all intents and purposes a military aircraft'.[7] That awkward solution provided a way around the immediate imbroglio.

New Zealand was ambivalent about the issue. While it would infringe their sovereignty, an American tourist development at McMurdo would probably use Christchurch as a transit point, with international tourists likely to spend money touring New Zealand as well. Meanwhile, a New Zealand cabinet minister flew over America's South Pole base in a US Army Globemaster, which dropped supplies of fuel and food to the scientists below. The politician took the opportunity to add something to the blossoming array of parachuted stores, dropping what he believed would be 'the first N.Z. flag at the South Pole'.[8] In fact, a New Zealand flag had been among the UN member flags that Byrd had dropped in February 1947. The latest flag was a futile attempt to assert a sovereignty that, in practice, no longer existed.

Australia faced an equally serious challenge to its sovereignty, with three Russian bases and one American base scheduled for establishment in its territory for the IGY. The prospect of the Russian arrival, in particular, had prompted the Australian government to expand its own presence on the continent. It had taken nearly a decade to get Mawson Base established in 1954. It was located in the western part of the Australian territory, at about 63° E, to ward off the Norwegians, who had a stronger claim to possession of that region. Australia's Antarctic chief Phillip Law later recalled how the 'spirit of the day' was 'all concerned with planting flags and declaring sovereignty over new areas and beating the Russians and Americans and others to these things'.[9] He had convinced the government to establish Mawson, on the understanding it was just for the duration of the IGY. But the imminent arrival of the Russians ensured that Mawson would remain much longer on territory that Australia regarded as its own, but that the United States persisted in calling 'Wilkes Land'.

As the Russian ships approached the Antarctic coast in January 1956, looking for a suitable site for their main base, the Australians expanded their own presence by establishing a base on the coast near the Vestfold Hills, at about 78° E. Dufek had sent the *Glacier* on a survey of the same coastline, during which several stops were made to allow the American flag to be hoisted onshore. The Americans landed on a group of rocky islets on 18 March 1956, only to find that the Russians had preceded them by nine days and left a note recording their visit. The Russians, in turn, had been preceded by Law nearly two months before, with Law leaving a note of his own, which declared, to whomsoever should read it, 'Welcome to Australian Antarctic Territory! The first landing in this place was made from the ship *Kista Dan*.'[10] In reinforcing Australia's claim to the territory, Law was aware that precedence could be crucial if the matter was ever referred to an international court.

The Russians finally settled on a site on the coast at about 93° E and began unloading men and material. The base was named 'Mirny', to commemorate the name of Bellingshausen's ship and thereby connect the present Soviet activity with the discoveries of the old Russian empire. In Russian, *mirny* meant 'peaceful', which fitted well with current Soviet foreign policy. The coast on which Mirny was located was named by the Russians as 'Pravda Coast', which means 'truth', while the main street of the 'settlement' was named after Lenin. It had a line of houses, along with a hospital, a laundry, a bathhouse, a canteen and even a pigsty.

The Russians were still unloading their ships when Law arrived in the *Kista Dan* on 30 January 1956. He met with the Russian scientific leader, Mikhail Somov, and presented him with a recently published map of the Australian Sector. It was done ostensibly in a spirit of cooperation but with the unspoken intention of making clear to Somov that he was on territory claimed by Australia and that its principal geographic features had already been named. Later, when the main Russian expedition ship called at Adelaide on its way back to Russia, Law flew from Melbourne to join with Mawson in presenting its personnel with the reports of Mawson's 1929–31 voyages that had been published to date, and to give a lecture to the Russians on the work of the various Australian expeditions from 1911 onwards. Of course, none of this political theatre deflected the Soviet Union from exploring the Australian Sector, surveying its coastline and naming its features. Law privately conceded that such work provided Russia with 'a strong claim to certain areas of territory', should they ever wish to exercise it.[11]

The United States was also trying to limit the rights that the Russians might be able to assert. Byrd was in the Antarctic when the Russians arrived to set up Mirny. In a carefully calculated move of his own, he sent a message of welcome to Somov, offering American cooperation. At the same time, Byrd informed him that American aircraft had flown in the vicinity of the two sites where the Russians planned to establish their inland bases and had found them suitable. Byrd wanted to show the Russians that the Americans had seen the sites first, which might 'some day play a role in the complex problem of deciding claims to the Antarctic'.

In fact, the routes of the American flights suggested they were hundreds of kilometres away from the prospective Russian bases. Byrd had planned to fly over the Pole of Inaccessibility to pre-empt the Russians but had been forced by bad weather to fly over the South Pole instead. The flights were all part of a rushed photo-reconnaissance of as much of the continent as the Americans could manage, before the Russians arrived with their own aerial mapping plans. Such was the urgency that Dufek ordered the American aircraft to keep flying from the ice runway at McMurdo despite signs of melting; there was a possibility that the runway, and any aircraft on it, might simply float off into the Ross Sea.[12]

Both Russia and America wanted to have free rein over the entire continent, and both regarded their own explorers as the discoverers of Antarctica. Both took symbolic possession of the continent by establishing bases – at the South Pole and the Pole of Inaccessibility respectively. While the Americans claimed to have preceded the Russians to their inland bases, the Russians did likewise with the Wilkes Base, near the Windmill Islands at about 111° E, some 800 kilometres from Mirny. When three American naval ships arrived to build the base in January 1957, they discovered a cairn left the previous November by Russian explorers from Mirny. The Russians had landed there by aircraft to explore and map the surrounding area; they left a vodka bottle with a message claiming to have 'discovered' the region. Determined not to be outdone, the Americans added a note to the bottle, which pointed out that the bay had been discovered by American fliers during Operation Highjump in 1947, and that American surveyors had landed there the following year to establish ground control points. A copy of the resulting map, which had been published just prior to the arrival of the Russians, was added to the vodka bottle, which was duly returned to the cairn.[13] And so the circus continued into the IGY, which was meant to be marked by scientific cooperation rather than territorial rivalry.

The rush of base-building was matched by a flood of philatelic issues, as nations continued to use stamps to assert their sovereignty. Many also established post offices at their new bases to demonstrate their administration of the area. Such was the public interest that the US Navy took hundreds of thousands of philatelic covers to Antarctica in late 1955, only to find that the sailors manning the several post offices could not process the four tons of mail before the ships left for home. The letters remained in the Antarctic over winter, with sailors processing them as time allowed.[14]

Most Antarctic stamps were shameless examples of political propaganda, whether it was a Norwegian stamp displaying a map of Antarctica with Queen Maud Land prominently marked, or New Zealand stamps showing a map of the Ross Dependency and the British explorers whose work underpinned New Zealand sovereignty. Others were more subtle, such as the French stamp in 1956 that showed the newly named '*Terres Australes et Antarctiques Françaises*' and their abundant penguins and sea elephants. It combined an assertion of French sovereignty with the implicit suggestion that its control would conserve the otherwise threatened wildlife.[15]

Australian External Affairs minister Richard Casey took a close interest in such assertions of sovereignty. In June 1956, he photographed the relevant portion of the globe so that a map could be drawn showing the relationship between Australia and its Antarctic territory. Originally done to accompany a newspaper article, Casey had the map reduced in size for use on a stamp. The space between Australia and Antarctica was foreshortened to give a misleading impression of the distance between the two continents. Casey thought it 'would have some educational value within Australia – and also overseas'. When concerns were raised about the map's suitability as a stamp, Casey stressed its 'considerable political advantage', noting that there 'is going to be a good deal of politics connected with the Antarctic in the next few years – and we rather badly need some publicity of the sort that such a stamp would provide'.

The pressure worked. A stamp was designed to Casey's specifications, including both a map and a scene showing the Australian flag being flown by Law in the Vestfold Hills in 1954. The stamps were issued in early 1957 for overseas airmail letters, since it was 'more politically valuable . . . to have this carried on letters going to other countries'. Casey later confided to a colleague that it had all been done 'for what might be called propaganda purposes'. Cheaper versions of the stamp would later be issued for circulation within Australia.[16]

Amid the continuing uncertainty about the Soviet presence, and the territorial implications of the IGY activity, Law pushed for greater Australian activity. He predicted that there could be a quick carve-up of the continent in the wake of the IGY, with the United States making 'extensive territorial claims which will cut right across the sector principle'. This could provoke the Soviet Union into calling for the continent to come under the control of the United Nations. Law suggested that Australia's best hope lay with the United States making a territorial claim, followed by a process of 'horse-trading' with Australia, during which Australia could concede 'vast spaces which appear as important concessions to our opponents but which have little real value'. In such a situation, Australia needed to know which parts were most valuable to retain. For this, more research needed to be quickly done.[17]

The men at Mawson Base had done almost all they could to explore the immediate area. They had just one small Beaver plane that had gone to the limit of its 640-kilometre range from the base. Any further exploration would require a larger aircraft and additional ground transport. But Casey preferred to increase activity at the small Davis Base near the Vestfold Hills, and considered establishing another base even further east, to the immediate south of Australia, from where a Russian submarine or missile base might otherwise threaten Australia. Spreading the Australian presence further along the coastline would also be the best means of reinforcing Australian sovereignty over the whole territory.[18]

Despite Casey's view, Law continued to call for an expansion of activity at Mawson, along with the possible establishment of another base in Oates Land, at the eastern extremity of the Australian territory, thousands of kilometres from Mawson. This area, argued Law, was 'one of the few remaining parts of Australian Antarctic Territory about which we have no information'. Along with Mawson, he had been scanning Norwegian and American aerial photographs to find the most suitable sites for bases, so that Australia could secure them before its rivals did. He was particularly interested in rocky outcrops near safe harbours, so as to avoid the problems of building a base amidst accumulating snow on shifting ice.

Law thought he had discerned a suitable site in Oates Land, but it would require a second ship to supply it, which would have serious budgetary implications. That, in turn, would limit what might be done on land. An economical solution was possible if the United States, once the IGY had ended, handed over its small base in the Windmill Islands, which was almost directly south of Perth. If the United States offered it to Australia, Casey was advised by his officials, Australia should accept it. The officials argued that it was better for 'political reasons' to have 'several small stations' strung along the coastline of Australia's territory.[19] Yet it would take more than several bases to ensure Australia's possession.

Securing the effective possession of a place by occupation was only part of the process. Law was concerned that Australia was not doing enough to convince the world that it was in rightful possession of the territory. He complained to a friend in May 1957 that 'no-one on the official side seems very interested in really publicizing our work', although he took some solace from the issue of the Antarctic stamps and the forthcoming production of a book 'which should help to inform other countries of our efforts'. It was not sufficient. Law tried to get America's *Polar Record* to give greater coverage to Australian activities, urging the Department of External Affairs to take additional steps to 'more effectively demonstrate that we consider our Antarctic possessions an integral part of Australia'. Among other things, he wanted more stamps, a booklet for schools, greater detail about the territory in the *Commonwealth Year Book*, the commissioning of an official history, the appointment of an administrator for the territory and the issuing of regulations for mining licenses in the Antarctic.[20] Law was frustrated further when the navy refused to deploy the aircraft carrier HMAS *Melbourne* for a summer of photographic flights, so that Australia could claim to know its territory better than others.[21] Knowing a place was a necessary part of being recognised as its rightful possessor.

The IGY provided an ideal opportunity for nations to have their maps and names accepted by the many scientific parties heading to the Antarctic. The American Geographical Society had provided maps of the Antarctic for Byrd's first expedition in 1928. Now the society's cartographer, William Briesemeister, revised the outdated map for the use of IGY expeditions. All those Anglo-American discussions between Brian Roberts and Harold Saunders proved their worth, as Briesemeister was able to refer to the resulting 1953 British gazetteer of names and the publications of the US Board on Geographic Names. Before actually placing particular names on the map, Briesemeister had them checked again by the US board, with the American recommendations being generally 'adopted through-out'.[22] The board then published its own gazetteer of Antarctic names in 1956, which listed every placename in Antarctica, noting who discovered and named it and whether any other names had been used.[23] Briesemeister's revised map was published in 1958. He incorporated the most recent discoveries and names of the Argentinians and Australians so that his would be the most up-to-date map available for IGY parties.[24] It might then become the standard map, with the approved American names being accepted by other nations.

Australia had other ideas. It had aspired to have its 1939 map become the standard map and wanted to update it with the latest discoveries and names. However, the arrival of the Russians and the rising influence of scientists during the IGY complicated matters. Scientists from ten of the twelve IGY nations had met in The Hague in February 1958 under the auspices of the International Council of Scientific Unions, where they agreed to establish a Special Committee on Antarctic Research – later renamed as the Scientific Committee on Antarctic Research (SCAR) – which would propose and coordinate scientific research in the Antarctic. Later that year, a SCAR conference in Moscow heard a Russian delegate announce that the Soviet Union was planning to map the entire continent. When the Australian delegate asked for the plan to be deferred, the Russians insisted that they would map one-third of the continent over the next few years, assuring the meeting that it was a 'purely scientific question and no attempt would be made to mark boundaries on the map'. Australia and other claimant nations were not reassured.[25]

While SCAR was proposing to coordinate mapping in the Antarctic, Australia was determined to use maps and naming to support its territorial claim. In December 1958, Law confided to a meeting of the Executive Planning Committee, chaired by Casey, that he had 'warned both U.K. and U.S. authorities . . . of the problems and difficulties that would arise if SCAR entered into mapping'. Casey agreed, noting that 'if other countries were permitted to do mapping in our Territory we gave them a great advantage'. He was particularly concerned about the Russians producing a superior map of Australia's territory. It was beyond Australia's resources to compete, and Casey welcomed any cooperation from the Americans so that Australia could produce a map just of 'the coastline and a certain distance inland from it'.

His more pugnacious colleague William Wentworth wanted the mapping to encompass the expanse of the polar icecap as well, noting that 'vast open spaces' looked 'impressive' when laid out on a map. But Australian cartographer Bruce Lambert advised that even the mapping of the coastline and immediate hinterland would take seven to ten years to complete. As a possible solution to Australia's conundrum, Wentworth suggested that it could establish an Antarctic Mapping Centre as an international service, thereby circumventing both the SCAR and the Russian initiatives.[26]

If there was going to be an international map of Antarctica, Casey wanted it to have all the Australian names that Mawson had bestowed during his expeditions. Otherwise, the map would be dominated by the discoveries and names of the contemporaneous Norwegians and the more recent American and Russian explorers. Casey was already concerned about a recent American map that was 'most ungenerous' about Australian discoveries. Mawson agreed that the American map was 'ingeniously contrived . . . to greatly exaggerate the U.S.A.'s contribution', which had only involved 'cursory inspections from the air of the vast interior'.[27]

In September 1958, Law asked Mawson for the photos and charts from his 1929 voyage so that Law could align features with the names that Mawson had given them. The request came too late. The seventy-six-year-old Mawson died of a stroke on 14 October 1958, leaving many of the results from his voyages unpublished and his papers in a state of some confusion. His death sparked a rush by Casey and Law to have the final volumes published, particularly the geographical volume.[28] As Law explained after lunching with Mawson's widow, Australia's territorial claim was based largely on Mawson's voyages, which made it 'most important' that the maps 'should be accurately drawn as soon as possible'. Casey reinforced the urgency, telling Lady Mawson that the Russians had been 'producing their own maps and putting their own names to features which they claim to have discovered'. Australia needed to provide 'incontrovertible evidence of Australian prior discovery if we are fully to protect our sovereignty'.[29]

Australian cartographers also had to clarify what Mawson had seen and named so that the current crop of Australian explorers would not overlay his discoveries with their own. There would be no easy resolution. The records of his voyages were less than ideal, and there continued to be dithering among Australian officials and politicians. It was not helped by Law looking elsewhere for a job, as he applied unsuccessfully to be vice-chancellor at different universities. He was unsure whether there would be much future for his Antarctic division and he was 'extremely discouraged' by his long-running battle to have his scientific responsibilities, and those of his division, recognised by the bureaucrats in Canberra.[30]

By April 1959, Australia's Executive Planning Committee met in Melbourne to hear Casey, Lambert and the distracted Law discuss the vexed question of mapping. Lambert urged that any mapping 'must be done in 1959 and 1960', with Casey agreeing that 'politically, the best efforts possible would have to be made in mapping'. That would require more effort than Australia was capable of mounting. By leaving the inland icecap to the Russians, Australia was able to concentrate on small-scale mapping of coastal areas. However, surveyors mapping the crevasse-ridden coast would have to be flown in to different areas with dogs and sledges.[31]

Meanwhile, Australia faced opposition to the idea of an International Antarctic Mapping Centre being established in Canberra. Neither Britain nor the United States wanted an international centre making maps that might endanger their own discoveries and names. The most they would concede was that Australia could provide a secretariat for the SCAR working group on cartography, which was meant to establish standards and exchange information between the Antarctic Mapping Centres in the various SCAR countries. It would be part of the secretariat's task to maintain a map of the Antarctic on a scale of 1:10,000,000, which could include only a handful of names. The Australian Antarctic Mapping Centre and the associated secretariat would have an initial staff of just three, with Casey hoping vainly that it might one day develop into the desired international centre.[32]

Australia was far from alone in its rush to map and name as much of its territory as it could. At the urging of Brian Roberts, Britain had embarked on a two-year aerial survey of the Falkland Islands Dependencies. It was designed to produce the most accurate and comprehensive map of the territory claimed by Britain, Argentina and Chile, the control of which was also desired by the United States.

Apart from mapping, creating more bases, issuing more stamps and supporting an enhanced scientific program, Britain was going to capture the attention of the world with an expedition that combined scientific endeavour with the first dramatic crossing of the continent. Going by way of the South Pole, it would be reminiscent of the feats of Scott and Shackleton, and it would provide an economical way for Britain to compete with the United States and the Soviet Union on the Antarctic stage.

The plan involved establishing a base at Vahsel Bay on the Weddell Sea in late 1955, an advance base about 440 kilometres inland, and another base on Ross Island in January 1957. It was planned that Fuchs would take seven assorted motorised vehicles, led by two dog teams, across the continent, while Hillary would strike out from New Zealand's Ross Island base to establish depots along a route towards the South Pole. Hillary was meant to stop short of the South Pole, in order to allow Fuchs to have the glory of being the first person since Scott to have reached the South Pole over land. However, the plan had not taken Hillary's ambition into account, or the problems that Fuchs would encounter with his tracked vehicles.

After leaving his Vahsel Bay base in October 1957, Fuchs was forced to abandon three of his vehicles as he encountered a succession of crevasses and ice ridges. Setting off from Ross Island, Hillary had an easier time laying his depots on the polar plateau, the last of which was about 800 kilometres from the pole. Rather than waiting for Fuchs, Hillary kept going, expecting that they would meet before he reached the pole.

Looking on from afar, the press began to depict the expedition as a race 'to the bottom of the world'. London's *Daily Mail* added to the frenzy by flying one of its reporters to the South Pole to await Fuchs' arrival. The expedition committee in London deplored the sensationalism, reminding the world that it was 'undertaking a serious scientific programme', while the New Zealand committee declared that there was 'no question of a race for the Pole'. But the conqueror of Everest was not going to be denied a second triumph. With the world watching, Hillary pushed all the way to the pole, reaching it on 4 January 1958.[33] Once again, a British explorer had been trumped in a race to the South Pole.

Concerned by the delays to Fuchs' party, Hillary then suggested to the organising committee that Fuchs be flown out when he reached the pole; he could return the following year to complete the journey and its program of seismic readings. However, Fuchs, who finally reached the pole on 19 January, insisted on persevering all the way to the Ross Sea. He was determined to complete Shackleton's ill-fated plan to cross the continent, and the London committee gave him its full support. After all, the whole point of the expedition was for Britain to counter the weight of America's Antarctic effort with an expedition that captured world attention and emphasised the long history of British involvement with the continent.

The leaking to the press of the cables from Hillary and Fuchs certainly grabbed public attention, while Fuchs' eventual arrival at Ross Island – after a ninety-nine-day journey – was more of an anticlimax. Yet he and the rest of the British team were still given a hero's welcome when they arrived back in London. For a relatively small amount of money, the British and New Zealanders had reinforced their tenuous territorial claims with a feat that harkened back to past glories.[34] But it was hardly sufficient to secure their title to territories that were being beset by expeditions from so many other countries.

It was the imminent arrival of these expeditions, and the fear of Russian bases remaining in Antarctica after the conclusion of the IGY, that prompted the United States and the seven claimant nations to put proposals for internationalisation back onto the diplomatic table. In February 1956, the staunchly anti-communist Secretary of State John Foster Dulles met in Washington with ambassadors from Britain, Australia, New Zealand and South Africa to discuss ways of 'countering Soviet penetration' of the Antarctic. While conceding that the United States had potential territorial conflicts with the four Commonwealth countries, Dulles agreed on the need 'to keep the Antarctic in friendly hands.' He was confident that any differences between them should 'not prevent . . . the reaching of a common position in regard to the Soviet'.[35]

That optimistic view soon dissipated when the Soviets arrived and established Mirny in 1955. By June 1956, an official of the

Australian Department of External Affairs conceded that it was 'too late now to exclude the Soviet Union completely from the Antarctic' and that Moscow might very well assert territorial claims based upon its past discoveries and 'the very substantial scientific work it is now doing'. It was more important to prevent any future arrivals from making claims, and for Australia to support a settlement that would give part of the continent 'to every one of the present claimants, including the Soviet Union'.[36]

With Russian bases on Australian territory, and with the threat of India taking the Antarctic question to the United Nations General Assembly, Australia sought to develop a scheme for an international regime that would open the Antarctic to other nations for scientific purposes while preserving Australia's sovereignty. Australian diplomats recommended that international recognition of Australian sovereignty should be extracted as the 'price' of agreeing to a system of international control for Antarctica. Giving other nations 'rights of exploration, scientific research and commercial exploitation' and demilitarising the continent could provide sufficient inducement for them to agree to such a regime. The changing reality on the ice had finally forced some Australian officials to accept the idea of internationalisation, albeit as the least worst option. One even suggested that Australia could relinquish its sovereignty altogether if there was 'a system of international control which would thereby ensure our security, rights of scientific research and commercial exploitation'.[37] However, the Australian government still saw the Russian presence as a strategic threat.

When Casey had talks with State Department officials in November 1956, he warned darkly of his concern that Russian research in the Southern Ocean was gathering information for a submarine base that 'would threaten Australia and command the whole South Pacific and Indian oceans'. In order to thwart such a threat, Casey argued that the United States should make a claim to Marie Byrd Land and engage in 'largely notional' activities, as Australia was doing in its territory. By not making a claim, and by refusing to recognise the Australian claim, the United States was making it easier for Russia to also refuse to recognise the Australian claim, which thereby allowed its bases to remain in the Australian territory after the end of the IGY. However, the Americans did not credit the Australian fears, and they were not going to limit their continental aspirations for the sake of assuaging them.[38]

Ever since the war, Australia had been forthright about its sovereignty and adamantly opposed to internationalisation. Yet it had been weak on the implementation of practical measures to reinforce its sovereignty. By mid-1957, Australia was being forced to adjust its territorial ambitions to the physical realities on the ground. When Casey went to Britain and the United States in July, he found that the British, New Zealanders and Americans were all moving toward 'some form of international arrangement' that would attempt to exclude the Russians. According to an Australian diplomat, James Plimsoll, Australia also had to move in that direction if it wanted to influence the outcome of the present developments.

Plimsoll had suggested as early as 1953 that Australia should support an international authority in the Antarctic that would include the Soviet Union, provided that the Russians agreed to demilitarise their bases and allow them to be inspected. Now he urged the importance of reaching agreement before minerals were discovered and countries such as China, Japan and India made Antarctic claims of their own. His advice was supported by a major reassessment of Australian policy by the Department of External Affairs, which cautiously suggested to Casey that the government consider 'some international regime under which, preferably with our sovereignty preserved, the Antarctic could be regarded by international consent as a demilitarized zone and made subject to a system of international inspection'. Most importantly, it argued that the 'retention of sovereignty . . . is not essential' for the protection of Australia's 'political and strategic interests'.[39]

Casey refused to accept the departmental advice. Nearly thirty years of his official and political life had been spent supporting the exploration and claiming of the Australian Antarctic Territory, and the former First World War officer was loath to signal a retreat. But a decision could not be deferred. British Prime Minister Harold Macmillan and Defence Secretary Lord Carrington were due to meet with Australian ministers in Canberra, and the Antarctic was high on the agenda.[40]

The confusion that beset the Australian and British governments was patently clear when Macmillan and Menzies met in Canberra on 31 January 1958. While Australia was anxious to retain its sovereignty and wary of any international regime, Britain was 'looking for the best way of avoiding trouble in the Antarctic'. Macmillan confided to Menzies and Casey that Britain wanted a solution to its 'difficulties' with Argentina and Chile, and acknowledged the 'impossibility of . . . trying to sustain a claim [to the Falkland Islands Dependencies] when no one in the United Kingdom would support the use of force for that purpose'. As for the Russians, Macmillan was resigned to their continuing presence and thought the best solution was to devise 'an arrangement under which they would make less trouble'.

In contrast, Menzies feared that an international agreement would detract from Australian sovereignty and might provoke the Russians to claim part of the Australian territory. Moreover, while demilitarisation was 'a good objective', it was not sufficiently 'precise and real'. Casey tried to impress upon Macmillan the importance of the Antarctic to Australia, both for weather forecasting and for defence. He did not see any hurry for an international regime, nor 'any reason for Australia to give up the attributes of sovereignty'.[41]

There was just as much confusion in Washington. While the State Department wanted the Russians to attend the prospective Antarctic conference, the Defense Department was implacably opposed. With the seven claimant nations also pushing or pulling in different directions, forging an agreement that was acceptable to all parties would be a herculean task. The responsibility for negotiating an Antarctic treaty was given to Paul Daniels, a State Department official who had worked as a diplomat in several Latin American countries before his retirement in 1953. This experience would have recommended him for the job, since Argentina and Chile were likely to prove particularly difficult to convince of the treaty's merits. It was up to Daniels to find a way through the labyrinth of competing interests and fierce rivalries. His first task was to keep congressmen from talking about America's potential territorial claims, so as not to alarm other claimants. He also had to get the State and Defense departments to agree on a common approach to the question of Russia's participation.[42]

Daniels and State Department legal adviser Loftus Becker went to the Pentagon on 30 January 1958 in an attempt to resolve their differences. While the US Navy's judge advocate, Admiral Chester Ward, wanted to force the Russians out of the Antarctic by means of a blockade and not 'worry so much about starting a third World War over Antarctica', Daniels counselled a more cautious approach that recognised the new reality: the Russians were likely to remain and there was 'no practical way to get rid of them'. He argued that the question had now become one of 'how best to control their continued presence', and suggested that 'it might be easier to control the Russians if they were in a regime than if they were out of one'.

As for the question of the United States annexing part of the Antarctic, the Joint Chiefs of Staff wanted America to make a claim 'throughout all parts of Antarctica, including areas presently claimed [by other countries], wherever the US has a basis for a claim', while the State Department preferred to 'reserve rights throughout the entire continent and to propose an international regime in which the legal status quo would be frozen'. The fall-back position of the State Department was to make a claim only in the unclaimed area and to reserve its rights elsewhere, while pushing for an international regime.[43]

Although the meeting at the Pentagon ended without any backdown by the Defense Department, Daniels pressed ahead with his efforts to get support for an Antarctic conference that would be limited to the twelve IGY nations. Such a conference would be attended by the seven claimant nations – Britain, Australia, New Zealand, Argentina, Chile, Norway and France – along with the United States, the Soviet Union, Japan, South Africa and Belgium. Just six days after the meeting with Ward, Daniels sought the endorsement of the Operations Coordinating Board, which had been established by President Eisenhower to implement decisions of the National Security Council. The board met weekly at the State Department and included representatives from the State Department, the Defense Department, the CIA and the United States Information Agency, along with security officials from the White House. Although the Defense representative noted that the Joint Chiefs were 'reluctant to agree to inclusion of the USSR in the administration of Antarctica', the meeting gave its general concurrence to Daniels' proposals. In the game of the Cold War, the board saw the 'great value' that the United States might gain by taking the 'initiative to form an international administration for the benefit of all nations'. Daniels was allowed to continue his talks with Britain, Australia and New Zealand, and to begin 'broad discussions with other nations'.[44]

Convincing various departments in Washington to agree on the future of Antarctica was hard enough. Convincing the claimant nations was even harder. When Daniels attempted to get Britain, Australia and New Zealand to agree on the terms of an approach to the other four claimant powers, the Australian government proved particularly difficult. Whereas the United States wanted to range over all the Antarctic and exploit any resources it discovered, the Australian government wanted to retain the exclusive right to exploit any resources in its territory and opposed the idea of an international authority regulating such development. Australia also wanted to be able to reinforce its territorial title after a treaty had been signed, rather than agree to a 'standstill' condition in the treaty so far as its title was concerned. It was paranoid about the Russian presence in its territory and wanted any treaty to somehow keep the Russians out.

Weeks of discussion, and a constant flow of cables to and from the four nation's respective capitals, were unable to resolve their differences. Although Britain wanted to reach a unified approach, the United States and New Zealand wanted to move on regardless and approach the other claimants. They were concerned about Russia leading an initiative of its own, perhaps by joining with India and other non-aligned nations, to bring the Antarctic under the purview of the United Nations.[45]

In early March 1958, the Australian government came under pressure from the United States and Britain to modify its position so that agreement could be reached. Macmillan convinced Menzies to allow the four-power talks to resume in Washington, with Menzies authorising the Australian delegation 'to consider some modification of positions'. At the same time, Dulles took advantage of a conference in the Philippines to meet with Casey. Over lunch in Manila, he urged agreement on a treaty while there was still time. According to Dulles, the Antarctic was likely to become of 'great significance' during the next half-century, and this could be the 'last opportunity to reach some international agreement before vested interests grew up that would make agreement impossible'.

Dulles was resigned to the presence of the Russians in the Antarctic and seized of the importance of reaching agreement with them. First he had to break down the resistance of the Australians and force them to face the reality of their position. There was no point talking about national sovereignty in the Antarctic, argued Dulles, since both the United States and Russia were in a position to make their own claims of sovereignty in the Australian territory. Indeed, he continued, if an agreement could not be reached, the United States 'would certainly make heavy claims' that would challenge Australia's sovereignty. He also warned Casey that international law did not accept the so-called 'sector principle', which underpinned the Australian claim. Nor did international law necessarily support Australia's claim just because the Australians had been occupying the territory a few years longer than the Americans or Russians.[46]

Although Australia was now on notice that its political position had become untenable, Casey refused to concede the new Antarctic reality. He still argued that any post-IGY arrangement should cover just scientific cooperation and demilitarisation. However, the Australian opposition was being whittled down by pressure from Washington and London, and by the threat to Australian sovereignty that was sure to come from any involvement of the non-aligned nations at the United Nations. Casey confided to the South African high commissioner at the end of March that he 'trembled to think what would happen' if the Antarctic question 'were to be thrown into the ring at the United Nations'.[47]

So Australia reluctantly supported the note that the State Department sent to the eleven other IGY nations in April, which asked for their views on international scientific cooperation, demilitarisation and the freezing of claims as part of a treaty. The talks that had been held in Washington for several months between the State Department and diplomats from Britain, Australia and New Zealand had been kept strictly secret. The world knew only that the three Commonwealth countries had been talking amongst themselves, not that this had been done on the initiative of the United States.[48]

In issuing its invitation, Washington made clear that it 'has had, and . . . continues to have, direct and substantial rights and interests in Antarctica'. Indeed, over the past 150 years, many parts of the Antarctic had been 'discovered, sighted, explored, and claimed on behalf of the United States by nationals of the United States and by expeditions carrying the flag of the United States'. Although substantial rights and claims arose from these activities, the United States believed that 'the interests of mankind would best be served . . . if the countries which have a direct interest in Antarctica were to join together in the conclusion of a treaty'. In other words, the United States was not a Johnny-come-lately. It had as much sovereignty to lose as the seven claimant nations.

When Eisenhower announced the conference on 3 May, it was all about ensuring that the 'vast uninhabited wastes of Antarctica shall be used only for peaceful purposes' and not 'become an object of political conflict'. The American aim, he declared, was to have the continent 'open to all nations to conduct scientific or other peaceful activities there'.[49] They were laudable objectives, although they concealed a darker American ambition to have unfettered access to the entire continent so that any of its hidden resources might be exploited without regard to the rights of the supposedly sovereign powers.

The State Department had done sufficient groundwork to know that ten of the invitations would receive a positive response. But it could not be certain of the Soviet reaction, and there was some confusion in Washington as to what it should do in the event of the Russians refusing to attend.[50] In fact, the Russians readily agreed to attend the conference and to participate in the secret preparatory talks that would decide some of the contentious issues in advance. However, the Russians did not want the talks or the conference to deal with the issue of territorial claims, which Moscow wanted to leave for another conference that additional countries could attend. The Soviet Union wanted the talks to be restricted to questions of procedure rather than of substance, and for the conference to be restricted to the questions of scientific cooperation and peaceful development.

While the Australians continued to be hesitant about the idea of the treaty 'freezing' their territorial claim and demanded 'very definite advantages' in return, the French were opposed altogether to anything that might conceivably infringe on what they regarded as their sovereignty over Adélie Land. Paris was concerned that other nations might 'cause irreversible damage' to the French claim if they were allowed to establish bases in Adélie Land during the operation of the treaty, which would cause a 'new status quo [to be] superimposed at some future date on the former status quo'. Chile also thought it was 'highly dangerous' for other nations to become signatories to the treaty in later years, since that might lead to the new nations becoming a majority and changing the treaty to 'strike out the claims clause'.[51]

The deep divisions between the twelve nations saw the planned date for the conference pushed back from 8 September to 23 October 1958. On 14 August, the Soviet representative again argued for the discussion not to concern the question of territorial claims, and for other nations who might want to do scientific research in the future to be invited to the conference, so they would not feel that the twelve IGY nations were attempting to 'monopolize Antarctic scientific activities'. Presumably, the Soviet Union had in mind its Eastern European allies, which might then operate as a voting bloc at the conference. There was no way that the other participants were going to agree to this. Daniels sought a way through this morass with a discussion paper on 'freezing the legal status quo', which effectively put the question aside so as 'not to complicate problems in the Antarctic but to simplify them'. This caused problems with the Russians, who felt that the 'freezing of claims' would mean the *de jure* recognition of such claims, which it opposed.

As the talks dragged on without resolution, Daniels held secret 'breakout' talks at the Australian and Chilean embassies without the Russian, French, Belgian, Norwegian or South African representatives. The meetings were meant to break down some of the differences and present a more united front at the joint meetings. At one of these meetings, Daniels proposed that they no longer refer to the 'freezing of claims' and talk instead about their intention to 'preserve the existing legal status quo', without actually defining it. While the different talks continued, the Russians proposed to the SCAR meeting in Moscow that the IGY be extended for another year, perhaps so that some of its allies could engage in Antarctic research and earn a seat at the treaty conference table.[52]

The Soviet delegation at the SCAR meeting announced plans to establish two new bases in the Antarctic, and its intention to 'carry out trans-continental explorations'. This was an interesting development, since it indicated that the international scientific community was emerging as an independent Antarctic participant that might rival the role of governments. Confirmation of this was seen when Casey suggested to an Australian SCAR delegate, Professor Keith Bullen, that he should keep in touch with the Department of External Affairs, only to be told very firmly by Bullen that he attended SCAR meetings as a scientist rather than as a representative of the Australian government.[53]

In Washington, Daniels was frustrated at not knowing much of what had occurred at the Moscow SCAR meeting and asked the various diplomats to question their scientists. He was also angry at not knowing whether the IGY would be extended for another year, telling his fellow diplomats that he 'deplored the fact that these matters were being decided by scientists and that very little information seemed to filter through to Governments about what they were doing'. When the SCAR meeting was held in Canberra in 1959, Daniels asked the American Ambassador to 'report whatever information it can properly obtain . . . and any conclusions reached', noting that 'its activities are of great interest to this Government'. The Chileans were similarly suspicious of SCAR and wanted the treaty parties to create an alternative scientific organisation that had representatives from 'all governments with a scientific interest in Antarctica'. The New Zealand government was much more sanguine, suggesting that SCAR might even 'be given certain coordinating functions', which could have the beneficial effect of making 'the Antarctic treaty itself more acceptable' to world opinion.[54]

While the diplomatic whispering continued in the carpeted corridors of Washington, Law predicted that the eventual signing of a treaty would see 'international territorial competition . . . replaced largely by scientific competition', as the United States and the Soviet Union competed to 'demonstrate their respective scientific and technological excellence for purposes of prestige and propaganda'. He suggested that the Russian announcement of two additional bases would force the United States to maintain a high level of scientific activity; it would probably also cause France, Japan, Norway and Belgium to remain in the Antarctic after 1959. 'Never again will Antarctica be deserted,' declared Law.

Indeed, he predicted a time when the Antarctic would see the 'establishment of centres of population in which both men and women lead reasonably normal lives'. Now was the time, Law argued, 'to tackle the long-term projects which will ensure that we are still in the van of Antarctic progress'.[55] In contrast, other officials hoped that the signing of a treaty might allow Australia to cut back its activity, since 'there would be no . . . need to "occupy" the Australian Antarctic Territory in the legal sense'.[56] Similar arguments occurred among officials of other claimant nations; they would not be resolved until the precise nature of the treaty was known.

By October 1958, there was still no treaty conference in sight. At the regular meetings of the twelve nations, the divisions over substantive issues were as deep as ever. Even when they held secret meetings between just some representatives, it still remained difficult to reach agreement. On the issue of allowing non-IGY nations to sign the treaty at a later time, the United States feared that its influence might be diminished by new members, while other nations were concerned that the Americas would simply establish a presence on the continent anyway. On the issue of demilitarisation, Australia argued for the military to be excluded altogether from the Antarctic, while the United States, Chile and Argentina wanted their armed forces to continue organising logistics. The Chileans regarded any demilitarisation clause as an attack upon their sovereignty, since they saw their Antarctic territory as an integral 'part of the metropolitan territory' and not an overseas dependency. The Americans also wanted the demilitarisation clause to operate only during peacetime, so that it could still establish military bases on the Antarctic Peninsula during wartime. The representatives could not even agree on the area to be covered by the treaty. They discussed whether it should include the surrounding seas, and where the boundary was to be set – at 60° S or at the 'Antarctic Convergence', the area where the cold Antarctic waters met the warmer waters further north.

There had been some urgency to reach agreement and set a date for the conference, as it was feared that the United Nations might intervene and cause the claimant nations to lose all that they were trying to protect. When that threat diminished in late September, after India withdrew its call for United Nations intervention, the sense of urgency dissipated. The conference date was postponed again to an indeterminate time in 1959.[57]

By the end of March 1959, after forty formal meetings and many more informal ones, there was still no prospect of a conference being called. The delegates had been averse to holding a conference until agreement had been reached on the substantive matters and a successful conference outcome was assured. However, such was the frustration with the interminable discussions that Australia proposed to Daniels that a conference be called anyway, even though it would end in failure. Once it was out of the way, it would be possible to 'reach real agreement after the exclusion of the USSR'.[58] But the whole point was to have the Russians sign the treaty, which would decrease the chances of conflict. So more meetings were held, in the hope that an informal understanding might still be reached. No one wanted to gather for a conference that would founder because of intractable differences, yet that is almost what happened when the conference finally began in Washington on 15 October 1959.

As had been expected, the Argentine and Chilean delegations were particularly sensitive about any clauses in the treaty relating to questions of sovereignty. Any suggestion that either country's sovereignty was liable to be infringed provoked a passionate response from its people and politicians. As one Argentine petition read, its 'national territory is one and indivisible, and never will there be an Argentine, worthy of the name, who will give up one single centimeter of the area of his fatherland'. The Chileans likewise maintained that the 'national patrimony . . . has to be maintained intact.'[59] Two concerns were that other nations might have the right to inspect Chile's bases and to undertake scientific research in its territory. The French were similarly reluctant to agree to anything that might have the slightest impact on their sovereignty in the Antarctic. France had lost Vietnam after a long war and was struggling to retain its grip on Algeria. It would not lightly give up its hold on the penguins of Adélie Land.

These impasses were only overcome by a series of painstaking informal meetings that finally brought agreement on the precise wording for a treaty. Although it was signed by the conference delegates on 1 December 1959, it would not come into force until it had been formally ratified by their respective governments.[60]

On the vexed issue of sovereignty and territorial claims, the Antarctic Treaty ostensibly 'froze' the status quo. The signatories agreed that there would be no renunciation of the rights and claims that had already been asserted, and that no further claims, or extensions of existing ones, could be made. The claimants were reassured by a provision stipulating that activities carried out while the treaty was in force could not be used to assert or support a claim. Other reassuring provisions ensured the demilitarisation of the Antarctic, the inspection of each other's bases and the sharing of scientific knowledge. The treaty also allowed other nations to become signatories if they embarked on significant research in the Antarctic. Of course, the delay in holding the conference meant that all the activities by nations during the IGY did lend support to their claims, as did subsequent activities until the treaty finally came into force on 23 June 1961.

Australia might have been reassured by the terms of the treaty and have felt secure about its sovereignty, but the United States and the Soviet Union now had bases in Australian territory, and both had done more than Australia to explore that part of the Antarctic. Both those nations continued their mantras of not recognising the claims of other nations while reserving their own rights in the Antarctic.

Significantly, although the Soviet Union had previously argued that its rights were based on the discoveries of Bellingshausen, it now declared that they were based on the 'discoveries and explorations of Russian navigators and scientists'.[61] The Russians were clearly aware that all their recent activity had immeasurably strengthened the rights that Bellingshausen had created by his circumnavigation of the continent and that had long since disappeared through Russia's failure to follow them up.

The rights of the United States, based upon the activities of the sealers in the early nineteenth century and the later official expedition of Charles Wilkes, had similarly eroded. Now American and Russian scientists and explorers had created new rights, based upon all their activities for the IGY. More recent entrants, such as Japan and Belgium, had also arrived in the Antarctic to shore up the rights they had established decades earlier. Despite optimistic comments about the treaty, the future of the continent remained very much in contention.

CHAPTER 21

'Who shall own the Antarctic?'

1961–2012

With his ship wreathed in ice, Captain James Cook came tantalisingly close to Antarctica without ever seeing it. In Cook's view, there was nothing tantalising about a continent that was beset by blizzards and defended by ramparts of ice. Such a forbidding land could never be an asset to England's burgeoning empire. Less than two centuries later, Antarctica had become permanently occupied, and there was a sometimes fierce contest for its possession. The Antarctic Treaty of 1959 was supposed to end that rivalry and transform the continent into a place of peaceful cooperation. The treaty certainly fostered cooperation but it could not end the territorial struggle. Moreover, there were new participants who wanted to assert their own rights to the Antarctic. The control of the continent became more contested than ever before.

When the diplomats and foreign ministers completed their handshaking and back-slapping at the end of the tortuous treaty conference in Washington, there was an awkward two-year hiatus before all twelve countries ratified it. Britain was the first to do so. The British had been concerned that their early ratification would alarm the Argentinians and Chileans, who might presume that Britain had the most to gain from the treaty and that they, therefore, had the most to lose. But the British were also concerned that the South Americans would regard a quick ratification by the Soviet Union as an even greater cause for alarm, so much so that it might turn them against the treaty altogether.[1] So Britain went ahead and ratified it on 31 May 1960, just as the US Senate was about to hold hearings on the issue.

Although America had taken the initiative in calling the conference, there were some in Congress who feared the treaty's consequences. Opponents of ratification included Senator Harry Byrd and Senator Thomas Dodd; the latter complained the treaty would 'spread the disease of communism even to the penguins'.[2]

Senator Clair Engle, a Democrat from California, was just as trenchant in his opposition. In a statement to the Committee on Foreign Relations on 14 June 1960, he attacked the Eisenhower administration for neglecting to make any territorial claims, despite the fact that America had 'the legal right to territorial sovereignty over a large portion of Antarctica'. Engle told his fellow senators that the United States 'shouldn't just sit down with the best hand in the poker game and just throw in our hands'. He lauded Antarctica's potential as 'a long-range missile base', as a repository for nuclear waste and as a testing ground for nuclear explosions, which might also 'open up harbors or melt the icecap'.

Engle was supported by Senator Ernest Gruening, the former Interior Department official who had been involved with the United States Antarctic Service expedition in 1939. Gruening claimed that the United States had explored eighty per cent of the Antarctic and been responsible for 'practically all the mapping that has been done there'. He feared that ratification would 'foreclose the assertion of the rights we have and can claim' in this 'treasure house'. A New York congressman, John Pillion, chimed in with a call for the Russians to be told that their continued presence 'constitutes a trespass.' He argued that their scientific activities were a diversion 'from the strategic problem – who shall own the Antarctic?'[3]

Anxious that the ratification not be derailed, the State Department sent the chair of the Antarctic Treaty conference, Herman Phleger, who was also a former State Department legal adviser, to laud the treaty's benefits. By allowing for inspection of Soviet bases, Phleger argued that it would provide 'a valuable source of practical experience' for the ongoing talks with Russia about 'nuclear testing, surprise attack, and general disarmament'. It also provided a precedent for dealing with sovereignty in outer space. At the time, the Soviet Union seemed likely to beat America to the moon. If the United States tried to 'claim all of Antarctica' simply on the basis of having 'discovered it and . . . flown over it', said Phleger, Russia might do likewise with the moon.

Moreover, trying to claim all of the Antarctic would upset America's friends and allies. On the other hand, if it restricted itself to the unclaimed portion, the United States would have just twenty per cent of the continent. It would be far better, argued Phleger, for the United States to annex nothing and retain 'the claim which we have maintained to date, that we have a right in all of Antarctica'.[4] Two months later, Congress agreed on ratification, making the United States the fifth nation to do so. It was closely followed by Norway, France, New Zealand and Russia. The last three to ratify were Australia, Argentina and Chile, which all did so on 23 June 1961.

For the United States, the signing of the treaty ended the indecision about whether to make a territorial claim. Now American officials could maintain their long-held position of not recognising the claims of other nations while reserving their own rights, which extended 'throughout Antarctica'. In a secret statement of American objectives, the State Department noted in February 1962 that scientific knowledge had become the primary resource to be exploited in the Antarctic, which meant that American policy should pursue a 'long-term program of scientific observations and studies'. And the United States had to occupy a 'position of leadership' so that it could enhance its 'ability to "have things our own way"'. This meant seeing off the competition from the Soviet Union.

It also meant maintaining permanent occupation of the McMurdo, Byrd and South Pole bases, with the last being important for scientific studies and 'for its value . . . to United States prestige in Antarctic affairs'. The State Department also suggested the establishment of a base in Ellsworth Land and another on what it called the 'Palmer Peninsula', both places where the United States might mount claims based upon historical discovery.[5] Ellsworth Base was established in January 1963, with the buildings being flown in from McMurdo, while Palmer Base was established in 1968.[6]

Whereas more fortunate nations were able to secure positions on rock to build their bases, others were forced to abandon and rebuild bases that were built on ice. Britain's Halley Base, built on an ice shelf flowing into the Weddell Sea, faced a particular challenge. With more than a metre of snow accumulating every year, the first Halley Base soon disappeared below the surface. Having been established in 1956, the base was nearly twenty metres below the surface and moving inexorably towards the sea by the time it was abandoned in 1967. In its last years, scientists had to use long ladders to descend down an ice shaft to reach their buried accommodation building, which was slowly being crushed by the pressure of the ice.

With the warmth of the building melting the surrounding ice, the living conditions for Halley's twenty-one inhabitants were abominable: 'Walls buckled and crumbled, melt water poured through the roof. Drainage gutters flanked the walls. Plastic sheets hung between the ceilings and bits of string were hung about to direct drips into buckets.' Its replacement lasted just six years, while two successive replacements lasted ten and nine years respectively. The fifth incarnation of Halley Base was built in 1992, with its buildings about five metres above the ice on supports that could be jacked up each year to keep clear of the accumulating snow.[7] Even that was not sufficient to ensure the survival of the buildings. In the summer of 2011–12 a new set of buildings was erected, which had jackable supports on skis so that they could be kept clear of the snow and relocated as necessary.

The cost of constantly rebuilding the base was justified by its strategic location, at the eastern edge of Britain's Antarctic territory and set between an American and an Argentine base. The scientific results from the base also more than justified the expense. Among the observations begun when the base was established in 1956 was the measurement of ozone in the upper atmosphere. By the late 1970s, the readings showed alarming changes in the ozone levels each spring. Scientists could not be certain whether it was caused by a faulty instrument or reflected a real and worrying transformation of the stratosphere, particularly when an orbiting satellite taking ozone measurements from above failed to discern any changes. A new instrument installed at Halley in 1982 confirmed the scientists' worst fears, with the readings being backed up by news that the satellite had been set to ignore measurements that seemed too extreme.

Unfortunately, the ozone depletion was extreme, with the ozone layer so thin each spring that it constituted a virtual hole that encompassed an area as big as the Antarctic. The gas used in the world's fridges, air conditioners and aerosols had risen to the upper atmosphere, where the sun had converted it to chlorine, which broke down the ozone. The discovery of the 'hole' came just in time, and governments began to coordinate the withdrawal of the gas from use so that the ozone depletion could be halted and the layer allowed to recover. The alternative was too terrible to contemplate, since the depleted ozone permitted the entry of ultraviolet radiation that was dangerous to humans and devastating to plants.[8]

Australia's two bases were better placed. Although it had considered closing one after the signing of the treaty, Australia soon realised that the territorial rivalry would not end.[9] Instead of reducing its activity, Australia took over America's Wilkes base in the Windmill Islands, partly from a fear that otherwise the Russians would do so.[10] As the Australian cabinet was advised in November 1960, its Antarctic territory 'will remain internationally disputed territory', and all its activities 'will need to be governed by our territorial and international interests'.[11]

That was also true of other nations, as Australia discovered during the takeover of Wilkes Base. The State Department told Australian officials that it wanted to give the impression the handover was being done in a spirit of 'cooperation, goodwill, etc.' and not as 'an American withdrawal or "give away"'.[12] However, Australia's Antarctic chief Phillip Law was determined that Australia should be seen as the dominant power in its own territory.

Although a few Americans would remain at the well-equipped base after the handover, and an American would be second in charge, Law was adamant that it would be an Australian base and not a joint one. Arriving at Wilkes on board the chartered Danish icebreaker *Magga Dan* on 24 January 1959, Law was immediately embroiled in questions of sovereignty when he incorrectly flew the Australian flag above the Stars and Stripes on the vessel's foremast. The position of the American flag was questioned by an American scientist on board, so it was taken down altogether.[13] From there, matters only worsened.

When the American relief ship USS *Staten Island* arrived on 2 February, Law suggested that the American flag flying above the base should be hauled down at the end of the changeover ceremony. Although he had no specific instructions from Canberra, it seemed the obvious procedure since it was 'going to be purely an Australian station'. When the captain of the *Staten Island* demurred, Law suggested that both flags could be 'rigged before the ceremony and left up throughout this period, so that the question of raising or lowering would not arise'.

When it was time for the *Magga Dan* to depart, Law had still not received clear instructions from Canberra. So the frustrated director ordered that both flags should remain flying for the following twelve months. The veteran British explorer Sir Raymond Priestley was a guest on the *Staten Island* and complained later about Law's 'arrogance'. In his defence, Law maintained that relations with the Americans had been 'excellent' throughout, and particularly so during the changeover party, when Australian champagne was drunk and Law entertained the Americans with his accordion. Law would later recall that the flag incident made him realise 'how ruthless the Americans were'. Despite Law's wish to have it as a purely Australian base, it was marked on American maps as a joint facility and the two national flags remained flying until the small American contingent withdrew two years later.[14]

Law got his revenge in 1968, when a new Australian base was built three miles away to replace the American buildings. He ensured that the name Wilkes would not be perpetuated, noting how the naming of the base had led people to assume wrongly that the American explorer had discovered that part of Antarctica. The Americans had recently reinforced that impression by carrying out 'saturation naming' in the immediate area to ensure that all geographic features had American names, 'whether explored by the Americans or not'. Law now wanted an Australian name for the new base so that the 'brief chapter . . . of American activities . . . could be closed and a clean page of purely Australian activity . . . could be started'. Australia should take the 'opportunity to put an Australian name on the map', declared Law, in the same way that the South Africans had renamed the base they had taken over from the Norwegians. It would show the world that 'Australian activities in this region far outweigh . . . anything done by the Americans'.[15] Law won out and the base was renamed 'Casey'.

The Argentinians were similarly forthright when the United States handed over Ellsworth Base on the Weddell Sea in 1959. The Americans wanted Ellsworth, like Wilkes, to be listed as a joint facility. However, since it was located in Argentine Antarctica, the American scientists complained that they were compelled to use Argentine call signs for their amateur radio equipment and were 'treated as employees of the Argentine Antarctic Institute'. This prompted the State Department to make clear to Buenos Aires that it 'expected the joint character of the scientific program at Ellsworth to be beyond question'. But Argentina refused to do anything that might detract from its sovereignty.

Both countries were in a bind. The United States wanted the joint facility as an economical way of maintaining its presence in that part of the continent, while the Argentinians wanted the token

American presence to deter the Russians and to act as an implicit recognition of Argentina's claim. In the event, the Antarctic ice solved the problem by slowly submerging the buildings, forcing Ellsworth Base to close in 1962 before it was completely swallowed.[16]

Just prior to the treaty discussions, Argentina had expanded its presence to eight bases. It also had twenty-eight *refugios*, which usually comprised one or two huts capable of temporarily housing about four men. The annual supply voyages maintained the huts and replenished their emergency supplies of food and fuel. They were there to provide accommodation for scientists in the summer and to act as way-stations for exploration parties or as refuges for parties seeking to escape the Antarctic's sudden blizzards. However, their primary purpose, as an American observer noted, was to 'provide evidence of possession, "occupation", "administration", and exploration, to bolster Argentina's position vis-à-vis sovereignty claims'. Some were also gradually enlarged, with the erection of additional buildings, the construction of wharves and the provision of facilities that made them suited to permanent occupation.[17] All this was done as part of Argentina's long-term strategy of gradually increasing its grip on the territory.

As well as increasing its presence, Argentina continued to perform symbolic acts designed to uphold its sovereignty. In August 1973, the incoming president of Argentina, Raúl Lastiri, bundled all his cabinet members and armed forces commanders into the presidential jet and flew them to the Marambio Base on Seymour Island, off the tip of the Antarctic Peninsula, from where he made a broadcast to the nation, declaring that his presence, albeit for three hours, 'reaffirms our national sovereignty over these southern regions'.[18]

Just as potent was the birth of Emilio Palma at the nearby Esperanza Base at Hope Bay in January 1978, making him the first person to be born on the continent. His father was the base's army commander, whose heavily pregnant wife had been flown in to give birth on the continent. The Hope Bay base was where Argentine troops had fired shots at a British landing party in 1952, and which had as its motto '*Permanencia, un acto de sacrifice*' (Permanence, an act of sacrifice). The birth was a powerful symbolic action by Argentina, and several more would follow in later years.

It was just part of the political theatre being played out at Esperanza Base, which was designed to have the characteristics of an Argentine hamlet. Personnel were encouraged to bring their families; a school was established the same year that Emilio was born, and a radio station started transmission the following year. It was not until 1984 that a Chilean child was born in the Antarctic, and then it was at their base on King George Island rather than on the Antarctic mainland. It helped to reinforce the Chilean claim to the island, which was densely packed with competing bases. The Chilean settlement was complete with a school, gym and supermarket, while the Russians would later build a Russian Orthodox church as part of their base on the island.[19]

With a claim to nearly half the continent, the Australians tried to outdo their rivals by securing the few areas of exposed rock, leaving any rival bases to be buried by windswept snow. Law was particularly anxious to find any rocky areas in Oates Land, at the eastern end of Australia's territory. But each attempt since 1947 had been thwarted by the thickness of the ice or the inclemency of the weather. Law was aware that American DC-3s had flown along the coastline in 1946–47, but their photographs were useless for mapping as they had made no landings to obtain astrofixes.[20]

The plucky Australian finally reached Oates Land in 1959, during the latter part of the *Magga Dan*'s voyage, when he was able to make two flights in a small Auster floatplane during which he photographed the area's main coastal features with a heavy camera held out of the aircraft's open window. At the end of the first flight, neither Law nor his pilot could see the ship. They faced the prospect of crash-landing the float plane on the ice. Fortunately, they were guided back by sailors on the deck with binoculars, with the pilot being forced to land in the forty metres of ice-free sea opened up at the stern of the slow-moving ship.

While Law was aloft, a ground party went ashore to climb to the summit of a coastal peak, where they left a pickle jar in a cairn of rocks, complete with an Australian flag and an account of their visit. An Australian flag was left flying from the peak. Unknown to Law, however, the Russians had been there the year before and had made an aerial survey by helicopter from which the first maps of Oates Land had been produced.[21]

The 1960s were frustrating years for Law. He lost his only influential ally in the Australian government. Richard Casey resigned as External Affairs minister in February 1960, after returning from the Antarctic Treaty conference in Washington and being appointed to the British House of Lords. In February 1965, Law proposed freeing the division from the shackles of the Department of External Affairs and creating a semi-governmental Antarctic Institute. His proposals were repeatedly rejected. Prime Minister Menzies had little interest in the Antarctic, and Law complained that requests for 'explicit directions as to the fundamental objectives of Australia's efforts in Antarctica' were never answered.[22]

Blocked at every turn, the embittered Law resigned as director in March 1966. As confirmation of the government's lack of interest, no permanent replacement was appointed until 1970. Despite Law's departure, the Department of External Affairs still pushed for the division to undertake pure research, warning that Australia's title would be put at risk if the Russians were seen as 'doing the only worthwhile work in Australian Antarctic Territory'.[23] In 1968, the division was shifted from External Affairs to the Department of Supply, and moved again in 1972 to the Department of Science. The latter change could have presaged a transformation but instead saw the minister for science, Bill Morrison, a former diplomat, stipulate that scientific activity should be of practical benefit to the Australian people. He also relocated the division from Melbourne to Hobart.

Law was outraged. He had continued to be involved in Antarctic affairs as a member of the government's placenames committee, and now launched a public attack on Morrison's proposal, arguing that Australia was not in Antarctica for 'scientific reasons' but to 'maintain a position of vantage in an area in which . . . national territorial aspirations are still clouded in uncertainty'.[24] For Law, science was just something to keep personnel busy at Australian bases, and scientists were attracted there because 'all the easy things are still there waiting just to be skimmed off'. Law recalled how he appointed biologists 'because with the seals and penguins lying round, obviously you had to do something'.[25]

It might have been expected that the Antarctic Treaty would neutralise mapping as a means of reinforcing sovereignty but this continued in new guises. Nations no longer competed to compile a standard map of Antarctica on which their names and discoveries would be privileged, but the scientists at the SCAR meeting in Moscow in 1958 had decided that they would establish a working group on cartography. With Australian cartographer Bruce Lambert as chairman, it would not do mapping of its own. Rather, the working group would coordinate the mapping activities of member nations;

a standard map might then emerge. Each of the SCAR nations had an Antarctic mapping centre, and these used the SCAR working group to exchange copies of their maps and charts. To ensure that their own discoveries and names would be prominently displayed on any joint map, nations used their Antarctic mapping centres to scatter national names on their individual maps, in the hope they would be adopted by other centres. Several countries also published Antarctic gazetteers with the same aim in mind.[26]

New Zealand believed that mapping was the key to protecting its title to the Ross Dependency and maintaining a high level of public support for the country's Antarctic program. As one official argued in July 1960, 'the mapping of territory betokens occupation and substantial national interest', while any diminution of the mapping program 'would be construed publically and politically as partial withdrawal from Antarctica'. Ironically, the program was organised in cooperation with the Americans at McMurdo, despite the fact that the United States was New Zealand's main rival for control of the Ross Dependency. The United States undertook the aerial surveys of areas that New Zealand ground parties were mapping; each country then used the other's data to compile its own maps.[27] It seemed the sort of cooperation that the Antarctic Treaty was intended to promote.

However, it was not cooperation between equals. New Zealand was heavily dependent on the United States for logistical support, and when that support was withdrawn in 1965, when the United States closed its joint base with New Zealand at Cape Hallett, the New Zealand activity at Cape Hallett came to an abrupt end. The New Zealand scientists were left in the lurch. Rather than having so many permanent bases, the United States planned to have some temporary bases that could be abandoned before they had to be rebuilt. If New Zealand's scientists objected to the closure of Hallett, they were threatened with having the US logistical support withdrawn for their activities elsewhere. The New Zealanders were described by one senior American official as being 'too nationalistic' and tending 'to introduce politics into the Antarctic', as if it had ever been a politics-free zone.[28]

Prior to the Antarctic Treaty, Australia had made urgent efforts to gather the geographic results of Mawson's voyages in 1929–31, which comprised the legal basis for its subsequent annexation of the Australian Antarctic Territory. The government wanted the maps and journal entries to prove that Mawson had preceded other explorers. However, even Australian officials had doubts about some of Mawson's supposed discoveries, particularly his claim to have discovered Princess Elizabeth Land in late December 1929, when it was clear that Mawson's ship had been too far from the coast for him to have seen it.

One of Mawson's friends, the geographer A. Grenfell Price, was given the task of writing the geographical volume. He accepted all Mawson's claims, while disparaging the work of the Norwegians. His assessment was challenged by the Antarctic Division's cartographer, Graeme McKinnon, who proposed that Price should suggest that Mawson had been misled by a mirage when he claimed to have seen the coast. Price conceded that Mawson had 'wanted to secure Princess Elizabeth Land on the grounds of discovery and we have to report his claim', but was relieved that 'we can escape in a mirage'.[29]

Meanwhile, Australian surveyors gradually charted more than 6000 kilometres of the Australian Antarctic Territory coastline and mapped its mountain ranges and glaciers. Law later recalled that it was 'a bit of a race against time because we were racing the Russians on this'. Although the Russians redid much of the Australian work in the Prince Charles Mountains area, Law was not concerned since the Australian names for the most significant features were firmly in place. They included the region's tallest mountain, the 3355 metre Mount Menzies.[30]

The Soviets were more anxious about catching up with the Americans. They began as soon as they landed at Mirny in 1956, using air-survey cameras to photograph much of East Antarctica. During that first year, they claimed to have 'discovered and named 186 new geographical objects'. By 1978, Soviet scientists were able to declare that they had named about 800 features and placed them on maps. Like the United States, Britain and Australia, Russia aspired to have its maps – complete with Russian names – accepted by other nations as the standard maps of particular regions and the continent as a whole. To this end, Moscow produced an atlas of the Antarctic in 1969, becoming the first nation to have done so.

That same year, the United States published a gazetteer of Antarctic placenames, which was greeted warmly in Moscow because it had 700 Soviet names listed among the total of 10,000 names. This was cited as evidence that 'Soviet scientists . . . have taken a leading role in the study of the icy continent and the Southern Ocean', with the names being chosen to 'commemorate important events in the history of our motherland or honor the memory of our leading scientists, writers, polar explorers and members of Soviet Antarctic expeditions who perished on the icy continent'. They included such names as the 'Russian Mountains' and the 'Soviet Plateau'.[31]

The maps and names helped create a sense of Russian possession in those areas of the Antarctic where Soviet scientists had been particularly active. That sense of possession was enhanced by the work of Russian historians, who had researched the voyage of Bellingshausen and found evidence that showed him to be the discoverer of Antarctica. These documents had been published in 1951 and were used to support the legitimacy of Russia's presence on the continent. The original documents were also translated and widely disseminated overseas, including at Soviet exhibitions in London and Paris.

Although the documentary evidence was incomplete, the British and American evidence concerning the voyages of Bransfield and Palmer was even more so, and Russia's claims about Bellingshausen were gradually accepted by many Antarctic historians. In 1962, the US Navy published maps showing early voyages to Antarctica, which credited Bellingshausen as being the first to sight the continent. A British article also gave credit to Bellingshausen, which prompted Vladimir Lebedev to hail the 'new spirit of cooperation and goodwill in the solution of controversial points in the history of Antarctica'. SCAR seemed to provide a way of sorting through the competing claims and reaching a considered judgement – or so Lebedev hoped.[32]

In fact, the history of the continent's discovery remains a contested space. In his history of Antarctica, first published in 1986, American writer Stephen Pyne has Bellingshausen 'probably sighting the continent in the vicinity of Queen Maud Land' and later having 'possibly spied the mainland' in the vicinity of the Antarctic Peninsula. No dates are given, nor any precedence acknowledged. Palmer fares little better. Pyne has the American sealer being dispatched 'on a voyage from the South Shetlands to the Antarctic Peninsula', but again no dates are given, nor is any confirmation that he saw or reached the peninsula. Bransfield fares worst of all, with Pyne merely noting that the English naval officer 'hastily organized an expedition . . . to the islands in order to claim them for Britain'. Bransfield then drops out of the history, with no indication that he led the expedition or saw the continent. Pyne bestows more credit to the American sealer John Davis for making 'the first documented landing on the continent', and to the American Charles Wilkes for having 'first proclaimed an "Antarctic continent"'.[33]

In a more recent publication, British author David McGonigal conceded that Bellingshausen had 'probably seen the icy fringe of Antarctica', but it was the British naval officer Bransfield who had 'sighted rocky mountains'; Bellingshausen had merely 'glimpsed ice'. As for Palmer, any sighting he made was ten months after Bransfield.[34] American journalist Walter Sullivan was right when he predicted in 1957 that it was 'likely that the question of who discovered Antarctica may never be settled'. The answer to the question did not matter, argued Sullivan, since the 'ultimate disposition' of Antarctica will be decided instead by evidence of 'occupation'. And in this the United States was clearly pre-eminent.[35]

The most contested space in terms of naming was the Antarctic Peninsula, which was known variously as the Palmer Peninsula, Graham Land, O'Higgins Land and San Martin Land. The Soviet Union suggested that the neutral name 'Antarctic Peninsula' should be adopted but it was rebuffed by Britain and the United States.[36] Roberts and Saunders had delayed discussing this issue for nearly two decades and concentrated on settling the names of lesser features. In August 1961, Roberts went to Washington to try to reach agreement with Saunders and the Advisory Committee on Antarctic Names. Roberts suggested that 'Trinity Peninsula' be the name for the entire peninsula, while 'Graham Land' should become the name for the northern portion and 'Palmer Land' for the southern portion. The Americans responded by suggesting 'Antarctic Peninsula', with 'Graham Land' and 'Palmer Land' as its subdivisions. But this was not acceptable to the British. It was not until 1964 that the two finally agreed to the original American suggestion.[37] Of course, that did not satisfy Argentina and Chile, which continued to use their own names.

Naming and mapping were not the only ways for nations to preserve their historical association with the Antarctic. Another means was through the restoration and preservation of historic sites, which reminded the world of a nation's activity there. Even as the Treaty Conference was about to assemble in Washington, the New Zealanders were moving to protect the huts of the early British explorers in the Ross Dependency and affix commemorative plaques to their exteriors. Borchgrevink's hut at Cape Adare had been relatively protected from human interference because of its isolation, but the huts of Scott and Shackleton on Ross Island were vulnerable to souvenir hunters from the nearby American base at McMurdo.[38] In fact, the proximity of the American base saw Scott's hut 'surrounded by stores, boxes, crates, old machinery etc.' and a fuel line passing within a metre of it. The New Zealanders had to appeal to the United States for help to ensure that the hut and the nearby commemorative cross were protected.[39]

With its continent-wide ambitions, Washington wanted to downplay such historical associations because of their links with sovereignty. When the question was discussed at the first consultative meeting of treaty powers in Canberra in 1961, Britain tried unsuccessfully to get agreement on the preservation of historic sites, such as 'huts, memorials, commemorative cairns and emblems of sovereignty'. All such relics provided evidence of exploration and occupation, which ensured that the issue was vigorously discussed by the various delegations The American delegates worried that it might 'stir up sensitivities related to the claims of sovereignty'.[40]

At the fifth consultative meeting of treaty powers, held in Paris in 1968, it was finally agreed that they would all compile a list of historic monuments and sites that needed to be protected. Brian Roberts was taken aback by the resulting Chilean list, which, according to Roberts, included some places that no longer existed and others where no location was specified. It also included inhabited bases and refuge huts, which gave the Chilean list 'a distinctly political flavor'. Among the 'monuments' was 'a Red Wooden Cross and electric light fittings' and a statue of the Virgin near the Chilean base on Greenwich Island. It was not only the British who were upset by the list, with the Argentinians threatening to submit an even longer list of their own. In order to reduce the scope for controversy, Britain suggested that items proposed as monuments would be accepted simply on the nomination of the proposing nation.[41]

This caused nations to compete in compiling long lists, with little regard to the intrinsic historical significance of the items. Once they were listed, such monuments had to be preserved and protected for all time, wherever they were located. When the Argentinians listed the flagpole erected in 1965 by the first Argentinian expedition to arrive overland at the South Pole, the Americans were required to keep the flagpole in place as a reminder of the Argentinian achievement.

Being kept *in situ* was everything. Thus, the Australian government refused suggestions in 1992 that Mawson's hut at Commonwealth Bay should be removed to Australia, arguing that it would 'detract from its symbolism as a link with our Antarctic past'.[42]

Another way of commemorating history was through stamps, which continued to be used to assert ownership. Australia planned to issue four stamps in 1959, one of which would celebrate the supposed achievement of Mawson and Edgeworth David in being the first to reach the South Magnetic Pole, while three others would show contemporary activities connected to maps of the Australian Antarctic Territory. The issue of the stamps was delayed for a time in early 1959, after Casey feared it might be regarded as provocative while the treaty talks were continuing in Washington.

It was delayed again in October because it coincided with the holding of the conference. Australia did not want to upset other countries with stamps that made such a blatant assertion of sovereignty when they were discussing the freezing of sovereignty. As soon as the conference concluded, Casey called on the post office to issue the stamps prior to the departure of the next Australian expedition in December. He denied that the designs were provocative and noted that France and Norway had recently issued stamps of their own.[43] And so it went on, despite calls by the Universal Postal Union to avoid using stamps to support contentious territorial claims and use them instead to strengthen the 'bonds of international friendship'.[44]

The establishment of post offices at Antarctic bases was also used to reinforce territorial claims. Australia continued to do this at its three Antarctic bases, which all had post offices. However, Russia's Mirny base was located in Australia's territory and also had a post office from which mail was posted with Russian stamps and Mirny postmarks. When such mail was given to Australian officials for onward transmission, it was treated as 'having been posted on board ship while on the high seas'. Australia thereby avoided giving any recognition to the operation of a foreign post office in Australian territory.[45]

Such informal arrangements had also worked well in New Zealand's Ross Dependency, where a New Zealand base was adjacent to the much larger McMurdo base of the United States. The US Navy's post office at McMurdo agreed to sell New Zealand stamps and covers to American personnel, while the New Zealanders accepted mail with US stamps affixed.

Britain was in the most difficult position, as it was contesting the Antarctic Peninsula with Chile and Argentina. It wanted to use the first consultative meeting of treaty powers, scheduled for Canberra in 1961, to agree on which post offices 'should be recognized as legally operating'. It also wanted nations not to use 'controversial stamps or slogans'. Deciding on which post offices were 'legal' was an anathema to the United States, which declared that it would 'operate post offices wherever we please in Antarctica'. Britain could hardly complain. It had been first to use stamps and post offices to buttress its sovereignty. They would remain a popular way for nations to promote their territorial claims.[46]

While stamps allowed nations to broadcast their claims to the world, their public-relations task took an unexpected turn when tourists began visiting. In December 1956, a Chilean aircraft took the first ever group of sixty-six tourists on a scenic flight over Chilean-occupied parts of the Antarctica Peninsula. Two years later, tourists were enlisted by Argentina to reinforce its claim to the same peninsula. In the summer of 1957–58, the Argentine navy transport ship *Ara Les Eclaireurs* sailed from Buenos Aires with about a hundred tourists; it would make two voyages to resupply Argentina's bases on the peninsula, the South Shetlands and South Orkneys.

Amongst the penguins and the seals and the icebergs, the tourists were shown the extent of Argentina's occupation. At Deception Island, where a British ship was at anchor, the two captains 'exchanged the usual formal notes, each welcoming the other to its "territorial waters" in the Antarctic'. The presence of tourists in the Falkland Islands Dependencies, and the propaganda use that was being made of them by Argentina, provoked a strong response from Britain, which reminded the world of its sovereignty over Deception Island. Not to be outdone, the Argentine government replied that it had been 'a tourist voyage . . . to a zone considered by Argentina to be under Argentina's exclusive sovereignty'. Undaunted, both Chilean and Argentine vessels returned in early 1959 with two further shiploads of tourists.[47]

The development of tourism took a new form in January 1966, when the New York-based travel company of Lars-Eric Lindblad chartered the Argentine naval ship *Lapataia* to take fifty-eight American tourists on a cruise from Ushuaia to the South Shetlands and Hope Bay. The group included an eighty-six-year-old woman from Washington. 'To have the Antarctic fall upon such evil days!' expostulated the American explorer Richard Black. Lindblad reported by radio how the ship had anchored off Argentina's Groussac Station, where the tourists were able to go ashore to visit the nearby penguin rookery. They had 'a wonderful time', said Lindblad, 'picking up penguins, photographing them and had tobogganing parties on the snow covered hills'.

As a result of the tourist initiative, Lindblad was proposed for membership of the New York Explorers' Club, which had been established in the early 1900s as a meeting place and sponsor for explorers. Now it was suggested that the 'future of the Club could well be tied in to scientific tourism or exploring trips for the non-professional explorers and their wives, as well as the professionals'. The explorer Finn Ronne led the Lindblad tour, which was pitched to those who were prepared to participate in a scientific program; they were given a list of books to read before departure. While it was suggested that these tourists bring warm underwear and a big woollen scarf, the men were also advised to pack a dark suit and the women 'a couple of nice cocktail dresses'.[48] As they frolicked among the penguins, and later sipped cocktails in the ship's bar, the elderly woman from Washington and her companions were inadvertently stirring up questions of sovereignty that were supposed to have been resolved by the Antarctic Treaty.

The visit of the American tourists to an Argentine base located in a territory claimed by both Argentina and Britain raised all sorts of jurisdictional problems that had not been contemplated when the Antarctic Treaty had been signed just a few years before. Although New Zealand was concerned that it raised 'in an acute form the vexed questions of sovereignty . . . and criminal jurisdiction', there was some confidence in Wellington that the 'costs and practical difficulties are so great' that there was not likely to be 'anything but a small trickle of tourists in the foreseeable future'.

Rather than trying to tackle the jurisdictional problems head-on, the treaty powers instead drew up a voluntary code of conduct for tourists and tour companies.[49] The diplomats needed to hurry. Just two years later, Lindblad extended his operations from the Antarctic Peninsula to McMurdo Sound. Tourists were drawn to the area by its association with Scott, Amundsen and Shackleton, and by the haunting presence of their historic huts.

This time, Lindblad chartered the Danish ship *Magga Dan*, leaving from Lyttelton near Christchurch for the long voyage across the Southern Ocean.[50] It was much longer than going from South America to the Antarctic Peninsula, and the seas could be as rough as those of the Drake Passage. It would be quicker if tourists could be flown to McMurdo and meet with a waiting ship, which might also serve as a floating hotel. There had been a proposal by Qantas in 1963 to do just that but it had come to nothing. It required the assistance of the American authorities who controlled the McMurdo landing strip, and that was not forthcoming.[51] Instead, Air New Zealand and Qantas began flights over the Ross Sea and McMurdo Sound in 1977. The flights came to an abrupt end when an Air New Zealand DC-10 crashed into Mount Erebus on Ross Island on 28 November 1979, killing all 257 people on board. Qantas would not resume its Antarctic flights until 1994.

The tragedy on Mount Erebus caused a serious disruption to the scientific programs conducted at the nearby New Zealand and American bases. Less serious disruptions occurred elsewhere, whenever a tourist ship disgorged its passengers at a scientific base. By 1987, America's National Science Foundation was concerned that its bases were facing an 'avalanche of tourism' that was getting 'totally out of hand', with nearly 3000 tourists expected during the coming summer season. Small scientific bases might see a shipload of tourists suddenly arrive and swarm across vulnerable landscapes and penguin rookeries.

The head of polar programs at the National Science Foundation, Dr Peter Wilkniss, was concerned that the treaty was not coping with this new threat to the Antarctic, where tourists were outnumbering scientists and other official inhabitants. He told a New Zealand journalist that it marked 'the dawn of the commercial age in Antarctica'. With several thousand tourists visiting the Antarctic Peninsula each summer, it became known as the 'Antarctic Riviera'. When a single cruise ship brought about 1000 people to the peninsula in the summer of 1987–88, the United States informed Argentina that they would not be permitted to visit America's Palmer Base.[52] Of course, with no recognised sovereignty in the Antarctic, the tourist ships could go where they pleased. Scientists had to rely on the voluntary cooperation of the tour companies, which also cooperated with each other so that two ships would not arrive together and dispel the sense of wilderness.[53] In 2011, the largest cruise ships were banned from Antarctic waters by the International Maritime Organization.

One tour company decided to put the absence of sovereignty to the test. In November 1987, an old DC-4 aircraft lumbered into view across the windswept and slightly corrugated field of ice near the base of the majestic, 4897 metre-high Mount Vinson, the highest mountain in the Antarctic. The landing place lay in territory contested by Chile and Britain. After an historic eleven-hour flight by the propeller-driven aircraft, British pilot Giles Kershaw managed to set down safely and unload supplies for the first commercial base ever established in the Antarctic. Run by a Canadian company, the Antarctic Airways flight was a direct challenge to those governments who purported to possess the territory, as well as to the other Antarctic Treaty signatories who supposedly administered the continent.

Effectively, the bluff of the signatories had been called. Since no sovereignty was recognised in the Antarctic, people could establish commercial operations without reference to any government. In this case, the site was chosen so that the DC-4 could bring passengers all the way from Argentina, who would then be offloaded into eight-seater, ski-fitted Beaver aircraft for onward transport to the South Pole or elsewhere. Some of the early passengers were adventurers intent on mountaineering or skiing, others were tourists keen to visit the South Pole, while others were scientists wanting to travel to one of the nearby bases on the Weddell Sea coast. The owners of the venture said they wanted to make access to Antarctica 'available to private individuals at an affordable cost'.[54]

Antarctic Airways put the continent on the agenda of thrill-seeking adventurers who wanted to climb the highest mountain on each continent, to ski unassisted to the South Pole or simply to fly to the South Pole for the briefest of stopovers. These were mainly personal quests. Rather than attempting to assert sovereignty, they were implicitly challenging the sovereignty of Antarctic nations, and perhaps suggesting that the continent belonged to all nations. By 1998, more than 400 mountaineers had climbed Mount Vinson, courtesy of Antarctic Airways.[55]

In January 2004 a team of eight Palestinians and Israelis climbed a mountain on the Antarctic Peninsula that they promptly named the 'Mountain of Palestinian–Israeli Friendship'.[56] In 1992, four American women planned to traverse the continent via the South

Pole but had to be content to end their trek there. British adventurer Ranulph Fiennes and companion Michael Stroud went further that same year, making an unassisted trek across the continent to McMurdo via the South Pole; they fell just short of Ross Island and had to be airlifted out. Fiennes tried again in 1996 and was forced to retire with kidney stones, while his Norwegian rival Børge Ousland completed the crossing alone and unassisted. A British father-and-son team had the curious distinction of becoming the first diabetics to reach the South Pole by skis and sledges, with the father also being the oldest person to have done so. An American woman took her two children and a British couple on foot to the South Pole in December 2004. Another group ignored opposition from the Chilean and US governments and took nearly two months to ski to the South Pole from the Patriot Hills, beginning each day's trek with a reading from Scott's diary.[57]

Some adventurers came to grief and had to be rescued. Some were beyond rescue, like the nature photographer frozen to death while photographing penguins in a blizzard, and the three skydivers whose parachutes failed to open when they dropped in on the South Pole.[58] Another couple sailed to the Antarctic and allowed their small boat to be locked in for the winter, declaring in a book of their experiences that 'Antarctica belongs to no-one'.[59] That sentiment was also expressed by a group of adventurers in 1986 who encountered hostility from scientists at McMurdo when they sought to follow in the footsteps of Scott. One riposted that they had given 'two fingers to anybody who thought they owned the place'.[60]

Although some of the treaty nations viewed adventure tourism with alarm, and most scientists did not welcome the burden of hosting mass tourist parties or the prospect of rescuing them in the field, some countries saw it as an opportunity to show the world that they were the sovereign power in a particular territory. When a chartered Argentine ship took American tourists to the Antarctic Peninsula, it provided a chance for Argentina to show off its bases and tell outsiders about its possession of the place.

There was also a very real economic benefit. Ever since 1956, New Zealand had been profiting by having American flights and ships call there on their way to the McMurdo base. Now it watched enviously as Australia and Chile, where three cruise ships were based, developed plans for Antarctic tourism. In September 1988, the director of the New Zealand Tourist and Publicity Department,

Neil Plimmer, recommended that New Zealand should 'share in the benefits of Antarctic tourism' by consolidating 'Christchurch's claim as an Antarctic gateway'. Plimmer noted that tourism had become the world's biggest industry. Moreover, tourism, rather than minerals, seemed likely to become the greatest producer of wealth in the Antarctic, which he described as 'the earth's last major tourism frontier'. By encouraging tourism in the Ross Dependency, New Zealand would enjoy economic benefits and raise the 'international profile of the New Zealand claim to the territory'.[61] Another New Zealand official was so attracted by the potential of tourism that he argued it should be regarded as equal to science when deciding priorities in the Antarctic.[62]

One way of using tourism to reinforce New Zealand's sovereignty was to upgrade the Antarctic exhibits at the Canterbury Museum in Christchurch, which would show New Zealanders – and international tourists transiting through Christchurch – the history of the country's involvement with the Ross Dependency. It was part of making Christchurch 'the "Capital" of Antarctica', with America's National Science Foundation having its Antarctic headquarters there, along with the New Zealand Antarctic Division.

While aircraft could make direct flights from Christchurch to the landing strip at McMurdo, the harbour facilities at nearby Lyttelton would be developed to accommodate cruise ships leaving for the Ross Dependency. Plimmer had accompanied New Zealand's deputy prime minister on a visit to McMurdo over the summer, where New Zealand and American bases sat in uneasy proximity to each other. It was clear to Plimmer that 'control is being consolidated around sites of national activity'. He was concerned that tourists might get the wrong impression by seeing the American flag flying over McMurdo, which gave the 'appearance of practical national control . . . over it and its immediate environs'. The Americans had also placed buildings and a flagpole on Marble Point, on the continental coast across from the McMurdo base, which they used as a refuelling station for helicopters heading to inland field stations.

Marble Point had been identified as an ideal site for a sealed runway, but they had never developed it. Instead, they had 'effectively "claimed" Marble Point', noted Plimmer, thereby denying it as a base and airfield site to any of America's territorial rivals. They had also denied it to New Zealand as an airfield for tourists. With this example in mind, Plimmer urged his government to locate future scientific activities in locations that had a 'high tourism potential', by which it could 'claim' the sites for their 'future potential'. He suggested that one such place could be Cape Roberts, which soon after became the site for a New Zealand tide gauge. Plimmer also wanted further restoration work done on the Scott and Shackleton huts, in order to 'reinforce the New Zealand connection and also to establish that New Zealand tourism is adopting a strongly conservationist approach to Antarctic tourism'.[63]

Whether or not he realised it, Plimmer was proposing a new way of looking at sovereignty in the Antarctic. Although New Zealand still asserted its sovereignty over the Ross Dependency, he was suggesting that sovereignty over places such as the American McMurdo base and its surrounds had effectively been assumed by the United States. As a result, New Zealand would have to look elsewhere to establish a wharf and airfield facilities.

A planner with the Tourist and Publicity Department, Jeff Robertson, took up Plimmer's arguments, noting the importance of occupying sites with tourism potential and thereby achieving 'effective sovereignty' over them. But he warned that there were likely to be conflicts with 'scientific agencies, which have had sole possession of the Antarctic for thirty years' and whose first inclination was to restrict tourists by 'rationing Base visits, closing sites or wildlife areas, [and] denying the use of facilities'.[64]

It was not just the scientific community that was developing a sense of possession in the Antarctic. Environmental groups were making demands of their own about what activities should be permitted there. They became particularly alarmed about the possible environmental hazards posed by tourism following the sinking of the Argentine naval ship *Bahia Paraiso* on 28 January 1989. A new territorial rivalry seemed to be emerging, not between nations but between the scientific community and environmental groups and the Antarctic tourist industry and their customers.

The *Bahia Paraiso* came to grief off the Antarctic Peninsula, as it was entering Arthur Harbor on Anvers Island with a party of eighty-one tourists. They had been planning to visit America's Palmer Base, but their vessel shuddered to a halt on a reef, which gashed a hole in the ship's side. An estimated 600,000 litres of diesel fuel poured into the icy waters, sending a slick over many square kilometres of sea, which would destroy much of the marine life and many of the birds and mammals that lived off it. Although the ship sank and was never recovered, the 234 passengers and crew managed to escape and find shelter at Palmer Base, where the scientists had the burden of hosting them until they could be collected by other cruise ships.

The sinking prompted environmental groups to call for tougher rules to manage the increase in Antarctic tourism, just as tourism companies were planning more inventive ways to bring ever greater numbers to the continent. There was already a forty-person hotel at a Chilean base on the peninsula, while other tourists were flown in from South America to a landing strip, from where they took helicopter rides to nearby wildlife colonies. Tourists were also flown from South America to join cruise ships on the peninsula, thereby avoiding the often stormy voyage across the Drake Passage. Environmentalists called for the Antarctic to be regarded as an 'area where wilderness values were paramount'.[65]

The call was a timely one. In May 1989 an Australian business-man was planning to build a five-storey hotel next to a runway capable of landing jumbo jets. It was estimated that the develop-ment, if approved, would attract an additional 16,000 tourists to the Antarctic each year. But it never went ahead.[66] There was increas-ing concern about the particular environmental hazards of human activity in polar areas. While the United States had established a nuclear power station at McMurdo and Britain had considered detonating a hydrogen bomb on the Antarctic Peninsula to scare away the Argentinians, there was a heightened environmental sensi-bility by the 1980s. The sinking of the *Bahia Paraiso* had helped to foster that sensibility. But it was the grounding on an Alaskan reef two months later of the mammoth oil tanker *Exxon Valdez* that really alerted the world to the dangers of oil spills in remote polar regions. Thousands of square miles of sea and 1300 miles of coast-line were covered by oil, causing an unprecedented environmental disaster. The consequent clean-up cost billions of dollars and caused problems of its own. Translated to the more isolated and colder Antarctic, the damage and cost would have been much greater.

The *Exxon Valdez* disaster could not have come at a worse time for those who wanted to explore for minerals and oil in the Antarctic. With no sovereignty being recognised in the Antarctic, it was potentially open to any mining company to explore for minerals and exploit what was found. At the same time, undertaking geological surveys was a useful way for governments to protect their territorial titles.

In 1957, New Zealand had conducted a geological survey of the Ross Dependency to reinforce its sovereignty and give it the right to exploit any mineral resources that were found. The government had been urged on by the nation's Antarctic Society, which argued that a survey would 'firmly establish our right to exploit it when the time comes. This is urgent. If we do not do it someone else will.'[67] Although nothing valuable was found, companies wanted to join in the exploration. In 1969, one company asked the New Zealand government whether there were any 'legal obstacles' to exploring in the Ross Dependency, while another sought 'exclusive rights to explore, prospect and develop a large area of the Ross Dependency for petroleum, coal and all other minerals'. New Zealand wanted to raise the issue at the next consultative meeting of treaty nations in 1970, but was opposed by Australia and Argentina because of the difficult sovereignty questions.[68] Only Japan expressed enthusiasm to discuss the issue.[69]

The mining issue was put on the agenda for discussion in Wellington in 1972; it was feared that the discovery of oil or mineral deposits would spell the end of the treaty. As one delegate observed, once 'a big mineral discovery is made – then it will be every man for himself'.[70] Although no agreement was reached, several treaty nations wanted exploration to be permitted. The oil crisis of October 1973 gave added force to their arguments, as did the discovery that same year of gas reserves off Antarctica by an American deep-sea drilling rig, the *Glomar Challenger*, and the discovery by British Petroleum of potential oil reserves south of the Falkland Islands.[71] With a huge oil and gas deposit being developed on the North Alaskan coast, some 400 kilometres north of the Arctic Circle, there were calls from non-treaty nations, led by Sri Lanka, for the internationalisation of the Antarctic under the control of the United Nations so that all could share in the possible harvest. With the Antarctic oil reserves believed to be much larger than those of Alaska, several developing nations argued that the Antarctic should be regarded as the common heritage of mankind, as the world's oceans were.[72]

While Australia, Argentina and Chile argued that only territorial claimants should benefit from any mineral resources, the United States, Russia and Japan also wanted to exploit the Antarctic.

With the United States enjoying a technological advantage in deep-sea oil drilling, it was keen to proceed quickly to an agreement. Other countries wanted to delay, in some cases to allow them time to catch up with the Americans.[73] In 1975, New Zealand's Labour government proposed a permanent moratorium on mining and the creation of a world park, but it failed to get support from other treaty nations. The subsequent National Party government reversed that position when it came to power in 1977.

For its part, New Zealand wanted to benefit 'to the maximum extent' from any deposits found in the Ross Dependency, but it was prepared to share the profits with non-treaty nations. New Zealand expanded its search for such deposits, conscious that its rights would be all the stronger for doing so. At the same time, the prospect of finding oil or minerals made the New Zealand government amenable to conceding part of its supposed sovereignty.[74] It wanted to avoid a rush by oil companies to the Antarctic that would see New Zealand at the back of the pack.

But the oil companies were already there. America's *Glomar Challenger* had found indications of oil in the Ross Sea, the Japanese research ship *Hakurei Maru* was based in McMurdo to investigate the undersea resources, and the Germans were on their way.[75] With two oil companies on the State Department's Antarctic Advisory Committee, the 'prospect of enormous commercial payoffs . . . is a genie that's out of the bottle', observed one State Department official. The question had become 'whether the Antarctic continent will remain a laboratory for scientific research or be exploited by rivals for vast natural resources'.[76]

New Zealand tried to stall for time, arguing that an environmental regime should be put in place before exploration began. It tried to stifle the enthusiasm by downplaying the riches that might be won, while at the same time stressing the need to protect the environment.[77] In stalling for time, New Zealand was anxious to improve its chances of securing those riches for itself. As diplomat Chris Beeby noted in 1982, New Zealand had 'exercised sovereignty over the Ross Dependency for nearly sixty years' and contributed to science and the protection of the environment for more than twenty-five years. As a result, argued Beeby, 'New Zealand is entitled to expect a fair share of any benefits that may flow from mining on the continent.'[78]

Beeby was well-placed to promote New Zealand's interests when the treaty nations made him chair of a consultative conference tasked in 1982 with finding a way to balance exploitation with protection of the environment and the preservation of sovereignty. The informal discussions began with a twelve-day meeting in Wellington in January 1983, after which Beeby was optimistic that the delegates were aware of the 'political urgency' of reaching agreement in the face of pressure from developing countries.[79] Indeed, a meeting of non-aligned countries in Delhi just two months later agreed that the exploitation of Antarctic resources should be 'for the benefit of all mankind'.[80]

It was not just developing nations whose interest in the Antarctic was sparked by the prospect of finding minerals or oil. While China and India signed the Antarctic Treaty in 1983, Germany, Italy, Spain, Finland and Sweden were among the developed countries who signed in the early 1980s. Swedish diplomat Bo Johnson explained his country's accession to the treaty by noting that the 'need for resources, and more resources, is the theme of the day'; Sweden planned to 'reconnect' with its 'scientific tradition in the Antarctic area' so that it could share in the 'possible future exploitation of Antarctic resources'.[81] Although these various moves put the treaty nations on notice, it would take six years of difficult discussions before agreement would be reached.

In June 1988, the Convention on the Regulation of Antarctic Mineral Resource Activities was finally adopted. Seemingly designed to protect the Antarctic environment, it was really intended to establish procedures for the exploration and exploitation of oil and mineral deposits. Before it could come into effect, however, the convention required ratification by the various governments involved. After the years of negotiation, this was assumed to be almost automatic.

But environmental groups and their supporters now had a sense of ownership over the Antarctic, and they used their influence to pressure their respective governments against ratification. Events moved in their favour. Just six days after the ratification measure was introduced into the British House of Lords, the *Exxon Valdez* struck the Alaskan reef, adding to the earlier concern over the *Bahia Paraiso*. Opposition to the minerals convention spread as quickly as the tanker's oil slick. In the United States, Senator Al Gore called for mining to be banned in the Antarctic and the continent to be declared 'a global ecological commons'.

The New Zealand government back-pedaled as fast as it could. While still supporting the minerals convention, it also wanted the creation of what it called an 'Antarctic Park'. Then it back-pedaled further and said it would not ratify the convention, and would instead push for a moratorium on mining, while leaving open the option of one day supporting the convention. The Australian government of Bob Hawke went further, announcing in May 1989 that it would not ratify the minerals convention.[82] Hawke went to Paris to meet with the French prime minister, Michel Rocard, with both leaders agreeing to oppose the convention. In the face of this, the convention could not come into force.[83]

While the treaty nations had been moving inexorably towards an agreement on mining, environmental groups were just as surely moving to thwart them. More than 200 such groups, from Greenpeace to the World Wildlife Fund, joined together to form the Antarctic and Southern Ocean Coalition (ASOC). It was led by the American environmentalist Jim Barnes, who campaigned against the minerals regime and called for Antarctica to be made a world park.[84]

Greenpeace became an Antarctic actor in its own right in 1987, when it established a small base at Cape Evans on Ross Island, where Scott had erected his hut in 1911. It was part of the campaign to have the Antarctic declared a world park, which would be 'dedicated to international scientific research, in which wilderness values are paramount'. The organisation intended to remain at Cape Evans 'to provide a continuous presence against possible minerals exploitation'.[85] Greenpeace also used the inspection provisions in the Antarctic Treaty to inspect other bases and to educate base personnel on their environmental responsibilities.

It did not have to look far to find problems, as the Americans and New Zealanders were dumping their sewerage and rubbish in the sea. The Americans had also disposed of radioactive waste in the ice. In January 1989, Greenpeace members went to the French base in Adélie Land, where an international landing strip was being built on the site of a penguin rookery in contravention of the agreed measures for the protection of Antarctic wildlife. The airstrip would enable a greater number of personnel to remain during the summer season for a longer period of time. Greenpeace brought the French transgression to world attention by camping on the half-formed runway, which highlighted the irony of a base being expanded partly to study the adjacent wildlife, only to adversely impact their habitat.[86] Several years later, France finally abandoned its half-completed project. The signing of the Madrid Protocol on Environmental Protection in October 1991 gave Antarctica a mining-free reprieve of fifty years, prompting Greenpeace to pack up its base at Cape Evans.

A similar tussle erupted over the exploitation of Antarctica's living resources, which comprised everything from whales, seals and penguins to fish, squid and krill. Some fared better than others. Penguins had never been exploited much in Antarctica, other than as food for explorers and their dogs or as exhibits for distant zoos and museums. Whales and seals had been heavily killed, almost to the point of extinction in the case of some species. Fish, squid and krill had been neglected until recent times, when overexploitation of other oceans led some nations to focus on the abundant resources in the Southern Ocean.

Krill, in particular, had been targeted by the Soviet Union since 1961. One Soviet writer listed the 'more efficient utilization of biological resources' as one of the main aims of the Soviet presence in Antarctica.[87] Japan and several other countries joined the Soviet Union in experimenting with krill harvesting and processing. By the mid-1970s, the total catch only amounted to about 20,000 tons.[88] These small creatures provided food for whales, seals and penguins, and it was believed that the sharp decline in whale numbers had resulted in a consequent explosion in krill stocks. Estimates varied widely, but the potential annual catch of krill on a sustainable basis was said to be about 100 million tons, which was more than twice the annual catch of marine life in the world's oceans. Similar potential was believed to exist with deep-sea Antarctic squid.[89]

By the early 1970s, the treaty nations had begun discussing ways of conserving such 'biological resources', which was code for exploiting them in a sustainable way, all the while trying to deflect the criticism they received from the increasingly influential environmental movement. When a conference was held in London in February 1972 to discuss the conservation of seals in the Antarctic, many of the American delegates were environmentalists. Yet the conference still approved the killing of some 200,000 seals on the Antarctic sea ice; those on the ice shelves remained safe from exploitation. The plan sparked outrage among conservationists, although there was no great interest by any parties to harvest seals.[90] There was much more interest in the size of fish and krill stocks, and in what a sustainable fishing level might be. Further scientific investigation would be required before agreement could be reached on their exploitation, which meant that treaty nations shifted more of their attention offshore so that they might eventually share in the harvest. They were also impelled to do so in order to retain their influence in the Antarctic and to bolster their territorial rights and claims, which, under the UN Law of the Sea Convention, could now extend 320 kilometres offshore. By 1982, the treaty powers had agreed to a convention to preserve marine resources in Antarctic waters and to ascertain the sustainable levels of their exploitation.[91]

For fifty years, the Antarctic Treaty has preserved peace on the continent and served as an example of cooperation. The risk of territorial rivalries erupting into armed conflict has been averted by the spirit of amity that it promotes. Even when Argentina invaded the Falkland Islands in 1982, the conflict did not spread to the Antarctic. Beneath the surface, however, the rivalries have continued, with the competition being complicated by the addition of new and powerful participants, such as China. The prospect of oil and mineral deposits has attracted the attention of many resource-starved nations.

At the same time, scientists have sought to control the continent so that its relatively pristine state is retained for their investigations. They have been joined by environmentalists, who want the Antarctic to be a 'world park' and have been prepared to set up their own base to promote their aim. Adventurers have ignored questions of sovereignty, flying in to test their limits in the icy wilderness. The largest group by far has been the tourists, who want to share in the continent's magic and mystery but inevitably diminish it by their presence.

For centuries, the Antarctic defied man's approach. Now its dangers and its terrors have been largely conquered. Only its future remains unknown.

EPILOGUE

From ancient times, the defeat of a territory's inhabitants usually invested the victor with the right to occupy that territory. But how was that to operate in the Antarctic where there were no people who could be demeaned and dispossessed? There were just the penguins to play the part of indigenous people in the imagination of explorers. Whether being fed to dogs, strangled for science or collected for zoos, the fate of the hapless creatures was used to confirm the victory of the human interlopers and often their ownership of the penguin's territory.

That ownership was reinforced by engendering a sense that the territory had been conquered. Explorers frequently described their expeditions in terms of conquest, as they launched 'assaults' on the South Pole and fought 'battles' with the penguins. There was an implicit suggestion that the dispossession of the penguins somehow justified the takeover of the territory, although it was more often nature itself that was regarded as the foe that had to be defeated.

Being able to defend a conquered territory is a necessary pre-condition for a nation to have its ownership recognised. This caused problems in the Antarctic, where the British in particular struggled to defend their claim to the Falkland Islands Dependencies from incursions by both Argentina and Chile. Shows of force by the various sides were insufficient to expel one rival or another. Other claimants were similarly unsuccessful in defending their supposed sovereignty.

As a result, when permanent bases began to be established from the 1940s onwards, there were cases where several nations contested the same territory. Some tried to assert their superiority over their rivals by describing them as insufficiently committed to scientific inquiry, as the British did of the Argentinians and the Chileans; or by suggesting that their scientific activities were merely a cover for other, more nefarious activities, as the Americans, Australians and others did of the Russians; or by alleging that their rivals were insufficiently protective of the wildlife, as the British did of the Norwegians, Japanese and others. It was a way of saying that their own presence, and therefore their right to the territory, was superior to that of their rivals.

In other times and places, foundation stories were developed to justify the occupation of a particular place and the displacement of the pre-existing people. Although the Antarctic had no pre-existing people, foundation stories were used to justify the occupation of particular places. Russia justified its belated involvement by pointing to Bellingshausen as the explorer who first sighted the Antarctic; nations such as Britain and France pointed to the discoveries of their explorers; the United States pointed to the voyages of early sealers such as Nathaniel Palmer, along with the discoveries of Charles Wilkes and his naming of the continent.

Such foundation stories were used to create and reinforce the moral claim that nations need to justify their occupation, both to their own citizens and the world at large.

The preservation of historic huts and other sites added an important physical dimension to the foundation stories, which is why claimant nations were adamant about the preservation of the sites when other nations began to establish bases on the continent. For example, the Russians might have more bases in the Australian Antarctic Territory, and have carried out more scientific research there, but Australia could take some comfort from the existence of Mawson's carefully preserved hut at Commonwealth Bay. Whatever the Russians might do, the hut was a potent reminder that the Australian involvement with the territory had preceded that of the Russians by several decades.

In other parts of the world, conquerors of a new territory would usually buttress their claim by tilling its soil, fencing fields, building houses and otherwise developing its resources. That did not seem possible in the Antarctic, although some nations tried to do so. The whaling industry operated in Antarctic seas, but never managed to have shore stations on the continent. There was talk of harvesting penguins as food for a fur-farming enterprise, but it never came to anything. Science was the only industry that was ongoing on the continent itself.

The nature of the Antarctic environment seemed to preclude doing much more in the way of asserting effective proprietorship. For decades it was believed that the permanent inhabitation of the Antarctic was impossible, although Borchgrevink's British expedition had wintered over at Cape Adare in 1899 and Argentina had been in permanent occupation of Laurie Island since 1904. The prevailing view about Antarctica's suitability for settlement began to change following Byrd's establishment of Little America and its successor 'villages', which suggested that permanent settlements might be possible on the continent itself.

By the 1970s, Argentina and Chile had women give birth at their Antarctic bases, although the families did not remain in Antarctica. They also tried to give their bases the appearance of being normal villages. The Argentinians and Chileans were particularly keen to do this, since they maintained that their Antarctic territories were an integral part of their homelands. Their bases consequently projected an impression of normality, sometimes coming complete with a bank, post office, hospital, church, school, radio station and even a bar and a simple supermarket.

The American McMurdo base was the largest in Antarctica and also resembled a small town, with laid-out streets, a cinema and a chapel. But the inhabitants of all the bases were temporary sojourners who invariably left when their tour of duty was done.

It is unlikely that any nation will ever have sufficient people in Antarctica to put their territorial claims beyond challenge. The seven claimant nations – Britain, Norway, Australia, New Zealand, France, Chile and Argentina – had certainly not managed to do so by the time of the International Geophysical Year in 1957, when their claims had received little international recognition. And they have not done so since. Now those claims are being challenged by the presence of many more nations, as well as by environmental groups such as Greenpeace, scientific groups such as SCAR and tourist and resource companies. Antarctica's ownership will be difficult to resolve.

The desire to achieve exclusive possession of territory in the Antarctic led to its tentative settlement and the intensive exploration of its mostly empty wastes. While governments sought to claim the Antarctic, the search by scientists for the continent's many secrets will continue for as long as there is knowledge, strategic advantage or possible profits to be won. In recent decades, some of the knowledge is being sought for what it might tell us about our likely climate in the coming century. Captain Cook could not have imagined that insights into the future of life on Earth might be found locked in the ice of the Antarctic, or that its ownership would continue to be a matter of international contention more than two centuries after his landmark voyage.

ENDNOTES

CHAPTER 1 – 1770s

1. Alexander Dalrymple, *An Historical Collection of the Several Voyages and Discoveries in the South Pacific Ocean*, Vol. 1, London, 1770, p. xxviii.

2. A translation of Bougainville's account of the voyage was published in London in 1772 by J. R. Forster, a scientist who would accompany Cook that same year on his second voyage around the world. See Louis de Bougainville, *A Voyage Round the World*, facsimile edition, Da Capo Press, New York, 1967.

3. J. C. Beaglehole's edited volumes of Cook's journals, together with his authoritative biography, remain the standard works on the life and voyages of the explorer. See J. C. Beaglehole (ed.), *The Journals of Captain James Cook on His Voyages of Discovery*, 3 vols, Hakluyt Society, Cambridge, 1961; J. C. Beaglehole, *The Life of Captain James Cook*, Adam and Charles Black, London, 1974.

4. Beaglehole, *The Life of Captain James Cook*, pp. 239, 276.

5. V. L. Lebedev, 'Geographical Observations in the Antarctic made by the Expeditions of Cook 1772–1775 and Bellingshausen–Lazarev 1819–1821', *Antarctica: Commission Reports, 1960*, Academy of Sciences of the U.S.S.R. Interdepartmental Commission on Antarctic Research, Moscow, 1961, p. 4.

6. David McGonigal (ed.), *Antarctica: Secrets of the Southern Continent*, Simon & Schuster, Sydney, 2008, pp. 133–134.

7. Beverley Hooper (ed.), *With Captain James Cook in the Antarctic and Pacific: The private journal of James Burney, Second Lieutenant of the Adventure on Cook's second voyage 1772–1773*, National Library of Australia, Canberra, 1975, p. 27.

8. Journal of John Elliott, January 1773, in Christine Holmes (ed.), *Captain Cook's Second Voyage: The journals of Lieutenants Elliott and Pickersgill*, Caliban Books, London, 1984, p. 14.

9. Hooper (ed.), *With Captain James Cook in the Antarctic and Pacific*, pp. 27–32.

10. Nicholas Thomas, *Discoveries: The voyages of Captain Cook*, Allen Lane, London, 2003, p. xix.

11. George Forster (edited by Nicholas Thomas et al.), *A Voyage Round the World*, vol. 1, University of Hawai'i Press, Honolulu, 2000, p. 295.

12. Forster, *A Voyage Round the World*, vol. 1, p. 294.

13. Beaglehole, *The Life of Captain James Cook*, p. 365.

14. Martin Dugard, *Farther Than Any Man: The Rise and Fall of Captain James Cook*, Allen & Unwin, Sydney, 2001, pp. 190–191.

15. Letter, Cook to Admiralty Secretary, 22 March 1775, in Beaglehole (ed.), *The Journals of Captain James Cook on His Voyages of Discovery*, vol. 2, p. 693.

16. Dugard, *Farther Than Any Man*, p. 209.

17. Beaglehole (ed.), *The Journals of Captain James Cook on His Voyages of Discovery*, vol. 2, p. 325.

18. Beaglehole, *The Life of Captain James Cook*, pp. 367–368.

19. Beaglehole (ed.), *The Journals of Captain James Cook on His Voyages of Discovery*, vol. 2, p. 604.

20 Beaglehole (ed.), *The Journals of Captain James Cook on His Voyages of Discovery*, vol. 2, pp. 605–606.

21 Journal of John Elliott, January 1775, in Holmes (ed.), *Captain Cook's Second Voyage*, pp. 40–41.

22 Beaglehole (ed.), *The Journals of Captain James Cook on His Voyages of Discovery*, vol. 2, pp. 617–626, 692.

23 Beaglehole (ed.), *The Journals of Captain James Cook on His Voyages of Discovery*, vol. 2, pp. 621–626; Michael Hoare (ed.), *The* Resolution *Journal of Johann Reinhold Forster 1772–1775*, vol. IV, Hakluyt Society, London, 1982, p. 715.

24 Letter, Cook to Admiralty Secretary, 22 March 1775, in Beaglehole (ed.), *The Journals of Captain James Cook on His Voyages of Discovery*, vol. 2, p. 692.

25 Beaglehole (ed.), *The Journals of Captain James Cook on His Voyages of Discovery*, vol. 2, p. 625.

26 Hoare (ed.), *The* Resolution *Journal of Johann Reinhold Forster 1772–1775*, p. 716.

27 Beaglehole (ed.), *The Journals of Captain James Cook on His Voyages of Discovery*, vol. 2, p. 622.

28 Beaglehole (ed.), *The Journals of Captain James Cook on His Voyages of Discovery*, vol. 2, p. 625.

29 Frank Debenham (ed.), *The Voyage of Captain Bellingshausen to the Antarctic Seas, 1819–1921*, Hakluyt Society, London, 1945, p. 91.

30 Beaglehole (ed.), *The Journals of Captain James Cook on His Voyages of Discovery*, vol. 2, pp. 626, 629.

31 Beaglehole (ed.), *The Journals of Captain James Cook on His Voyages of Discovery*, vol. 2, pp. 636–637.

32 Beaglehole (ed.), *The Journals of Captain James Cook on His Voyages of Discovery*, vol. 2, p. 766.

33 Beaglehole (ed.), *The Journals of Captain James Cook on His Voyages of Discovery*, vol. 2, pp. 636–637.

34 Beaglehole (ed.), *The Journals of Captain James Cook on His Voyages of Discovery*, vol. 2, Appendix VI, pp. 870–871.

35 Beaglehole (ed.), *The Journals of Captain James Cook on His Voyages of Discovery*, vol. 2, pp. 637–638.

36 Beaglehole (ed.), *The Journals of Captain James Cook on His Voyages of Discovery*, vol. 2, p. 632.

37 Beaglehole (ed.), *The Journals of Captain James Cook on His Voyages of Discovery*, vol. 2, p. 643.

38 Letter, Cook to Admiralty Secretary, 22 March 1775, Beaglehole (ed.), *The Journals of Captain James Cook on His Voyages of Discovery*, vol. 2, p. 693.

CHAPTER 2 – 1780–1820

1 Instructions from the Minister of the Navy, in Debenham (ed.), *The Voyage of Captain Bellingshausen to the Antarctic Seas, 1819–1921*, p. 14.

2 Debenham (ed.), *The Voyage of Captain Bellingshausen to the Antarctic Seas, 1819–1921*, p. 12.

3 Debenham (ed.), *The Voyage of Captain Bellingshausen to the Antarctic Seas, 1819–1921*, p. 26.

4 Debenham (ed.), *The Voyage of Captain Bellingshausen to the Antarctic Seas*, 1819–1921, p. 33; Robert Cushman Murphy, 'Captain Bellingshausen's Voyage 1819–1821', *Geographical Review*, vol. 37, no. 2, April 1947, p. 305;

Hugh Robert Mill, 'Bellingshausen's Antarctic Voyage', *Geographical Journal*, vol. 21, no. 2, February 1903, pp. 152–153.

5   Debenham (ed.), *The Voyage of Captain Bellingshausen to the Antarctic Seas, 1819–1921*, p. 92; Mill, 'Bellingshausen's Antarctic Voyage', p. 153.

6   Debenham (ed.), *The Voyage of Captain Bellingshausen to the Antarctic Seas, 1819–1921*, p. 117.

7   V. L. Lebedev, 'Geographical Observations in the Antarctic made by the Expeditions of Cook 1772–1775 and Bellingshausen–Lazarev 1819–1821', *Antarctica: Commission Reports, 1960*, Academy of Sciences of the U.S.S.R. Interdepartmental Commission on Antarctic Research, Moscow, 1961, p. 14.

8   Debenham (ed.), *The Voyage of Captain Bellingshausen to the Antarctic Seas, 1819–1921*, p. 128.

9   R. J. Campbell (ed.), *The Discovery of the South Shetland Islands: The Voyages of the Brig Williams, 1819–1820*, Hakluyt Society, London, 2000, pp. 27–28, 40–51, 64–65; A. G. E. Jones, 'Captain William Smith and the Discovery of New South Shetland', *Geographical Journal*, vol. 141, no. 3, November 1975, p. 454.

10   Campbell (ed.), *The Discovery of the South Shetland Islands*, pp. 40–55, 59.

11   Campbell (ed.), *The Discovery of the South Shetland Islands*, pp. 60–61.

12   Jones, 'Captain William Smith and the Discovery of New South Shetland', p. 455.

13   Campbell (ed.), *The Discovery of the South Shetland Islands*, pp. 70–71.

14   'The First American Discoveries in the Antarctic, 1819', *American Historical Review*, vol. 16, no. 4, July 1911, pp. 794–798; Philip Mitterling, *America in the Antarctic to 1840*, University of Illinois, Urbana, 1959, pp. 31–35.

15   'The First American Discoveries in the Antarctic, 1819', *American Historical Review*, vol. 16, no. 4, July 1911, pp. 794–798.

16   Campbell (ed.), *The Discovery of the South Shetland Islands*, pp. 73–75, 79–81, 85–86, 117.

17   Campbell (ed.), *The Discovery of the South Shetland Islands*, pp. 73–75, 79–81, 85–86, 112; Mitterling, *America in the Antarctic to 1840*, pp. 42–43.

18   Campbell (ed.), *The Discovery of the South Shetland Islands*, p. 88.

19   Campbell (ed.), *The Discovery of the South Shetland Islands*, p. 88.

20   Campbell (ed.), *The Discovery of the South Shetland Islands*, pp. 73–75, 80, 89.

21   Mitterling, *America in the Antarctic to 1840*, pp. 24–35.

22   Mitterling, *America in the Antarctic to 1840*, pp. 31–35; 'The First American Discoveries in the Antarctic, 1819', pp. 794–798.

23   Campbell (ed.), *The Discovery of the South Shetland Islands*, pp. 51, 65, 75.

24   Campbell (ed.), *The Discovery of the South Shetland Islands*, pp. 82–83.

25   Mill, 'Bellingshausen's Antarctic Voyage', p. 156.

26   Debenham (ed.), *The Voyage of Captain Bellingshausen to the Antarctic Seas 1819–1821*, pp. 421, 423.

27   Debenham (ed.), *The Voyage of Captain Bellingshausen to the Antarctic Seas 1819–1821*, p. 410.

28   Debenham (ed.), *The Voyage of Captain Bellingshausen to the Antarctic Seas 1819–1821*, pp. 411–412.

29   Debenham (ed.), *The Voyage of Captain Bellingshausen to the Antarctic Seas 1819–1821*, pp. 419–420.

30 Debenham (ed.), *The Voyage of Captain Bellingshausen to the Antarctic Seas 1819–1821*, pp. 419–420.

31 Debenham (ed.), *The Voyage of Captain Bellingshausen to the Antarctic Seas 1819–1821*, p. 421.

32 Debenham (ed.), *The Voyage of Captain Bellingshausen to the Antarctic Seas 1819–1821*, p. 16.

33 Debenham (ed.), *The Voyage of Captain Bellingshausen to the Antarctic Seas 1819–1821*, pp. 421, 424–427.

34 Edouard Stackpole, *The Voyage of the* Huron *and the* Huntress *The American Sealers and the Discovery of the Continent of Antarctica*, Marine Historical Association, Mystic, 1955, pp. 10–20.

35 Debenham (ed.), *The Voyage of Captain Bellingshausen to the Antarctic Seas 1819–1821*, p. 425.

36 Stackpole, *The Voyage of the* Huron *and the* Huntress, pp. 44–46.

37 Debenham (ed.), *The Voyage of Captain Bellingshausen to the Antarctic Seas 1819–1821*, pp. 425–426.

38 Edmund Fanning, *Voyages Round the World*, Collins and Hannay, New York, 1833.

39 William Hobbs, 'Review of *The Voyage of Captain Bellingshausen to the Antarctic Seas, 1819–1821*, by Frank Debenham', *American Historical Review*, vol. 53, no. 1, October 1947, p. 107.

40 Stackpole, *The Voyage of the* Huron *and the* Huntress, pp. 60–61.

41 The American geographer Professor William Hobbs was Palmer's foremost advocate during the mid-twentieth century, arguing in several articles, conference papers and books that Fanning's account of the discussion was 'more complete' than Bellingshausen's. See William Hobbs, 'Review of *The Voyage of Captain Bellingshausen to the Antarctic Seas, 1819–1821*, by Frank Debenham', p. 107.

42 Stackpole, *The Voyage of the* Huron *and the* Huntress, p. 51.

43 Mitterling is probably correct in suggesting that Davis was 'using the word continent merely to designate a body of land larger than a small island' (Mitterling, *America in the Antarctic to 1840*, p. 55).

CHAPTER 3 – 1821–1838

1 Stackpole, *The Voyage of the* Huron *and the* Huntress, p. 51.

2 Lebedev, 'Geographical Observations in the Antarctic made by the Expeditions of Cook 1772–1775 and Bellingshausen–Lazarev 1819–1821', *Antarctica: Commission Reports, 1960*, p. 6.

3 Stackpole, *The Voyage of the* Huron *and the* Huntress, p. 65.

4 Stackpole, *The Voyage of the* Huron *and the* Huntress, p. 78.

5 The British map can be seen in Campbell (ed.), *The Discovery of the South Shetland Islands*, pp. 76–77.

6 Campbell (ed.), *The Discovery of the South Shetland Islands*, p. 82.

7 V. L. Lebedev, 'Who Discovered Antarctica?', *Antarctica: Commission Reports, 1961*, Academy of Sciences of the U.S.S.R. Interdepartmental Commission on Antarctic Research, Moscow, 1962.

8 Debenham (ed.), *The Voyage of Captain Bellingshausen to the Antarctic Seas, 1819–1921*, p. 117.

9 Mitterling, *America in the Antarctic to 1840*, p. 56–59.

10 Introduction by Boggs, in Richard Kane, 'The Earliest American Sealers in the Antarctic', 17 February 1954, Department of State, Bureau of Intelligence

and Research, Office of the Geographer, Records Relating to Antarctica and Antarctic Exploration, 1930–1955, Box #6, 'The First American Sealers in the Antarctic 1812–1819' folder, NARA.

11 James Weddell, *A Voyage Towards the South Pole Performed in the Years 1822–24*, (second edition), Longman, Rees, Orme, Brown and Green, London, 1827, p. 2.

12 The pugnacious American geologist William Herbert Hobbs was so sceptical of Weddell's account of his voyage into the usually ice-choked sea that he described Weddell as a 'fake explorer'. The allegation sparked a furious argument with a British geographer, Arthur Hinks. See William Herbert Hobbs, 'The Pack-Ice of the Weddell Sea', *Annals of the Association of American Geographers*, vol. 29, no. 2, June 1939.

13 Weddell, *A Voyage Towards the South Pole Performed in the Years 1822–24*, p. 44.

14 William Stanton, *The Great United States Exploring Expedition of 1838–1842*, University of California Press, Berkeley, 1975, p. 2; Captain Benjamin Morrell, *A Narrative of Four Voyages to the South Sea, North and South Pacific Ocean, Chinese Sea, Ethiopic and Southern Atlantic Ocean, Indian and Antarctic Ocean, from the Year 1822 to 1831*, J. & J. Harper, New York, 1832, pp. 30–67, 254; Mitterling, *America in the Antarctic to 1840*, pp. 60–66.

15 Weddell, *A Voyage Towards the South Pole Performed in the Years 1822–24*, pp. 42–43.

16 'The South Sea Surveying and Exploring Expedition: Its origin, organization, equipment, purposes, results, and termination', by Titian Ramsay Peale, c. 1885, Box 1/2, United States Exploring Expedition 1835–1885, SIA; Mitterling, *America in the Antarctic to 1840*, pp. 67–81.

17 Stanton, *The Great United States Exploring Expedition of 1838–1842*, pp. 13–15.

18 Mitterling, *America in the Antarctic to 1840*, pp. 82–87.

19 William Lenz, 'Narratives of Exploration, Sea Fiction, Mariners' Chronicles, and the Rise of American Nationalism: "To Cast Anchor on that Point Where All Meridians Terminate" ', *American Studies*, vol. 32, no. 2, Fall 1991, p. 54.

20 Mitterling, *America in the Antarctic to 1840*, pp. 91, 96; Daniel McKinley, *James Eights 1798–1882: Antarctic Explorer, Albany Naturalist, His Life, His Times, His Works*, New York State Museum Bulletin 505, Albany, 2005, pp. 40–41.

21 'On the Expediency of Fitting Out Vessels of the Navy for an Exploration of the Pacific Ocean and South Seas', 25 March 1828, *American State Papers: Naval Affairs*, vol. 3, pp. 189–197.

22 'On the Expediency of Fitting Out Vessels of the Navy for an Exploration of the Pacific Ocean and South Seas', pp. 189–197.

23 'On the Expediency of Fitting Out Vessels of the Navy for an Exploration of the Pacific Ocean and South Seas', pp. 189–197.

24 W. H. B. Webster, *Narrative of a Voyage to the Southern Atlantic Ocean, in the Years 1828, 29, 30, performed in H.M. Sloop Chanticleer, under the Command of the Late Captain Henry Foster, F.R.S. &'c by order of the Lord Commissioners of the Admiralty*, Richard Bentley, London, 1834, vol. 1, pp. 1–3, and vol. 2, pp. 372–82.

25 Webster, *Narrative of a Voyage to the Southern Atlantic Ocean*, vol. 1, pp. 136–137; William Herbert Hobbs, 'The Discoveries of Antarctica within the American Sector, as Revealed by Maps and Documents', *Transactions of the American Philosophical Society*, vol. XXXI, Part 1, January 1939, pp. 50–52.

26 Webster, *Narrative of a Voyage to the Southern Atlantic Ocean*, vol. 1, pp. 147, 157, 159.

27 McKinley, *James Eights 1798–1882*, pp. 101–102.

28 'Authorization of the Naval Exploring Expedition in the South Seas and Pacific Ocean, and of the Purchase and Payment for Astronomical and Other Instruments for the Same', 17 March 1830, *American State Papers: Naval Affairs*, vol. 3, pp. 546–560.

29 McKinley, *James Eights 1798–1882*, pp. 41–42.

30 Lenz, 'Narratives of Exploration, Sea Fiction, Mariners' Chronicles, and the Rise of American Nationalism', p. 54.

31 'Information Collected by the Navy Department Relating to Islands, Reefs, Shoals, Etc., in the Pacific Ocean and South Seas, and Showing the Expediency of an Exploring Expedition in that Ocean and those Seas by the Navy', 29 January 1835, *American State Papers: Naval Affairs*, vol. 4, pp. 688–700.

32 'Authorization of the Naval Exploring Expedition in the South Seas and Pacific Ocean, and of the Purchase and Payment for Astronomical and Other Instruments for the Same', 17 March 1830, *American State Papers: Naval Affairs*, vol. 3, pp. 546–560.

33 'Authorization of the Naval Exploring Expedition in the South Seas and Pacific Ocean, and of the Purchase and Payment for Astronomical and Other Instruments for the Same', 17 March 1830, *American State Papers: Naval Affairs*, vol. 3, pp. 546–560.

34 'On the Policy and Objects of the Exploring Expedition to the Pacific Ocean and South Seas', 23 February 1829, *American State Papers: Naval Affairs*, vol. 3, pp. 336–343.

35 'Exploring Expedition to the Pacific Ocean and South Seas', 16 February 1829, *American State Papers: Naval Affairs*, vol. 3, pp. 308–317.

36 'On the Policy and Objects of the Exploring Expedition to the Pacific Ocean and South Seas', 23 February 1829, *American State Papers: Naval Affairs*, vol. 3, pp. 336–343.

37 'On the Policy and Objects of the Exploring Expedition to the Pacific Ocean and South Seas', 23 February 1829, *American State Papers: Naval Affairs*, vol. 3, pp. 336–343; Char Miller, 'South Sea Fur Company and Exploring Expedition', in *Encyclopedia of Earth*, 1 August 2009, www.eoearth.org; Char Miller, 'James Eights', in *Encyclopedia of Earth*, 3 March 2009, www.eoearth. org; For the best account of Eights, see McKinley, *James Eights 1798–1882*; McKinley has questioned the claims regarding Eights' association with drugs and the suggestion that Eights was later passed over for the Wilkes expedition because of being homosexual. See McKinley, *James Eights 1798–1882*, p. 395.

38 McKinley, *James Eights 1798–1882*, pp. 40, 45.

39 McKinley, *James Eights 1798–1882*, pp. 46–47, 53–54.

40 Fanning, *Voyages Round the World*, pp. 476, 480; 'Information Collected by the Navy Department Relating to Islands, Reefs, Shoals, Etc., in the Pacific Ocean and South Seas, and Showing the Expediency of an Exploring Expedition in that Ocean and those Seas by the Navy', 29 January 1835, *American State Papers: Naval Affairs*, vol. 4, pp. 688–700.

41 McKinley, *James Eights 1798–1882*, pp. 93–94.

42 McKinley, *James Eights 1798–1882*, pp. 93–94; Fanning, *Voyages Round the World*, pp. 476, 478–489, 487–488; Miller, 'James Eights'.

43 J. N. Reynolds, *Voyage of the United States Frigate Potomac 1831–4*, Harper & Brothers, New York, 1835, pp. ii, 480–514.

44 For some sense of the excitement surrounding the work of these geographical societies, see 'A Sketch of the Progress of Geography; – and of the Labours of the Royal Geographical Society, during the year 1836–7', *Journal of the Royal Geographical Society of London*, vol. 7, 1837.

45 Fanning, *Voyages Round the World*, pp. 475–476.

46 Morrell, *A Narrative of Four Voyages*, pp. 29, 68–69; William Lenz, *The Poetics of the Antarctic*, Garland Publishing, New York, 1995, pp. 20–21.

47 'On the Expediency and Importance of Authorizing a Naval Expedition to Explore the Pacific Ocean and South Seas', 7 February 1835, *American State Papers: Naval Affairs*, vol. 4, pp. 707–715; 'On the Expediency of Authorizing an Exploring Expedition, by Vessels of the Navy, to the Pacific Ocean and South Seas', 21 March 1836, *American State Papers: Naval Affairs*, vol. 4, pp. 867–873.

48 'On the Expediency and Importance of Authorizing a Naval Expedition to Explore the Pacific Ocean and South Seas', 7 February 1835, *American State Papers: Naval Affairs*, vol. 4, pp. 707–715; 'Journal of a Voyage towards the South Pole on Board the Brig "Tula", under the Command of John Biscoe, with the Cutter "Lively" in Company' [extract], in George Murray (ed.), *The Antarctic Manual, for the use of the Expedition of 1901*, Royal Geographical Society, London, 1901 [facsimile edition by Explorer Books, Palistow, no date], pp. 331–332.

49 *Hobart Town Courier*, Hobart, 30 August 1833.

50 McGonigal (ed.), *Antarctica*, pp. 276–277; 'On the Expediency and Importance of Authorizing a Naval Expedition to Explore the Pacific Ocean and South Seas', 7 February 1835, *American State Papers: Naval Affairs*, vol. 4, pp. 707–715; John Biscoe and Messrs Enderby, 'Recent Discoveries in the Antarctic Ocean, from the Log-book of the Brig Tula, commanded by Mr. John Biscoe, R.N.', *Journal of the Royal Geographical Society of London*, vol. 3, 1833; John Cumpston, 'The Antarctic Landfalls of John Biscoe, 1831', *The Geographical Journal*, vol. 129, no. 2, June 1963.

51 'On the Expediency of Authorizing an Exploring Expedition, by Vessels of the Navy, to the Pacific Ocean and South Seas', 21 March 1836, *American State Papers: Naval Affairs*, vol. 4, pp. 867–873.

52 J. N. Reynolds, *Address on the Subject of a Surveying and Exploring Expedition to the Pacific Ocean and South Seas*, Harper and Brothers, New York, 1836, pp. 21–22, 70.

53 Reynolds, *Address on the Subject of a Surveying and Exploring Expedition to the Pacific Ocean and South Seas*, pp. 42–44, 70–71.

54 Reynolds, *Address on the Subject of a Surveying and Exploring Expedition to the Pacific Ocean and South Seas*, p. 96.

55 Reynolds, *Address on the Subject of a Surveying and Exploring Expedition to the Pacific Ocean and South Seas*, pp. 74, 86, 99.

56 Reynolds, *Address on the Subject of a Surveying and Exploring Expedition to the Pacific Ocean and South Seas*, p. 93–99.

57 J. N. Reynolds, *Pacific and Indian Oceans: The South Sea Surveying and Exploring Expedition: Its Inception, Progress, and Objects*, Harper and Brothers, New York, 1841, pp. 399.

58 McKinley, *James Eights 1798–1882*, pp. 240–42, 246.

59 Mitterling, *America in the Antarctic to 1840*, pp. 108–109.

60 Interestingly, the Naval Lyceum was the only organisation to suggest that the expedition should determine whether there was an Antarctic continent, and to predict that its discovery could shed light on the 'general theory of climate' and provide information about 'the distribution of heat on the Globe'. McKinley, *James Eights 1798–1882*, pp. 242, 253; Mitterling, *America in the Antarctic to 1840*, pp. 109–110; Reynolds, *Pacific and Indian Oceans*, pp. vi–viii.

61 Mitterling, *America in the Antarctic to 1840*, pp. 112–14.

62 Mitterling, *America in the Antarctic to 1840*, pp. 108–109; Reynolds, *Pacific and Indian Oceans*, pp. vi–viii.

63 Reynolds, *Pacific and Indian Oceans*, pp. 304–21, 337.

64 Reynolds, *Pacific and Indian Oceans*, pp. 374, 382–384.

65 Reynolds, *Pacific and Indian Oceans*, pp. 345–359.

66 Reynolds, *Pacific and Indian Oceans*, pp. 398, 406.

67 Reynolds, *Pacific and Indian Oceans*, pp. 410–420.

68 Reynolds, *Pacific and Indian Oceans*, pp. 455–456; Stanton, *The Great United States Exploring Expedition of 1838–1842*, p. 68; Mitterling, *America in the Antarctic to 1840*, Chapter 8.

69 Reynolds, *Pacific and Indian Oceans*, pp. i, 503, 509–510.

70 Reynolds, *Pacific and Indian Oceans*, p. i.

CHAPTER 4 – 1839–1843

1 Helen Rosenman (trans. & ed.), *An Account in Two Volumes of Two Voyages to the South Seas*, by Dumont d'Urville, vol. 1, Melbourne University Press, Melbourne, 1987, pp. xli–xlii.

2 Rosenman, *An Account in Two Volumes of Two Voyages to the South Seas*, vol. 1, pp. xlv–xlviii; John Dunmore, *Visions and Realities: France in the Pacific 1695–1995*, Heritage Press, Waikanae, 1997, pp. 158–165.

3 Rosenman, *An Account in Two Volumes of Two Voyages to the South Seas*, vol. 1, pp. xlix–li and vol. 2, pp. 322–324.

4 Rosenman, *An Account in Two Volumes of Two Voyages to the South Seas*, vol. 2, pp. 324–325.

5 Rosenman, *An Account in Two Volumes of Two Voyages to the South Seas*, vol. 2, pp. 317–321, 324–329.

6 Rosenman, *An Account in Two Volumes of Two Voyages to the South Seas*, vol. 2, p. 326.

7 Rosenman, *An Account in Two Volumes of Two Voyages to the South Seas*, vol. 2, p. 335.

8 Stanton, *The Great United States Exploring Expedition of 1838–1842*, p. 173.

9 Rosenman, *An Account in Two Volumes of Two Voyages to the South Seas*, vol. 2, pp. 335–345.

10 Rosenman, *An Account in Two Volumes of Two Voyages to the South Seas*, vol. 2, p. 344–347.

11 Rosenman, *An Account in Two Volumes of Two Voyages to the South Seas*, vol. 2, p. 347–351.

12 Rosenman, *An Account in Two Volumes of Two Voyages to the South Seas*, vol. 2, p. 350.

13 Rosenman, *An Account in Two Volumes of Two Voyages to the South Seas*, vol. 2, pp. 356–369, 566–567.

14 Rosenman, *An Account in Two Volumes of Two Voyages to the South Seas*, vol. 2, pp. 318–321, 389–445.

15 Rosenman, *An Account in Two Volumes of Two Voyages to the South Seas*, vol. 2, pp. 447–449, 575.
16 Rosenman, *An Account in Two Volumes of Two Voyages to the South Seas*, vol. 2, pp. 451–452; Mitterling, *America in the Antarctic to 1840*, pp. 136–140.
17 Rosenman, *An Account in Two Volumes of Two Voyages to the South Seas*, vol. 2, pp. 458, 461–463.
18 Rosenman, *An Account in Two Volumes of Two Voyages to the South Seas*, vol. 2, p. 465; McGonigal, *Antarctica: Secrets of the Southern Continent*, p. 278; Charles Enderby, 'Discoveries in the Antarctic Ocean, in February, 1839', *Journal of the Royal Geographical Society of London*, vol. 9, 1839.
19 Rosenman, *An Account in Two Volumes of Two Voyages to the South Seas*, vol. 2, pp. 465–469.
20 Rosenman, *An Account in Two Volumes of Two Voyages to the South Seas*, vol. 2, pp. 470–473, 277–278.
21 Rosenman, *An Account in Two Volumes of Two Voyages to the South Seas*, vol. 2, pp. 473–478.
22 Rosenman, *An Account in Two Volumes of Two Voyages to the South Seas*, vol. 2, pp. 486–487; Charles Wilkes, *Narrative of the United States Exploring Expedition*, [First published 1845] Gregg Press, New Jersey, 1970, vol. 1, p. xxx.
23 Wilkes, *Narrative of the United States Exploring Expedition*, vol. 1, pp. xxv–xxxi.
24 Wilkes, *Narrative of the United States Exploring Expedition*, vol. 1, pp. 394–396; Stanton, *The Great United States Exploring Expedition of 1838–1842*, pp. 92–98.
25 Mitterling, *America in the Antarctic to 1840*, pp. 130–135; Stanton, *The Great United States Exploring Expedition of 1838–1842*, pp. 95–104.
26 Stanton, *The Great United States Exploring Expedition of 1838–1842*, pp. 107–115.
27 Mitterling, *America in the Antarctic to 1840*, pp. 137–140; Stanton, *The Great United States Exploring Expedition of 1838–1842*, pp. 143–149.
28 Stanton, *The Great United States Exploring Expedition of 1838–1842*, pp. 150–160.
29 Stanton, *The Great United States Exploring Expedition of 1838–1842*, pp. 161–168.
30 Stanton, *The Great United States Exploring Expedition of 1838–1842*, pp. 169–175; Mitterling, *America in the Antarctic to 1840*, pp. 145–146.
31 Stanton, *The Great United States Exploring Expedition of 1838–1842*, pp. 175–180.
32 Stanton, *The Great United States Exploring Expedition of 1838–1842*, pp. 173, 180–185; Mitterling, *America in the Antarctic to 1840*, p. 144.
33 Stanton, *The Great United States Exploring Expedition of 1838–1842*, pp. 180–185.
34 Reynolds, *Pacific and Indian Oceans*, p. ix.
35 Rosenman, *An Account in Two Volumes of Two Voyages to the South Seas*, vol. 2, p. 489.
36 Rosenman, *An Account in Two Volumes of Two Voyages to the South Seas*, vol. 2, pp. 493–495, 524, 529–530, 577.
37 Explaining the breach of his instructions, Wilkes told the navy secretary that it was done as a matter of courtesy to Ross, who had earlier helped him when he was purchasing instruments for the expedition in London. See Mitterling, *America in the Antarctic to 1840*, p. 155. Copies of Wilkes' letter and chart

can be found in Captain Sir James Clark Ross, *A Voyage of Discovery and Research in the Southern and Antarctic Regions During the Years 1839–43*, vol. 1, [first published 1847] David and Charles Reprints, Newton Abbot, 1969, pp. 346–352.

38 Mitterling, *America in the Antarctic to 1840*, p. 155; Ross, *A Voyage of Discovery and Research in the Southern and Antarctic Regions During the Years 1839–43*, vol. 1, pp. 133–134.

39 M. J. Ross, *Polar Pioneers: John Ross and James Clark Ross*, McGill-Queen's University Press, Montreal, 1994, pp. 199–204; Charles Enderby, 'Discoveries in the Antarctic Ocean, in February, 1839', *Journal of the Royal Geographical Society of London*, vol. 9, 1839; Ross, *A Voyage of Discovery and Research in the Southern and Antarctic Regions During the Years 1839–43*, vol. 1, pp. xxv–xxvi, 117.

40 Ross, *A Voyage of Discovery and Research in the Southern and Antarctic Regions During the Years 1839–43*, vol. 1, pp. 182–190, 349.

41 Ross, *A Voyage of Discovery and Research in the Southern and Antarctic Regions During the Years 1839–43*, vol. 1, pp. 210–261, 279–85; Ross, *Polar Pioneers*, pp. 229–232.

42 Ross, *A Voyage of Discovery and Research in the Southern and Antarctic Regions During the Years 1839–43*, vol. 1, pp. 210–261, 279–285.

43 Ross, *A Voyage of Discovery and Research in the Southern and Antarctic Regions During the Years 1839–43*, vol. 2, pp. 364–366.

44 A. H. Markham, 'Antarctic Exploration', *North American Review*, vol. 164, no. 485, April 1897, pp. 434, 436.

45 Wilkes, *Narrative of the United States Exploring Expedition*, vol. 2, pp. 360–361.

46 Rosenman, *An Account in Two Volumes of Two Voyages to the South Seas*, vol. 2, p. 489.

47 Ross, *A Voyage of Discovery and Research in the Southern and Antarctic Regions During the Years 1839–43*, vol. 1, pp. 285–299.

CHAPTER 5 – 1843–1895

1 Rosenman, *An Account in Two Volumes of Two Voyages to the South Seas*, vol. 1, pp. lii–liii.

2 Mitterling, *America in the Antarctic to 1840*, pp. 160–161; Stanton, *The Great United States Exploring Expedition of 1838–1842*, pp. 278–289; 'The South Sea Surveying and Exploring Expedition: Its origin, organization, equipment, purposes, results, and termination', by Titian Ramsay Peale, c. 1885, Box 1/2, United States Exploring Expedition 1835–1885, SIA.

3 Mitterling, *America in the Antarctic to 1840*, pp. 162–165; Stanton, *The Great United States Exploring Expedition of 1838–1842*, pp. 283–289.

4 Mitterling, *America in the Antarctic to 1840*, pp. 159–163; Stanton, *The Great United States Exploring Expedition of 1838–1842*, p. 272; Ross, *A Voyage of Discovery and Research in the Southern and Antarctic Regions During the Years 1839–43*, vol. 2, pp. 66–67; Ross, *Polar Pioneers*, p. 235.

5 J. Gordon Hayes, *Antarctica: A Treatise on the Southern Continent*, Richards Press, London, 1928, pp. 116–119.

6 Ross, *Polar Pioneers*, p. 250.

7 Ross, *A Voyage of Discovery and Research in the Southern and Antarctic Regions During the Years 1839–43*, vol. 1, pp. 168–169, 191–192, 266.

8 Ross, *A Voyage of Discovery and Research in the Southern and Antarctic Regions During the Years 1839–43*, vol. 2, pp. 327.

9   McGonigal, *Antarctica*, pp. 182–195; William Mills, *Exploring Polar Frontiers: A Historical Encyclopedia*, vol. 1, ABC-Clio, Santa Barbara, 2003, pp. 160–161.

10   Ross, *Polar Pioneers*, pp. 271–357; David Stam and Deidre Stam, *Books on Ice: British & American Literature of Polar Exploration*, Grolier Club, New York, p. 29.

11   McGonigal, *Antarctica*, pp. 288–289.

12   Klaus Barthelmess, "A Century of German Interests in Modern Whaling, 1860s–1960s', in Bjorn Basberg et al. (eds), *Whaling and History: Perspectives on the Evolution of the Industry*, Whaling Museum, Sandefjord, 1993, p. 122; Mills, *Exploring Polar Frontiers*, vol. 1, p. 169; Karl Fricker, *The Antarctic Regions*, Swan Sonnenschein & Co., London, 1904, pp. 119–121.

13   Fricker, *The Antarctic Regions*, p. 123.

14   Lynette Cole, 'Proposals for the First Australian Antarctic Expedition', *Monash Publications in Geography*, Monash University, Melbourne, 1990, pp. 19–20.

15   Cole, 'Proposals for the First Australian Antarctic Expedition', pp. 19–20.

16   Cole, 'Proposals for the First Australian Antarctic Expedition', pp. 22–25, 28.

17   Lance Davis and Robert Gallman, 'American Whaling, 1820–1900: Dominance and Decline', and Gordon Jackson, 'Why Did the British Not Catch Rorquals in the Nineteenth Century?', in Basberg et al. (eds), *Whaling and History*, pp. 65–72, 116–117.

18   W. G. Burn Murdoch, *From Edinburgh to the Antarctic*, [First published 1894] Paradigm Press, Bungay, 1984, pp. xi–xii.

19   J. N. Tønnessen and A. O. Johnsen, *The History of Modern Whaling* [abridged and translated; first published in Norwegian in 4 vols, 1959–1970], C. Hurst & Co., London, 1982, pp. 149–152; Fricker, *The Antarctic Regions*, pp. 125–129; Klaus Barthelmess, "A Century of German Interests in Modern Whaling, 1860s–1960s', in Basberg, et al. (eds), *Whaling and History: Perspectives on the Evolution of the Industry*, p. 123.

20   Tønnessen and Johnsen, *The History of Modern Whaling*, pp. 153–155; Michael Rosove, *Let Heroes Speak: Antarctic Explorers, 1772–1922*, Naval Institute Press, Annapolis, 2000, pp. 61–62; H. J. Bull, *The Cruise of the 'Antarctic' to the South Polar Regions*, Edward Arnold, London, 1896 [Facsimile edition, Paradigm Press, Bungay, 1984], pp. 80, 82, 104–105.

21   Tønnessen and Johnsen, *The History of Modern Whaling*, pp. 153–155; Rosove, *Let Heroes Speak*, pp. 61–62, 65–66.

22   Bull, *The Cruise of the 'Antarctic' to the South Polar Regions*, p. 233.

23   Tønnessen and Johnsen, *The History of Modern Whaling*, pp. 153–155; Rosove, *Let Heroes Speak*, pp. 61–62, 65–66; Bull, *The Cruise of the 'Antarctic' to the South Polar Regions*, p. 233.

24   Bull, *The Cruise of the 'Antarctic' to the South Polar Regions*, pp. 221–222.

CHAPTER 6 – 1895–1906

1   Peter Speak, *William Speirs Bruce: Polar Explorer and Scottish Nationalist*, National Museums of Scotland Publishing, Edinburgh, 2003, pp. 36–37; Murdoch, *From Edinburgh to the Antarctic*, pp. 363–364.

2   *Oxford Dictionary of National Biography*, s. v. 'Markham'.

3   Clements Markham, *Antarctic Obsession: A personal narrative of the origins of the British National Antarctic Expedition 1901–1904* [edited by Clive Holland], Bluntisham Books, Alburgh, 1986, pp. 2–5.

4   John Murray, 'The Renewal of Antarctic Exploration', *Geographical Journal*, vol. 111, no. 1, January 1894, pp. 1–42.
5   Murray, 'The Renewal of Antarctic Exploration', p. 36.
6   Report by Research Department, Foreign Office, 1 May 1945, A4311/365/8, NAA.
7   Robert Headland, 'Geographical Discoveries in Antarctica by the Whaling Industry', in Bjorn Basberg et al. (eds), *Whaling and History: Perspectives on the Evolution of the Industry*, Whaling Museum, Sandefjord, 1993, pp. 192–193; Hugh Robert Mill, 'The Geographical Work of the Future', *Scottish Geographical Magazine*, February 1895.
8   Fricker, *The Antarctic Regions*, pp. 278–280; McGonigal, *Antarctica*, pp. 300–301.
9   'Plans for Dr. Cook's Proposed Antarctic Expedition and Story of the Eskimos and Dogs', c. 1894, Writings, Container 12, Frederick Albert Cook Papers, LoC; Cook's account of the *Belgica* expedition can be found in Frederick Cook, *Through the First Antarctic Night 1898–1899*, William Heinemann, London, 1900.
10 Brigadier General Greely, 'Antarctica', *Cosmopolitan*, New York, July 1894.
11 For the American imperial expansion at the turn of the twentieth century, and the racial thinking that underpinned it, see James Bradley, *The Imperial Cruise: A Secret History of Empire and War*, Little Brown, New York, 2009.
12 'Peeps into the Beyond: Reminiscences of Voyages of Exploration', undated typescript by Frederick Cook, Writings, Container 12, Cook Papers, LoC.
13 McGonigal, *Antarctica*, pp. 292–293.
14 'Peeps into the Beyond: Reminiscences of Voyages of Exploration', undated typescript by Frederick Cook, Writings, Container 12, Cook Papers, LoC; McGonigal, *Antarctica*, pp. 292–293.
15 McGonigal, *Antarctica*, pp. 292–293.
16 'Peeps into the Beyond: Reminiscences of Voyages of Exploration', undated typescript by Frederick Cook, Writings, Container 12, Cook Papers, LoC.
17 Untitled and undated account by Cook, c. 1927. Writings, Container 9, Cook Papers, LoC.
18 Cook, *Through the First Antarctic Night 1898–1899*, pp. 457–463.
19 Untitled and undated account by Cook, c. 1927, Writings, Container 9, Cook Papers, LoC.
20 'Peeps into the Beyond: Reminiscences of Voyages of Exploration', undated typescript by Frederick Cook, Writings, Container 12, Cook Papers, LoC.
21 C. E. Borchgrevink, *First on the Antarctic Continent, Being an Account of the British Antarctic Expedition 1898–1900*, George Newnes Limited, London, 1901.
22 *Daily News*, London, 10 August 1898; *Daily Chronicle*, London, 20 August 1898; Bernacchi diary, 22 August 1898 – 17 February 1899, MS 232/1/1/1, Bernacchi Papers, CM; T. H. Baughman, *Pilgrims on the Ice: Robert Falcon Scott's First Antarctic Expedition*, University of Nebraska Press, Lincoln, 1999, p. 8; letter, Borchgrevink to Evans, 17 December 1930, M 1/150/2/9/31 Part 1, ANZ.
23 Bernacchi diary, 22 August 1898 – 17 February 1899, MS 232/1/1/1, Bernacchi Papers, CM.
24 Borchgrevink, *First on the Antarctic Continent*, p. 84.
25 McGonigal, *Antarctica*, pp. 294–295; Borchgrevink, *First on the Antarctic Continent*, pp. 6–7, 84, 99, 258.

26 Louis Bernacchi, *To the South Polar Regions: Expedition of 1898–1900*, Hurst and Blackett, London, 1901, p. 84; Bernacchi diary, 1 March 1899–6 August 1899, MS 232/1/2/2, Bernacchi Papers, CM.

27 *Strand Magazine*, London, September 1900; Bernacchi diary, 1 March 1899–6 August 1899, MS 232/1/2/2, Bernacchi Papers, CM.

28 Bernacchi, *To the South Polar Regions*, pp. ix–x.

29 Borchgrevink, *First on the Antarctic Continent*, p. 7; Bernacchi, *To the South Polar Regions*, pp. 185–190; McGonigal (ed.), *Antarctica: Secrets of the Southern Continent*, pp. 294–295.

30 Letter Borchgrevink to Evans, 17 December 1930, M 1/150/2/9/31 Part 1, ANZ; McGonigal, *Antarctica*, p. 295.

31 Bernacchi, *To the South Polar Regions*, pp. 282–283.

32 Fricker, *The Antarctic Regions*, pp. 278–280.

33 Fricker, *The Antarctic Regions*, pp. 278–280; Erich von Drygalski, *The Southern Ice-Continent: The German South Polar Expedition aboard the Gauss 1901–1903*, Bluntisham Books, Bluntisham, 1989, pp. iii, 3–15; McGonigal, *Antarctica*, pp. 300–301.

34 Markham, *Antarctic Obsession*, pp. 8–10, 13, 23, 65, 71, 75; *Westminster Gazette*, London, 28 March 1899.

35 Baughman, *Pilgrims on the Ice*, pp. 19–20.

36 Markham's lecture in Berlin was reprinted as Clements Markham, 'The Antarctic Expeditions', *Geographical Journal*, vol. XIV, no. 5, November 1899; Markham, *Antarctic Obsession*, pp. 10–11; Erich Von Drygalski, 'The German Antarctic Expedition', *Geographical Journal*, vol. XVIII, no. 3, September 1901.

37 Peter Speak (ed.), *The Log of the* Scotia *Expedition, 1902–4*, Edinburgh University Press, Edinburgh, 1992, p. 29.

38 Markham, *Antarctic Obsession*, pp. 27–28.

39 Speak, *William Speirs Bruce*, pp. 69–75.

40 Markham, *Antarctic Obsession*, pp. 32–35, 41–43.

41 Markham, *Antarctic Obsession*, pp. 43–47.

42 Markham, *Antarctic Obsession*, p. 121.

43 Letter, Ford to his sister, 7 November 1901, MS 797/80/68/3, Ford Papers, AWMM.

44 Robert Scott, *The Voyage of the 'Discovery'*, Macmillan, London, 1905, vol. 1, pp. 148, 280–281, and vol. 2; McGonigal, *Antarctica*, pp. 296–299; British National Antarctic Expedition, Ephemera, 1902–1904, MS 259, CM.

45 Baughman, *Pilgrims on the Ice: Robert Falcon Scott's First Antarctic Expedition*, p. 135.

46 Robert Scott, *The Voyage of the 'Discovery'*, Macmillan, London, 1905, vol. 1, pp. 408–409; McGonigal, *Antarctica*, pp. 296–299; Max Jones (ed.), Introduction to *Journals: Captain Scott's Last Expedition*, Oxford University Press, Oxford, 2005, pp. xxii–xxiii; David Yelverton, *Antarctica Unveiled: Scott's First Expedition and the Quest for the Unknown Continent*, University Press of Colorado, Boulder, 2000, p. 223; Roland Huntford, *Scott and Amundsen*, Hodder and Stoughton, London, 1979, Chapters 10–12.

47 Memo, Thomas to Colbeck, 5 February 1904, MS 151, William Colbeck Papers, CM; A. G. E. Jones, *Harry Mackay, Master of the Terra Nova*, Raven Press, Christchurch, no date, reprinted from *Antarctic*, vol. 6, no. 9, March 1973.

48 Louis Bernacchi, 'Topography of South Victoria Land (Antarctic)', read at the Royal Geographical Society, 18 March 1901, in Murray (ed.), *The Antarctic Manual, for the use of the Expedition of 1901*, pp. 497, 514.

49 Clements Markham, 'The First Year's Work of the National Antarctic Expeditions', *Geographical Journal*, vol. XXII, no. 1, July 1903, p. 18; Robert Scott, *The Voyage of the 'Discovery'*, pp. 102, 124.

50 *Slough Observer*, 25 February 1905, MS 797/76/114/1, C. R. Ford Papers, AWMM.

51 Yelverton, *Antarctica Unveiled*, pp. 329–330.

52 Erich Von Drygalski, 'The German Antarctic Expedition', *Geographical Journal*, vol. XXIV, no. 2, August 1904; McGonigal, *Antarctica*, pp. 300–301; Drygalski, *The Southern Ice-Continent*, p. 239.

53 Drygalski, *The Southern Ice-Continent*, p. 372.

54 Erich Von Drygalski, 'The German Antarctic Expedition', *Geographical Journal*, vol. XXIV, no. 2, August 1904.

55 Christer Lindberg, 'Otto Nordenskjöld: Ethnographer' in Aant Elzinga et al. (eds), *Antarctic Challenges: Historical and Current Perspectives on Otto Nordenskjöld's Antarctic Expedition 1901–1903*, Royal Society of Arts and Sciences, Göteborg, 2004; Anders Karlqvist (ed.), *Sweden and Antarctica*, Swedish Polar Research Secretariat, Stockholm, 1985, pp. 17–37; McGonigal, *Antarctica*, pp. 302–303.

56 Jean Charcot, 'The French Antarctic Expedition', *Geographical Journal*, vol. 26, no. 5, November 1905; McGonigal, *Antarctica*, p. 306.

57 Lisbeth Lewander, 'Gender Aspects in the Narratives of Otto Nordenskjöld's Antarctic Expedition', in Elzinga et al. (eds), *Antarctic Challenges*, p. 115.

58 Lewander, 'Gender Aspects in the Narratives of Otto Nordenskjöld's Antarctic Expedition', p. 115.

59 Speak, *William Speirs Bruce*, pp. 75–81.

60 Speak (ed.), *The Log of the* Scotia *Expedition, 1902–4*, pp. 39, 59, 80, 196.

61 Speak (ed.), *The Log of the* Scotia *Expedition, 1902–4*, pp. 147–151, 160, 202.

62 Speak (ed.), *The Log of the* Scotia *Expedition, 1902–4*, pp. 146–147, 203.

63 Speak (ed.), *The Log of the* Scotia *Expedition, 1902–4*, pp. 175, 209, 215–224.

64 Speak (ed.), *The Log of the* Scotia *Expedition, 1902–4*, pp. 224, 237.

65 Letters, MacGregor to Foreign Office, 26 March 1904; Foreign Office to Haggard, 26 April 1904, in Speak (ed.), *The Log of the* Scotia *Expedition, 1902–4*, pp. 291–293.

CHAPTER 7 – 1907–1912

1 Jean Charcot, *The Voyage of the 'Pourquoi-Pas?': The Journal of the Second French South Polar Expedition, 1908–1910'*, Australian National University Press, Canberra, 1978, p. 32; Robert Headland, 'Whalers and Explorers', in Jan Erik Ringstad (ed.), *Whaling and History II: New Perspectives*, Whaling Museum, Sandefjord, 2006, p. 50.

2 Tønnessen and Johnsen, *The History of Modern Whaling*, pp. 158, 164–165; Robert Headland, 'Geographical Discoveries in Antarctica by the Whaling

Industry', in Bjorn Basberg et al. (eds), *Whaling and History: Perspectives on the Evolution of the Industry*, Whaling Museum, Sandefjord, 1993, pp. 193–195; Charcot, *The Voyage of the 'Pourquoi-Pas?'*, p. 42.

3   Jackson, 'Why Did the British Not Catch Rorquals in the Nineteenth Century?', in Bjorn Basberg et al. (eds), *Whaling and History*, pp. 116–117.

4   Wray Vamplew, *Salveson of Leith*, Scottish Academic Press, Edinburgh, 1975, pp. 136–138.

5   Klaus Barthelmess, 'An International Campaign against Whaling and Sealing prior to World War One', in Jan Erik Ringstad (ed.), *Whaling and History II: New perspectives*, Whaling Museum, Sandefjord, 2006, pp. 153–161.

6   Tønnessen and Johnsen, *The History of Modern Whaling*, pp. 158, 165–167.

7   'Territorial Claims in the Antarctic', report by Research Department, Foreign Office, 1 May 1945, A4311/365/8, NAA.

8   Tønnessen and Johnsen, *The History of Modern Whaling*, p. 165.

9   'Territorial Claims in the Antarctic', report by Research Department, Foreign Office, 1 May 1945, A4311/365/8, NAA.

10 Jorge Guzman Gutiérrez, 'Whales and Whaling in Chile', in Ringstad (ed.), *Whaling and History II*, pp. 69–73.

11 'British Policy in the Antarctic', memorandum by Inter-Departmental Committee, May 1926, ADM 116/2386/377, NA.

12 Tønnessen and Johnsen, *The History of Modern Whaling*, p. 169.

13 'British Policy in the Antarctic', memorandum by Inter-Departmental Committee, May 1926, ADM 116/2386/377, NA.

14 For Charcot's account of the voyage, see Charcot, *The Voyage of the 'Pourquoi-Pas?'*; J. B. Charcot, 'The Second French Antarctic Expedition', *Geographical Journal*, vol. XXXVII, no. 3, March 1911, p. 241; Hayes, *Antarctica*, pp. 135–139; McGonigal (ed.), *Antarctica*, pp. 306–307.

15 Yelverton, *Antarctica Unveiled*, p. 337.

16 Yelverton, *Antarctica Unveiled*, pp. 334–346; letter [copy], Shackleton to Scott, 17 May 1907, MS 276/1/1/8a, Bernacchi Papers, CM.

17 Roland Huntford, *Shackleton*, Hodder and Stoughton, London, 1985, pp. 174–184.

18 Ernest Shackleton, *The Heart of the Antarctic*, William Heinemann, London, 1910, p. 3.

19 *Argus*, Melbourne, 7 January 1897.

20 David Burke, *Body at the Melbourne Club: Bertram Armytage, Antarctica's forgotten man*, Wakefield Press, Adelaide, 2009, p. 48.

21 Letters, David to Lyne, 16 December 1907; Shackleton to Deakin, 23 December 1907, A2/1909/2497, NAA; Huntford, *Shackleton*, pp. 182, 185, 187–189; Shackleton, *The Heart of the Antarctic*, p. 2.

22 Huntford, *Shackleton*, pp. 189, 199.

23 'New Zealand Antarctic Post Offices, King Edward VII Land', extract from P.M.G.'s report for 1907–08, AAMF/W3118/3/1955/2876, ANZ.

24 *Hansard*, Senate, 6 February 1908, A2/1909/2497, NAA.

25 William Ronson, 'Stamps of the Arctic and of the Antarctic', *Explorers Journal*, June 1962; 'Territorial Claims in the Antarctic', report by Research Department, Foreign Office, 1 May 1945, A4311/365/8, NAA.

26 Huntford, *Shackleton*, p. 312.

27 Harboard diary, 1 January 1908, Arthur Harboard Papers, MS 330, CM.

28 Harboard diary, 6 and 7 January 1908, Arthur Harboard Papers, MS 330, CM.

29 *Nimrod* Logbook, January 1908–March 1909, Henrik Bull Papers, MS 315, CM; Yelverton, *Antarctica Unveiled*, pp. 346–347; Huntford, *Shackleton*, pp. 190–207.

30 Yelverton, *Antarctica Unveiled*, pp. 346–347; Huntford, *Shackleton*, pp. 190–207.

31 Letter, Scott to Bernacchi, 25 March 1908, MS 276/1/1/8, Bernacchi Papers, CM.

32 Huntford, *Scott and Amundsen*, p. 239.

33 Harboard diary, 29 and 30 January 1908, 21 and 27 December 1909 and 1 January 1910, Arthur Harboard Papers, MS 330, CM.

34 Harboard diary, 1 February 1908, Arthur Harboard Papers, MS 330, CM.

35 Huntford, *Shackleton*, pp. 239–240.

36 Huntford, *Shackleton*, Chapter XXIV.

37 Huntford, *Shackleton*, pp. 264–272; Shackleton, *The Heart of the Antarctic*, pp. 200–209.

38 See, for instance, a letter by Phillip Law along these lines: letter, Law to Landy, 31 December 2001, MS 9458/1/150, Law Papers, NLA; Huntford, *Shackleton*, pp. 310–311.

39 Shackleton, *The Heart of the Antarctic*, p. 210.

40 Huntford, *Shackleton*, p. 272; Hugh Robert Mill, *The Life of Sir Ernest Shackleton*, William Heinemann, London, 1923, p. 144.

41 Shackleton, *The Heart of the Antarctic*, p. 310.

42 Mill, *The Life of Sir Ernest Shackleton*, pp. 156–180; Yelverton, *Antarctica Unveiled*, p. 348.

43 Huntford, *Scott and Amundsen*, pp. 247–248.

44 Jones (ed.), *Journals: Captain Scott's Last Expedition*, pp. xxv–xxvi.

45 Huntford, *Scott and Amundsen*, pp. 215–220; telegrams, James Gordon Bennett, *New York Herald*, to Cook, 2 and 3 September 1909, and other documents in Correspondence, Container 2, Frederick Albert Cook Papers, LoC.

46 Letters, Heinemann to Cook, and Curtis Brown to Cook, both dated 2 September 1909, and Hallett to Cook, 8 September 1909, and other documents in Correspondence, Container 2, Frederick Albert Cook Papers, LoC.

47 Yelverton, *Antarctica Unveiled*, p. 348; McGonigal, *Antarctica*, pp. 320–321.

48 'The Indomitable Pathfinder, Amundsen', Typescript by Cook, c. 1929, Writings, Container 9, Cook Papers, LoC; Huntford, *Scott and Amundsen*, pp. 88–114, 265, 294–295.

49 *Bulletin of the American Geographical Society*, vol. XLIII, 1911; Huntford, *Scott and Amundsen*, p. 222; Wilhelm Filchner, *To the Sixth Continent: The second German south polar expedition*, Bluntisham Books, Bluntisham, 1994, p. 4; *New York Times*, New York, 12 March 1910.

50 Hugh Robert Mill, *The Life of Sir Ernest Shackleton*, William Heinemann, London, 1923, p. 184; *Scotsman*, Edinburgh, 10 January 1910; *Glasgow Herald*, 11 January 1910; *West of Scotland Notes*, [undated] pp. 263–265, HH1/1936, Scottish National Antarctic Expedition Papers, NAS.

51 Edward Wilson, *Diary of the Terra Nova Expedition to the Antarctic 1910–1912*, Blandford Press, London, 1972, p. xix; Huntford, *Scott and Amundsen*, pp. 268–269.

52 Letter, Shackleton to Scott, 21 February 1910, MS 367/17/2/D, SPRI. I am grateful to Peter FitzSimons for bringing this reference to my attention. Huntford, *Scott and Amundsen*, pp. 324–325.

53 Huntford, *Scott and Amundsen*, pp. 282–283.
54 Huntford, *Scott and Amundsen*, pp. 286–287.
55 Huntford, *Shackleton*, p. 329.
56 Jones (ed.), *Journals: Captain Scott's Last Expedition*, p. xxvi; Huntford, *Scott and Amundsen*, pp. 317–322.
57 Peter FitzSimons, *Mawson and the Ice Men of the Heroic Age: Scott, Shackleton and Amundsen*, William Heinemann, Sydney, 2011, pp. 235–236.
58 Crane, *Scott of the Antarctic*, pp. 441–445.
59 Roald Amundsen, *The South Pole: An account of the Norwegian Antarctic expedition in the 'Fram', 1910–1912*, vol. 1, C. Hurst, London, 1976, pp. 203–205; Raymond Priestley, *Antarctic Adventure: Scott's northern party*, Melbourne University Press, Melbourne, 1974, pp. 40–41; Wilson, *Diary of the Terra Nova Expedition to the Antarctic 1910–1912*, p. 107.
60 Jones (ed.), *Journals: Captain Scott's last expedition*, p. 135.
61 Amundsen, *The South Pole*, vol. 1, pp. 378–389, vol. 2, pp. 113–114; Huntford, *Scott and Amundsen*, pp. 487–495.
62 Amundsen, *The South Pole*, vol. 2, pp. 125–132; Huntford, *Scott and Amundsen*, pp. 487–495; Newspaper cuttings, c. 9 March 1912, Newspaper Cuttings Book, AAD; lecture by Amundsen to the Berlin Geographical Society, 9 October 1912, *Bulletin of the American Geographical Society*, vol. XLIV, 1912, pp. 822–838.
63 Huntford, *Scott and Amundsen*, pp. 334, 418–425.
64 Crane, *Scott of the Antarctic*, pp. 414–419; Huntford, *Scott and Amundsen*, p. 513.
65 Wilson, *Diary of the Terra Nova Expedition to the Antarctic 1910–1912*, pp. 231–233.
66 Huntford, *Scott and Amundsen*, pp. 515–517.
67 Huntford, *Scott and Amundsen*, pp. 545–560; [no author] *Captain Scott's Message to England*, St Catherine's Press, London, 1913.
68 Huntford, *Scott and Amundsen*, pp. 518-545; Roald Amundsen, *My Life as an Explorer*, William Heinemann, London, 1927, pp. 72–73; newspaper cuttings, c. 9 March 1912, Newspaper Cuttings Book, AAD.
69 'Captain Roald Amundsen and the Society', *Journal of the Royal Geographical Society*, December 1927, pp. 572–575.
70 Huntford, *Scott and Amundsen*; [no author] *Captain Scott's Message to England*, St Catherine's Press, London, 1913. A recent defence of Scott was provided by David Crane's *Scott of the Antarctic*.

CHAPTER 8 – 1912–1918

1   For details of Mawson's private life, see Philip Ayres, *Mawson: A life*, Melbourne University Press, Melbourne, 1999.
2   *Advertiser*, Adelaide, 12 January 1911; *Sydney Morning Herald*, Sydney, 8 September 1911; Ayres, *Mawson*, p. 43
3   Ayres, *Mawson*, pp. 44, 53; *Daily Telegraph*, Sydney, 14 January 1911.
4   *Register*, Adelaide, 19 January 1911.
5   Douglas Mawson, 'The Australasian Antarctic Expedition', *Geographical Journal*, June 1911; Ayres, *Mawson*, pp. 44–53, 55; Huntford, *Shackleton*, pp. 338–339.
6   Ayres, *Mawson*, pp. 44–53; Huntford, *Shackleton*, pp. 338–339.

7   Newspaper cuttings, c. 1914, Newspaper Cuttings Book, AAD.
8   Douglas Mawson, *The Home of the Blizzard, Being the Story of the Australasian Antarctic Expedition, 1911–1914*, vol. 1, William Heinemann, London, 1915, pp. 23–24.
9   Ayres, *Mawson*, p. 52; 'Personal Diary of Stanley Taylor, Fireman on the "Aurora" ', AAD.
10   *Register*, Adelaide, 18 November 1911.
11   Fred Jacka and Eleanor Jacka (eds.), *Mawson's Antarctic Diaries*, Unwin Hyman, London, 1988, pp. xxxv–xxxvi.
12   Percival Gray, '*Antarctic Voyages': Diary aboard the Aurora, 1911–14*, 3 January 1912, AAD.
13   Mawson, *The Home of the Blizzard*, vol. 1, pp. 61–62.
14   Charles Laseron, *South with Mawson*, Australasian Publishing, Sydney, 1947, p. 61.
15   Mawson, *The Home of the Blizzard*, vol. 1, pp. 239–242, 296; Ayres, *Mawson*, pp. 73–75; Jacka and Jacka (eds.), *Mawson's Antarctic Diaries*, pp. 153–154, 158, 181; Beau Riffenburgh, *Racing with Death: Douglas Mawson – Antarctic Explorer*, Bloomsbury, London, 2008, pp. 136–137.
16   Riffenburgh, *Racing with Death*, pp. 119–127.
17   Riffenburgh, *Racing with Death*, pp. 128–130; Ayres, *Mawson*, pp. 73–75; Jacka and Jacka (eds.), *Mawson's Antarctic Diaries*, pp. 153–158.
18   Riffenburgh, *Racing with Death*, pp. 131–133.
19   Ayres, *Mawson*, pp. 78–79; Jacka and Jacka (eds.), *Mawson's Antarctic Diaries*, pp. 159–171.
20   Jacka and Jacka (eds.), *Mawson's Antarctic Diaries*, pp. 186, 200; Mawson, *The Home of the Blizzard*, vol. 1, pp. 77–78 and vol. 2, pp. 102–105, 123–124.
21   'Personal Diary of Stanley Taylor', p. 83, AAD.
22   Mawson, *The Home of the Blizzard*, vol. 2, p. 135.
23   Mawson, *The Home of the Blizzard*, vol. 1, p. 271; Jacka and Jacka (eds.), *Mawson's Antarctic Diaries*, p. 171.
24   Jacka and Jacka (eds.), *Mawson's Antarctic Diaries*, p. 162.
25   Newspaper cuttings, c. 1914, Newspaper Cuttings Book, Australian AAD.
26   Newspaper cutting, c. March 1914, Newspaper Cuttings Book, AAD.
27   Newspaper cutting, c. February 1914, Newspaper Cuttings Book, AAD.
28   Riffenburgh, *Racing with Death*, pp. 178–180.
29   Mawson, *The Home of the Blizzard*, vol. 1, pp. 264–265; Jacka and Jacka (eds.), *Mawson's Antarctic Diaries*, pp. 161–162.
30   Ayres, *Mawson*, p. 80.
31   Tim Jarvis, *Mawson: Life and death in Antarctica*, Miegunyah Press, Carlton, 2008, pp. 212–213.
32   Newspaper cutting, c. February 1914, Newspaper Cuttings Book, AAD.
33   'Territorial Claims in the Antarctic', report by Research Department, Foreign Office, 1 May 1945, A4311/365/8, NAA; Newspaper cuttings, c. 1914, Newspaper Cuttings Book, AAD.
34   'Capt. Scott's Expedition: Lecture Tour, 1913–14, by Commander E.R.G.R. Evans, C.B., R.N.', PRG 523, Series 11/1, Mawson Papers, SLSA; Ayres, *Mawson*, pp. 106–110; Riffenburgh, *Racing with Death*, pp. 182–184.
35   Filchner, *To the Sixth Continent: the second German south polar expedition*, pp. 194–195, 201–214, 227–235.

36 For Filchner's account of the German expedition, see Filchner, *To the Sixth Continent*; *New York Times*, 8 January 1913.

37 *Sydney Morning Herald*, Sydney, 1 December 1910, 8 February 1911; McGonigal, *Antarctica*, p. 321; Shirase Expedition Supporters Association, *The Japanese South Polar Expedition 1910–12, A Record of Antarctica*, Erskine Press and Bluntisham Books, Norwich and Bluntisham, 2012, pp. 15, 22–23, 45.

38 *Sydney Morning Herald*, Sydney, 2 May 1911; *Cairns Post*, Cairns, 15 February 1913;

39 *Sydney Morning Herald*, Sydney, 1 July and 16 November 1911; *Argus*, Melbourne, 13 November 1911; Shirase Expedition Supporters Association, *The Japanese South Polar Expedition 1910–12*, pp. 27, 42, 83, 88.

40 Shirase Expedition Supporters Association, *The Japanese South Polar Expedition 1910–12*, pp. 92–94.

41 *Sydney Morning Herald*, 25 March and 5 April 1912; *New York Times*, New York, 25 March 1912; McGonigal, *Antarctica*, p. 321; Shirase Expedition Supporters Association, *The Japanese South Polar Expedition 1910–12*, pp. 172–173, 396–397.

42 Shirase Expedition Supporters Association, *The Japanese South Polar Expedition 1910–12*, pp. 200, 205, 217–218, 235, 238, 315–316, 319.

43 'Territorial Claims in the Antarctic', report by Research Department, Foreign Office, 1 May 1945, A4311/365/8, NAA.

44 Letters, Ikeda to President, RGS, 18 August and 17 September 1912, Keltie to Colles, 27 March 1914; postcard, Ikeda to President, RGS, 20 August 1912, provided courtesy of Hilary Shibata, SPRI; Shirase Expedition Supporters Association, *The Japanese South Polar Expedition 1910–12*, p. 321.

45 Letters, Newberry to Robbins, 8 March 1906, and Hays to Secretary, American Geographical Society, 20 May 1909, 'Wilkes Land controversy' folder, AGS; Edwin Swift Balch, 'Why America Should Re-Explore Wilkes Land', *Proceedings of the American Philosophical Society*, vol. 48, no. 191, April 1909.

46 Balch, 'Why America Should Re-Explore Wilkes Land'.

47 Letter, Littlehales to Adams, 22 October 1909, 'Wilkes Land controversy' folder; letter, Robbins to Clarkson, 19 November 1909, 'Wilkes Land controversy' folder, AGS.

48 Letter, Huntington to Secretary of the Navy, 7 December 1909, 'Wilkes Land controversy' folder, AGS.

49 Letter, Wainwright to James, 1 April 1910, 'Wilkes Land controversy' folder, AGS.

50 Letter, Balch to Adams, 18 February 1914, 'Wilkes Land controversy' folder, AGS; 'Antarctic Names', Edwin Swift Balch, *Bulletin of the American Geographical Society*, vol. XLIV, 1912, pp. 561–581.

51 Cited in Hayes, *Antarctica: A Treatise on the Southern Continent*, p. 364.

52 *Bulletin of the American Geographical Society*, vol. XLIII, 1911.

53 Huntford, *Shackleton*, p. 350.

54 Hugh Robert Mill, 'Ten Years of Antarctic Exploration', *Geographical Journal*, vol. 39, no. 4, April 1912, p. 375.

55 William Bruce, *Polar Exploration*, Williams and Norgate, London, 1911, pp. 236, 253.

56 Huntford, *Shackleton*, p. 362; Ernest Shackleton, *South: The Story of Shackleton's Last Expedition 1914–1917*, Century Publishing, London, 1983, pp. xi–xiii.

57 Newspaper cuttings, c. 1914, Newspaper Cuttings Book, AAD.
58 Shackleton, *South*, p. xiii.
59 When an Austrian member of Filchner's party announced that he was going back in the *Deutschland* to lead an expedition of his own to Vahsel Bay and demanded that Shackleton go elsewhere, Shackleton refused to budge. In the event, the Austrian expedition never sailed, being overtaken by the outbreak of war.
60 Shackleton, *South*, p. xiv–xv; Huntford, *Shackleton*, p. 368.
61 Unknown author, 'British Imperial Trans-Antarctic Expedition', unpublished notes, 5 April 1916. MS 377, CM; Huntford, *Shackleton*, p. 366.
62 Notes by Churchill, 23 January and 7 February 1914, ADM 1/8368/29, NA.
63 Huntford, *Shackleton*, pp. 364, 383.
64 Huntford, *Shackleton*, pp. 390–392.

CHAPTER 9 – 1919–1926

1 Memo, Amery to Milner, 13 June 1919, AMEL 1/3/42, Leo Amery Papers, CAC.
2 Memo, Amery to Milner, 13 June 1919, AMEL 1/3/42, Leo Amery Papers, CAC.
3 Memo, Amery to Milner, 13 June 1919, AMEL 1/3/42, Leo Amery Papers, CAC.
4 Huntford, *Shackleton*, pp. 673–685.
5 Margery and James Fisher, *Shackleton*, Barrie, London, 1957, pp. 442–458; 'The Voyage of the "Quest" ', *Geographical Review*, New York, vol. XIV, 1924, p. 484.
6 Huntford, *Shackleton*, pp. 451–452, 639.
7 Undated newspaper cuttings, c. 1919, MS 883/31/2, Frank Hurley Papers, NLA; *New York Times*, 24 and 26 January and 28 October 1920; Simon Nasht, *The Last Explorer: Hubert Wilkins – Australia's unknown hero*, second edition, Hachette, Sydney, 2006, p. 94.
8 'Territorial Claims in the Antarctic Regions', report compiled in the Hydrographic Department, 1919, ADM 1/8565/226, NA.
9 'Territorial Claims in the Antarctic Regions', report compiled in the Hydrographic Department, 1919; minute, Learmonth to DCNS, 3 January 1920, ADM 1/8565/226, NA.
10 Memorandum, Amery to Governors General of Australia and New Zealand, 6 February 1920, CO 886/9/22, NA; *Sydney Morning Herald*, 14 and 23 August 1919.
11 'Future Policy of Empire in Antarctic Regions', memo by Shepherd, 12 January 1921, and other documents in this file, A981/ANT4/Part 1, NAA.
12 Cable, Hughes to Millen, 21 October 1920, A981/ANT4/Part 1, NAA.
13 'Future Policy of Empire in Antarctic Regions', memo by Shepherd, 12 January 1921, and other documents in this file, A981/ANT4/Part 1, NAA.
14 *Argus*, Melbourne, 3 January 1921.
15 Cable, Hughes to Millen, 29 January 1921; minutes of meeting at Colonial Office, 2 February 1921, A981/ANT4/Part 1, NAA.
16 'Memorandum on Control of the Antarctic', March 1921, CO 886/9/5; note, Learmonth to Director, Naval Intelligence, 10 May 1921, ADM 1/8565/226, NA.
17 Letters, Greene to Colonial Office, 23 October 1911, Mallett to Under Secretary of State, Colonial Office, 23 November 1911, Colonial Office to Foreign Office, 13 December 1911; dispatches, Mallett to Bertie, 18 December 1911,

and Bertie to Foreign Office, 19 April 1912, CO 537/1080, CO 537/1080, NA.

18 Letter, Foreign Office to Dominions Office, 4 November 1925, CO 537/1093, NA.
19 'Memorandum on Control of the Antarctic', March 1921, CO 886/9/5; note, Learmonth to Director, Naval Intelligence, 10 May 1921, ADM 1/8565/226, NA.
20 Letter, Marsh to Hughes, 7 June 1921, A981/ANT4/Part 1, NAA.
21 Undated newspaper cuttings, c. 1919, MS 883/31/2, Frank Hurley Papers, NLA.
22 *New York Times*, 24 December 1920.
23 Nasht, *The Last Explorer*, p. 97.
24 Nasht, *The Last Explorer*, pp. 93–102; McGonigal, *Antarctica* p. 333; further details of the expedition are on the website of the Scott Polar Research Institute.
25 For details on the selection of Marr and Mooney, see the website www.scouting.milestones.btinternet.co.uk/marr.htm.
26 *New York Times*, 18 September 1921; Huntford, *Shackleton*, p. 683.
27 Huntford, *Shackleton*, pp. 688–690; undated newspaper cutting, c. January 1922, MS 883/31/2, Frank Hurley Papers, NLA; Fisher, *Shackleton*, pp. 479–483.
28 Newspaper cutting, c. February 1922, MS 59, CCC; Marr, *Into the Frozen South*, pp. 101–102, 186–197; Huntford, *Shackleton*, pp. 688–691; Fisher, *Shackleton*, pp. 482–483.
29 Cable, Churchill to Jellicoe, 28 June 1922, 'Antarctic and Arctic Regions, Control of,' folder, G48/1/A/3, ANZ.
30 Cable, Jellicoe to Colonial Secretary, 29 July 1922; letter, Devonshire to Jellicoe, 21 November 1922, 'Antarctic and Arctic Regions, Control of,' folder, G48/1/A/3, ANZ.
31 Letter, Devonshire to Jellicoe, 1 February 1923, 'Antarctic and Arctic Regions, Control of,' folder, G48/1/A/3, ANZ.
32 Cable, Jellicoe to Secretary of State, Colonial Office, 29 July 1922; letter, Duke of Devonshire to Jellicoe, 21 November 1922, 'Antarctic and Arctic Regions, Control of,' folder, G48/1/A/3, ANZ; *Dominion*, Wellington, 14 August 1923.
33 For the correspondence between the French and British governments on this issue in 1911–12, see CO 537/1080, NA.
34 Report to President by Daladier, 21 November 1924, M1/1207/25/1982, ANZ.
35 Memo by Learmonth, 17 September 1924, ADM 116/2386; 'British Policy in the Antarctic', memo by Dominions Office, August 1925, CO 537/1081, NA.
36 Telegram, Governor General to Amery, 4 December 1924, ADM 116/2386/49, NA; cable, Governor General to Amery, 16 February 1925, A981/ANT4/Part 4, NAA.
37 *Dominion*, Wellington, 17 February 1925.
38 Telegram, Amery to Governor General, 18 February 1925, ADM 116/2386/114, NA.
39 'The French Claim to Part of the Antarctic Continent', memorandum by the Hydrographic Department, Admiralty, January 1925, ADM 116/2386/57, NA.
40 *New York Times*, 6 April 1929.

41 According to the *New York Times*, the undiscovered continent could cover an area half as large as the United States. *New York Times*, 12 June 1925.

42 *New York Times*, 26 April and 12 June 1925; *Popular Science*, New York, July 1925; Lisle Rose, *Explorer: The Life of Richard E. Byrd*, University of Missouri Press, Columbia, 2008, Chap. 3; Jeff Maynard, *Wings of Ice*, Vintage Books, Sydney 2010, pp. 40–44.

43 Letter, Vogt to Chamberlain, 24 February 1925, ADM 116/2386/125, NA.

44 Note by Douglas, 16 March 1925, ADM 116/2386/125; letter, Batterbee to Under Secretary of State, Foreign Office, 29 May 1925, ADM 116/2386/167, NA.

45 'Adelie Land', memo by Henderson, 21 April 1925, A981/ANT4/Part 4, NAA.

46 Memo by the Australian National Research Council, 1925, ADM 116/2386/321, NA.

47 Minutes of Deputation from the Australian National Research Council, 3 July 1925, A981/ANT4/Part 4, NAA.

48 Letter, Forster to Amery, 16 September 1925, ADM 116/2386/318; 'Notes on the Australian National Research Council's Memorandum Respecting the "Australian Sector" of the Antarctic', by Hydrographic Department, January 1926, ADM 116/2386/331, NA; despatch, Amery to Lord Stonehaven, 24 December 1925, A981/ANT4/Part 4, NAA.

49 Letter, Batterbee to Secretary, Admiralty, 29 May 1925; note by Douglas, 18 June 1925, ADM 116/2386/157; letter, Walker to Batterbee, 15 July 1925; minute, Batterbee to Davis,15 July 1925, CO 537/1075, NA.

50 Letter, Davis to Foreign Office, 29 August 1925, CO 537/1075; 'On the Validity of the French Territorial Claims in the Antarctic', memo by Hydrographic Department, October 1925, CO 537/1081, NA.

51 Letter, Villiers to Dominions Office, 4 November 1925, CO 537/1093, NA; see also minute by Douglas, 4 February 1926, ADM 116/2386/230, NA.

52 Minute, Batterbee to Davis, 26 January 1926, CO 537/1093; 'British Policy in the Antarctic', memo prepared by the Inter-Departmental Committee, May 1926, ADM 116/2386/377, NA.

53 *Mercury*, Hobart, 10 May 1924.

54 *Mercury*, Hobart, 16 and 20 May 1924.

55 *Mercury*, Hobart, 20 May 1924.

56 *Mercury*, Hobart, 28 May 1924; *Weekly Press*, Christchurch, 18 March 1926.

57 *Weekly Press*, Christchurch, 18 March 1926.

58 Letter, Fergusson to Amery, 14 April 1925, 'Antarctic and Arctic Regions, Control of,' folder, G48/1/A/3, ANZ.

59 Letter, Andvig to New Zealand High Commissioner, 16 September 1925; letter, Andvig to Colonial Office, 26 September 1925, 'Antarctic and Arctic Regions, Control of,' folder, G48/1/A/3, ANZ.

60 Letters, Melsom and Melsom to Governor of the Falkland Islands, 21 September 1925, Melsom and Melsom to Colonial Office, 10 October and 11 November 1925, Grindle to Melsom and Melsom, 6 and 25 November 1925, and Amery to Fergusson, 11 January 1926, 'Antarctic and Arctic Regions, Control of,' folder, G48/1/A/3, ANZ.

61 Letter, Henderson to Secretary, Prime Minister's Department, 27 February 1924; 'Control of Ross Sea in the Antarctic', memo, 29 March 1924, A981/ANT4, Part 2, NAA.

62 Letter, Harding to Secretary, Admiralty, 23 March 1926; note by Douglas, 3 May 1926, ADM 116/2386, NA.

63 'British Policy in the Antarctic', memo prepared by the Inter-Departmental Committee, May 1926, ADM 116/2386/377, NA.

64 Minutes, Committee on British Policy in the Antarctic, 10, 17 and 18 November 1926, CAB 32/51, NA.

65 'Report of the Committee on British Policy in the Antarctic', 19 November 1926, CAB 32/51, NA.

66 'Report of the Committee on British Policy in the Antarctic', 19 November 1926, CAB 32/51, NA.

67 John Barnes and David Nicholson (eds), *The Leo Amery Diaries, Vol. 1: 1896–1029*, Hutchinson, London, 1980, p. 482.

CHAPTER 10 – 1926–1928

1 Letter, Vogt to Chamberlain, 13 May 1927, ADM 116/2386/464, NA.

2 Note by Douglas, 13 June 1927, ADM 116/2386; 'Notes on the Norwegian Territorial Claims in the Antarctic', Admiralty memo, 7 July 1927, ADM 116/2386/469; letter, Foreign Office to Vogt, August 1927, ADM 116/2386/502, NA; draft note, British Foreign Office to Norwegian Minister, September 1927, M 1/1209/25/2029, ANZ.

3 Memorandum, Acting Prime Minister to Governor-General, 14 January 1927, G 48/1/A/3(1), ANZ.

4 Memo, Acting Prime Minister to Governor-General, 14 January 1927, G 48/1/A/3(1), ANZ; *Argus*, Melbourne, 23 March 1927; letter, Dixon to Casey, 30 April 1927, A981/ANT4/Part 4, NAA.

5 Kyvind Tofte, 'Report of Expedition to Peter Island in the Antarctic, 1927', Whaling Museum, Sandefjord; Robert Headland, 'Geographical Discoveries in Antarctica by the Whaling Industry', in Bjorn Basberg, Jan Erik Ringstad and Einar Wexelsen (eds), *Whaling and History: Perspectives on the Evolution of the Industry*, Whaling Museum, Sandefjord, 1993, p. 197.

6 Lars Christensen, *Such Is the Antarctic*, Hodder and Stoughton, London, 1935, pp. 17–18.

7 Christensen, *Such Is the Antarctic*, p. 32.

8 'Bouvet Island', *Geographical Journal*, vol. 72, no. 6, December 1928, p. 537.

9 Note by Douglas, 15 November 1927, ADM 116/2386/532, NA.

10 Headland, 'Geographical Discoveries in Antarctica by the Whaling Industry', in Basberg et al. (eds), *Whaling and History*, p. 197; 'Bouvet Island', *Geographical Review*, vol. 19, no. 3, July 1929.

11 Articles by Bjarne Aagaard, 17–23 March 1928, Newspaper cutting book relating to Bouvet Island, WM.

12 *Manchester Guardian*, Manchester, *Evening News*, *Daily Express* and *Daily Sketch*, London, 20 January 1928.

13 *Times*, London, 24 and 25 January and 30 April 1928; Articles by Bjarne Aagaard, 17–23 March 1928, Newspaper cutting book relating to Bouvet Island, WM.

14 'Polar Regions', *Geographical Record*, vol. 18, no. 4, October 1928,

15 'Territorial Claims in the Antarctic', report by Research Department, Foreign Office, 1 May 1945, A4311/365/8, NAA.

16 'Territorial Claims in the Antarctic', report by Research Department, Foreign Office, 1 May 1945, A4311/365/8, NAA.

17 Noel Barrett, *Was Australian Antarctic Won Fairly?*, Honours Thesis, Bachelor of Antarctic Studies, University of Tasmania, November 2007, p. 29.

18 Headland, 'Geographical Discoveries in Antarctica by the Whaling Industry', in Basberg et al. (eds), *Whaling and History*, p. 197; Christensen, *Such Is the Antarctic*, p. 33.

19 Rose, *Explorer*, pp. 7–39.

20 'Polar Lands and Explorers', by Frederick Dellenbaugh, *Geographical Review*, vol. XVI, 1926; 'The Polar Flights of Byrd and Amundsen', *Geographical Review*, vol. XVI, 1926; Vilhjalmur Stefansson, *The Adventure of Wrangel Island*, Macmillan, New York, 1925; D. M. LeBourdais, *Stefansson: Ambassador of the North*, Harvest house, Montreal, 1963, pp. 158–172.

21 Rose, *Explorer*, pp. 60–100; Maynard, *Wings of Ice*, pp. 40–44; 'The Amundsen-Ellsworth Polar Flight', *Geographical Review*, New York, vol. XV, 1925, p. 665.

22 Rose, *Explorer*, pp. 101–116; *New York Times*, 28 March 1926; telegrams, Byrd to Bowman, 9 January 1926, Byrd to E. S. Evans, c. January 1926; letter, Byrd to Bowman, 28 January 1926, 'Byrd, R. E., 1926' folder, AGS; Maynard, *Wings of Ice*, p. 77.

23 Rose, *Explorer*, pp. 116–123; Maynard, *Wings of Ice*, pp. 109–111.

24 Letters, Byrd to Bowman, 24 November 1926, and Bowman to Byrd, 29 November 1926, 'Byrd, R. E., 1926' folder, AGS.

25 Rose, *Explorer*, pp. 123–146.

26 Richard E. Byrd, *Skyward*, Putnam, New York, 1928, pp. 222–278; Rose, *Explorer*, pp. 157–165.

27 Letter, Byrd to Bowman, 15 January 1927, 'Byrd, R. E., 1927–28' folder, AGS.

28 Rose, *Explorer*, p. 147.

29 Rose, *Explorer*, p. 174.

30 Byrd, *Skyward*, p. 300.

31 Letter, Joerg to Drygalski, 4 August 1926, 'Erich von Drygalski, Antarctic' folder; letters, Bowman to Byrd, 20 August, 22 September and 20 December 1926, 'Byrd, R. E., 1926' folder, AGS.

32 Byrd, *Skyward*, pp. 305, 317.

33 Letters, Bowman to Byrd, 3 January, 16 February and 7 June 1927; cable, Bowman to Byrd, 8 July 1927, 'Byrd, R. E., 1927–28' folder, AGS.

34 H. H. Clayton, 'Argentine Interest in Antarctic Exploration', *Geographical Review*, vol. XV, 1925, p. 667; memo to Coulter and Pickering, 1 September 1926, enclosing copy of letter from Antonio Pauly, 'Expeditions and Explorers: Arctic and Antarctic – Miscellaneous' Folder, AGS.

35 *Niagara Falls Gazette*, Niagara Falls, 9 April 1927.

36 Letters, Byrd to Bowman, 25 July 1927, and Bowman to Byrd, 28 July 1927, 'Byrd, R. E., 1927–28' folder, AGS.

37 *New York Times*, 5 August 1927; letter, Byrd to Bowman, 6 August 1927, and Bowman to Byrd, 12 August 1927, 'Byrd, R. E., 1927–28' folder, American Geographical Society, New York; Rose, *Explorer*, Chap. 6.

38 Letters, Byrd to Bowman, 14 August 1927, 17 and 22 September 1927 and 13 February 1928, 6 and 19 April 1928 and 3 May 1928, and Bowman to Byrd, 19 and 27 September 1927 and 10 April 1928, 'Byrd, R. E., 1927–28' folder, AGS.

39 Byrd, *Skyward*, p. 303.

40 Nasht, *The Last Explorer*, pp. 160–173; W. J. Hudson and Jane North (eds.), *My Dear P.M.: R.G. Casey's Letters to S. M. Bruce 1924–1929*, Australian Government Publishing Service, Canberra, 1980, pp. 78–79, 178–179, 341–342.

41 Hudson and North (eds.), *My Dear P.M.*, pp. 341–342.
42 *Times*, London, 8 June and 10 September 1928.
43 Nasht, *The Last Explorer*, pp. 174–178; *Times*, London, 7 June 1928.
44 Memo, Dominions Secretary to Bruce, 3 August 1928, A2910/417/15/9 Part 1, NAA; Dispatch, Foreign Office to Chiltern, 4 September 1928, M 1/1218/25/2296 Part 3, ANZ.
45 Cited in Maynard, *Wings of Ice*, p. 186.
46 Nasht, *The Last Explorer*, pp. 179–180.
47 Nasht, *The Last Explorer*, pp. 181–183; 'Policy in the Antarctic', Memo for the Imperial Conference, September 1930, A981/ANT4, Part 8, NAA.
48 Rose, *Explorer*, pp. 225–226.
49 Cables, Amery to Governor-General, 6 November 1928, and Governor-General to Amery, 8 November 1928, N 1/463/16/8/13, ANZ.
50 'Territorial Claims in the Antarctic', report by Research Department, Foreign Office, 1 May 1945, A4311/365/8, NAA; Dispatch, Foreign Office to Chiltern, 4 September 1928, M 1/1218/25/2296 Part 3, ANZ.

CHAPTER 11 – 1929–1930

1   Letter, Bowman to Byrd, 26 September 1928, 'Byrd, R. E., 1927–28' folder, AGS.
2   Memorandum by Bowman, undated, 'Expeditions – A.G.S.: Byrd Antarctic Expedition, 1928–1930' Folder, AGS.
3   Navy press release, 28 June 1929, Byrd Papers, RG 56.1, Box 8, Folder 292, BPRC.
4   Richard Evelyn Byrd, 'The Conquest of Antarctica by Air', *National Geographic Magazine*, vol. LVIII, no. 2, August 1930, pp. 127, 168.
5   Letter, Byrd to Bowman, 9 October 1928, 'Byrd, R. E., 1927–28' folder, AGS.
6   Letters, Casey to Bruce, 11 April and 9 and 16 May 1929, Hudson and North (eds), *My Dear P.M.*, pp. 492, 510 and 514.
7   'Policy in the Antarctic', memo for the Imperial Conference, September 1930, A981/ANT4, Part 8, NAA.
8   Letters, Casey to Bruce, 11 April, 16 May and 6 June 1929, Hudson and North (eds), *My Dear P.M.*, pp. 492, 514 and 518–519.
9   'Policy in the Antarctic', memo for the Imperial Conference, September 1930, A981/ANT4, Part 8; 'Territorial Claims in the Antarctic', report by Research Department, Foreign Office, 1 May 1945, A4311/365/8, NAA; Nasht, *The Last Explorer*, pp. 204–207.
10 Letter, Byrd to Weyland, 28 September 1928, Byrd Papers, Folder I-4, DCL.
11 Byrd, 'The Conquest of Antarctica by Air', p. 198; letters, Byrd to Bowman, 3 and 24 May 1928, and Bowman to Byrd, 15 May and 18 June 1928, 'Byrd, R. E., 1927–28' folder, AGS.
12 Wallace West, *Paramount Newsreel Men with Admiral Byrd in Little America*, Whitman Publishing, Racine, 1934, p. 70; Byrd, 'The Conquest of Antarctica by Air', p. 207.
13 Byrd, 'The Conquest of Antarctica by Air', pp. 216–217; Richard Evelyn Byrd, *Little America*, Putnam, New York, 1930, pp. 341–342, 345.
14 Lowell Thomas and Lowell Thomas Jr, *Famous First Flights That Changed History*, Lyons Press, Guildford, Connecticut, 2004, p. 219.
15 Radiograms, [copies] Sulzberger to Byrd, 20 November 1929, and Byrd to Sulzberger, 22 November 1929, 'Expeditions – A.G.S.: Byrd Antarctic

Expedition, 1928–1930' Folder, AGS; Byrd, 'The Conquest of Antarctica by Air', pp. 219.

16 Byrd, *Little America*, pp. 351–353, 357.

17 *New York Times*, 8 December 1929.

18 *New York Times*, 20 December 1929.

19 *New York Times*, 1 December 1929.

20 Byrd, *Little America*, pp. 359, 407–408.

21 Newspaper cutting, c. 10 March 1930, Scrap Book, OV-1/I-101, Bernt Balchen Papers, LoC.

22 West, *Paramount Newsreel Men with Admiral Byrd in Little America*, p. 20; Byrd, *Little America*, pp. 155–157.

23 Byrd, *Little America*, pp. 22, 272.

24 Despatch, Passfield to Dominion Governments, 14 January 1930, M 1/1218/25/2296 Part 3, ANZ; 'Territorial Claims in the Antarctic', report by Research Department, Foreign Office, 1 May 1945, A4311/365/8, NAA.

25 Letters, Cook to Loper, 5 and 29 January 1900, Box II: 14, Folder 1; letter, Balch to Loper, 22 February 1904, Box II: 10, Folder 3, Palmer-Loper Families papers, LoC.

26 See letters by Balch to *Science*, vol. 18, Nos. 445 and 453, 10 July and 4 September 1903; Edwin Swift Balch, 'Antarctic Nomenclature', *Bulletin of the American Geographical Society*, vol. 37, no. 12, 1905; 'Stonington Antarctic Explorers', *Bulletin of the American Geographical Society*, vol. XLI, no. 8, 1909; 'Palmer Land', *Bulletin of the American Geographical Society*, vol. 43, no. 4, 1911; 'The First Sighting of West Antarctica', *Geographical Review*, vol. 15, no. 4, 1911.

27 John Randolph Spears, *Captain Nathaniel Brown Palmer*, Macmillan, New York, 1922; letters, John Spears to Mrs Loper, 14 and 31 March, 25 April and 7, 20 and 24 May 1921, and Loper to Spears, 21 March 1921, Box II: 6, Folder 12, Palmer-Loper Families papers, LoC.

28 Frank Williams, 'Lawrence Martin, 1880–1955', *Annals of the Association of American Geographers*, vol. 46, no. 3, September 1956.

29 Letters, Putnam to Loper, 30 September 1927, and Martin to Loper, 6 December 1928, Box II: 8, Folder 1, Palmer-Loper Families papers, LoC.

30 Letters, Casey to Bruce, 30 May and 4 July 1929, in Hudson and North (eds), *My Dear P.M.*, pp. 516 and 534.

31 Despatch, Amery to Governor-General, 5 January 1927, CP 46/2/41; 'British Policy in the Antarctic', memorandum by Davis to Comptroller General of Customs, 16 February 1927; letters, Deane to Masson, 21 March 1927, and Masson to Deane, 1 and 25 July 1927, A981/ANT4/Part 4; minute by Henderson, 6 December 1928, A4311/362/5, NAA.

32 'Greenland: Correspondence (September, 1919 – September, 1920) with the Government of the Dominion of Canada as to the Recognition of Danish Sovereignty over Greenland', CO 886/9/6, NA; D. A. Nichols, 'Greenland, our North-Eastern Neighbour', *Canadian Geographical Journal*, vol. XXII, no. 1, January 1941; Gustav Smedal, *Acquisition of Sovereignty over Polar Areas*, Translated from Norwegian by Chr. Meyer, Oslo, 1930.

33 See documents in A4311/362/5, NAA.

34 Letter, Casey to Bruce, 10 January 1929, A461/J413/1; also see documents in A4311/362/5, NAA.

35 Letter, Casey to Bruce, 6 June 1929, in Hudson and North (eds), *My Dear P.M.*, p. 519.

36 Letter, Mawson to Bruce, 31 January 1929, A461/J413/1, NAA.
37 *Times*, London, 20 January 1928.
38 Cable, Casey to External Affairs, 20 February 1929, A461/J413/1, NAA.
39 *Hansard*, 21 February 1929, p. 461; 'Antarctic Expedition', draft press release, 7 March 1929, A461/J413/1, NAA.
40 Ayres, *Mawson*, p. 166.
41 Jacka and Jacka (eds), *Mawson's Antarctic Diaries*, p. 252.
42 Memo by Henderson, c. November 1929, A461/B413/4, NAA.
43 Manuscript by Henderson, 8 February 1960, A981/ANT22, NAA.
44 'Manuscript of A. Grenfell Price's book, "Antarctic Research Expedition 1929–1931"', PRG 523/15/2, Mawson Papers, SLSA.
45 Jacka and Jacka (eds), *Mawson's Antarctic Diaries*, pp. 252–253; Harold Fletcher, *Antarctic Days with Mawson: A personal account of the British, Australian and New Zealand Antarctic Research Expedition of 1929–31*, Angus and Robertson, Sydney, 1984, p. 44.
46 Jacka and Jacka (eds), *Mawson's Antarctic Diaries*, p. 310.
47 *Daily News*, London, 10 October 1929.
48 Cables, Casey to Trumble, 11 October 1929, and Casey to Mawson, 12 October 1929, A2908/1/E6, NAA.
49 Christensen, *Such is the Antarctic*, p. 161.
50 Cable, Casey to Mawson, 15 October 1929, A2908/1/E6, NAA, Canberra;
51 'Policy in the Antarctic', memo for the Imperial Conference, September 1930, A981/ANT4, Part 8, NAA.
52 Jacka and Jacka (eds), *Mawson's Antarctic Diaries*, pp. 255–256.
53 Barrett, *Was Australian Antarctic Won Fairly?*, p. 25.
54 Christensen, *Such is the Antarctic*, pp. 154, 168–170; Hjalmar Riiser-Larsen, 'The "Norvegia" Antarctic Expedition of 1929–1930', *Geographical Review*, vol. 20, no. 4, October 1930; Manuscript by W. Henderson, 8 February 1960, A981/ANT22, NAA.
55 Jacka and Jacka (eds), *Mawson's Antarctic Diaries*, pp. 288–289.
56 Jacka and Jacka (eds), *Mawson's Antarctic Diaries*, pp. 293, 298.
57 'Territorial Claims in the Antarctic', report by Research Department, Foreign Office, 1 May 1945, A4311/365/8, NAA; Jacka and Jacka (eds), *Mawson's Antarctic Diaries*, pp. 254–346.
58 Jacka and Jacka (eds), *Mawson's Antarctic Diaries*, p. 304.
59 Jacka and Jacka (eds), *Mawson's Antarctic Diaries*, p. 310.
60 Jacka and Jacka (eds), *Mawson's Antarctic Diaries*, pp. 311–312.
61 Barrett, *Was Australian Antarctic Won Fairly?*, p. 33; Jacka and Jacka (eds), *Mawson's Antarctic Diaries*, pp. 313–315; Fletcher, *Antarctic Days with Mawson*, pp. 162–163.
62 Christensen, *Such Is the Antarctic*, p. 173; Barrett, *Was Australian Antarctic Won Fairly?*, p. 33; Jacka and Jacka (eds), *Mawson's Antarctic Diaries*, pp. 316–317; Fletcher, *Antarctic Days with Mawson*, pp. 167–170; B.A.N.Z. Antarctic Research Expedition: Report on Geographic Discoveries and Proclamations by Mawson, 13 January 1930, ADM 1/8827, NA.
63 Jacka and Jacka (eds), *Mawson's Antarctic Diaries*, pp. 317–321.
64 Christensen, *Such Is the Antarctic*, p. 172; B.A.N.Z. 'Antarctic Research Expedition: Report on Geographic Discoveries and Proclamations by Mawson', 13 January 1930, p. 2, ADM 1/8827, NA.
65 Jacka and Jacka (eds), *Mawson's Antarctic Diaries*, pp. 324–325; Fletcher, *Antarctic Days with Mawson*, p. 181.

66 Hjalmar Riiser-Larsen, 'The "Norvegia" Antarctic Expedition of 1929–1930', *Geographical Review*, vol. 20, no. 4, October 1930.

CHAPTER 12 – 1931–1933

1 Gunnar Isachsen, 'Norwegian Explorations in the Antarctic, 1930–1931', *Geographical Review*, vol. XXII, no. 1, January 1932, p. 83.
2 Manuscript by W. Henderson, 8 February 1960, A981/ANT22, NAA; Christensen, *Such Is the Antarctic*, p. 40.
3 Isachsen, 'Norwegian Explorations in the Antarctic, 1930–1931', p. 84.
4 Manuscript by W. Henderson, 8 February 1960, A981/ANT22, NAA; Christensen, *Such Is the Antarctic*, p. 173.
5 *Dundee Courier and Advertiser*, Dundee, 6 April 1929.
6 Isachsen, 'Norwegian Explorations in the Antarctic, 1930–1931', pp. 85–86; Christensen, *Such Is the Antarctic*, pp. 198–199.
7 Isachsen, 'Norwegian Explorations in the Antarctic, 1930–1931', pp. 86–87, 93; memo, Wingfield to Henderson, 19 May 1931, ADM 1/8753/221, NA.
8 Christensen, *Such Is the Antarctic*, p. 211.
9 Isachsen, 'Norwegian Explorations in the Antarctic, 1930–1931', pp. 93–96; Christensen, *Such Is the Antarctic*, pp. 202–203, 210–211.
10 Isachsen, 'Norwegian Explorations in the Antarctic, 1930–1931', pp. 93–96.
11 Christensen, *Such Is the Antarctic*, p. 154.
12 'Report by Sir Douglas Mawson on the Work of the Expedition in R.S.S. "Discovery" during the Season, 1929–1930', A461/A413/4, NAA; Manuscript by Henderson, 8 February 1960, A981/ANT22, NAA.
13 Letters, Passfield to Scullin, 6 March 1930, and Scullin to Passfield, 10 May 1930, A461/F413/4, NAA.
14 'Policy in the Antarctic', memo for the Imperial Conference, September 1930; report by Committee on Polar Questions, Imperial Conference, 30 October 1930, A981/ANT4, Part 8, NAA.
15 Manuscript by Henderson, 8 February 1960, A981/ANT22, NAA.
16 Jacka and Jacka (eds), *Mawson's Antarctic Diaries*, p. 352.
17 Memo by Officer for Scullin, 8 July 1931, p. 2, A981/ANT4, Part 8, NAA.
18 Minutes of the Antarctic Committee, 9 August and 26 September 1930, in Manuscript by Henderson, 8 February 1960, A981/ANT22, NAA.
19 Memo, Mawson to Strahan, 22 November 1930; letter, Strahan to Holtz, 24 February 1931, A461/L413/2, NAA.
20 Minutes of the Antarctic Committee, 9 August and 26 September 1930, in Manuscript by Henderson, 8 February 1960, A981/ANT22, NAA.
21 Fletcher, *Antarctic Days with Mawson*, p. 229.
22 Stuart Campbell, Diary: '"Canopy of Ice": Second Voyage of the British, Australian, New Zealand Antarctic Research Expedition 1929–1931, Under the Command of Sir Douglas Mawson aboard S.Y. Discovery', AAD; Jacka and Jacka (eds), *Mawson's Antarctic Diaries*, pp. 362–63.
23 Jacka and Jacka (eds), *Mawson's Antarctic Diaries*, p. 364; letter, Casey to Prime Minister's Department, 8 January 1931, in Manuscript by Henderson, 8 February 1960, A981/ANT22, NAA.
24 Campbell diary, 28 January 1930, AAD.
25 Ayres, *Mawson*, p. 197; Campbell diary, 5 January 1931, AAD; Fletcher, *Antarctic Days with Mawson*, pp. 265–266.

26 Copies of the various BANZARE proclamations can be found in 'Proclamations read by Sir Douglas Mawson', 1929–1931, A981/ANT22, NAA; Campbell diary, 5 January 1931, AAD; Tom Griffiths, *Slicing the Silence: Voyaging to Antarctica*, Harvard University Press, Cambridge, 2007, pp. 119–120; Fletcher, *Antarctic Days with Mawson*, p. 266.

27 Campbell diary, 6 February 1931, AAD; Fletcher, *Antarctic Days with Mawson*, p. 290.

28 *Sun*, Melbourne, 18 February and 19 March 1930; Headland, 'Whalers and Explorers', in Ringstad (ed.), *Whaling and History II: New Perspectives*, p. 53.

29 Campbell diary, 7–8 February 1931, AAD.

30 Jacka and Jacka (eds), *Mawson's Antarctic Diaries*, pp. 374, 377–378; Campbell diary, 11–13 February 1931, AAD.

31 Jacka and Jacka (eds), *Mawson's Antarctic Diaries*, pp. 379–380; Campbell diary, 13 February 1931, AAD.

32 Campbell diary, 18 February 1931, AAD; Jacka and Jacka (eds), *Mawson's Antarctic Diaries*, p. 380–382; Fletcher, *Antarctic Days with Mawson*, p. 301.

33 Wireless message from Mawson, 16 March 1931, A981/ANT4, Part 8, NAA.

34 Letter, Mawson to Amery, 7 May 1931, AMEL 2/1/21, Leo Amery Papers, CAC.

35 Memos, Wingfield to Henderson, 11 March and 27 May 1931, and other documents in this file, ADM 1/8753/221, NA.

36 Manuscript by W. Henderson, 8 February 1960, A981/ANT22, NAA.

37 For a copy of the poster of *Siege of the South*, see Jacka and Jacka (eds), *Mawson's Antarctic Diaries*, p. 376; undated, draft script for a film of the BANZARE expedition, PRG 523, Series 11/1, Mawson Papers, SLSA.

38 Letter, Scullin to Dominions Secretary, 13 July 1931, A981/ANT4, Part 8, NAA; letter, Law to editor of the *Age*, 24 November 1988, MS 9458/1/100, Law Papers, NLA.

39 Letter, Casey to Bruce, 10 January 1929, enclosing minutes of the Inter-departmental Committee on the Antarctic, 8 January 1929, A461/J413/1, NAA.

40 *The Antarctic Pilot, comprising the Coasts of Antarctica and all Islands Southward of the Usual Routes of Vessels*, Admiralty Hydrographic Department, London, 1930, Davis Papers, AAD.

41 Isachsen, 'Norwegian Explorations in the Antarctic, 1930–1931', p. 93.

42 Christensen, *Such Is the Antarctic*, pp. 210–211.

43 Christensen, *Such Is the Antarctic*, pp. 222–223.

44 Douglas Mawson, 'The B.A.N.Z. Antarctic Research Expedition, 1929–31', *Geographical Journal*, vol. LXXX, no. 2, August 1932.

45 Mawson, 'The B.A.N.Z. Antarctic Research Expedition, 1929–31', p. 129.

46 Minutes of the Polar Committee, 5 October 1933, M 1/1218/25/2296 Part 3, ANZ.

47 *Hansard*, 26 May 1933, pp. 1950–1955.

48 *Hansard*, 26 May 1933, pp. 1950–1952, 1957.

49 *Hansard*, 26 May 1933, pp. 1952, 1956, 2020.

50 Cable, Commonwealth Government to Australian High Commission, 19 August 1936, A2910/404/16/1 Part 1, NAA.

51 Christensen, *Such Is the Antarctic*, pp. 214–221

CHAPTER 13 – 1934–1936

1 Newspaper cuttings, 24 June and 8 July 1930, Clippings 1920s–1930s, Byrd Folder, EC.
2 *New York Times*, 23 April 1930.
3 Letters, Byrd to Pond, 9 and 24 December 1931, Byrd Papers, I-2, DCL.
4 Letter, Byrd to Harry Byrd, 17 September 1931, Byrd Papers, RG 56.1, Box 1, Folder 37, BPRC.
5 Memo, Byrd to Walden, 22 August 1930, Byrd Papers, I-2, DCL.
6 Newspaper cutting, 8 July 1930, Clippings 1920s–1930s, Byrd Folder, EC.
7 Letter, Byrd to Harry Byrd, 8 February 1931, Byrd Papers, RG 56.1, Box 1, Folder 37, BPRC.
8 Letters, Byrd to Eleanor Roosevelt, 17 September 1931, and Byrd to Harry Byrd, 3 and 16 November 1931, Byrd Papers, RG 56.1, Box 1, Folder 37, BPRC.
9 Undated newspaper cutting, c. 23 June 1930, Scrap Book, OV-1/I-113, Bernt Balchen Papers, LoC.
10 Undated newspaper cutting, c. 19 June 1930, Scrap Book, OV-1/I-113, Bernt Balchen Papers, LoC.
11 Undated newspaper cutting from the *New York Times*, c. 1931, Laurence Gould folder, EC.
12 *New York Times*, 24 February 1931.
13 Letter, Byrd to Bowman, 24 February 1931, 'Byrd, R. E., 1930–35' folder, AGS.
14 Letter, Bowman to Byrd, 26 February 1931, 'Byrd, R. E., 1930–35' folder, AGS.
15 Letters, Bowman to Byrd, 18 and 20 March 1931, 'Byrd, R. E., 1930–35' folder, AGS; *Detroit Times*, Detroit, 24 November 1929.
16 Letter, Bowman to Ranck, 7 February 1929, 'Wilkins Hearst Antarctic Expedition 1929–30' folder, AGS.
17 *New York Times*, 6 February 1932; For an account of Watkins' expedition, see Jeremy Scott, *Dancing on Ice: A 1930s Arctic Adventure*, Old Street Publishing, London, 2010.
18 Memorandum by Bowman, undated, 'Expeditions – A.G.S.: Byrd Antarctic Expedition, 1928–1930' Folder, AGS.
19 *New York Times*, 27 July 1932; letters, Byrd to Bowman, 11 August and 13 October 1932, 'Byrd, R. E., 1930–35' folder, AGS; Rose, *Explorer*, Chap. 10.
20 *Time*, New York, 2 January 1933; letters, Byrd to Harry Byrd, 24, 28 and 30 January 1933, Byrd Papers, RG 56.1, Box 1, Folder 39, BPRC; Rose, *Explorer*, Chap. 10.
21 Letters, Harry Byrd to Byrd, 31 January and 27 February 1933, Byrd Papers, RG 56.1, Box 1, Folder 39, BPRC.
22 Letters, Byrd to Bowman, 21 April 1933, and Bowman to Byrd, 11 May 1933, 'Byrd, R. E., 1930–35' folder, AGS.
23 Minutes of the Polar Committee, 5 October 1933, M 1/1218/25/2296 Part 3, ANZ.
24 Launcelot Fleming, Colin Bertram and Brian Roberts, 'Three Antarctic Years: The British Graham Land Expedition of 1934–1937', *Canadian Geographical Journal*, vol. XXII, no. 1, January 1941; John Rymill, *Southern Lights: The Official Account of the British Graham Land Expedition 1934–1937*, Chatto and Windus, London, 1938, pp. 26–31.
25 J. R. Rymill, 'British Graham Land Expedition, 1934-37', *Geographical Journal*, Vol. 91, Nos. 4 and 5, April and May 1938.

26 Letter, Ellsworth to Secretary, Explorers Club, 5 February 1930, enclosing cutting from *San Diego Union*, 4 February 1930, Ellsworth Folder, EC; *Boy's Life*, April 1928.

27 *New York Times Magazine*, New York, 29 May 1932; *Little America Times*, 31 December 1934, Byrd Folder, EC; Lincoln Ellsworth, *Beyond Horizons*, Doubleday, Doran & Company, New York, 1938, pp. 27, 91.

28 Letters, Bowman to Sverdrup, 9 March 1931, and Sverdrup to Bowman, 25 March 1931; cables, Ellsworth to Christensen, 1 May 1931, Ellsworth to Riiser-Larsen, 9 May 1931 and Riiser-Larsen to Ellsworth, 12 May 1931; undated memorandum, 'Ellsworth Antarctic Expedition, 1932–1933', probably by Bowman, 'Expeditions – A.G.S.: Ellsworth Trans-Antarctic flight expedition, 1933' Folder, AGS.

29 *New York Times*, 1 March 1935; Ellsworth, *Beyond Horizons*, p. 255; Nasht, *The Last Explorer*, pp. 257–259.

30 *New York Times*, 18 and 21 April 1932; *Herald Tribune*, New York, 18 April 1932.

31 Letter, Bowman to Ellsworth, 19 July 1933, 'Expeditions – A.G.S.: Ellsworth Trans-Antarctic flight expedition, 1933' Folder, AGS.

32 'Ellsworth Trans-Antarctic Flight Expedition', memo, probably by Bowman, c. December 1933, 'Expeditions – A.G.S.: Ellsworth Trans-Antarctic flight expedition, 1933' Folder, AGS.

33 'Ross Dependency: American Expeditions to the Dependency and Correspondence Relating to these Expeditions', undated memorandum, c. 1956, M 1/1209/25/2029, ANZ; 'Territorial Claims in the Antarctic', report by Research Department, Foreign Office, 1 May 1945, A4311/365/8, NAA.

34 'Territorial Claims in the Antarctic', report by Research Department, Foreign Office, 1 May 1945, A4311/365/8, NAA.

35 Ellsworth, *Beyond Horizons*, pp. 265–268.

36 Ellsworth, *Beyond Horizons*, pp. 271–290; cablegrams, Wilkins to Bowman, 29 December 1934, and Ellsworth to Bowman, 15 January 1935, 'Expeditions – A.G.S.: Ellsworth Trans-Antarctic flight expedition, 1933' Folder, AGS.

37 *Little America Times*, 31 January 1935, Ellsworth Folder, EC.

38 *New York Times*, 1 March 1935.

39 *Little America Times*, 30 April 1935, Balchen Scrap Book Number Two, OV-2, II-1A, Bernt Balchen Papers, LoC.

40 Ellsworth, *Beyond Horizons*, pp. 298–310.

41 Ellsworth, *Beyond Horizons*, pp. 310–320.

42 Ellsworth, *Beyond Horizons*, pp. 319–323.

43 Ellsworth, *Beyond Horizons*, pp. 323–325.

44 Ellsworth, *Beyond Horizons*, pp. 327–345.

45 'Territorial Claims in the Antarctic', report by Research Department, Foreign Office, 1 May 1945, A4311/365/8, NAA.

46 'Ross Dependency: American Expeditions to the Dependency and Correspondence Relating to these Expeditions', undated memo, c. 1956, M 1/1209/25/2029, ANZ; Ellsworth, *Beyond Horizons*, p. 362; *Little America Times*, 31 January 1935, Ellsworth Folder, EC.

47 Letters, Byrd to Bowman, 24 July and 8 August 1933, and Bowman to Byrd, 5 August 1933, 'Byrd, R. E., 1930–35' folder, AGS; letters, Harry Byrd to Byrd, 2 and 14 August 1933, Byrd Papers, RG.1, Box 1, Folder 39, BPRC.

48 Letters, Byrd to Bowman, 8 August and 1 September 1933; 'The Scientific Work of the Byrd Antarctic Expedition, 1928–30 and Suggestions on a Scientific

Program for the Byrd Antarctic Expedition of 1933–34', memorandum by Bowman, 20 August 1933, 'Byrd, R. E., 1930–35' folder, AGS.

49 Extract from *New York World-Telegram*, 7 September 1933, M 1/1218/25/2296 Part 3, ANZ, Wellington; Rose, *Explorer*, pp. 313–314.

50 Letter, Byrd to Bowman, 21 September 1933, and Bowman to Byrd, 9 October 1933, 'Byrd, R. E., 1930–35' folder, AGS.

51 'Ross Dependency: American Expeditions to the Dependency and Correspondence Relating to these Expeditions', undated memo, c. 1956, M 1/1209/25/2029, ANZ.

52 'Ross Dependency: American Expeditions to the Dependency and Correspondence Relating to these Expeditions', undated memo, c. 1956, M 1/1209/25/2029, ANZ.

53 Richard Evelyn Byrd, *Antarctic Discovery: The Story of the Second Byrd Antarctic Expedition*, Putnam, London, 1936, pp. 8, 17–18.

54 Byrd, *Antarctic Discovery*, pp. 77, 104, 121.

55 Byrd, *Antarctic Discovery*, pp. 160–163, 170; Rose, *Explorer*, pp. 287–289, 345.

56 *New York Times*, 6 February 1932.

57 Stam, *Books on Ice*, pp. 117–118.

58 Byrd, *Antarctic Discovery*, pp. 172–176, 234–248; Rose, *Explorer*, pp. 357–374.

59 Byrd, *Antarctic Discovery*, pp. 274, 302–307, 317–320, 331.

60 *Little America Times*, 31 December 1934, Byrd Folder, EC.

61 Letter, Bowman to Mrs Byrd, 19 December 1934, 'Byrd, R. E., 1930–35' folder, AGS.

62 Letter, Byrd to Bowman, 8 August 1933, 'Byrd, R. E., 1930–35' folder, AGS.

63 Letter, Shook to Governor-General, 21 January 1936; telegram, Dominions Secretary to Governor-General, 20 November 1934, M 1/1218/25/2296 Part 3, ANZ; 'Ross Dependency: American Expeditions to the Dependency and Correspondence Relating to these Expeditions', undated memo, c. 1956, M 1/1209/25/2029, ANZ; Rose, *Explorer*, p. 332.

64 'Ross Dependency: American Expeditions to the Dependency and Correspondence Relating to these Expeditions', undated memo, c. 1956, M 1/1209/25/2029; memo, Forbes to Governor-General, 7 December 1934, M 1/1218/25/2296 Part 3, ANZ.

65 *Little America Times*, New York, 31 March 1935. Byrd Folder, EC; notice from C. F. Anderson, 27 January 1935, in 'Diary of a Voyage to Antarctica, 1935', NZMS 661, William Loudon Papers, ACL.

66 Note, Lindsay to Hull, 27 December 1934; memo, Forbes to Governor-General, 7 December 1934, M 1/1218/25/2296 Part 3, ANZ.

67 Dispatch, Dominions Secretary to Governor-General, 18 December 1934, M 1/1218/25/2296 Part 3, ANZ.

68 Rose, *Explorer*, p. 381.

69 *Little America Times*, New York, 28 February 1935. Byrd Folder, EC; *Dominion*, Wellington, 2 March 1935.

70 *Dominion*, Wellington, 6 March 1935.

71 *Little America Times*, New York, 31 May 1935; program of a Testimonial Dinner for Byrd, 5 June 1936, Byrd Folder, EC; Rose, *Explorer*, p. 384.

72 Letter, Byrd to Bowman, 10 May 1936, 'Byrd, R. E., 1930–35' folder, AGS.

73 *Business Machines*, New York, 12 June 1936; Program of a Testimonial Dinner for Byrd, 5 June 1936, Byrd Folder, EC.

74 *Dominion*, Wellington, 22 February 1936; 'Charles Cheney Hyde', *Political Science Quarterly*, vol. 67, no. 2, June 1952.

75 Letter, [unclear] to Viereck, 2 January 1936, Byrd Papers, RG 56.1, Box 8, Folder 292, BPRC.

76 Rose, *Explorer*, pp. 317, 384–386; 'The Second Byrd Antarctic Expedition, 1933–1935', probably by Bertrand, c. 1954, Department of State, Bureau of Intelligence and Research, Office of the Geographer, Records Relating to Antarctica and Antarctic Exploration, 1930–1955, Box #7, 'The Second Byrd Antarctic Expedition, 1933–1935' folder, NARA.

CHAPTER 14 – 1937–1938

1 Vilhjalmur Stefansson, *The Friendly Arctic: The Story of Five Years in Polar Regions*, Harrap, London, 1921.

2 Barthelmess, 'A Century of German Interests in Modern Whaling, 1860s–1960s', in Basberg, *Whaling and History: Perspectives on the Evolution of the Industry*, pp. 129–131.

3 'Situation in the Antarctic', memo for Imperial Conference, 4 February 1937, M 1/1209/25/2029, ANZ.

4 Gustav Smedal, *Acquisition of Sovereignty over Polar Areas*, J. Dybwad, Oslo, 1931, pp. 36–37.

5 Secret memorandum (draft) to Cornish, c. December 1937, A981/ANT26, NAA.

6 Caroline Mikkelsen, the wife of the *Thorshavn*'s captain, is often claimed to have been the first woman when she stepped ashore in February 1935, but it is now known that she landed on an offshore island. *Cape Times*, Cape Town, 28 December 1936 and 18 February 1937; *New York Sun*, 13 February 1937; 'Territorial Claims in the Antarctic', report by Research Department, Foreign Office, 1 May 1945, A4311/365/8, NAA; F. I. Norman, J. A. E. Gibson and J. S. Burgess, 'Klarius Mikkelsen's 1935 landing in the Vestfold Hills, East Antarctica: some fiction and some facts', *Polar Record*, vol. 34, no. 191, 1998, pp. 295–296.

7 Memo, Cumpston to Acting Secretary, 10 May 1937, A981/ANT 48, Part 3, NAA.

8 'Adelie Land', memo by Cumpston, 15 January 1937; cable, Hodgson to Department of External Affairs, 1 May 1937; memo, Cumpston to Acting Secretary, Department of External Affairs, 10 May 1937, A981/ANT 48, Part 3, NAA.

9 Letter, Mawson to Peterson, 26 July 1937; memo, Stirling to Hodgson, 1 September 1937; letter, Hodgson to Cornish, 24 December 1937; and Secret memo (draft) to Cornish, c. December 1937, A981/ANT26, NAA.

10 *Herald*, Melbourne, 22 June 1938.

11 M. Ruth Megaw, 'The Scramble for the Pacific: Anglo-United States Rivalry in the 1930s', *Historical Studies*, Vol. 17, No. 69, 1977.

12 *Evening Post*, Wellington, 6 July 1938; Cabinet Submission by Hughes, 28 June 1938, A4311/365/9/1, NAA; Newspaper cutting, 22 June 1938, J. K. Davis, D.26 folder, Davis Papers, AAD.

13 Letters, Waesche to Kellogg, 3 March 1939 and Kellogg to Waesche, 8 March 1939, RG 126/9/13/9, Part #1, 'Antarctica, Industries, Whaling' File, NARA.

14 Congressional Record – House, 11 March 1938, p. 4364; *Science*, 3 December 1937.

15 J. K. W. and W. O. F., 'Obituary: Lawrence Martin', *Geographical Review*, vol. 45, no. 4, October 1955; Frank E. Williams, 'Lawrence Martin, 1880–1955', *Annals of the Association of American Geographers*, vol. 46, no. 3, September 1956; letter, Martin to Loper, 11 November 1937, Box II: 8, Folder 1, Palmer-Loper Families papers, LoC.

16 *Science*, 3 December 1937 and 18 February 1938; letter, Martin to Loper, 9 February 1938, Box II: 8, Folder 1, Palmer-Loper Families papers, LoC; *New York Evening Sun*, 3 June 1938.

17 *New York Times*, 17 October 1909.

18 Letter, Hobbs to Harry Byrd, 6 July 1939, Byrd Papers, RG 56.1, Box 1, Folder 43, BPRC.

19 Laurence Gould, 'Obituary: William Herbert Hobbs', *Geographical Review*, vol. 43, no. 3, July 1953; Robert Burnett Hall, 'William Herbert Hobbs, 1864–1953', *Annals of the Association of American Geographers*, vol. 43, no. 4, December 1953; Clifford Wilcox, 'World War 1 and the Attack on Professors of German at the University of Michigan', *History of Education Quarterly*, vol. 33, no. 1, Spring, 1993.

20 Letters, Hobbs to Loper, 10 September 1937 and Martin to Loper, 23 September 1937, and other documents in these papers, Box II: 14, Folder 3, Palmer-Loper Families papers, LoC.

21 Letters, Hobbs to Loper, 6, 8 and 9 October 1937, 28 February and 3 and 18 March 1938, Box II: 14, Folder 3, Palmer-Loper Families papers, LoC.

22 William Herbert Hobbs, 'The Pack-Ice of the Weddell Sea', *Annals of the Association of American Geographers*, vol. 29, no. 2, June 1939.

23 William Herbert Hobbs, 'The Discoveries of Antarctica within the American Sector, as Revealed by Maps and Documents', *Transactions of the American Philosophical Society*, vol. XXXI, Part 1, January 1939.

24 *New York Evening Sun*, New York, 3 June 1938; undated newspaper cutting, c. April 1938, Box II: 19, Folder 6, Palmer-Loper Families papers, LoC.

25 For a sample of the British responses, see R. N. Rudmose Brown, 'Antarctic History: A Reply to Professor W. H. Hobbs', *Scottish Geographical Magazine*, vol. 55, May 1939; Arthur Hinks, 'Review: On Some Misrepresentations of Antarctic History', *Geographical Journal*, vol. 94, no. 4, October 1939; R. T. Gould, 'The Charting of the South Shetlands, 1819–28', *Mariner's Mirror*, vol. 17, no. 3, July 1941; for two American views of Hobbs, see letters, Birdseye to Bowman, 15 May 1939, and Bowman to Birdseye, 19 May 1939, RG 126/9/13/2, Part #1, 'Administrative, Islands, Palmer' File; letter, Byrd to Gruening, 24 May 1939, RG 126/9/13/2, Part 2, 'Administrative, General, 8 May 1939 to 28 November 1939' File, NARA.

26 Letter, Byrd to Harold Byrd, 8 June 1937, Byrd Papers, RG 56.1, Box 1, Folder 41, BPRC.

27 Rose, *Explorer*, pp. 386–398; letter, Byrd to Harold Byrd, 18 June 1937, Byrd Papers, RG 56.1, Box 1, Folder 41, BPRC.

28 Memo, Black to Gruening, 4 May 1938; letters, Black to Gruening, 6 and 7 May 1938, RG 126/9/13/2, Part 1, 'Administrative, General, 4 May 1938 to 6 May 1939' File, NARA.

29 Memo, Black to Gruening, 4 May 1938; letters, Black to Gruening, 6 and 7 May 1938, RG 126/9/13/2, Part 1, 'Administrative, General, 4 May 1938 to 6 May 1939' File, NARA.

30 *New York Times*, 6 May 1938; Newspaper cutting, 6 August 1938, RG 126/9/13/11, 'Publicity, Publications, Press Clippings, Ellsworth Expeditions' File, NARA.

31 Letter, Redmond to Wright, 21 June 1938, 'Expeditions: Ellsworth Antarctic Expedition, 1938–' Folder, AGS.

32 *New York Times*, 6 May 1938.

33 'History and Current Status of Claims in Antarctica', Secret report by Office of Intelligence Research, 24 November 1947, pp. 64–65, Department of State, Bureau of Intelligence and Research, Office of the Geographer, Records Relating to Antarctica and Antarctic Exploration, 1930–1955, Box #3, 'Antarctica: The Fischer Study' folder, NARA.

34 Letters, Redmond to Wright, 21 June 1938, and Wood to Redmond, 23 June 1938, 'Expeditions: Ellsworth Antarctic Expedition, 1938–' Folder, AGS.

35 Newspaper cutting, 6 August 1938, RG 126/9/13/11, 'Publicity, Publications, Press Clippings, Ellsworth Expeditions' File, NARA.

36 Letter, Wilkins to Casey, 6 August 1938; telegram, Wilkins to Casey, c. August 1938; memo, Hodgson to Stirling, 18 November 1938, A981/ANT22, NAA; Newspaper cutting, 31 August 1938, J. K. Davis, D.26 folder, Davis Papers, AAD.

37 Telegram, Wilkins to Casey, 6 September 1938; letter, Hodgson to Wilkins, 12 September 1938, A981/ANT22, NAA.

38 Letter, Wilkins to Hodgson, 16 September 1938; 'Map of the Antarctic', undated and unsigned memorandum, c. August 1938; memo, Hodgson to Stirling, 18 November 1938, A981/ANT22, NAA.

39 Letter, Stirling to Hodgson, 19 October 1938; memo, Hodgson to Stirling, 18 November 1938, A981/ANT22, NAA.

40 'History and Current Status of Claims in Antarctica', Secret report by Office of Intelligence Research, 24 November 1947, pp. 64–65, Department of State, Bureau of Intelligence and Research, Office of the Geographer, Records Relating to Antarctica and Antarctic Exploration, 1930–1955, Box #3, 'Antarctica: The Fischer Study' folder, NARA.

41 Lincoln Ellsworth, 'My Four Antarctic Expeditions', *National Geographic Magazine*, Washington, July 1939; Nasht, *The Last Explorer*, p. 271.

42 Speech by Ellsworth, 5 December 1944, Ellsworth Folder, EC.

43 'Ellsworth Antarctic Expedition 1938–39: Extracts from Report (Sir Hubert Wilkins)', A981/ANT22, NAA.

44 'Ellsworth Antarctic Expedition 1938–39: Extracts from Report (Sir Hubert Wilkins)', A981/ANT22, NAA; Nasht, *The Last Explorer*, pp. 171–172.

45 'Ellsworth Antarctic Expedition 1938–39: Extracts from Report (Sir Hubert Wilkins)', A981/ANT22, NAA.

46 Lincoln Ellsworth, 'My Four Antarctic Expeditions', *National Geographic Magazine*, July 1939; 'Ellsworth Antarctic Expedition 1938–39: Extracts from Report (Sir Hubert Wilkins)', A981/ANT22, NAA; *New York Times*, 13 and 16 January 1939.

47 Confidential memo by Black, 1 May 1939, RG 126/9/13/2, Ellsworth folder, NARA; Radio message, Wilkins to Hodgson, 13 January 1939; letter, Watt to Mawson, 6 February 1939, and other documents in A981/ANT22, NAA.

48 Newspaper cutting, 27 January 1939, Davis papers, AAD; letter, Mawson to his wife, 30 January 1939, PRG 523/3/4/7, Mawson Papers, SLSA.

49 Letter, Mawson to Hodgson, 3 February 1939, A981/ANT22, NAA.

50 Letter, Head of Marine Branch to Davis, 7 February 1939; newspaper cutting, c. 9 February 1939, Davis papers, AAD; *Mercury*, Hobart, 10 February 1939.

51 Newspaper cutting, 3 March 1939, Davis papers, AAD; letter, Mawson to his wife, 30 January 1939, PRG 523/3/4/7; letter, Mawson to his wife, 1 March 1939, PRG 523/3/3/7, Mawson Papers, SLSA.

52 Memo, Hodgson to Stirling, London, 17 May 1939, A981/ANT22; 'Territorial Claims in the Antarctic', report by Research Department, Foreign Office, 1 May 1945, A4311/365/8, NAA.

53 *Sydney Morning Herald*, Sydney, 11 February 1939.

54 *New York Times*, 23 January and 4 February 1939; *Herald*, Melbourne, 16 February 1939; *Sydney Morning Herald*, Sydney, 17 February 1939.

55 *Sydney Morning Herald*, Sydney, 7 February 1939; *New York Times*, 9 February 1939; letter, Officer to Hodgson, 6 May 1938; 'Antarctic', memo by Officer, c. February 1939; memo, Officer to Hodgson, 9 February 1939; telegram, Hodgson to Officer, 10 February 1939, A981/ANT22, NAA.

56 *New York Times*, 1 March 1939; Newspaper cutting, c. 1 March 1939, RG 126/9/13/11, 'Publicity, Publications, Press Clippings, Ellsworth Expeditions' File, NARA.

57 'The German Antarctic Expedition of 1938–1939', Box 2601, 'ONI: German-Antarctic Expedition' folder, NARA.

58 *New York Times*, 1 March 1939.

CHAPTER 15 – 1939–1941

1 Letter, Black to Gruening, 18 November 1938; memo, Roosevelt to Welles, 7 January 1939, RG 126/9/13/2, Part 1, 'Administrative, General, 4 May 1938 to 6 May 1939' File, NARA.

2 Rose, *Explorer*, pp. 405–408.

3 'Conference on cooperative government plans in the Antarctic', memo by Black, 17 February 1939; 'United States Government colonization in the Antarctic', confidential memo by Black, 21 February 1939, RG 126/9/13/2, Part 1, 'Administrative, General, 4 May 1938 to 6 May 1939' File, NARA.

4 United States Government colonization in the Antarctic', confidential memo by Black, 21 February 1939, RG 126/9/13/2, Part 1, 'Administrative, General, 4 May 1938 to 6 May 1939' File, NARA.

5 Memo, Black to Gruening, 16 March 1939, RG 126/9/13/2, Part 1, 'Administrative, General, 4 May 1938 to 6 May 1939' File, NARA.

6 'United States Government colonization in the Antarctic', confidential memo by Black, 21 February 1939, RG 126/9/13/2, Part 1, 'Administrative, General, 4 May 1938 to 6 May 1939' File, NARA.

7 'United States Government colonization in the Antarctic', confidential memo by Black, 21 February 1939, RG 126/9/13/2, Part 1, 'Administrative, General, 4 May 1938 to 6 May 1939' File, NARA.

8 Letter, Siple to Gruening, 8 March 1939, RG 126/9/13/1, Part #1, 'Administrative, Islands, Heard' File, NARA.

9 'United States Government colonization in the Antarctic', confidential memorandum by Black, 21 February 1939, RG 126/9/13/2, Part 1, 'Administrative, General, 4 May 1938 to 6 May 1939' File, NARA.

10 Letter, Siple to Gruening, 8 March 1939, RG 126/9/13/1, Part #1, 'Administrative, Islands, Heard' File, NARA.

11 'The German Antarctic Expedition of 1938–1939', [Condensed translation of 'Die Deutsche Antarktische Expedition 1938–1939', vol. 1, Leipzig, 1942] 15

November 1946, Records of the Army Chief, Assistant Chief of Staff (G-2), Intelligence Administrative Div., Document Library Branch, Publications ("P") Files, 1946–51, Box 2601, 'ONI: German-Antarctic Expedition' folder, NARA.

12 'The German Antarctic Expedition of 1938–1939', [Condensed translation of 'Die Deutsche Antarktische Expedition 1938–1939', vol. 1, Leipzig, 1942] 15 November 1946, Records of the Army Chief, Assistant Chief of Staff (G-2), Intelligence Administrative Div., Document Library Branch, Publications ("P") Files, 1946–51, Box 2601, 'ONI: German-Antarctic Expedition' folder, NARA.

13 Memo, Black to Gruening, 10 March 1939, RG 126/9/13/3, Part #1, 'Administrative, Expeditions, German' File, NARA.

14 Letter, Black to Ronne, 17 March 1939, RG 126/9/13/2, Part 1, 'Administrative, General, 4 May 1938 to 6 May 1939' File, NARA.

15 Telegram, Byrd to Harry Byrd, 4 April 1939; letters, Byrd to Harry Byrd, 4 April 1939, and Harry Byrd to Byrd, 6 April 1939, Byrd Papers, RG 56.1, Box 1, Folder 43, BPRC.

16 Letters, Black to Gruening, 21 March 1939; Black to Ronne, Wade and Siple, 27 March 1939; Ronne to Black, 28 March 1939; Black to Wade, 4 April 1939, RG 126/9/13/2, Part 1, 'Administrative, General, 4 May 1938 to 6 May 1939' File, NARA.

17 Letter, Wade to Black, 1 April 1939, RG 126/9/13/2, Part 1, 'Administrative, General, 4 May 1938 to 6 May 1939' File, NARA.

18 Letter, Black to Gruening, 21 March 1939, RG 126/9/13/2, Part 1, 'Administrative, General, 4 May 1938 to 6 May 1939' File, NARA.

19 New York Times, 13 April 1939; letter, Geist to Secretary of State, 14 April 1939, RG 126/9/13/3, Part #1, 'Administrative, Expeditions, German' File, NARA.

20 Speech by Ellsworth to the American Polar Society, 5 December 1944, Ellsworth Folder, EC.

21 New York Times, 19 April 1939; New York Herald Tribune, 19 April 1939; letters, Black to Hatch, 18 April 1939 and Black to Wade, 25 April 1939, RG 126/9/13/2, Part 1, 'Administrative, General, 4 May 1938 to 6 May 1939' File, NARA.

22 Memorandum of Conference, 27 April 1939, RG 126/9/13/2, Part 1, 'Administrative, General, 4 May 1938 to 6 May 1939' File, NARA.

23 Letter, Byrd to Black, 18 May 1939, RG 126/9/13/2, Part #1, Ellsworth folder, NARA.

24 Rose, Explorer, pp. 411–412.

25 Kenneth S. Davis, FDR: Into the Storm, 1937–1940, A History, Random House, New York, 1993, pp. 446–458.

26 Press release by Ickes, 3 June 1939; memo, Gruening to Ickes, 6 July 1939, RG 126/9/13/2, Part 2, 'Administrative, General, 8 May 1939 to 28 November 1939' File, NARA.

27 Letter, Byrd to Harold Byrd, 13 June 1939, Byrd Papers, RG 56.1, Box 1, Folder 29, BPRC.

28 Memo, Gruening to Burlew, 9 June 1939, RG 126/9/13/3, Part #1, 'Administrative, Expeditions, German' File, NARA.

29 Letter, Burlew to Woodrum, 12 June 1939, RG 126/9/13/3, Part #1, 'Administrative, Expeditions, German' File, NARA.

30 Letters, Black to Korff, 20 June 1939, and Gruening to Black, 23 June 1939; memo, Gruening to Burlew, 22 June 1939, RG 126/9/13/2, Part 2,

'Administrative, General, 8 May 1939 to 28 November 1939' File, NARA; Magazine cutting, c. June 1939, RG 126/9/13/3, Part #1, 'Administrative, Expeditions, German' File, NARA; *New York Times*, New York, 24 June 1939.

31 Letters, Gruening to Black, 24 June 1939, and Black to Korff, 20 June 1939, RG 126/9/13/2, Part 2, 'Administrative, General, 8 May 1939 to 28 November 1939' File, NARA.

32 Telegram, Harry Byrd to Byrd, 30 June 1939, Byrd Papers, RG 56.1, Box 1, Folder 43, BPRC.

33 Memo, Gruening to Ickes, 5 July 1939, RG 126/9/13/2, Part 2, 'Administrative, General, 8 May 1939 to 28 November 1939' File, NARA.

34 Memo, Gruening to Ickes, 6 July 1939, RG 126/9/13/2, Part 2, 'Administrative, General, 8 May 1939 to 28 November 1939' File, NARA.

35 *New York Times*, New York, 7 July 1939; letter, Roosevelt to Ickes, 7 July 1939, RG 126/9/13/2, Part 2, 'Administrative, General, 8 May 1939 to 28 November 1939' File, NARA.

36 *New York Times*, 8 July 1939.

37 *New York Times*, 8 July 1939.

38 *New York Times*, 8 July 1939; *Washington Times-Herald*, 10 July 1939.

39 *Washington Post*, 10 July 1939; *New York Times*, 14 July 1939; for some of the critical reaction, see Rose, *Explorer*, p. 411.

40 Letter, Roosevelt to Byrd, 12 July 1939, RG 126/9/13/2, Part 2, 'Administrative, General, 8 May 1939 to 28 November 1939' File, NARA.

41 Letter [not sent], Gruening to Byrd, 29 May 1939, RG 126/9/13/2, Part 2, 'Administrative, General, 8 May 1939 to 28 November 1939' File, NARA.

42 Memoranda, Gruening to Watson, 13 July 1939, and Roosevelt to Gruening, 17 July 1939, RG 126/9/13/2, Part 2, 'Administrative, General, 8 May 1939 to 28 November 1939' File, NARA.

43 Letter, Wilkins to McGregor, 25 July 1939; letter [not sent], Hodgson to McGregor, 28 September 1939, A981/ANT 45, NAA.

44 *Daily Telegraph*, Sydney, 4 August 1939.

45 *Washington Post*, Washington, 25 July 1939.

46 *Washington Daily News*, Washington, 24 July 1939; undated newspaper cutting, c. July 1939, RG 126/9/13/11, 'Publicity – Publications, Press Clippings' File, NARA.

47 Letter, Byrd to Gruening, 18 July 1939; memo, Byrd to United States Antarctic Service Committee, 26 July 1939, RG 126/9/13/3, Part #1, 'Appropriations, Estimates, 1939' File, NARA; letters, Byrd to Hampton, 18 August 1939, and attached memo, and Byrd to Black, 18 August 1939, RG 126/9/13/2, Part 2, 'Administrative, General, 8 May 1939 to 28 November 1939' File, NARA.

48 Letter, Gruening to Byrd, 6 October 1939, RG 126/9/13/3, Part #1, 'Appropriations, Estimates, 1939' File, NARA.

49 Minutes, Executive Committee of the United States Antarctic Service, 4 October 1939; letter, Byrd to Gruening, 12 October 1939, RG 126/9/13/3, Part #1, 'Appropriations, Estimates, 1939' File, NARA; letter, Byrd to Gruening, 26 October 1939, RG 126/9/13/3, Part #1, 'Administrative, Islands, Heard' File, NARA; Radiogram, Byrd to Roosevelt, 26 November 1939, RG 126/9/13/2, Part 2, 'Administrative, General, 8 May 1939 to 28 November 1939' File, NARA; letter, Byrd to Gruening, 12 October 1939, RG 126/9/13/13, Part #1, 'Antarctica, Supplies and Equipment, Airplanes' File, NARA.

50 Letter, Helm to Executive Committee, 14 February 1940, RG 126/9/13/11, Part #1, 'Antarctica, Publicity, Photographs' File, NARA.

51 Dean Freitag and J. Stephen Dibbern, 'Dr Poulter's Antarctic Snow Cruiser', *Polar Record*, vol. 23, no. 143.

52 Minutes, Executive Committee of the United States Antarctic Service, 4 October 1939, RG 126/9/13/3, Part #1, 'Appropriations, Estimates, 1939' File, NARA; letter, Hawthorne to Byrd, 27 September 1939, 2 April 1945, RG 126/9/13/11, 'Antarctica, Publicity, General' File, NARA.

53 *New York Times*, New York, 19 November 1939.

54 *Washington Post*, Washington, 25 July 1939; *New York Times*, New York, 29 July 1939; minutes of a Conference of the National Research Council on the Scientific Work of the United States Antarctic Expedition, 28 July 1939, 'Expeditions. U.S. Antarctic Expedition' Folder, AGS.

55 Rose, *Explorer*, pp. 412–413; letter, Roosevelt to Byrd, 25 November 1939, RG 126/9/13/2, Part 2, 'Administrative, General, 8 May 1939 to 28 November 1939' File, NARA.

56 Letter, Roosevelt to Byrd, 25 November 1939, RG 126/9/13/2, Part 2, 'Administrative, General, 8 May 1939 to 28 November 1939' File, NARA.

57 Letter, Roosevelt to Byrd, 25 November 1939, RG 126/9/13/2, Part 2, 'Administrative, General, 8 May 1939 to 28 November 1939' File, NARA.

58 Letter, Black to Hampton, 30 January 1940, RG 126/9/13/2, Part 3, 'Antarctica, Administrative, General' File, NARA.

59 Letter, Dawson, to Byrd, 30 November 1939, RG 126/9/13/2, Part 3, 'Antarctica, Administrative, General' File, NARA.

60 Minutes, Executive Committee of the United States Antarctic Service, 5 June 1940, RG 126/9/13/2, Part #1, 'Administrative, Minutes of Executive Committee' File, NARA.

61 'General Information. The United States Antarctic Service', Press release, March 1940, RG 126/9/13/11, Part #1, 'Antarctica, Publicity, Publications, General' File, NARA.

62 Tim Baughman (ed.), *Ice: The Antarctic Diary of Charles F. Passel*, Texas Tech University Press, Lubbock, 1995, p. 46.

63 'General Information. The United States Antarctic Service', Press release, March 1940, RG 126/9/13/11, Part #1, 'Antarctica, Publicity, Publications, General' File, NARA.

64 Rose, *Explorer*, pp. 414–417; Roger Hawthorne, 'Exploratory Flights of Admiral Byrd (1940)', *Proceedings of the American Philosophical Society*, vol. 89, no. 1, April 1945, pp. 398a-398e.

65 Memo, Ickes to Roosevelt, 29 May 1940, RG 126/9/13/2, Part 3, 'Antarctica, Administrative, General' File, NARA; Rose, *Explorer*, pp. 416–417.

66 Cable, Black to Executive Committee, 14 December 1940, RG 126/9/13/2, Part 3, 'Antarctica, Administrative, General' File, NARA.

67 Rose, *Explorer*, pp. 413–414.

68 Newspaper cutting, 15 May 1940, RG 126/9/13/11, 'Publicity – Publications, Press Clippings' File, NARA; *Washington Post*, Washington, 15 May 1940.

69 Minutes, Executive Committee of the United States Antarctic Service, 5 June 1940, RG 126/9/13/2, Part #1, 'Administrative, Minutes of Executive Committee' File, NARA.

70 Minutes, Executive Committee of the United States Antarctic Service, 5 June 1940, RG 126/9/13/2, Part #1, 'Administrative, Minutes of Executive Committee' File, NARA.

71 Newspaper cutting, 15 May 1940, RG 126/9/13/11, 'Publicity – Publications, Press Clippings' File, NARA; letter, Roosevelt to Taylor, 27 May 1940, RG 126/9/13/3, Part #1, 'Administrative, Islands, Heard' File, NARA.

72　Minutes, Executive Committee of the United States Antarctic Service, 5 June 1940, RG 126/9/13/2, Part #1, 'Administrative, Minutes of Executive Committee' File, NARA.

73　Memo, Ickes to Roosevelt, 29 May 1940, RG 126/9/13/2, Part 3, 'Antarctica, Administrative, General' File, NARA.

74　Minutes, Executive Committee of the United States Antarctic Service, 5 June 1940, RG 126/9/13/2, Part #1, 'Administrative, Minutes of Executive Committee' File, NARA.

CHAPTER 16 - 1941-1945

1　Letter, Emerson to Collins, 15 August 1940, RG 126/9/13/7, Part #1, 'Antarctica, General, General' File, NARA.

2　Letter, Roosevelt to Spinden, 22 January 1940, and other documents in Franklin D. Roosevelt Folder, EC.

3　Minutes, Executive Committee of the United States Antarctic Service, 20 September 1940, RG 126/9/13/2, Part #1, 'Administrative, Minutes of Executive Committee' File; memorandum, Judge Advocate General to Chief of the Bureau of Aeronautics, 4 October 1940, RG 126/9/13/13, Part #1, 'Antarctica, Supplies and Equipment, Airplanes' File; memo, Emerson to MacDonald, 31 October 1940, and other documents in this file, RG 126/9/13/2, Part #1, Evacuation File, NARA.

4　Radiogram, Berlin to Executive Committee, c. 13 November 1940; press release, 21 November 1940; memoranda, Hampton to Johnson, 3 December 1940, and Johnson to Hampton, 12 December 1940, RG 126/9/13/2, Part 3, 'Antarctica, Administrative, General' File, NARA.

5　'History and Current Status of Claims in Antarctica', Secret report by Office of Intelligence Research, 24 November 1947, Department of State, Bureau of Intelligence and Research, Office of the Geographer, Records Relating to Antarctica and Antarctic Exploration, 1930–1955, Box #3, 'Antarctica: The Fischer Study' folder, NARA.

6　Letter, Lystad to Hampton, 29 March 1941, RG 126/9/13/2, Part 3, 'Antarctica, Administrative, General' File; and 'Report on Evacuation East Base, Antarctica, Return of Bear and North Star', Press release, March 1941, RG 126/9/13/2, Part #1, Evacuation File, NARA; R. A. J. English, 'Preliminary Account of the United States Antarctic Expedition, 1939–1941', *Geographical Review*, vol. 31, no. 3, July 1941, pp. 477–478.

7　'Report on Evacuation East Base, Antarctica, Return of Bear and North Star', Press release, March 1941; minutes of Executive Committee, 20 March 1941, RG 126/9/13/2, Part #1, Evacuation File, NARA; Richard Black, 'Geographical Operations from East Base, United States Antarctic Service Expedition, 1939–1941', *Proceedings of the American Philosophical Society*, vol. 89, no. 1, April 1945, pp. 11–12.

8　Letter, Black to Executive Committee, 27 May 1941, RG 126/9/13/2, Part 3, 'Antarctica, Administrative, General' File, NARA.

9　*Washington Herald*, 17 May 1941.

10　Letter, English to Rawson, 13 January 1940, and other documents in RG 126/9/13/11, Part #1, 'Antarctica, Publicity, Publications, General' File, NARA.

11　English, 'Preliminary Account of the United States Antarctic Expedition, 1939–1941'.

12　Memorandum to the Director, Division of Territories and Island Territories, 31 December 1940, RG 126/9/13/6, Part #2, 'Antarctica, Employees, General' File, NARA.

13 Cable, Black to Executive Committee, 14 December 1940, RG 126/9/13/2, Part 3, 'Antarctica, Administrative, General' File, NARA.

14 Magazine cutting, undated, c. 1941, Clippings – 1940s and later, Byrd Folder, EC.

15 Memo, Hodgson to Stirling, 16 May 1940, A2910/404/16/1 Part 1, NAA.

16 Executive Committee Minutes, 5 September and 4 November 1941, RG 126/9/13/2, Part #1, 'Administrative, Minutes of Executive Committee' File, NARA.

17 Memorandum, Gilmour to Hampton, 24 August 1942, RG 126/9/13/6, Part #2, 'Antarctica, Employees, General' File, NARA.

18 'Sailing Directions for Antarctica, 1943', United States Navy Department Hydrographic Office, p. 9, Box 1, Robert B. Klaverkamp Antarctic Collection, SIA.

19 'Territorial Claims in the Antarctic', report by Research Department, Foreign Office, 1 May 1945, A4311/365/8, NAA.

20 Executive Committee Minutes, 5 September 1941, RG 126/9/13/2, Part #1, 'Administrative, Minutes of Executive Committee' File, NARA.

21 Letter, Welch to Larus, 2 April 1945, RG 126/9/13/11, 'Antarctica, Publicity, General' File, NARA.

22 Executive Committee Minutes, 20 September 1940 and 5 September and 4 November 1941, RG 126/9/13/2, Part #1, 'Administrative, Minutes of Executive Committee' File, NARA.

23 Executive Committee Minutes, 5 September and 4 November 1941, RG 126/9/13/2, Part #1, 'Administrative, Minutes of Executive Committee' File, NARA.

24 Reports on Scientific Results of the United States Antarctic Service Expedition, 1939–1941, *Proceedings of the American Philosophical Society*, vol. 89, no. 1, April 1945.

25 William Herbert Hobbs, 'The Discovery of Wilkes Land, Antarctica', *Proceedings of the American Philosophical Society*, vol. 82, 1940.

26 Lawrence Martin, 'Antarctica Discovered by a Connecticut Yankee, Captain Nathaniel Brown Parker', *Geographical Review*, vol. XXX, no. 4, October 1940.

27 'Centenary Celebration. The Wilkes Exploring Expedition of the United States Navy 1838–1840 and Symposium on American Polar Exploration', program of the American Philosophical Society, 23–24 February 1940, Box II: 8, Folder 1, Palmer-Loper Families papers, LoC.

28 G. R. Crone et al., 'Obituary: Arthur Robert Hinks, C.B.E., F.R.S. Secretary, 1915–45', *Geographical Journal*, vol. 105, no. 3/4, March-April 1945.

29 Arthur Hinks, 'The Log of the Hero', *Geographical Journal*, vol. 96, no. 6, December 1940; William Herbert Hobbs, 'Early Maps of Antarctic Land, True and False', *Papers of the Michigan Academy of Science, Arts and Letters*, vol. 26, 1940.

30 Arthur Hinks, 'Antarctica Discovered: A Reply', *Geographical Review*, vol. 31, no. 3, July 1941.

31 Edouard Stackpole, *The Voyage of the* Huron *and the* Huntress, pp. 28–32.

32 McKinley, *James Eights 1798–1882*, pp. 386–387, 390.

33 *New York Times*, 25 July 1939.

34 *Buenos Aires Herald*, 8 August 1939, cited in 'Territorial Claims in the Antarctic', report by Research Department, Foreign Office, 1 May 1945, A4311/365/8, NAA.

35 *New York Times*, 25 July 1939.

36 Argentine Decree No. 61,852.M.97, 30 April 1940, A981/ANT 45, NAA; *New York Times*, 22 May 1940.

37 Dispatch, Department of External Affairs to Australian Chancery, Tokyo, 8 August 1941, A981/ANT 45, NAA; letters, Senoret to Halifax, 11 November 1940, and Balfour to Subercaseaux, 25 February 1941; dispatch, Ovey to Halifax, 25 November 1940, M 1/1209/25/2029, ANZ.

38 'Territorial Claims in the Antarctic', report by Research Department, Foreign Office, 1 May 1945, A4311/365/8, NAA, Canberra; letter, Ovey to Eden, 14 November 1941, A981/ANT 45, NAA.

39 Letter, Roberts to Mossop, 28 August 1944, ADM 1/16123, NA; letter, Browne to Secretary, Admiralty, 1 December 1941, and other documents in ADM 116, NA; 'Territorial Claims in the Antarctic', report by Research Department, Foreign Office, 1 May 1945, A4311/365/8, NAA.

40 Adrian John Howkins, *Frozen Empires: A history of the Antarctic sovereignty dispute between Britain, Argentina and Chile, 1939–1959*, PhD thesis, University of Texas at Austin, 2008, p. 72.

41 Note, Eden to Hadow, 27 June 1942, A981/ANT 45; 'Territorial Claims in the Antarctic', report by Research Department, Foreign Office, 1 May 1945, A4311/365/8, NAA.

42 'Territorial Claims in the Antarctic', report by Research Department, Foreign Office, 1 May 1945, A4311/365/8, NAA; note by J. C. Mossop, 22 April 1942, ADM 116, NA.

43 'Territorial Claims in the Antarctic', report by Research Department, Foreign Office, 1 May 1945, A4311/365/8, NAA.

44 Note by Mossop, 15 September 1943, ADM 1/13321, NA.

45 'Territorial Claims in the Antarctic', report by Research Department, Foreign Office, 1 May 1945, A4311/365/8, NAA; note by Mossop, 15 September 1943, ADM 1/13321, NA; letters, Black to Department of State, 10 February 1945, and Thoron to Black, 4 April 1945, RG 126/9/13/2, Part 3, 'Antarctica, Administrative, General' File, NARA.

46 Note by Mossop, 15 September 1943, ADM 1/13321, NA; medical report, Operation Tabarin, 1944–1946, by Back, May 1946, C.O. 78/218/88027/15, NA; cable, Dominions Secretary to External Affairs Minister, 14 December 1946, N 2/15/08/37/3, ANZ; Klaus Dodds, *Pink Ice: Britain and the South Atlantic Empire*, I. B. Taurus, London, 2002, pp. 14–16; 'Territorial Claims in the Antarctic', report by Research Department, Foreign Office, 1 May 1945, A4311/365/8, NAA.

47 Dodds, *Pink Ice*, pp. 15–16; 'Territorial Claims in the Antarctic', report by Research Department, Foreign Office, 1 May 1945, A4311/365/8, NAA.

48 Dodds, *Pink Ice*, p. 15; medical report, Operation Tabarin, 1944–1946, by Back, May 1946; medical report on Lieut. Cdr. J. W. S. Marr, R.N.V.R. by Back, 8 February 1945, C.O. 78/218/88027/15, NA; note, Acheson to Secretary, Admiralty, 8 September 1944, ADM1/18114, NA; cable, Dominions Secretary to External Affairs Minister, 14 December 1946, N 2/15/08/37/3, ANZ; 'Territorial Claims in the Antarctic', report by Research Department, Foreign Office, 1 May 1945, A4311/365/8, NAA.

49 'Territorial Claims in the Antarctic', report by Research Department, Foreign Office, 1 May 1945, A4311/365/8, NAA.
50 Memos, Santiago Chancery to Foreign Office, 13 November 1944 and 12 January 1945, ADM 1/16124, NA.
51 Report of the Sub-committee appointed to consider the future of the Committee, 21 November 1944; minutes of the "Discovery" Committee, 6 December 1944; letter, Smith to Under Secretary, Colonial Office, December 1944, A3317/22/1945, NAA.
52 Letter, Smith to Under Secretary, Colonial Office, December 1944; letter, Wordie to Hayward, 18 January 1945; letter, Smith to Secretary, South African Antarctic Research Committee, February 1945, A3317/22/1945, NAA.

CHAPTER 17 – 1945–1947

1 Letters, Southern to Truman, 9 July 1945 and Fahy to Southern, 19 July 1945, RG 126/9/13/2, Part #1, 'Administrative, Scientific Works, General' File, NARA.
2 Letters, May to U.S. Antarctic Service, 12 February 1946 and Tyrell to May, 20 February 1946, RG 126/9/13/2, Part #1, 'Administrative, Scientific Works, General' File, NARA.
3 Rose, *Explorer*, pp. 420–421, 426–427.
4 Rose, *Explorer*, pp. 426–428; 'Report of Operation Highjump: U.S. Navy Antarctic Development Project 1947', RG 126/9/13/12, 'Antarctica, Accounts, Reports, Operation, High-Jump' File, NARA; Richard Byrd, 'Our Navy Explores Antarctica', *National Geographic Magazine*, vol. XCII, no. 4, October 1947.
5 Rose, *Explorer*, pp. 428–429.
6 *New Zealand Herald*, Auckland, 14 November 1946; *Herald*, Melbourne, 7 December 1946; 'Report of Operation Highjump: U.S. Navy Antarctic Development Project 1947', RG 126/9/13/12, 'Antarctica, Accounts, Reports, Operation, High-Jump' File, NARA.
7 *Dominion*, Wellington, 9 December 1946.
8 *Truth*, Auckland, 18 December 1946; *New Zealand Herald*, Auckland, 10 December 1946; see also, *Daily Times*, Otago, 26 December 1946.
9 *Dominion*, Wellington, 7 December 1946; *Southern Cross*, Wellington, 10 December 1946; *Gisborne Herald*, Gisborne, 14 April 1947.
10 Letters, Marsden to Faulkner, 11 November 1946, and Marsden to Taylor, 16 November 1946, N 2/15/08/37/3, ANZ.
11 Minutes of an Informal Meeting, 17 January 1947, N 2/15/08/37/3, ANZ.
12 Cable, Beasley to External Affairs, 1 November 1946, A5954/2311/1, NAA.
13 *Herald*, Melbourne, 16 November 1946.
14 David Day, *Chifley*, HarperCollins, Sydney, 2001, p. 433.
15 Memo, Cumpston to Dunk, 3 December 1946, A6348/A21/1, NAA.
16 Memorandum, Dunk to External Affairs Officer, 20 June 1947, A1068/A47/26/20; memo, Hay to Cumpston, 18 November 1947, A6348/A21/1, NAA.
17 'Notes on the Australian Antarctic Territory', memo by Department of External Affairs, 21 November 1946, A5954/2311/1; and 'Australian Antarctic Territory: Inter-Departmental Meeting to discuss future Exploration and Exploitation of Resources', 2 December 1946, A2908/W26 Part 1, NAA.
18 Letter, Mawson to Campbell, 4 November 1948, Davis Papers, AAD.

19 'Australian Antarctic Territory: Inter-Departmental Meeting to discuss future Exploration and Exploitation of Resources', 2 December 1946, A2908/ W26 Part 1; minute of Defence Committee Meeting, 13 December 1946, A5954/2311/1, NAA; *Age*, Melbourne, 20 December 1946.

20 'H.M.A.S. Wyatt Earp (Ex-H.M.A.S. Wongala)', Paper by Naval Archives, 16 May 1962, Davis Papers, AAD.

21 Statement by Chifley, 16 January 1947, A5954/2311/1, NAA.

22 *Herald*, Melbourne, 17 January 1947.

23 Cable, Parry to Naval Intelligence Office, Wellington, 15 November 1946, N 2/15/08/37/3, ANZ.

24 Cable, Dominions Secretary to NZ External Affairs Minister, 14 December 1946, N 2/15/08/37/3, ANZ; Howkins, *Frozen Empires*, p. 99.

25 'Statement by Foreign Office Legal Adviser on the necessity of physical occupation as a means of securing sovereignty in the Polar Regions', c. 31 October 1946, A5954/2311/1, NAA; See also letter (copy), Foreign Office to Admiralty, 7 October 1946, N 2/15/08/37/3, ANZ.

26 *ONI Review*, February 1947, N 2/15/08/37/3, ANZ.

27 Note, Day to Secretary of External Affairs, 28 October 1946, M 1/1209/ 25/2029, ANZ.

28 Letter, Cumpston to Australian Embassy, Washington, 10 June 1947, A3300/541A, NAA.

29 Memo, Cumpston to Australian Chancery, Washington, 25 April 1947, A3300/541A, NAA; *Weekly Notes*, 15 April 1947, N 2/15/08/37/3, ANZ, Wellington.

30 Letter, Cumpston to Australian Embassy, Washington, 10 June 1947, A3300/541A, NAA.

31 *Weekly Notes*, 8 April 1947, N 2/15/08/37/3, ANZ; letter, Cumpston to Australian Embassy, Washington, 30 April 1947, A3300/541A, NAA.

32 *Weekly Notes*, 22 July 1947, N 2/15/08/37/3, ANZ.

33 'Proposed Expedition to Antarctica', prospectus by Ronne, 4 July 1945, RU 192, Box 581/179983, SIA.

34 Letters, Bowman to Wright, 21 July 1945, Ronne to Wright, 11 August 1945, Wright to Bowman, 21 August 1945 and Bowman to Wright, 25 August 1945, Cabot to Wright, 30 August 1945, and Wright to Cabot, 4 September 1945, 'Expeditions: Ronne Antarctic Expedition – Correspondence' folder, AGS.

35 Letter, Wright to Forrestal, 19 October 1945, 'Expeditions: Ronne Antarctic Expedition – Correspondence' folder, AGS.

36 Letter, Ronne to Wright, 26 November 1945, 'Expeditions: Ronne Antarctic Expedition – Correspondence' folder, AGS; memo by Wetmore, 29 November 1945, RU 192, Box 581/179983, SIA.

37 Letters, Ronne to Wright, 7 January 1945 and c. 1 June 1946, 'Expeditions: Ronne Antarctic Expedition – Correspondence' folder, AGS; letter, Fisher to Wetmore, 23 January 1946, RU 192, Box 581/179983, SIA.

38 Letter, Ronne to Gould, 22 April 1946, Stefansson MSS, Gould Papers, Box 1, Folder 8, DCL; letters, Ronne to Eisenhart 1 June 1946, and Ronne to Wright, 6 and 12 June 1946, and Byrd to Chairman of the House Naval Affairs Committee, undated, 'Expeditions: Ronne Antarctic Expedition – Correspondence' folder, AGS; memorandum by Wetmore, 3 July 1946; letters, Eklund to Wetmore, 3 September 1946, and Wetmore to Day, 13 September 1946, RU 192, Box 581/179983, SIA.

39 Letter, Wright to Redmond, 20 September 1946, 'Expeditions: Ronne Antarctic Expedition – Correspondence' folder, AGS.

40 Letter, British Ambassador to Acting Secretary of State, 24 September 1946, RG 126/9/13/2, Part 3, 'Antarctica, Administrative, General' File, NARA.

41 Memoranda by R. E. James, 7 October 1946, RG 126/9/13/2, Part #2, and 7 October 1946, RG 126/9/13/2, Part 3, 'Antarctica, Administrative, General' File, NARA.

42 Memorandum of Conversation by Ronhovde, 10 October 1946, Department of State, Bureau of Intelligence and Research, Office of the Geographer, Records Relating to Antarctica and Antarctic Exploration, 1930–1955, Box #3, 'Ronne Antarctic Research Expedition, 1947–1948' folder; letter, Everson to Wailes, 17 December 1946, RG 126/9/13/2, Part 3, 'Antarctica, Administrative, General' File, NARA; *New York Times*, 23 December 1946.

43 Finn Ronne, *Antarctic Conquest*, Putnam, New York, 1949, pp. 31, 34–35.

44 Letter, Ronne to Wright, 10 November 1946, 'Expeditions: Ronne Antarctic Expedition – Correspondence' folder, AGS; letter, Gould to Ronne, 18 November 1946, Stefansson MSS, Laurence McKinley Gould Papers, Box 1, Folder 8, DCL.

45 Letter, Ronne to Wetmore, 10 January 1947, RU 192, Box 581/179983, SIA.

46 Letter, Ronne to Wright, 2 March 1947, 'Expeditions: Ronne Antarctic Expedition – dinner and meeting of welcome' folder, AGS.

47 *Washington Post*, Washington, 5 March 1947.

48 Letter, Mclean to Schmitt, 19 January 1947, RU 192, Box 581/179983, SIA.

49 Memorandum, Gerberich to Hall, Wells, Trueblood and Briggs, 25 September 1946, Department of State, Bureau of Intelligence and Research, Office of the Geographer, Records Relating to Antarctica and Antarctic Exploration, 1930–1955, Box #3, 'Ronne Antarctic Research Expedition, 1947–1948' folder, NARA.

50 Memorandum, Secretary of State to Postmaster General, 19 January 1953; letter, Ronhovde to Raymond, 6 February 1953, Department of State, Bureau of Intelligence and Research, Office of the Geographer, Records Relating to Antarctica and Antarctic Exploration, 1930–1955, Box #3, 'Ronne, Comdr. Finn – Proposed Antarctic Expedition' folder, NARA.

51 Memo, Acting Secretary of State to Secretary of the Interior, 21 March 1947, RG 126/9/13/2, Part 3, 'Antarctica, Administrative, General' File, NARA; cablegram, Bowers to Secretary of State, 2 April 1947, Department of State, Bureau of Intelligence and Research, Office of the Geographer, Records Relating to Antarctica and Antarctic Exploration, 1930–1955, Box #3, 'Ronne Antarctic Research Expedition, 1947–1948' folder, NARA; *Star*, Washington, 19 March 1947; Ronne, *Antarctic Conquest*, p. 61.

52 'History and Current Status of Claims in Antarctica', Secret report by Office of Intelligence Research, 24 November 1947, Department of State, Bureau of Intelligence and Research, Office of the Geographer, Records Relating to Antarctica and Antarctic Exploration, 1930–1955, Box #3, 'Antarctica: The Fischer Study' folder, NARA; 'Revised Political Instructions to the Leader of the Falkland Islands Dependencies Survey, January 1947', A2908/W26 Part 1, NAA.

53 *Weekly Notes*, 18 February 1947, N 2/15/08/37/3, ANZ.

54 'History and Current Status of Claims in Antarctica', Secret report by Office of Intelligence Research, 24 November 1947, p. 44, Department of State, Bureau

of Intelligence and Research, Office of the Geographer, Records Relating to Antarctica and Antarctic Exploration, 1930–1955, Box #3, 'Antarctica: The Fischer Study' folder, NARA.

55 *Star-Sun*, Christchurch, 3 June 1947.
56 'Report of Operation Highjump: U.S. Navy Antarctic Development Project 1947', p. 6, RG 126/9/13/12, 'Antarctica, Accounts, Reports, Operation, High-Jump' File, NARA.
57 *Dominion*, Wellington, 13 February 1947.
58 *Evening Post*, Wellington, 4 March 1947.
59 *Dominion*, Wellington, 11 March 1947.
60 *Dominion* and *Evening Post*, both Wellington, 14 March 1947; see also, 'Summary of Discussions between Admiral Byrd and the New Zealand Authorities', 13 March 1947, Davis Papers, 1944–47 folder, AAD; For a biography of Peter Fraser, see Michael Bassett and Michael King, *Tomorrow comes the song: A life of Peter Fraser*, Penguin, Auckland, 2000.
61 Minutes, Antarctic Technical Sub-Committee, 18 March 1947, N 2/15/08/37/3, ANZ.
62 *Evening Post*, Wellington, 10 February 1947; 'Summary of Discussions between Admiral Byrd and the New Zealand Authorities', 13 March 1947, Davis Papers, 1944–47 folder, AAD.
63 *New Zealand Herald*, Auckland, 12 April 1947.
64 *Southern Cross*, Wellington, 16 April 1947.
65 Memo, Shanahan to Chiefs of Staff, 31 August 1948; 'Strategic Importance of Antarctica', memo by Chiefs of Staff Committee, 23 September 1948, N 2/15/08/37/3, ANZ.
66 'Papers on Proposed Antarctic Expedition: The Potential Value to New Zealand of Whaling and Allied Activities of the Antarctic', by Sherland, 17 February 1947, N 2/15/08/37/3, ANZ.
67 'Paper on Proposed Antarctic Expedition', by sub-committee of the Antarctic Committee, c. March 1947, N 2/15/08/37/3, ANZ.
68 'Strategic Importance of Antarctica', memo by Chiefs of Staff Committee, 23 September 1948, N 2/15/08/37/3, ANZ.
69 Letters, Australian High Commissioner to Addison, 2 January and 18 February 1947; telegram, Australian High Commission to External Affairs, 28 January 1947, A2908/W26 Part 1, NAA.
70 Cable, Burton to Shedden, 27 March 1947, A5954/2311/1, NAA.
71 *Dominion*, Wellington, 28 February 1947; *Herald*, Melbourne, 11 March 1947.
72 Letters, Davis to Cotton, 19 March 1947, Burton to Davis, 6 April 1947, Carne to Davis, 19 April 1947 and Davis to Carne, 22 April 1947, Davis Papers, 1944–47 folder, AAD.
73 Letter, Mawson to his wife, 25 April 1947, PRG 523/3/6/7, Mawson Papers, SLSA.
74 Executive Planning Committee Minutes, 5 May 1947, Davis Papers, 1944–47 folder, AAD.
75 Letters, Davis to Campbell, 14 July 1947, and Campbell to Davis, 15 July 1947; Committee of Australian National Antarctic Research Expedition Minutes, 23 July 1947, Davis Papers, 1944–47 folder; and 'Australian National Antarctic Research Expedition 1947, Operation Orders and Instructions', Department of External Affairs, c. August 1947, AAD.

76 Cabinet memo by Chifley, c. October 1947; cable, Burton to Shedden, 27 March 1947; memo, Shedden to Dedman, 26 May 1947; cables, Australian High Commissioner to Evatt, 24 December 1947, and South African Prime Minister to Evatt, 6 January 1948, A5954/2311/1, NAA.

77 Memo, Burton to Cumpston, 25 September 1947, A6348/A21/1, NAA.

78 *Daily Telegraph*, Sydney, 15 November 1947; *Argus* and *Age*, both Melbourne, 5 January 1948.

79 Cabinet memorandum no. 1275E, by Chifley, c. October 1947, A5954/2311/1; and 'Declaration to be made by Leader of Expedition to Heard Island at Formal ceremony on Arrival' c. October 1947, A6348/A21/1, NAA.

80 *Age*, Melbourne, 5 January 1948.

81 'H.M.A.S. Wyatt Earp (Ex-H.M.A.S. Wongala)', Paper by Naval Archives, 16 May 1962, Davis Papers, AAD.

82 Captain W. F. Cook, 'H.M.A.S. "Wyatt Earp", Australian National Antarctic Research Expedition 1947–1948', *Naval Historical Review*, December 1978.

83 Message, Ronne to Secretary of State, 2 June 1947, Department of State, Office of the Geographer, Records relating to Antarctica and Antarctic Exploration, 1930–1955, Box #2, 'Antarctic Expedition – Finn Ronne Proposal' folder, NARA.

84 Memo, Black to Committee on Geographical Exploration, 17 July 1947; memo for the Record by Simpson, 2 September 1947; memo by Davis, 5 September 1947, and other documents in Department of State, Office of the Geographer, Records relating to Antarctica and Antarctic Exploration, 1930–1955, Box #2, 'Antarctic Expedition – Finn Ronne Proposal' folder, NARA.

85 Memo, Cruzen to Executive Director, Joint Research and Development Board (Committee on Geographical Exploration), 25 August 1947, and other documents in Department of State, Office of the Geographer, Records relating to Antarctica and Antarctic Exploration, 1930–1955, Box #2, 'Antarctic Expedition – Finn Ronne Proposal' folder, NARA.

86 Memo, Piggot to Executive Director, Com. on Geographical Exploration, 26 July 1947, Department of State, Office of the Geographer, Records relating to Antarctica and Antarctic Exploration, 1930–1955, Box #2, 'Antarctic Expedition – Finn Ronne Proposal' folder, NARA.

87 'Territorial Claims in Antarctica', Secret map of Antarctica by the Map Branch, CIA, October 1947, and issued by Department of State, 4 August 1948, Department of State, Bureau of Intelligence and Research, Office of the Geographer, Records Relating to Antarctica and Antarctic Exploration, 1930–1955, Box #3, 'Map "Territorial Claims in Antarctica"' folder, NARA.

88 'History and Current Status of Claims in Antarctica', Secret report by Office of Intelligence Research, 24 November 1947, pp. 8–9, 31–35, Department of State, Bureau of Intelligence and Research, Office of the Geographer, Records Relating to Antarctica and Antarctic Exploration, 1930–1955, Box #3, 'Antarctica: The Fischer Study' folder, NARA.

CHAPTER 18 – 1948–1951

1 Program of event to welcome members of the Ronne Expedition, 16 April 1948, 'Expeditions: Ronne Antarctic Expedition – dinner and meeting of welcome' folder, AGS.

2 'Palmer Land – Disputed Area of the Antarctic', memorandum by Ronne, undated, c. 1948, 'Expeditions: Ronne Antarctic Expedition – dinner and meeting of welcome' folder, AGS; Ronne, *Antarctic Conquest*, p. 288.

3 Letter, Ronne to Wright, 14 March 1948, 'Expeditions: Ronne Antarctic Expedition – dinner and meeting of welcome' folder, AGS.

4 Letter, Gould to Wright, 20 April 1948, 'Expeditions: Ronne Antarctic Expedition – dinner and meeting of welcome' folder; program for Ronne Reception, 16 April 1948, 'Expeditions: Ronne Antarctic expedition – publication of results' Folder, AGS; Finn Ronne, 'Antarctica – One Continent', *Explorers Journal*, Summer-Autumn, 1948.

5 'Palmer Land – Disputed Area of the Antarctic', memorandum by Ronne, undated, c. 1948, 'Expeditions: Ronne Antarctic Expedition – dinner and meeting of welcome' folder, AGS.

6 Program for Ronne Reception, 16 April 1948, 'Expeditions: Ronne Antarctic expedition – publication of results' Folder; letter, Gould to Wright, 20 April 1948, 'Expeditions: Ronne Antarctic Expedition – dinner and meeting of welcome' folder, AGS; Invitation, 15 April 1948; invitation to Dr Alexander Wetmore, 16 April 1948, RU 192, Box 581/179983, SIA; letter, Ronne to Gould, 29 April 1948, Stefansson MSS, Gould Papers, Box 1, Folder 8, DCL.

7 Memo, Briesemeister to Wright, 25 April 1948; letter, Wright to Boardman, 29 April 1948, 'Expeditions: Ronne Antarctic Expedition – dinner and meeting of welcome' folder, AGS; Finn Ronne, 'Antarctica – One Continent', *Explorers Journal*, Summer-Autumn, 1948; Ronne, *Antarctic Conquest*, p. xx.

8 Memo, Briesemeister to Wright, 25 April 1948, 'Expeditions: Ronne Antarctic Expedition – dinner and meeting of welcome' folder, AGS, New York.

9 Letter, Gould to Wright, 20 April 1948, 'Expeditions: Ronne Antarctic Expedition – dinner and meeting of welcome' folder, AGS.

10 Letter, Eisenhart to Wright, 21 September 1948, 'Expeditions: Ronne Antarctic expedition – publication of results' Folder, AGS.

11 Letter, Ronne to Wright, 14 October 1948, 'Expeditions: Ronne Antarctic expedition – publication of results' Folder, AGS; letter, Ronne to Gould, 11 June 1950, Stefansson MSS, Laurence McKinley Gould Papers, Box 1, Folder 9, DCL; Richard Byrd, 'Our Navy Explores Antarctica', *National Geographic Magazine*, October 1947.

12 Letter, Ronne to Wright, 14 October 1948, 'Expeditions: Ronne Antarctic expedition – publication of results' Folder, AGS.

13 Letter, Ronne to Gould, 11 June 1950, Stefansson MSS, Gould Papers, Box 1, Folder 9, DCL.

14 Byrd, 'Our Navy Explores Antarctica', *National Geographic Magazine*, p. 434.

15 Letter, Byrd to Wright, 14 April 1948, 'Expeditions: Ronne Antarctic Expedition – dinner and meeting of welcome' folder, AGS.

16 Letter, Byrd to Wright, 14 April 1948, 'Expeditions: Ronne Antarctic Expedition – dinner and meeting of welcome' folder, AGS; letter, Ronne to Gould, 2 November 1948, Stefansson MSS, Laurence McKinley Gould Papers, Box 1, Folder 8, DCL.

17 Memo, Boggs to Hulley and Green, 31 August 1948, enclosing proposal by Ronne, 26 August 1948, Department of State, Bureau of Intelligence and Research, Office of the Geographer, Records Relating to Antarctica and Antarctic Exploration, 1930–1955, Box #3, 'Ronne Antarctic Research Expedition, 1947–1948' folder, NARA.

18 Letter, Department of State to Krug, 8 June 1948, RG 126/9/13/2, Part 3, 'Antarctica, Administrative, General' File, NARA.

19   Letter, Ronne to Marshall, 16 December 1948, Department of State, Bureau of Intelligence and Research, Office of the Geographer, Records Relating to Antarctica and Antarctic Exploration, 1930–1955, Box #3, 'Ronne Antarctic Research Expedition, 1947–1948' folder, NARA.

20   Rose, *Explorer*, pp. 431–433.

21   'Antarctic Research: Elements of a Coordinated Program', report by the National Academy of Sciences, 2 May 1949, Department of State, Bureau of Intelligence and Research, Office of the Geographer, Records Relating to Antarctica and Antarctic Exploration, 1930–1955, Box #6, 'Antarctic Research: Elements of a Coordinated Program' folder, NARA.

22   Letter, Ronne to Gould, 12 April 1949, Stefansson MSS, Gould Papers, Box 1, Folder 9, DCL.

23   Letter, Case to Gould, 18 July 1949, Stefansson MSS, Gould Papers, Box 1, Folder 9, DCL; Ray Josephs, 'Beyond the World's Last Frontier', *Argosy*, April 1949.

24   Memorandum of Conversation, Boggs and Tison, 22 August 1949, Department of State, Bureau of Intelligence and Research, Office of the Geographer, Records Relating to Antarctica and Antarctic Exploration, 1930–1955, Box #3, 'Ronne Antarctic Research Expedition, 1947–1948' folder, NARA.

25   Letter, Boggs to Ronne, 25 August 1949, Department of State, Bureau of Intelligence and Research, Office of the Geographer, Records Relating to Antarctica and Antarctic Exploration, 1930–1955, Box #3, 'Ronne Antarctic Research Expedition, 1947–1948' folder, NARA; 'Antarctic Research: Elements of a Coordinated Program', report by the National Academy of Sciences, 2 May 1949, Department of State, Bureau of Intelligence and Research, Office of the Geographer, Records Relating to Antarctica and Antarctic Exploration, 1930–1955, Box #6, 'Antarctic Research: Elements of a Coordinated Program' folder, NARA.

26   Memorandum of Conversation, Ronne and Green, 19 October 1949, Department of State, Bureau of Intelligence and Research, Office of the Geographer, Records Relating to Antarctica and Antarctic Exploration, 1930–1955, Box #3, 'Ronne Antarctic Research Expedition, 1947–1948' folder, NARA.

27   Finn Ronne, 'Ronne Antarctic Research Expedition 1946–1948', *Geographical Review*, vol. 38, no. 3, July 1948; Finn Ronne, 'Antarctic Mapping and Aerial Photography', *Scientific Monthly*, vol. LXXI, no. 5, November 1950.

28   Cables, Commonwealth Relations Secretary to Evatt, 28 December 1947, and Cumpston to Department of External Affairs, 16 February 1948, A5954/2311/1, NAA.

29   *Argus*, Melbourne, 7 and 21 February 1948; *Age* and *Herald*, Melbourne, 21 February 1948; *Dominion*, Wellington, 4 January 1949; cables, Commonwealth Relations Secretary to Department of External Affairs, 16 and 25 February 1948, and Australian High Commissioner to Department of External Affairs, 26 February 1948, A5954/2311/1, NAA.

30   Cable, Cumpston to Department of External Affairs, 9 March 1948, A5954/2311/1, NAA.

31   Cable, Commonwealth Relations Secretary to Department of External Affairs, 9 March 1948, A5954/2311/1, NAA.

32   Note by Bennett, 30 December 1946, CO 537/2459, NA.

33 Letter, Tennant to Cunningham, 5 May 1948, ADM 1/21126, NA.
34 Memorandum, Shanahan to Naval Secretary, 25 August 1948, N 2/15/08/37/3, ANZ.
35 Cables, Addison to Evatt, 17 February and 6 March 1948, and Australian Embassy to External Affairs, 2 March 1948, A5954/2311/1, NAA.
36 *Times*, London, 19 January 1949.
37 Cable, South African Government to Addison, 9 March 1948, A5954/2311/1, NAA.
38 Cable, Fraser to Addison, 11 March 1948, A5954/2311/1, NAA.
39 Cables, Fraser to Addison, 5 and 11 March 1948, A5954/2311/1, NAA.
40 *Dominion*, Wellington, 11 February 1948.
41 Cable, Evatt to Addison, 11 March 1948, A5954/2311/1, NAA.
42 Cables, Addison to Australian Government, 17 March and 24 July 1948, A5954/2311/1, NAA.
43 Cable, Department of External Affairs to Addison, 30 July 1948, A5954/2311/1, NAA.
44 *Argus*, Melbourne, 4 August 1948; telegram, Secretary of State, Commonwealth Relations, to Minister of External Affairs, 26 November 1948, N 2/15/08/37/3, ANZ.
45 Memorandum, Noel-Baker to New Zealand Government, 5 January 1949, N 1/202/8/37/3, ANZ.
46 Memo, McIntosh to Naval Secretary, 25 March 1949, and other documents in N 1/202/8/37/3, ANZ.
47 Diary by Stuart Campbell, 8–22 February 1948, MS9458, Box 48, Law Papers, NLA; Cook, 'H.M.A.S. "Wyatt Earp", Australian National Antarctic Research Expedition 1947–1948', *Naval Historical Review*.
48 Diary by Stuart Campbell, 10–13 March 1948, MS9458, Box 48, Law Papers, NLA; Kathleen Ralston, 'The Wyatt Earp's Voyages of Reconnaissance of the Australian Antarctic Territory, 1947–48', *Journal of Australian Studies*, March 1995.
49 *Herald*, Melbourne, 30 August 1948.
50 Letter, Davis to Mawson, 22 June 1948, Davis Papers, AAD.
51 Minutes, Planning Committee, Australian National Antarctic Research Expedition, 18 May 1948, Davis Papers, AAD.
52 'Australian National Antarctic Research Expedition 1949–50, Operation Orders and Instructions', Department of External Affairs, AAD; Minutes, Antarctic Committee, 28 September 1948, Davis Papers, AAD.
53 *Herald*, Melbourne, 1 December 1948.
54 Minutes, Antarctic Committee, 28 September 1948, Davis Papers, AAD.
55 Cabinet Agendum No. 1275F, by Dr Evatt, c. March 1948, A1068/A47/26/23, NAA; Agenda for Meeting of Planning Committee, Australian National Antarctic Research Expedition, 18 May 1948, Davis Papers, AAD.
56 Letters, Campbell to Burton, 5 July 1948, Campbell to Mawson, 13 October 1948, Law to Colin [unclear], 27 October 1948, and Mawson to Campbell, 4 November 1948, MS 9458/1/193, Law Papers, NLA.
57 Memo, Burton to Campbell, 8 December 1948, MS 9458/1/193, Law Papers, NLA.
58 Letter, Burton to Law, 14 December 1948, teleprinter message, Campbell to Burton, 15 December 1948 and memorandum, Campbell to Burton, 16 December 1948, MS 9458/1/193, Law Papers, NLA.
59 Law would continue to argue without success for such an institute and museum. See memo, Law to Secretary, Department of External Affairs, 11 July 1949, MS 9458/1/193, Law Papers, NLA.

60 'Lecture – Royal Empire Society – 7th July 1949', 'Speech to Luncheon "Carry On Club"', 21 September 1949; 'Legacy Club Luncheon', talk by Law, c. 1949, MS 9458/4/3, Law Papers, NLA.

61 *Age*, Melbourne, 1 April 1949; Newspaper cutting, 10 December 1948, Davis Papers, AAD.

62 'Australian Interests in the Antarctic', memorandum for Spender, 25 January 1950, A1838/1495/4 Part 1, NAA; minutes of Meeting, 18 May 1950, MS 9458/1/193; resolution by the Australian Antarctic Executive Committee, undated, c. 1950, MS 9458/1/200, Law Papers, NLA.

63 'Antarctica', undated and unsigned memorandum, c. 1950, A1838/1495/4 Part 1, NAA.

64 'Russian Place-Names in the Antarctic Given by Thaddeus Bellingshausen', Agenda paper APC(50)9, Antarctic Place-Names Committee, 1950, P1469/0/127/2 Part 1, NAA.

65 Memorandum, Costello to Secretary of External Affairs, 7 October 1949, N 1/202/8/37/3, ANZ.

66 Minute, S. W. to Kevin, 17 June 1950; letter, Coodes to Secretary, External Affairs, 27 June 1950, A1838/1495/4 Part 1, NAA.

67 Resolution by the Australian Antarctic Executive Committee, c. 1950, MS 9458/1/200, Law Papers, NLA.

68 Letters, Mawson to Law, 30 August 1950, and Davis to Law, 18 September 1950, Davis Papers, AAD.

69 Letter, Edwards to Mighell, 19 August 1946; telegrams, Dominions Office to Australian and New Zealand Governments, 21 August 1946, New Zealand Government to Dominions Office, 22 August 1946, Australian Government to Dominions Office, 27 August 1946; memo, McCarthy to Strahan, 25 September 1946; dispatch, Dunk to External Affairs Officer, 6 November 1946, A2908/W26 Part 1, NAA; *Newsweek*, New York, 9 September 1946.

70 *Nippon Times*, Tokyo, 27 June 1947; *New Zealand Herald*, Auckland, 4 November 1947; Newspaper cutting, c. 1950, A1838/479/3/4/1 Part 6, NAA.

71 Memo, Salisbury to Menzies, 16 January 1952, A1838/479/3/4/1 Part 6, NAA.

72 'Japanese Antarctic Claims', memo, Mallaby to Stirling, 8 August 1947, and other documents in CO 537/2470, NA.

73 'Report on Antarctic Whaling Expeditions', Edwards to Mighell, 6 December 1946; letter, Dunbabin to Bonney, 8 January 1947, A2908/W26 Part 1, NAA; Tonnessen and Johnsen, *The History of Modern Whaling*, Chaps. 27–29.

74 Tonnessen and Johnsen, *The History of Modern Whaling*, pp. 749, 753.

CHAPTER 19 – 1952–1956

1 *Sydney Morning Herald*, Sydney, 4 February 1952; *Age*, Melbourne, 5 February 1952; Vivian Fuchs, *Of Ice and Men: The Story of the British Antarctic Survey 1943–73*, Anthony Nelson, Oswestry, 1982, pp. 164–166.

2 Fuchs, *Of Ice and Men*, pp. 164–166.

3 *New York Times*, 7, 20 and 21 February 1953; *Times*, London, 13 and 21 February 1953.

4 *New York Times*, 22, 24 and 27 February 1953, 11 December 1953 and 6 March 1954; *Times*, London, 23 and 24 February 1953, 26 March 1953, 18 February 1954 and 5 and 8 March 1954.

5 Draft Cabinet Paper, c. July 1954, CO 1024/132, NA.

6 Memo, Cranborne to Curtin, 8 August 1944, A989/1944/45/10; 'Territorial Claims in the Antarctic', report by Research Department, Foreign Office, 1 May 1945, A4311/365/8, NAA.
7 Minutes of Antarctic Place-Names Committee, 5 October 1950, P1469/0/127/2 Part 1, NAA.
8 Minutes of Antarctic Place-Names Committee, 5 October 1950, P1469/0/127/2 Part 1, NAA.
9 Minutes of Antarctic Place-Names Committee, 5 October 1950 and 2 November 1950, P1469/0/127/2 Part 1, NAA.
10 'Progress Report on the work on Place-Names in the Antarctic', by Roberts, 12 March 1953, P1469/0/127/2 Part 2, NAA.
11 Note, Morris to Martin, 28 July 1953, 'Plans for a Trans-Antarctic Journey', by V. E. Fuchs, undated; extract from Notes of a Meeting of the Polar Committee held at the Commonwealth Relations Office, 24 March 1953, CO 1024/60, NA; Vivian Fuchs, A Time to Speak: An autobiography, Anthony Nelson, Oswestry, 1990, pp. 218–222.
12 Memo, Newell to Admiralty Board, 11 May 1954, ADM 1/26146, NA; memorandum, Corner to Secretary of External Affairs, 16 September 1953, N 1/202/8/37/3, ANZ; see documents in CO 1024/60, NA.
13 Minute, Attorney-General to Menzies, 15 August 1955, A4940/C1438, NAA.
14 Memo, Wilson to Secretary, Admiralty 19 January 1955, ADM 1/26146, NA.
15 Minute, Attorney-General to Menzies, 15 August 1955; cabinet minute, 16 August 1955, A4940/C1438, NAA.
16 'Text of Communique Issued on Renewal of Tripartite Naval Declarations on Antarctica, 26th November, 1953', N 1/512/16/31/8, ANZ.
17 Notes, Morris to Martin, 16 July 1954, and Salisbury to Alexander, 20 August 1954, CO 1024/132, NA.
18 Letters, Thomas to Eden, 16 November 1954, Eden to Thomas, 23 November 1954, Thomas to Macmillan, 1 December 1954, Macmillan to Thomas, 7 December 1954, and Thomas to Eden, 23 December 1954, ADM 1/25577, NA.
19 Letters, Eden to Thomas, 23 November 1954, Macmillan to Eden, 23 December 1954, Lennox-Boyd to Thomas, 12 January 1955; cable, Arthur to Colonial Secretary, 30 September 1954, ADM 1/25577, NA.
20 Unsigned minute, 21 January 1955, and 'Antarctica C(55)56', draft cabinet paper, c. February 1955, ADM 1/25577, NA.
21 'Antarctica', memorandum by Eden, draft cabinet paper, c. February 1955, ADM 1/25577, NA.
22 Minute by Naime, 26 August 1955 and secret message, Admiralty to Commander in Chief, America and West Indies, 6 September 1955, ADM 1/26148, NA; memo, Vile to Arthur, 24 October 1955; extract from C.O.S.(55) 83rd Meeting, 11/10/55, CO 1024/133, NA.
23 Memo, Boggs to Matthews, 24 February 1953; memorandum of conversation, Ronne, Boggs, Ronhovde and Hilliker, 25 February 1953, Department of State, Bureau of Intelligence and Research, Office of the Geographer, Records Relating to Antarctica and Antarctic Exploration, 1930–1955, Box #3, 'Ronne, Comdr. Finn – Proposed Antarctic Expedition' folder, NARA.
24 'Department's Proposed Preliminary Position on Proposed Antarctic Expedition', memo by Hilliker, 3 April 1953, Department of State, Bureau of Intelligence and Research, Office of the Geographer, Records Relating to Antarctica and Antarctic Exploration, 1930–1955, Box #3, 'Ronne, Comdr. Finn – Proposed Antarctic Expedition' folder, NARA.

25 Letter, Ronne to Gould, 10 May 1954, Stefansson MSS, Gould Papers, Box 1, Folder 9, DCL.

26 Letter drafted by Hilliker for reply by Eisenhower to Case, 5 January 1954, and 'S.3381: A Bill to authorize the President to provide assistance to an expedition to the Antarctic in furtherance of the interests of the United States', 29 April 1954, Department of State, Bureau of Intelligence and Research, Office of the Geographer, Records Relating to Antarctica and Antarctic Exploration, 1930–1955, Box #3, 'Ronne, Comdr. Finn – Proposed Antarctic Expedition' folder, NARA.

27 Statement of Captain Finn Ronne before the Armed Services Committee of the United States Senate, c. May 1954, Stefansson MSS, Gould Papers, Box 1, Folder 9, DCL.

28 Letter, Ronne to Gould, 3 May 1954, and other documents, in Stefansson MSS, Gould Papers, Box 1, Folder 9, DCL.

29 Letter, Ronne to Gould, 10 May 1954, Stefansson MSS, Gould Papers, Box 1, Folder 9, DCL.

30 Memorandum, Barbour to Murphy, 14 June 1954, in United States Department of State, *Foreign Relations of the United States, 1952–1954, Volume 1, Part 2, General: Economic and Political Matters*, U.S. Government Printing Office, Washington, pp. 1741–1742.

31 Draft Statement of Policy Proposed by the National Security council, 28 June 1954, in United States Department of State, *Volume 1, Part 2, General: Economic and Political Matters*, U.S. Government Printing Office, Washington, *Foreign Relations of the United States, 1952–1954*, pp. 1744–1756.

32 Memorandum of discussion at the 206th Meeting of the National Security Council on Thursday, July 15, 1954, in United States Department of State, *Foreign Relations of the United States, 1952–1954, Volume 1, Part 2, General: Economic and Political Matters*, U.S. Government Printing Office, Washington, pp. 1744–1756.

33 Statement by Case, 5 August 1954, Stefansson MSS, Gould Papers, Box 1, Folder 9, DCL.

34 Letter, Ronne to Gould, 5 August 1954, Stefansson MSS, Gould Papers, Box 1, Folder 9, DCL; letter, Byrd to Harold Byrd, 6 July 1954, Byrd Papers, RG 56.1, Box, 1, Folder 31, BPRC; Rose, *Explorer*, pp. 440–442.

35 Letters, Black to Case, 10 July 1954, and Ronne to Gould, 13 July 1954, Stefansson MSS, Gould Papers, Box 1, Folder 9, DCL.

36 Letter, Gould to Dufek, 19 October 1954, Stefansson MSS, Laurence McKinley Gould Papers, Box 1, Folder 4, DCL.

37 *New York Times*, 16 January and 16 February 1955.

38 Cable, Acting Secretary of State to US Embassy, Argentina, 22 October 1954, in United States Department of State, *Foreign Relations of the United States, 1952–1954*, pp. 1764–1765.

39 'Joint Resolution: Declaring the right of sovereignty of the United States over certain areas of the Antarctic Continent, and for other purposes', by Tollefson, 5 January 1955, Box II: 19, Folder 6, Palmer-Loper Families papers, LoC.

40 Letters, Ronne to Gould, 25 December 1954, 1 February 1955 and 30 March 1955, Stefansson MSS, Gould Papers, Box 1, Folder 9, DCL.

41 Transcript of interview with Phillip Law, TRC 351, NLA.

42 'Naming Antarctic Features', article by Law, undated, MS 9458/1/155, Law Papers, NLA.

43 Minutes, Australian Committee on Antarctic Names, 21 October 1952, P1469/0/127/2 Part 3, NAA.

44 'The Problem of Place Names in Antarctica', paper by Law, 22 August 1956,

MS 9458/6/11; 'Naming Antarctic Features', article by Law, undated, MS 9458/1/155, Law Papers, NLA.

45 Letter, Law to Secretary, External Affairs, 31 August 1951; cabinet agendum by Casey, 6 October 1951, B1387/22/1996/1069 Part 1, NAA.

46 Letter, Law to Liotard, 8 October 1951, and other documents in B1387/22/1996/1069 Part 1, NAA.

47 Teleprinter message, Holland to Law, 8 January 1952; note of telephone conversation between Law and Taylor, 30 January 1952, and other documents in B1387/22/1996/1069 Part 1, NAA.

48 Letter, Law to Davis, 11 February 1953, Davis Papers, AAD; letters, Casey to Law, 30 July 1953, Law to Casey, 31 July and 4 August 1953; note, Casey to Waller, 24 August 1953; Executive Planning Committee Paper 53(1): Draft Cabinet Submission, c. November 1953, A10299/A8, NAA.

49 *Age*, Melbourne, 21 March 1953; *Herald*, Melbourne, 28 March 1953.

50 *Sunday Herald*, Sydney, 30 November 1952.

51 *Herald*, Melbourne, 28 March 1953.

52 *Age*, Melbourne, 5 January 1954; 'Australian Expedition Leaves for Antarctica', by Hungerford, Australian News and Information Bureau, c. January 1954, N 1/512/16/31/8, ANZ.

53 Transcript of interview with Phillip Law, TRC 351, NLA.

54 Memos, Waller to Law, 26 May 1954, Law to Secretary, External Affairs, 23 September 1954; note, Law to Casey, 22 October 1954; press release, c. November 1955; note for Public Relations File, 13 December 1955, B1387/22/1996/1089, NAA.

55 Letters, Law to Director, News and Information Bureau, 4 August 1955, P1469/0/134/1 Part 1, Law to Secretary, External Affairs, 3 September 1954; notes, Law to Waller, 15 October 1954 and 28 September 1955, B1387/22/1996/1097, NAA.

56 Letter, Law to Hawes, 28 November 1955, and other documents in B1387/1996/1090, NAA.

57 Memo, Law to Holland, 23 December 1955, P1469/0/134/1 Part 1, NAA.

58 Letter, Casey to Campbell, 8 May 1956; note, Casey to Law, 16 July 1956, P1469/0/134/1 Part 2, NAA.

59 Draft memo, [unclear] to Law, 16 December 1955, P1469/0/134/1 Part 2, NAA.

60 'Public Relations and the Antarctic Division', memo by Law to Secretary, External Affairs, 10 May 1956, P1469/0/134/1 Part 2, NAA.

61 Memo, White to Minister for Scientific and Industrial Research, 15 July 1953, CAB 409/1/1, Part 1, ANZ.

62 Memo, Shanahan to Secretary, DSIR, 5 October 1953, and Hicks, 21 October 1953, N 1/202/8/37/3, ANZ.

63 Letter, Fuchs to Odell, 19 October 1954, MS 2003/101/7, J. H. Rose Papers, AWMM.

64 Minutes of the First Meeting of the Auckland Committee for the Discussion of Antarctic Matters, 2 December 1954, MS 966/1, AWMM; letter, Packard to Odell, 10 December 1954, MS 2003/101/7, J. H. Rose Papers, AWMM.

65 Letter, Odell to Rose, 17 December 1954; submission by Deputation of the New Zealand Antarctic Society and its Supporters to the Hon. The Minister of External Affairs, 14 January 1955, MS 2003/101/7, J. H. Rose Papers, AWMM; *New York Times*, 10 January 1955; minutes of the First Meeting of the Auckland Branch of the New Zealand Antarctic Society, 22 February 1955, MS 966/1, Auckland Committee for Discussion of the Antarctic Papers, AWMM.

66 Memorandum, McIntosh to Macdonald, 11 January 1955, CAB 409/1/1, Part 1, ANZ.

67 Memo, Shanahan to Macdonald, 19 January 1955; cable, Macdonald to Holland, 19 January 1955, CAB 409/1/1, Part 1, ANZ; letter, Rose to Falla, 4 March 1955, MS 2003/101/7, J. H. Rose Papers, AWMM; *Herald*, Melbourne, 10 March 1955; *Auckland Star*, Auckland, 12 March 1955; letter, Odell to Rose, 23 March 1955, MS 2003/101/7, J. H. Rose Papers, AWMM.

68 Memo, Shanahan to Macdonald, 16 March 1955; cabinet memo by Macdonald, 1 April 1955, CAB 409/1/1, Part 1, ANZ.

69 Memo, Shanahan to Macdonald, 5 April 1955; cabinet memo by Algie, 15 April 1955, CAB 409/1/1, Part 1, ANZ.

70 Letter, Hillary to Helm, 13 July 1955, MS 162/13/44, CM.

71 Background paper (restricted), Ross Sea Committee, c. June 1955, MS 162/3/10, CM.

72 Cabinet memo by Algie and Macdonald, 5 August 1955, CAB 409/1/1, Part 1, ANZ.

73 Cabinet memo by Holyoake, 20 April 1956; 'Antarctica – Joint United States/ New Zealand Base at Cape Adare', cabinet memo by Algie and Macdonald, 27 April 1956, CAB 409/1/1, Part 1, ANZ.

74 'Operation Deepfreeze II – Facilities in New Zealand', cabinet memo by Macdonald, 19 July 1956, CAB 409/1/1, Part 1, ANZ.

75 Memoranda, Laking to McFarlane, 18 October 1956, and Laking to Algie, 30 May 1956, AMF/W3118/4/1955/2876/3, ANZ; memoranda by McFarlane, 16 February and 19 July 1955, McFarlane to Postmaster-General, 21 November 1955; letters, Helm to McFarlane, 21 June 1955, and McFarlane to Smith, 1 December 1955, AAMF/W3118/3/1955/2876/1, ANZ; *New Zealand Herald*, Auckland, 24 November 1956; *New York Times*, 10 February 1957.

76 Tønnessen and Johnsen, *The History of Modern Whaling*, p. 749.

CHAPTER 20 – 1957–1960

1 Rose, *Explorer*, pp. 453–462; letters, Ronne to Gould, 13 February 1956, Box 1, Folder 10, and Gould to Byrd, 7 August and 28 November 1956, and Byrd to Gould, 17 August 1956; memo, Byrd to Chief of Naval Operations, 20 August 1956, Gould Papers, Box 1, Folder 3, DCL.

2 *Time*, New York, 31 December 1956.

3 Memorandum by Ronne, 6 May 1955, Gould Papers, Box 1, Folder 10, DCL.

4 *New York Times Magazine*, 30 December 1956 and 14 January 1957; letter, Dufek to Gould, 5 January 1959, Stefansson MSS, Gould Papers, Box 1, Folder 6, DCL; Sullivan's account of Operation Deep Freeze can be found in Walter Sullivan, *Quest for a Continent*, McGraw-Hill, New York, 1957; *Polar Record*, New York, December 1956.

5 Memo by Department of External Affairs, 4 October 1957, N 1/513/16/31/16; memo by Chiefs of Staff, 16 July 1958, AAEG 6956/W3252/1/TKY5/A/1 Part 5, ANZ; *New York Times*, 10 February 1957; For the unsuccessful attempts by New Zealand to prevent the United States establishing a post office in the Ross Dependency, see docs in AAMF/W3118/3/1955/2876, ANZ.

6 *New York Times*, 16 October and 29 November 1957; letters, Gould to Dufek, 16 October and 19 December 1957, and Dufek to Gould, 31 October 1957, Stefansson MSS, Gould Papers, Box 1, Folder 5, DCL.

7 Memos, Ruegg to Scott, 31 October 1957, and Scott to Ruegg, 6 November 1957, M 1/1209/25/2029, ANZ.

8   Roneod letter by New Zealand MP, 23 October 1957, CAB 409/1/1, Part 1, ANZ.
9   Interview with Phillip Law by Jill Cassidy, 10 July 1991, MS 9458/1/166, Law Papers, NLA.
10   *Polar Record*, New York, June 1956, p. 19; V. G. Kort, 'Report on the Naval Antarctic Expedition of the U.S.S.R. Academy of Sciences', *Accounts and Materials of the Complex Antarctic Expedition of the USSR Academy of Sciences*, USSR Academy of Sciences, Moscow, 1956, A1838/1495/1/9/7 Annex, NAA; 'A.N.A.R.E. Exploration of Wilkes Land', paper by Law, c. 1957, MS 9458/6/11, Law Papers, NLA.
11   V. F. Burhanov, 'Report on the Research Work in the Antarctic during the Season of 1955–1956', *Accounts and Materials of the Complex Antarctic Expedition of the USSR Academy of Sciences*, USSR Academy of Sciences, Moscow, 1956, A1838/1495/1/9/7 Annex, NAA; V. A. Bugaev (ed.), *Soviet Antarctic Research 1956–1966: Proceedings of the All-Union Conference on Antarctic Research 1966*, Academy of Sciences of the USSR, Moscow, 1967; A. V. Nudel'man, *Soviet Antarctic Expeditions 1955–1959*, USSR Academy of Sciences, Moscow, 1959, p. 10, 14; *New York Times*, 8 September 1957; transcript of interview with Phillip Law, TRC 351, NLA; 'Report of Visit to U.S.S.R. Base at Mirny', by Law, c. 1956, MS 9458/6/11, Law Papers, NLA.
12   *Polar Record*, New York, June 1956, p. 8; *Pegasus*, Fairchild Engine and Airplane Corporation, New York, c. 1956.
13   *Polar Record*, New York, December 1957, p. 13.
14   *Polar Record*, New York, June 1956.
15   *Polar Record*, New York, June 1956, p. 34, December 1956, p. 30 and June 1957, p. 29.
16   Letters, Casey to Davidson, 9 July and 4 October 1956, Davidson to Casey, 6 May 1958 and 16 January 1959, and Casey to Holt, 11 February 1957; note, Casey to Kevin, 22 October 1956; press release by Davidson, 22 January 1957; memo, Hill to Casey, 4 December 1958, A10302/1959/57C, NAA.
17   Memo, Law to Kevin, 29 November 1956, A1838/1495/3/2/1 Part 2, NAA.
18   Memos, Law to Casey, 4 December 1956, Casey to Kevin, 6 December 1956, and Tange to Secretary, Department of Defence, 18 July 1956, A1838/1495/3/2/1 Part 2, NAA.
19   Memo by Law, 14 December 1956; memo, Kevin to Casey, 15 December 1956, A1838/1495/3/2/1 Part 2, NAA.
20   Letters, Law to Goldie, 16 May 1957, Law to Wilkins, 21 June 1957; memo, Law to Secretary, External Affairs, 16 May 1957, P1469/0/134/1 Part 2, NAA.
21   Minutes, Executive Planning Committee, 25 November 1957, A1838/1495/3/4/1 Part 4, NAA.
22   William Briesemeister, 'New Four-Sheet Planning Map of Antarctica for the International Geophysical Year 1957–1958', *Bulletin No. 26*, Geography and Map Division, Special Libraries Association, December 1956, 'Antarctica – IGY map notes' folder, AGS.
23   Evelyn Stefansson, 'Antarctic Names – A Review', *Bulletin No. 26*, Geography and Map Division, Special Libraries Association, December 1956, 'Antarctica – IGY map notes' folder, AGS.
24   Letter, Briesemeister to Argentine Antarctic Institute, 23 September 1958, 'Antarctica – 1958 revision of Map' folder, AGS.
25   Minutes, Executive Planning Committee, 7 November 1958; minutes, Sub-Committee on Air Photography and Mapping, 18 November 1958, A1838/1495/3/4/1 Part 4, NAA.

26 Minutes, Executive Planning Committee, 16 December 1958, A1838/1495/3/4/2, NAA.

27 Letters, Casey to Mawson, 13 May 1958, and Mawson to Casey, 1 June 1958, PRG 523/7/12/13, Mawson Papers, SLSA.

28 Letters, Law to Mawson, 5 September 1958, PRG 523/7/13/13, Mawson Papers, SLSA.

29 Letters, Casey to Lady Mawson, 27 January 1959, PRG523/7/3/13, Price to Lady Mawson, 24 March 1959, PRG 523/7/9/13, Law to Lady Mawson, 8 December 1958, Casey to Mawson, 13 May 1958, Casey to Lady Mawson, 22 December 1958, PRG 523/7/12/13, Mawson Papers, SLSA; see also, documents in B1387/23/1996/822, NAA.

30 Letter, Law to Secretary, Monash University, 25 March 1959; memo, Law to Secretary, Department of External Affairs, 22 April 1959, Law 1/4, Law Papers, NLA.

31 Minutes, Executive Planning Committee, 27 April 1959, A1838/ 1495/3/4/1 Part 4, NAA.

32 Minutes, Executive Planning Committee, 27 April and 7 September 1959, A1838/1495/3/4/1 Part 4, NAA.

33 *New York Times*, 23 December 1957; minutes of the Second AGM of the Trans-Antarctic Expedition, London, 20 December 1957, MS 162/3/9, Robert Falla Papers, CM; letter, Hillary to manager, H. Walker Ltd, January 1958, MS 515, CM; McGonigal, *Antarctica*, pp. 351–352.

34 Minutes, Committee of Management of the Trans-Antarctic Expedition, 6 and 13 January 1958, MS 162/3/10, CM.

35 Agenda Paper, Commonwealth Prime Ministers' Conference, 1956, A1838/1495/3/2/1 Part 2, NAA.

36 Memos, Plimsoll to Kevin, 18 June 1956, and Kevin to Tange, 22 June 1956, A1838/1495/3/2/1 Part 2, NAA.

37 Memos, Tange to Secretary, Department of Defence, 18 July 1956, and Cooper to Kevin, 16 August 1956, A1838/1495/3/2/1 Part 2, NAA.

38 Final draft of Joint Intelligence Committee Paper, 7 November 1956; cable, Australian Embassy to External Affairs, 10 November 1956; note, Cooper to Kevin, 10 December 1956, A1838/1495/3/2/1 Part 2, NAA.

39 Personal message, Secretary of State for Commonwealth Relations to Casey, 3 July 1957; letter, Plimsoll to Tange, 12 July 1957, A1838/1495/3/2/1 Part 5, NAA.

40 Cables, Casey to Spender, 21 January 1958, External Affairs to Australian Embassy, 10 January 1958, External Affairs, London to External Affairs, Canberra, 23 January 1958, and Booker to External Affairs, 28 January 1958, A3092/221/16/1/2 Part 1, NAA.

41 'Unofficial Record of Discussions with Mr. Macmillan on the Antarctic', 31 January 1958, A1838/1495/3/2/1 Part 12, NAA.

42 Secret memo, O'Connor to Daniels, 22 January 1958, Department of State, Bureau of Inter-American Affairs, Office of the Deputy Assistant Secretary, Office files, 1956–59, Box 25, Antarctica file, NARA.

43 Memorandum of Conversation, 30 January 1958, Department of State, Bureau of Inter-American Affairs, Office of the Deputy Assistant Secretary, Office files, 1956–59, Box 25, Antarctica file, NARA.

44 Secret memorandum, Richards to Daniels, 5 February 1958, Department of State, Bureau of Inter-American Affairs, Office of the Deputy Assistant Secretary, Office files, 1956–59, Box 25, Antarctica file, NARA.

45 Cable, Booker to External Affairs, 10 March 1958, A1838/1495/3/2/1 Part 12, NAA.
46 Personal messages, Macmillan to Menzies, 11 March 1958, and Menzies to Macmillan, 14 March 1958; cables, Casey to External Affairs, 11 March 1958 and External Affairs to Australian Embassy, Washington, 20 March 1958, A1838/1495/3/2/1 Part 12, NAA.
47 Cable, Australian Embassy to External Affairs, 17 March 1958; record of a conversation between Casey and Hamilton, 31 March 1958, A1838/1495/3/2/1 Part 12, NAA.
48 Cable, External Affairs to Australian High Commissions, New Delhi, Ottawa, Karachi, Colombo, Kuala Lumpur, Accra, 25 April 1958, A1838/1495/3/2/1 Part 12, NAA.
49 Telex, Tange to Casey, 2 May 1958; cable, Australian Embassy to External Affairs, 3 May 1958, A1838/1495/3/2/1 Part 12, NAA.
50 Memorandum, Snow to Daniels, 9 May 1958, Department of State, Bureau of Inter-American Affairs, Office of the Deputy Assistant Secretary, Office files, 1956–59, Box 25, Antarctica file, NARA.
51 Memos, White to Tokyo Embassy, 11, 17 and 18 July and 14 August 1958; memo, Scott to External Affairs, 1 August 1958, AAEG 6956/W3252/1/ TKY5/A/1 Part 5, ANZ.
52 Memos, White to Tokyo Embassy, 18 July and 14 and 27 August 1958, and Scott to External Affairs, 1 August 1958, AAEG 6956/W3252/1/TKY5/A/1 Part 5, ANZ.
53 Minutes, Executive Planning Committee, 16 December 1958, A1838/1495/ 3/4/2, NAA.
54 Memos, White to Tokyo Embassy, 27 August and 8 September 1958 and 26 February 1959, and Craw to White, 2 October 1958, AAEG 6956/W3252/1/ TKY5/A/1 Part 5, ANZ, Wellington; letter, Sebald to Daniels, 15 January 1959, and other documents in this file, State Department, Bureau of East Asian and Pacific Affairs, Country Dir. For Australia, New Zealand and Pacific Islands, Box 2, 'Antarctica Operation, Australia, 1959 Aust. Desk File' folder, NARA.
55 Memo by Law, c. October 1958, A1838/1495/3/4/1 Part 4, NAA.
56 Memo, Kevin to Casey, 5 November 1958, A1838/1495/3/4/1 Part 4, NAA.
57 Memos, White to Tokyo Embassy, 8 and 23 September and 24 October 1958 and 25 February 1959, and Craw to White, 2 October 1958, AAEG 6956/ W3252/1/TKY5/A/1 Part 5, ANZ.
58 Memorandum, Prince to Robertson and Mein, 31 March 1959, State Department, Bureau of East Asian and Pacific Affairs, Country Dir. For Australia, New Zealand and Pacific Islands, Box 2, 'Antarctica Operation, Australia, 1959 Aust. Desk File' folder, NARA.
59 Robert Hayton, 'The "American" Antarctic', *American Society of International Law*, vol. 50, no. 3, July 1956, p. 607.
60 'The Antarctic Conference – Washington 1959: Delegation Report', by Casey, M4081/6/1, NAA.
61 Boczek, 'The Soviet Union and the Antarctic Regime', p. 841.

CHAPTER 21 – 1961–2012

1 Letter, Molyneux to Acting Secretary, Prime Minister's Department, 24 May 1960, A1209/1960/597, NAA.
2 Boczek, 'The Soviet Union and the Antarctic Regime', p. 839.
3 *Antarctic Treaty: Hearings before the Committee on Foreign Relations,*

United States Senate, 14 June 1960, United States Government Printing Office, Washington, 1960.

4 *Antarctic Treaty: Hearings before the Committee on Foreign Relations, United States Senate, 14 June 1960*, United States Government Printing Office, Washington, 1960.

5 'Statement of U.S. Objectives regarding Antarctica and Courses of Action during the next several years', 14 February 1962, Department of State, Bureau of Inter-American Affairs, Records relating to Argentina, 1956–64, Box 5/331, NARA.

6 Albert Crary, 'Antarctica – A Frontier of Science', *Explorers Journal*, September 1964.

7 Margaret Florio, 'The Little Known Heroes of Halley Bay', *Explorers Journal*, Spring 1994.

8 Florio, 'The Little Known Heroes of Halley Bay'.

9 Minutes, Executive Planning Committee, 7 September 1959, A1838/1495/3/4/1 Part 4, NAA.

10 Letters, Casey to Hamilton, 2 April 1958, and Law to Hamilton, 22 April 1958, A1838/1495/3/4/1 Part 4, NAA.

11 Cabinet Submission by Gorton, 22 November 1960, A1838/1495/3/4/30 Part 3, NAA.

12 Cable, Australian Embassy to External Affairs, 25 and 26 February 1958, A1838/1495/3/2/1 Part 2, NAA.

13 Memo by Law, 28 September 1959, MS 9458/1/204, Law Papers, NLA; Kathleen Ralston, *Phillip Law: The Antarctic Exploration Years, 1954–66*, Ausinfo, Canberra, 1998, pp. 116–131; transcript of interview with Phillip Law, TRC 351, NLA.

14 Memo by Law, 28 September 1959, MS 9458/1/204, Law Papers, NLA; Antarctic Diary of Raymond Priestley, [Deep Freeze IV: 15 December 1958 – 13 February 1959] Davis Papers, D24 folder, AAD; Ralston, *Phillip Law*, pp. 116–131; transcript of interview with Phillip Law, TRC 351, NLA.

15 Letter, Law to Hasluck, 7 October 1968, MS 9458/1/124, Law Papers, NLA.

16 Memo, Fisher to O'Connor, 19 February 1960, and other documents in Department of State, Bureau of Inter-American Affairs, Records Relating to Argentina 1956–1964, Box 1/331, NARA.

17 'Report of Ben L. Stotts, United States Observer with Argentine Antarctic Expedition, 1957–58', pp. 46–47, SPRI.

18 Memorandum of conversation, Berasategui and Mills, 21 January 1963, Department of State, Bureau of Inter-American Affairs, Records relating to Argentina, 1956–64, Box 6/356, NARA; cable, New Zealand Legation, Washington to Foreign Affairs, 10 August 1973, ABHS 18069/W5402/4/BRU/322/1/1 Part 3, ANZ; *Polar Times*, New York, December 1973, p. 16.

19 *Polar Times*, New York, June 1985, p. 10.

20 'Civic Reception, Hobart, 1959', talk by Law, MS 9458/4/3, Law Papers, NLA.

21 Ralston, *Phillip Law*, pp. 125–31.

22 Memo by Law, 5 February 1965; 'Some Notes on the Scientific Work of the Antarctic Division', note by Law, c. 1965; 'Antarctic Division – Scientific Branch', memo by Law, c. April 1965, and other documents in A1838/1495/3/4/30 Part 3, NAA.

23 Memo, McIntyre to Public Service Board, 25 November 1966, A1838/1495/3/4/30 Part 4, NAA.

24 Michael Stoddart and Marcus Haward, 'Science', in Haward and Griffiths (eds.), *Australian and the Antarctic Treaty System*, pp. 148–149; *Herald*, Melbourne, 8 March 1974; *Age*, Melbourne, 10 June 1975.

25 Interview with Law by Jill Cassidy, 10 July 1991, MS 9458/1/166, Law Papers, NLA.

26 'Surveying the Last Continent', lecture by Law, 17 March 1969, MS 9458, Box 46, Law Papers, NLA.

27 Memo, Joiner to Minister for Scientific and Industrial Research, 20 July 1960, AALJ 7291/W3508/270/1/275 Pt. 1, ANZ.

28 'Visit of Dr T. O. Jones', note for file, 17 July 1964, AAOQ/W3305/30/28/1 Part 2, ANZ.

29 Letters, McKinnon to Price to 5 January 1962, and Price to McKinnon, 11 January and 12 February 1962, B1387/23/1996/822, NAA.

30 Transcript of interview with Phillip Law, TRC 351, NLA.

31 E. S. Korotkevich and L. I. Dubrovin, 'Two Decades of Soviet Research in the Antarctic'; L. I. Dubrovin and M. A. Preobrazhenskaya, 'Russian Names in the Toponymy of the Antarctic' in G. A. Avsyuk (ed.), *The Antarctic Committee Reports No. 17: Main Results of Twenty Years' Research in the Antarctic*, Moscow, 1978, pp. 12, 17, 275–279.

32 V. L. Lebedev, 'Geographical Observations in the Antarctic made by the Expeditions of Cook 1772–1775 and Bellingshausen–Lazarev 1819–1821', *Antarctica: Commission Reports, 1960*, Academy of Sciences of the U.S.S.R. Interdepartmental Commission on Antarctic Research; V. L. Lebedev, 'Who Discovered Antarctica?', *Antarctica: Commission Reports, 1961*, Academy of Sciences of the U.S.S.R. Interdepartmental Commission on Antarctic Research; V. L. Lebedev, 'A New Basis for the Solution of Controversial Aspects of Antarctic History', *Antarctica: Commission Reports, 1962*, Academy of Sciences of the U.S.S.R. Interdepartmental Commission on Antarctic Research.

33 Pyne, *The Ice*, pp. 75–79.

34 McGonigal, *Antarctica*, p. 273.

35 Sullivan, *Quest for a Continent*, p. 27.

36 V. L. Lebedev, 'A New Basis for the Solution of Controversial Aspects of Antarctic History', *Antarctica: Commission Reports, 1962*, Academy of Sciences of the U.S.S.R. Interdepartmental Commission on Antarctic Research, p. 182.

37 Minutes of Advisory Committee on Antarctic Names, Board on Geographic Names, 8 August 1961; letter, Burrill to Roberts, 10 April 1962, A1838/1495/1/8 Part 7, NAA; *Polar Times*, New York, June 1964, p. 1.

38 Letter, Quartermain to Goldsmith, 4 September 1959; report by Roberts, c. 1959, N 1/513/16/31/16, ANZ.

39 Aide memoire, New Zealand to United States, 5 April 1963, ABHS 18069/ W5402/4/BRU/322/1/1 Part 1, ANZ.

40 'Memorandum Reporting Debates, Discussions, and Negotiations at the First Consultative Meeting under the Antarctic Treaty, Canberra, Australia, July 10–24, 1961', State Department, Bureau of East Asian and Pacific Affairs, Country Dir. For Australia, New Zealand and Pacific Islands, Box 6, 'Antarctica – Australia, 1961–62 Aust. Desk Files' folder, NARA.

41 Letter, Roberts to Svenne, 17 September 1970, A1838/1495/3/2/17 Part 3; note, Chilean Embassy to External Affairs, 6 August 1970, A1838/1495//3/2/17 Part 2, NAA.

42 'List of Historic Monuments Identified and Described by the Proposing Government or Governments', AAAC7922/W5158/24/2280/2/Part 3, ANZ; letter, Kelly to Langmore, 15 December 1992, AATJ 7495/W5621/88/ BD/13/9/7/6 Part 1, ANZ.

43 Letter, Davidson to Casey, 16 January 1959, and other documents in A10302/1959/57C, NAA.

44 Memo, Stradwick to External Affairs, 3 May 1961, and other documents in AAMF/W3118/5/1961/327/4, ANZ.

45 Memo, Stradwick to External Affairs, 3 May 1961, and other documents in AAMF/W3118/5/1961/327/4, ANZ.

46 Memo, Post and Telegraph Department to External Affairs, 4 July 1961, AAMF/W3118/5/1961/327/4, ANZ; memo, Hamilton to External Affairs, 18 May 1962, A1838/1495/3/2/13 Part 1, NAA; 'Memorandum Reporting Debates, Discussions; negotiations at the First Consultative Meeting under the Antarctic Treaty, Canberra, Australia, July 10–24, 1961', State Department, Bureau of East Asian and Pacific Affairs, Country Dir. For Australia, New Zealand and Pacific Islands, Box 6, 'Antarctica – Australia, 1961–62 Aust. Desk Files' folder, NARA.

47 'Report of Ben L. Stotts, United States Observer with Argentine Antarctic Expedition, 1957–58', p. 80, SPRI; 'Chronological List of Antarctic Expeditions and Related Historical Events', extract by R. K. Headland, 1989, AATJ 7495/ W5621/88/BD/13/9/7/6 Part 1, ANZ; *Polar Record*, New York, June 1958, p. 26, and December 1958, p. 28.

48 Letter, Black to Law, 14 April 1966, MS 9458/1/38, Law Papers, NLA; 'Explorers Club – Proposal for Membership of Lars-Eric Lindblad', 10 January 1966; letter, Sexton to Admissions Committee 13 December 1965; 'Antarctic Expedition 1966, with Captain Finn Ronne', travel brochure, Lars-Eric Lindblad folder, EC; *Polar Record*, New York, June 1966, p. 9.

49 'Chronological List of Antarctic Expeditions and Related Historical Events', extract by R. K. Headland, 1989, AATJ 7495/W5621/88/BD/13/9/7/6 Part 1, ANZ, Wellington; memo, Bullock to Australian Embassy, Brussels, 23 May 1966, and Horne to External Affairs, 19 July 1966, A1838/1495/3/2/15 Part 2, NAA.

50 *Polar Record*, New York, December 1967, p. 7.

51 Teleprinter message, External Affairs to Pyman, 30 July 1963, A1838/1495/3/10 Part 2, NAA.

52 *Post*, Wellington, 25 November 1987; *Time*, New York, 16 January 1990.

53 Letter, Bowden to Law, 26 January 2003, MS 9458/1/149, Law Papers, NLA.

54 *Flight International*, 23 January 1988; *Bulletin*, Sydney, 9 February 1988.

55 Damien Gildea, *The Antarctic Mountaineering Chronology*, self-published, Goulburn, 1998.

56 *Guardian*, London, 19 January 2004.

57 *Explorers Journal*, New York, Spring 2003, Winter 2003/04; Joseph Murphy, *South to the Pole by Ski: Nine Men and Two Women Pioneer a New Route to the South Pole*, Marlor Press, St Paul, 1990; Nancy Loewen and Ann Bancroft, *Four to the Pole!: The American Women's Expedition to Antarctica, 1992–93*, Shoe String Press, North Haven, 2001; Ranulph Fiennes, *Mind over Matter: The Epic Crossing of the Antarctic Continent*, Delacorte Press, New York, 1994; *Bulletin*, Sydney, 9 February 1988; *Polar Times*, Spring-Summer 1997, p. 5.

58 *Polar Times*, Spring-Summer 1998, p. 19.

59 Deborah Shapiro and Rolf Bjelke, *Time on Ice: A Winter Voyage to Antarctica*, McGraw-Hill, New York, pp. 245, 247.

60 *Bulletin*, Sydney, 9 February 1988.

61 'Antarctic Tourism – Background and Prospects for New Zealand', New Zealand Tourist and Publicity Department, September 1988, AAAC7922/ W5158/24/2280/2/ Part 3, ANZ.

62 Letter, Matheson to Beeby, 27 September 1989, AAAC7922/W5158/24/2280/2/ Part 3, ANZ.

63 Letters, Plimmer to Hunt, 14 October 1988 and 15 February 1989, AAAC7922/ W5158/23/2280/2/Part 1, ANZ.

64 'Managing Tourism in Antarctica' and 'Antarctic Tourism: Investigation Proposal', memos by Robertson, c. 1989, AAAC 7922/W5158/23/2280/2 Parts 2 and 3, ANZ.

65 'Tourism in the Antarctic', ASOC Information Paper, 12 May 1989, AAAC 7922/W5158/23/2280/2 Part 2, ANZ; *Christchurch Star*, Christchurch, 18 April 1989; Robert Headland, 'Historical Development of Antarctic Tourism', *Annals of Tourism Research*, vol. 21, no. 2, pp. 269–280; Kees Bastmeijer and Ricardo Roura, 'Regulating Antarctic Tourism and the Precautionary Principle', *American Journal of International Law*, vol. 98, no. 4, October 2004.

66 *Southland Times*, Invercargill, 29 May 1989.

67 Cabinet memo by Algie, 27 June 1957, CAB 409/1/1, Part 1, ANZ.

68 Memo, Craw to NZ High Commissioner, 30 September 1969, AAOQ/ W3305/30/28/1 Part 2, ANZ; memo, Dobson to Australian Embassy, Washington, 11 June 1970, A1838/1495/3/2/17 Part 2, NAA.

69 R. B. Thomson, *NZARP 1965–1988*, July 1991, AAYY/W4899/40, ANZ.

70 *Auckland Star*, Auckland, 3 November 1973.

71 *New Zealand Herald*, Auckland, 17 April 1989.

72 Memo, Gilchrist to Minister of Foreign Affairs, 5 February 1976, A1838/1495/3/ 2/19 Part 5, NAA; *New Zealand Herald*, Auckland, 27 July 1977.

73 Report, Australian Delegation, Eighth Antarctic Treaty Consultative Meeting, Oslo, 9–20 June 1975, A1838/1495/3/2/19 Part5, NAA.

74 Cabinet memo by Minister of Foreign Affairs, 10 March 1977, AATJ 7428/ W3566/1294/73/1/11 Part 1, ANZ

75 *Evening Post*, Wellington, 10 January 1983.

76 *US News and World Report*, 24 January 1983.

77 'Extract from Brief prepared for Prime Minister's Visit to Antarctica, 19–21 January, 1982', Ministry of Foreign Affairs, 13 January 1982, AATJ 7428/ W3566/1294/73/1/11 Part 1, ANZ.

78 Chris Beeby, 'Towards an Antarctic mineral resources regime', *New Zealand International Review*, May/June 1982.

79 'Informal Meeting on Antarctic Mineral Resources, Wellington, 17–28 January 1983', memo by Secretary for Foreign Affairs, undated, AATJ 7428/ W3566/1295/73/1/11 Part 2, ANZ.

80 'International Constraints', seminar paper by Keith Brennan, at seminar *The Antarctic – Preferred Futures, Constraints and Choices*, Wellington, 17–18 June 1983, AATJ 7428/1295/73/1/11/1 Part 2, ANZ.

81 Bo Johnson, 'Some Swedish Viewpoints on the Antarctic Treaty System' in Anders Karlqvist, *Sweden and Antarctica*, SPRI, pp. 71–77.

82 Minutes of Cabinet Policy Committee, 19 July 1989; 'Antarctica: Environmental Policy', cabinet decision, 26 February 1990, AATJ 7452/ W5354/489/RPG2/7 Part 2; 'White Paper on Antarctic Environment', August 1989, Press Statement by Palmer, 6 July 1990; transcript, 'TVNZ Jo Malcolm interview with Prime Minister', 23 August 1990, AAAC7922/ W5158/24/2280/2/Part 3, ANZ.

83 Catherine Redgwell, 'Antarctica', *International and Comparative Law Quarterly*, vol. 39, no. 2, April 1990, pp. 474–481; interview by the author with former Australian Prime Minister, Bob Hawke, June 2011; Andrew Jackson and Peter Boyce, 'Mining and "World Park Antarctica", 1982–1991', in Marcas Haward and Tom Griffith (eds.), *Australia and the Antarctic Treaty System: 50 Years of Influence*, UNSW Press, Sydney, 2011, pp. 243–273.

84 *Eco*, vol. XXIII, no. 1, AATJ 7428/W4838/341/73/1/11/1/1 Part 1, ANZ.

85 Greenpeace, *1991/92 Antarctic Expedition Report*, Greenpeace International, Amsterdam, October 1992. p. 1.

86 Greenpeace International, 'Report on a visit to Dumont d'Urville, Antarctica', and Pierre Jouventin and Vincent Bretagnolle, 'French biologists reply to Greenpeace report', *Polar Record*, vol. 26, no. 156, pp. 51–54, 1990.

87 E. I. Tolstikov, 'Soviet Scientists in the Antarctic in 1956–1966', in V. A. Bugaev (ed.), *Soviet Antarctic Research 1956–1966: Proceedings of the All-Union Conference on Antarctic Research 1966*, Academy of Sciences of the USSR, Moscow, 1967.

88 G. C. Eddie, *The Harvesting of Krill*, Food and Agriculture Organization, Rome, 1977.

89 'The Strategic and Economic Significance of Antarctica', External Intelligence Bureau, August 1977, AATJ 7428/W3566/1294/73/1/11 Part 1, ANZ.

90 Memo, Hughes to Foreign Affairs, 4 February 1972; 'Report of the New Zealand Delegation to the Conference on the Conservation of Antarctic Seals, London, 3–11 February 1972', by Farrell; letters, Quirk to Minister for External Affairs, 19 May 1972, and Sinclair to Quirk, 30 May 1972, A1838/1495/1/1/2 Part 3, NAA; report, Australian Delegation, Eighth Antarctic Treaty Consultative Meeting, Oslo, 9–20 June 1975, A1838/1495/3/2/19 Part5, NAA.

91 For the Australian reaction, see Cabinet Submission by Peacock, 20 May 1977; notes on Cabinet Submission No. 1327, by Farrell and McCay, 6 July 1977, and other documents in A10756/LC720 Part 1, NAA.

SELECT BIBLIOGRAPHY

MANUSCRIPT SOURCES

AAD   Australian Antarctic Division, Hobart
ACL   Auckland Central Library
AGS   American Geographical Society, New York
ANZ   Archives New Zealand, Christchurch and Wellington
ASOC   Antarctic and Southern Ocean Coalition
ATL   Alexander Turnbull Library, Wellington
AWMM   Auckland War Memorial Museum
BPRC   Byrd Polar Research Center, Ohio State University, Columbus
CAC   Churchill Archives Centre, Cambridge
CCC   Christchurch Central Library
CM   Canterbury Museum, Christchurch
DCL   Dartmouth College Library, Hanover, New Hampshire
EC   Explorers' Club, New York
LoC   Library of Congress, Washington
ML   Mitchell Library, Sydney
NA   National Archives, London
NAA   National Archives of Australia, Canberra and Hobart
NARA   National Archives and Records Administration, Maryland
NAS   National Archives of Scotland, Edinburgh
NLA   National Library of Australia, Canberra
RGS   Royal Geographical Society, London
RL   Roosevelt Library, Hyde Park
SIA   Smithsonian Institution Archives, Washington
SLSA   State Library of South Australia, Adelaide
SLT   State Library of Tasmania, Hobart
SLV   State Library of Victoria, Melbourne
SPRI   Scott Polar Research Institute, Cambridge
WM   Whaling Museum, Sandefjord, Norway

CONTEMPORARY SOURCES

BOOKS

Roald Amundsen, *My Life as an Explorer*, William Heinemann, London, 1927
Roald Amundsen, *The South Pole: An Account of the Norwegian Antarctic Expedition in the "Fram," 1910–1912*, [first published, 1912] C. Hurst, London, 1976
Edwin Swift Balch, *Antarctica*, Allen, Lane & Scott, Philadelphia, 1902
J. C. Beaglehole (ed.), *The Journals of Captain James Cook on His Voyages of Discovery*, vol. 2, Hakluyt Society, Cambridge, 1961
Louis Bernacchi, *To The South Polar Regions: Expedition of 1898–1900*, Hurst and Blackett, London, 1901

C. E. Borchgrevink, *First on the Antarctic Continent, Being an Account of the British Antarctic Expedition 1898–1900*, George Newnes Limited, London, 1901

R. N. Rudmose Brown, R. C. Mossman and J. H. Harvey Pirie, *The Voyage of the "Scotia", Being the Record of a Voyage of Exploration in Antarctic Seas*, William Blackwood and Sons, Edinburgh, 1906

William Bruce, *Polar Exploration*, Williams and Norgate, London, 1911

V. A. Bugaev, *Soviet Antarctic Research 1956–1966: Proceedings of the All–Union Conference on Antarctic Research 1966*, [Translated from Russian], Israeli Program for Scientific Translations, Jerusalem, 1970

H. J. Bull, *The Cruise of the 'Antarctic' to the South Polar Regions*, [Originally published 1896], Paradigm Press, Bungay, 1984

Richard E. Byrd, *Alone*, Queen Anne Press, London, 1987

Richard E. Byrd, *Antarctic Discovery: The Story of the Second Byrd Antarctic Expedition*, Putnam, London, 1936

Richard E. Byrd, *Little America: Aerial Exploration in the Antarctic, The Flight to the South Pole*, Putnam, New York, 1930

Richard E. Byrd, *Skyward*, Putnam, New York, 1928

R. J. Campbell (ed.), *The Discovery of the South Shetland Islands 1819–1820: The Voyages of the Brig* Williams *1819–1820 as recorded in contemporary documents and the Journal of Midshipman C.W. Poynter*, Hakluyt Society, London, 2000

Jean Charcot, *The Voyage of the 'Pourquoi–Pas?': The Journal of the Second French South Polar Expedition, 1908–1910*, Australian National University Press, Canberra, 1978

Lars Christensen, *Such Is the Antarctic*, Hodder and Stoughton, London, 1935

Frederick Cook, *Through the First Antarctic Night 1898–1899: A Narrative of the Voyage of the "Belgica" among newly discovered lands and over an unknown sea about the South Pole*, William Heinemann, London, 1900

John K. Davis, *With the "Aurora" in the Antarctic 1911–1914*, Andrew Melrose, London, 1919

Frank Debenham (ed.), *The Voyage of Captain Bellingshausen to the Antarctic Seas 1819–1821*, 2 vols, Hakluyt Society, London, 1945

Erich von Drygalski, *The Southern Ice-Continent: The German South Polar Expedition aboard the* Gauss *1901–1903*, Translated by M. M. Raraty, Bluntisham Books, Bluntisham, 1989

Lincoln Ellsworth, *Beyond Horizons*, Doubleday, Doran & Company, New York, 1938

Captain Edmund Fanning, *Voyages and Discoveries in the South Seas 1792–1832*, Collins and Hannay, New York, 1833

Wilhelm Filchner, *To the Sixth Continent: The Second German South Polar Expedition*, Bluntisham Books, Bluntisham, 1994

Vivian Fuchs, *Antarctic Adventure*, Cassell, London, 1959

Adrien de Gerlache, *Voyage de la Belgica: Quinze Mois dans L'Antarctique*, Imprimerie Scientifique, Brussels, 1902

Laurence McKinley Gould, *Cold: The Record of an Antarctic Sledge Journey*, Brewer, Warren & Putnam, New York, 1931

Michael Hoare (ed.), *The* Resolution *Journal of Johann Reinhold Forster 1772–1775*, vol. IV, Hakluyt Society, London, 1982

Frank Hurley, *Argonauts of the South: Being a Narrative of Voyagings and Polar Seas and Adventures in the Antarctic with Sir Douglas Mawson and Sir Ernest Shackletom*, G. P. Putnam's Sons, New York, 1925

Leonard Huxley (ed.), *Scott's Last Expedition*, 2 vols, Smith, Elder & Co., London, 1913

Fred Jacka and Eleanor Jacka (eds.), *Mawson's Antarctic Diaries*, Unwin Hyman, London, 1988

W. L. G. Joerg, *The Work of the Byrd Antarctic Expedition 1928–1930*, American Geographical Society, New York, 1930

Max Jones (ed.), *Journals: Captain Scott's Last Expedition*, Oxford University Press, Oxford, 2005

Clements Markham, *Antarctic Obsession: A personal narrative of the origins of the British National Antarctic Expedition 1901–1904*, Bluntisham Books, Alburgh, 1986

J. W. S. Marr, *Into the Frozen South*, Funk and Wagnalls, New York, 1923

Douglas Mawson, *The Home of the Blizzard, Being the Story of the Australasian Antarctic Expedition, 1911–1914*, 2 vols, William Heinemann, London, 1915

Hugh Robert Mill, *The Life of Sir Ernest Shackleton*, William Heinemann, London, 1923

Hugh Robert Mill, *The Siege of the South Pole: The Story of Antarctic Exploration*, Alston Rivers, London, 1905

Otto G. Nordenskjöld and Johan Gunnar Andersson, *Antarctica: or, Two years Amongst the Ice of the South Pole*, Hurst and Blackett, London, 1905

A. V. Nudel'man, *Soviet Antarctic Expeditions 1955–1959*, [Translated from Russian], Israeli Program for Scientific Translations, Jerusalem, 1966

J. N. Reynolds, *Address on the Subject of a Surveying and Exploring Expedition to the Pacific Ocean and South Seas*, Harper and Brothers, New York, 1836

J. N. Reynolds, *Pacific and Indian Oceans: The South Sea Surveying and Exploring Expedition: Its Inception, Progress, and Objects*, Harper and Brothers, New York, 1841

Finn Ronne, *Antarctic Conquest: The Story of the Ronne Expedition 1946–1948*, G. P. Putnam's Sons, New York, 1949

Helen Rosenman (trans. & ed.), *An Account in Two Volumes of Two Voyages to the South Seas*, by Dumont d'Urville, Melbourne University Press, Melbourne, 1987

Captain Sir James Clark Ross, *A Voyage of Discovery and Research in the Southern and Antarctic Regions during the years 1839–43*, 2 vols, [first published 1847] David and Charles Reprints, Newton Abbot, 1969

John Rymill, *Southern Lights: The Official Account of the British Graham Land Expedition 1934–1937*, Chatto and Windus, London, 1938

Robert Scott, *The Voyage of the 'Discovery'*, 2 vols, Macmillan, London, 1905

Ernest Shackleton, *The Heart of the Antarctic*, William Heinemann, London, 1910

Ernest Shackleton, *South: The Story of Shackleton's Last Expedition 1914–1917*, Century Publishing, London, 1983

Shirase Expedition Supporters Association, *The Japanese South Polar Expedition 1910–12, A Record of Antarctica*, [Originally published in Japanese, 1913, translated by Lara Dagnell and Hilary Shibata], Erskine Press and Bluntisham Books, Norwich and Bluntisham, 2012

Peter Speak (ed.), *The Log of the* Scotia *Expedition, 1902–4*, Edinburgh University Press, Edinburgh, 1992

John Randolph Spears, *Captain Nathaniel Brown Palmer*, Macmillan, New York, 1922

Walter Sullivan, *Quest for a Continent*, McGraw–Hill, New York, 1957

Nicholas Thomas et al (eds.), *A Voyage Round the World*, by George Foster, 2 vols, University of Hawai'i Press, Honolulu, 2000

W. H. B. Webster, *Narrative of a Voyage to the Southern Atlantic Ocean, in the Years 1828, 29, 30, performed in H.M. Sloop Chanticleer, under the Command of the Late Captain Henry Foster*, 2 vols, Richard Bentley, London, 1834

James Weddell, *A Voyage Towards the South Pole Performed in the Years 1822–24, Containing an Examination of the Antarctic Sea*, [first published 1825] David and Charles Reprints, Newton Abbot, 1970

Wallace West, *Paramount Newsreel Men with Admiral Byrd in Little America*, Whitman Publishing Company, Racine, 1934

Charles Wilkes, *Narrative of the United States Exploring Expedition*, 5 vols, [Originally published 1845] Gregg Press, New Jersey, 1970

BOOKLETS, PAMPHLETS, REPORTS, ETC.

[no author] *Captain Scott's Message to England*, St Catherine's Press, London, 1913

E. P. Bayliss and J. S. Cumpston, *Handbook and Index to accompany a Map of Antarctica*, Department of the Interior, Canberra, 1939

Lars Christensen, *My Last Expedition to the Antarctic 1936–1937: A Lecture delivered before the Norwegian Geographical Society, September 22nd, 1937*, Johan Grundt Tanum, Oslo, 1938

Expedition report: Greenpeace Antarctic Expedition 1989/90, Greenpeace International, Amsterdam, c. 1990

Anders Karlqvist (ed.), *Sweden and Antarctica*, Swedish Polar Research Secretariat, Stockholm, 1985

Reports on Scientific Results of the United States Antarctic Service Expedition 1939–1941, American Philosophical Society, Philadelphia, 1945

SECONDARY SOURCES

BOOKS

Susan Barr, *Norway – A Consistent Polar Nation?*, Kolofon, Oslo, 2003

Bjorn Basberg, Jan Erik Ringstad and Einar Wexelsen (eds), *Whaling and History: Perspectives on the Evolution of the Industry*, Whaling Museum, Sandefjord, 1993

T. H. Baughman, *Pilgrims on the Ice: Robert Falcon Scott's First Antarctic Expedition*, University of Nebraska Press, Lincoln, 1999

J. C. Beaglehole, *The Life of Captain James Cook*, Adam and Charles Black, London, 1974

Kenneth Bertrand, *Americans in Antarctica 1775–1948*, American Geographical Society, New York, 1971

David Crane, *Scott of the Antarctic*, HarperCollins, London, 2005

David Day, *Conquest: How societies overwhelm others*, Oxford University Press, New York, 2008

Frank Debenham, *Antarctica: The Story of a Continent*, Herbert Jenkins, London, 1959

Klaus Dodds, *Pink Ice: Britain and the South Atlantic Empire*, I. B. Tauris, London, 2002

Martin Dugard, *Farther than Any Man: The Rise and Fall of Captain James Cook*, Allen and Unwin, Sydney, 2001

Vivian Fuchs, *Of Ice and Men: The Story of the British Antarctic Survey 1943–73*, Anthony Nelson, Oswestry, 1982

Vivian Fuchs, *A Time to Speak: An autobiography*, Anthony Nelson, Oswestry, 1990

Tom Griffiths, *Slicing the Silence: Voyaging to Antarctica*, Harvard University Press, Cambridge, 2007

Alan Gurney, *The Race to the White Continent*, Norton, New York, 2000

David Harrowfield, *Call of the Ice: Fifty years of New Zealand in Antarctica*, David Bateman, Auckland, 2007

J. Gordon Hayes, *Antarctica: A Treatise on the Southern Continent*, Richards Press, London, 1928

William H. Hobbs, *Explorers of the Antarctic*, House of Field, New York, 1941

Roland Huntford, *Scott and Amundsen*, Hodder and Stoughton, London, 1979

Roland Huntford, *Shackleton*, Hodder and Stoughton, London, 1985

Tim Jarvis, *Mawson: Life and Death in Antarctica*, Miegunyah Press, Carlton, 2008

Max Jones, *The Last Great Quest: Captain Scott's Antarctic Sacrifice*, Oxford University Press, Oxford, 2003

Christopher C. Joyner and Ethel R. Theis, *Eagle Over The Ice: The U.S. in the Antarctic*, University Press of New England, Hanover, 1997

Daniel McKinley, *James Eights 1798–1882: Antarctic Explorer, Albany Naturalist, His Life, His Times, His Works*, New York State Museum, Albany, 2005

Geoffrey Martin, *The Life and Thought of Isaiah Bowman*, Archon Books, Hamden, 1980

Philip Mitterling, *America in the Antarctic to 1840*, University of Illinois Press, Urbana, 1959

Simon Nasht, *The Last Explorer: Hubert Wilkins – Australia's Unknown Hero*, Second Edition, Hachette, Sydney, 2006

Stephen Pyne, *The Ice*, Phoenix, London, 2004

Kathleen Ralston, *Phillip Law: The Antarctic Exploration Years 1954–66*, AusInfo, Canberra, 1998

Beau Riffenburgh, *Racing with Death: Douglas Mawson – Antarctic Explorer*, Bloomsbury, London, 2008

Jan Erik Ringstad (ed.), *Whaling and History II: New Perspectives*, Whaling Museum, Sandefjord, 2006

Lisle A. Rose, *Explorer: The Life of Richard E. Byrd*, University of Missouri Press, Columbus, 2008

M. J. Ross, *Polar Pioneers: John Ross and James Clark Ross*, McGill–Queen's University Press, Montreal, 1994

Peter Speak, *William Speirs Bruce: Polar Explorer and Scottish Nationalist*, National Museums of Scotland Publishing, Edinburgh, 2003

Francis Spufford, *I May Be Some Time: Ice and the English Imagination*, Faber and Faber, London, 1996

Edouard Stackpole, *The Voyage of the* Huron *and the* Huntress: *The American Sealers and the Discovery of the Continent of Antarctica*, Marine Historical Association, Mystic, 1955

William Stanton, *The Great United States Exploring Expedition of 1838–1842*, University of California Press, Berkeley, 1975

J. N. Tønnessen and A. O. Johnsen, *The History of Modern Whaling*, [abridged and translated; first published in Norwegian in 4 vols, 1959–70] C. Hurst & Co., London, 1982

David E. Yelverton, *Antarctica Unveiled: Scott's First Expedition and the Quest for the Unknown Continent*, University Press of Colorado, Boulder, 2000

JOURNAL ARTICLES

Edwin Swift Balch, 'Antarctic Names', *Bulletin of the American Geographical Society*, vol. 44, 1912

Edwin Swift Balch, 'Why America Should Re–Explore Wilkes Land', *Proceedings of the American Philosophical Society*, vol. 48, no. 191, April 1909

John Biscoe and Messrs Enderby, 'Recent Discoveries in the Antarctic Ocean, from the Log–book of the Brig Tula, commanded by Mr. John Biscoe, R. N.', *Journal of the Royal Geographical Society of London*, vol. 3, 1833

Boleslaw Boczek, 'The Soviet Union and the Antarctic Regime', *American Journal of International Law*, vol. 78, no. 4, October 1984

R. N. Rudmose Brown, 'Antarctic History: A Reply to Professor W. H. Hobbs', *Scottish Geographical Magazine*, vol. 55, May 1939

Richard Byrd, 'The Conquest of Antarctica by Air', *National Geographic Magazine*, August 1930

Richard Byrd, 'Exploring the Ice Age in Antarctica', *National Geographic Magazine*, October 1935

Richard Byrd, 'Our Navy Explores Antarctica', *National Geographic Magazine*, October 1947

Jean Charcot, 'The Second French Antarctic Expedition', *Geographical Journal*, vol. 37, no. 3, March 1911

Jean Charcot, 'The French Antarctic Expedition', *Geographical Journal*, vol. 26, no. 5, November 1905

W. F. Cook, 'H.M.A.S. "Wyatt Earp"', Australian National Antarctic Research Expedition 1947–1948', *Naval Historical Review*, December 1978

Mary E. Cooley, 'The Exploring Expedition in the Pacific', *Proceedings of the American Philosophical Society*, vol. 82, 1940

Erich Von Drygalski, 'The German Antarctic Expedition', *Geographical Journal*, vol. XVIII, no. 3, September 1901

Erich Von Drygalski, 'The German Antarctic Expedition', *Geographical Journal*, vol. XXIV, no. 2, August 1904

Lincoln Ellsworth, 'The First Crossing of Antarctica: A paper read at the Evening Meeting of the Society on 30 November 1936', *Geographical Journal*, vol. LXXXIX, no. 3, March 1937

Lincoln Ellsworth, 'My Four Antarctic Expeditions', *National Geographic Magazine*, July 1939

Laurence Gould, 'Strategy and Politics in the Polar Areas', *Annals of the American Academy of Political and Social Science*, vol. 255, January 1948

Arthur Hinks, 'Antarctica Discovered: A Reply', *Geographical Review*, vol. 31, no. 3, July 1941

Arthur Hinks, 'The Log of the Hero', *Geographical Journal*, vol. 96, no. 6, December 1940

Arthur Hinks, 'Review: On Some Misrepresentations of Antarctic History', *Geographical Journal*, vol. 94, no. 4, October 1939

William Herbert Hobbs, 'Antarctic Names', *Proceedings of the Sixth Pacific Science Congress*, 1939

William Herbert Hobbs, 'The Discoveries of Antarctica within the American Sector, as Revealed by Maps and Documents', *Transactions of the American Philosophical Society*, vol. XXXI, Part 1, January 1939

William Herbert Hobbs, 'The Discovery of Wilkes Land, Antarctica', *Proceedings of the American Philosophical Society*, vol. 82, 1940

William Herbert Hobbs, 'Early Maps of Antarctic Land, True and False', *Papers of the Michigan Academy of Science, Arts and Letters*, vol. 26, 1940

Gunnar Isachsen, 'Norwegian Explorations in the Antarctic, 1930–1931', *Geographical Review*, vol. XXII, no. 1, January 1932

Gunnar Isachsen, 'Modern Norwegian Whaling in the Antarctic', *Geographical Review*, vol. 19, no. 3, July 1929.

A. G. E. Jones, 'Captain William Smith and the Discovery of New South Shetland', *Geographical Journal*, vol. 141, no. 3, November 1975

Clements Markham, 'Address to the Royal Geographical Society, 1904', *Geographical Journal*, vol. XXIV, no. 1, July 1904

Clements Markham, 'Address to the Royal Geographical Society, 1905', *Geographical Journal*, vol. XXVI, no. 1, July 1905

Clements Markham, 'The Antarctic Expeditions', *Geographical Journal*, vol. XIV, no. 5, November 1899

Clements Markham, 'The First Year's Work of the National Antarctic Expeditions', *Geographical Journal*, vol. XXII, no. 1, July 1903

Lawrence Martin, 'Antarctica Discovered by a Connecticut Yankee, Captain Nathaniel Brown Palmer', *Geographical Review*, vol. XXX, no. 4, October 1940

Lawrence Martin, 'The Geography of the Monroe Doctrine and the Limits of the Western Hemisphere', *Geographical Review*, vol. 30, no. 3, July 1940

Hugh Robert Mill, 'Bellingshausen's Antarctic Voyage', *Geographical Journal*, vol. 21, no. 2, February 1903

Hugh Robert Mill, 'Ten Years of Antarctic Exploration', *Geographical Journal*, vol. 39, no. 4, April 1912

Dr Otto Nordenskjöld, 'The Swedish Antarctic Expedition', *Geographical Journal*, vol. XXIV, no. 1, July 1904

F. I. Norman, J. A. E. Gibson and J. S. Burgess, 'Klarius Mikkelsen's 1935 landing in the Vestfold Hills, East Antarctica: some fiction and some facts', *Polar Record*, vol. 34, no. 191, 1998

Kathleen Ralston, 'The Wyatt Earp's Voyages of Reconnaissance of the Australian Antarctic Territory, 1947–48', *Journal of Australian Studies*, March 1995

Catherine Redgwell, 'Antarctica', *International and Comparative Law Quarterly*, vol. 39, no. 2, April 1990

Hjalmar Riiser–Larsen, 'The "Norvegia" Antarctic Expedition of 1929–1930', *Geographical Review*, vol. 20, no. 4, October 1930

Finn Ronne, 'Antarctic Mapping and Aerial Photography', *Scientific Monthly*, vol. LXXI, no. 5, November 1950

Finn Ronne, 'Ronne Antarctic Research Expedition 1946–1948', *Geographical Review*, vol. 38, no. 3, July 1948

Captain Harold E. Saunders, 'The Flight of Admiral Byrd to the South Pole and the Exploration of Marie Byrd Land', *Proceedings of the American Philosophical Society*, vol. 82, 1940

Commander Robert Scott, 'The National Antarctic Expedition', *Geographical Journal*, vol. XXIV, no. 1, July 1904

Mikhail M. Somov, 'Journey into the Inaccessible', *UNESCO Courier*, January 1962

THESES

Noel Barrett, *Was Australian Antarctic Won Fairly?*, Honours Thesis, Bachelor of Antarctic Studies, University of Tasmania, November 2007

Irina Gan, *Red Antarctic: Soviet Interests in the South Polar Region Prior to the Antarctic Treaty*, PhD, University of Tasmania, 2009

Adrian John Howkins, *Frozen Empires: A history of the Antarctic sovereignty dispute between Britain, Argentina and Chile, 1939–1959*, PhD thesis, University of Texas at Austin, 2008

INDEX